D1415492

The Adolescent

Development, Relationships, and Culture
Sixth Edition

F. PHILIP RICE
University of Maine

Allyn and Bacon
Boston•London•Sydney•Toronto

Copyright © 1990, 1987, 1984, 1981, 1978, 1975 by Allyn and Bacon
A Division of Simon & Schuster, Inc.
160 Gould Street, Needham Heights, Massachusetts 02194

All rights reserved. No part of the material protected by this copyright notice may be reproduced or utilized in any form or by any means, electronic or mechanical, including photocopying, recording, or by any information storage and retrieval system, without the written permission of the copyright owner.

Series Editor: Diane McOscar
Production Administrator: Rowena Dores
Senior Editorial Assistant: Laura Frankenthaler
Manufacturing Buyer: Bill Alberti
Cover Administrator: Linda K. Dickinson

Chapter Opening Photo Credits: Chapter 1—Frederic Utter; Chapter 2—Robert Harbison; Chapter 3—© The Christian Science Monitor; Chapter 4—© Frank Siteman; Chapter 5—Robert Harbison; Chapter 6—Marc P. Anderson; Chapter 7—© The Christian Science Monitor/R. Norman Matheny; Chapter 8—Ulrike Welsch; Chapter 9—Michael Kagan/Monkmeyer Press Photo Service; Chapter 10—H. Armstrong Roberts; Chapter 11—© Eric Kroll/Taurus Photos Inc.; Chapter 12—Steve Woit; Chapter 13—© Frank Siteman; Chapter 14—Robert Harbison; Chapter 15—Globe Photos; Chapter 16—© The Christian Science Monitor/Peter Main; Chapter 17—© Frank Siteman; Chapter 18—© Frank Siteman; Chapter 19—Ken Karp; Chapter 20—© Frank Siteman.

Library of Congress Cataloging-in-Publication Data

Rice, F. Philip.
    The adolescent : development, relationships, and culture / F.
Philip Rice.—6th ed.
      p.   cm.
    Includes bibliographical references.
    ISBN 0-205-12310-4
    1. Youth—United States—Social conditions.   2. Adolescent
psychology.   3. Adolescence.   I. Title
HQ796.R543   1990
305.23'5—dc20
                                       89-27502
                                          CIP

Printed in the United States of America

10 9 8 7 6 5 4 3 2   94 93 92 91 90

Brief Contents

Contents

PART IV   EMOTIONAL

Preface

I have been absolutely delighted at the positive response of professors and students from across the world who use this textbook. Some of the professors have used the text in all of its editions and have made valuable suggestions that have been incorporated in the text to make it as useful as possible.

What can be said about a book that is now in its sixth edition? Certainly the subject of adolescent psychology continues to be interesting and challenging. The subject is constantly changing, always surprising, fascinating, and mind-boggling. Adolescents are always on the growing edge of change and challenge. To be a part of these changes and to reflect the adolescents' world is an exciting experience.

In trying to reflect the life and world of adolescents, I have tried to incorporate some very important features into this edition.

Up-to-Date References One important feature is the *newness* of this edition. Forty-five percent of the 1210 research references, or 549 in all, are completely new. Practically all of this data base comes from journal articles published in the 1980s. To keep this material as up-to-date as possible, hundreds of older references have been deleted.

Visual Appeal Much attention has been given to making this edition as visually appealing as possible. A textbook should not only be pedagogically sound, it should also be pleasant and attractive to use. The new two-color design and the extensive use of photographs, figures, graphs, and tables enhance the learning process.

Topics of Current Interest A number of very current topics are presented. These include such widely diverse subjects as Southeast-Asian adolescents, divorce and family disorganization and their effects on adolescents, use of steroids by athletes, date rape, school-based birth control clinics, AIDS, sexual violence in the media, the latest trends in contemporary music, and eating disorders.

Highlight Special boxed sections called *Highlight* pinpoint topics of special interest. Over twenty new highlights have been added. These include such widely different topics as menstrual irregularities in athletes, family factors in obesity, health concerns of adolescents, cognitive development and sexual behavior, gender differences in formal operations, five theories about causes of anorexia, factors contributing to adolescent loneliness, the exclusion of intimacy, parental control techniques, Gilligan's theory of sex differences in moral reasoning, middle-class parenting and underachievement, and male-female graduates—7 months later.

Broad Research Base   The discussions are substantiated with 1210 citations, most of which are original research studies; however, the findings are incorporated into the discussion. The emphasis is on discussing the subjects, not summarizing one research study after the other.

Manageable Length   There is a tendency for each edition of a textbook to become more lengthy than the previous one. Sometimes this expansion gets out of hand. To avoid this, the sixth edition contains twenty chapters, two fewer than the previous edition. Chapters 1 and 2 have been combined and rewritten into one on the important subject of "Profiles of Adolescents in Contemporary Society." The chapter on religion has been incorporated into Chapter 18 on "The Development of Moral Judgment, Character, Values, Beliefs, and Behavior."

Pedagogical Aids   The book has been written with the teaching-learning process in mind. Each chapter begins with a detailed outline. Key terms have been placed in the margins and in a glossary at the end of the book. Each chapter includes a detailed summary. Discussion questions with each chapter may be used in class discussions or in essay assignments. Extensive bibliographies for each chapter enable students and instructors to do extra reading on each subject, as desired. A completely revised instructor's manual, including test questions, is available for teachers. A *unique and helpful feature is the italicizing of key phrases and sentences in each paragraph.* This enables students to review the most important thoughts without having to underline with a magic marker.

There are some other outstanding features of this book that have been continued in this edition.

Eclectic Orientation   The book presents not one theory of adolescence but many, with the contributions, strengths, and weaknesses of each discussed.

Comprehensive Coverage   The book is as comprehensive as possible within the confines of one text. The adolescent has been placed within the context of contemporary society. The book includes both theory and life experiences of adolescents and discusses physical, intellectual, emotional, social, familial, moral, educational, and vocational aspects of adolescent development and behavior.

Adolescents in Contemporary Society   How modern society and social forces shape the lives of adolescents today is an important focus. Adolescents are discussed in social context, not as though they were isolated from the social forces around them.

Cultural Diversity   Adolescents are not all alike any more than adults are. A wide variety of ethnic, racial, and cultural groups are discussed.

Adolescent Society and Culture   This book includes not only adolescent development and relationships but also group life and culture. Subjects include cultural versus subcultural societies, dress, argot, and group life in and out of school. The importance of the automobile and music in the life of adolescents are also emphasized.

Gender Issues and Concerns   Gender issues are raised in relation to a wide variety of topics: physical attributes and body image, cognitive abilities and intelligence, eating disorders, social development and dating, concepts of masculinity and femininity and sex roles, sexual values and behavior, education, work and vocation, and others.

Personal Applications   The discussion questions at the end of each chapter are designed to bring out student attitudes, feelings, and responses to the subjects discussed. Students are encouraged to reflect on their adolescent years, to talk about adolescents they know (either their own friends or children), and to react in a critical way to the issues discussed.

ACKNOWLEDGMENTS

I would like to acknowledge the special help of the following people who have offered valuable guidance in writing this book: Tracy L. Cross, Louisiana Tech University; Dan Gallagher, Salisbury State University; Charles W. Good, West Chester University; Richard Hagen, The Florida State University; Victoria Molfese, Southern Illinois University at Carbondale; and LeAdelle Phelps, University of Missouri—Columbia.

About the Author

The eclectic approach to adolescent psychology that is reflected in this book has been possible because of the wide background of education and experience of the author, F. Philip Rice. Dr. Rice is currently Professor of Psychology at the University of Maine, with major responsibility for teaching Psychology of Adolescence as well as other courses in psychology. In addition, he is in private practice as a Marriage and Family Counselor. He has had a total of twenty-five years experience as a college professor and as a therapist in private practice.

For seven years he was Family Life Specialist for the state of Maine, with major responsibilities in family life education. In that position, Dr. Rice conducted workshops, seminars, classes, forums, and conferences for youth leaders, parents, teachers, social workers, church leaders, and adolescents themselves to develop greater understanding of today's adolescents and to improve parent-teen relationships. Dr. Rice received the Distinguished Service Award from the University of Maine for his work in this regard.

Dr. Rice has a master's degree in Psychology from New York University and a doctorate in Family Relations and Child Development from Teachers College, Columbia University.

Dr. Rice's active private practice has given him a wide background of clinical experience from which to draw in making this book as helpful as possible.

Dr. Rice is the author of twenty-seven books, including eleven college textbooks, such as *Human Sexuality, Intimate Relationships, Marriages, and Families,* and *Adult Development and Aging.*

CHAPTER

1

Profiles of Adolescents in Contemporary Society

Research indicates that adults generally dislike and mistrust adolescents more than any other age group (Willis, 1981). This negative attitude is based on stereotypes. All adolescents are viewed as being alike, and these views often focus on the delinquent, addicted, or disturbed minority.

This chapter examines positive and negative views of adolescents. It also includes a discussion of selected societal influences: technological and social change, urbanization, materialism and poverty, mass communications, social and emotional stress, family disorganization, and life events and stress. How these societal influences affect the lives of adolescents is also discussed. A look backward to the Roaring Twenties in the United States will reveal that attitudes and relationships have not changed. Adults were as critical in those days as they are today, and youths were as rebellious and conformist, moral and immoral, as they are today.

POSITIVE AND NEGATIVE VIEWS OF ADOLESCENTS

The Problem with Stereotypes

stereotypes

What do you think of when you think of adolescents? Is it true that adolescents are loud, vulgar, ill-mannered, immoral, ungrateful, irresponsible, sexually promiscuous, untidy, rebellious, or lazy? Such adjectives are supposed to be accurate descriptions of adolescents. Actually, they reflect **stereotypes**—broad, over-simplified images of this age group. A *stereotype represents a commonly held conception or idea about a group of persons*, but it may not be accurate. It is usually based on prejudiced attitudes and feelings about specific persons that are applied to a whole group. To say that all adolescents are lazy because a 15-year-old boy named George is lazy is simply not true and is grossly unfair to the large group of youths who are not lazy at all.

Many adults are concerned that today's youth are all problem children who are more interested in having a good time than in growing up, and whose chief delights are sexual indulgence and attending rock concerts to smoke marijuana and listen to shocking music. From some of the publicity young people receive, it appears that many adults not only mistrust adolescents, they also dislike them. An article about youth in the professional journal *Adolescence* was titled: "Why are they so obnoxious?" (Newman, 1985). The article describes adolescents' unwillingness to listen to what adults tell them, their bravado and claim to know everything, their immaturity and refusal to accept responsibility for their own actions, their inability to think logically, their social ineptness, their egocentrism and selfishness, their conformity to peer pressure, their inability to make good moral judgments, and their rebelliousness. The article affirms that adolescents are sometimes hard to live with, but it also emphasizes that not all adolescents are difficult in all of these ways, and some are not difficult in these ways at all. If an adolescent is always obnoxious and adults are always exasperated, this is a departure from the norm, and therapy may be needed to break the deadlock (Newman, 1985).

The point is we cannot place all adolescents in narrow categories and say this is the way they are. How many adults would say it is appropriate to describe all adults, all men, all women, or all elderly as obnoxious? Adolescents are as diverse in personality and behavior as adults. Any generalization about adolescents immediately calls for an opposite one. Adolescents are maddeningly self-centered yet capable of impressive feats of altruism. Their attention wanders like a butterfly, yet they can spend hours concentrating on something of real interest. They are often lazy and rude, but when you least expect it, they can be loving and helpful (Csizkszentmihalyi and Larson, 1984).

This unpredictability, this shifting from black to white and from hot to cold, is what adolescence is all about. The study of adolescents is a study of contrasts, change, experimentation, and growth. This fluctuation allows freedom to alter the course of life while growing into adulthood. This is, after all, the important task during this stage of life.

HIGHLIGHT   Historical Perceptions of Youth

Negative perceptions of adolescents have been prevalent throughout history. During the eighth century B.C., Hesiod provided the following description of youth:

> I see no hope for the future of your people if they are dependent on the frivolous youth of today, for certainly all youth are reckless beyond words. . . . When I was a boy, we were taught to be discreet and respectful of elders, but the present youth are exceedingly wise and impatient of restraint.

Complaints about youth were echoed by Loring in the eighteenth century:

> When children and young people are suffered to haunt the taverns, get into vile company, rabble up and down in the evening, when they should be at home to attend family worship; in the dark and silent night, when they should be in their beds, when they are let alone to take

other sinful courses without check or restraint, they are then on the high road to ruin.

Literature from the nineteenth century repeatedly referred to youth as "disorderly" and "disobedient." Burton wrote:

> It must be confessed that an irreverent, unruly spirit has come to be a prevalent, an outrageous evil among the young people of our land. . . . Some of the good old people make facetious complaint on this. . . . "There is as much family government now as there used to be in our young days," they said, "only it has changed hands."

SOURCE: Manning, M. L. (1983, Winter). "Three Myths Concerning Adolescence," *Adolescence* 18: 824; Loring, I. (1718). *Duty and Interests of Young Persons* (Boston), p. 18; Burton, W. (1863). *Helps to Education* (Crosby and Nichols), pp. 38–39.

Adolescent Values

Reference has already been made to common negative stereotypes of adolescents. When considered alone these present a very lopsided picture. Studies of adolescents' values, however, reveal some very positive images. A 1981 study of 200 students at Temple University revealed that 63 percent anticipated that family life would be their major source of life satisfaction in the future (McFalls et al., 1985). Occupation was listed second, with 20 percent of the students anticipating that it would be their major source of life satisfaction.

In comparing the results of the 1981 survey with a similar survey in 1969, there was an interesting increase in the number of respondents who chose religion as their number one life satisfaction. This finding reflects the spread of new religious cults, plus a resurgence in mainline denominations, as well as considerable growth in student religious organizations on campus (Lloyd, 1981).

As seen in table 1-1, however, there was a decrease in the percentage of students indicating community or national affairs as a chief source of satisfaction. In answer to those who charge that adolescents only want to have a good time, the percentage of those indicating recreation as a major source of satisfaction actually decreased from 6 percent to 3 percent from 1969 to 1981. Adolescents had become more family and religiously oriented over these years (McFalls et al., 1985).

A different approach to the study of adolescent values was used in a study of English-speaking youths attending schools in Austria, France, Switzerland, and West Germany (Simmons and Wade, 1985). The adolescents were asked to complete the sentence, "The sort of person I would most like to be like . . . ."A number of youth indicated that they would not really like to be anyone but themselves. Others named famous persons that personified their ideals. Others wanted particular careers, ranging from singers to archaeologists. Some adolescents emphasized materialism: "I'd like to have lots of money, so I'd be rich." Others

TABLE 1-1

Anticipated major sources of life satisfaction.

LIFE SATISFACTION	1969	1981
1. Family	53%	63%
2. Occupation	24%	20%
3. Religion	1%	9%
4. Recreation	6%	3%
5. Community Affairs	6%	1%
6. National Affairs	10%	6%

Adapted from: McFalls, J. A., Jr., Jones, B. J., Gallagher, B. J. III., and Rivera, J. (1985). "Political Orientation and Occupational Values of College Youth, 1969 and 1981: A Shift Toward Uniformity." *Adolescence*, 20, 697–713.

emphasized physical appearance and popularity: "I would like to have a lot of girl and boyfriends. It also wouldn't be amiss if I were slimmer and prettier" (p. 896). Seventeen percent of respondents expressed ideals that went beyond popularity and good looks, such as to be friendly, courteous, or good humored. Eighteen percent wanted to be honest, reliable, industrious, and kind. One Swiss boy wrote:

> I'd like to be a person who is respected, open, friendly, helpful, etc., simply a person in whom others can take pleasure, a real human being. I know I won't succeed in all that 100%, but I'd like to and give myself a lot of trouble to be a person whom other people like to be with—someone they can talk to, a prototype of a true friend and helper (p. 896).

Still other adolescents emphasized the importance of social justice and human brotherhood:

> I would like to be able to bring happiness to people who are less fortunate . . . I would like to be someone who could love everyone equally, without taking any notice of his race, nor his color, nor his social class (p. 897).

It is apparent that idealism was revealed in these statements of adolescents from around the world (Simmons and Wade, 1985).

Activism and Powerlessness

The 1960s and early 1970s witnessed the peak of youth **activism** and social protest. There were two overriding issues that spearheaded the movement: civil rights and Vietnam. Students from all over the country marched in support of Martin Luther King, Jr., traveled to mass rallies in Washington, D. C., protested at the Democratic National Convention in Chicago, or held rallies and protests in towns and on college campuses. When the United States attacked Cambodia in 1970, there were antiwar protests on campuses throughout the United States.

activism

Youthful idealism and concern about social problems is still much in evidence. A survey of 446 undergraduate students at a midwestern university yielded five items that 75 percent of the subjects rates as serious or very serious problems today (Roscoe, 1985). The five issues were *drug use, pollution, hunger, threat of nuclear war,* and *poverty.* An additional six issues were considered serious to very serious by at least 50 percent of the participants. Those six issues were *nuclear accidents, conventional war, government corruption, lack of education, sickness and disease,* and *racial discrimination.* Table 1-2 shows the results of the survey. However, even though students say these problems are serious concerns, only a small minority think their actions can help solve them. The others withdraw from the issues, feeling powerless to do anything about them.

The journalist Paul Loeb met with students in more than 100 colleges across the United States to talk about social activism. Students at Fairfield University, an affluent Catholic school in Connecticut, agreed that crumbling houses and boarded up storefronts in the adjacent city of Bridgeport made poor places to live. One student suggested that improved local education might help: "Starting

Although today's youth are not activist rebels like those of the late 1960s and early 1970s, various issues, including abortion, still act as catalysts that bring adolescents together to work for a cause. (AP/Wide World Photos)

kids off right is really important," he said, but added, "But it's not my job to do it" (Loeb, 1988, p. 60). Nearly one-half of the students that Loeb interviewed across the country believed that atomic war was a reasonable likelihood within the course of their lives, but only a handful thought their actions could prevent it.

privatism   Schroth (1982) has suggested that the erosion of political activism and declining interest in community and national affairs has resulted in **privatism**, a tendency to narrow the world, their experience, to pull into their rooms and "shut the door," and to hide from the rough-and-tumble of political responsibility. Along with this has come a decline in knowledge about community and national affairs and a decrease in popularity of government-related occupations (McFalls, Jones, Gallagher, and Rivera, 1985).

While activism has declined noticeably, there are still thousands of adolescents who want to express their idealism by going into vocations "to help other people," such as social service or teaching. A survey of 200 students at Temple University revealed significant numbers who wanted to go into people-oriented vocations (McFalls et al., 1985). Altogether, only 15 percent of students classified as politically conservative said they wanted to enter people-oriented vocations. This contrasted with 36 percent of radical students who wanted to enter people-oriented occupations "to help others" or "work with people."

TABLE 1-2

Perceptions of social issues by adolescents.

| | PERCENTAGE OF RESPONSES | | | |
Issue	Not a Problem	Somewhat a Problem	Serious Problem	Very Serious Problem
Drug Use	1	10	41	48
Pollution	1	16	52	31
Hunger	2	15	38	45
Nuclear War	5	13	22	60
Poverty	1	21	49	29
Nuclear Accidents	6	27	27	40
Conventional War	7	31	36	26
Government Corruption	4	37	40	19
Lack of Education	4	39	39	18
Sickness and Disease	7	38	40	15
Racial Discrimination	5	45	36	14
Sexual Discrimination	6	52	30	12
Communism	17	41	30	12
Overpopulation	12	47	28	13
Religious Discrimination	31	51	14	4
Age Discrimination	14	69	15	2

From: Roscoe, B. (1985). "Social Issues as Social Problems: Adolescents' Perceptions." *Adolescence*, 20, 377–383.

There are also still islands of activism on some college campuses. At Texas University, Oberlin College, and Brandeis University, the South African divestment movement has spurred marches of up to 1,000 students, with 1,000 arrested at Cornell University in 1985. Deciding that its presence caused the university "too much trouble," the CIA abandoned recruiting at the University of Colorado, Boulder, following a three-year campaign and 700 arrests. Anti-CIA protests have spread to other campuses. In February 1988, a national activist convention at Rutgers University drew more than 700 students representing 130 schools from 41 states. However, students who are not involved generally regard marchers and petitioners as too serious, frivolous, snobby, preachy, ignorant, complicated, emotional, in-groupy, and demanding. "They all wear black." "They all dress alike." Uninvolved students think of student activists as refugees from the 1960s (Loeb, 1988).

Cynicism and Optimism

Some adolescents are cynical and distrustful of other people. Bachman and colleagues (1987) found that only one-fourth of high school seniors said that people could be trusted, another one-fourth were undecided, and about one-half felt that "you can't be too careful" (p. 36). There was good reason for this uncertainty. One in six reported having been threatened by someone with a weapon, one in four said that an unarmed person threatened him or her with injury, and one in six said that someone injured him or her on purpose without using a weapon.

As today's youth look ahead, many see a bleak future for the country and the world. Pessimism is higher than it was a decade ago. More than one-half of high school seniors agreed that things will get worse in the rest of the world in the next five years, and one-third believed things will get worse in the country. Yet, when it comes to their own lives, adolescents are increasingly optimistic (Otto, 1988). Nine out of ten high school seniors believed that things would get better for them, and only one out of thirty-five thought that their lives would get worse (Bachman et al., 1987). These attitudes reflect the halo effect characteristic of many adolescents—bad things happen to others but not to them. *Adolescents are characteristically optimistic about their personal futures and lives, though cynical and skeptical about the rest of the world.*

Parental Relationships

One of the stereotypes of adolescents is that as a group they are in mass rebellion against their parents and parental values. This is simply not true. There is no question that adolescence is a time for children to consolidate their growing independence. Dalsimer (1986) insists:

> With the onset of puberty . . . it becomes essential that parents be relinquished as the primary objects of love. This constitutes one of the most painful but also one of the most significant, psychological tasks of adolescence (p. 6).

Without such emotional weaning and learning to make decisions and to assume responsibility for their own lives, adolescents cannot grow as mature adults.

There is a difference, however, between establishing emotional and social independence and rejecting parents and parental values. A survey of 6,000 adolescents from ten nations found few adolescents who were alienated from their parents (Atkinson, 1988a,b). Instead, *today's youth were shown to have great respect for their parents.* In the United States, only 7 percent of adolescents said they thought their parents were ashamed of them or would be disappointed in them in the future (Atkinson, 1988a,b). There were, however, 13 percent who very often felt their mother was no good and 15 percent who felt their father was no good. Not all parents received a score of approval.

An extensive national survey of a probability sample of 1,500 students in grades 7 through 12 revealed widespread agreement with parental values (National Association of Secondary School Principals, 1984). In eight major issue areas—*drugs, education, work, politics, choice of friends, religion, sex,* and *dress styles*—a clear majority of students said they agreed with their parents' views. Table 1-3 shows the percentage of students agreeing with their mothers and fathers on these issues.

Overall, the evidence suggests that adolescents still turn to parents for guidance and share parental values on major issues. The concept of parent-child alienation as a usual feature of adolescence is a myth (Rutter, 1980).

■ **TABLE 1-3**

Percent of adolescents grades 7 to 12 agreeing with parents on various issues.

AREAS	PERCENT AGREEING WITH MOTHER	PERCENT AGREEING WITH FATHER
1. Drugs	82.6	75.6
2. Education	81.2	74.6
3. Work	80.4	73.0
4. Politics	77.6	69.2
5. Choice of Friends	74.4	66.8
6. Religion	74.0	65.5
7. Sex	69.4	62.4
8. Clothing	64.5	53.0

Adapted from: National Association of Secondary School Principals. (1984). *The Mood of American Youth.* Reston, VA.: National Association of Secondary School Principals.

Responsibility and Irresponsibility ■

Adolescents are sometimes accused of being irresponsible and lazy (Cole, 1980).

"What are you doing?"
"Nothing,"
"What would you like to do?"
"Nothing."

Here is an example of a typical fatherly complaint about his son's lack of helpfulness around the house:

He never does anything. He even complains if I ask him to take out the trash. He'll lie on the couch and watch his mother work and never volunteer to lift a finger to help (Author's counseling notes).

One mother describes her two college-aged sons: "Both dropped out of college. They came home to live with me, but they aren't working. They go out nights, and sleep and hang around the house during the day watching television. The worst part of it is, they don't contribute a cent. I'm supporting them, and they don't even help out around the house."

But this example may be contrasted with that of Octavio, a 17-year-old Hispanic youth. His mother needs the money he makes working, but he also wants to stay in school. He goes to school in the South Bronx but works packing boxes in a perfume factory in Brooklyn. He has seven classes in a row from 7:45 P.M. to 2:30 P.M., but he has to be at work by 3:00 so he cannot each lunch. When he gets home at 9 P.M., he is often too tired to do his homework and thus is embarrassed to go to class the next day ("Report Finds Teenagers 'Chasing the American Dream,'" 1981, p. 1).

Most adolescents dislike helping parents around the house, but they want to work at jobs outside the home. Three-fourths of today's high school seniors hold a part-time job during the school year (Bachman et al., 1987; Johnston, O'Malley, and Bachman, 1987). The proportion of high school students who work has been rising steadily, and, generally speaking, working students have had the support of parents, teachers, and social scientists. "Working is good for them," the conventional wisdom seemed to argue (Otto, 1988).

With the blessing of society, our nation's youth have gone to work. Among high school seniors, one of three males works at least 20 hours a week, and one of four females does the same (Bachman et al., 1987). They're working half-time while going to school full-time!

There are some authorities, however, who are beginning to feel that many adolescents are devoting too much time to jobs and not enough to school. Greenberger and Steinberg (1981), for example, conclude that when high school students work more than 15 to 20 hours a week, the disadvantages include diminished involvement with school, family, and peers and increased use of cigarettes, alcohol, marijuana, and other drugs (Steinberg et al., 1982).

Some adolescents today grow up so used to working after school and on weekends that they never have any leisure time for extracurricular activities, for healthy recreation, or for just having fun with peers. When they become adults they are workaholics, never learning how to relax or to play. Such habits can be very detrimental to marital and familial relationships.

The proportion of high school students who work has been rising steadily, and some authorities feel that too much time is devoted to work and not enough time is devoted to school. (Robert Harbison)

SOCIETAL INFLUENCES ON THE ADOLESCENT

Selected Influences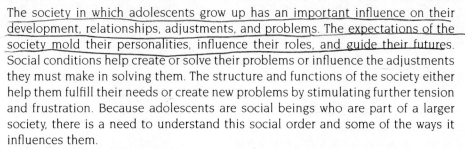

The society in which adolescents grow up has an important influence on their development, relationships, adjustments, and problems. The expectations of the society mold their personalities, influence their roles, and guide their futures. Social conditions help create or solve their problems or influence the adjustments they must make in solving them. The structure and functions of the society either help them fulfill their needs or create new problems by stimulating further tension and frustration. Because adolescents are social beings who are part of a larger society, there is a need to understand this social order and some of the ways it influences them.

A truly comprehensive examination of the many facets of U.S. society and the numerous ways they influence adolescents would require volumes. Instead, discussion is confined to seven important influences on today's adolescents: *technological and social change, urbanization, materialism and poverty, mass communications, social and emotional stress, family disorganization,* and *life events and stress.* Other influences, such as peers, the school, and churches, will be discussed in later chapters.

Technological and Social Change

The adolescent of today lives in a society undergoing intensive and rapid technological change. Probably no other society has so revered technological innovation or placed less restraint upon it than modern U.S. culture. Since the turn of the century, it has witnessed unprecedented advances: the introduction of electricity, radio, television, the automobile, airplane, atomic energy, rocketry, computers, lasers, and robots. Each new invention stimulates in turn a series of additional technological changes.

In every culture, technological innovation becomes the stimulus and the motor for social change as well. Consider the automobile as a modern example. The development of the motor car changed patterns of work and residence, making it possible for people to live dozens of miles from their jobs. Whole patterns of family living changed, with the family becoming more mobile and its members more separated. The automobile made possible the regional consolidation of schools, with adolescents attending with hundreds of others from a wide geographic area. The automobile transformed the rural United States into a sprawling complex of turnpikes and freeways. It was instrumental in encouraging urban blight as middle-class families retreated to the suburbs, leaving the minority poor to inhabit the largest cities. Thus, each new technological invention has consequences for social living. A series of technological inventions necessitates an increasing number of social adjustments.

For the most part, these changes have been unplanned and unguided. Social transformations have occurred as a haphazard result of technological progress. It is difficult to guide, predict, or alter the future directions of these changes. The growth of the megalopolis, the sprawling urban complex of cities reaching out to touch each other has obliterated the countryside and polluted the environment. Not only has the physical environment become completely altered and almost unmanageable, but the social climate has suffered as well. The faster the city grows, the more difficult it is for people to exert any control over their physical environment or their social order. These rapid technological and social changes have profound effects upon the adolescent. Five of these effects will be discussed here.

The past grows increasingly distant from the present. The more rapid and drastic are the social changes, the more different are standards and patterns of life from those of previous years. This makes the adolescent feel that anything old is also outmoded and irrelevant, so that it ought not to be allowed to exert much influence over today's life.

The future grows more remote, uncertain, and unpredictable, so the adolescent feels less secure about tomorrow. When standards, customs, mores, social structures, conditions, and functions are changing rapidly, it becomes hard to predict what life will be like in the years to come and more difficult to prepare for that future. The adolescent is pushed into living more in the present than in the future. "Why worry about tomorrow? I can't know what tomorrow will bring. All I can do is to live day by day."

Rapid change weakens the roles and functions of the family. Fewer sons and daughters follow their parents' occupations, for example. Also, education has become largely nonfamilial. Emotional ties are loosened by geographic mobility. Fewer interpersonal contacts result in a decrease or affective interchange—socialization and emotional and morale-building functions. As a result the nuclear family is less able to fulfill its affective functions and disintegrates under the strain, as documented by the high divorce rate and the growing number of one-parent families.

Cultural confusion with shifting beliefs, attitudes, values, mores, and standards results in stress, conflict, and personality disturbance in the lives of young people. In a world of pluralistic standards, changing customs, and uncertain values, it becomes difficult for adolescents to know how to live and what to believe. Uncertainty and conflict create disturbing internal stress. When everyone in a culture accepts the same ideas and values, adolescents find it easier and more secure to know and accept the status quo; but when they are confronted with changing, conflicting ideas and values, they feel forced to shift about, trying to find meaning for themselves.

One result of change is a spiritual vacuum in which adolescents have difficulty finding identity. They ask: "Can I commit my life to anything? Is there anything in human culture today worth saving, worth committing myself to?" Among some of the young, this pain comes close to being a mass neurosis: a lack of faith in self, an emptiness of spirit, a lack of order and direction. As one youth expressed it longingly, "The answer must be out there somewhere."

Increasing technology and social complexity have increased the period of adolescent dependency. It is more difficult for adolescents to graduate from high school and get well-paying jobs. "High-tech" positions require special training. The National Commission on Excellence in Education (1983) suggests that if American adolescents are to grow up being competitive with their peers in other technological nations, they will have to spend more days and years in school, spend more hours doing homework, and tackle more complex information.

The need for education has increased and requires more years of preparation, so the period of dependency upon parents has lengthened. Since 1969, the proportion of young people in the United States between the ages of twenty and twenty-nine living at home has increased by 25 percent (Goleman, 1980). The result has been delayed independence and maturity (Chance, 1988).

Urbanization

As people leave their farms and move to the cities in increasing numbers, their lives are drastically altered. For one thing, *the sheer size of the city makes personal, close relationships more difficult.* Neighbors remain strangers. Affectional needs may not be met. The individual feels isolated and alone in a city with millions of people.

There are urban high schools today with student enrollments exceeding five thousand. How can the adolescent in this educational complex find identity or any sense of belonging (Garbarino, 1980)?

Urbanization creates impersonalization in the family also. Home, school, and work may be separated by great distances. One or both parents may commute into the city to work, leaving at dawn, returning at dusk. Adolescents ride the school bus to the consolidated high school, seldom seeing their parents during daylight hours, at least in the winter. It becomes harder for family members to be together or to relate to each other personally when they seldom see one another or spend much time together. One result may be a household of strangers who live together but do not really know one another.

Urbanization also creates a host of social problems: overcrowding, poverty, slums, gangs, delinquency, and other problems that go with city life. Cities have a way of altering the lives of people, imposing stresses, strain, temptations, and problems on the children and youths growing up within their confines. Not every effect of city life is negative. Sometimes the city may offer superior educational opportunities, recreational facilities, or cultural influences. But as more and more cities become dangerous and depersonalizing, the social disadvantages of living there increasingly outweigh the advantages.

Materialism and Poverty

Today's youth have grown up in a time of affluence unprecedented in the history of the world, with the majority of adolescents sharing in the benefits of this prosperity and a minority, by comparison, becoming poorer than ever. Money is at hand because parents seem to offer an ample supply, or adolescents are able to earn part of it themselves. One-half of young men and one-third of young women who work part-time earn more than $50 a week. Most of these earnings are "fun money" with little contributed toward family expenses or saved for future education. The biggest expense of males is for automobiles (Otto, 1988). The affluence of today's generation has a number of consequences.

Today's youths constitute a huge consumers' market. Business caters directly to them; clothes, cosmetics, automobiles, records, stereos, skis, snowmobiles, motorcycles, magazines, grooming aids, sports equipment, cigarettes, and thousands of other items are given the hard sell to attract the dollars of increasing numbers of youths.

■ **The affluent generation**

Reprinted from Farrow, P. (Spring 1978). "The Presymposial State," *Andover Review* 5: 30. Copyright © by The Trustees of Phillips Academy. Used by permission.

A major segment of the youth culture has become a status-conscious, prestige-seeking culture. Today's youth have become concerned about self—how best to get a good job and satisfy their own material needs (Otto, 1988; Yankelovich, 1981). The emphasis is on earning a big salary and winning the struggle for status, position, and material advancement (Balswick and Balswick, 1980; Rubenstein, 1981). In his discussion with students across the country, Loeb found many youths whose immediate goal in life was to earn over $50,000 a year. There were some whose goal was to earn over six figures (Loeb, 1988).

Other studies reaffirm this increased emphasis on materialism. In the past 10 to 12 years, there has been a dramatic decline in the importance of **intrinsic values** of work, such as the desire for self-expression or the need to be creative, use one's abilities, and work with people to help them. These intrinsic values have been partially replaced by **extrinsic values** such as the importance of achieving status and security through earning money (McFalls et al., 1985). Bachman et al. (1987) found that the majority of high school seniors expected to earn more than their parents and that having a lot of money was important or very important to them. Two-thirds felt that a house of their own, a big yard, and a well-kept garden and lawn were quite important or extremely important. Nine out of 10 said it was important for them to be able to give their children even better opportunities than they had (Bachman et al., 1987).

intrinsic values

extrinsic values

Given the realities of the world, large numbers of youths will be disappointed when their immediate accomplishments do not measure up to their expectations. One father explained:

> My daughter is an honor student. When she graduated from college she honestly thought that she was going to earn $40,000 a year immediately. Actually, she's earning about $18,000. She can barely pay her rent, never mind buying a new car. She complains constantly that she never has any money (Author's counseling notes).

One of the problems is that such adolescents grew up in families where parents have taken a lifetime to earn what they have. Their children expect to start at where their parents are now, and become disillusioned when they are not able.

Those families who have not been able to keep up with the struggle for money, status, and prestige seem poorer than ever. As a result, their adolescents feel abandoned and rejected. Adolescents who come from extremely poor families (and these families make up at least 13 percent of the population) are nonjoiners in school activities, are seldom elected to positions of prestige, and often seek status through anti-social behavior (U.S. Bureau of the Census, *Statistical Abstract of the United States,* 1987). These youths struggle for identity and sometimes become problems because they have to find an identity that middle-class society rejects.

A certain percentage of middle-class and upper middle-class youth have rebelled against the overemphasis upon materialism and seem to want the other extreme. These adolescents are more content with very few material possessions, emphasizing instead relationships with other people and with the world of nature. Some are experimenting with various forms of group life, emphasizing love and togetherness in their relationships. A minority have joined punk rock groups who are openly rebelling against what they feel are hypocritical, superficial, and false values and undesirable priorities and goals of society.

Affluence has created an opportunity for leisure for the young, which some use in the pursuit of hedonistic pastimes. This is especially true of those from wealthy families who discount the need for work involvement and grow up bored (Norman, 1984). However, leisure is also a problem to the dropout or to the unemployed or disenfranchised of any social class (U.S. Dept. of Labor, 1980).

Mass Communications

The mass media are partly responsible for creating the generation of consuming adolescents described. Today's child has been surrounded, as no other generation before, by messages on signs, billboards, in newspapers, magazines, radio, and television, urging the purchase of the newest antiperspirant, breakfast food, or shaving cream.

In 1984, 98 percent of U.S. households had television and home radios. Thirteen percent of all households had videocassette recorders (VCRs). Some 7.6 million VCRs alone were sold in 1984, bringing the number in U.S. homes to 17 million (Doan, 1985). Adolescents can now record television programs and rent movies for home use. Some experts worry that rental movies will expose more youths to violent and sexually explicit films. Others contend that the hours spent in front of yet another video attraction will cut further into study and exercise time.

The mass media have also created an age of instant news: television viewers share in the experiences of starving Africans, terrorist bombings, and massive earthquakes. Today's youth have not just heard about killing; they have seen and reacted to it in the nightly news. They have been bombarded with sensory information that affects the realm of emotion and feeling, as well as cognitive perception. The insistent beat of global communication not only transforms the mind but also motivates the will and stirs the emotions to action.

As a result some youths are skeptical about what they are told. They have learned to believe what they see happening rather than naively to accept what they are told is true. They have learned to see through false promises, to distinguish thought from action, and sham, pretense, and hypocrisy from sincerity and true concern.

Social and Emotional Stress

Today's adolescents have been exposed year after year to physical violence and disturbances in the world: the murder or attempted assassination of national leaders, the bombing of embassies, terrorism on a global scale, and war in over a dozen countries. It includes constant exposure to violence on television and in the press. It includes the constant threat of nuclear war.

National studies reveal that many children and youth are afraid of the nuclear threat. When asked, "What does the word 'nuclear' bring to mind?" one high school student replied: "Danger, death, sadness, explosion, cancer, children, waste, bombs, pollution, terrible" (Yudkin, 1984, p. 20). Children report nightmares in which everyone is being blown up except themselves, leaving them alone and helpless. When students from 130 high schools across the country were surveyed, more than one-third believed that "nuclear or biological annihilation will probably be the fate of all mankind within my lifetime" (Yudkin, 1984, p. 20).

The most disturbing change in recent years relates to mortality factors. When young people die, they die violent deaths. Among adolescents aged 15 to 24 who die, 77 percent die violently. Death from accidents, suicides, and homicides has passed disease as the leading cause of death for youth (Diegmueller, 1987). Young people are the only age group in the United States that have not enjoyed improved health status over the past 30 years. Death by communicable disease has decreased appreciably, but the rise in violent deaths has more than offset the reduction in deaths due to disease.

An analysis of the extent and variety of adolescent victimization as reported in newspapers in Great Britain revealed the causes of physical injury, death, and mental hurt. The results are shown in table 1-4 (Falchikov, 1986).

The FBI Uniform Crime Reports for 1986 (Diegmueller, 1987) indicate that one-half of all homicides and suicides occur in the 15-to-24-year-old age group. From 1950 to 1980, homicides increased threefold and suicides increased more than fourfold for this age group. Yet, most violent deaths among young people occur on highways. Two-thirds of their violent deaths involve car wrecks.

■ **TABLE 1-4**

Newspaper adolescent "victim" categories: outcomes and causes.

CAUSES OF PHYSICAL INJURY (PERCENT)		CAUSES OF DEATH (PERCENT)		CAUSES OF MENTAL HURT (PERCENT)	
Gun attack abroad	14.0	Car accidents	11.6	Accusations of	
Rape and sexual		Suicide	9.3	murder	2.3
assault	9.3	Careless driving	7.0	Grief at death of	
Attempted murder	4.7	Violent attack	4.7	parents	2.3
Car and motorcycle		Drowning	2.3	Homelessness	2.3
accidents	4.7	Murder	2.3	Loss of cash	2.3
Freak whirlwind	4.7	Total	37.2	Total	9.2
Violent attack	4.7				
The Atomic Age	2.3				
Cervical cancer	2.3				
Falling tree	2.3				
Political action					
abroad	2.3				
Soccer					
hooliganism	2.3				
Total	53.6				

From: Falchikov, N. (1986). "Images of Adolescence: An Investigation into the Accuracy of the Image of Adolescence Constructed by British Newspapers." *Journal of Adolescence*, 9, 167–180.

There is a link between alcohol and adolescent suicides, homicides, and fatal accidents (Diegmueller, 1987). In some areas, the percentage of teen suicides who had been drinking prior to their deaths increased from 13 percent in the period 1968 to 1972 to 46 percent a decade later (Otto, 1988). The equation becomes even more deadly when firearms are involved. The most common method of teen suicide among those with significant alcohol content is use of a firearm. Homicides, suicides, automobile accidents, firearms, and alcohol, are pernicious threats to our nation's youth. They represent the most serious forms of problem behavior when found in combination.

From a psychological point of view, stress creates upset and insecurity; continued stress can result in disturbed behavior. Not all behavior of adolescents is disturbed, nor do all youths have emotional problems, but widespread mental illness, alcoholism, drug abuse, vandalism, suicide, homicide, and various other forms of acting out behavior among youths indicate that many have psychological problems. Psychiatrist Miller (1974) suggests that social stresses are partly responsible for adolescent problems:

The Spartans exposed their young to physical stress in order to toughen their society. This was a conscious decision, but eventually so much was demanded that by killing its young the society destroyed itself. Social stress applied to youth may produce similar effects in the Western world. Because of this it is very difficult for parents and other adults to know how much an adolescent's behavior is a function of family interaction and how much depends on stress in society-at-large. . . . This has been called a permissive society. . . . Society might more appropriately be considered confused and anxiety-ridden. (p. 123)

Miller goes on to suggest that young people need release from the tension created by these social pressures, primarily through goal-directed, constructive outlets. If constructive outlets are not provided, youths react with rage and anger—or with withdrawal. Some express their rage through vandalism or heated protest. Others withdraw and become drop-outs. In both cases the causes are the same: too much exposure to too much stress over too long a time.

Whether or not it is a unique attitude, today's youths find it hard to accept reassurances of a secure future. It is not surprising that they sometimes participate in meaningless and sometimes destructive violence against public institutions and buildings or in drug parties that turn off everyday sights and sounds. Such self-destructive behavior is symbolic of a sense of uselessness and despair.

HIGHLIGHT   The Threat of Nuclear War

On October 17, 1981, members of the Children's Campaign for Nuclear Disarmament (CCND) stood in front of the White House and read nearly 3,000 letters from children. One of these letters read:

I am 10 years old. I think nuclear war is bad because many innocent people will die. The world could even be destroyed. I don't want to die. I don't want my family to die. I want to live and grow up. Please stop nuclear bombs. Please work to bring peace.

Source: (Yudkin, 1984, p. 24)

Family Disorganization

Part of adolescents' emotional stress arises not from society but from within their own families. The United States now has the highest divorce rate of any country. According to 1985 figures, about one-half of the marriages of couples now 25 to 40 years of age will end in divorce (Norton and Moorman, 1987). Nearly two out of three of these divorces involve couples with children. The high divorce and separation rate, plus a rise in out-of-wedlock births, means that over one-half of all children born in the 1980s will spend a considerable amount of time living with only one parent (Hofferth, 1985). This usually means less contact with and support from their natural fathers (Amato, 1988). If parents remarry, the children have the added task of learning to live with a stepparent (Cherlin and McCarthy, 1985; Peterson and Zill, 1986).

Coming from a broken home has differential effects on adolescents (Wallerstein and Kelly, 1980). Some adolescents blame themselves and feel guilty and upset about the divorce (Young, 1980). However, the effect of divorce can be positive if it ends turmoil and upset in the family. Some adolescents whose parents have been divorced report that parental conflict and tension beforehand was more stressful than the divorce itself. These adolescents report fear of physical violence, social embarrassment because of parental strife, upset over financial hardships because of separations, and anxiety and confusion because of successive separations and reconciliations of parents. In such cases, divorce comes almost as a relief from years of strife. Thus, parental separation, as such, does not always result in traumatic experiences for children (Baydar, 1988).

The overall effect of divorce depends on the conditions of the divorce and on events before and after it (Bridgwater, 1984; Hodges, Tierney, and Buchsbaum, 1984). When there is little fighting between parents during and after the divorce, when the separation is amicable, and when the children have free access to both parents and a lot of support from parents, siblings, and friends, upset is kept to a minimum. Joint custody of children means that both parents are involved in parenting (Lowery and Settle, 1985), which has a positive effect (Bowman and Ahrons, 1985). The situation is different in a bitterly fought divorce involving disputes over property, alimony, child custody, and other matters. Children are particularly affected if parents try to get them to take sides or exploit them as pawns, scapegoats, go-betweens, spies, informers, manipulators, and allies in punishing the other parent. Postdivorce conflicts that go on for years increase children's anxiety (Booth, Brinkerhoff, and White, 1984; Johnston, Gonzalez and Campbell, 1987), irritability, aggressiveness, and a wide range of behavior disorders, neurotic conflicts, and psychotic breakdowns (Guidubaldi et al., 1986).

Several studies of children and adolescents found that those who had experienced father loss through divorce demonstrated significantly lower self-concepts than those who were from intact families (Boyd, Nunn, and Parish, 1983). This was true whether the mother had remarried or not. Whether these behaviors continue over the long-term is a matter of dispute (Amato, 1988; Kalter, 1983; Parish and Wigle, 1985). Another study (Parish, 1981) of college students revealed

Most youths face problems during adolescence; these stressful events include parental breakup, school problems, disappointments with relationships, a death in the family, and health problems. (Mimi Forsyth/Monkmeyer Press Photo Service)

that their evaluations of their parents were much lower after divorce, indicating they blamed their parents for what had happened. Divorce has also been found to be a factor in adolescents' leaving home (Moore and Hotch, 1982), in fewer years of schooling (Keith and Finlay, 1988; Krein and Beller, 1988), and in lower economic attainment (Mueller and Cooper, 1986). Research, however, casts some doubt on the claim that the divorce of parents is a cause of delinquency. There are too many variables to single out divorce as the reason. We know only that, other things being equal, a happy, unbroken home is better for adolescents than a happy, broken home and that both are better than an unhappy, unbroken home or an unhappy broken home. *When there is upset and conflict in the family of the adolescent, whether the parents divorce or remain unhappily married, the effect is disturbing* (Demo and Acock, 1988; Peterson and Zill, 1986). This is one reason why so many youths seek love, companionship, warmth, and intimacy with others outside their own families.

Life Events and Stress

There are other events in an adolescent's life besides social violence and family disruption that create stress: failure in school, being arrested by the police, getting into drugs or alcohol, losing a job, breaking up with a close girlfriend or boyfriend, getting pregnant, getting badly hurt or sick, or moving to a new home. Most youths face one or more of these problems during their adolescence or have close friends who do (Johnson, 1986). Table 1-5 lists various life change events and arranges them in order of decreasing stress as rated by adolescents on the *Adolescent Life Change Event Scale* (Yeaworth et al., 1980). A family member dying is

▓ TABLE 1-5

Adolescent life change event scale (ALCES).

RANK	LIFE CHANGE EVENT	LIFE CHANGE UNIT[a]
1	A parent dying	98
2	Brother or sister dying	95
3	Close friend dying	92
4	Parents getting divorced or separated	86
5	Failing one or more subjects in school	86
6	Being arrested by the police	85
7	Flunking a grade in school	84
8	Family member (other than yourself) having trouble with alcohol	79
9	Getting into drugs or alcohol	77
10	Losing a favorite pet	77
11	Parent or relative in your family (other than yourself) getting very sick	77
12	Losing a job	74
13	Breaking up with a close girlfriend or boyfriend	74
14	Quitting school	73
15	Close girlfriend getting pregnant	69
16	Parent losing a job	69
17	Getting badly hurt or sick	64
18	Hassling with parents	64
19	Trouble with teacher or principal	63
20	Having problems with any of the following: acne, overweight, underweight, too tall, too short	63
21	Starting a new school	57
22	Moving to a new home	51
23	Change in physical appearance (braces, glasses)	47
24	Hassling with brother or sister	46
25	Starting menstrual periods (for girls)	45
26	Having someone new move in with your family (grandparent, adopted brother or sister, or other)	35
27	Starting a job	34
28	Mother getting pregnant	31
29	Starting to date	31
30	Making new friends	27
31	Brother or sister getting married	26

[a]Figures rounded to the nearest whole number.

From: Yeaworth, R. C., York, J., Hassey, M. A., Ingle, M. E., and Goodwin, T. (Spring 1980). "The Development of an Adolescent Life Change Event Scale," *Adolescence*, 15, 93.

rated as most stressful, followed by parents getting divorced or separated. Problems at school, with the police, with drugs, at work, with girlfriends or boyfriends, or with health are also ranked high on the scale. Another study, with college undergraduates, revealed that death, illness, or accident of a loved one, followed by ill health, disappointments in friendships or love affairs, and being cut off from others were among the most disturbing events in life (Tolor, 1983).

ADOLESCENTS IN A PREVIOUS ERA: THE ROARING TWENTIES

Is the present situation unique? Or has there always been adult-youth conflict and tension? One way to find an answer is to take a look at adult-adolescent relationships in former times. The 1920s in the United States have been selected because of several parallels to current times.

Flaming Youth

flaming youth

In describing adult views of youth in the 1920s in *Wild Kids*, F. R. Donovan uses an expression that was then very much in vogue: **flaming youth.** Headlines read: "The Revolt of Youth," "Is Modern Youth Going to the Devil?" and "They Are Hell Bent." A suspected increase in juvenile delinquency brought such headlines as "80% of Crimes Committed by Boys." (The Children's Bureau subsequently reported some slight increase during World War I but an overall decrease for the period 1913 to 1923 and in some cases a reduction for 1924 and 1925) (Donovan, 1967, pp. 188, 189.) Although there was much talk of juvenile delinquency, most of the concern was with immorality and defiance of authority rather than with crime. Juveniles were said to have adopted a horrifying moral code of their own based on promiscuous sex, excessive drinking, indecent dress for the girls (the flapper dresses and short skirts), and lewd dancing (like the Charleston). The little hussies also painted their faces and puffed daringly on cigarettes. *Century Magazine* printed an article in 1921 that read in part:

> It seems that the young people have taken the bit between their teeth and are running wild. They are wholly contemptuous of the traditional controls and show no disposition to impose a speed limit upon themselves. Fond parents, maiden aunts, all the amateur censors of morals are at their wits' ends. They are shouting voluminous warnings after the runaways, but the pace only gets hotter. And the end is not in sight. . . .
>
> The elders of today are convinced that never before have the established and responsible members of society had to remonstrate against so many anarchic notions and such alarming behavior. No age, they say, has had on its hands such a problem of reckless and rebellious youth. (Davis, 1944)

Characteristically, the youths of that day also talked back in their own defense. College kids in particular were adept at throwing the ball back to their elders:

> I would like to observe that the older generation had certainly pretty much ruined this world before passing it on to us. They give us this Thing, knocked to pieces,

leaky, red-hot, threatening to blow up; and then they are surprised that we don't accept it with the same attitude of pretty, decorous enthusiasm with which they received it 'way back in the eighteen-nineties, nicely painted, smoothly running, practically foolproof. (Donovan, 1967, p. 195)

Sex Magazines and Movies

Nearly as much trash was written and sold in the 1920s as today. There was a bumper crop of sex magazines, confession magazines, and lurid motion picture magazines. A leading pulp magazine of the day, *Telling Tales*, featured these four stories: "Indolent Kisses," "Primitive Love," "Watch Your Step-Ins," and "Innocents Astray." The movies were doing a booming business with sex films. Clara Bow was the "It" girl. If you had "It" (sex appeal), you were in. If you did not have "It," you were out.

Psychologist Dorothy Bromley reflected the feelings of many adults of the 1920s when she wrote in her study, "Youth and Sex":

> The movies' direct influence on the new sex mores . . . is generally known. . . . For young men and girls who have not yet had time to discover the comparative scale of values which life offers, the lush sensuality of these shows, night after night, may be very disturbing. The movies have taken off the bed-room doors for young people and turned life into a French peep-show. (Bromley, 1967, p. 198)

Perhaps she had just as much basis for complaint as adults do today. Some of the movie titles were: *Sinners in Silk*, *Women Who Give*, *The Price She Paid*, *Queen of Sin*, *Rouged Lips*, and *Name the Man—a Story of Betrayed Womanhood*. A movie entitled *Flaming Youth* was advertised as offering "neckers, petters, white kisses, red kisses, pleasure mad daughters, sensation craving mothers. . . . the truth, bold, naked, sensational" (Donovan, 1967, p. 199).

The success of such sex exploitation movies prompted the office of Postmaster General Hayes under President Harding to promulgate a movie code that made it mandatory for every movie to have a moral ending. As a result movies continued to show all kinds of violence, crime, and sexual misconduct so long as virtue triumphed in the end.

Styles of Clothing and Dance

Apparently adults were also having trouble with youthful styles and fashions. The president of the University of Florida declared: "The rolled hose and short skirts are born of the Devil and his angels and are carrying the present and future generations to chaos and destruction" (Donovan, 1967, p. 202). As a result of the short skirts, one thousand clergymen were asked what they felt the standards were for moral dress. A special committee designed a "moral gown" with hemlines 7½ inches from the floor. (It was endorsed by ministers of fifteen denominations.) A number of state legislators proposed fines and imprisonment and laws to make short skirts illegal. None of these proposals worked: the brazen flapper continued to flaunt her kneecaps, and she won her freedom. (The revolt was over when mothers, following their daughters, started exposing their adult calves.)

There was a great deal of criticism of the dancing of the twenties, which was called by some "a syncopated embrace." It was performed to the primitive strains of the saxophone rather than the romantic melodies of the violin. The *Catholic Telegraph* said: "The music is sensuous, the embracing of the partners—the female only half dressed—is absolutely indecent" (Donovan, 1967, p. 204).

Problem Social Behavior

Parents were concerned about the social behavior of their youths. Petting parties had replaced the "spooning" of the previous generation. Boys and girls petted openly between and after dances, retiring to dark corners, lawns, or parks. One study revealed that one-half of all youths believed that nine out of every ten boys and girls of high school age had petting parties (Donovan, 1967, p. 204).

The use of contraceptives by youths of the twenties was a major scandal. Even the best hotels provided a slot machine in men's washrooms that sold contraceptive devices for a quarter.

Youthful drinking was another controversial aspect of adolescent behavior during the Roaring Twenties. Prohibition started with the Volstead Act on January 16, 1920. For a few years, drinking among young people declined. Then the speakeasy came into being. Many were expensive; the most famous, the Stork Club, catered chiefly to boys from the Ivy League colleges, to whom the proprietor sent cards of admission. Roadhouses opened everywhere and were hangouts for prostitutes. Rebellious youths carried the hip flask filled with liquor stolen from papa's bootleg liquor cabinet. One judge complained that "no petting party, no roadhouse toot, no joy ride from the prying eye of Main Street, is complete unless the boys carry flasks" (Donovan, 1967, p. 213).

Demise of Flaming Youth

Gradually the reverberations from the antics of "flaming youth" subsided. (The Great Depression probably eliminated some excesses: it was too expensive to party all the time.) H. L. Mencken, a cynic and liberal of his day, wrote a discourse in 1931 on the demise of flaming youth:

> The moral divagations of the youth of today do not differ three percent from those of the youth of yesterday. When I was a youngster . . . with Victoria in full blast upon her throne, great numbers of boys were diligent lushers, just as they are now: the only difference I can make out is that they drank beer . . . whereas they now have to put up with bootleg gin, which often makes them sick. . . . There was necking too. . . . In case the business goes farther than mere necking there is some ground, of course, for sociologists to intervene, but I doubt that it goes further today any oftener than it did yesterday. (Donovan, 1967, p. 214)

SUMMARY

A stereotype represents a commonly held conception or idea about a group of persons. Stereotypes are sometimes applied to adolescents, so that they are described according to preconceived ideas that are applied to all. But adolescents are as different as any other group of persons. The study of adolescents is a study of contrasts, change, and growth.

Studies of values of adolescents reveal some very positive images. One study found that the majority of adolescents said their major source of life satisfaction in the future would be their family life. There has also been an increase in interest in religion and a decrease in interest in community or national affairs and in recreation as a major source of life satisfaction. Other studies have revealed high idealism among many adolescents.

There has, however, been a decrease in activism as adolescents have become more unwilling to do something about world problems. They recognize serious concerns but feel there is nothing they can do to change things. This reflects an increase in cynicism and distrust in other people.

As a group, however, adolescents are not in mass rebellion against their parents and parental values. Most youth have great respect for their parents and show widespread agreement with parental values.

Adolescents are sometimes accused of being irresponsible and lazy. Many do not like to help out with chores around the house, but three-fourths of high school seniors have part-time jobs during the school year. Many work more than 15 to 20 hours a week in addition to going to school full-time, leading some authorities to feel they work too much, to the detriment of their school work, family life, and social life.

There are a number of important societal influences on adolescents. Those discussed in this chapter are technological and social change, urbanization, materialism and poverty, mass communications, social and emotional stress, family disorganization, and stress from life events.

Adults of every era tend to think their young people are problems and that the present generation is worse than any before or after. During the 1920s, adults called adolescents "flaming youth" and criticized the sex magazines and movies, styles of clothing and dance, and problem social behavior of their adolescents. The antics of youth subsided when the Depression eliminated some of the excesses.

SELECTED READINGS: ADOLESCENTS IN PREVIOUS ERAS
Colonial America

The puritan ethic of colonial America emphasized the importance of children obeying their parents. The goal of discipline was to break the child's will and to force children to submit to their superiors. The following rules for proper behavior were derived from English guides and were first reprinted in the colonies in 1715. Moody's version appeared in Boston in 1772 (Moody, 1772).

THE GOOD MANNERS CHECKLIST*
When at Home

1. Make a bow always when you come home, and be immediately uncovered. (remove headgear)

---

* From Moody, Eleazar. (1772). *The School of Good Manners, Composed for the Help of Parents in Teaching Their Children How to Carry It in Their Places During Their Minority* (Boston). Reprinted in *Children and Youth in America: A Documentary History*, Vol. I: 1600–1865, ed. Robert H. Bremner et al. (1970). (Cambridge, Mass.: Harvard University Press), pp. 33–34.

2. Never sit in the presence of thy parents without bidding, tho' no stranger be present.
3. If thou passest by thy parents, and any place where thou seest them, when either by themselves or with company, bow towards them.
4. If thou art going to speak to thy parents, and see them engaged in discourse with company, draw back and leave thy business until afterwards; but if thou must speak, be sure to whisper.
5. Never speak to thy parents without some title of respect, viz., Sir, Madam, etc.
6. Dispute not, nor delay to obey thy parents' commands.
7. Go not out of doors without thy parents' leave, and return within the time by them limited.
8. Come not into the room where thy parents are with strangers, unless thou art called, and then decently; and at bidding go out; or if strangers come in while thou art with them, it is manners with a bow to withdraw.
9. Use respectful and courteous but not insulting or domineering carriage or language toward the servants.
10. Quarrel not nor contend with thy brethren or sisters, but live in love, peace, and unity.
11. Grumble not nor be discontented at anything thy parents appoint, speak, or do.
12. Bear with meekness and patience, and without murmuring or sullenness, thy parents' reproofs or corrections: Nay, tho' it should so happen that they be causeless or undeserved.

In spite of the efforts of adults to control completely their children's behavior, the naturally high spirits and mischievousness of the young resulted in some "unseemly" behavior. The following letter to the editor might have been written today instead of in 1723 ("A Letter to the Editor," 1723).

TO OLD JANUS THE COURANTEER   March 11, 1723
SIR,

The extraordinary disturbance made at Mr. Gatchell's Dancing School in Hanover Street |Boston| may be thought worth taking notice of in your paper. On Thursday the 28th of February, a company of young lads who were denied admittance, after firing several volleys of oaths and curses, threatening to kill Mr. Gatchell and using abundance of obscene discourse not fit to be mentioned, they fell upon the glass windows, shattered them all to pieces, and broke one of the iron bars. On Monday night last, ten of them were brought before a Justice of the Peace, who was obliged to remove from his house to the Town-house, by reason of the great concourse of people. The lads owned they were there, but denied the fact. However, several witnesses being sworn against them, they were bound over to answer it at the sessions. 'Tis now grown too common for our children and youth to swear and curse in the streets, and to abuse with foul language, not only one another but their superiors. And this growing wickedness is certainly in great measure owing to the many servants brought from other countries, who seldom fail of ruining most of the children in the families where they live. But I leave others to propose a method for preventing or punishing these enormities and remain, Sir,

YOUR HUMBLE SERVANT, etc.

Nineteenth-Century Industrial United States

The way of life prescribed for young people in the nineteenth century was based on the ethic of thrift and unrelenting work. As a consequence, the transition from childhood to adulthood was brief and early compared with that of today. The Harvard student body was made up largely of boys aged fourteen and fifteen. Marriage by eighteen was the rule rather than the exception for young women. A British traveler comments on the early maturity of youth in the United States during the middle of the nineteenth century and on the materialistic philosophy by which they lived (Grattan, 1859).

BORN MIDDLE-AGED*
All Business

. . . Children soon go from the nursery to the schoolhouse. If they are boys they run through their boyhood with marvelous rapidity. A "Boston boy" is a melancholy picture of prematurity. It might be almost said that every man is born middle-aged in that and every other great city of the Union. The principal business of life seems to be to grow old as fast as possible. The boy, the youth, the young man are only anxious to hurry on to the gravity and the care of "the vale of tears." There is a velocity in their movements, as though the hill they mount were a mere molehill, and that their downward course commenced before the youth of other countries had gained a third of the upward path. The toils of life—the destiny of the poorer classes in Europe—form the free choice of the rich man of America, always excepting the indolent Southern planters.

The boys are sent to college at fourteen. They leave it with their degrees at about seventeen. They are then launched at once into life, either as merchants or attorneys' clerks, medical students or adventurers in the Western states of the Union, or in foreign countries. The interval between their leaving school and commencing their business career offers no occupation to give either gracefulness or strength to body or mind. Athletic games and the bolder field sports being unknown . . . I doubt if there exists an American gentleman who could take a horse over a three-foot rail in England or an Irish potato trench. Yet they constantly talk of such or such a one being "a good rider."

Young men made up of such materials as I describe are not young men at all. . . . Their chief ambition is to grow bald or gray. They are thought nothing of till that consummation happens. They think nothing of themselves. They know that till they become rich they have no influence; and there is nothing more absurd than those meetings called "Young Men's Conventions." They are a mockery. No act of theirs can be valid, for their title is a false one. The class I treat of feels this. They as soon as possible plunge into the cares of the world. They follow business like drudges, and politics with fierce ardor. They marry. They renounce partygoing. They give up all pretension in dress. They cannot force wrinkles and crow's-feet on their faces, but they assume and soon acquire a pursed-up, keen, and haggard look. Their air, manners, and conversation are alike contracted. They have no breadth, either of shoulders, information, or ambition. Their physical powers are subdued, and their mental capability cribbed into narrow limits. There is constant

---

* By Thomas C. Gratton.

activity going on in one small portion of the brain; all the rest is stagnant. The money-making faculty alone is cultivated. They are incapable of acquiring general knowledge on a broad or liberal scale. All is confined to trade, finance, law, and small, local, provincial information. Art, science, literature are nearly dead letters to them. But the foregoing opinions must be taken like all those given wholesale and on general concerns, with the usual "grain of salt," in this case a very large one.

Before the Civil War, most lived on farms where life was hard. Almost all work was done by hand. The young had to help along with adults, and the day was long. John Muir, a naturalist and writer, describes his boyhood on the farm (Muir, 1923).

FROM SUNUP TO SUNDOWN*

The summer work, on the contrary, was deadly heavy, especially harvesting and corn-hoeing. All the ground had to be hoed over for the first few years, before father bought cultivators or small weedcovering plows, and we were not allowed a moment's rest. The hoes had to be kept working up and down as steadily as if they were moved by machinery. Plowing for winter wheat was comparatively easy, when we walked barefooted in the furrows, while the fine autumn tints kindled in the woods and the hillsides were covered with golden pumpkins.

In summer the chores were grinding scythes, feeding the animals, chopping stove-wood, and carrying water up the hill from the spring on the edge of the meadow, etc. Then breakfast, and to the harvest or hayfield. I was foolishly ambitious to be first in mowing and cradling, and by the time I was sixteen led all the hired men. An hour was allowed at noon for dinner and more chores. We stayed in the field until dark, then supper, and still more chores, family worship, and to bed, making altogether a hard, sweaty day of about sixteen or seventeen hours. Think of that, ye blessed eight-hour-day laborers!

In winter father came to the foot of the stairs and called us at six o'clock to feed the horses and cattle, grind axes, bring in wood, and do any other chores required, then breakfast, and out to work in the mealy, frosty snow by daybreak, chopping, fencing, etc. So in general our winter work was about as restless and trying as that of the long-day summer. No matter what the weather, there was always something to do. During heavy rains or snowstorms we worked in the barn, shelling corn, fanning wheat, thrashing with the flail, making axe-handles or ox-yokes, mending things, or sprouting and sorting potatoes in the cellar.

The Industrial Revolution, with its need for cheap labor combined with the puritan gospel of work, provided a perfect rationale for exploitation of the young. Working conditions were unregulated, and it was not unusual for girls to work in textile mills for twelve or fourteen hours a day. They usually stayed in boardinghouses

---

* From *The Story of My Boyhood and Youth* by John Muir. Copyright 1912 and 1913 by the Atlantic Monthly Company. Copyright 1913 by John Muir. Copyright 1916 by Houghton Mifflin Company. Copyright renewed 1940 and 1941 by Wanda Muir Hanna. Reprinted by permission of Houghton Mifflin Company.

in town to be close to their work. The following excerpt describes a visit to the textile mills of New England ("A New Kind of Feudalism," 1836).

A NEW KIND OF FEUDALISM

We have lately visited the cities of Lowell [Massachusetts] and Manchester, New Hampshire, and have had an opportunity of examining the factory system more closely than before. In Lowell live between seven and eight thousand young women, who are generally daughters of farmers of the different states of New England; some of them are members of families that were rich the generation before. . . .

The operatives work thirteen hours a day in the summer time, and from daylight to dark in the winter. At half past four in the morning the factory bell rings, and at five the girls must be in the mills. A clerk, placed as a watch, observes those who are a few minutes behind the time, and effectual means are taken to stimulate to punctuality. This is the morning commencement of the industrial discipline (should we not rather say industrial tyranny?), which is established in these associations of this moral and Christian community. At seven the girls are allowed thirty minutes for breakfast, and at noon thirty minutes more for dinner, except during the first quarter of the year, when the time is extended to forty-five minutes. But within this time they must hurry to their boarding houses and return to the factory, and that through the hot sun, or the rain and cold. A meal eaten under such circumstances must be quite unfavorable to digestion and health, as any medical man will inform us. At seven o'clock in the evening the factory bell sounds the close of the day's work.

Thus thirteen hours per day of close attention and monotonous labor are exacted from the young women in these manufactories. . . . So fatigued—we should say, exhausted and worn out, but we wish to speak of the system in the simplest language—are numbers of the girls, that they go to bed soon after their evening meal, and endeavor by a comparatively long sleep to relieve their weakened frames for the toils of the coming day. When capital has got thirteen hours of labor daily out of a being, it can get nothing more.

Now let us examine the nature of the labor itself and the conditions under which it is performed. Enter with us into the large rooms, when the looms are at work. The largest that we saw is in the Amoskeag Mills at Manchester. It is 400 feet long and about 70 broad; there are 500 looms and 21,000 spindles in it. The din and clatter of these 500 looms under full operation struck us on first entering as something frightful and infernal, for it seemed such an atrocious violation of one of the faculties of the human soul, the sense of hearing. After a while we became somewhat inured to it, and by speaking quite close to the ear of an operative and quite loud, we could hold a conversation and make the inquiries we wished.

The girls attend upon an average three looms; many attend four, but this requires a very active person and the most unremitting care. However, a great many do it. Attention to two is as much as should be demanded of an operative. This gives us some idea of the application required during the thirteen hours of daily labor. The atmosphere of such a room cannot of course be pure; on the contrary it is charged with cotton filaments and dust, which, we are told, are very injurious to the lungs. On entering the room, although the day was warm, we remarked that the windows were down; we asked the reason, and a young woman answered very naively, and without seeming to be in the least aware that this privation of fresh air was anything else than perfectly natural, that "when the wind blew, the threads did not work so well." After we had been in the room for fifteen or twenty minutes, we found ourselves, as did the persons who accompanied us, in quite a perspiration, produced by a certain moisture which we observed in the air, as well as by the heat. . . .

The young women sleep upon an average six in a room, three beds to a room. There is no privacy, no retirement here; it is almost impossible to read or write alone, as the parlor is full and so many sleep in the same chamber. A young women remarked to us, that if she had a letter to write, she did it on the head of a bandbox, sitting on a trunk, as there was not space for a table. So live and toil the young women of our country in the boarding houses and manufactories which the rich and influential of our land have built for them.

Students of every generation find social evils and causes to protest against. If these causes are antiestablishment, society finds ways to punish its youth for their radicalism. During the early nineteenth century, students protested against slavery and spearheaded the abolition movement. The following excerpt describes student involvement in the effort to abolish slavery. One result of the efforts described was the student founding of Oberlin Institute (later a college) in Ohio and of other schools (Martineau, 1837).

THE STUDENT ABOLITION MOVEMENT*

The students of Lane Seminary, near Cincinnati, of which Dr. Beecher is the president, became interested in the subject |abolition| three or four years ago, and formed themselves into an Abolition Society, debating the question and taking in newspapers. This was prohibited by the tutors but persevered in by the young men, who conceived that this was a matter with which the professors had no right to meddle. Banishment was decreed, and all submitted to expulsion but fourteen. Of course, each of the dispersed young men became the nucleus of an Abolition Society and gained influence by persecution. It was necessary for them to provide means to finish their education.

One of them, Amos Dresser, |moved about| (as is usual in the sparsely peopled West), traveling in a gig and selling Scott's Bible to raise money for his educational purposes. He reached Nashville in Tennessee and there fell under suspicion of abolition treason, his baggage being searched and a whole abolition newspaper and a part of another being found among the packing-stuff of his Bibles. There was also an unsubstantiated rumor of his having been seen conversing with slaves.

He was brought to trial by the Committee of Vigilance, seven elders of the Presbyterian Church at Nashville being among his judges. After much debate as to whether he should be hanged, or flogged with more or fewer lashes, he was condemned to receive twenty lashes with a cowhide in the marketplace of Nashville. He was immediately conducted there, made to kneel down on the flint pavement, and punished according to his sentence, the mayor of Nashville presiding

---

* By Harriet Martineau.

and the public executioner being the agent. He was warned to leave the city within twenty-four hours, but was told by some charitable person who had the bravery to take him in, wash his stripes, and furnish him with a disguise that it would not be safe to remain so long. He stole away immediately, in his dreaded condition, on foot, and when his story was authenticated had heard nothing of his horse, gig, and Bibles, which he values at three hundred dollars.

The Jitterbug Era

Every adult generation criticizes its young for their music. Today's grandparents criticize their adolescent grandchildren for liking modern music and for their desire to attend rock concerts, forgetting that they themselves loved to go to big-band concerts to hear jazz and swing during the jitterbug era. The following excerpt from *The New York Times* in 1943 describes the gathering to hear Harry James, the new big-band idol and trumpeter, in concert in New York (Berger, 1943).

GATHERING OF THE HEPCATS*

The peculiar behavior of jitterbugs, chiefly but not entirely adolescents, who have swarmed to the Paramount Theater [in New York City] to sigh and all but swoon over the trumpeting of the band leader Harry James, continued yesterday to the disgust and amazement of police and puzzled adult passersby.

Yesterday, as on Tuesday, lines formed outside the theater in the predawn hours. Some of the boys and girls were there at four o'clock in the morning. By 9 A.M. the line reached westward to Eighth Avenue and doubled back on itself along its entire length to Seventh. Thirty patrolmen . . . and three mounted policemen rode herd on the jitterbugs. The children were good-natured and never disorderly, but their tenseness and their strange yearning for "hot music" bewildered the police.

Most of the jitterbugs wore the strange garb affected by the breed. Some were no more than twelve or thirteen years old, which is under legal age for admission to a theater without adult escort. The police cut some 75 minors out of line and sent them home. A police sergeant estimated that some 7,500 children were in line by 9 o'clock. The figure included those who were admitted at 7:30 A.M., which is one hour ahead of regular opening time. During this period, when the jitterbugs are in full swing, the theater gives seven shows a day instead of five.

The children all seemed clean, bright-faced, and alert, but they also seemed inarticulate when they were asked what brought in such swarms to hear a trumpeter.

"You can't really tell what it is," the consensus seemed to be. "It's only that shivers run down your spine when that trumpet gets hot."

In the line, questioning developed, were children from fairly remote communities in New Jersey and Westchester County. Some had written to the theater a week in advance to learn what time each show went on. Many brought their lunch or lived on chocolate bars in order to stay through three, four, or five shows.

---

* Berger, Meyer. (1943, April 23). "Jitterbugs Again Swarm to See Their 'Hot Music' Idol in Person," *The New York Times*. Copyright © 1943 by The New York Times Company. Reprinted by permission.

. . . A *clean blond youth* [20 years old], who is a machinist's helper, confided that he had sacrificed eleven hours' work at 75 cents an hour in order to sit all day listening to the jitterbug music. [Another boy] . . . , wearing the most extreme cut and rig of the jitterbug—the porkpie hat, the fingertip coat, and the tight-bottomed trousers, said he had begged his boss in a Harlem . . . grocery store to let him off for the day. He lost five dollars in salary, but said it was worth it.

. . . Children who had sat through several performances on Tuesday waited all day at the stage door for a glimpse of Harry James, who is a rather ordinary-looking chap, . . . but their god of the moment.

"We just want to see him, maybe shake his hand," one of the girl devotees told reporters simply. "He's wonderful."

This seemed to be the general attitude. It was carried one degree further by a girl who stood in silent worship before the trumpeter's picture in the lobby. . . .

Inside the theater observers noted the adolescents in a semihypnotic state when James appeared on stage bathed in a mystic blue light. Girls whispered his name, shifted restlessly in their seats, clasped their hands tightly.

When children in the audience were asked why they were so moved at sight of Mr. James and by the sounds from his trumpet, they seemed puzzled. To them the answer was simple.

"He gets you," they'd say, "but you feel it more when you're up close in the front rows. It does something to your blood. If you were a hepcat, you'd understand."

The music from the trumpet seemed quite ordinary, no different from any blare and bray of the usual jazz band, but this apparently was due to some defect in the adult makeup. The children could not understand why adults were so unmoved by it.

At some points in the program the entire audience clapped hands or stamped with their feet in strange beat, following the trumpet's and the saxophones' rhythm. They swayed or bobbed in their seats and you could hear the children nearby breathe, "Come on Harry," an appeal to the trumpeter.

DISCUSSION QUESTIONS

1. How do adults today generally feel about adolescents? Answer the question by describing the attitudes of some adults whom you know.

2. Why do some adults dislike adolescents?

3. Describe the values of some adolescents whom you know. What values would you affirm yourself, and which ones would you personally reject?

4. Is there much youth activism on this campus? Why? or Why not? Why do some youth feel they cannot do anything personally about social problems? Do you feel the individual makes any differences in changing things?

5. Would you describe your personal feelings

about the world as cynical or optimistic? Explain. How would you describe your feelings about your own personal future?

6. Describe your relationships with your parents. What parental values do you accept and what ones do you reject? Explain.

7. In what ways are the adolescents whom you know responsible and in what ways are they irresponsible?

8. What have been the most important social changes during the years you have been growing up? (Consider important changes in customs, manners, mores, values, attitudes, habit systems, and activities in your personal life and in social groups, organizations, and institutions.) How have these changes affected your life?

9. In what ways have television, radio, movies, and other mass media influenced (1) your outlook on life and society and (2) your own personality and emotional security?

10. Do you feel or not feel that there has been a great deal of stress in your life as you have grown up? What have been the major sources of that stress? How has it affected you?

11. In what ways were the "Roaring Twenties" similar to life today?

12. Compare the rules of etiquette in "The Good Manners Checklist" with the rules parents establish for adolescents today. What system do you feel is better for the adolescent?

13. Comment on the life of youths in the nineteenth century as revealed in the passages that describe life in the rural United States and in the factories of New England. How did adolescent life then compare to now? Were there any advantages to this type of life over the lives of adolescents today?

BIBLIOGRAPHY

Amato, P. R. (1988). "Long-term Implications of Parental Divorce for Adult Self-Concept." *Journal of Family Issues*, 9, 201–213.

Atkinson, R. (1988a). "Respectful, Dutiful Teenagers." *Psychology Today*, 22, 22–26.

Atkinson, R. (1988b). *Teenage World: Adolescent Self-Image in Ten Countries*. New York: Plenum.

Bachman, J. G., Johnston, L. D., and O'Malley, P. M. (1987). *Monitoring the Future: Questionnaire Responses from the Nation's High School Seniors, 1986*. Ann Arbor, MI.: Institute for Social Research.

Balswick, J. K., and Balswick, J. (Fall, 1980). "Where Have All the Alienated Students Gone?" *Adolescence*, 15, 691–697.

Baydar, N. (1988). "Effects of Parental Separation and Reentry Into Union on the Emotional Well-Being of Children." *Journal of Marriage and the Family*, 50, 967–981.

Berger, M. (April 23, 1943) "Jitterbugs Again Swarm to See Their 'Hot Music' Idol in Person." *New York Times*, p. 19.

Booth, A., Brinkerhoff, D. B., and White, L. K. (February, 1984). "The Impact of Parental Divorce on Courtship." *Journal of Marriage and the Family*, 46, 85–94.

Bowman, M. E., and Ahrons, C. R. (May, 1985). "Impact of Legal Custody Status on Fathers' Parenting Postdivorce." *Journal of Marriage and the Family*, 47, 481–488.

Boyd, D., Nunn, G., and Parish, T. (1983). "Effects of Marital Status and Parental Marital Status on Evaluation of Self and Parents." *Journal of Social Psychology*, 119, 229–234.

Bridgwater, C. (July, 1984). "Divorce: The Long-term Effects on Children." *Psychology Today*, 18, 9.

Bromley, Dorothy. (1967). "Youth and Sex." In F. R. Donovan. *Wild Kids*. Harrisburg, Pa.: Stackpole Co.

Chance, P. (1988). "Fast Track to Puberty." *Psychology Today*, 22, 26.

Cherlin, A., and McCarthy, J. (February, 1985). "Remarried Couple Households: Data from the June 1980 Current Population Survey." *Journal of Marriage and the Family*, 47, 23–30.

Cole, S. (July, 1980). "Send Our Children to Work?" *Psychology Today*, 44ff.

Csizkszentmihalyi, M., and Larson, R. (1984). *Being Adolescent*. New York: Basic Books.

Dalsimer, K. (1986). *Female Adolescence*. New Haven: Yale University Press.

Davis, Katherine. (1944). "Adolescence and the Social Structures." *Annals of the American Academy of Political and Social Science*, 263, 1–168.

Demo, D. H., and Acock, A. C. (1988). "The Impact of Divorce on Children." *Journal of Marriage and the Family*, 50, 619–648.

Diegmueller, K. (1987). "The Violent Killings of Youths: An Adolescent Fact of Death." *Insight*, 3, 18–20.

Doan, M. (January, 1985). "As the Video Craze Captures U.S. Families." *U.S. News & World Report*, 28, 58, 59.

Donovan, F. R. (1967). *Wild Kids*. Harrisburg, Pa: Stackpole Co.

Falchikov, N. (1986). "Images of Adolescence: An Investigation into the Accuracy of the Image of Adolescence, Constructed by British Newspapers." *Journal of Adolescence*, 9, 167–180.

Farrow, P. (Spring, 1978). "The Presymposial State." *Andover Review*, 5, 14–37.

Garbarino, J. (February, 1980). "Some Thoughts on School Size and Its Effects on Adolescent Development." *Journal of Youth and Adolescence*, 9, 19–31.

Goleman, D. (August, 1980). "Leaving Home: Is There a Right Time to Go?" *Psychology Today*, 52ff.

Grattan, T. C. (1859). *Civilized America*. Vol. 2. London: Bradbury and Evans.

Greenberger, E., and Steinberg, L. (1981). "The Workplace as a Context for the Socialization of Youth." *Journal of Youth and Adolescence*, 10, 185–210.

Guidubaldi, J., Cleminshaw, H. K., Perry, J. D., Nastasi, B. K., and Lightel, J. (1986). "The Role of Selected Family Environment Factors in Children's Post-Divorce Adjustment." *Family Relations*, 35, 141–151.

Hodges, W. F., Tierney, C. W., and Buchsbaum, H. K. (August, 1984). "The Cumulative Effect of Stress on Preschool Children of Divorced and Intact Families." *Journal of Marriage and the Family* 46, 611–617.

Hofferth, S. L. (February 1985). "Updating Children's Life Course." *Journal of Marriage and the Family*, 47, 93–115.

Johnson, J. H. (1986). *Life Events As Stressors in Childhood and Adolescence*. Beverly Hills, CA.: Sage.

Johnston, J. R., Gonzalez, R., and Campbell, L.E.G. (1987). "Ongoing Postdivorce Conflict and Child Disturbance." *Journal of Abnormal Child Psychology*, 15, 443–509.

Johnston, L. D., O'Malley, P. M., and Bachman, J. G. (1987). *National Trends in Drug Use and Related Factors Among American High School Students and Young Adults, 1975–1986*. Washington, D. C.: U.S. Government Printing Office.

Kalter, N. (1983). "How Children Perceive Divorce." *Medical Aspects of Human Sexuality*, 17, 18–45.

Keith, V. M., and Finlay, B. (1988). "The Impact of Parental Divorce on Children's Educational Attainment, Marital Timing, and Likelihood of Divorce." *Journal of Marriage and the Family*, 50, 797–809.

Krein, S. F., and Beller, A. H. (1988). "Educational Attainment of Children from Single-Parent Families: Differences by Exposure, Gender, and Race." *Demography*, 25, 221.

"A Letter to the Editor." (March 11, 1723). *New England Courant*.

Lloyd, L. (April 26, 1981). "College Students Flock Back to Church." *Philadelphia Inquirer*, 1, 10.

Loeb, P. (1988). "Willful Unconcern." *Psychology Today*, 22, 59–62.

Lowery, C. R., and Settle, S. A. (1985). "Effects of Divorce on Children: Differential Impact of Custody and Visitation Patterns." *Family Relations*, 34, 455–463.

Manning, M. L. (Winter, 1983). "Three Myths Concerning Adolescence." *Adolescence*, 18, 823–829.

Martineau, H. (1837). *Society in America*. New York and London: Sanders and Otley.

McFalls, J. A., Jones, B. J., Gallagher, B. J. III, and Rivera, J. (1985). "Political Orientation and Occupational Values of College Youth, 1969 and 1981: A Shift Toward Uniformity." *Adolescence*, 20, 696–713.

Miller, D. (1974). *Adolescence: Psychology, Psychopathology, and Psychotherapy*. New York: Jason Aronson.

Moody, Eleazar. (1970). *The School of Good Manners, Composed for the Help of Parents in Teaching Their Children How to Carry It in Their Places During Their Minority*. Boston, 1772, pp. 17–19. Reprinted in *Children and Youth in America: A Documentary History*. Vol. 1, 1600–1865. Edited by Robert H. Bremner et al. Cambridge, Mass.: Harvard University Press.

Moore, D., and Hotch, D. F. (April, 1982). "Parent-Adolescent Separation: The Role of Parental Divorce." *Journal of Youth and Adolescence*, 11, 115–119.

Mueller, D. P., and Cooper, P. W. (1986). "Children of Single Parent Families: How They Fare as Young Adults." *Family Relations*, 35, 169–176.

Muir, John (1923). *The Story of My Boyhood and Youth*. Boston: Houghton Mifflin.

The National Association of Secondary School Principals (1984). *The Mood of American Youth*. Reston, VA.: The National Association of Secondary School Principals.

National Commission on Excellence in Education (1983). *A Nation at Risk: The Imperative for Educational Reform*. Washington, D. C.: U.S. Government Printing Office.

"A New Kind of Feudalism." (November 14, 1836). *Harbinger*.

Newman, J. (1985). "Adolescents: Why They Can Be So Obnoxious." *Adolescence*, 20, 635–646.

Norman, M. (December, 1984). "Growing Up Rich: Problems in the Fast Lane." *Psychology Today*, 18, 70.

Norton, A. J., and Moorman, J. E. (1987). "Current Trends in Marriage and Divorce Among American Women." *Journal of Marriage and the Family*, 49, 3–14.

Otto, L. B. (1988). "America's Youth: A Changing Profile." *Family Relations*, 37, 385–391.

Parish, T. S. (Fall, 1981). "The Impact of Divorce on the Family." *Adolescence*, 16, 577–580.

Parish, T. S., and Wigle, S. E. (Spring, 1985). "A Longitudinal Study of the Impact of Parental Divorce on Adolescents' Evaluation of Self and Parents." *Adolescence*, 20, 239–244.

Peterson, J. L., and Zill, N. (1986). "Marital Disruption, Parent-Child Relationships and Behavior Problems in Children." *Journal of Marriage and the Family*, 48, 295–307.

"Report Finds Teenagers 'Chasing the American Dream.'" (Fall 1981): T.C. *Today*, 10, 1, 2.

Roscoe, B. (1985). "Social Issues as Social Problems: Adolescents' Perceptions." *Adolescence*, 20, 377–383.

Rubenstein, C. (May 1981). "Money and Self-Esteem, Relationships, Secrecy, Envy, and Satisfaction." *Psychology Today*, 29ff.

Rutter, M. (1980). *Changing Youth in a Changing Society*. Cambridge, MA.: Harvard University Press.

Schroth, R. (November-December, 1982). "Hope for an Unnamed Generation." *Academe*, 16–20.

Simmons, C. V., and Wade, W. B. (1985). "A Comparative Study of Young People's Ideals in Five Countries." *Adolescence*, 20, 889–898.

Steinberg, L., Greenberger, E., Garduque, L., Ruggiero, M., and Vaux, A. (1982). "Effects of Early Work Experience on Adolescent Development." *Developmental Psychology*, 18, 385–395.

Tolor, A. (Fall, 1983). "A Perception of Quality of Life of College Students and Their Faculty," *Adolescence* 18, 585–594.

U.S. Bureau of the Census (1987). *Statistical Abstract of the United States*, 1987. Washington, D. C.: U.S. Government Printing Office.

Wallerstein, J. B., and Kelly, J. S. (1980). *Surviving the Breakup: How Children and Parents Cope with Divorce*. New York: Basic Books.

Willis, M. R. (Winter, 1981). "The Maligning of Adolescence: Why?" *Adolescence*, 16, 953–958.

Yankelovich, D. (April, 1981). "New Rules in American Life: Searching for Self-Fulfillment in a World Turned Upside Down." *Psychology Today*, 35ff.

Yeaworth, R. C., York. J., Hassey, M. A., Ingle, M. E., and Goodwin, T. (Spring, 1980). "The Development of an Adolescent Life Change Event Scale." *Adolescence*, 15, 91–97.

Young, D. M. (Winter, 1980). "A Court-Mandated Workshop for Adolescent Children of Divorcing Parents: A Program Evaluation." *Adolescence*, 15, 763–774.

Yudkin, M. (April, 1984). "When Kids Think the Unthinkable." *Psychology Today*, 18, 18–25.

CHAPTER

2

Cultural Diversity

One of the greatest myths about adolescents is that they are all alike. This is not true. Adolescents cannot be discussed as one homogeneous group any more than any other age group. Not only do they come from a wide variety of ethnic and cultural backgrounds, but the environments in which they are raised are different, and the circumstances of their lives are quite variable.

Many sections of this book refer to cultural differences among adolescents. Differences between low socioeconomic status and middle-class adolescents are highlighted, as are some differences between black and white adolescents. Unfortunately, however, much of the research with adolescents has been conducted with white, middle-class youths. Although these are the majority, they are not representative of all. So before we get into more detailed discussion of various aspects of adolescence, it seems appropriate to select some representative minority groups to emphasize the wide cultural diversity that exists among them.

The discussion concerns six major groups: (1) low socioeconomic status adolescents of whatever race or national origin, (2) black adolescents, (3) Mexican-American adolescents, (4) Chinese-American adolescents, (5) Native American adolescents and (6) Southeast Asian adolescents. The chapter begins with a definition of low socioeconomic status. Who are the low socioeconomic status young people? What are the special limitations imposed upon their lives? How is the cycle of poverty and deprivation perpetuated from generation to generation? The chapter goes on to discuss some of the characteristics and problems of low socioeconomic status adolescents.

Following this general discussion of low socioeconomic status adolescents, the chapter discusses in detail black, Mexican-American, Chinese-American, Native American, and Southeast Asian adolescents. Such factors as discrimination, segregation, housing, education, employment, and income are explored. Some of the parental and cultural values of Mexican-American, Chinese-American, Native American, and Southeast Asian adolescents are highlighted to show the difficulties in socialization and the cultural conflicts that beset youths of these four minority groups.

The low socioeconomic status category cuts across many national and ethnic boundaries, reaching into 13 percent of U.S. homes. Black adolescents constitute the largest single minority group; Mexican-Americans comprise the second largest minority group. Puerto Rican Americans, the third largest minority, are not included in this discussion. Instead, Native American adolescents have been selected because they constitute the most deprived minority group and because, as the only native Americans, they too need to be better understood. Chinese-Americans are included as representative of the total group of Asian-Americans. Southeast Asians are our newest immigrants and have special problems as refugees from war.

LOW SOCIOECONOMIC STATUS ADOLESCENTS

low
socioeconomic
status
Various terms have been applied to youths who are of lower social classes and also poor: disadvantaged, culturally deprived, educationally deprived, low socioeconomic status, and working class. The term **low socioeconomic status** has been

selected here because it refers to two important aspects of the living condition: low social class and status, including cultural deprivation, and low income. Obviously, not all "lower-class" youths are poor, nor are all low-income youths culturally deprived, even though the two aspects frequently go together. However, this chapter emphasizes both lower social class and low income.

Low socioeconomic status adolescents grow up in 13 percent of American families classified as poor (U.S. Dept. of Commerce, 1987). In comparison with the general population, they are more often from non-white families; have less education, fewer wage earners, and more female heads; and are from larger than average families. They reside more often in the South, in farm areas, or in cities and less often in rural nonfarm or suburban areas. By definition, they are also culturally deprived, with only limited access to leisure facilities, educational advantages, work opportunities, health and medical care, proper living conditions, and many of the values, attitudes, customs, institutions, and organizations characteristic of the large masses of middle-class Americans.

Limitations of Low Socioeconomic Status

These circumstances impose four important limitations upon the lives of low socioeconomic status adolescents.

Limited Alternatives   These youth have not been exposed to a variety of social and cultural settings. Vocationally they have fewer opportunities, confront less complex situations on the job, and have fewer, less diverse standards to meet. Socially they are the nonjoiners, seldom going beyond the borders of kinship and neighborhood groups. Their limited experience and knowledge make it difficult to get out of or go beyond the narrow world in which they were brought up. Limited vision and experience limit the possibilities and opportunities in their lives.

Helplessness, Powerlessness   In the working world, their skills are limited, they can exercise little autonomy or influence in improving their conditions, they have little opportunity or knowledge to receive additional training, and they are the most easily replaced workers. They have little political or social influence in their communities and, sometimes, inadequate legal protection of their rights as citizens.

Deprivation   They are aware of the affluence around them and the achievements of and benefits received by others, but their situation makes them constantly aware of their own abject status and "failure," resulting in bitterness, embarrassed withdrawal and isolation, or social deviation and rebellion.

Insecurity   They are at the mercy of life's unpredictable events: sickness, loss of work, injury, legal problems, school difficulties, family difficulties, and others. They strive for security because they never feel certain about their own lives. They strive just to provide themselves with the basic necessities of life (Dill et al., 1980).

Cycle of Poverty and Deprivation

The net effect of the limitations imposed upon the lives of low socioeconomic status youths is to perpetuate poverty and cultural deprivation. Figure 2-1 illustrates this cycle of poverty and cultural deprivation.

The cycle begins at the top with the low level of education. Moving clockwise, little education results in a low income, which results in a low level of living, which results in limited ability to manage or control the external environment (the limited alternatives and powerlessness already mentioned). In turn the adolescents are socialized to expect low education, level of living, and powerlessness; their whole orientation serves to perpetuate the life-style to which they have become accustomed.

FIGURE 2-1

The cycle of poverty and cultural deprivation.

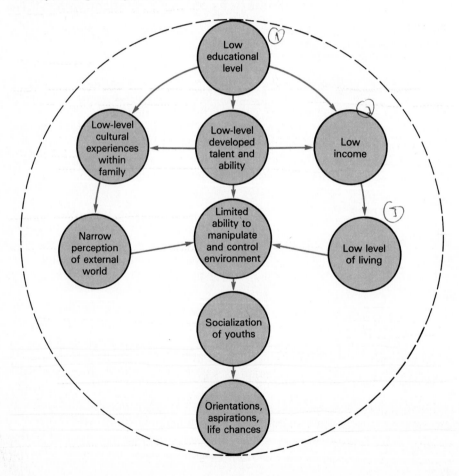

Starting at the top again and moving counterclockwise, the low level of education results in a low level of developed talent and ability and a low level of cultural experiences in the family. This in turn results in a narrow perception of the external world, which, along with the low level of living, contributes to limited ability to manage and control their environment. Because of the limitations imposed upon them, parents in turn teach their children not to expect a very high income, level of living, or much education. Low socioeconomic status adolescents tend to be caught in a self-perpetuating cycle of poverty and cultural deprivation.

Family Instability

Partly as a result of hasty early marriages (Booth and Edwards, 1985), economic struggles, and a long list of other factors, low socioeconomic status families are much more unstable than higher-class ones (Larson, 1984). The rates of divorce and separation increase as one goes down the socioeconomic scale (Rank, 1987). Illegitimacy rates also are higher among those of lower socioeconomic status groups, particularly among non-whites (Gabriel and McAnarney, 1983; Roosa, Fitzgerald and Carlson, 1982). Table 2-1 shows the rates. These figures are of concern because they represent a large number of youths growing up without the benefit of a stable, two-parent family.

Female-Headed Household

Female-headed households are prevalent and persistent among the poor (Franklin, 1988; Scheirer, 1983). Research indicates that although a single-parent family may not be entirely disadvantageous (a father may be a financial burden or a source of friction), the overall effects of the absence or only occasional presence of a father are detrimental to the emotional and social development of some adolescents. The difficulties appear in oedipal conflict, overdependence on the mother, and lack of models in the development of masculine and feminine roles. There also may be more unsatisfactory peer-group relations than among other youths and more feelings of inferiority and insecurity. There is evidence that some adolescents react as if it is their fault that their father is absent. Sometimes they have a poor self image and feel unlovable and self-derogating (Watson and Protinsky,

TABLE 2-1

Birthrate of unmarried women, 15 to 44 years as percentage of all births in racial groups, 1950–1984.

GROUP	1984	1981	1975	1970	1965	1960	1950
All unmarried females	31.0	29.6	24.5	26.4	23.5	21.6	14.1
Whites	20.1	18.2	12.4	13.8	11.6	9.2	6.1
Non-Whites	71.4	75.4	79.0	89.9	97.6	98.3	71.2

From: U.S. Bureau of the Census, Department of Commerce (1987). Statistical Abstract of the United States, 1987 (Washington, D.C.: U.S. Government Printing Office), p. 61.

1988). These young people may see the love relationship between sexes as irregular and unstable. In addition, most young adults raised by single parents (primarily single mothers) tend to have lower educational, occupational, and economic attainment (Krein, 1986; Mueller and Cooper, 1986).

Working Mothers

Large numbers of low socioeconomic status mothers must work, even in intact families (Slesinger, 1980). A part-time work commitment apparently has a relatively stable and positive effect upon girls from intact working-class families. What about mothers who work full time? Girls from these low socioeconomic status families often show strong affection for and strong dependency on the mother. They may show premature seriousness, somewhat more responsibility for housekeeping tasks than do adolescents of nonworking mothers, and intense loyalty and strong emotional ties to the family. Like middle-class girls, however, they do not spend their leisure time with their family. They find a boyfriend and emotional satisfaction outside the family.

What is the effect of maternal employment on adolescent boys? The boys of part-time working mothers of the working-class group exhibit patterns that resemble those of the girls in this group: they are often active, responsible, and mature. But the sons of full-time working mothers become more concerned with financial problems and may feel that their mother's working implies something is wrong with the father as provider. The father does not serve as an effective ideal, and the son less often chooses the father as a model (Carlson and Iovini, 1985). Some of these boys are rebellious toward adult authority and show signs of poor ego integration. They usually date heavily, which may reflect a lack of emotional security derived from the family. They do not have part-time jobs as often as other boys, nor do they have many organizational ties or leisure engagements.

Child-Rearing Goals and Philosophies

Lower socioeconomic status families tend to be hierarchical, evidencing rigid parental relationships with adolescents. The parents are repeatedly seen as closed or inaccessible to the adolescent's communication. The atmosphere is one of imperatives and absolutes, physical violence, and psychological distance, if not rejection, by the adults. Parent-child interaction patterns are rigid and oriented toward maintaining order, obedience, and discipline (Jacob, 1974). The discipline seems to be impulsive, harsh, inconsistent, and to emphasize physical punishment (even of adolescents) rather than verbal explanations and requests (Gecas and Nye, 1974). As a group, adolescents from low socioeconomic status families report more problems with parents than do those from more privileged families (Harper and Collins, 1975).

It is certain that such parents mean well. They usually want to bring up their children to live decent, obedient, honest lives. They want their children to rise above them economically, and a good report card from school seems to promise upward movement. There is a great deal of concern over obedience, respect for adults, conformity to externally imposed standards, and staying out of trouble.

The lower-class parent is concerned with overt behavior, with the immediate situation, and not with what behavior means in terms of future development. There is little concern for personality growth or for desirable child-rearing goals such as the development of creativity, curiosity, independence, or self-direction. Greater family control is exercised over adolescent daughters than sons, which is why many girls use marriage as an escape from home (Gecas and Nye, 1974).

In large families especially, parents seem to lack the time and will to control and give attention to their children as they get older. The mother is preoccupied with a new baby, leaving the adolescents feeling left out and rejected. When problems arise with the adolescents, the parents feel hurt, bewildered, and powerless to remedy the situation. Frequently the attitude of parents is, "We've done the best we could. You've made your bed; now you'll have to lie in it. There is nothing I can do." Their fatalistic attitude of accepting what comes is evident in the child-rearing task.

Among lower socioeconomic status youths, physical, social, and emotional emancipation from the family comes early and is often abrupt and psychologically premature. Adolescents do not yet feel ready or prepared to take their place in an adult world. Their social and emotional needs foster excessively dependent relationships with peers during the transition period from youth to adulthood.

Peer Orientation

Because adolescents from low socioeconomic status families tend to maintain weaker ties with parents than do youths from middle-class families, they form stronger, more lasting peer relationships. Those who report a low evaluation of parents and low self-esteem tend to be more peer oriented than those who have a high evaluation of parents (DiCindio, et al., 1983). This may be for at least two reasons.

One, *adolescents do not gain status through their familial identifications*. Their parents may be "nobodies"; they do not feel important because their mothers or fathers are professors, doctors, and business people. They feel keenly their parents' lack of status in the community, and therefore, their own lack of status. If their mother has a bad reputation in the adult society, the adolescents' status is likewise threatened. Thus, the adolescents can establish status only in relationship to their friends, by being tougher, wilder, sexier, funnier, or more daring than others. It has been found that adolescent boys with inadequate fathers have a special need to find peer approval as good guys or tough guys (Starr, 1981). Juvenile gangs evolve partly out of a need for status, identity, and recognition. Particular groups are formed on the basis of ethnic identity, a neighborhood locale, or a common purpose. When a group in an achievement-oriented society cannot gain status in socially acceptable ways, theft, extortion, narcotics, assault, sex, vandalism, or other antisocial expressions may become the means of gaining status and recognition. The peer group replaces the family as the adolescent's primary reference group.

The importance of the peer group apparently carries into adulthood. The tendency to seek friendships with those outside the family continues as part of the leisure pattern of the low socioeconomic status male, who prefers going "out with the boys." Such associations give him the same feelings of status, security, and virility that he needed in his youth. The more he is criticized by his wife, rejected by his children, or in other ways loses status at home, the more he turns to his buddies for recognition.

The second reason why low socioeconomic status adolescents become more peer oriented than parent oriented is their need for security. Physically, and perhaps psychologically, adults have left them. They feel a lack of communication and contact with adults and turn to their peers to find physical protection, mutual security, and emotional satisfaction. In the ghetto they need their gangs to protect lives; outside crime neighborhoods, they need their gangs for companionship, direction, and fulfillment.

Social Outcasts

Many low socioeconomic status adolescents are socialized differently from middle-class youths. They have their own manner of dress, speech, and behavior. Those who seem loud, ill mannered, or aggressive are scorned by middle-class society. Low self-esteem, shyness, and withdrawal keep others away from many social functions and groups. Inappropriate clothing and inadequate neatness and cleanliness invite criticism.

Ordinarily school is an important part of the social world of the adolescent. But prejudicial treatment by middle-class adults and students makes the low socioeconomic status adolescents social outcasts. They are likely to find themselves more and more socially isolated as they proceed through the grades and as a result tend to seek friendships with out-of-school youths. Sometimes the association with other out-of-school youths influences adolescents to drop out of school.

Mental Health

The lack of emotional security and stability in lower-class homes and particular patterns of child rearing gives rise to a high rate of psychological problems and mental illness among adolescents (See special issue: Journal of Adolescence (June 1988), 11). The incidence of schizophrenia, the most common psychosis of adolescents as well as adults, is significantly associated with social class. Furthermore, once hospitalized, low socioeconomic status adolescents are less likely to receive adequate treatment; are less often accepted for psychotherapy (partly due to a lower IQ level); are assigned less skilled staff members; are treated for shorter periods with less intensive techniques; and are less likely to improve in psychotherapy (Riessman et al., 1964).

BLACK ADOLESCENTS

Legacy of Discrimination

For generations, black families, especially those of lower class, were forced to assume an inferior role in order to get along in white society. Getting along in those days meant sitting in the back of the bus, avoiding all "white only" restaurants, rest rooms, recreational facilities, theaters, and playgrounds. Black parents had to teach their children the black role. As one mother bluntly put it, "You have to let them know before they get out of their own backyard." Black children left their homes for school at their peril if they had not learned where they could sit and what they could or could not do if they got hungry or thirsty. At five, just as surely as at fifteen or twenty-five, they had to know their place. Also one of the important lessons to learn was that no matter how unjustly they were treated, they must control anger and conceal hostility. They must be subservient, polite in the face of provocation, and walk with eyes straight ahead, unmoved by taunts and jeers. Above all, they must ignore insults and never argue or get in a fight with a white person. Black parents felt they must use severe measures to inculcate fear in their children as their best protection, or else white society would punish them more severely.

Richard Wright wrote of his "first lesson in how to live as a Negro." He had become involved in a fight with white boys who threw bottles at him and his friends; he was badly cut.

> I sat brooding on my front steps, nursing my wound and waiting for my mother to come home from work. . . . I could just feel in my bones that she would understand. . . . I grabbed her hand and babbled out the whole story. She examined my wound, then slapped me.
>
> "How come yuh didn't hide?" she asked me. "How come yuh always fightin?"
>
> I was outraged and bawled. Between sobs I told her that I didn't have any trees or hedges to hide behind. . . .
>
> She grabbed a barrel stave, dragged me home, stripped me naked, and beat me till I had a fever of one hundred and two. She would smack my rump with the stave, and, while the skin was still smarting, impart to me gems of Jim Crow wisdom. I was never to throw cinders any more. . . . I was never, never under any conditions to fight white folks again. And they were absolutely right in clouting me with the broken milk bottle. (Wright, 1937)

Not all black families used these means to protect their children from the wrath of whites. Upper-class families told their children to avoid fights or brawls with whites, not because it was dangerous but because it was beneath their social status. These families tried to isolate their children from racial discrimination as much as possible by outsegregating the white segregationists.

New Image

The image of blacks has been changing. A series of sweeping judicial decisions that promised to desegregate their lives; the emergence of a significant black middle class; the rise of political leadership among blacks; enfranchisement; the legalization and regulation of fair employment practices; and determined efforts to discover their uniqueness, their heritage, and their culture have contributed to the formation of a new image of black people in the minds of white and black alike. With a newly gained confidence and sense of security, young blacks no longer give the impression that they feel inferior or that they are a helpless

Black adolescents are gradually overcoming the legacy of prejudice and discrimination against them. (© Frank Siteman)

minority (Barnes and Farrier, 1985). More and more, black adolescents are accepting the fact that they are human beings of worth, with a positive identity, united with each other in proclaiming their admission into the human race and into middle-class culture (Mboya, 1986).

Contemporary Segregation

On May 17, 1954, the U.S. Supreme Court overruled the principle of "separate but equal" opportunity in education (Merritt, 1983). In 1956 Dr. Martin Luther King, Jr., launched his passive resistance movement against the segregated bus system of Montgomery, Alabama. Although the court battles have been fought and won, there is still considerable differential between white and black income, education, and other standards of living, and segregation continues to be a fact of life.

Unequal Education

In spite of the legal efforts to ensure equal education for all citizens, black adolescents still do not enjoy that privilege. In terms of the total number of years of schooling, young blacks have almost caught up with whites. If only those in the 25-to-29-year-old age group are considered, the educational attainment of these young non-whites almost equals the attainment of all races together. Figure 2-2 shows the improvement between 1960 and 1985. If quality of education is considered, however, blacks still lag far behind whites.

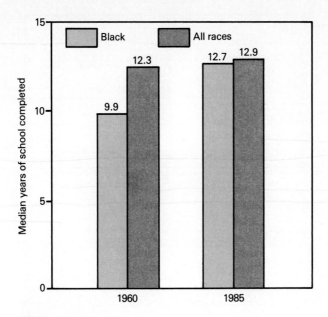

FIGURE 2-2

Educational attainment, blacks and all races combined, ages 25 to 29, 1960–1985.

From: U.S. Bureau of the Census, Department of Commerce. (1987). *Statistical Abstract of the United States*, 1987 (Washington, D.C.: U.S. Government Printing Office).

Unemployment Rates

When the unemployment rates of non-white and white teenagers are compared, the differences are striking (Billingsley, 1988). As can be seen in figure 2-3, *non-white teenagers have a far greater unemployment rate than their white contemporaries*: 48 percent of non-white teenagers seeking employment in 1985 could not find jobs. Many jobless youths were wandering the streets with nothing to do.

Income

In spite of the fact that the income of both whites and blacks has been increasing, *the income gap between whites and non-whites has widened*, not closed (U.S. Department of Commerce, 1987). In every occupational category, blacks are paid less than whites for the same work. Unequal income, unequal education, segregation, and discrimination are still a reality. Legally, black adolescents should have equal rights with white youths; in actuality, complete equality is still a goal to be attained.

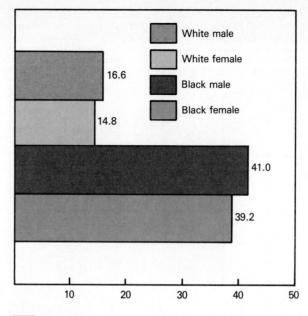

White male
White female
Black male
Black female

16.6
14.8
41.0
39.2

10   20   30   40   50

FIGURE 2-3

Non-white and white unemployment rates, ages 16 to 19, 1985.

From: U.S. Bureau of Census, Department of Commerce. (1987). *Statistical Abstract of the United States,* 1987 (Washington, D.C.: U.S. Government Printing Office).

Black Family Strengths

Many of the problems that beset the black family are due to racial discrimination and the economic conditions under which many live (Crawley, 1988). Black families show a number of positive characteristics that have enabled them to function and survive in a hostile social environment (Broman, 1988; Bryant and Coleman, 1988; Gary et al., 1983). These characteristics are:

① **Strong Kinship Bonds**   Extended families are common (Ball, 1983). Blacks are exposed to far more stress than whites, but family members rely on one another for care, strength, and mutual support (Ball, 1983, McAdoo, 1982; Taylor, 1985;1986).

② **A Favorable Attitude toward the Elderly**   At all socioeconomic levels, blacks have a more favorable attitude toward the elderly than do whites (Register, 1981).

③ **Adaptable Roles**   Husband-wife relationships in more black families are egalitarian, with black husbands sharing significantly in the performance of

HIGHLIGHT   Those Who Make It

In spite of prejudices and handicaps that they face, some black adolescents do achieve a high level of academic and social success. One study of rural, black adolescents from the Southeast showed that those who succeeded had several characteristics in common:

1. Close and supportive family networks with strong direction from parents.
2. Highly developed social network outside of family.
3. Strong identification with positive role models.
4. Active participation in school and church activities with limited activity in community activities.
5. Positive educational experiences, with school providing the major social outlet.
6. Strong future orientation based on realism.
7. High educational and occupational goals and expectations.

8. Moderate to highly conservative moral attitudes.
9. Strong religious convictions.
10. Positive but realistic view of self with the ability to accept responsibility for self and behavior, the ability to lead and follow, and an internal locus of control.
11. Well-developed outside interests although limited in scope.
12. Limited degree of black consciousness or of racial identity (that is, race was not an important factor in their social interactions).
13. Well-developed views on the nature of success.

SOURCE: Lee, C. C. (Spring 1985) "Successful Rural Black Adolescents: A Psychological Profile," *Adolescence* 20: 140.

household tasks (Hill, 1971). Roles of all family members are flexible. An uncle or grandfather can assume the vacated position of a father or an absent mother.

Strong Achievement Orientation   Most blacks have a high motivation to get ahead and have pride in their own accomplishments and those of black people generally.

Strong Religious Orientation   Religion has been a source of solace for downtrodden people, as well as a vehicle for rebellion and social advancement.

MEXICAN-AMERICAN ADOLESCENTS

Mexican-Americans constitute the second largest minority group in the United States. Figure 2-4 shows the relative population of different minority groups. Adolescents 15 to 19 years of age constitute about 11 percent of the total Mexican-American population, or over 700,000 (U.S. Dept. of Commerce, 1987). About 87 percent reside in Arizona, California, Colorado, New Mexico, and Texas; the vast majority live in California and Texas.

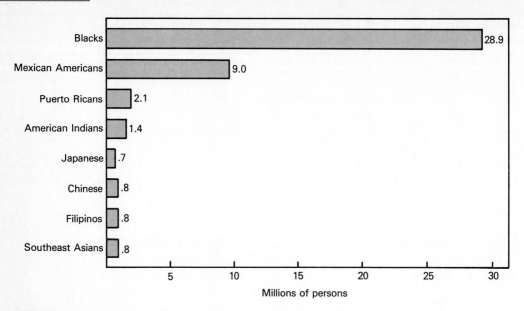

FIGURE 2-4

Size of selected disadvantaged minority groups in the United States, 1985.

From: U.S. Bureau of the Census, Department of Commerce. (1987). *Statistical Abstract of the United States, 1987.* (Washington, D.C.: U.S. Government Printing Office).

Nomenclature

Chicano

Various terms are used to describe Mexican-Americans. The preferences vary by region, ranging from *Latin American* in Texas, *Spanish-American* in New Mexico, and *Mexican* in Arizona and eastern Colorado, to *Mexican-American* and **Chicano** in California. The term *Chicano* has been associated with working-class males who have been struggling for fair economic treatment. "Chicano power" has been the slogan of this group.

Segregation and Housing

colonias or barrios

Mexican-American youths, like white youths, are primarily urbanized: 79 percent live in urban areas. Many live in cities and go to work as migrant workers on farms. About 75 percent of all Mexican-Americans are segregated in residential ghettos called **colonias or barrios** ("neighborhoods"). Some Mexican-Americans, however, in such cities as Los Angeles have been able to move to areas outside the central city.

Lack of Acculturation

acculturation

One result of physical segregation is social isolation, making **acculturation**, or the process of adopting the cultural patterns or traits of majority groups, difficult. Mexican-Americans do not participate in politics to any significant extent. Youths have a poor record of registering to vote, more so than either **Anglos** or blacks.

Anglos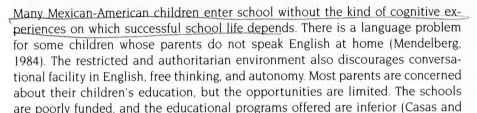

Education

Many Mexican-American children enter school without the kind of cognitive experiences on which successful school life depends. There is a language problem for some children whose parents do not speak English at home (Mendelberg, 1984). The restricted and authoritarian environment also discourages conversational facility in English, free thinking, and autonomy. Most parents are concerned about their children's education, but the opportunities are limited. The schools are poorly funded, and the educational programs offered are inferior (Casas and Ponterotto, 1984).

Another factor in the poor scholastic performance of Mexican-American adolescents is the teacher. Many Anglo teachers are hostile to Mexican-American children, especially if they persist in speaking Spanish or if they speak with a considerable accent. The teachers often do not understand Spanish or Mexican-American culture and the sociocultural factors affecting the classroom behavior of the children.

Under these circumstances, it is not surprising that scholastic performance is poorer than that of Anglo-American children. Table 2-2 shows the percentage of Spanish-Americans and Anglo-Americans aged 25 and older with fewer than five years of school or with four years or more of high school.

Families

Mexican-American families tend to be larger than Anglo-American ones, averaging one more child per family than Anglos (Jorgensen and Adams, 1988). It has been shown that students with more siblings have less chance of realizing their occupational aspirations than do those from smaller families. Mexican-American boys with four or more siblings show as much as ten points lower IQ than those with no sibling or only one.

Favoring Mexican-American families is the fact that the marriages are much more stable than either those of Anglos or blacks. The greater stability holds true even when statistical allowances are made for differences in age, age at first marriage, education, and place of residence (Staples and Mirande, 1980). Apparently the tradi-

TABLE 2-2

Percentage of people aged 25 or older with designated years of schooling, 1985.

AGE	SPANISH-AMERICANS	ANGLO-AMERICANS
Less than five years of school	13.5	2.2
Four years of high school or more	47.4	75.5

From: U.S. Bureau of the Census, Department of Commerce. (1987). *Statistical Abstract of the United States, 1987* (Washington, DC.: U.S. Government Printing Office).

Mexican-Americans constitute the second largest minority group in the United States. Although traditionally they have had stable marriages and highly cohesive families, there is some evidence that this emphasis on family is declining as the wives and mothers are now going to work outside the home. (© Frank Siteman)

tional, paternalistic Mexican-American family is highly cohesive. The mother is especially close to the children and plays an important role in their care (Martinez, 1988; Serrano, 1984). Extended families are common (Markides et al., 1983). There is some evidence, however, that the traditional emphasis on the family is beginning to decline. Whereas Mexican-American women formerly found their major role to be that of wives and mothers, more are now going to work outside the home. This is particularly true among many college-educated wives and among those with preschool-aged children. What effect these changes will have on marital stability remains to be seen.

Socialization of Adolescents

Mexican-American parents emphasize some values that hinder the advancement of adolescents in an individualistic, highly competitive, materialistic society. An emphasis on family ties and dependency, authority, honor, masculinity, living in the present, and politeness are not conducive to independence, achievement, deferred gratification, and success. For example, the older son's role is an extension of that of the father: protector, orderer, and guardian of the younger children. Excessive family dependency hinders the development of initiative and autonomy, particularly when sons are overindulged and given much social freedom but little motivation to succeed educationally and occupationally. Girls are closely supervised and taught primarily to take their place in the home. The emphasis on honor and respectful conduct leads to extraordinary courtesy and politeness. Young people are taught to show respect, obedience, and humility. (In traditional homes the answer to the parent's call is *mande usted*—"at your command.") Therefore, in school or work, adolescents are not prodded to take risks but to be careful not to bring shame upon themselves or their families. They are inclined to adopt in wholesale fashion their parents' commitments to occupational and ideological choices and activities (Abraham, 1986). This is one reason why comparisons between Mexican-American and Anglo-American adolescents show that the latter are much more competitive. Mexican-Americans are concerned with personal gain but more often avoid competitive behavior. Furthermore, children are not expected to defer gratification but to live in the present. Such an orientation is not conducive to upward mobility. The lack of independence training in the family, the negative self-identity of many Mexican-American youths, and the prejudicial treatment in the schools also interfere with achievement.

HIGHLIGHT   Glimpses of the Mexican-American Family

The following excerpt describes family life in Mexican-American families residing on Thirty-second Street in Chicago.

> The kinship network on 32nd street can best be termed an "expanded family." While many relatives of varying generations tend to live nearby and interact continuously, each household is comprised of a nuclear family unit. In Mexico, particularly among the urban poor, the ties of kinship have been augmented to include *compadres* (fictive kin) through treating the godparents of the children as part of the expanded family network. . . . The relationship between the godparents of a child's baptism and the child's parents remains particularly important for many families.
>
> Having a large, close family that can be augmented by *compadres* who can and will readily help in time of need is very highly valued. . . . In such a family . . . members lend each other money, locate a car mechanic, and help out in innumerable situations.

> Those families who do not have relatives or *compadres* on whom to rely must turn to public welfare in time of financial problems or must ask for support, thereby publicly acknowledging their humiliation. The neighborhood is attuned to such events, and news of them is quickly shared. . . .
>
> The role of the Mexican father/husband has been described as one of domination and control over his wife and daughters.* . . . He alone must be responsible for supporting his family and must not publicly appear to become dependent on a working wife. The husband/father as the family head and the son as an independent young man both expect to be served by the women in the household and to come and go as they please. . . . Men are taught that cooking, washing clothes, and cleaning are women's and

---

* (which he is expected to exercise in a just, dignified, and fair manner, showing honor and respect for other family members.)

not men's work. . . . A man who does "woman's work" must be unable to find a woman to do that work, and therefore less than a man, or must be unduly controlled by his woman. This male dependence actually gives a woman a significant source of power.

While a husband may have extramarital affairs, he should not publicly flaunt them because it would demonstrate lack of respect for his wife. . . . The sexual purity of women—the faithfulness of a wife to her husband or the virginity of an unmarried woman—is symbolized by the Virgin Mother. The honor of a man is besmirched if a daughter is not a virgin at marriage or a wife is unfaithful. . . .

Most families are concerned with the movements of their daughters, but cannot completely restrict their activities, though a few families do attempt to retain tight control.

Parents are faced with . . . an unresolvable dilemma. If they follow the traditional honor-based code and refuse to allow their daughter to go out unsupervised, then her virginity remains publicly unquestioned and the honor of her family is upheld. . . . But if they closely supervise her activities, they risk alienating her.

Unable to resolve the dilemma with their parents, many young women marry in order to leave home. Marriage is one of the few culturally legitimate means for young women to leave home and still maintain their honor and that of their families. . . .

Motherhood is the most culturally acceptable identity available to women. The role of independent career women is not culturally acceptable.

The husband-wife bond is based on procreation and expression of love but little on companionship. . . . Most socializing occurs in single-sex groups, and the expanded family network fulfills companionship functions. But children's ties with their mothers are natural and lifelong: they never become distant with age, as do ties with their fathers, who discipline them and control them. . . .

Though it is becoming more common for young women to desire to limit family size, in part because of the expense of bringing up children, older people and many younger ones see this not only as tampering with "God's will" but also as comparing things that cannot be compared: economics and family. For most, social and economic success are not valued above motherhood.

SOURCE: From *Honor and the American Dream: Culture and Identity in a Chicano Community* by Ruth Horowitz. Copyright © 1983 by Rutgers, the State University of New Jersey.

Heterosexual Relationships

machismo When the male reaches adolescence, he is expected to take an interest in females and talk and act in the sexual sphere to demonstrate his virility. There are "bad" girls whom he can exploit for sexual purposes to prove his **machismo** (manhood), and "good" girls whom he can idealize and one of whom he can eventually marry. Dating is frowned upon, but the practice is difficult to suppress in the United States. However, a matchmaker or *portador* is still called into service when mate selection reaches a serious stage. Some youths prefer to bypass the elaborate ritual of courtship and the expenses of the wedding by eloping.

Sex Education ◼

The importance of modesty is highly emphasized, especially for girls, who are not supposed to learn about sexual relations by either conversation or experience. The result is a very low level of scientific knowledge about human sexuality (Scott et al., 1988). Mothers do not discuss sex with daughters or usually even menstruation. The daughter is left to cope alone with menstruation and sex in marriage. As a result, the honeymoon period and early days of marriage are upsetting, often painful experiences for them. Because of the negative, repressive attitudes they learn, it is difficult for wives to care much about sex or enjoy it as much as their husbands. However, repressive attitudes have resulted in a low level of premarital pregnancies among Mexican-American women ("Most First Births . . . ," 1987).

Sex education for males is learned primarily from other male friends and from experience. Boys tell one another about and seek experiences with "bad" girls and prostitutes who help them learn about the physical aspects of sex. Such education is also negative and exploitative, for males learn to use females rather than to share companionship, love, and sex with them.

CHINESE-AMERICAN ADOLESCENTS

Asian Groups ◼

There are over 3.7 million Asian-Americans in the United States: Chinese, 806,000; Filipinos, 774,700; Japanese, 701,000; Asian Indians, 361,500; Koreans, 354,600; Vietnamese, 261,700; and others 466,500. "Others" comprises three groups: Indochinese (Thais and Cambodians), Indonesians, and Pacific Islanders (Hawaiians, Samoans, Guamanians, Polynesians, and Tongans) (U.S. Dept. of Commerce, 1985). This section will focus on the largest group of adolescents with Asian heritage: the Chinese-Americans.

Immigration ◼

A minority of modern Chinese-Americans are descendants of Chinese who immigrated to the United States during the period of open immigration from 1820 to 1882. After 1882, a series of exclusion acts were passed that restricted Asian immigration. As a result, during a number of years, more Chinese left than entered the United States. It was not until 1965 that the national origin quota system that discriminated against Asians was abolished. Now, each country is given an equal quota of 20,000 immigrants yearly (McLeod, 1981). Since that time, Chinese have immigrated in large numbers according to their quotas on a first-come, first-served basis (Sih and Allen, 1976).

Traditionally Chinese males entered the United States without their wives and children. Custom required that a man marry before he left China and that his wife remain in the house of her husband's parents. The man's duty was to send money to his patiently waiting family and to return home eventually. Frequently years passed before he returned. Many hoped to earn enough to bring their families to the United States. But under the Immigration Act of 1882, no Chinese women, except a minority of exempt classes and wives of U.S. citizens, were

Contemporary Chinese-American youths are more vocal, and more inclined to speak out and rebel against authority than previous generations. (Robert Harbison)

permitted to enter. This restriction continued until 1943. As a result, Chinese men who remained abroad were condemned to a life without intimate family relations. They joined together in clans and secret societies that provided a sense of family and solidarity. Some engaged in gambling, opium smoking, and prostitution and were stereotyped by white Americans as lowly, immoral, and dangerous. In 1930, there were four Chinese males to every Chinese female in the United States. Today the ratio is almost equal.

Family and Children

Well-educated Chinese American immigrants have lower rates of divorce, mental illness and public assistance—and higher family income—than the general U.S. population (McLeod, 1986). In comparison to other minorities, Chinese Americans have more conservative sexual values, a lower fertility rate, fewer out-of-wedlock births, and more conservative attitudes toward the role of women (Monahan, 1977; Braun and Chao, 1978). Most Chinese-Americans today have a strong sense of family ties. They have a high sense of duty to family, feel responsible for relatives, and express self-blame when a young person fails to live up to expectations. A child who misbehaves brings shame to the family name.

Philosophies and methods of child rearing depend on the degree of acculturation. Traditional approaches use authoritarian methods: a strict interpretation of good and bad behavior, the limitation of social interaction, firm discipline involving physical punishment, little verbal communication other than commands or scoldings, the expectation of obedience and conformity, and the absence of overt parental praise.

Americanized Chinese parents use different approaches. The parents are nurturant and expose their children to more varied experiences than immigrant families. They use more verbal praise, talk and joke more with their children, and give them more freedom and choice in decision making. Chinese mothers play a significant role in decision making and discipline in the family. They consider teaching to be an important part of their maternal role and give regular formal instruction to children at home (Stewart and Stewart, 1975).

Chinese children are taught that everyone has to work for the welfare of the family. They are given a great deal of responsibility and assigned specific chores. Adolescents are responsible for supervising young children and for work around the house or in the family business.

Youth

Traditionally rebellion among Chinese youths was almost unknown. Respect for elders was so deeply ingrained that youth never questioned their parents' authority or broke rules that would bring dishonor on their families. If parents forbid something, it was wrong.

Contemporary Chinese-American youths are more vocal than previous generations, more inclined to speak out and to rebel against authority. As youths became more disaffiliated from parents, antisocial behavior increased. Young and newly arrived immigrants from Hong Kong and Taiwan and American-born Chinese school dropouts became estranged from both Chinatown's leaders and white America. Many became involved in radical political protest and others in delinquent activity. Some adolescent gangs became tied to organized adult crime (Sih and Allen, 1976).

Education

Chinese-Americans have always stressed the importance of education and hard work as the means of getting ahead. Parents who are shopkeepers or farmers urge their children to go to college to be professionals. The emphasis is on the technical professions such as engineering, pharmacy, and dentistry. More than one-third of today's Asian immigrants have a college degree, almost double the rate among white Americans. So great is the drive for educational accomplishment that Asian-Americans now outscore all other groups on college-entrance math exams and are overrepresented at top universities such as Harvard, Princeton, University of California at Berkeley, Brown, MIT, and California Institute of Technology. Such academic and occupational success has earned Asian-Americans the title of "model minority" (McLeod, 1986).

The primary educational problem for Chinese youths, especially the foreign born, is to learn English. Apparently no one has devised an effective way to teach English to Chinese young people. It is an extremely difficult task, yet youths suffer if they cannot communicate. Without English fluency, they are forced to remain within the confines of the Chinatown job market: in restaurants, garment factories, or low-grade office jobs.

Prejudices

Racial prejudices are still important limiting factors in the lives of Chinese-Americans. Some employers like to hire Chinese persons because of their reputation of being hard working and dependable. But often the jobs are low paying. In seeking more desirable employment, many Chinese feel they do not have an equal chance with Anglo-Americans. A successful engineer may still be labeled a "Chinese engineer," whereas one hardly hears reference to a German or Swedish engineer. Frequent reminders of their racial origin makes some Chinese-Americans feel that they are not fully accepted as Americans (Sih and Allen, 1976). "In the past we had the coolie who slaved," said Tim Tso, president of the Organization of Chinese Americans of Northern Virginia. "Today we have the high-tech coolie" (McLeod, 1986).

Housing

Nowhere is racial discrimination more evident than in segregated housing. Large numbers of Chinese are forced to live in the Chinatowns of San Francisco, Chicago, New York, or Boston. The social conditions in which some live are appalling. Whole families live in rundown, overcrowded, cramped, rat- and roach-infested tenements owned by absentee landlords who charge high rents and have no interest in doing repairs.

Health

Partly because of superstitions, more traditional Chinese are reluctant to seek health care. There are strong taboos against hospitals. One result is that the incidence of tuberculosis and many other diseases is higher among Chinese than among Anglos. Local clinics, partly staffed by Chinese-speaking personnel, help to overcome reluctance to obtain care (Huang and Grachow, n.d.).

Women

The complexities of acculturation have produced many identity conflicts in Chinese-Americans. Young Chinese women are undergoing such a crisis. They seek equal opportunities and reject the traditional image of Asian women as docile, submissive dolls or exotic sex objects. They want equality of social and economic status but do not want to abandon their Chinese cultural heritage, and they resent being "too Americanized" (Sih and Allen, 1976). Many second-generation Chinese are ashamed of their heritage, but by the third generation, they make determined efforts to recapture and preserve their heritage.

NATIVE AMERICAN ADOLESCENTS

Population, Distribution, and Relocation

The number of Native Americans of all ages in the United States is dependent upon the definition of what constitutes a Native American. At the present time, the Bureau of Indian Affairs (BIA) defines Native Americans as those with one-fourth or more Indian blood. The latest census figures (1987) indicate that 1,534,000 persons identify themselves as Native Americans (U.S. Dept. of Commerce, 1987). No one knows with certainty how many of these have at least one-fourth Indian ancestry. The bureau is concerned primarily with those Native Americans living on or near land under some form of federal supervision. In 1987 this included approximately 861,500 persons. This leaves over 672,500 who have migrated off reservations. In spite of this large overflow, the number living on reservations continues to increase.

Of the total population of Native Americans, 45 percent live in the West and Southwest: Arizona, New Mexico, California, and Oklahoma. Arizona and Oklahoma represent two extremes in tribal representation. Arizona has the largest number and the largest single tribe, the Navaho, lives on the largest reservation in the United States, most of which lies within Arizona. Oklahoma, in contrast, has the largest number of tribes, about sixty. This land was once Indian Territory, to which Native Americans from all over the country were moved when their tribal lands were coveted by whites. Because the Indians were newcomers, living on land next to their white neighbors (who had also recently immigrated), most Oklahoma Indians lived among the general population, although there are some remote reservations in the state. In states such as New Mexico and the Dakotas, the majority of the Native American population is still confined to original reservations. In other states, such as North Carolina, California, and New York, the majority either resisted movement to reservations or now live on land where government control has terminated. Table 2-3 shows the population of the largest Indian reservations in the United States (Information Please Almanac, 1988).

Since the beginning of World War II, *there has been a rapid migration of* Native Americans to urban areas, (Red Horse, et al., 1979). In 1940 only 7.2 percent of the total Native American population was urban; in 1980, 45 percent was urban. This rapid migration was partly the result of youths' leaving reservations during World War II to

■ **TABLE 2-3**

Population of largest Indian reservations, 1987.

Navajo (Ariz., N.M., Utah)	173,018	Rosebud (S.D.)	11,685	Zuni (N.M.)	8,135
		Gila River (Ariz.)	10,688	Pawnee (Okla.)	7,657
Cherokee (Okla.)	58,232	Papago-Sells (Ariz.)	10,138	Northern Pueblos	
Creek (Okla.)	54,606	Turtle Mountain		(N.M.)	7,651
Choctaw (Okla.)	21,858	(N.D.)	9,889	Shawnee	
Pine Ridge (S.D.)	19,246	Hopi (Ariz.)	9,040	(Okla., Texas)	7,263
Southern Pueblos		Standing Rock		Blackfeet (Mont.)	7,193
(N.M.)	17,079	(N.D., S.D.)	8,612	Yakima (Wash.)	6,846
Chicksaw (Okla.)	11,780	Fort Apache (Ariz.)	8,421	Wind River (Wyo.)	5,124

NOTE: The Bureau of Indian Affairs lists 861,500 Indians residing on or near Federal reservations as of January 1987. The total Indian population of the United States, according to the 1980 updated census, is 1,534,000, including Aleuts and Eskimos. *Source:* Department of the Interior, Bureau of Indian Affairs. 1. 1984 data.

From: *The 1988* Information Please Almanac. Copyright © 1987 by Houghton Mifflin Company. Reprinted by permission of Houghton Mifflin Company.

join the armed services or of adults' going to work in wartime factories. The government encouraged migration and offered assistance through a relocation program that sought to promote rapid integration into American life. But this relocation created many problems. In their study of 120 urban Native American families, Miller (1975) and her Native American researchers discovered that: (1) one-third were female-headed, (2) 27 percent were receiving public welfare; (3) they had an average of three children; and (4) only one-third had an adequate income. A follow-up study revealed that 40 percent had returned to the reservation (Miller, 1980). Some returned because of dislike for the city, others went back because they could not cope with its demands.

Native Americans in cities are not integrated but are an alienated, invisible minority group. Urbanization has increased their level of income, rate of employment, quality of housing, and "perceived quality of life," but it has not been a panacea for poverty, discrimination, and alienation. For example, for Native Americans who already had problems with alcoholism or crime, moving to the city increased these problems. Many Native Americans go to the city with the promise of better job opportunities, income, medical care, housing, environment, and more recreational opportunities. Sometimes friends or relatives already in the city urge them to move. It has been estimated, however, that if comparable job opportunities could be found in and around reservations, 75 percent would return to the reservations (Clinton et al., 1975). The problem is twofold: lack of assimilation into the white culture and active discrimination against Native Americans in economic affairs and interpersonal relationships. Whites and Native Americans say they support assimilation, but whites will not tolerate cultural differences, and Native Americans want to preserve traditional ways (Chadwick and Stauss, 1975).

The federal relocation program and its effects highlights one of the major problems of contemporary Native American youths: the problem of cultural conflict between the way of life on reservations and the way of life in urban America. This conflict will be examined in greater detail in a later section.

Health and Standard of Living

Native Americans have the highest birthrate, the highest death rate, and the shortest life expectancy of any other group in the United States (Hill and Spector, 1974). They are afflicted with all major diseases to a much greater degree than other Americans. They suffer more from hunger and malnutrition than does any other group in the United States. Accidents, cirrhosis of the liver (attributable to poor nutrition and excessive drinking), and homicide are nearly triple the national rate. Suicide is the leading cause of death among Native American youths 15 to 19 years old, with a rate five times the national average (NIMH, 1973). The rate varies tremendously from tribe to tribe, however (Dizmang et al, 1974; Shore, 1975). Native Americans have a lower standard of living than any other minority group in the United States, with unemployment high and income low. Approximately 75 percent live below the poverty level (U.S. Bureau of the Census, *Statistical Abstract of the United States*, 1987). Unemployment on some reservations runs as high as 80 to

90 percent. In most Native American communities, the pattern is one of bare subsistence, with the result that some of the worst slums in the United States are on reservations.

Education

The record of education is one of broken promises, inadequate resources, the poorest teachers, and, worst, the use of education as a tool to destroy culture and way of life. Altogether, over two-thirds of Native American children not in public schools attend boarding schools, living away from their homes and families (Farris and Farris, 1976). Life at boarding schools is regimented. Estranged from family, regimented by an alien culture, and unable to talk to teachers (who do not know dialects), academic performance is poor.

In addition, the BIA operates a number of day schools located on or near the reservations. These schools present problems also. Physical facilities are notoriously inadequate, texts and supplies are scarce and outdated, and little money is available to hire competent staff. The schools conduct all classes in English, yet some of the children speak little or no English. The dropout rate is very high.

At the secondary level the school curriculum is the standard white one. A report on education in Native American schools in Alaska said that "education which gives the Indian, Eskimo, and Aleut knowledge of—and therefore pride in—their historic and cultural heritage is nonexistent" (Henninger and Esposito, 1971).

The Indian Education Act of 1972 (Known as Title IV) resulted in some improvements. A study of Native American boarding schools revealed that more than half the teachers had taken one or more courses related to Native American tribes, cultures, and history. Several schools had started courses in Native American history, tribal governments, and art and craftwork. In addition, many tribes

---

HIGHLIGHT   The People without a History

The late Senator Robert F. Kennedy related this experience:

We were in Idaho the other day and I was asking the superintendent of schools, where they had 80 percent Indian children, whether they taught anything about Indian history or Indian culture. The tribe was a very famous tribe, the Shoshone, which had a considerable history, and he said, "There isn't any history to this tribe. . . ." So I asked him if there were any books in the library where all these children could go and read about Indian history, and he said, "Yes," and we went to the library. There was only one book and the book was entitled, "Captive of the Delawares." It showed a white child being scalped by an Indian.

FROM: Cahn, E. S. (Ed.). (1969). *Our Brother's Keeper* (New York: World Publishing), p. 35.

are trying to gain control over their schools, with school boards made up of tribal appointees (Chavers, 1975).

Many problems remain. Some tribes want to keep the boarding schools open to enable them to send problem students to them. Some students are given a choice between reform school or boarding school. Offenses run the gamut from creating disturbances to murder (Chavers, 1975). In other cases, children are taken out of the homes of alcoholic parents and sent to boarding schools (Shore, 1975). These conditions create havoc with the educational process in boarding schools.

One hopeful sign is the rise in the number of Native American young people going to college. Today, one in four Native American youth has had some college education. Nationwide, increasing numbers have acquired advanced degrees (U.S. Bureau of the Census, *Statistical Abstract of the United States*, 1987).

Family Life

There is no such institution as a Native American family. There are only tribes and family structure and values will differ from tribe to tribe. Despite the attempt to impose Western family models on them, various family forms still exist among *matrilineal* the different tribal groups (Unger, 1977). Some families are **matrilineal** (with descent through the mother's line) (Keshna, 1980). For many Native Americans, the extended family is the basic unit for carrying out family functions. This is often true despite the absence of extended kin in the same household. Children may be raised by relatives residing in different, noncontiguous households. The existence of multiple households sharing family functions is quite common. Red Horse et al. (1979) discovered one community where 92 percent of the elderly population resided in independent households but maintained close functional contact with their children, grandchildren, and great grandchildren. They fulfilled traditional family roles on a daily basis.

Children

Most Native Americans view children as assets to the family. Children are taught that family and tribe are of the utmost importance. Grandmothers are very important, and the aged in general are looked up to for wisdom and counsel. The aged occupy the important position of relating traditions, beliefs, and customs through the role of storyteller (Backup, 1979). Children are taught to be independent (there are no rigid schedules for eating and sleeping) and to be patient and unassuming. They are taught not to show emotions but to maintain a rather severe reserve. The ability to endure pain, hardship, hunger, and frustration is emphasized, as are bravery and courage.

Cultural Conflict

Native Americans are making a determined effort to retain and to teach their cultural values to their young people. Religion has always been important, but many practices were banned when the federal government conducted its sixty-year (1870–1930) program of enforced enculturation ("The Denial of Indian Civil and Religious Rights," 1975).

Puberty rites or equivalent rites of passage are still practiced by some tribes and form part of religious rituals. When the federal government banned all Indian assemblies during the years 1870–1930, except between July 1 and July 4, the Apache changed the individual rite that marked a girl's first menstruation to a group rite in which all girls who had come of age during the year participated. The mandatory rite marks a transition in status from childhood to adulthood and makes her eligible for marriage. Navaho boys and girls go through a religious ceremony at about the time of appearance of secondary sex characteristics. Through this ceremony, they are introduced to full participation in ceremonial life. In addition, females go through a four-day ritual at the time of first and second menstruation, after which they attain the status of women.

Most important, *Native American values are at variance with Anglo-American culture.* The Native American is present oriented, concerned with decisions about the concrete present and not concerned about the future or with time. White people are future oriented, concerned about time and planning ahead. Native Americans see human life as being in harmony with nature. Whites tend to seek conquest over nature. Native American life is group oriented, emphasizing cooperation, while white people emphasize individualism and competition.

As *a result of conflicting cultures, Native American youths today are faced with a dilemma*: *whether to accommodate themselves to the white world and learn to compete in it or to retain traditional customs and values and live apart from the white world.* Over 150 years of determined government effort has not succeeded in destroying Native American culture and society. Yet the longer Native American youths are isolated, the greater their chances are of remaining the most deprived minority in the United States. Certainly one answer is to help all to appreciate and understand the values of Native American culture and the importance of preserving a rich heritage. The adolescent who is proud of being a Native American, as many are, and who is respected by white society, can contribute richly to a Western world that prides itself on being the world's melting pot. America's original inhabitants have never been accepted as an important segment of American life. As a consequence, most contemporary Native American youths suffer psychological strain under the impact of cultural change. Progress has been slow because they are caught between two cultures and immobilized from going in either direction easily. The following poem, "Thoughts to Ponder," was written by Marie Ann Begay, a Navaho, while completing her senior year at Del Norte High School in Albuquerque, New Mexico:

> Sitting here
> A thought came into my mind
> Living in two worlds—
> That seems hard sometimes,
> Especially if you are an Indian.
> You feel like two persons
> Trying to struggle for something
> That you don't care about at times.

I ask myself what I am doing here,
But all odds add up to my own benefits
And a look at the new side.
Even though I should be
Riding or running in the open countryside
With the fresh clean air racing along with me,
Seeing the rain fall in the distance
And thunder that shakes the earth—

But here I am sitting trying to get
What I think is good for an Indian
Who's trying to make it
In the White Men's world and his own.

SOUTHEAST-ASIAN ADOLESCENTS*

Southeast-Asian adolescents, new to America, are confronted with three special types of stress: physiological and emotional upheavals as adolescents, social and psychological adjustments as refugees, and intercultural conflicts caused by the immense value-system differences between Asian and American cultures. As a unique group of youth, they are in tumultuous transitions. Many of them are faced with the difficult tasks of recovering from old wounds caused by the trauma of war, struggling with daily survival issues at home and in school, and establishing a new identity that is acceptable to their family members and to the host country.

Background

The Southeast-Asian refugee exodus from the countries of Vietnam, Cambodia (now Kampuchea), and Laos is one of the largest refugee movements in modern history. The total Southeast Asian refugee population in the United States was 711,001 as of September 1984 (Office of Refugee Resettlement, 1985). This group now constitutes one of the largest Asian-origin groups in the United States (Rumbaut and Weeks, 1985).

There have been two major "waves" of Southeast-Asian refugee settlement in the United States: from 1975 to 1977 and from 1978 to the present. Major political, economic, and sociocultural differences exist between these two waves of refugees. The first group of refugees admitted to the United States was almost all Vietnamese. They were generally well-educated, young, urban dwellers, in good health, and in the company of family (Montero, 1979). The second wave of refugees included much greater proportion of Hmong, Khmer, Lao, and Chinese-Vietnamese ethnic groups. They were generally less well-educated, less literate, and of rural origin. Escape attempts from the countries of origin were typically long and traumatic (Kinzie et al., 1984; Knoll, 1982).

* Adapted from: Lee, E. (June 1988). "Cultural Factors in Working With Southeast Asian Refugee Adolescents." *Journal of Adolescence,* 11, 167–179. Used by permission.

Many of those who suffered from the trauma of war were children and youths. Among the first wave of 130,000 refugees admitted to the United States in May 1975, 46 percent were younger than 18, and 50 percent of those who entered between January and May 1982 were 19 or younger (Office of Refugee Settlement, 1982). A research study of 40,000 Southeast-Asian refugees in San Diego County showed a very young population, with a median age of 18 years, and 44 percent being children under the age of 18. Its age-sex structure is typical of that of populations of developing countries and reflects high dependency and fertility ratios (Rumbaut and Weeks, 1985).

Acculturation Stress

Unfortunately, in spite of the large numbers of refugee children and youths, very limited studies have been conducted solely on this population (Charron and Ness, 1983; Harding and Looney, 1977; Williams and Westermeyer, 1983). Acculturation is a multifaceted phenomenon composed of numerous dimensions and factors. The acculturation rate of Southeast-Asian refugee adolescents is influenced by

HIGHLIGHT   Comparison of Traditional Asian Values and Urban Industrial Values

TRADITIONAL ASIAN VALUES	URBAN INDUSTRIAL VALUES
Group/community emphasis	Individual emphasis
Extended family	Nuclear family/blended family
Interdependence	Independence
Person-to-person orientation	Person-to-object orientation
Past→present→future	Future→present→past
Age	Youth
Conformity/cooperation	Competition
Harmony with nature	Conquest over nature
Fatalism	Master of one's own fate
Logic of the heart	Logic of the mind
Balance	Change
Patience/modesty	Aggression/assertion
Pragmatic outlook	Theoretical outlook
Suppression of emotion	Expression of emotion
Rigidity of role and status	Flexibility of role and state

←──────────────────────────────────────→

Eastern   Western

From: Lee, E. (June 1988). "Cultural Factors in Working With Southeast Asian Refugee Adolescents." *Journal of Adolescence*, 11, 167–179. Used by permission.

five different cultures that are in continuous interplay with each other: (1) the Southeast-Asian culture, (2) the American culture, (3) the refugee culture, (4) the adolescent culture in America, and (5) the refugee adolescent culture.

Many Southeast-Asian adolescents are confronted with the traditional values from the old country, the contemporary values from the new country, and the transitional values that represent a mixture of some traditional and contemporary traits (Tobin and Friedman, 1984).

As indicated in the highlight section, *there are major differences between the traditional Asian values and the contemporary urban industrial values.* The degree of acculturation of each individual refugee adolescent depends upon the following variables: (1) years in the United States, (2) cultural compatibility of the country of origin and the "host community", (3) age at time of immigration, (4) language usage at home, (5) school environment, and (6) acculturation rate of parents and family members.

Acculturation stress is not solely induced by the process of acculturation but also by the difference perceived by their friends and family members. A Vietnamese adolescent girl may be perceived as "too Vietnamese" by her American friends, "too old-fashioned" by her Vietnamese peers, and "too American" by her parents. Her American friends may expect her to go out after school, to date American boys, to drive a car, and to be more independent. Her parents may expect her to speak only Vietnamese at home, to take care of grandparents and younger siblings after school, to clean the house, and to marry someone chosen by the family. Many deal with the conflict by rejecting the new and the old cultures and establishing a "third culture" with a combination of the two with their refugee experiences.

Life-Cycle Stress

Adolescents who are refugees and from other cultures have special developmental tasks confronting them. Three issues are critical in adolescent development: *separation and individuation, identity, and sexual role formation* (Tobin and Friedman, 1984). It is important to assess each developmental task in the context of the refugee experience and the cultural experience of the world of Southeast Asians.

Separation and Individuation   Peter Blos describes adolescence as a second period of separation and individuation (Blos, 1964). Separation lies at the core of refugee experience. With no alternatives, to be a refugee is to be separated from family members, peers, community, and possessions. Individuation and separation are threatening issues for refugee adolescents and their families as the adolescents' growing psychological autonomy and widening circle of activities and relationships are likely to reawaken painful memories of previous separation (Tobin and Friedman, 1984). For many unaccompanied refugee adolescents, the "premature" physical separation from their family members does not diminish the psychological attachment to their parents. Many are struggling with conflicting feelings of resentment (being abandoned and unprotected) and gratitude (being chosen to come to the United States).

Southeast-Asian refugee adolescents are additionally prone to doubts and guilt concerning the separation issue. Many came from traditional extended Asian families where three or four generations lived together. Sons and daughters are expected to take care of their parents until they die. Their wishes of moving and living on their own like their American peers are in considerable conflict with their parental expectations.

Identity   Erikson describes the concept of identity versus role confusion in adolescents (Erikson, 1959). If identity is difficult for adolescents growing up in stable and protective societies, it is certainly much more so for refugee adolescents. Establishing a strong sense of self-identity is far too difficult for many refugee youths. Traumatic experiences—such as the removal from family homes and community, disintegration of the family unit, suspension of schooling, witnessing death and torture, competition for food due to starvation, and forced internment in labor camps—destroyed most of the physical and emotional connections they had before the war. The process of escape also intensifies their awareness of change in self, others, and the outside world. The sudden recognition that life is dangerous and one cannot always trust others or protect loved ones creates overpowering emotions of fear, rage, and shame. The uncertainty of "being processed" in the refugee camp also intensifies loss of individual identity, as part of a massive refugee population.

For many refugee adolescents, constructing a new identity after their arrival in this country is not easy. Many adolescents are forced to become "adults" to take care of their family members. They may perceive themselves as older or more "mature" than American friends of the same age. They do not feel accepted or connected with the American adolescent culture. In addition, because of racism, and the unpopularity of the Vietnam War in this country, Southeast-Asian adolescents may try to avoid contacts with Americans. Furthermore, the refugee adolescents' experience of discontinuity with their own culture creates a new identity crisis. Their experience of cultural discontent is not so much because they come to this country from another culture as because the culture they come from may seem to them failed and irrelevant. They all too often feel that their culture of origin is their parents' culture but not their own. The greatest threat to identity in refugee adolescents, thus, is not the feeling of belonging to two cultures but the feeling of belonging to none (Tobin and Friedman, 1984).

Sexual Role Formation   For most refugee adolescents, resolving the competitive and affectionate feelings toward their parents is not an easy task. Preoccupied with their own survival, many refugee parents may be physically and emotionally unavailable for their adolescent children. In addition, many parents, especially the fathers, still suffer from the guilt of having failed to protect their families from suffering during the war. Many are burdened by depression and other forms of emotional difficulties and are unaware of the difficulties of adolescent identity struggles. In addition, the low educational achievement, low socioeconomic status, inability to speak English, and lack of understanding of American culture serve to make Southeast-Asian parents appear to their adolescent children as hopelessly inappropriate role models for forming sexual and occupational identities. Instead of serving as objects of competition and identification, they become objects of pity and shame.

■ Family Stress

In comparison with other family life-cycle stages, *families migrating when their children are adolescents may have more stress because they will have less time together as a unit before the children move out on their own*. Thus, the family must struggle with multiple transitions and generational conflicts at once. In addition, the distance from the grandparental generation left behind may be particularly distressing as grandparents become ill, disappear, or die. The parents may experience severe stress in not being able to fulfill their obligation to their parents in the country of origin and their adolescent children in the new country (McGoldrick, 1982).

The following are some major sources of family stress in Southeast-Asian refugee families with adolescents:

1. *Intergenerational conflicts* caused by disparity between the adolescents' and the parents' values and expectations. Southeast Asian parents expect their children to be quiet, obedient, polite, humble, hard-working, and respectful to them and other extended family members. Good sons and daughters are expected to take care of younger siblings and aged parents and bring honor to the family. Such value orientation is not only different but very opposite to the American values, which have strong emphasis on independence, self-reliance, assertiveness, "open-communication," and competition. Three major intergenerational conflicts deserve special attention:
   a. *Conflicts concerning dating and marriage*. Many parents still insist in taking an active part in the choice and approval of dating and marital partners of their children. Many adolescents are being pressured to date and marry within their own ethnic group (Tobin and Friedman, 1984).
   b. *Conflicts concerning career choices*. Some career plans of their children are expected and are acceptable and some are not to Southeast-Asian parents. They highly value professional careers such as medicine, law, engineering, and so forth. Parents usually disapprove of nonprofessional jobs such as factory worker, sales, and careers in music or writing.
   c. *Conflicts caused by role reversal*. Southeast-Asian refugee adolescents usually are much more educated than their parents, who had little or no opportunity to attend school. In addition, many monolingual parents depend on their "English-speaking" adolescents as the "cultural brokers" to deal with the outside world. Such dependence can evoke anger and resentment on both parts and may lead to prolonged family stress.
2. *Special family stress resulting from the trauma of war.* Like the families of survivors of the Nazi holocaust, many families, especially the families from Cambodia, experienced tremendous suffering and losses. Managing rage, aggression, despair, guilt, and grief is an enormous problem for the survivors. Life during the war and the escape process did not afford the survivors adequate opportunities for expression of these feelings. During the post-migration period, many express these repressed emotions in the form of somatization, nightmares, compulsive work, drug abuse, and physical abuse of family members. Parental fighting sometimes takes the form of uncontrollable rage, followed

usually by outbursts of tears and self-pity. Adolescent children often feel the intense obligation to compensate for their parents' helplessness and sorrow.

Assessment of Strengths

In addition to the assessment of stress, careful assessment of strengths, such as adaptation, coping, and problem-solving, is very important. Southeast-Asian families arrive in the United States with many problems associated with their refugee experience. They also bring thousands of years of Asian culture and culturally specific coping strategies in response to stress. Despite the hardships of the refugee experience, many refugees manage to endure and cope effectively without serious psychological problems. Family strengths, such as the support of extended family members and siblings, the strong sense of obligation and self-sacrifice, the strong focus on educational achievement, the strong work ethic, and the loyalty of family members and friends, can be respected (Lee, 1982). Furthermore, religious beliefs in Buddhism provide strength to endure suffering caused by war and trauma.

The support system in the refugee community also plays an important role in determining the facility with which each family resolves transition. Many refugee youths are in frequent contact with community education and social service agencies. Being cut off from their families, villages, and countries, Southeast-Asian refugees feel an urgent need to cluster together and to form community organizations as secondary sources of security.

SUMMARY

This chapter has described six groups of adolescents: (1) those who are of low socioeconomic status of whatever race or national origin, (2) blacks, (3) Mexican-Americans, (4) Chinese-Americans, (5) Native Americans, and (6) Southeast Asians.

Low socioeconomic status youths refer to those who are both culturally deprived and with low income. There are four limitations on their lives. They have limited experience and opportunities. They have little autonomy or influence, which gives a sense of helplessness and powerlessness. They feel a sense of failure because of their status amid those who are more affluent. They are insecure, at the mercy of life's unpredictable events. The net effect of these limitations is to perpetuate a cycle of poverty and cultural deprivation.

There are other important characteristics. Their families are more unstable, resulting in large numbers of female-headed households. Parents tend to be authoritarian, impulsive, harsh, and rigid in disciplining children, more concerned with overt behavior and keeping children out of trouble than with personality growth. Adolescents usually leave the family early and abruptly to try to take their place in the adult world, usually becoming dependent on peers as parental ties weaken. The fact that they are socialized differently, with their own language, manners, dress, and behavior, invites criticism from middle-class society.

Black adolescents are gradually overcoming the legacy of prejudices and discrimination against them. A series of legal decisions that promise equality have helped in this struggle. Nevertheless, blacks still live in segregated neighborhoods and have not achieved equality of education, rates of employment, and income, although some achieve a high level of success in spite of the handicaps they face.

The majority of Mexican-American adolescents live in urban areas in segregated ghettos called *colonias* or *barrios*, experiencing a high degree of social isolation from white society. In general, their scholastic achievement is below average, partly because of language problems.

Mexican-American families tend to be more stable than either white or black families. Members of the extended family, including relatives and godparents, depend closely upon one another for help. Accepting welfare is an admission of failure. The husband-father role is a difficult one. He alone must be the dominant, controlling figure in his family, the sole supporter (wives are discouraged from working outside the home), and responsible for protecting his honor and that of his wife and daughters. Sons are expected to be autonomous and independent like their father, so they spend most of their time outside the home with peers.

Men are allowed to have premarital and extramarital affairs, but women are to be chaste before marriage and faithful after marriage. Traditional families try to protect the virginity of their daughters, sometimes chaperoning them whenever they leave the house. Dating is discouraged. Sex education is inadequate. The Virgin Mother is the ideal, symbolizing purity and motherhood, which are highly prized. Motherhood is the most acceptable identity for women, which is why family planning is frowned upon. The husband-wife bond is based upon procreation and love, with little companionship. Most socializing occurs in single-sex groups.

By tradition, Chinese men immigrated to the United States without their wives, expecting to rejoin them later. A series of expulsion acts restricting additional Asian immigration kept families separated, so for years there were many more Chinese men than women in the United States. Today the ratio is almost equal.

Chinese-Americans have a strong sense of duty to family. Filial piety emphasizes obedience to parents with firm discipline and little verbal communication except commands or scoldings. Americanized parents are more nurturant, allowing more freedom in decision making. But as youth become disaffiliated from parents, antisocial behavior, including delinquency, increases.

Chinese-Americans have always stressed the importance of education. The primary educational problem is teaching English to Chinese young people. Racial prejudices are still important limiting factors in their lives.

Racial discrimination is most evident in segregated housing within the ghettos of the Chinatowns. Taboos against hospitals prevent some from getting adequate health care. Chinese-American females have rejected the image of Asian women as docile, submissive dolls or as erotic sex objects and are striving for equal social and economic status without becoming too Americanized.

A little over half of the 1.5 million citizens who identify themselves as Native Americans live on or near reservations. Half dwell in the western and southwestern part of the United States. Since World War II, large numbers have migrated to urban areas, encouraged by the government, which has tried to promote enforced acculturation and rapid integration into American life.

Native Americans are severely handicapped by discrimination. They are the most deprived minority in the United States, having the highest birthrate, the highest death rate, and the shortest life expectancy of any other group in the United States. They are afflicted with all major diseases to a much greater degree than other Americans and suffer from hunger and malnutrition. They have a lower standard of living than any other minority group; 75 percent of the families live below the poverty level. Education, whether in boarding schools away from home, in day schools (supposedly near reservations), or in regular public schools with white children, are of poor quality, with not enough teachers understanding, appreciating, or teaching Native American culture. From the beginning, the government used education as a means of waging cultural war against the Native American.

There have been a few improvements. Some teachers are now taking courses relating to Indian tribes, culture, and history or are Native Americans themselves. Parents are supposed to be involved in policy making in the schools. More schools are closer to home. And an increasing number of Native American young people are going to college.

The primary problem is still cultural conflict between the white world and Native American customs and ways. This conflict will not be resolved until whites and Native Americans develop a greater understanding and appreciation of Native American culture and the importance of preserving a rich heritage.

Southeast-Asian adolescents are a unique group because they are refugees from war. As a unique group, they are in tumultuous transitions. They are recovering from the wounds of war, struggling with daily survival issues at home and in school, and establishing a new identity that is acceptable to their family members and to the host country. The stresses that they face include the difficulties of acculturation, since there are major differences between traditional Asian values and contemporary urban industrial values; life-cycle stresses as they seek to solve the problems of individuation and separation from parents; identity and sexual role formation; and family stresses. Family stresses arise because of intergenerational conflicts caused by the disparity between adolescents' and parents' values. Conflicts arise over dating and marriage, career choices, and role reversal. Special family stresses are also the result of the trauma of war.

Strengths include years of Asian culture, family solidarity, religious beliefs, and the support system in the refugee community.

DISCUSSION QUESTIONS

1. Are poor people that way because they are lazy? Why or why not?
2. Is it possible for adolescents from poor families to break the cycle of poverty and deprivation? If so, how?
3. Can children be well adjusted growing up in a female-headed household?
4. Do low socioeconomic status adolescents consider themselves social outcasts? Why or why not?
5. Is education the answer to the black adolescent's situation?
6. If the law says that blacks must have equality of opportunity in education and employment, why is there still so much discrepancy between blacks and whites?
7. What factors in the family relationships of Mexican-Americans contribute to occupational success? What factors contribute to occupational failure of adolescents from those families?
8. What do you think of the traditional Mexican-American family? What aspects do you approve of, and what do you disapprove of? What other ethnic groups in the United States have philo-

sophies of family living similar to those of the Mexican-Americans?

9. What do you admire most about the family relationships of Chinese-Americans? What do you admire the least?

10. Why is delinquency on the increase among Chinese-American adolescents?

11. Describe a Chinese-American family and/or students whom you know.

12. Why are Native Americans the most deprived minority in the United States?

13. Do you know any Native-American families and/or adolescents? Describe them and what you admire most about them, their way of life, and ideas. Describe what you admire the least.

14. Should Native-American adolescents be taught the ways of whites? Why or why not?

15. Why did the government use education to acculturate the Indians and destroy their culture?

16. What would likely happen to Indians who were moved from the reservations to the city?

17. Is it possible to be Indian in a white world? Why or why not?

18. Are there any Southeast-Asian families in your community? What are the attitudes of other people toward them?

19. What special problems do Southeast Asians in this country face? What helps do they have in solving them? What are the great hindrances to solving them?

BIBLIOGRAPHY

Abraham, K. G. (1986). "Ego-Identity Differences among Anglo-American and Mexican-American Adolescents." *Journal of Adolescence*, 9, 151–166.

Backup, R. (1979). "Implementing Quality Care for the American Indian Patient." *Washington State Journal of Nursing* (Special supplement), 20–24.

Ball, R. E. (1983). "Marital Status, Household Structure, and Life Satisfaction of Black Women." *Social Problems*, 30, 400–409.

Billingsley, A. (1988). "The Impact of Technology on Afro-American Families." *Family Relations*, 37, 420–425.

Blos, P. (1964). "The Second Individuation Process of Adolescence." *The Psychoanalytical Study of the Child*, 2, 410–418.

Booth, A., and Edwards, J. N. (1985). "Age at Marriage and Marital Instability." *Journal of Marriage and the Family*, 47, 67–75.

Braun, J., and Chao, H. (1978). "Attitudes Toward Women: a Comparison of Asian-born Chinese and American Caucasians." *Psychology of Women Quarterly*, 2, 195–201.

Broman, C. L. (1988). "Satisfaction Among Blacks: The Significance of Marriage and Parenthood." *Journal of Marriage and the Family*, 50, 45–51.

Bryant, Z. L., and Coleman, M. (1988). "The Black Family as Portrayed in Introductory Marriage and Family Textbooks." *Family Relations*, 37, 255–259.

Cahn, E. S., ed. (1969). *Our Brother's Keeper: The Indian in White America*. New York: World Publishing Co.

Carlson, J. M., and Iovini, J. (Spring, 1985). "The Transmission of Racial Attitudes from Fathers to Sons: A Study of Blacks and Whites." *Adolescence*, 20, 233–237.

Casas, J. M., and Ponterotto, J. G. (February, 1984). "Profiling an Invisible Minority in Higher Education: The Chicana." *Personnel and Guidance Journal*, 62, 349–353.

Chadwick, B. A., and Stauss, J. H. (1975). "The Assimilation of American Indians into Urban Society: The Seattle Case." *Human Organization*, 34, 359–369.

Charron, D., and Ness, R. (1983). "Emotional Distress among Vietnamese Adolescents: A Statewide Survey." *Journal of Refugee Resettlement*, 1, 7–15.

Chavers, D. (1975). "New Directions in Indian Education." *Indian Histories*, 4, 43–46.

Clinton, L., et al. (1975). "Urban Relocation Reconsidered: Antecedents of Employment among Indian Males." *Rural Sociology*, 40, 117–133.

Crawley, B. (1988). "Black Families in a Neo-Conservative Era." *Family Relations*, 37, 415–419.

"The Denial of Indian Civil and Religious Rights." (1975) *Indian Historian*, 8, 43–46.

DiCindio, L. A., Floyd, H. H., Wilcox, J., and McSeveney, D. R. (Summer, 1983). "Race Effects in a Model of Parent-Peer Orientation." *Adolescence*, 18, 369–379.

Dill, D., Feld, E., Martin, J., Beukema, S., and Belle, D. (1980). "The Impact of the Environment on the Coping Effects of Low-income Mothers." *Family Relations*, 29, 503–509.

Dizmang, L. H., et al. (1974). "Adolescent Suicide at an Indian Reservation." *American Journal of Orthopsychiatry* 44, 43–49.

Erikson, E. H. (1959). *Identity and Life Cycle*. New York: International University Press.

Farris, C. E., and Farris, L. S. (1976). "Indian Children: The Struggle for Survival." *Social Work*, 21, 386–389.

Franklin, D. L. (1988). "The Impact of Early Childbearing on Developmental Outcomes: The Case of Black Adolescent Parenting." *Family Relations*, 37, 268–274.

Gabriel, A., and McAnarney, E. R. (Fall, 1983). "Parenthood in Two Subcultures: White, Middle-Class Couples and Black, Low-Income Adolescents in Rochester, New York." *Adolescence*, 18, 595–608.

Gary, L. et al. (1986). "Strong Black Families: Models of Program Development for Black Families." In *Family Strengths 7: Vital Connections*, edited by S. Van Zandt et al. Lincoln, Nebraska: Center for Family Strengths, 453–468.

Gecas, V., and Nye, F. I. (1974). "Sex and Class Differences in Parent-Child Interaction: A Test of Kahn's Hypothesis." *Journal of Marriage and the Family*, 36, 742–749.

Harper, J., and Collins, J. K. (1975). "A Different Survey of the Problems of Privileged and Underprivileged Adolescents." *Journal of Youth and Adolescence*, 4, 349–358.

Henninger, D., and Esposito, N. (1971). "Indian Schools." In *America's Other Youth: Growing Up Poor.* Edited by D. Gottlieb and A. L. Heinsohn. Englewood Cliffs, N.J.: Prentice-Hall.

Hill, C., and Spector, M. (1974). "Natality and Mortality of American Indians Compared With U.S. Whites and Non-whites." *Health Services and Mental Health Administration Reports*, 68.

Hill, R. B. (1971). *The Strengths of Black Families*. New York: Emerson Hall.

Horowitz, R. (1983). *Honor and the American Dream*. Brunswick, N.J.: Rutgers University Press.

Huang, C., and Grachow, F. n.d. "The Dilemma of Health Services in Chinatown." New York: Department of Health.

Information Please Almanac, Atlas, and Yearbook, 1988. 41st edition. Boston: Houghton Mifflin Co., 1988.

Jacob, T. (1974). "Patterns of Family Conflict and Dominance as a Function of Child Age and Social Class." *Developmental Psychology*, 10, 1–12.

Jorgensen, S. R., and Adams, R. P. (1988). "Predicting Mexican-American Family Planning Intentions: An Application and Test of a Social Psychological Model." *Journal of Marriage and the Family*, 560, 107–119.

Keshna, R. (1980). "Relevancy of Tribal Interests and Tribal Diversity in Determining the Educational Needs of American Indians." In *Conference on the Education and Occupational Needs of American Indian Work.* Washington, D. C.: U.S. Department of Education, National Institute of Education.

Kinze, J. D., Frederickson, R. H., Ben, R., Fleck, J., and Karls, W. (1984). "Post-Traumatic Stress Disorder among Survivors of Cambodian Concentration Camps." *American Journal of Psychiatry*, 141, 645–650.

Knoll, T. (1982). *Becoming Americans*. Portland: Coast to Coast Books.

Krein, S. F. (1986). "Growing Up in a Single Parent Family: The Effect on Education and Earnings of Young Men." *Family Relations*, 35, 161–168.

Larson, J. H. (October, 1984). "The Effect of Husband's Employment on Marital and Family Relations in Blue-Collar Families." *Family Relations*, 33, 503–511.

Lee, C. C. (Spring, 1985). "Successful Rural Black Adolescents: A Psychological Profile." *Adolescence*, 20, 130–142.

Lee, E. (1982). "A Social Systems Approach to Assessment and Treatment for Chinese American Families." In *Ethnicity and Family Therapy*, edited by M. McGoldrick, J. Pearce, and J. Giordana. New York: Guilford Press.

Lee, E. (1988). "Cultural Factors in Working with Southeast Asian Refugee Adolescents." *Journal of Adolescence*, 11, 167–179.

Lee, E. and Chan, F. (1985). "The Use of Diagnostic Interview Schedule with Vietnamese Refugees." *Asian American Psychological Association Journal* 1, 36–39.

Markides, K. S., Hoppe, S. V., Martin, H. W., and Timbers, D. M. (1983). "Sample Representativeness in a Three-Generation Study of Mexican Americans." *Journal of Marriage and the Family*, 45, 911–916.

Martinez, E. A. (1988). "Child Behavior in American/Chicano Families: Maternal Teaching and Child-Rearing Practices." *Family Relations*, 37, 275–280.

Mboya, M. M. (1986). "Black Adolescents: A Descriptive Study of Their Self-Concepts and Academic Achievement." *Adolescence*, 21, 689–696.

McAdoo, H. P. (1982). "Stress Absorbing Systems in Black Families." *Family Relations*, 31, 479–488.

McGoldrick, M. (1982). "Ethnicity and Family Therapy." In *Ethnicity and Family Therapy*, edited by M. McGoldrick, J. Pearce, and J. Giordana. New York: Guilford Press.

McLeod, B. (1986). "The Oriental Express." *Psychology Today*, 20, 48–52.

Mendelberg, H. E. (Spring, 1984). "Split and Continuity in Language Use of Mexican-American Adolescents of Migrant Origin." *Adolescence*, 19, 171–182.

Merrit, R. (Spring, 1983). "Comparison of Tolerance of White Graduates of Racially Integrated and Racially Segregated Schools." *Adolescence*, 18, 67–70.

Miller, D. (1975). *American Indian Socialization to Urban Life*. San Francisco: Institute for Scientific Analysis.

Miller, D. (1980). "The Native American Family: The Urban Way." In *Families Today*, edited by E. Corfman. Washington, D. C.: U.S. Government Printing Office, 441–484.

Monahan, T. (1977). "Illegitimacy by Race and Mixture of Race." *International Journal of Sociology of the Family*, 7, 45–54.

Montero, D. (1979). *Vietnamese Americans: Patterns of Resettlement and Socioeconomic Adaptation in the United States*. Boulder, CO.: Westview Press.

"Most First Births are Marital Among Young Women of Mexican Origin" (1987). *Family Planning Perspectives*, 19, 30.

Mueller, D. P., and Cooper, P. W. (1986). "Children of Single Parent Families: How They Fare as Young Adults." *Family Relations*, 35, 169–176.

National Institute of Mental Health (1973). *Suicide, Homicide, and Alcoholism among American Indians: Guidelines for Help*. Washington, D. C.: U.S. Government Printing Office.

Office of Refugee Resettlement (1982, 1985). *Refugee Resettlement Program: Report to the Congress*. Washington, D. C.: U.S. Government Printing Office.

Rank, M. R. (1987). "The Formation and Dissolution of Marriages in the Welfare Population." *Journal of Marriage and the Family*, 49, 15–20.

Red Horse, J. G., Lewis, R., Feit, M., and Decker, J. (1979). "Family Behavior of Urban American Indians." *Social Casework*, 59, 67–72.

Register, J. C. (1981). "Aging and Race: A Black-white Comparative Analysis." *The Gerontologist*, 21, 438–443.

Riessman, F., et al., eds. (1964). *Mental Health of the Poor*. London: Free Press of Glencoe.

Roosa, M. W., Fitzgerald, M. E., and Carlson, N. A. (1982). "A Comparison of Teenage and Other Mothers: A Systems Analysis." *Journal of Marriage and the Family*, 44, 367—377.

Rumbaut, R. G., and Weeks., Jr. (1985). *Fertility and Adaptation among Indochinese Refugees in the United States*. Research Paper No. 3. San Diego: University of California, San Diego, Indochinese Health and Adaptation Research Project.

Scheirer, M. A. (November, 1983). "Household Structure among Welfare Families: Correlates and Consequences." *Journal of Marriage and the Family*, 45, 761–771.

Scott, C. S., Shifman, L., Orr, L., Owen, R. G., and Fawcett, N. (1988). "Hispanic and Black American Adolescents' Beliefs Relating to Sexuality and Contraception. *Adolescence*, 23, 667–668.

Serrano, R. G. (Fall, 1984). "Mexican-American Self-Disclosure in Friendship Formation." *Adolescence*, 19, 539–549.

Shore, J. H. (1975). "American Indian Suicide: Fact and Fantasy." *Psychiatry*, 28, 86–91.

Sih, P. K. T., and Allen, L. B. (1976). *The Chinese in America*. New York: St. John's University Press.

Slesinger, D. P. (1980). "Rapid Changes in Household Composition Among Low-Income Mothers." *Family Relations*, 29, 221–228.

Special Issue: Mental Health Research and Service Issues for Minority Youth (June, 1988). *Journal of Adolescence*, 11.

Staples, R., and Mirande, A. (1980). "Racial and Cultural Variations Among American Families: A Decennial Review of the Literature on Minority Families." *Journal of Marriage and the Family*, 42, 887–903.

Starr, J. M. (1981). "Adolescents and Resistance to Schooling: A Dialectic." *Youth and Society*, 13, 189–227.

Stewart, M., and Stewart, S. (September, 1975).

"Teaching-Learning Interactions in Chinese American and Anglo American Families: Study in Cognitive Development and Ethnicity." Unpublished paper.

Taylor, R. J. (1985). "The Extended Family as a Source of Support to Elderly Blacks." *The Gerontologist*, 25, 488–495.

Taylor, R. J. (1986). "Receipt of Support from Family among Black Americans: Demographic and Familial Differences." *Journal of Marriage and the Family*, 48, 67–77.

Tobin, J. J., and Friedman, J. (1984). "Intercultural and Developmental Stresses Confronting Southeast Asian Refugee Adolescents." *Journal of Operational Psychiatry*, 15, 39–45.

Unger, S. (1977). *The Destruction of American Families.* New York: Association on American Indian Affairs.

U.S. Bureau of the Census (1985). *Statistical Abstract of the United States*, 1985. Washington, D. C.: U.S. Government Printing Office.

U.S. Bureau of the Census (1987). *Statistical Abstract of the United States*, 1987. Washington, D. C.: U.S. Government Printing Office.

Watson, M. F., and Protinsky, H. O. (1988). "Black Adolescent Identity Development: Effects of Perceived Family Structure." *Family Relations*, 37, 288–292.

Williams, C., and Westermeyer, J. (1983). Psychiatric Problems among Adolescent Southeast Asian Refugees. *Journal of Nervous and Mental Disease*, 171, 79–85.

Wright, R. (1937). "The Ethics of Living Jim Crow." *American Stuff.* New York: Harper & Row.

CHAPTER

3

Multidisciplinary Views of Adolescence

read
↓

The important task of this chapter is to answer the question: What is adolescence? The answer may be found in one of a number of ways: by trying to define adolescence and related concepts such as maturity, puberty, pubescence, teenager, juvenile, and youth. This method is used as the chapter begins with some brief definitions.

Another way to answer the question is to approach it from various points of view: from the studies of the biologist, psychiatrist, psychologist, sociologist, anthropologist, and social psychologist. This chapter presents the views of a few representative and influential writers from each of these disciplines: biological views—G. Stanley Hall and Arnold Gesell; psychoanalytical views—Sigmund Freud and Anna Freud; sociopsychoanalytical views—Erik Erikson and James Marcia; sociological views—Allison Davis, Albert Bandura and Richard H. Walters; anthropological views—Margaret Mead and Ruth Benedict; psychosocial views—Robert Havighurst and Kurt Lewin; and a social cognition view—Robert Selman. By understanding various viewpoints, readers will gain a truer, more complete picture of the numerous aspects of adolescence.

DEFINING TERMS

adolescence The word **adolescence** comes from the Latin verb *adolescere*, which means "to grow" or "to grow to maturity" (Golinko, 1984). It is defined as a period of growth between childhood and adulthood (deBrun, 1981). There is a general disagreement about when it begins and ends, especially because the period has been prolonged in Western culture. For most people, adolescence is an intermediate stage between being a child and being an adult (Matter, 1984). The transition from one stage to the other is gradual and uncertain: the beginning and the end are somewhat blurred, and the time span is not the same for every person, but most adolescents eventually become mature adults. In this sense, adolescence is likened to a bridge between childhood and adulthood over which individuals must pass before they are to take their places as mature, responsible, creative adults.

maturity **Maturity** is that age, state, or condition of life at which a person is considered fully developed physically, emotionally, socially, intellectually, and spiritually. The balance of all these characteristics is not always achieved simultaneously. A person may be mature physically but not emotionally. Conversely, there are some individuals who are intellectually quite mature but have not attained full spiritual and moral growth. Young persons who become physically mature at age fourteen may have a lot of growing up to do before they are mature in other ways as well.

puberty **Puberty** is the period during which a person reaches sexual maturity and becomes capable of begetting or bearing offspring. Puberty can be used in a fairly narrow sense to denote only that age when a person first becomes sexually capable of having children. In a broader sense (and the sense in which it is used in this book), puberty is used to denote the several years during which physical changes relative to sexual maturation are taking place: those years during which the mature primary and secondary sexual characteristics develop. The first two years of puberty are spent in preparing the body for reproduction, and the last two years are spent in completing it. The first part of puberty overlaps childhood and adolescence, and the last part coincides with the first several years of adolescence.

Pubescence should be used synonymously with *puberty* to denote the whole period during which sexual maturation takes place. Literally, it means becoming hairy or downy, describing one of the important physical changes that occur during puberty. So a *pubescent* child is one who is arriving at or has arrived at puberty.

pubescence

The term **teenager,** in a strict sense, means only those in the teen years: thirteen to nineteen years of age. However, because children (especially girls) sometimes mature physically before thirteen years of age, there are some discrepancies. An eleven-year-old girl may look and act like a teenager, but a fifteen-year-old boy, if not yet sexually mature, may still act and look like a child.

teenager

The word *teenager* is of fairly recent origin. It first appeared in the *Reader's Guide to Periodical Literature* in the 1943–1945 issue. Subsequently, the term has become popular in the lay vocabulary. It is a word to which many youths object because of its negative emotional connotations: wild, delinquent, incorrigible, immoral. Margaret Mead objects to the term because it is too restrictive in terms of age (thirteen to nineteen years). She objects to it for emotional reasons also. There are many different types of teenagers: scholarly, intellectual teenagers; cool teenagers. The term will be avoided in this book, where the designation *adolescent* is preferred.

The word **juvenile** is generally used in a legal sense: one who is not yet considered an adult in the eyes of the law, in most states anyone up to eighteen years of age. The legal rights of eighteen-year-olds are confusing, however, for they vary from state to state. The Twenty-sixth Amendment gave them the right to vote, and in some areas they are called for jury duty. They may obtain credit in their own name at some stores or banks, but at others they have to obtain cosigners, even though they are legally responsible for their own debts. Many landlords still require parents to cosign leases. Most states now require youths to be twenty-one years of age to purchase alcoholic beverages. In Colorado, eighteen-year-olds can sign some contracts but not others; they can marry without parental consent; they can leave home at age sixteen but do not attain full legal rights until age twenty-one. The net result is confusion over their identities. When do they fully become adults? Some adolescents feel they have to wait too many years to "get into the club" ("Legal Rights . . . ," 1976). One author suggests the law recognize an intermediate legal status between ages fifteen and eighteen when adolescents are accorded more rights than children but fewer than those of adults (Heyneman, 1976). Keniston (1970) suggests that because of the prolongation of adolescence, we should conceptualize a new stage of life, that of *youth,* which he defines as a developmental period that would follow adolescence. In general terminology, however, *youth* refers to the younger generation, usually adolescence (Sebald, 1984). It is used in this latter sense in this book.

juvenile

BIOLOGICAL VIEWS OF ADOLESCENCE

A strictly biological view of adolescence would emphasize this period as one of physical and sexual maturation during which important growth changes take place in the child's body. Any biological definition would outline in detail these physical, sexual, and physiological changes; their reasons (when known); and their consequences.

This biological view would also emphasize biogenetic factors as the primary cause of any behavioral and psychological change in the adolescent. Growth and behavior are under the control of internal maturational forces, leaving little room for environmental influences. Development occurs in an almost inevitable, universal pattern, regardless of sociocultural environment.

Hall and Recapitulation Theory

One of the most influential exponents of a biological theory was G. Stanley Hall (1846–1924), the first Ph.D. in psychology in the United States and the founder of the child-study movement in North America. He was the first to advance a psychology of adolescence in his two-volume treatise on the subject (Hall, 1904). According to Hall, during its development, each human organism relives each of the stages that occurred in human evolutionary development. He outlined four major stages: *infancy* (first four years), during which the child reenacts the animal stage of development; *childhood* (five to seven), which corresponds to the cave-dwelling and hunting-fishing epoch of human history (because this is a time the child plays hide and seek, cowboys and Indians, and uses toy weapons); *youth* (eight to twelve), the preadolescent stage of development during which the child recapitulates the life of savagery but is predisposed to learn to read, write, draw, manipulate numbers, and to learn languages, manual training, music, and other subjects through routine practice and discipline; and *puberty* (thirteen to twenty-four), the period of adolescence.

Hall described adolescence as the period corresponding to the time when the human race was in a turbulent, transitional stage, a time of great "storm and stress." Like some theorists today, *Hall said that puberty is a time of great upset, emotional maladjustment, and instability in which the adolescent's moods oscillate between energy and indifference, gaiety and depression, or egotism and bashfulness.* The end of adolescence marks a new birth in which higher, more completely human traits are born, a time corresponding to the beginning of modern civilization.

Hall's views exerted a marked influence upon the study of adolescence for many years (Hall and Lindzay, 1970). Because the theory held that development was controlled from within, parents were cautioned not to interfere but to let the child pass from one stage to the other. Such a view was comforting to parents who found their children difficult at one stage; they always had the hope that the next stage would be better. One difficulty was that serious, abnormal disturbances at adolescence were sometimes accepted as normal.

Hall's view of adolescence has since been severely criticized on a number of points: (1) his biological, genetic explanation of behavior allows no room for the role of environment; (2) he felt that behavior at each stage is universal, unchangeable, and predisposed by biological drives, a tenet since refuted by cultural anthropologists; (3) he felt parents must be permissive and tolerate socially unacceptable behavior during the various stages of development; and (4) he overemphasized adolescence as an inevitable period of "storm and stress," a point that also has been refuted by demonstrations that adolescence in some cultures is not at all stormy. Even in our culture, current evidence suggests that the rate of emotional disturbance among adolescents does not differ significantly from that of the population at large (Ellis, 1979). (See the section on anthropological views.) In spite of criticisms of his theory, Hall's influence is still felt in some circles today.

Arnold Gesell: Spiral Growth Patterns

Gesell (1880–1961) is known for observations of human development from birth to adolescence that he and his staff made at the Yale Clinic of Child Development and later at the Gesell Institute of Child Development. His best-known book on adolescence is *Youth: The Years from Ten to Sixteen* (Gesell and Ames, 1956).

Gesell was interested mainly in the behavioral manifestations of development and personality. He observed the actions and behavior of children and youths at different ages and constructed descriptive summaries of growth gradients grouped in stages and cycles of development. In his summaries he described what he felt were the norms of behavior in their chronological sequence.

Several explanations, implications, and criticisms need to be discussed for an understanding of Gesell's theory. It is essentially a biologically oriented theory, for maturation is mediated by genes and biology that determine the order of appearance of behavioral traits and developmental trends. Thus, abilities and skills appear without the influence of special training or practice.

This concept implies a sort of biological determinism that prevents teachers and parents from doing anything to influence development. Because maturation is regarded as a natural ripening process, it is assumed that time alone will solve most of the minor problems that arise in raising children. Difficulties and deviations will be outgrown, so parents are advised against emotional methods of discipline (Gesell and Ames, 1956).

Gesell did try to allow for individual differences, accepting that each child is born unique, with his or her own "genetic factors or individual constitution and innate maturation sequences" (Gesell and Ames, 1956, p. 22). But he emphasized that "acculturation can never transcend maturation" because maturation is of primary importance. In spite of accepting individual differences and the influence of environment on individual development, he nevertheless considered many of the principles, trends, and sequences to be universal among humans. This concept partly contradicts the findings of cultural anthropology and social and educational psychology, which emphasize significant, culturally determined individual differences (Gesell and Ames, 1956, p. 41).

Gesell tried to emphasize that changes are gradual and overlap, but his descriptions often indicate profound and sudden changes from one age to the next. He emphasized also that development is not only upward but also spiral, characterized by both upward and downward gradients that cause some repetition at different ages. Thus, freckles are evident at both sixteen and twelve; both the eleven- and fifteen-year-old are rebellious and quarrelsome, whereas the twelve- and sixteen-year-old are fairly stable.

One of the chief criticisms of Gesell's work concerns his sample. He drew his conclusions from boys and girls of favorable socioeconomic status, of a high to superior level of school population in New Haven, Connecticut. He contended that such a homogeneous sample would not lead to false generalizations. However, even when only physical factors are considered, children differ so greatly in the level and timing of growth that it is difficult to establish norms for any age level. Nevertheless, Gesell's books have been used by thousands of parents and exerted tremendous influence on child-rearing practices during the 1940s and 1950s. The books were considered the "child-development bibles" for many students and teachers during these years.

PSYCHOANALYTICAL VIEWS OF ADOLESCENCE

Sigmund Freud

Freud (1856–1939) was not much involved with theories on adolescence, for he considered the early years of a child's life to be the formative ones. But he did deal briefly with adolescence in his *Three Essays on the Theory of Sexuality* (Freud, 1953). He described adolescence as a period of sexual excitement, anxiety, and sometimes personality disturbance. According to Freud, puberty is the culmination of a series of changes destined to give infantile sexual life its final, normal form. During the period of infancy, when pleasure is linked with oral activities

oral stage   (*oral stage*), children employ a sexual object outside their own bodies: their mother's breasts. From this object they derive physical satisfaction, warmth, pleasure, and security. While the mother feeds her infants, she also cuddles, caresses, kisses, and rocks them.

Gradually children's pleasures become autoerotic; that is, they begin to derive pleasure and satisfaction from activities that they can carry on by themselves. As they give up sucking at their mother's breasts, they find they can still derive pleasure from oral activities in which they can engage without the need of their mother. They learn to feed themselves, for example. Later, much concern and

anal stage   pleasure centers around anal activities and elimination (the **anal stage,** around age two to three). This period is followed by a developing interest in their own

phallic stage   bodies and in the examination of their sex organs during the **phallic stage** (ages four, five) of development.

period of latency   During the next stage, which Freud termed the **period of latency** (roughly from six years of age to puberty), children's sexual interests are not as intense, and they continue to relate to other people who help them and who satisfy their needs for love. Their source of pleasure gradually shifts from self to other persons. They become more interested in cultivating the friendship of others, especially those of the same sex.

genital stage   At puberty (the **genital stage**) this process of "object finding" is brought to completion. Along with maturation of the external and internal sexual organs comes a strong desire for resolution of the sexual tension that follows. This resolution demands a love object; therefore, Freud theorizes, adolescents are drawn to a member of the opposite sex who can resolve their tensions.

Freud stresses that the sexual aim of the adolescent is different from that of the child. The child seeks physical pleasure and psychic satisfaction through bodily contact and the stimulation of the erotogenic zones, and the pleasure derived becomes an end in itself. But at the onset of adolescence, the sexual aim changes. Now the aim is not only for erotogenic stimulation (which Freud calls *fore-pleasure*) but also for orgastic satisfaction. The sexual stimulation of the erotogenic zones of the body is no longer an end in itself but a preparation for the greater satisfaction of orgasm in intercourse:

> Fore-pleasure is thus the same pleasure that has already been produced, although on a smaller scale, by the infantile sexual instinct; end-pleasure is something new. . . . The formula for the new function of the erotogenic zones therefore: they are used to make possible, through the medium of the fore-pleasure which can be derived from them (as it was during infantile life), the production of the greater pleasure of satisfaction. (Freud, 1953, p. 210)

Freud also writes of the pleasure of orgasm:

> This last pleasure is the highest in intensity, and its mechanism differs from that of the earlier pleasure. It is brought about entirely by discharge: it is wholly a pleasure of satisfaction and with it the tension of the libido is for the time being extinguished. (Freud, 1953, p. 210)

Freud emphasizes two important elements of the sexual aim at adolescence, and with these some differences between men and women. One element is *physical and sensual*. In men this aim consists of the desire to produce sexual products, accompanied by physical pleasure. In women the desire for physical satisfaction and the release of sexual tension is still there but without the discharge of physical products. This desire in women is historically more repressed than in men, for the inhibitions to sexuality (shame, disgust, and so on) are developed earlier and more intensely in girls than in boys. However, there is a physical element to sexual desire in both men and women.

The second element of the sexual aim at adolescence is *psychic*; it is the affectionate component, which is more pronounced in females and which is similar to the infant's expression of sexuality. In other words the adolescent desires emotional satisfaction as well as physical release. This need for affection is especially prevalent in females, but satisfying the need is an important goal of all adolescent sexual striving. Freud would also emphasize that a normal sexual life is assured only when there is a convergence of the affectionate and the sensual currents, both being directed toward the sexual object and sexual aim. *The desire for true affection and for the release of sexual tension combined are the underlying normal needs that motivate the individual to seek out a love object.*

An *important part of the maturing process at adolescence is the loosening of the child's emotional ties with parents.* During the process of development, children's sexual impulses are directed toward their parents, with the son being drawn toward his mother and the daughter toward her father. Freud also speaks of a second Oedipal situation at adolescence, when a boy may fall in love with his mother and a young girl may fall in love with her father (Freud, 1925). However, a natural and socially reinforced barrier against incest restrains this expression of sexuality, so adolescents seek to loosen their connections with their families. As they overcome and

A desire for true affection is an underlying normal need motivating an adolescent to seek out a love object. (Robert Harbison)

repudiate their incestuous fantasies, adolescents also complete "one of the most painful, psychical achievements of the pubertal period . . . : detachment from parental authority" (Freud, 1953, p. 227). This is done by withdrawing their affection from their parents and transferring it to their peers. Blos referred to this emotional loss as the "mourning of separation" (Blos, 1979).

individuation   Subsequent theorists refer to the process of **individuation,** which involves a differentiation of an individual's behavior, feelings, judgments, and thoughts from those of parents. At the same time, the parent-child relationship moves toward growing cooperation, equality, and mutuality as the child becomes an autonomous person within the family context (Mazor and Enright, 1988).

Freud assumes that object-choice during adolescence must find its way to the opposite sex. There is a need to establish heterosexual friendships as one moves away from the homosexual attachments of childhood. Freud sees no harm in sentimental friendships with others of one's own sex, provided there is no permanent inversion or reversal of the sexual role and choice of the sexual object. Although reversal of sexual roles and sexual objects is frequent, Freud regards the reversal as a deviation from normal sexual life to be avoided if possible (Freud, 1953).

Anna Freud

Anna Freud (1895–1982) was more concerned with the period of adolescence than her father was and elaborated more on the process of adolescent development and the changes in the psychic structure of the child at puberty (Freud, 1946, 1958).

She characterized adolescence as a period of internal conflict, psychic disequilibrium, and erratic behavior. Adolescents are, on the one hand, egoistic, regarding themselves as the sole object of interest and the center of the universe, but, on the other hand, also capable of self-sacrifice and devotion. They form passionate love relations, only to break them off suddenly. They sometimes desire complete social involvement and group participation and at other times solitude. They oscillate between blind submission to and rebellion against authority. They are selfish and material minded but also full of lofty idealism. They are ascetic yet indulgent, inconsiderate of others yet touchy themselves. They oscillate between light-hearted optimism and blackest pessimism, between indefatigable enthusiasm and sluggishness and apathy (Freud, 1946).

descript. of adoles.

The reasons for this conflicting behavior are the psychic disequilibrium and internal conflict that accompanies sexual maturation at puberty (Blos, 1979). At puberty, the most obvious change is an increase in the instinctual drives (which have their source in the id). This is due partly to physical sexual maturation, with its accompanying interest in genitality and the flare-up of genital impulses. But the increase in instinctual drives at puberty also has a physical base not confined solely to the sexual life. Aggressive impulses are intensified, hunger becomes voracity, naughtiness sometimes erupts into criminal behavior. Oral and anal interests, long submerged, appear. Habits of cleanliness give way to dirt and disorder. Modesty and sympathy are replaced by exhibitionism and brutality. Anna Freud compared this increase in instinctual forces at puberty to the similar condition of early infancy. Early infantile sexuality and rebellious aggression are "resuscitated" at puberty (Freud, 1946, p. 159).

Because the impulses of the ***id*** increase at adolescence, they present a direct challenge to the individual's ego and superego. By ***ego*** Anna Freud means the sum of those mental processes that aim at safeguarding mental function. The ego is the evaluative, reasoning power of the individual. By ***superego*** Anna Freud means the ego-ideal and the conscience that result from the incorporation of the social values of the same-sexed parent. Therefore the renewed vigor of the instincts at adolescence directly challenges the reasoning abilities and the powers of conscience of the individual. The careful balance achieved between these psychic powers during latency is overthrown as open warfare breaks out between the id and superego. The ego, which previously has been able to enforce a truce, has as much trouble keeping the peace now as does a weak-willed parent when confronted by two strong-willed children who are quarreling. If the ego allies itself completely with the id, "no trace will be left of the previous character of the individual and the entrance into adult life will be marked by a riot of uninhibited gratification of instinct" (Freud, 1946, p. 163). If the ego sides completely with the superego, the character of the individual of the latency period will declare itself once and for all, with the id impulses confined within the narrow limits prescribed for the child but with the need for a constant expenditure of psychic energy on anticathexes (emotionally charged activities), defense mechanisms, and emotional sympathy to hold the id in check.

id

ego

superego

defense
mechanisms

Unless this id-ego-superego conflict is resolved at adolescence, the consequences can be emotionally devastating to the individual. Anna Freud discusses how the ego employs indiscriminately all the methods of defense (in psychological terms, the **_defense mechanisms_**) to win the battle. The ego represses, displaces, denies, and reverses the instincts and turns them against the self; it produces phobias and hysterical symptoms and builds anxiety by means of obsessional thinking and behavior. According to Anna Freud, the rise of asceticism and intellectualism at adolescence is a symptom of mistrust of all instinctual wishes. (See also the section on Piaget in chapter 6.) The accentuation of neurotic symptoms and inhibitions during adolescence signals the partial success of the ego and superego but at the expense of the individual. Anna Freud does feel, however, that harmony among the id, ego, and superego is possible and does occur finally in most normal adolescents if the superego is sufficiently developed during the latent period—but not to inhibit the instincts too much, causing extreme guilt and anxiety—and if the ego is sufficiently strong and wise to mediate the conflict (Freud, 1946).

SOCIOPSYCHOANALYTICAL VIEWS OF ADOLESCENCE

Erik Erikson: Ego Identity

Erikson (b. 1902) modified Freud's theory of psychosexual development as a result of findings of modern sociopsychology and anthropology and described eight stages of human development (Erikson, 1950, 1968, 1982). In each of the eight stages the individual has a psychosocial task to master. The confrontation with each task produces conflict, with two possible outcomes. If the conflict during the stage is successfully resolved, a positive quality is built into the personality and further development takes place. If the conflict persists or is unsatisfactorily resolved, the ego is damaged because a negative quality is incorporated into it. Therefore, according to Erikson, the overall task of the individual is to acquire a positive ego identity as he or she moves from one stage to the next. The positive solution of the task, each with its negative counterpart, is listed below for each period (Erikson, 1950, 1959):

1. Infancy: Achieving trust versus mistrust.
2. Early childhood: Achieving autonomy versus shame and doubt.
3. Play age: Achieving initiative versus guilt.
4. School age: Achieving industry versus inferiority.
5. Adolescence: Achieving identity versus identity diffusion.
6. Young adult: Achieving intimacy versus isolation.
7. Adulthood: Achieving generativity versus stagnation.
8. Mature age: Achieving ego integrity versus disgust, despair.

Because this chapter is concerned only with the adolescent period, discussion will be limited to the adolescent task of establishing ego identity. Erikson emphasizes several aspects of this process.

Identity formation neither begins nor ends with adolescence. It is a lifelong process, largely unconscious to the individual. Its roots go back in childhood to the experience of mutuality between the mothering adult and mothered children. As children reach out to their first love objects, they begin to find self-realization coupled with mutual recognition. Their identity formations continue through a process of selection and assimilation of childhood identifications, which in turn depend upon parental, peer, and society's identification of them as important persons. The community both molds and gives recognition to newly emerging individuals. The child in the multiplicity of successive and tentative identifications begins early to build up expectations of what it will be like to be older and what it will feel like to have been younger—expectations that become part of an identity as they are, step by step, verified in decisive experiences of psychosocial fittedness. Thus, *the process of identity formation emerges as an evolving configuration gradually established by successive ego syntheses and resyntheses throughout childhood* (Erikson, 1959).

Erikson emphasizes that adolescence is a normative crisis, a normal phase of increased conflict, characterized by a fluctuation of ego strength. The experimenting individual becomes the victim of an identity consciousness that is the basis for the self-consciousness of youth. It is during this time that the individual must establish a sense of *personal identity* and avoid the dangers of *role diffusion* and *identity diffusion.* To establish identity requires individual effort in evaluating personal assets and liabilities and in learning how to use these in working to achieve a clearer concept of who one is and what one wants to be and become. Erikson feels that during adolescence there must be an integration of all converging identity elements and a resolution of conflict that he divided into seven major parts.

Temporal Perspective versus Time Confusion. This means gaining a sense of time and of the continuity of life so that one can coordinate the past and the future and gain some concept of how long it takes to achieve one's life plans. It means learning to estimate and allocate one's time. Research has shown that a true sense of time does not develop until relatively late in adolescence—around fifteen or sixteen (Gallatin, 1975).

Self-Certainty versus Self-Consciousness This means developing self-confidence based upon past experiences so that one believes in oneself and feels that one has a reasonable chance of accomplishing future aims. To do this adolescents go through a period of increasing self-awareness and self-consciousness, especially in relation to their physical self-image and social relationships. When development follows a relatively normal course, children acquire confidence in themselves and their abilities. They develop confidence in their ability to cope in the present and in anticipation of future success (Randolph and Dye, 1981).

Role Experimentation versus Role Fixation Adolescents have an opportunity to try out the different roles they are to play in society. They can experiment with many different identities, with different personality characteristics, with a variety of ways of talking and acting, with different ideas, philosophies, and goals, or with different types of relationships. Identity comes through opportunities for such experimentation. Those who have developed too much inner restraint and guilt, who have lost initiative, or who prematurely experience role fixation never really find out who they are (Erikson, 1968).

Apprenticeship versus Work Paralysis   Similarly, the adolescent has an opportunity to explore and try out different occupations before deciding on a vocation. Once entered, one's job plays a large part in determining identity (Erikson, 1968). Furthermore, a negative self-image in the form of inferiority feelings can prevent one from mustering the necessary energy to succeed at school or on the job.

Sexual Polarization versus Bisexual Confusion   Adolescents continue to attempt to define what it means to be "male" and "female." Erikson feels it is important that adolescents develop a clear identification with one sex or the other as a basis for future heterosexual intimacy and as a basis for a firm identity. Furthermore, he emphasizes that for communities to function properly, men and women must be willing to assume their "proper roles"; sexual polarization, then, is necessary (Erikson, 1968). Much of present-day analysis (and some criticism) of Erikson relates to his emphasis on the need for sexual polarization.

Leadership and Followership versus Authority Confusion   As adolescents expand their social horizons through education, work, apprenticeship, social groups, and new friends and contacts, they begin to learn to take leadership responsibilities as well as how to follow others. But at the same time they discover there are competing claims on their allegiance. The state, employer, sweetheart, parents, and friends all make demands, with the result that adolescents experience confusion in relation to authority. To whom should they listen? Whom should they follow? To whom should they give their primary allegiance? Sorting out the answers requires an examination of personal values and priorities.

Ideological Commitment versus Confusion of Values   This conflict is closely related to all the others because construction of an ideology guides other aspects of behavior. Erikson refers to this struggle as the "search for fidelity" (Erikson, 1968). Erikson emphasizes that individuals need something to believe in, to join, to follow, something to which to relate and to devote oneself (Logan, 1980).

If the individual is able to resolve these seven conflicts, a firm identity emerges. The crisis is past when he or she no longer has to question at every moment his or her own identity, when he or she has subordinated childhood identity and found a new self-identification (Erikson, 1950).

Erikson acknowledges that finding an acceptable identity is much more difficult during a period of rapid social change because the older generation is no longer able to provide adequate role models for the younger generation.

One interesting aspect of Erikson's theory is his concept of adolescence as a *psychosocial moratorium,* a societally sanctioned intermediary period between childhood and adulthood, during which the individual through free role experimentation may find a niche in some section of society (Erikson, 1959). Adolescence becomes a period of standing back, of analyzing, and of trying various roles

psychosocial moratorium

without the responsibility for assuming any one role. Erikson acknowledges that the duration and intensity of adolescence vary in different societies, but that near the end of adolescence a failure to establish identity results in deep suffering for the adolescent because of a diffusion of roles. Such role diffusion may be responsible for the appearance of previously latent psychological disturbances.

The adolescent who fails in the search for an identity will experience self-doubt, role diffusion, and role confusion; such an individual may indulge in a self-destructive, one-sided preoccupation or activity. He or she will continue to be morbidly preoccupied with the opinions of others or may turn to the other extreme of no longer caring what others think. He or she may withdraw or turn to drugs or alcohol in order to relieve the anxiety that role diffusion creates. Ego diffusion and personality confusion can be observed in the chronic delinquent and in psychotic personality disorganization (Muuss, 1988, p. 63).*

Erikson emphasizes that *whereas the identity crisis is most pronounced at adolescence, a redefinition of one's ego identity may also take place at other periods of life*: when individuals leave home, get their first job, marry, become parents, get divorced, change occupations, become unemployed, become seriously ill, are widowed, or retire. The extent to which individuals are able to cope with these other changes in identity is determined partly by the success with which they have first mastered the adolescent identity crises (Erikson, 1959).

Since Erikson introduced his theory, numerous research studies have validated, clarified, or questioned his ideas (particularly those related to female subjects) (Adams, 1977; Adams and Shea, 1979; Anderson and Fleming, 1986; Bourne, 1978a, 1978b; Cote, 1986; Josselson, 1982; Juhasz, 1982; Logan, 1978;

---

* From Muuss, R.E. (1988). *Theories of Adolescence*, 5th ed. Copyright© McGraw Hill Publishing Company. Used by permission.

Identity, described as a total concept of self, is personal as well as social; this social aspect includes one's collective identity. (© The Christian Science Monitor/Barth Falkenberg)

Matteson, 1977; McClain, 1975; Morgan and Farber, 1982; Newman and Newman, 1978a, 1978b; Newman and Newman, 1988; Onyehalu, 1981; Orlofsky, 1978; Raphael, 1977, 1978, 1979; Rosenthal, Gurney, and Moore, 1981; Rothman, 1978; St. Clair and Day, 1979; Waterman and Goldman, 1976; Waterman and Nevid, 1977).

Identity has many components (Rogow, Marcia, and Slugoski, 1983)—*physical, sexual, social, vocational, moral, ideological,* and *psychological* characteristics—that make up the total self (Grotevant, Thorbecke, and Meyer, 1982; LaVoie, 1976; Miller, 1978; Newman and Newman, 1978a; Raphael, 1979; Waterman, 1982; Waterman and Nevid, 1977). Thus, individuals may be identified by their physical appearance and traits; by their gender as well as their sex roles; by their social characteristics, social relationships, and membership in groups; by their vocations and work; by their religious and political affiliations and ideologies; and by the characteristics of their psychological adjustment and extent of their personality synthesis. *Identity may be described in terms of the total concept of self.* It is personal because it is a sense of "I-ness," but it is also social, for it includes "we-ness," or one's collective identity (Adams, 1977). Adolescents who have a positive identity have developed a sense of being all right, of accepting themselves. Furthermore, identity development is associated with the development of intimacy. Adolescents are attracted to those with identity statuses similar to themselves (Goldman et al., 1980). Identity achievement also helps in developing committed relationships: intimacy alters identity—it helps people grow (Kacerguis and Adams, 1980).

Some adolescents adopt negative identities, defined self-images contrary to the cultural values of the community:

> "Failure," "good-for-nothing," "juvenile delinquent," "hood," and "greaser" are labels the adult society commonly applies to certain adolescents. In the absence of any indication of the possibilities of success or contribution to the society, the young person accepts these negative labels as his/her self-definition and proceeds to validate this identity by continuing to behave in ways that will strengthen it. (Newman and Newman, 1978b, p. 313)

Protinsky (1988) found that adolescents who exhibit behavioral problems score much lower on measures of general identity than those who do not have such problems.

Other adolescents will behave in ways to reduce temporarily the anxiety of an uncertain or incomplete identity (Logan, 1978). Some will try to *escape* through intense immediate experiences such as drug abuse, wild parties, rock concerts, or fast rides in cars. These emotional experiences temporarily blot out the search for identity. Others *substitute temporary identities* by becoming a joiner, a goof-off, a clown, a bully, a pool shark, a ladies' man. Some seek to *strengthen their identity* temporarily through petty crime, vandalism, competitive sports, popularity contests, or short-term expedients. The person who becomes a bigot, who takes a stance against minorities, or who becomes a superpatriot seeks to build a temporary "fortress identity." *Ensuring a meaningless identity* by engaging in such fads as participating in trivia contests is another possibility. For some youths, a meaningless identity is better than no identity at all.

Some aspects of identity are more easily formed than others. Physical and sexual identities seem to be established earliest. Young adolescents are concerned with their body image before they become interested in choosing a vocation or examining their moral values and ideologies. Similarly, they must deal with their own sexual identities both before and after puberty (Waterman and Nevid, 1977).

Vocational, ideological, and moral identities are established more slowly (Logan, 1983). These identities depend upon adolescents' having reached the formal operation stage of cognitive growth and development that enables them to explore alternative ideas and courses of action. (See the discussion on Piaget in chapter 6.) In addition, reformulation of these identities requires a high degree of independence of thought. The exploration of occupational alternatives is the most immediate and concrete task as adolescents finish high school or enter college. Religious and political ideologies are examined during late adolescence, especially the college years, but identities in these areas may be in a state of flux for years (Raphael, 1979).

There does seem to be some difference between males and females in identity achievement (Kroger, 1986). More females than males, for example, experience a crisis in sexual identity, probably because standards for female sexual behavior are still more restrictive than those for males, even though society is moving in the direction of a single standard (Waterman and Nevid, 1977). At the same time, more females than males solve this crisis and achieve sexual identity. Males less often question the sexual ideologies of their society.

In spite of the increasing emphasis on careers for women, *more females than males have trouble establishing occupational identities.* One reason may be that college is still more conducive to ego development in males than in females, especially in terms of making vocational decisions and preparing for an occupation. Also, at this period when female roles are in a state of flux, women are experiencing conflict in gaining a sense of confidence and worthiness as females. However, a low level of anxiety about themselves and their roles indicates that increasing numbers are solving their identity crisis. Females raised by mothers who encourage independence are those most likely to find their identities apart from family living (Newman and Newman, 1978a). One study found that high school girls whose parents were divorced were significantly more likely to be identity achievers than were those from unbroken homes. The authors conclude:

> These findings suggest that the security of the traditional family may not provide the optimal setting for the adolescent female to engage in the processes leading to identity achievement. In addition, the finding of higher identity achievement among girls from broken homes adds to the growing body of evidence that divorce does not necessarily have adverse effects on the adolescent, and, in fact, may be associated with better adjustment of the adolescent. (St. Clair and Day, 1979, p. 324)

James Marcia

Among the many studies of Erikson's concepts, those by James Marcia have been particularly influential (Bernard, 1981; Marcia, 1966, 1967, 1976; Marcia and Friedman, 1970; Toder and Marcia, 1973). According to Marcia, the criteria used to establish the attainment of a mature identity are two variables, *crisis* and *commitment*, in relation to occupational choice, religion, and political ideology. "Crisis refers to the adolescent's period of engagement in choosing among meaningful alternatives; commitment refers to the degree of personal investment the individual exhibits" (Marcia, 1966). A *mature identity is achieved when the individual has experienced a crisis and has become committed to an occupation and ideology.*

identity diffused Marcia's research revealed four basic types of persons (Marcia, 1966). **Identity**
or identity **diffused** or **identity confused** subjects have not experienced a crisis period, nor
confused have they made any commitment. They have not decided on an occupation nor are they much concerned about it. They are either uninterested in ideological matters or feel one outlook is as good as another and therefore may sample them all. One author reports:

> Perhaps the word which best characterizes the diffusion subject is "withdrawal."
> . . . The most frequent response to stress is withdrawal. Related to this is the
> finding that . . . diffusions have shown the lowest level of intimacy with same- and
> opposite-sex friends or else appeared to lack any significant social relationship.
> (Bourne, 1978b).

foreclosure   **Foreclosure** subjects have not experienced a crisis, but they have made commitments to occupations and ideologies that are not the result of their own searching but ready-made and handed down to them, frequently from parents. They often have identified closely with same-sex parents (Cella, DeWolfe, and Fitzgibbon, 1987). They become what others intend them to become, without really deciding for themselves (White, 1980). Foreclosure subjects are typified by youths who adopt their parents' religion, follow the vocation their parents select for them, or submerge themselves in conformity to peer groups. Their foreclosure status is often a symptom of neurotic dependence (Cote and Levine, 1983). Such subjects score high on authoritarianism and intolerance, show a high degree of conformity and conventionality, and are usually satisfied with their college education (Bourne, 1978a; Josselson, 1982; Marcia, 1967). When put under stress, however, they perform poorly. Their security lies in avoiding change or stress. As Keniston writes, the "total lack of conflict during adolescence is an ominous sign that the individual's psychological maturity may not be progressing" (Keniston, 1971, p. 364).

It has been suggested also that foreclosure is a means of reducing anxiety. Persons who are too uncomfortable with uncertainty make choices without a lengthy process of consideration. They often marry while still in school, as well as make early decisions about vocations without lengthy consideration (Lutes, 1981).

The question needs to be asked, however: Do individuals in cultures that neither encourage nor support identity crises have an identity? Of course, but it is a foreclosed one. An identity does not have to be achieved in these cultures to be functional. Going through the decision-making process necessary to achieve an identity can be a painful, unrewarding experience if no cultural support is given for the crisis. It is certainly easier to remain foreclosed in a foreclosure society (Rowe and Marcia, 1980).

   Moratorium subjects are involved in continual crises. They are actively search-   *moratorium*
ing out various alternatives but have not made any permanent commitments. As
a consequence, such persons seem confused, unstable, and discontented. They
are often rebellious and uncooperative and score low on authoritarianism. Because they experience crises, they tend to be anxious. These adolescents generally
have fairly permissive parents, are uncertain they have selected the right major
in college, and may be unhappy with their college experience and education.
Others show a high level of authority conflict, so that part of their crisis is an
attempt to disengage themselves from their parents (Bourne, 1978b). However,
using adolescence as a period of moratorium can be an advantage. Muuss writes:

> If adolescents, while experimenting with moratorium issues, have sufficient op-
> portunity to search, experiment, play the field, and try on different roles, there is
> a very good chance that they will find themselves, develop an identity, and emerge
> with commitments to politics, religion, a vocational goal and a more clearly de-
> fined sex role and sex preference. These final commitments are frequently less
> radical than some of the tentative and exploratory commitments during the mora-
> torium. According to Marcia, moratorium is truly an essential and necessary pre-
> requisite for identity achievement (Muuss, 1988, p. 72).*

   Moratorium females score high on measures of cognitive complexity, tolerance of ambiguity, intelligence, and social class. These high-scoring females are
those who are best able to explore alternatives and to use a moratorium period
in a constructive way (Raphael, 1977, 1978).

   Entering college increases the number of adolescents in a state of moratorium. This is because at college these students are more actively and thoughtfully
confronted with the crisis of making an occupational commitment and because
they are stimulated to rethink their ideologies. As a result, many adolescents
change their occupational plans during college.

   The college environment favors male over female development in helping
develop identities. This is partly explained by Toder and Marcia: "It would appear
that there is still more social support for the male while he breaks away from
parental values and experiments with new roles than there is for the female who
can, apparently, count on less support" (Toder and Marcia, 1973).

   Identity achieved subjects have experienced a psychological moratorium,   *identity achieved*
have resolved their identity crisis by carefully evaluating various alternatives and
choices, and have come to conclusions and decisions on their own. They have
been highly motivated to achieve and are able to do so not so much because of
great ability as because they have attained higher levels of intrapsychic integration and social adaptation (Bourne, 1978b). Once an identity has been achieved,
there is self-acceptance, a stable self-definition, and a commitment to a vocation,
religion, and political ideology. There is harmony within oneself and an acceptance of capacities, opportunities, and limitations. There is a more realistic con-

---

* From Muuss, R.E. (1988). *Theories of Adolescence*, 5th ed. Copyright © McGraw Hill Publishing
Company. Used by permission.

cept of goals (Marcia, 1966, 1967; Marcia and Friedman, 1970). Although these individuals are more advanced in their ego development, they are not necessarily free of all anxiety, however (Adams and Shea, 1979). Once committed to specific goals, they still worry about achieving them (Rothman, 1984).

Prior to the women's movement, identity-achieved females showed fewer positive traits than did males. Identity-achieved females, for example, showed lowest in self-esteem of all the four groups studied, with foreclosure females showing the highest self-esteem. Identity-achieved females also showed considerable anxiety, indicating that they were achieving identity status through an occupation (they were also majoring in more difficult subjects), but in opposition to stereotyped, cultural expectations, and with consequent feelings of anxiety and lowered self-esteem because of perceived social stigmas (Marcia and Friedman, 1970). Studies after 1972, however, indicate this is slowly changing, with female identity achievers scoring higher in self-esteem and showing less anxiety. One study showed that college females reported significantly less ego diffusion than males within every age group (17 to 20 years) (Josselson, 1982). A 1981 study showed that women who had achieved identity were those who were functioning at the highest ego levels (Ginsburg and Orlofsky, 1981). A 1982 study showed that women holding nontraditional views of women's roles had achieved a clearer sense of identity than those with traditional views (Stein and Weston, 1982). They showed the positive psychological growth that Erikson suggested is necessary for mental health. It is evident that females increasingly are able to be self-actualizing and to find their identity through occupations and to experience more self-satisfaction and self-esteem while doing do.

Research with high school students indicates that few have achieved identity by the time of graduation (Rahael and Xelowski, 1980). Living at home and possessing limited life and work experiences are not conducive to identity achievement. Some students miss out on a moratorium and have made commitments of a sort, which are often superficial:

> I thought about various jobs when I was in grade 11. Now I know I want to be a nurse. No I can't imagine anything causing me to change my mind. (Raphael and Xelowski, 1980, p. 385).

> I thought earlier this year about interior decorating, but now I want to be a secretary and will stay with that until I have a child. (Ibid.)

Are these individuals identity achieved? It is doubtful. Even at the college level, 80 percent of students change their major during their four years. In general, however, *the percentage of adolescents who are identity achievers increases with age* (Fregeau and Barker, 1986).

SOCIOLOGICAL VIEWS OF ADOLESCENCE

In studying adolescence, the sociologist focuses on the social environment as the determinant of adolescent development (Hall and Lindzay, 1970). The sociologist recognizes the existence of biological and intrapersonal psychological processes but chooses to study the interaction between the adolescent and society.

Allison Davis: Socialized Anxiety

In "Socialization and Adolescent Personality" (Davis, 1944), Allison Davis (b. 1902) defines **socialization** as the process by which individuals learn and adopt the ways, ideas, beliefs, values, and norms of their culture and make them part of their personalities. Davis sees the process of maturation during adolescence as the process of becoming socialized.

socialization

According to Davis, each society defines the goals, values, and behaviors it desires of its members. Socially acceptable behavior is rewarded; unacceptable behavior is punished. Repeated punishment for unacceptable behavior induces what Davis calls "socialized anxiety," which becomes the negative motivation for socialization to take place. Once socialized anxiety has been induced in children, they seek to show behavior that minimizes it. If socialized anxiety is too strong, it can have an inhibiting or disorganizing effect. If socialized anxiety is too weak, the attainment of maturity is not likely either. Therefore it is important that a correct amount be present (Davis, 1944).

Davis emphasizes that middle-class and lower-class cultures have different expectations of their adolescents. Middle-class cultures emphasize prestige, social position, success, status, and morality. These expectations give rise to more social anxiety in their adolescents than is evident in the lower-class adolescent. The social anxiety generated in turn motivates the middle-class youngster to strive even more for socially desirable goals.

Lower-class cultures do not put so much emphasis on long-term goals, success, status, and a postponement of short-term pleasures like sex expression. Low socioeconomic status adolescents do not develop the kind of social anxiety that motivates them to succeed according to middle-class standards. They see no point in postponing many sexual or recreational pleasures, for they do not expect to receive the rewards of a middle-class culture anyhow (Davis, 1944).

Davis's views are important because they emphasize that society influences what adolescents are, what their problems are, and what they become. The sociological view alone, however, does not explain why youths from even the poorest families sometimes succeed according to middle-class standards. Davis's view must be considered alongside the views of other disciplines.

Albert Bandura and Richard H. Walters: Social Learning Theory

Social learning theory is concerned with the relationship between social and environmental factors and their influence on behavior. Because Bandura (b. 1925) and Walters (1918–1967) have been more concerned with the application of that theory to adolescence than have other social learning theorists, the major focus here will be on their work. Their views are outlined in four major books (Bandura, 1969, 1973; Bandura and Walters, 1959, 1963) and in numerous articles and research studies (Bandura, 1964, 1965, 1971; Bandura and Kupers, 1964; Bandura and McDonald, 1963; Ban-

One way children learn is by observing the behavior of others and imitating this pattern; this process is called *modeling*. (© Frank Siteman)

dura and Mischel, 1965; Bandura and Perloff, 1967; Bandura, Ross, and Ross, 1963a, 1963b; Bandura and Whalen, 1966).

modeling   Bandura and Walters emphasize that children learn through observing the behavior of others and by imitating this pattern, a process referred to as ***modeling***. Modeling then becomes a socialization process by which habitual response patterns develop (Bandura and Walters, 1959; McDonald, 1977). As children grow, they imitate different models from their social environment. In many studies, parents are listed as the most significant adults in the lives of adolescents (Blyth, Hill, and Thiel, 1982; Galbo, 1983). Siblings are also mentioned as significant others, as are extended family members such as aunts and uncles. Nonrelated significant adults include ministers and youth ministers found within the church setting, teachers, or neighbors.

Different studies reveal varying results, however, depending on the group surveyed. Adolescents from working-class families less frequently mention mothers or fathers. College-age adolescents often mention faculty members and friends as significant others in their lives (Galbo, 1984). Studies of role models among black youths suggest a preference for movie stars or athletes (Oberle, Stowers, and Folk, 1978). Investigations among Native American youths reveal the importance of parents and close family members (Lafromboise, Dauphinais, and Rowe, 1978).

When family influence declines, entertainment heroes and peers become increasingly important as models, especially in influencing verbal expressions, hair styles, clothing, music, and basic social values of all adolescents. Imitation is important in learning such complex social behaviors as self-control, altruism, aggression, and sexual behavior or in learning such motor skills as handwriting, driving a car, or operating a machine. Bandura (1962) showed, for example, that Guatemalan natives could learn to operate a cotton textile machine by observing the correct operation of the machine for a number of days.

Bandura showed also that when children watched unusually aggressive behavior in a real-life model or a model in a film or cartoon, many of the children's responses were accurate imitations of the aggressive acts of the real-life model or the person in the film. The cartoon model elicited less precise imitation (Bandura, Ross, and Ross, 1963). Walters found similar results among high school students, young women, and male hospital attendants (Bandura and Walters, 1959, 1963). This research has led to much concern about the effects on children and adolescents from watching aggressive behavior on television screens: "exposure to filmed aggression heightens aggressive reactions" (Bandura, Ross, and Ross, 1963a). (See also chapter 18.) This finding has been substantiated (Tooth, 1985).

Bandura and Walters showed that a number of factors in the home situation contribute to effective socialization. One is early dependency of children on parents, so that children desire approval and affection. In studies of adolescent aggression, Bandura and Walters (1959) showed that aggressive boys were less dependent on their fathers, more rejected by their fathers, and their fathers spent less time with them than did the fathers of less aggressive boys.

Another home factor that contributes to socialization is the exertion of socialization pressure in the form of demands, restrictions, and limitations: in other words, discipline. The parents of less aggressive sons limited the amount of aggression they would tolerate, used more reasoning as a disciplinary method, and had higher expectations of the boys than did the parents of aggressive sons. Aggressive sons were encouraged to show aggression outside the home toward other children: to stand up for their rights, to use their fists. The fathers of aggressive boys seemed to get vicarious enjoyment from their sons' aggressive acts and were more permissive of their sons' sexual behavior. As a result these boys had greater sexual experience than did other boys (Bandura and Walters, 1959).

The parents of the aggressive boys were also more punitive when the aggressive behavior was directed toward them. They used more physical discipline, isolation, deprivation of privileges, and less reasoning. The more the boys were punished physically at home for aggressive behavior, the more aggressive they became. Thus, they learned aggression by modeling the behavior of the punishing parent. Bandura and Perloff (1967, p. 43) write: "When a parent punishes his child physically for having aggressed toward peers, for example, the intended outcome of this training is that the child should refrain from hitting others. The child, however, is also learning from parental demonstration how to aggress physically."

The conscience development of the aggressive boys also differed from that of the less aggressive sons. The behavior of the latter was controlled by guilt and internal avoidance, whereas if the aggressive sons were inhibited at all, it was by fear of punishment rather than by guilt and internal controls. Because aggressive

reinforcement

sons did not have as close emotional relationships with their parents, especially with fathers, their conscience development suffered.

Most social learning theorists emphasize the role of **reinforcement,** or the responses of others, in influencing future behavior. Bandura expands on this idea, speaking of **vicarious reinforcement** and **self-reinforcement.** Vicarious reinforcement consists of the positive or negative consequences that one observes others'

vicarious reinforcement

experience. Observing that others are rewarded for aggressive behavior increases the possibility that the observer will also show aggression. Bandura and Perloff (1967) observed that self-reinforcement was as effective as external reinforcement

self-reinforcement

in influencing behavior. Once the performance of a desired response pattern, such as shooting and making baskets with a basketball, acquired a positive value, adolescents could administer their own reinforcement by producing the baskets and then feeling good afterward. Adolescents who set reasonable goal levels of performance and reach that level feel proud and satisfied internally and become decreasingly dependent on parents, teachers, and bosses to give them rewards.

Bandura questions the stage-theory assumption that adolescence is inevitably a period of "storm and stress, tension, rebellion" (Bandura, 1964). He feels that the description of turmoil, anxiety, sexual tensions, compulsive conformity, and acute identity crises applies to the actual behavior of only "the deviant ten percent of the adolescent population." Research tends to prove Bandura correct; data indicate that "the rate of emotional disturbance for adolescents does not differ significantly from the population at large" (Ellis, 1979, p. 101).

The work of social-learning theorists is of great importance in explaining human behavior. It is especially important in emphasizing that *what adults do and the role models they represent are far more important in influencing adolescent behavior than what they say.* Teachers and parents can best encourage human decency, altruism, moral values, and a social conscience by exhibiting these virtues themselves.

ANTHROPOLOGICAL VIEWS OF ADOLESCENCE

Margaret Mead and Ruth Benedict

cultural determinism

The theories of Margaret Mead (1901–1978), Ruth Benedict (1887–1948), and other cultural anthropologists have been called **cultural determinism** and **cultural relativism** because *anthropologists emphasize the importance of the social environment in determining the personality development of the child.* And because social institutions, economic patterns, habits, mores, rituals, and religious beliefs vary

cultural relativism

from society to society, culture is relative. The kinds of influences that mold the child depend on the culture in which the child grows up (Benedict, 1950; Mead, 1950, 1953).

The later writings of Mead (Mead, 1970, 1974) and others have undergone some modification; they show some recognition of universal aspects of development (incest taboos, for example) and more acknowledgment of the biological role in human development. Today extreme positions are generally disregarded by both geneticists and anthropologists.* They agree that a composite view that acknowledges both biogenetic factors and environmental forces comes closest to the truth.

What did Mead and Benedict have to say about adolescence?

Cultural Continuity versus Discontinuity

Anthropologists challenge the basic truths of all age and stage theories of child and adolescent development. Mead discovered, for example, that Samoan children follow a relatively continuous growth pattern, with no abrupt changes from one age to the other. They are not expected to behave one way as children, another way as adolescents, and yet another way as adults. They never have to change abruptly their ways of thinking or acting; they do not have to unlearn as adults what they learned as children, so adolescence does not represent an abrupt change or transition from one pattern of behavior to another. This principle of continuity of cultural conditioning may be illustrated with three examples by Benedict (1938) and Mead (1950).

First, the responsible roles of children in primitive societies are contrasted with the nonresponsible roles of children in Western culture. Children in primitive societies learn responsibility quite early. Play and work often involve the same activity; for example, by "playing" with a bow and arrow, a boy learns to hunt. His adult hunting "work" is a continuation of his youthful hunting "play." In contrast, children in Western culture must assume drastically different roles as they grow up: they shift from nonresponsible play to responsible work and must do it rather suddenly.

Second, the submissive role of children in Western culture is contrasted with the dominant role of children in primitive society. Children in Western culture must drop their childhood submission and adopt its opposite, dominance, as they become adults. Mead (1950) showed that the Samoan child is not taught submission as a child and then suddenly expected to become dominant upon reaching adulthood. On the contrary, the 6- or 7-year-old Samoan girl dominates her younger siblings and in turn is dominated by the older ones. The older she gets, the more she dominates and disciplines others and the fewer there are to dominate her (the parents never try to dominate her). When she becomes an adult, she does not experience the dominance-submission conflict of the adolescent in Western society.

Third, the similarity of sex roles of children and adults in primitive cultures is contrasted with the dissimilar sex roles of children and adults in Western culture. Mead indicates that the Samoan girl experiences no real discontinuity of sex roles as she passes from childhood to adulthood. She has the opportunity to experiment and become familiar with sex with almost no taboos (except against incest).

---

* For a critique of Mead see: Freeman, D. (1983). *Margaret Mead and Samoa: The Making and Unmaking of an Anthropological Myth*. Cambridge, MA.: Harvard University Press.

Therefore, by the time adulthood is reached, she is able to assume a sexual role in marriage very easily.

By contrast, in Western culture infant sexuality is denied and adolescent sexuality is repressed; sex is considered evil and dangerous. When adolescents mature sexually, they must unlearn those earlier attitudes and taboos and become sexually responsive adults.

Storm and Stress versus Cultural Conditioning

In *showing the continuity of development of children in some cultures in contrast to the discontinuity of development of children in Western culture,* anthropologists and some psychologists (Roll, 1980) cast doubt upon the universality of ages and stages of growth of children in all cultures. Only societies that emphasize discontinuity of behavior (one type of behavior as a child, another as an adult) are those described as "age-grade societies" (Benedict, 1938).

Anthropologists challenge the inevitability of the storm and stress of adolescence by minimizing the disturbance of physical changes and by emphasizing the interpretation given those changes. Menstruation is a case in point. One tribe may teach that the menstruating girl is a danger to the tribe (she may scare the game or dry up the well); another tribe may consider her condition a blessing (she could increase the food supply or the priest could obtain a blessing by touching her). A girl taught that menstruation is a positive good will react and act differently from a girl who is taught that it is a curse. Therefore, the stress and strains of pubescent physical changes may be the result of certain cultural interpretations of those changes and not due to any inherent biological tendencies.

Cross-Cultural Views on Parent-Adolescent Relations

Anthropologists describe many conditions in Western culture that create a generation gap, but *they deny the inevitability of that gap* (Mead, 1974). Rapidity of social change, pluralistic value systems, and modern technology make the world appear too complex and too unpredictable to adolescents to provide them with a stable frame of reference. Furthermore, early physiological puberty and the need for prolonged education allow many years for the development and assimilation of a peer-group culture in which adolescent values, customs, and mores may be in conflict with those in the adult world (Finkelstein and Gaier, 1983). Mead feels that close family ties should be loosened to give adolescents more freedom to make their own choices and live their own lives. By requiring less conformity and less dependency and by tolerating individual differences within the family, Mead feels that adolescent-parent conflict and tension can be minimized (Mead, 1950). Also, Mead feels that youths can be accepted into adult society at younger ages. Gainful employment, even part time, would promote greater financial independence. Parenthood should be postponed but not necessarily sex or marriage. (See also the section on Mead's two-stage marriage proposal in chapter 17). Adolescents should be given a greater voice in the social and political life of the community. These measures would eliminate some of the discontinuities of cultural conditioning of children growing up in Western society and would allow for a smoother, easier transition to adulthood.

PSYCHOSOCIAL VIEWS OF ADOLESCENCE

Havighurst: Developmental Tasks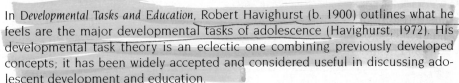

In *Developmental Tasks and Education,* Robert Havighurst (b. 1900) outlines what he feels are the major developmental tasks of adolescence (Havighurst, 1972). His developmental task theory is an eclectic one combining previously developed concepts; it has been widely accepted and considered useful in discussing adolescent development and education.

Havighurst sought to develop a psychosocial theory of adolescence by combining consideration of individuals' needs with societal demands. What individuals need and society demands constitute the ***developmental tasks.*** *They are the skills, knowledge, functions, and attitudes that individuals have to acquire at certain points in their lives through physical maturation, social expectations, and personal effort.* Mastery of the tasks at each stage of development results in adjustment and preparation for the harder tasks ahead. Mastery of adolescent tasks results in maturity. Failure to master the adolescent tasks results in anxiety, social disapproval, and inability to function as a mature person.

developmental tasks

According to Havighurst there is a teachable moment, a correct time for teaching any task. Some of the tasks arise out of biological changes, others from societal expectations at a given age, or the individual's motivation at certain times to do particular things. Furthermore, developmental tasks differ from culture to culture, depending on the relative importance of biological, psychological, and cultural elements in determining the tasks. If a task is determined primarily by biological factors, it may be almost universal; if determined by cultural elements, great differences in the nature of the task may exist from culture to culture. There are significant differences in developmental tasks in the upper, middle, and lower classes of the United States.

Havighurst (1972) outlined eight major tasks during the adolescent period:

1. Accepting one's physique and using the body effectively.
2. Achieving new and more mature relations with age-mates of both sexes.
3. Achieving a masculine or feminine social-sex role.
4. Achieving emotional independence from parents and other adults.
5. Preparing for an economic career.
6. Preparing for marriage and family life.
7. Desiring and achieving socially responsible behavior.
8. Acquiring a set of values and an ethical system as a guide to behavior—developing an ideology.

These eight developmental tasks need to be interpreted. What did Havighurst say about them (Havighurst, 1972)?

Accepting one's physique and using the body effectively. One of the characteristics of adolescents is their emerging, often extreme, self-consciousness about their physical selves as they reach sexual maturity. Adolescents need to accept their physique and the pattern of growth of their own body, to learn to care for their body, and to use the body effectively in sports and athletics, recreation, work, and everyday tasks (Havighurst, 1972).

Achieving new and more mature relations with age-mates of both sexes. Adolescents must move from the same-sex interests and playmates of middle childhood to establish heterosexual friendships. Becoming an adult means also learning social skills and behaviors required in group life (Havighurst, 1972).

Achieving a masculine or feminine social-sex role. What is a man? What is a woman? What are men and women supposed to look like? How are they supposed to behave? What are they supposed to be? Psychosexual social roles are established by each culture, but because masculine-feminine roles in Western culture are undergoing rapid changes, part of the maturing process for adolescents is to reexamine the changing sex roles of their culture and to decide what aspects they must adopt. (Havighurst, 1972).

Achieving emotional independence from parents and other adults. Adolescents must develop understanding, affection, and respect without emotional dependence. Adolescents who are rebellious and in conflict with their parents and other adults need to develop a greater understanding of themselves and adults and the reasons for their conflict (Finkelstein and Gaier, 1983).

Preparing for an economic career. One of the primary goals of adolescents is to decide what they want to become vocationally, to prepare for that career, and then to become economically emancipated from parents by earning their own living. Part of the task is to discover what they want out of life. Another aspect is to choose a career, become educated for it, and start to work in it.

Preparing for marriage and family life. Patterns of marriage and family living are being readjusted to changing economic, social, and religious characteristics of society. The majority of youths desire a happy marriage and parenthood as one important goal in life and need to develop the positive attitudes, social skills, emotional maturity, and necessary understanding to make marriage work.

Desiring and achieving socially responsible behavior. This goal includes the development of a social ideology that takes into account societal values. The goal also includes participation in the adult life of the community and nation. Many adolescents are disturbed by the ethical quality of their society. Some become radical activists; others join the ranks of the uncommitted who refuse to act. These adolescents struggle to find their place in society in a way that gives meaning to their lives (Havighurst, 1972).

Acquiring a set of values and an ethical system as a guide to behavior—developing an ideology. This goal includes the development of a sociopolitico-ethical ideology and the adoption and application of meaningful values, morals, and ideals in one's personal life.

Havighurst feels that many modern youths have not been able to achieve identity and therefore suffer from aimlessness and uncertainty. He says that the way most youths (especially boys) achieved identity in the first half of the twentieth century was through selecting and preparing for an occupation; work was the whole axis of life. Now, he feels, with the emphasis on expressive values, nothing has replaced occupational choice and preparation as the sure means of identity formation. Some adolescents, of course, would disagree; they would say that identity comes through a close, meaningful, loving relationship with another person, or persons, or through oneness with nature.

Kurt Lewin: Field Theory

Kurt Lewin's (1890–1947) theory of adolescent development is outlined in his article, "Field Theory and Experiment in Social Psychology: Concepts and Methods" (1939). His field theory explains and describes the behavior of individual adolescents in specific situations.

Lewin's (1939) core concept is "that behavior (B) is a function (f) of the person (P) and of his environment (E)" (p. 34). To understand an adolescent's behavior, one must consider the individual's personality and the environment as interdependent factors. The sum total of all environmental and personal factors in interaction is called the "life space" (LSp) or "the psychological Space." Behavior is a function of the life space, $B = f(LSp)$, which includes physical-environmental, social, and psychological factors such as needs, motives, and goals, all of which influence behavior. Lewin's field theory integrates biological and environmental factors in behavior without trying to judge which has the greater influence.

Lewin compares the life space of a child with that of the adult. The child's life space is structured by what is forbidden and is beyond his or her ability. As the child matures and becomes more capable, fewer restrictions are placed on freedom so the life space expands into new regions and experiences. By the time the child reaches adolescence, more regions have become accessible, but it is unclear which ones the adolescent is supposed to enter. Some regions may not be beyond the adolescent's ability but may not be explicitly allowed or forbidden. Thus, the life space remains undefined and unclear. The adult's space is considerably wider, but it is still bounded by activities beyond ability or forbidden by society. Figure 3-1 shows the life spaces of the child, adolescent, and adult.

According to Lewin, adolescence is a period of transition during which group membership changes from childhood to adulthood. The adolescent belongs partly to the child group and partly to the adult group. Muuss writes:

> Parents, teachers, and society reflect this lack of clearly defined group status; and their ambiguous feelings become obvious when they treat the adolescent at one time like a child and at another time like an adult. Difficulties arise because certain childish forms of behavior are no longer acceptable. At the same time some of the adult forms of behavior are not yet permitted either, or if they are permitted, they are new and strange to the adolescent. The adolescent is in a state of "social locomotion," moving into an unstructured social and psychological field. Goals are no longer clear, and the paths to them are ambiguous and full of uncertainties—the adolescent may no longer be certain that they even lead to the desired goals. (Muuss, 1982b, p. 147)

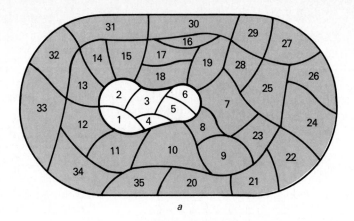

a

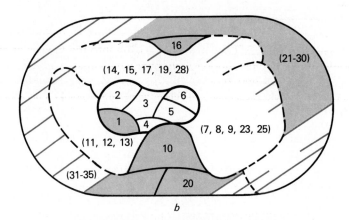

b

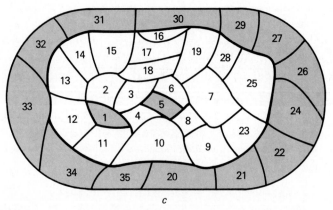

c

FIGURE 3-1

Life space of the child, adolescent, and adult.   The actual activity regions are represented. The accessible regions are blank; the inaccessible shaded. (*a*) The *space of free movement* of the *child* includes the regions 1–6 representing activities such as getting into the movies at children's rates, belonging to a boy's club, etc. The regions 7–35 are not accessible, representing activities such as driving a car, writing checks for purchases, political activities, performance of adults' occupations, etc. (b) The *space of free movement* of the *adolescent*. The space of free movement is greatly increased, including many regions which previously have not been accessible to the child, for instance, freedom to smoke, returning home late, driving a car (regions 7–9, 11–13, . . .). Certain regions accessible to the adult are clearly not accessible to the adolescent, such as voting (represented by regions 10 and 16). Certain regions accessible to the child have already become inaccessible, such as getting into the movies at children's rates, or behaving on too childish a level (region 1). The boundaries of these newly acquired portions of the space of free movement are only vaguely determined and in themselves generally less clearly and sharply differentiated than for an adult. In such cases the life space of the adolescent seems to be full of possibilities and at the same time of uncertainties. (c) The *adult space of free movement* is considerably wider, although it too is bounded by regions of activities inaccessible to the adult, such as shooting his enemy or entering activities beyond his social or intellectual capacity (represented by regions including 29–35). Some of the regions accessible to the child are not accessible to the adult, for instance, getting into the movies at children's rates, or doing things socially taboo for an adult which are permitted to the child (represented by regions 1 and 5).

From: Lewin, K. (1939). "Field Theory and Experiment in Social Psychology: Concepts and Methods." *American Journal of Sociology* 44:868–897. Used with permission of the University of Chicago Press.

This "lack of cognitive structures" helps explain uncertainty in adolescent behavior. Lewin refers to the adolescent as the "marginal man," represented in figure 3-2 by the overlapping area (A*d*) of the child region (C) and the adult region (A). *Being a marginal man implies that the adolescent may at times act more like a child, often when he or she wants to avoid adult responsibilities; at other times he or she acts more like an adult and requests adult privileges* (Muuss, 1988, p. 169).

One of the strengths of Lewin's field theory is that it assumes both personality and cultural differences, so it allows for wide individual variations in behavior. It also allows for varying lengths of the adolescent period from culture to culture and from social class to social class within a culture (Muuss, 1988).

A SOCIAL COGNITION VIEW OF ADOLESCENCE

Social Cognition

Social cognition can be defined as "how people think about other people and about themselves," or how people come to know their social world. It is concerned with the processes by which children and adolescents conceptualize and learn to understand others: their thoughts, emotions, intentions, social behavior, and general point of view. Implied in the concept of social cognition is an ability to make inferences about other people's capabilities, attributes, expectations, and potential reactions (Muuss, 1988).

social cognition

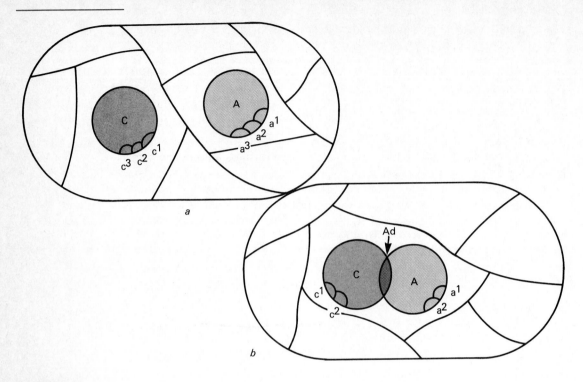

■ FIGURE 3-2

The marginal man.   The adolescent as a marginal man. (a) During childhood and adulthood the "adults" (A) and "children" (C) are viewed as relatively separated groups, the individual child (c^1, c^2) and the individual adult (a^1, a^2) being sure of their belonging to their respective groups. (b) The adolescent belonging to a group (Ad) which can be viewed as an overlapping region of the children's (C) and the adults' (A) group belonging to both of them, or as standing between them, not belonging to either one.

From: Lewin, K. (1939). "Field Theory and Experiment in Social Psychology: Concepts and Methods." *American Journal of Sociology* 44: 868–897. Used with permission of The University of Chicago Press.

The question arises as to whether social knowledge and physical knowledge are gained in the same way. Certainly much of both are acquired through observation, trial and error, exploration, direct first-hand experiences, and discovery. But gaining social knowledge is more difficult. Physical knowledge is objective and factual. Social knowledge may be quite arbitrary, determined by a specific social situation, as well as by social, cultural, and even subcultural definitions, requirements, and expectations. Moore (1979) writes:

Because of the arbitrary nature of social rules and social protocol, the child will have to acquire some social knowledge by direct instruction from adults or older children, by observing the behavior of mature people in the environment, or by experiencing approval and disapproval for appropriate and inappropriate behavior. (Moore 1979, p. 54)

Because social rules are less uniform, less specific, and more situation dependent than physical phenomena, they are less predictable and more complicated to understand.

What is the relationship between other cognitive abilities, such as intellectual problem-solving skills, or moral problem-solving skills, and social problem-solving skills? The person who has superior intellectual problem-solving skills does not necessarily have superior social problem-solving skills (Keating and Clark, 1980). An intellectually superior person may be socially inept, indicating that cognitive abilities involved in interpersonal relationships are not the same as those measured by a conventional IQ test. Social problem-solving skills may be learned or taught, separate from intellectual abilities. Shure and Spivak (1980) found that the improvement in social adjustment resulting from their interpersonal skills program was not a function of a child's level of intellectual functioning. Selman (1980) concludes: "The development of social conceptions, reasoning, thought—social cognition—is distinct from, though not unrelated to, the development of nonsocial cognition." There is some evidence, however, that persons who show superior ability in moral reasoning also show superior ability in social cognition (Muuss, 1982).

Robert Selman: Role Taking

Social cognition cannot be perceived as one uniform, theoretical construct. There are actually a variety of minitheories and constructions. One of the most useful is that of Robert Selman (1977, 1980) who has advanced a stage theory of social cognition outlining predictable stages in **social role taking.** He describes his role-taking concept as a form of social cognition intermediate between logical and moral thought. To Selman social role taking is the ability to understand the self and others as subjects, to react to others as like the self, and to react to the self's behavior from the other's point of view. Such an ability involves self-knowledge, perspective, empathy, moral reasoning, and interpersonal problem solving and increases with age into adolescence and into adulthood.

social role taking

Selman identifies five stages or developmental levels of social role taking (Muuss, 1982; Selman, 1977, 1980):

Stage 0. The egocentric undifferentiated stage (approximately age three to six).

Stage 1. The differentiated and subjective perspective-taking stage (age five to nine).

Stage 2. Self-reflective thinking or reciprocal perspective-taking stage (age seven to twelve).

Stage 3. The third person or mutual perspective-taking stage (age ten to fifteen).

Stage 4. The in-depth and societal perspective-taking stage (age twelve to adulthood).

These need to be explained in more detail. (See figure 3-3.)

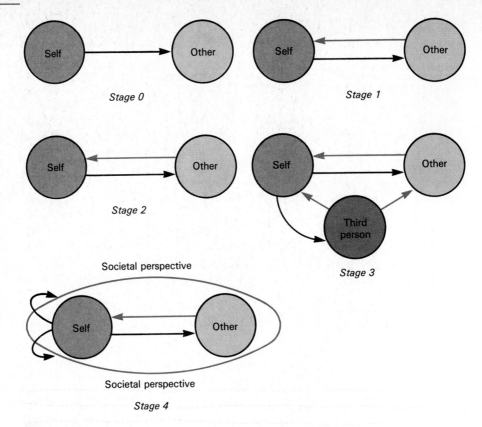

FIGURE 3-3

Selman's five stages of social role taking.   *Stage* 0. The other person is seen egocentrically, or undifferentiated from the self's own point of view. *Stage* 1. The other is seen as different from the self, but the other person's perception of the self is still undifferentiated. *Stage* 2. The self can take the perspective of another person and becomes aware that the other person can also take the perspective of the self. *Stage* 3. The self can view the self-other interaction from the perspective of a neutral third person. *Stage* 4. The self can take a generalized societal perspective of the self-other interaction.

From: Muuss, R. E. (1988). *Theories of Adolescence*, 5th ed. New York: McGraw Hill Publishing Company, pp. 249, 251, 254, 256, 258. Copyright© McGraw Hill Publishing Company. Used by permission.

>   *Stage 0. Egocentric Undifferentiated Stage of Social Perspective Taking (Age Three to Six)*   At the egocentric undifferentiated stage of social perspective taking, children cannot make a clear distinction between their own interpretation of a social situation and another point of view. Nor can they understand that their own perception may not be the correct or true perspective. Although children understand that each person can have different feelings, they

do not yet have the ability to determine how the thoughts and feelings of others might differ from their own (Muuss, 1988).

Stage 1. Differential or Subjective Perspective-taking Stage, or the Social-Informational Role-taking Stage (Approximately Age Five to Nine) Children at this stage begin to realize that another person can have cognitive or social perspectives different from their own. An awareness develops that others can interpret the same social situation differently. However, children are still unable to evaluate accurately what the other person's perspective looks like. In other words, they cannot maintain their own perspective and simultaneously assume the perspective of another.

There are three distinctive features of this level of social-perspective taking. First, the children become aware that they themselves and their own inner thoughts can be the object of another person's thinking, but they cannot judge accurately their own behavior as seen from the perspective of another person. Second, the stage 1 child, in contrast to the stage 0 child, distinguishes between unintentionality and intentionality of behavior and thus begins to consider personal reasons as causes of action. Third, stage 1 children are capable of inferring the other person's intentions, feelings, and thoughts. However, since they base their judgment of the feelings of others on physical observations, they are not always correct (Muuss, 1988).

Stage 2. Self-Reflective Thinking or Reciprocal Perspective Taking (Age Seven to Twelve) The preadolescent at stage 2 realizes that the other person thinks about his or her thinking and can take the subject's role. Thus, the change from stage 1 to stage 2 is the ability to mentally leave oneself and to take the perspective of another individual. Individuals can now become capable of making inferences about the perspectives of others; they can reflect about their own behavior and their own motivation as seen from the perspective of another person.

This ability introduces an awareness that no single individual's social perspective is necessarily correct or valid in an absolute sense. Another person's point of view may be as correct as one's own. However, the mutual role-taking ability that develops is only a two-way reciprocity; it is sequential but not yet simultaneous or mutual. The preadolescent thinks only within a two-person frame of reference—"I think—you think" and cannot take a more general third-person perspective (Muuss, 1982, 1988).

Stage 3. The Third Person or Mutual Perspective Taking Stage (Age Ten to Fifteen) The third-person perspective allows the adolescent to step abstractly outside an interpersonal interaction and simultaneously and mutually coordinate and consider the perspectives (and their interaction) of self and others (Selman, 1980). Furthermore, the ability to distinguish between one's own point of view and a more generalized perspective that might be taken by an "average" member of the group emerges. Friendship now is viewed not as a process of reciprocal backscratching but as a series of interactions over an extended period of time. Conflicts are seen as emerging possibly from different personality characteristics (Muuss, 1982).

Stage 4. In-depth and Societal Perspective-taking Stage (Adolescence to Adulthood)   There are two distinguishing features of adolescents' conception of other people. First, they become aware that motives, actions, thoughts, and feelings are shaped by psychological factors. This notion of psychological determinants now includes the idea of the unconscious processes, although adolescents may not express this awareness in psychological terminology. Second, they begin to appreciate the fact that a personality is a system of traits, beliefs, values, and attitudes with its own developmental history.

During adolescence the individual may move to a still higher and more abstract level of interpersonal perspective taking, which involves the coordination of all possible third-person perspectives—a societal perspective. The adolescent can conceptualize that each person can consider the shared point of view of the "generalized other"—that is, the social system—which, in turn, makes possible the accurate communication with an understanding of other people. Further, the idea of law and morality as a social system depends on the concept of consensual group perspective (Selman, 1980).

Selman emphasizes that not all adolescents or adults will reach stage 4 in social cognitive development. Stage 4 corresponds to Piaget's level of formal operations in logical reasoning and to Kohlberg's conventional and postconventional stages of moral development (Selman, 1977, 1980). Selman's theory implies a movement away from limited concern with the cognitive side of learning toward an inclusion of interpersonal, social cognitive awareness (Muuss, 1988).

SUMMARY

What about the various theories of adolescence? Which view or views are correct? Each view has contributed to an understanding of adolescence; each has an emphasis that is needed. Although no student of adolescent behavior today relies on Hall's recapitulation theory, many scholars would emphasize biogenetic factors as important determinants. Hereditary factors, biological drives, and physical changes exert a tremendous influence, although they are not the only factors influencing behavior. Gesell emphasized the importance of maturation in learning—an important emphasis—even though he neglected environmental contributions to personality growth. Sigmund Freud and Anna Freud made a significant contribution in their emphasis on sexual and psychic drives and needs. The desire to satisfy sexual instincts and psychic needs for affection are strong motivating factors in influencing adolescent behavior. Similarly, S. Freud's explanations of the need for emotional emancipation from parents, the need to establish heterosexual friendships with peers, and the need to find a love object for emotional fulfillment are helpful in understanding adolescent-parent-peer relationships. A. Freud's explanation of the psychic disequilibrium of adolescents helps us understand the causes of their erratic behavior. Erikson's explanation of the adolescent's need for identity and the process by which the adolescent forms identity has had a marked influence on adolescent theory and research for over twenty years. Marcia has helped to clarify Erikson's view and to show how it applies to various types of adolescents. Sociologists have made an important contribution in showing the influence of society and culture in the lives of youth, in describing the process by which socialization takes place, and in pointing to the cultural differences among adolescents of different ethnic, economic, and social backgrounds. Similarly, anthropologists have made the careful student aware that there are few universal patterns of development or behavior, so that general conclusions about adolescents should be formulated to take into account the cultural vantage point from which one speaks. By making cultural comparisons, anthropologists enable the student to see some of the positive and negative elements in each culture that become a help or a hindrance to the adolescent. Havighurst's outline of the developmental tasks of adolescence is helpful to youths themselves in discovering some of the things they need to accomplish to reach adulthood. The outline is also helpful to parents, educators, and adult leaders who seek to teach and guide adolescents on their road to maturity. Lewin's field theory emphasizes adolescence as the bridge between childhood and adulthood and the difficulty of bridging that gap. Selman's emphasis on the development of social cognition helps us understand the process by which people learn to understand themselves and others and to get along as social groups.

One view alone gives only a partial picture, for, after all, adolescents are biological, psychological, social and cultural beings; genetically controlled organisms, and psychologically and sociologically conditioned products of the family and society of which they are a part (Ellis, 1979). To understand adolescents, one must stand in many places and look from many points of view (Mead, 1974).

DISCUSSION QUESTIONS

1. What should be done in our society to enable adolescents to bridge the gap between childhood and adulthood and to grow up faster?

2. Are there adult privileges given adolescents that you feel should not be given? Are there adult privileges that are not given that should be?

3. Is adolescence a period of storm and stress? Explain.

4. What do you think of the views of Sigmund Freud?

5. Discuss one id-ego-superego conflict that might erupt during adolescence.

6. In what ways is adolescence a period of identity formation? How do adolescents go about forming an identity? What happens if they cannot "find themselves"? Is identity formation ever completed?

7. Of the four basic types of persons as outlined by Marcia (identity diffused, foreclosure, morato-

rium, and identity achieved), which would you rather be at this stage of your life? Why?

8. Is "socialized anxiety" positive?

9. What is your opinion about the influence of aggression on television on aggression in children and youth? Should children and adolescents be restricted from watching some programs? Explain.

10. Which of the eight psychosocial tasks as outlined by Havighurst do you feel are the most difficult to achieve? Explain.

11. In what ways is the adolescent the "marginal man" according to Lewin?

12. Explain stage 4 of Selman's developmental view of social cognition. How does Selman's theory contribute to an understanding of how people can learn to understand and get along with one another?

BIBLIOGRAPHY

Adams, G. R. (Summer, 1977). "Personal Identity Formation: A Synthesis of Cognitive and Ego Psychology." *Adolescence*, 12, 151–164.

Adams, G. R., and Shea, J. A. (March, 1979). "The Relationship between Identity Status, Locus of Control, and Ego Development." *Journal of Youth and Adolescence*, 8, 81–89.

Anderson, S. A., and Fleming, W. M. (1986). "Late Adolescents' Identity Formation: Individuation From the Family of Origin." *Adolescence*, 26, 785–796.

Baker, C. D. (December, 1983). "A 'Second Look' at Interviews with Adolescents." *Journal of Youth and Adolescence*, 12, 501–519.

Bandura, Albert. (1962). "Social Learning through Imitation." In *Nebraska Symposium on Motivation*. Edited by M. R. Jones. Lincoln: University of Nebraska Press.

_____ . (1964). "The Stormy Decade: Fact or Fiction?" *Psychology in the Schools* 1, 224–231.

_____ . (1965). "Behavioral Modifications through Modeling Procedures." In *Research in Behavior Modification*. Edited by L. Krasner and L. Ullmann. New York: Holt, Rinehart, and Winston.

_____ . (1969). *Principles of Behavior Modification*. New York: Holt, Rinehart and Winston.

_____ . (1971). "Vicarious and Self-Reinforcement Processes." In *The Nature of Reinforcement*. Edited by R. Glaser. New York: Academic Press.

_____ . (1973). *Aggression, a Social Learning Analysis*. Englewood Cliffs, N.J.: Prentice-Hall.

Bandura, Albert, and Kupers, C. J. (1964). "Transmission of Patterns of Self-Reinforcement through Modeling." *Journal of Abnormal and Social Psychology*, 69, 1–9.

Bandura, Albert, and McDonald, F. J. (1963). "Influence of Social Reinforcement and the Behavior of Models in Shaping Children's Moral Judgments." *Journal of Abnormal and Social Psychology*, 67, 274–281.

Bandura, Albert, and Mischel, W. (1965). "Modification of Self-Imposed Delay of Reward through Exposure to Live and Symbolic Models." *Journal of Personality and Social Psychology*, 2, 698–705.

Bandura, Albert, and Perloff, B. (1967). "Relative Efficacy of Self-Monitored and Externally Imposed Reinforcement Systems." *Journal of Personality and Social Psychology*, 7, 111–116.

Bandura, Albert; Ross, D.; and Ross, S. A. (1963a). "Invitation of Film-Mediated Aggressive Models." *Journal of Abnormal and Social Psychology*, 66, 3011.

_____ . (1963b). "Vicarious Reinforcement and Imitative Learning." *Journal of Abnormal and Social Psychology*, 67, 601–607.

Bandura, Albert, and Walters, R. H. (1959). *Adolescent Aggression*. New York: Ronald Press.

_____ . (1963). *Social Learning and Personality Development*. New York: Holt, Rinehart and Winston.

Bandura, Albert, and Whalen, C. K. (1966). "The Influence of Antecedent Reinforcement and Divergent Modeling Cues on Patterns of Self-Reward." *Journal of Personality and Social Psychology*, 3, 373–383.

Benedict, Ruth. (1938). "Continuities and Discontinuities in Cultural Conditioning." *Psychiatry*, 1, 161–167.

_____ . (1950). *Patterns of Culture*. New York: New American Library.

Bernard, H. S. (Summer, 1981). "Identity Formation during Late Adolescence: A Review of Some Empirical Findings." *Adolescence*, 16, 349–358.

Blos, P. (1972). "The Child Analyst Looks at the Young Adolescent." In *Twelve to Sixteen: Early Adolescence*. Edited by J. A. Kagan and Robert Coles. New York: W. W. Norton and Co.

Blos, P. (1979). *The Adolescent Passage: Developmental Issues*. New York: International Universities Press, 1979.

Blyth, D. A., Hill, J. P., and Thiel, K. S. (December, 1982). "Early Adolescents' Significant Others: Grade and Gender Differences in Perceived Relationships with Familial and Nonfamilial Adults and Young People." *Journal of Youth and Adolescence*, 11, 425–450.

Bourne, E. (September, 1978a). "The State of Research on Ego Identity: A Review and Appraisal. Part I." *Journal of Youth and Adolescence*, 7, 223–251.

_____ . (December, 1978b). "The State of Research on Ego Identity: A Review and Appraisal. Part II." *Journal of Youth and Adolescence*, 7, 371–392.

Cella, D. F., DeWolfe, A. S., and Fitzgibbon, M. (1987).

"Ego Identity Status, Identification, and Decision-Making Style in Late Adolescents." *Adolescence*, 22, 849–861.

Cote, J. E. (1986). "Identity Crisis Modality: A Technique for Assessing the Structure of the Identity Crisis." *Journal of Adolescence*, 9, 321–335.

Cote, J. E., and Levine, C. (February, 1983). "Marcia and Erikson: The Relationships among Ego Identity Status, Neuroticism, Dogmatism, and Purpose in Life." *Journal of Youth and Adolescence*, 12, 43–53.

Davis, Allison. (1944). "Socialization and Adolescent Personality." In *Adolescence*. Yearbook of the National Society for the Study of Education. Vol. 43, Part I.

deBrun, S. R. (Winter, 1981). "The Psycho-Social Dimensions of Preadolescence." *Adolescence*, 16, 913–918.

Ellis, E. H. (Spring, 1979). "Some Problems in the Study of Adolescent Development." *Adolescence*, 14, 101–109.

Erikson, Erik. (1950). *Childhood and Society*. New York: W. W. Norton & Co.

_____ . (1959). *Identity and the Life Cycle*. New York: International Universities Press.

_____ . (1968). *Identity: Youth and Crisis*. New York: W. W. Norton and Co.

_____ . (1982). *The Lifecycle Completed*. New York: W. W. Norton and Co.

Finkelstein, M. J., and Gaier, E. L. (Spring, 1983). "The Impact of Prolonged Student Status on Late Adolescent Development." *Adolescence*, 18, 115–129.

Freeman, D. (1983). *Margaret Mead and Samoa: The Making and Unmaking of an Anthropological Myth*. Cambridge, MA: Harvard University Press.

Fregeau, D. L., and Barker, M. (1986). "A Measurement of the Process of Adolescence: Standardization and Interpretation." *Adolescence*, 21, 913–919.

Freud, Anna. (1946). *The Ego and the Mechanism of Defence*. New York: International Universities Press.

_____ . (1958). *Psychoanalytic Study of the Child*. New York: International Universities Press.

Freud, S. A. (1925). "Three Contributions to the Sexual Theory." *Nervous and Mental Disease Monograph Series*, No. 7.

_____ . (1953). *A General Introduction to Psychoanalysis*. Translated by Joan Riviere. New York: Permabooks.

_____ . (1953) *Three Essays on the Theory of Sexuality*, vol. 7. London: Hogarth Press.

Galbo, J. J. (Summer, 1983). "Adolescent's Perceptions of Significant Adults." *Adolescence*, 18, 417–427.

_____ . (Winter, 1984). "Adolescent's Perceptions of Significant Adults: A Review of the Literature." *Adolescence*, 19, 951–970.

Gallatin, J. E. (1976). "Theories of Adolescence." In *Understanding Adolescence*. 3d ed. Edited by J. F. Adams. Boston, MA: Allyn and Bacon.

Gesell, Arnold, and Ames, L. B. (1956). *Youth: The Years from Ten to Sixteen*. New York: Harper & Row.

Ginsburg, S. D., and Orlofsky, J. L. (August, 1981). "Ego Identity Status, Ego Development, and Loss of Control in College Women." *Journal of Youth and Adolescence*, 10, 297–307.

Goldman, J. A., Rosenzweig, C. M., and Lutter, A. D. (April, 1980). "Effect of Similarity of Ego Identity Status on Interpersonal Attraction." *Journal of Youth and Adolescence*, 9, 153–162.

Golinko, B. E. (Fall, 1984). "Adolescence: Common Pathways through Life." *Adolescence*, 19, 749–751.

Grotevant, H. D., Thorbecke, W., and Meyer, M. L. (February, 1982). "An Extension of Marcia's Identity Status Interview into the Interpersonal Domain." *Journal of Youth and Adolescence*, 11, 33–47.

Hall, G. Stanley. (1904). *Adolescence: Its Psychology and Its Relation to Physiology, Anthropology, Sociology, Sex, Crime, Religion and Education*. 2 vols. New York: D. Appleton and Co.

Hall, G. Stanley, and Lindzay, G. (1970). *Theories of Personality*. 2d ed. New York: John Wiley & Sons.

Havighurst, R. J. (1972). *Developmental Tasks and Education*. 3d ed. New York: David McKay Co.

Heyneman, S. P. (December, 1976). "Continuing Issues in Adolescence: A Summary of Current Transition to Adulthood Debates." *Journal of Youth and Adolescence*, 5, 309–323.

Hummel, R., and Roselli, L. L. (Spring, 1983). "Identity Status and Academic Achievement in Female Adolescents." *Adolescence*, 18, 17–27.

Josselson, R. (August, 1982). "Personality Structure and Identity Status in Women as Viewed through Early Memories." *Journal of Youth and Adolescence*, 11, 293–299.

Juhasz, A. M. (Summer, 1982). "Youth, Identity and Values: Erikson's Historical Perspective." *Adolescence*, 17, 443–450.

Kacerguis, M. A., and Adams, G. R. (April, 1980).

"Erikson Stage Resolution: The Relationship between Identity and Intimacy." *Journal of Youth and Adolescence*, 9, 117–126.

Keating, D. P., and Clark, L. V. (1980). "Development of Physical and Social Reasoning in Adolescence." *Developmental Psychology*, 16, 23–30.

Keniston, K. (1971). "Youth: A New Stage of Life." *American Scholar*, 39 (1970): 4.

———. "The Tasks of Adolescence." In *Developmental Psychology Today*. Del Mar, Calif.: CRM Books.

Kroger, J. (1986). "The Relative Importance of Identity Status Interview Components: Replication and Extension." *Journal of Adolescence*, 9, 337–354.

Lafromboise, T., Dauphinais, P., and Rowe, W. (1978). "A Survey of Indian Students' Perceptions of the Counseling Experience." Paper presented at the annual meeting of the American Educational Research Association, Toronto, March 1978.

Lewin, K. (1939). "Field Theory and Experiment in Social Psychology: Concepts and Methods." *American Journal of Sociology*, 44, 868–897.

Logan, R. D. (Fall, 1978). "Identity Diffusion and Psycho-Social Defense Mechanisms." *Adolescence*, 13, 503–507.

———. (Summer, 1980). "Identity, Purity and Ecology." *Adolescence*, 15, 409–412.

———. (Winter, 1983). "A Re-Conceptualization of Erikson's Identity Stage." *Adolescence*, 18, 943–946.

Lutes, C. J. (Winter, 1981). "Early Marriage and Identity Foreclosure." *Adolescence*, 16, 809–830.

McBee, S. (April, 1985). "Heroes Are Back. Young Americans Tell Why." *U.S. News & World Report*, 22, pp. 44–48.

McDonald, G. W. (November, 1977). "Parental Identification by the Adolescent: Social Power Approach." *Journal of Marriage and the Family*, 39, 705–719.

Marcia, J. E. (1966). "Development and Validation of Ego Identity Status." *Journal of Personality and Social Psychology*, 3, 551–558.

———. (1967). "Ego Identity Status: Relationship to Change in Self-Esteem, 'General Maladjustment,' and Authoritarianism." *Journal of Personality*, 35, 118–133.

———. (1976). "Identity Six Years After: A Follow Up Study." *Journal of Youth and Adolescence*, 5, 145–160.

Marcia, J. E., and Friedman, M. L. (1970). "Ego Identity Status in College Women." *Journal of Personality*, 38, 249–263.

Matter, R. M. (Spring, 1984). "The Historical Emergence of Adolescence: Perspectives from Developmental Psychology and Adolescent Literature." *Adolescence*, 19, 131–142.

Matteson, D. R. (December, 1977). "Exploration and Commitment: Sex Differences and Methodological Problems in the Use of Identity Status Categories." *Journal of Youth and Adolescence*, 6, 353–374.

Mazor, A., and Enright, R. D. (1988). "The Development of the Individuation Process from a Social-Cognitive Perspective." *Journal of Adolescence*, 11, 29–47.

Mead, Margaret. (1950). *Coming of Age in Samoa*. New York: New American Library.

———. (1953). *Growing Up in New Guinea*. New York: New American Library.

———. (1970). *Culture and Commitment: A Study of the Generation Gap*. Garden City, N.Y.: Doubleday.

———. (1974). "Adolescence." In *Youth and Culture: A Human Development Approach*. Edited by H. V. Kraemer. Monterey, Calif.: Brooks/Cole Publishing Co.

Miller, J. P. (Summer, 1978). "Piaget, Kohlberg, and Erikson: Developmental Implications for Secondary Education." *Adolescence*, 13, 237–250.

Moore, S. G. (1979). "Social Cognition: Knowing about Others." *Young Children*, 34, 54–61.

Morgan, E., and Farber, B. A. (Spring, 1982). "Toward a Reformulation of the Eriksonian Model of Female Identity Development." *Adolescence*, 17, 199–211.

Muuss, R. E. (Fall, 1982). "Social Cognition: Robert Selman's Theory of Role Taking." *Adolescence*, 17, 499–525.

———. (1988). *Theories of Adolescence*. 5th ed. New York: McGraw Hill.

Newman, B. M., and Newman, P. R. (Spring, 1978a). "The Concept of Identity: Research and Theory." *Adolescence*, 13, 157–166.

Newman, P. R., and Newman, B. M. (Summer, 1978b). "Identity Formation and the College Experience." *Adolescence*, 13, 311–326.

———. (1988). "Differences Between Childhood and Adulthood: The Identity Watershed." *Adolescence*, 91, 551–557.

Oberle, W., Stowers, K. R., and Folk, N. W. (1978). "Place of Residence and the Role Model Preferences of Black Boys and Girls." *Adolescence*, 13, 13–20.

Onyehalu, A. S. (Fall, 1981). "Identity Crisis in Adolescence." *Adolescence*, 16, 629–632.

Orlofsky, J. L. (March, 1978). "Identity Formation, Achievement, and Fear of Success in College Men and Women." *Journal of Youth and Adolescence*, 7, 49–62.

Proefrock, D. W. (Winter, 1981). "Adolescence: Social Fact and Psychological Concept." *Adolescence*, 16, 851–858.

Protinsky, H. (1988). "Identity Formation: A Comparison of Problem and Nonproblem Adolescents." *Adolescence*, 23, 67–72.

Randolph, E. M., and Dye, C. A. (Winter, 1981). "The Peter Pan Profile Development of a Scale to Measure Reluctance to Grow Up." *Adolescence*, 16, 841–850.

Raphael, D. (March, 1977). "Identity Status in University Women: A Methodological Note." *Journal of Youth and Adolescence*, 6, 57–62.

_____ . (Winter, 1978). "Identity Status in High School Females." *Adolescence*, 13, 627–641.

_____ . (Spring, 1979). "Sequencing in Female Adolescents' Consideration of Occupational, Religious and Political Alternatives." *Adolescence*, 14, 73–80.

Raphael, D., and Xelowski, H. G. (October, 1980). "Identity Status in High School Students: Critique and a Revised Paradigm." *Journal of Youth and Adolescence*, 9, 383–389.

Roessler, R. T. (1971). "Sexuality and Identity: Masculine Differentiation and Feminine Constancy." *Adolescence*, 6, 187–196.

Rogow, A. M., Marcia, J. E., and Slugoski, B. R. (October, 1983). "The Relative Importance of Identity Status Interview Components." *Journal of Youth and Adolescence*, 12, 387–400.

Roll, E. J. (Fall, 1980). "Psychologists' Conflicts about the Inevitability of Conflict during Adolescence: An Attempt at Reconciliation." *Adolescence*, 15, 661–670.

Roscoe, B., and Peterson, K. L. (Summer 1984). "Older Adolescents: A Self-Report of Engagement in Developmental Tasks." *Adolescence*, 19, 391–396.

Rosenthal, D. A., Gurney, R. M., and Moore, S. M. (December, 1981). "From Trust to Intimacy: A New Inventory for Examining Erikson's Stages of Psychosocial Development." *Journal of Youth and Adolescence*, 10, 525–537.

Rothman, K. M. (March, 1978). "Multivariate Analysis of the Relationship of Psychosocial Crisis Variables to Ego Identity Status." *Journal of Youth and Adolescence*, 7, 93–105.

_____ . (Fall, 1984). "Multivariate Analysis of the Relationship of Personal Concerns to Adolescent Ego Identity Status." *Adolescence*, 19, 713–727.

Rowe, I., and Marcia, J. E. (April, 1980). "Ego Identity Status, Formal Operations, and Moral Development." *Journal of Youth and Adolescence*, 9, 87–99.

St. Clair, S., and Day, H. D. (September, 1979). "Ego Identity Status and Values among High School Females." *Journal of Youth and Adolescence*, 8, 317–326.

Sebald, H. (1984). *Adolescence: A Social Psychological Analysis.* 3d ed. Englewood Cliffs, N.J.: Prentice-Hall.

Selman, R. L. (1977). "A Structural-Developmental Model of Social Cognition: Implications for Intervention Research." *Counseling Psychologist*, 6, 3–6.

_____ . (1980). *The Growth of Interpersonal Understanding: Development and Clinical Analysis.* New York: Academic Press.

Shure, M. B., and Spivak, G. (1980). "Interpersonal Problem Solving as Mediator of Behavioral Adjustment in Preschool and Kindergarten Children." *Journal of Applied Developmental Psychology*, 1, 29–44.

Stein, S. L., and Weston, L. C. (Winter, 1982). "College Women's Attitudes toward Women and Identity Achievement." *Adolescence*, 17, 895–899.

Toder, N. L., and Marcia, J. E. (1973). "Ego Identity Status and Response to Conformity Pressure in College Women." *Journal of Personality and Social Psychology*, 26, 287–294.

Tooth, G. (February, 1985). "Why Children's TV Turns Off So Many Parents." *U.S. News & World Report*, 18, p. 65.

Waterman, A. S. (1982). "Identity Development from Adolescence to Adulthood: An Extension of Theory and a Review of Research." *Developmental Psychology*, 18, 341–358.

Waterman, C. K., and Nevid, J. S. (December, 1977). "Sex Differences in the Resolution of the Identity Crisis." *Journal of Youth and Adolescence*, 6, 337–342.

White, K. M. (Spring, 1980). "Problems and Characteristics of College Students." *Adolescence*, 15, 23–41.

CHAPTER 4

Sexual Maturation and Physical Growth

Adolescence has been described as a period of sexual maturation and physical growth. The purpose of this chapter is to discuss this maturation and growth: what changes take place and why, when, and how they occur.

THE ENDOCRINE GLANDS AND HYPOTHALAMUS

hormones   The endocrine glands (see figure 4-1) are ductless glands that secrete their biochemical substances, called **hormones** (meaning "I excite"), directly in the bloodstream. The hormones bathe every cell of the body, but each also has target organs on which it acts specifically. The hormones act as an internal communication system, telling the different cells what to do and when to act.

Because of their importance in human sexuality, three glands of the endocrine system are discussed in this section: the pituitary gland, the adrenal glands, and the gonads. The closely related hypothalamic region of the brain plays a role in regulating the secretions of the pituitary, so it is discussed here as well.

▮ FIGURE 4-1

The endocrine glands.

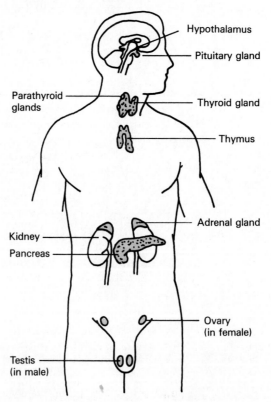

Adapted from Hole, J. W. (1987). *Human Anatomy and Physiology*, 4th ed. Copyright© 1987 Wm. C. Brown Publishers, Dubuque, Iowa. All rights reserved. Reprinted by permission.

Pituitary Gland

The **pituitary gland** is a small gland—about one-half inch long—weighing less than half a gram and is located in the skull at the base of the brain. It consists of three lobes: anterior, intermediary, and posterior. The anterior pituitary lobe is known as the master gland of the body, for it produces several hormones that control the action of the other glands. Not all the hormones secreted by the pituitary have been identified or their actions defined, but the best-known ones and their functions are described here.

    The growth hormone, referred to as **HGH (*human growth hormone*)** or SH (*somatotrophic hormone*), affects the growth and shaping of the skeleton. An excess causes *giantism*; a deficiency causes *dwarfism*. Sometimes an excess is secreted after normal bone growth has ceased, causing the bones of the hands and feet to lengthen disproportionately, the jaw to grow with the lower section projecting forward, and the teeth to become widely separated. The condition is known as *acromegaly* ("big extremities").

    Gonadotropic hormones are secreted by the anterior pituitary and are so named because they influence gonad functioning (Kulin, 1974; Kulin and Reiter, 1973). There are two gonadotropic hormones. **FSH (*follicle-stimulating hormone*)** and **LH (*luteinizing hormone*)** are secreted to stimulate the growth of the egg cells in the ovaries and sperm in the testes. FSH and LH in the female control the production and release of estrogen and progesterone by the ovary. LH in the male controls the production and release of testosterone by the testes (Rice, 1989).

    In addition to its secretion of growth hormones and gonadotropic hormones, the pituitary secretes a lactogenic hormone, **LTH (*luteotropic hormone*),** containing the hormone *prolactin*, which stimulates the secretion of milk by the mammary glands of the breast.

pituitary gland

human growth hormone (HGH)

gonadotropic hormones

follicle-stimulating hormone (FSH)

luteinizing hormone (LH)

luteotropic hormone (LTH)

Gonads

The **gonads,** or sex glands, secrete a number of sex hormones. The *ovaries* in the female secrete a whole group known as **estrogens** (meaning "producing mad desire") that stimulate the development of female sex characteristics such as breast development, the growth of pubic hair, and the distribution of fat on the body. These hormones also maintain the normal size and function of the uterus, its tubes, and the vagina; they maintain the normal condition and function of nasal and oral mucous membranes, control the growth of breast duct tissue, influence normal uterine contractions, and develop and maintain physical and mental health in other ways. Through negative feedback to the pituitary, they control the production of various pituitary hormones. Studies have also shown that estrogens influence olfactory sensitivity, which is greatest midway between menstrual periods when estrogen levels are the highest (McCary and McCary, 1982).

    A second female hormone, **progesterone**, is produced in the ovaries by a new cell growth, yellow in color, under the stimulus of LH from the pituitary, following the rupture of the ovum from the ovarian follicle. When an egg cell is discharged

gonads

estrogens

progesterone

corpus luteum

from a follicle in ovulation, the remaining follicular cells multiply rapidly and fill the cavity. This new cell growth becomes the ***corpus luteum*** ("yellow body"), which secretes progesterone for about thirteen days following ovulation. If the ovum has not been fertilized, the corpus luteum disintegrates, and the secretion of progesterone ceases until ovulation occurs again during the next cycle. If, however, the ovum is fertilized, and the corpus luteum does not degenerate, it continues to secrete progesterone and keep the *endometrium*, or uterine lining, ready to receive the fertilized egg. The corpus luteum continues to secrete progesterone for the first few months of pregnancy; after this time the *placenta* takes over the task of secreting both estrogen and progesterone for the remainder of the pregnancy.

Progesterone is an extremely important hormone. It controls the length of the menstrual cycle from ovulation until the next menstruation. It is of primary importance in preparing the uterus for pregnancy and maintaining the pregnancy itself. A proper amount of progesterone is necessary to inhibit premature uterine contractions; it is often prescribed when there is danger of spontaneous abortion. It also stimulates the mammary glands of the pregnant woman, causing enlargement of the breasts. In the nonpregnant female it keeps breast tissue firm and healthy and reduces the possibility of painful menstruation, premenstrual tension, and other gynecological problems (McCary and McCary, 1982).

testosterone

The *testes* in the male, under the stimulation of LH from the pituitary, begin the production of the androgenic hormone, ***testosterone.*** It is this male hormone that is responsible for the development and preservation of masculine secondary sexual characteristics, including facial and body hair, voice change, and muscular and skeletal development, and for the development of the other male sex organs: the seminal vesicles, prostate gland, epididymis, penis, and scrotum.

The estrogens and androgens are found in both boys and girls but in negligible amounts prior to puberty. They are produced by the adrenals and the gonads in moderately increasing amounts during childhood. As the ovaries mature, the production of ovarian estrogenic hormones increases dramatically and begins to show the cyclic variation in level during various stages of the menstrual cycle. The level of androgens in the girl's bloodstream increases only slightly. As the testes mature in the male, the production of testosterone increases dramatically, whereas the level of the estrogens in the boy's bloodstream increases only slightly. Figure 4-2 shows the increases in hormones at puberty. It is the ratio of the levels of the male to female hormones that is partly responsible for development of male or female characteristics. An imbalance in the natural hormonal state in a growing child can produce deviations in primary and secondary sexual characteristics and affect the development of expected masculine or feminine physical traits. A female with an excess of androgens may grow a mustache and body hair, develop masculine musculature and strength, or evidence an enlarged clitoris or other masculine characteristics. Athletes sometimes take male hormones (testos-

steroids

terone, also called ***steroids***) to increase their strength and endurance. A male with an excess of estrogens may evidence decreased potency and sex drive and an enlargement of the breasts.

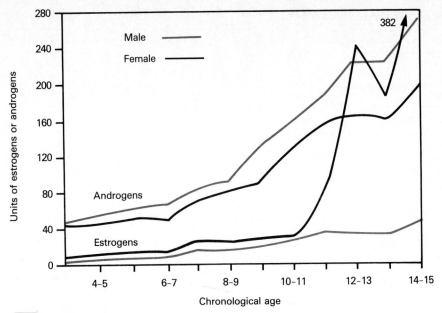

FIGURE 4-2

Hormone secretion with age.

Adrenals*

adrenal glands

The **adrenal glands** are located just above the kidneys. In the female, they produce androgens (masculinizing sex hormones) at low levels. The adrenal glands also secrete estrogen (feminizing sex hormone), partially replacing the loss of ovarian estrogen after menopause. In the male, the adrenals secrete both androgens and estrogens, with androgens produced in a greater amount.

Hypothalamus

hypothalamus

The **hypothalamus** is a small area of the forebrain about the size of a marble. It is the motivational and emotional control center of the brain, regulating such functions as eating, drinking, hormonal production, menstrual cycles, pregnancy, lactation (milk production), and sexual response and behavior. It contains both the pleasure and pain centers connected with sexual response. Electrical stimulation of the hypothalamus can produce sexual thoughts and feelings (Delgardo, 1969). Stimulation of the hypothalamus in male rats can produce extraordinary sexual interest and performance (Caggiula and Hoebel, 1966).

We are most concerned here with the role of the hypothalamus in hormonal production and regulation. A chemical called **GnRH (*gonadotropin-releasing hormone*)** is produced by the hypothalamus to control the secretion of LH and FSH. Thus, the hypothalamus plays an important role in regulating the pituitary. Let us see how this works in men and women.

gonadotropin-releasing hormone (GnRH)

---

* Part of the material on pages 121, 122, 123, 128, and 131 of this book has been taken from Rice, F. P. (1989), *Human Sexuality*. Copyright© 1989 by Wm. C. Brown Publishers. Reprinted by permission.

Sex Hormones in Males

spermatogenesis

The hypothalamus, pituitary gland, and testes function together in the male to control hormonal production. Under the influence of GnRH from the hypothalamus, the pituitary secretes FSH and LH. FSH stimulates sperm growth in the testes (**spermatogenesis**) as does LH. Without LH, sperm production does not go beyond the second cell division and second stage of growth. However, the chief function of LH is to stimulate the interstitial cells of the testes to produce testosterone (Winter and Fairman, 1972).

The level of testosterone is kept fairly constant by a phenomenon known as a *negative feedback loop* (see figure 4-3). The GnRH stimulates the production of LH, which, in turn, stimulates secretion of testosterone. As the level of testosterone builds, the hypothalamus, sensitive to the amount of testosterone present, reduces the production of GnRH, which, in turn, reduces the production of LH and

FIGURE 4-3

Negative feedback loops.

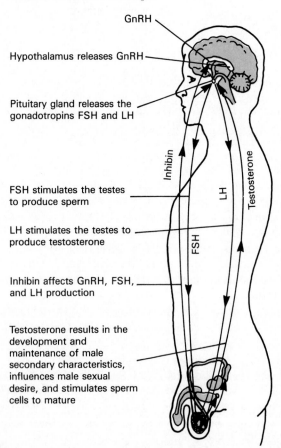

GnRH

Hypothalamus releases GnRH

Pituitary gland releases the gonadotropins FSH and LH

Inhibin

LH

Testosterone

FSH stimulates the testes to produce sperm

LH stimulates the testes to produce testosterone

FSH

Inhibin affects GnRH, FSH, and LH production

Testosterone results in the development and maintenance of male secondary characteristics, influences male sexual desire, and stimulates sperm cells to mature

testosterone. When the level of testosterone declines, the hypothalamus picks up this signal to increase secretion of GnRH, which stimulates greater production of LH and testosterone. The system acts much like a furnace with a thermostat to control the temperature of a room: an increase in temperature shuts the furnace down, a decrease turns it on.

An additional substance, **inhibin,** regulates FSH levels in another negative feedback loop (Hafez, 1980; Moodbidri et al., 1980). Inhibin is produced by the testes or, perhaps, by the sperm themselves. As the level of inhibin builds, FSH production is suppressed, which results in a decline of sperm production. With the discovery of inhibin, researchers have shown considerable interest in the possibility of using it as a male contraceptive because it inhibits sperm production. Whether the idea is practical remains to be seen (Rice, 1989).

inhibin

Sex Hormones in Females

The hypothalamus, pituitary gland, and ovaries also work together in a negative feedback loop to control hormonal production in females. GnRH from the hypothalamus stimulates the pituitary to produce FSH and LH. These hormones act upon the ovary to stimulate the growth of follicles and egg cells and the secretion of ovarian estrogen and progesterone. As the level of estrogen builds, it inhibits the production of GnRH, which, in turn, reduces the production of FSH (Rice, 1989).

The major difference between the hormonal systems of males and females is that the level of testosterone in males is fairly constant, whereas estrogen and progesterone secretion is cyclic in females. Estrogen and progesterone levels of females vary with different stages of the menstrual cycle, which is discussed in a subsequent section of this chapter.

MATURATION AND FUNCTIONS OF MALE SEX ORGANS

The primary male sex organs are the **testes, scrotum, epididymis, seminal vesicles, prostate gland, Cowper's glands, penis, vas deferens,** and **urethra.** They are depicted in figure 4-4.

A number of important changes occur in these organs during adolescence. The growth of the testes and scrotum accelerates, beginning at about age 11½, becoming fairly rapid by age 13½, and slowing thereafter. These ages are averages. Rapid growth may start between 9½ and 13½ years, ending between ages 13 and 17. During this time, the testes increase 2½ times in length and about 8½ times in weight. Before puberty the epididymis is relatively large in comparison with the testes; after maturity the epididymis is only about one-ninth the size of the testes.

testes

scrotum

epididymis

seminal vesicles

prostate gland

Cowper's glands

penis

vas deferens

urethra

Spermatogenesis

The most important change within the testes themselves is the development of mature sperm cells. This occurs when FSH and LH from the pituitary stimulate production and growth. The total process of *spermatogenesis*, from the time the primitive spermatogonium is formed until it grows into a mature sperm, is about ten days (McCary and McCary, 1982).

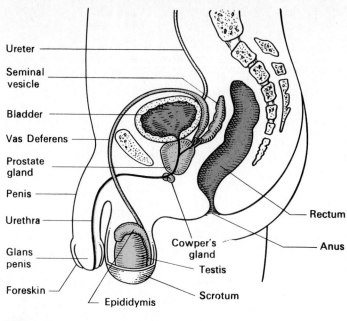

FIGURE 4-4

The male reproductive system.

Following spermatogenesis the sperm migrate by contraction of the seminiferous tubules to reach the epididymis where they may remain for as long as six weeks. Sperm are then transported by ciliary action through the epididymis into the vas deferens where many are stored. There they are conducted by ciliary action through the vas deferens, eventually reaching the seminal vesicle and prostate gland where they are made more mobile by the addition of the *seminal fluid*, passing with it through the urethra and out of the penis at each ejaculation. The seminal fluid, a highly alkaline, milky fluid, keeps the sperm alive, healthy, and mobile and serves as a vehicle for carrying the sperm out of the penis. About 70 percent of the seminal fluid comes from the seminal vesicles, the remaining 30 percent comes from the prostate glands (Spring-Mills and Hafez, 1980).

The Developing Penis

The penis doubles in length and girth during adolescence, with the most rapid growth taking place between ages fourteen and sixteen. Genital growth usually takes 3 years to reach the adult stage, but some males complete this development in 1.8 years and others take as many as 4.7 years. In the adult male, the flaccid (limp) penis averages from 3 to 4 inches in length and slightly over 1 inch in diameter. The tumescent (erect) penis, on the average, is 5½ to 6½ inches in length and 1½ inches in diameter; sizes vary tremendously from male to male (Gebhard and Johnson, 1979).

Adolescent boys are often concerned with the dimensions of their penis, for they associate masculinity and sexual capability with penis size (Henker, 1982). In fact the size of the flaccid penis has little to do with the size of the erect penis, for the small penis enlarges much more in proportion to its size than does the large penis. Moreover, the size of the erect penis has little to do with sexual capability, for the vagina has few nerve endings, and female sexual excitation comes primarily from stimulation of the external genitalia (Rowan, 1982). The degree of pleasure experienced by both the man and woman has nothing to do with the size of the male organ.

The head of the penis (*glans penis*) is covered by a loose fold of skin, the *prepuce* or *foreskin*, often removed surgically through *circumcision* for hygienic or religious reasons. Circumcision is not an obligatory health measure today as long as the foreskin can be retracted and the penis is kept clean. If the prepuce is not retracted and the glans washed, a cheeselike substance known as *smegma* collects, acting as a breeding ground for irritants and disease.

Erection of the penis is possible from infancy; it may be caused by tight clothing, local irritation, the need to urinate, or manual stimulation. Freud was the first to acknowledge infant sexuality and the likelihood that the small boy may gain pleasure from masturbation. Kinsey (1948) pointed out that young children sometimes masturbate to orgasm. However, ejaculation of semen does not occur prior to sexual maturity. (Chapter 15 provides information on masturbation during adolescence.)

Cowper's Glands

The Cowper's glands, which also mature at this time, secrete an alkaline fluid that lubricates and neutralizes the acidity of the urethra for easy and safe passage of the semen. This fluid may be observed at the opening of the glans during sexual excitement and before ejaculation. Because the fluid contains sperm in about 25 percent of cases examined, conception is possible whenever intercourse occurs, even if the male withdraws prior to ejaculation (McCary and McCary, 1982).

Nocturnal Emissions

Adolescent boys wonder and worry about **nocturnal emissions,** or so-called wet dreams. Kinsey (1948) reported that almost 100 percent of men have erotic dreams, and about 83 percent of them have dreams that culminate in orgasm. These dreams occur most frequently among males in their teens and twenties, but about half of all married men continue to have them. If nocturnal orgasms cause anxiety, adolescents should be reassured that such experiences are normal, that no harm comes from them, and that they should be accepted as part of their sexuality. Anxiety may be prevented if adolescents are prepared for nocturnal orgasms ahead of time (Paddack, 1987).

nocturnal emissions

Mood Changes

There is substantial evidence that men go through cycles of mood that affect their behavior (Parlee, 1978). But there is no evidence that these cycles correspond to fluctuations in the levels of testosterone. So many factors—weather, health, fatigue, time of week, social happenings—affect mood fluctuations that it is impossible to say they are based entirely upon physiological changes. There is evidence of some correlation between high levels of testosterone and increased aggression (Ehrhardt and Meyer-Bahlburg, 1981).

MATURATION AND FUNCTIONS OF FEMALE SEX ORGANS

ovaries

fallopian tubes

uterus

vagina

vulva

mons veneris

labia majora

labia minora

clitoris

vestibule

hymen

Bartholin's glands

The primary internal female sex organs are the **ovaries, fallopian tubes, uterus,** and **vagina.** The external female sex organs are known collectively as the **vulva.** They are the **mons veneris (mons pubis),** the **labia majora** (major or large outer lips), the **labia minora** (small inner lips), the **clitoris,** and the **vestibule** (the cleft region enclosed by the labia minora). The **hymen** is a fold of connective tissue that partly closes the vagina in the virginal female. The **Bartholin's gland,** situated on either side of the vaginal orifice, secrete a drop or so of fluid during sexual excitement. The female sexual organs are depicted in figure 4-5.

███ **FIGURE 4-5**

The female reproductive system.

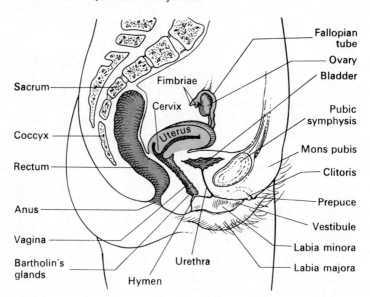

███ Vaginal Development

The vagina matures at puberty in a number of ways. It increases in length, and its mucous lining becomes thicker, more elastic, and turns a deeper color. The Bartholin's glands begin to secrete their fluids, and the inner walls of the vagina change their secretion from the alkaline reaction of childhood to an acid reaction in adolescence.

Changes in the Vulva and Uterus

The labia majora, practically nonexistent in childhood, enlarge greatly, as do the labia minora and the clitoris. The mons veneris becomes more prominent through the development of a fatty pad.

A dramatic change also takes place in the uterus, which doubles in length, showing a straight-line increase during the period from ten to eighteen years of age. The uterus of the mature nonpregnant female is a hollow, thick-walled, muscular organ shaped like a pear, about 3 inches long, 2½ inches at the top and narrowing to a diameter of 1 inch at the cervix (McCary and McCary, 1982).

Ovarian Changes

The ovaries increases greatly in size and weight. They ordinarily show a fairly steady growth from birth to about eight years of age. From eight to about the time of ovulation (twelve or thirteen years) the rate of growth accelerates somewhat, but the most rapid increase occurs after sexual maturity is reached. This is due, no doubt, to the maturation of the follicles within the ovary itself.

Every infant girl is born with about 400,000 follicles in each ovary. By the time puberty has been reached, this number has declined to about 80,000 in each ovary. Ordinarily, one follicle ripens into an ovum every twenty-eight days for a period of about thirty-eight years, which means that only about 495 have ripened during the woman's reproductive years (McCary and McCary, 1982).

Menarche

On the average the adolescent girl begins her menstrual cycle at twelve to thirteen years of age, although she may mature considerably earlier or later (nine to eighteen years is an extreme range). **Menarche** (the onset of menstruation) usually does not occur until after maximum growth rates in height and weight have

menarche

HIGHLIGHT Controversy over Change in Age of Menarche

J. M. Tanner (1962, 1968, 1970, 1972), the world's most noted specialist on physical growth in adolescence, has reported that the age of menarche declined an average of four months per decade, or a total of 3½ years, over the past century. He reported that the average age for menarche during the mid-1800s was 17 and 13½ during the mid-1900s. But recent evidence summarized by Bullough suggests that Tanner only had a single source to document his claim of age 17 for the 1800s. According to Bullough, other sources suggest an average age of 14, so that the change in age of menarche may be less pronounced. However, the overall finding that menarche occurs somewhat earlier is still valid.

Bullough, V. L. (1981). "Age at Menarche: A Misunderstanding." *Science,* 213: 365–366.

been achieved. Because of the superior nutrition and health care, girls start menstruating earlier today than in former generations (Bullough, 1981; Katcha-dourian, 1977; Roche, 1979). An increase in body fat may stimulate menarche; vigorous exercise tends to delay it (Stager, 1988).

The Menstrual Cycle

The menstrual cycle may vary in length from 20 to 40 days, averaging about 28 days (Vollman, 1977). However, there is considerable difference in the length of the cycle when different women are compared, and any one woman may show widespread variations. A regular cycle is quite rare.

The four phases of the menstrual cycle are: *follicular or proliferative phase, ovulatory phase, luteal or secretory phase*, and *menstrual phase* (see figure 4-6). The *follicular phase* extends from just after menstruation until a follicle ripens (sometimes more than one follicle ripens) and an egg or ovum matures. During this phase, the pituitary secretes some LH but relatively higher levels of FSH. FSH stimulates development of the follicles and one or more ova and induces the secretion of increasing levels of estrogen. When estrogen is at a peak, the hypothalamus acts upon the pituitary to reduce the level of FSH and to secrete a surge of LH. The increased estrogen level results in a thickening of the inner lining of the uterus (the endometrium)

FIGURE 4-6

The menstrual cycle.

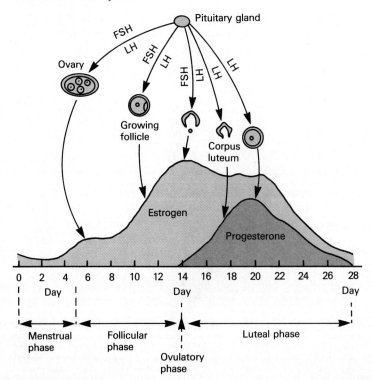

to receive a possible fertilized egg.

Approximately fourteen days before the onset of the next menstrual period, the spurt in LH production results in *ovulation*, during which a mature ovum erupts from its Graafian follicle and passes to the fimbriae or fingerlike projections of the fallopian tube. The ovulatory phase is the shortest of the cycle.

The *luteal phase* follows ovulation and continues to the beginning of the next menstrual period. During the luteal phase, LH secretion from the pituitary stimulates growth of the follicle from which the ovum has erupted. This follicle develops into the corpus luteum (meaning yellow body) that secretes progesterone during the remainder of this phase.

During the *menstrual phase* (see figures 4-6 and 4-7), the levels of estrogen and progesterone are at a minimum. This signals the hypothalamus to resume production of GnRH, which stimulates the pituitary to begin secretion of LH and FSH all over again.

One of the questions adolescents ask concerns the exact time ovulation occurs. *Ordinarily the time of ovulation is about fourteen days before the onset of the next menstrual period*, which would be on the fourteenth day of a twenty-eight-day cycle and on the seventeenth day of a thirty-one-day cycle. However, there is some evidence to show that girls have become pregnant on any one day of the cycle, including during menstruation itself, and that some girls may ovulate more than once during a cycle, possibly due to the stimulus of sexual excitement itself. With

■ FIGURE 4-7

Formation of the corpus luteum.

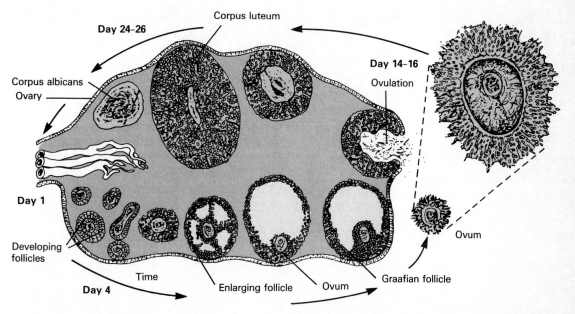

Adapted from Hole, J. W. (1987). *Human Anatomy and Physiology*, 4th ed. Copyright© 1987 Wm. C. Brown Publishers, Dubuque, Iowa. All rights reserved. Reprinted by permission.

the exact time of ovulation difficult to predict, *there are really no completely "safe" times during the month when a girl cannot become pregnant.*

anovulatory   A girl may menstruate **anovulatory** (without ovulation) when her menstrual cycle begins until the ovaries mature enough to discharge mature ova and until the endocrine glands secrete enough of their hormones to make ovulation possible. The first periods may be scanty and irregular, spaced at varying intervals until a rhythm is established. It is not uncommon for the flow to last only a day or so for the first few periods. Later it may last from two to seven days, with the mean usually about five days. The total amount of blood lost averages 1.5 ounces (three tablespoonsful). A normal range is from 1 to 5 ounces. Only part of the menstrual fluid is blood. The total discharge amounts to approximately one cupful (6 to 8 ounces) and is composed partly of mucus and broken-down cell tissue (McCary and McCary, 1982).

Menstrual Problems and Concerns

Beginning menstruation can be a traumatic event for some girls who are not prepared ahead of time (Pillemer et al., 1987). One sixteen-year-old commented:

> I was very frightened of the sexual changes that occurred in my body. The first change I noticed was my menstrual period. I was very frightened of the blood; I didn't know why it occurred. When I finally asked my mother, she did not really take the time to explain it to me, so I didn't really know just why or how it happened. (Dreyfus, 1976, p. 43)

Other girls are able to accept menstruation in a natural way because they have been taught what to expect. One girl remarked:

> I was aware of the changes that were going to take place in my body before they occurred. I was not really frightened of the changes in my body because I was told a lot about it by my next door neighbor and my mother. (Dreyfus, 1976, p. 42)

Still other girls are excited and happy that they are maturing. Such were the feelings of Anne Frank at age 14½:

> I think what is happening to me is so wonderful, and not only what can be seen on my body, but all that is taking place inside. I never discuss myself or any of these things with anybody; that is why I have to talk to myself about them.
>   Each time I have a period—and that has only been three times—I have the feeling that in spite of all the pain, unpleasantness, and nastiness, I have a sweet secret, and that is why, although it is nothing but a nuisance to me in a way, I always long for the time that I shall feel that secret within me again (Frank, 1953, p. 117).

Some writers suggest that menarche should be a time of celebration and congratulations. Logan, Calder, and Cohen (1980) write:

> Two elements of a tradition that seem most appropriate are a physical gesture such as a hug or a kiss and material token such as a present or a card. The

physical gesture would convey a message of support and of acceptance of the body. . . . A material token has two advantages. First, a present is already an established form of celebration of life. Second, her major reaction to it can be private. She can come back to it and reflect on it when *she* feels comfortable. (p. 267)

The author goes on to tell of a father who filled his daughter's room with flowers, which she found upon arrival from school.

Whether the adolescent girl experiences any menstrual problem will depend on both physical and emotional factors. Almost all girls experience variations of mood according to the stage of the menstrual cycle. For some women, the so-called **premenstrual syndrome (PMS)** includes unpleasant physical changes and mood swings (Hopson and Rosenfeld, 1984). There is a physical basis for these fluctuations. Depression, hostility, anxiety, and emotional upset are more evident just before and during the menstrual period when the female hormones are at their lowest levels. Feelings of joy are greatest midway between periods when the estrogen level is at its highest.

premenstrual syndrome (PMS)

Not all women exhibit symptoms, however. Keye (1983) reported that only 5 percent to 10 percent of the women in his study had premenstrual distress serious enough to interfere with functioning. Another research group that measured school grades found no effects of the menstrual cycle on academic performance (Walsh et al., 1981).

Premenstrual symptoms do not always occur and they vary from woman to woman. Some women are not bothered by them, others are bedridden. So many environmental factors can influence mood that it is a mistake to attribute all emotional fluctuations to female hormones. The truth of the matter is that both men and women experience biological and psychological cycles that depend upon everything from the weather to personal relationships with parents, teachers, or the opposite sex. Good and bad moods cannot be predicted solely on the basis of the time of month.

The young girl's attitudes and feelings about menstruation are also very important. A study of menarche experience of ninety-five women from twenty-three countries revealed that negative reactions to first menstruation were very common (Logan, 1980). In Asian countries especially, girls hear little about menstruation, so that 50 percent of Asian women reported embarrassment at menarche. Fifty percent of Japanese women were surprised. Only half of the Asian mothers spoke to their daughters prior to menarche; over one-half of the daughters felt inadequately prepared for their first period. Table 4-1 shows the emotional reactions of all ninety-five of the foreign women to menarche.

It is important, therefore, that women be prepared in a positive way for menstruation. The more knowledgeable they are prior to menarche, the more likely they will report a positive initial experience (Koff, Rierdan, and Sheingold, 1982; Ruble and Brooks-Gunn, 1982; Shandhon, 1988).

Unfortunately, many girls are negatively conditioned even before menses (Amann-Gainotti, 1986; Stubbs, 1982). One study of sixth to eighth graders in white middle- and upper-class schools revealed that menstruation was associated

TABLE 4-1

Emotional reactions of the foreign women to their menarche.

REACTION	PERCENTAGE SHOWING REACTION
Surprised	32
More grown up	24
Embarrassed	23
Sick	15
Frightened	15
Happy	15
More feminine	13
Different	13
Afraid everyone would know	12
Unclean	11
Proud	10
Worried about what to do	10
Sad	8
Closer to mother	5

From: Logan, D. D. (Summer 1980). "The Menarche Experience in Twenty-Three Foreign Countries," *Adolescence* 15: 254.

mainly with negative attitudes and expectations. Most believed that it was accompanied by physical discomforts, increased emotionality and mood changes, and disruption of activities and social life. Because some of the girls answering the questions had not yet menstruated, their responses reflected not actual experiences but negative cultural stereotypes and negative beliefs that they had learned. Their menstrual experiences were primed to become self-fulfilling prophecy (Clarke and Ruble, 1978).

One study of advertisements of menstrual products showed that the ads depicted menstruation as a "hygienic crisis" that is managed by an "effective security system" that affords protection and "peace of mind." Failure to provide adequate protection places the woman at risk for soiling, staining, embarrassment, and odor. Such ads encourage guilt and diminished self-esteem in the adolescent who experiences discomfort (Havens and Swenson, 1988).

Other researchers have demonstrated the relationship between sociopsychological factors and menstrual distress. One study showed that women who have more liberal attitudes about the role of women in society experience less psychological stress that may manifest itself in menstrual difficulties. Women in therapy who were encouraged to understand and appreciate their female role reported decreased menstrual symptomatology (Brattesani and Silverthorne, 1978). Warm, supportive family and peer relations also may be conducive to less stressful menstrual cycles and to fewer physical difficulties in general.

Some adolescent females experience physical difficulties with their menstrual periods (Huffman, 1986). These physical problems usually fall into one of four categories. *Dysmenorrhea* is painful or difficult menstruation: menstrual cramps or abdominal pain, with or without other symptoms such as backache, headache, vomiting, fatigue, irritability, sensitivity of the genitals or breasts, pain in the legs, swelling of the ankles, or skin irritations such as pimples. *Menhorrhagia* is excessive bleeding due to physical or emotional factors (Altchek, 1988). *Amenorrhea* is absence of flow. This may be due to a physical cause, such as vigorous exercise that changes the percentage of body fat (Andrews, 1982) and alters hormonal secretion (Bullen et al., 1981). It may also be caused by an endocrine disorder or a change of climate, overwork, emotional excitement, and other factors. *Metrorrhagia*—bleeding from the uterus at times other than during a menstrual period—is not common. It demands a medical checkup to determine physical and/or emotional causes.

Many questions arise concerning exercise, bathing, or swimming during the menstrual period. Exercise is not only possible but beneficial. Doctors may even prescribe certain exercises to relieve menstrual cramps. Bathing is desirable if the water is not too cold or hot; excessively cold water will stop the menstrual flow and sometimes cause cramps. Swimming is permissible if chilling or excessive fatigue are avoided. Authorities do not suggest forcing vigorous exercise during menstruation but emphasize that the continuation of normal professional and athletic activities during all phases of the menstrual cycle decreases the amount and intensity of menstrual discomfort.

HIGHLIGHT   Menstrual Irregularity in Athletes

Extensive research has established that amenorrhea or irregular menstruation is common in female athletes: ballet dancers, distance runners, swimmers, and others (Calabrese et al., 1983; Frisch et al., 1981; Baker et al., 1981). The current evidence, from both anecdotal and investigative sources, suggests that exercise-induced amenorrhea rapidly reverses once training is discontinued (Stager, 1984; Stager, Ritchie, Robertshaw, 1984). When physical training is reduced or stopped, either as a result of a vacation or an injury, amenorrheic athletes report a resumption of normal menstrual periodicity.

A study comparing ex-collegiate distance runners with current runners and sedentary controls showed that the ex-runners were similar to the control group in terms of the number of menses in the previous 12 months. Current runners reported significantly fewer menses than either of the other two groups. Further, the ex-athletes who experienced menstrual irregularity during training reported that the average (mean) time for resumption of normal menstruation was 1.7 months after training was terminated. No relationship was established between length of amenorrhea and the rate of resumption (Stager, Ritchie, Robertshaw, 1984).

DEVELOPMENT OF SECONDARY SEXUAL CHARACTERISTICS

Sexual maturation at puberty includes development not only of the reproductive organs but also of secondary sex characteristics. These include the appearance of body hair, voice changes, the development of mature male and female body contours, and other minor changes.

The sequence of development for boys and girls is given in table 4-2. The development of some of the primary sexual characteristics is also included to give a picture of the total sequence of development (primary characteristics are marked with an asterisk). The ages provided in the table are averages. Actual ages may extend several years before and after with individual differences having a hereditary base (Akinboye, 1984; Westney et al., 1984). Although the average girl matures about two years before the average boy, the rate of development is not always consistent. An early-maturing boy may be younger than a late-maturing girl. The mean age of menarche is 12.5; the mean age for first ejaculation of

▉ TABLE 4-2

Sequence of development of primary and secondary sexual characteristics.

BOYS	AGE SPAN		GIRLS
Beginning growth of testes, scrotum, pubic hair	11.5–13	10–11	Height spurt begins
Some pigmentation, nodulation of breasts (later disappears)			Slight growth of pubic hair
			Breasts, nipples elevated to form "bud" stage
Height spurt begins			
Beginning growth of penis*			
Development of straight, pigmented pubic hair	13–16	11–14	Straight, pigmented pubic hair
Early voice changes			Some deepening of voice
Rapid growth of penis, testes, scrotum, prostate, seminal vesicles*			Rapid growth of vagina, ovaries, labia, uterus*
First ejaculation of semen*			Kinky pubic hair
Kinky pubic hair			Age of maximum growth
Age of maximum growth			Further enlargement, pigmentation, elevation of nipple, areola to form "primary breast"
Beginning growth of axillary hair			
			Menarche*
Rapid growth of axillary hair	16–18	14–16	Growth of axillary hair
Marked voice change			Filling out of breasts to form adult conformation, secondary breast stage
Growth of beard			
Indentation of frontal hair line			

Note: Primary sexual characteristics are marked with an asterisk.

semen is 13.7. But it is untrue to refer to these ages as the norm. The age of sexual maturity extends over such a wide range (9 to 18 years is not unusual) that any ages within the range should be considered normal.

Males

The development of secondary sexual characteristics in boys is a gradual process. The development of pubic hair starts with sparse, straight hair at the base of the penis, and then the hair gradually becomes more profuse and curled, forming an inverse triangle and spreading up to the umbilicus. Figure 4-8 shows the developmental process (Katchadourian, 1977). Axillary hair usually first appears two years after the appearance of pubic hair, with the growth of the beard coming near the end of the total sequence, and the indentation of the hair line (this does not

FIGURE 4-8

Stages of pubic hair development in adolescent boys.   Stages are: (1) prepubertal (not shown) in which there is no true pubic hair; (2) sparse growth of downy hair mainly at base of penis; (3) pigmentation, coarsening, and curling with an increase in amount of hair; (4) adult hair, but limited in area; (5) adult hair with horizontal upper border and spread to thighs.
Adapted from: Tanner, J. M. (1962). *Growth at Adolescence*, 2d ed. (Oxford: Blackwell Scientific Publications) as reprinted in Katchadourian, H. (1977). *The Biology of Adolescence* (San Francisco: W. H. Freeman), p. 67.

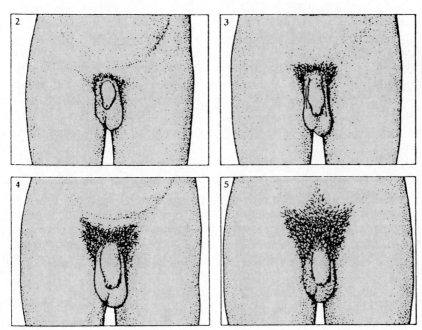

occur in girls) the final development. Muscular development, widening of the shoulders and chest, and other changes in body contours continue. Usually a boy has reached 98 percent of his adult height by 17¼ years of age, plus or minus ten months.

Changes in the boy's voice are due to the rapid growth of the larynx (the Adam's apple) and the lengthening of the vocal cords across it. The vocal cords nearly double in length, lowering the pitch one octave. Volume also increases, and the tonal quality is more pleasant. Roughness of tone and unexpected pitch changes may last until sixteen or eighteen years of age.

Before and during the period when sexual maturation takes place, some boys suffer what has been referred to as the locker room syndrome. The boy in middle school or junior high is herded into the shower after gym where he has to undress and bathe in front of others. The range in normal developmental rates is great enough so that some boys are completely underdeveloped, while others are ahead of their classmates. The boy with little pubic or axillary hair, no noticeable beard, an underdeveloped penis, or a childlike body feels immature in front of his more fully developed friends. Those who have started to develop may become self-conscious at their new sexual image. Involuntary erection in front of others is especially embarrassing. Boys with noticeable body odor are shunned by others, and they wonder why. Even little things become a source of embarrassment; an old pair of socks with holes or loud-colored underwear that invites negative comments. The desire to avoid critical comments leads some boys to become excessively modest or withdrawn and to retreat from the world through daydreaming. Some boys become hostile and defensive, ready to argue or fight at the slightest provocation; others become daring show-offs, exhibiting bravado to hide their anxieties and their lack of self-confidence.

One of the most immediate results of sexual maturation is a developing preoccupation with sex. Attention becomes focused on sex, new sexual sensations, and the opposite sex. One study of graffiti on the bathroom walls of junior high schools indicated that the greatest percentage of inscriptions were sex related. The graffiti of males were most often related to sexual activity, whereas those of females most often expressed sexual desire (Peretti et al., 1977). Adolescent boys and girls spend a lot of time thinking or dreaming about sex, reading sex-oriented literature, and talking about the opposite sex.

These awakening sexual interests motivate adolescent boys to devote much time and attention to grooming and clothes, to body building and care, or to various attempts to attract the attention of girls. Some boys become preoccupied with finding girls who are sexually cooperative, available as outlets for sexual tension. Others turn their attention on themselves through masturbation. Others partially sublimate their urges through sports, work, or other constructive outlets. Quite typically, there are wide variations in the strength of the sexual drive in adolescent boys, but most have to learn how to deal with their urges in socially acceptable ways. The developing male is usually able to adjust to these sexual changes and to come to grips with his feelings and urges only gradually. But sex remains a problem for most adolescent boys until they develop satisfying relationships with girls. (See chapter 15 on sexual behavior.)

Females

Development of pubic hair in girls is similar to that of boys (Faust, 1977). On the average girls are 11.9 years of age when straight, pigmented pubic hair begins to grow, first along the labia, then becomes more abundant and kinky, spreading over the mons in an inverse triangular pattern, and by late adolescence spreads to the medial surface of the thighs (Stubbs, 1982). Figure 4-9 shows the developmental sequence (Katchadourian, 1977).

Facial hair of girls appears first as a slight down on the upper lip, then spreads to the upper part of the cheeks, and finally to the sides and lower border of the chin. This hair is less pigmented and of finer texture than that of men, but brunettes may have a darker, heavier down than blonds. Axillary hair grows about two years after pubic hair and is generally coarser and darker in brunettes than in blonds. Body hair, especially on the arms and legs, is the last hair to develop. Ordinarily, girls do not have noticeable hair on their chests, shoulders, or backs except in cases of glandular disturbance.

FIGURE 4-9

Stages of pubic hair development in adolescent girls.
(1) prepubertal (not shown) in which there is no true pubic hair; (2) sparse growth of downy hair mainly at sides of labia; (3) pigmentation, coarsening, and curling with an increase in the amount of hair; (4) adult hair, but limited in area; (5) adult hair with horizontal upper border.
Adapted from: Tanner, J. M. (1962). *Growth at Adolescence*, 2d ed. (Oxford: Blackwell Scientific Publishers) as reprinted in Katchadourian, H. (1977). *The Biology of Adolescence* (San Francisco: W. H. Freeman), p. 57.

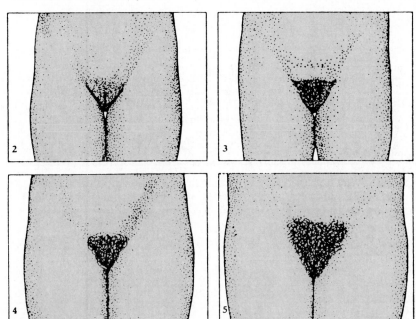

One of the most noticeable changes in girls is the development of the breasts. It takes place in five stages:

Prepubertal stage. Flat appearance.

Bud stage. Elevation, enlargement, and pigmentation of the nipple and surrounding areola, usually starting about two and a half years before menarche.

Primary stage. Increase in underlying fat surrounding the nipple and areola, causing the areola to project in a mound above the level of the chest wall.

Secondary or mature stage. Development of mammary gland tissue—larger, rounder breast. Areola recedes and is incorporated in the breast itself so that only the papilla (nipple) protrudes. This mature stage usually comes after menarche. Regardless of when development starts, it usually takes three years before the papilla projects out from the surrounding breast.

Adult stage. Completion of development.

Figure 4-10 shows the progress of breast development (Katchadourian, 1977).

Adolescent girls are concerned about the size and shape of their breasts. Some girls who are flat chested feel self-conscious because they are influenced by the "playboy" element in their society, which emphasizes fullness of breast as

---

HIGHLIGHT   Breast Concern

The adolescent girl's preoccupation with breast development and size is well illustrated in the following account:

> I was about six months younger than everyone else in my class . . . I would sit in the bathtub and look at my breasts and know that any day now, any second now, they would start growing like everyone else's. They didn't. "I want to buy a bra," I said to my mother one night. "What for?" she asked. . . . "Why not use a Band-Aid instead?" she would say. . . .
>
> I suppose that for most girls, breasts, brassieres, that entire thing, has more trauma, more to do with the coming of adolescence, with becoming a woman, than anything else. . . .
>
> I started with a 28 AA bra. . . . My first brassiere came from Robinson's Department Store in Beverly Hills. I went

> there alone, shaking, positive they would look me over and smile and tell me to come back next year. An actual fitter took me into the dressing room and stood over me while I took off my blouse and tried the first one on. The little puffs stood out on my chest. "Lean over," said the fitter. . . . I leaned over, with the fleeting hope that my breasts would miraculously fall out of my body and into the puffs. Nothing.
>
> "Don't worry about it," said my friend Libby some months later, when things had not improved. "You'll get them after you're married."
>
> . . . And I knew that no one would ever want to marry me. I had no breasts. I would never have breasts.

Ephron, N. (1975). *Crazy Salad* (New York: Knopf), pp. 4-6.

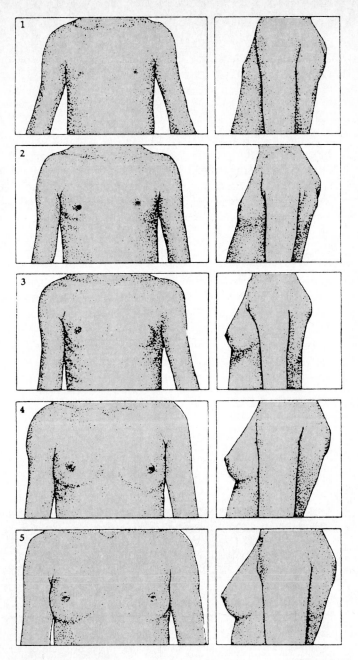

■■ FIGURE 4-10

Stages of breast development in adolescent girls.
Stages are: (1) prepubertal flat appearance like that of a
child; (2) small, raised breast bud; (3) general enlargement
and raising of breast and areola; (4) areola and papilla
(nipple) form contour separate from that of breast;
(5) adult breast—areola is in same contour as breast.
Adapted from: Tanner, J. M. (1962). *Growth at Adolescence*, 2d ed. (Oxford:
Blackwell Scientific Publishers) as reprinted in Katchadourian, H.
(1977). *The Biology of Adolescence* (San Francisco: W. H. Freeman), p. 55.

a mark of beauty and sexuality. Some adolescent girls go to the extremes of wearing padded bras, tight jerseys, or sweaters or even getting medical help to enlarge their breasts. Such girls find advertising promises to "put inches on your bosom in only a few days" appealing. Girls who have huge, pendulous breasts are also self-conscious when they suffer unkind remarks and stares.

Also of concern to girls are the changes that take place in body contours. The most noticeable change other than breast development is the widening and rounding of the hips. This is due to the broadening of the pelvis and the increased deposition of fat in the subcutaneous tissue of this area. These changes occur over about an eighteen-month period, usually starting at about the same time that the first breast buds appear. Whereas during this period girls are acquiring subcutaneous fat on their hips, boys seem to lose body fat across the hips at the same time. Girls stop growing in height, on the average, at 16¼, plus or minus thirteen months.

There is some evidence that adolescent girls become more concerned than boys about the physical changes taking place in their bodies. The principal reason is that society places great emphasis on a woman's physique. Women get rewards in society for their appearance. It follows, therefore, that a girl will be concerned about her body for it helps her to determine whether she fits in socially and what her self-concept will be. The adolescent girl's concern is with meeting cultural standards of physical appearance and obtaining the approval of friends. As a consequence, glamour and popularity become important concerns.

GROWTH IN HEIGHT AND WEIGHT

One of the earliest and most obvious physical changes of adolescence is the growth spurt that begins in early adolescence. This growth in height is accompanied by an increase in

Adolescence has been described as a period of sexual maturity and physical growth. (© Frank Siteman)

weight and changes in body proportion. These changes are determined through longitudinal studies of individual children who are measured year after year. The combined data provide a composite picture of growth trends in groups of children.

Growth Trends

Girls grow faster in height and weight at approximately 12 years of age; boys grow faster in height and weight at approximately 14 (see figure 4-11) (Tanner, 1972). Girls are usually shorter and lighter than boys during childhood; however, because they start to mature earlier, they average slightly taller than boys between 12 and 14 and heavier than boys between the ages of 10 and 14. Whereas girls have reached 98 percent of the adult height at 16¼ years, boys do not reach 98 percent of their adult height until 17¾ years. These rates vary for different individuals.

Determinants of Height

A number of factors are believed to be important in determining the total mature height of the individual (Eveleth and Tanner, 1976; Gertner, 1986). One of the most important factors is heredity. Tall parents tend to have tall children; short parents,

FIGURE 4-11

Increase in height.
Adapted from: Tanner, J. M. (1962). *Growth at Adolescence,* 2d ed. (Springfield, Ill.: Charles C. Thomas). Used by permission of the author.

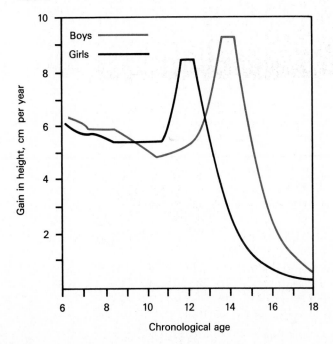

short children. The most important environmental factor is nutrition (Tanner, 1970). Children who are better nourished during the growth years become taller adults than less well-nourished persons. Studies have shown that children from higher socioeconomic groups grow taller than those from poorer families. The reason is poorer nutrition, not income, job, or education as such. Depression or war can affect growth because it affects nutrition. During the last years of World War II and for several years thereafter, growth retardation of children was widespread.

The age when sexual maturation begins also affects the total height finally achieved (Tanner, 1970). Boys and girls who are early maturers tend to be shorter as adults than those who are later maturers. Sexual maturation results in the secretion of sex hormones from the gonads; the hormones inhibit the pituitary from further production of HGH. A later maturer has a longer time to grow before the sex hormones stop the pituitary from stimulating further growth.

Furthermore, the growth achieved before puberty is of greater significance to total adult height than is the growth achieved during puberty. The adolescent growth spurt contributes, in absolute terms, relatively little to the postadolescent skeletal dimensions and only moderately to weight and strength.

Evidence indicates that the total process of growth is speeding up. Children and adolescents today experience the growth spurt earlier, grow faster, attain a greater total adult height, and attain this height earlier than did children and adolescents sixty or seventy years ago. The normal, healthy girl is ½ to 1 inch taller and reaches menarche ten months earlier than her mother. Girls at the turn of the century reached their adult height at eighteen or nineteen; the average today has dropped to sixteen. Tanner reports an increase in adult height of males of 2½ to 3½ inches during the last century. In 1880 males did not reach their final height until twenty-three to twenty-five years of age; today their adult height is reached at age eighteen (Tanner, 1968). The average height of U.S. sailors in the war of 1812 is estimated at 5 feet, 2 inches, which explains why the decks of the U.S.S. *Constitution* did not need to be more than five feet, six inches high.

Other dimensions, too, are larger today. The average male today wears a size 9 to 10B shoe; his grandfather was a size 7. The seats of the famous La Scala opera house in Milan, Italy, constructed in 1776, were eighteen inches wide; today comfortable seats need to be twenty-four inches wide. These accelerated growth *secular trend* patterns, referred to as the **secular trend,** are beginning to taper off, at least in the United States and some other developed countries. There is a limit to the ultimate size of human beings.

Some adolescents are dissatisfied with the height they attain. This is especially true of boys, many of whom tend to be shorter than they would like.

SUMMARY

Adolescence is a period of sexual maturation and physical growth. The changes that occur are triggered and controlled by the hypothalamus and endocrine glands, which secrete hormones that stimulate and regulate the growth and maturation process. The ovaries secrete the hormones estrogen and progesterone.

Estrogen stimulates the development of female sex characteristics, and progesterone regulates the menstrual cycle and acts upon the breasts. The testes secrete the male hormone testosterone, which stimulates the development of male sex characteristics.

Numerous changes occur in the male sex organs. The testes, scrotum, penis, prostate glands, and Cowper's glands enlarge. The testes begin the production of mature sperm (spermatogenesis).

Numerous changes occur in the female sex organs. The vagina, labia, clitoris, uterus, and Bartholin's glands enlarge and mature. The ovaries begin the production of mature ova. The menstrual cycle begins. Menarche can become an upsetting event for girls who are not prepared for it. Whether the adolescent girl experiences any menstrual problems will depend on physical and emotional factors.

Sexual maturation at puberty includes also the development of secondary sexual characteristics: the appearance of pubic hair, the height spurt, voice changes, muscular development, and the growth of axillary hair, including the beard, in men and the appearance of pubic hair, breasts, the rounded female figure, and the growth spurt in women. Boys and girls can become self-conscious about their development, especially if they do not believe their growth is normal.

Boys and girls mature at younger ages and are growing more than did those of previous generations. This trend, called the secular trend, is due primarily to better nutrition and health care.

DISCUSSION QUESTIONS

1. Should female athletes be allowed to take testosterone to improve their ability? What might be some of the effects?
2. What might be the effect on a male fetus if a woman took birth control pills after she was pregnant?
3. Is it possible to tell if a man is virile by his build or the size of his genitals?
4. Is it possible to tell if a woman is sexually responsive by her figure?
5. Is PMS (premenstrual syndrome) primarily a psychological problem?
6. To girls: When you first started to menstruate, did you understand what was happening? Were you prepared for it? How did you feel?
7. To boys: When you had your first nocturnal emission, did you understand what was happening? Were you prepared for it? How did you feel?
8. Comment on the attitudes in American society toward female breasts. What effect do these attitudes have upon adolescent girls? Boys?
9. When you were an adolescent, were you shorter or taller than your classmates? How did you feel? Explain.

BIBLIOGRAPHY

Akinboye, J. O. (Summer, 1984). "Secondary Sexual Characteristics and Normal Puberty in Nigerian and Zimbabwian Adolescents." *Adolescence*, 19, 483–492.

Altchek, A. (1988). "Abnormal Uterine Bleeding in Teenage Girls." *Medical Aspects of Human Sexuality*, 22, 82–88.

Amann-Gainotti, M. (1986). "Sexual Socialization During Early Adolescence: The Menarche." *Adolescence*, 83, 703–710.

Andrews, W. C. (October, 1982). "Jogger Amenorrhea." *Medical Aspects of Human Sexuality*, 16, 13–16.

Baker, E. R., Mathur, R. S., Kirk, R. F., et al. (1981). "Female Runners and Secondary Amenorrhea: Correlation with Age, Parity, Mileage and Plasma Hormonal and Sex Hormone-Binding Globulin Concentrations." *Fertility and Sterility*, 36, 183.

Brattesani, K., and Silverthorne, C. P. (October, 1978). "Social Psychological Factors of Menstrual Distress." *Journal of Social Psychology*, 106, 139–140.

Bullen, B. A., Skrinar, G. S., Beitins, I. Z., et al. (1981). "Endurance Training Effects on Plasma Hormonal Responsiveness and Sex Hormone Secretion." *Journal of Applied Physiological, Respiratory, Environmental Exercise Physiology*, 56, 1453.

Bullough, V. L. (1981). "Age at Menarche: A Misunderstanding." *Science*, 213, 365–366.

Caggiula, A. R., and Hoebel, B. G. (1966). "Copulation-Record Site in the Posterior Hypothalamus." *Science*, 153, 1284–1285.

Calabrese, L. H., Kirkendall, D. T., Floyd, M., et al. (1983). "Menstrual Abnormalities, Nutritional Patterns and Body Composition in Female Classic Ballet Dancers." *Physicians Sportsmedicine*, 11, 86.

Clarke, A. E., and Ruble, D. N. (March, 1978). "Young Adolescents' Beliefs Concerning Menstruation." *Child Development*, 49, 231–234.

Delgardo, J. M. R. (1960). *Physical Control of the Mind*. New York: Harper and Row.

Dreyfus, E. A. (1976). *Adolescence. Theory and Experience*. Columbus, Ohio: Charles E. Merrill Publishing Co.

Ehrhardt, A., and Meyer-Bahlburg, H. (1981). "Effects of Prenatal Sex Hormones on Gender-Related Behavior." *Science*, 211, 312–318.

Eveleth, P., and Tanner, J. (1976). *Worldwide Variations in Human Growth*. New York: Cambridge University Press.

Faust, M. (1977). "Somatic Development of Adolescent Girls." *Monographs of the Society for Research in Child Development*, 42, serial no. 169.

Frank, A. (1953). *The Diary of a Young Girl*. New York: Pocket Books.

Frisch, R.E., Gotz-Welbergen, A.V., McArthur, J. W., et al. (1981). "Delayed Menarche and Amenorrhea of College Athletes in Relation to Age of Onset of Training." *Journal of the American Medical Association*, 246, 1599.

Garrison, K. C. (1976). "Physiological Development." In *Understanding Adolescence*. 3d ed. Edited by J. F. Adams. Boston, Mass.: Allyn and Bacon.

Gebhard, P. H., and Johnson, A. B. (1979). *The Kinsey Data*. Philadelphia: W. B. Saunders Co.

Gertner, J. M. (1986). "Short Stature in Children." *Medical Aspects of Human Sexuality*, 20, 36–42.

Hafez, E. S. E. (Ed.). (1980). *Human Reproduction: Conception and Contraception*. Hagerstown, MD.: Harper and Row.

Havens, B., and Swenson, I. (1988). "Imagery Associated with Menstruation in Advertising Targeted to Adolescent Women." *Adolescence*, 23, 89–97.

Henker, F. O. (August, 1982). "Men's Concern about Penis Size." *Medical Aspects of Human Sexuality*, 16, 149.

Hopson, J., and Rosenfeld, A. (August, 1984). "PMS: Puzzling Monthly Symptoms." *Psychology Today*, 18, 30–35.

Huffman, J. W. (1986). "Teenagers' Gynecologic Problems." *Medical Aspects of Human Sexuality*, 20, 57–61.

Katchadourian, H. (1977). *The Biology of Adolescence*. San Francisco: W. H. Freeman.

Keye, W. R. (Fall, 1983). "Update: Premenstrual Syndrome." *Endocrine and Fertility Forum*, 6, 1–3.

Kinsey, Alfred, et al. (1948). *Sexual Behavior in the Human Male*. Philadelphia: W. B. Saunders Co.

Koff, E.; Rierdan, J.; and Sheingold, K. (February, 1982). "Memories of Menarche: Age, Preparation, and Prior Knowledge as Determinants of Initial Menstrual Experience." *Journal of Youth and Adolescence*, 11, 1–19.

Kulin, H. E. (1974). "The Physiology of Adolescence in Man." *Human Biology*, 46, 133–143.

Kulin, H. E., and Reiter, E. O. (1973). "Gonadotropins during Childhood and Adolescence: A Review." *Pediatrics*, 51, 260–271.

Logan, D. D.; Calder, J. A.; and Cohen, B. L. (1980). "Toward a Contemporary Tradition for Menarche." *Journal of Youth and Adolescence*, 9, 263–269.

McCary, J. L., and McCary, S. P. (1982). *McCary's Human Sexuality*. 4th ed. Belmont, Calif.: Wadsworth Publishing Co.

Masters, W. H., and Johnson, V. (1966). *Human Sexual Response*. Boston: Little, Brown.

Moodbidri. S. B., et al. (1980). "Measurement of Inhibin." *Archives of Andrology*, 5, 295–303.

Morris, N. M., and Udry, J. R. (June, 1980). "Validation of a Self-Administered Instrument to Assess Stage of Adolescent Development." *Journal of Youth and Adolescence*, 9, 271–280.

Paddack, C. (1987). "Preparing a Boy for Nocturnal Emissions." *Medical Aspects of Human Sexuality*, 21, 15, 16.

Parlee, M. B. (April, 1978). "The Rhythms in Men's Lives." *Psychology Today*, 82ff.

Peretti, P. O., et al. (Spring, 1977). "Graffiti and Adolescent Personality." *Adolescence*, 12, 31–42.

Petersen, A. C. (1979). "Can Puberty Come Any Earlier?" *Psychology Today*, 13, 45, 46.

Pillemer, D. B., Koff, E., Rhinehart, E. D., and Rierdan, J. (1987). "Flashbulb Memories of Menarche and Adult Menstrual Distress." *Journal of Adolescence*, 10, 187–199.

Rice, F. P. (1989). *Human Sexuality*. Dubuque, IA.: Wm. C. Brown Co.

Rierdan, J., and Koff, E. (February, 1980). "The Psychological Impact of Menarche: Integrative versus Disruptive Changes." *Journal of Youth and Adolescence*, 9, 49–58.

Roche, A. F., ed. (1979). "Secular Trends in Human Growth, Maturation, and Development." *Monographs of the Society for Research in Child Development*, 44, serial no. 179.

Rowan, R. L. (July, 1982). "Irrelevance of Penis Size." *Medical Aspects of Human Sexuality*, 16, 153, 156.

Ruble, D. N., and Brooks-Gunn, J. (1982). "The Experience of Menarche." *Child Development*, 53, 1557–1566.

Skandhan, K. P., Pandya, A. K., Skandhan, S., and Mehta, Y. B. (1988). "Menarche: Prior Knowledge and Experience." *Adolescence*, 89, 149–154.

Spring-Mills, E., and Hafez, E. S. (1980). "Male Accessory Sexual Organs." In E. S. Hafz (Ed.), *Human Reproduction*, pp. 60–90. New York: Harper and Row.

Stager, J. M. (1984). "Reversibility of Amenorrhea in Athletes: A Review." *Sports Medicine*, 1, 337.

_____ . (1988). "Menarche and Exercise." *Medical Aspects of Human Sexuality*, 22, 118, 133.

Stager, J. M., Ritchie, B. A., and Robertshaw, D. (1984). "Reversal of Oligo/Amenorrhea in Collegiate Distance Runners." *New England Journal of Medicine*, 310, 51.

Stubbs, M. L. (Spring, 1982). "Period Piece." *Adolescence*, 17, 45–55.

Tanner, J. M. (1962). *Growth of Adolescence*. Springfield, Ill.: Charles C. Thomas.

_____ . (1968). "Earlier Maturation in Man." *Scientific American*, 218, 21–27.

_____ . (1970). "Physical Growth." In *Carmichael's Manual of Child Psychology*. Vol. 1. 3d ed. Edited by P. H. Mussen. New York: John Wiley & Sons.

_____ . (1972). "Sequence, Tempo, and Individual Variation in Growth and Development of Boys and Girls Aged Twelve to Sixteen." *Twelve to Sixteen: Early Adolescence*. Edited by J. Kegan and Robert Coles. New York: W. W. Norton and Co.

Thomas, J. K. (1973). "Adolescent Endocrinology for Counselors of Adolescents." *Adolescence*, 8, 395–406.

Vollman, R. F. (1977). *The Menstrual Cycle*. Philadelphia: W. B. Saunders.

Walsh, R. N., et al. (1981). "The Menstrual Cycle, Sex, and Academic Performance." *Archives of General Psychiatry*, 38, 219–221.

Westney, O. I., Jenkins, R. R., Butts, J. D., and Williams, I. (Fall, 1984). *Adolescence*, 19, 557–568.

Winter, J. S. D., and Fairman, C. (1972). "Pituitary–Gonadal Relationships in Male Children and Adolescents." *Pediatric Research*, 6, 126–135.

CHAPTER

5

The Body Image

The adolescent's emotional reactions to physical changes are as important as the changes themselves. Adolescents become concerned about body image: physical attractiveness, body type, concepts of the ideal, body weight, and timing of their own development in relation to norms. This chapter discusses these and other health concerns along with two selected health problems: acne and nutrition.

THE BODY BEAUTIFUL

Physical Attractiveness

Physical attractiveness has an important relationship to the adolescent's positive self-evaluation, popularity, and peer acceptance. Physical attractiveness is an important ingredient in interpersonal attraction (Shea and Adams, 1984). It influences personality development, social relationships, and social behavior. Attractive adolescents are thought of in positive terms: warm, friendly, successful, desirable, and intelligent. Partly as a result of differential treatment, attractive adolescents appear to have higher self-perceptions and healthy personality attributes, to be better adjusted socially, and to possess a wider variety of interpersonal skills (Adams, 1980; Cash and Janda, 1984; Reis, Nezlek, and Wheeler, 1980).

Body Types

ectomorph
mesomorph
endomorph

Three body types have been identified: **ectomorph, mesomorph,** and **endomorph.** Most people are a mixture rather than a pure type, but identifying the pure types helps considerably in any discussion of general body build. Ectomorphs are tall, long, thin, and narrow, with slender, bony, basketball-player builds. Endomorphs are at the other extreme with soft, round, thick, large, wide, heavy trunks and limbs, and wrestler builds. The mesomorphs are between these two types. They have square, strong, tough, hard bodies, well muscled, with medium-length limbs and wide shoulders. They represent the athletic type of build and participate in strenuous physical activity more frequently than the others.

Body proportions of each type change as the individual grows older. Adolescents tend to grow up before they grow out, so they may be long, slim "bean poles" before they round out. Parts of their bodies grow disproportionately. Their hands, feet, and limbs grow faster than the trunks of their bodies so they may seem gangly, clumsy, and short-waisted. Parts of their faces, such as the nose or chin, may protrude from the relatively long heads until the flesh of the face fills in and the head becomes rounder. Gradually, however, the trunk lengthens, so that sitting height increases in relation to standing height (Eveleth, 1978). The waistline drops, the shoulders widen, the hips of the female broaden, and the body takes on a more mature appearance. The muscles of the limbs develop and flesh is added, so the hands and feet no longer seem out of proportion to the rest of the body. When growth is complete, the body seems back in balance again.

Concepts of the Ideal

Adolescents are affected profoundly by the images of ideal body builds taught by their culture (Collins, 1981). *Most adolescent boys and girls would prefer to be medium types* (Ogundari, 1985). Tall, skinny boys or girls are unhappy with themselves, as are short or fat adolescents. The female endomorph is especially miserable, for Western culture overemphasizes the slim, chic, well-proportioned feminine figure (Bozzi, 1985). The desire for thinness has almost become an obsession among females in our culture (Lundholm and Littrell, 1986). It is partly because of this obsession that anorexia nervosa and bulimia have become so common among adolescent girls (Grant and Fodor, 1986). (See Chapter 9 for a full discussion of eating disorders.) If a girl does not have a slim figure, she is likely to be ignored by boys and less likely to have dates. Such social rejection is hard to live with. This means that self-esteem and self-satisfaction are closely related to acceptance and satisfaction with a physical self (Jaquish and Savins-Williams, 1981; Padin, Lerner, and Spiro, 1981; Pomerantz, 1979; Stewart, 1982).

Studies of males provide further evidence of the social importance of physical attractiveness and of possessing an average physique. Tall men with good builds are considered more attractive than short men (Feingold, 1982). Men with muscular, mesomorphic body builds are more socially accepted than those with different builds (Tucker, 1982). College-aged men with a muscular build are more likely to be socially easygoing and optimistic about interacting with others than endomorphs and ectomorphs (Tucker, 1983). In another study, adolescents who rated themselves as unattractive were also likely to describe themselves as lonely (Moore and Schultz, 1983).

In one experimental test of body stereotyping, three groups of male adolescents were asked to view a series of pictures of men fitting the three body types. The males scored each picture on fifteen personality traits. The mesomorphic body type was associated with socially positive personality traits by all three age groups. Endomorph and ectomorph pictures were frequently associated with negative personality items (Lerner and Karabeneck, 1974). Phrases like "unpopular" and "doesn't have many friends" were more often associated with extreme ectomorphs and endomorphs. In view of these findings, it is not surprising that boys who deviate from the mesomorphic type are dissatisfied with their bodies and wish they were different.

Individual Body Characteristics

Adolescent girls in the sixth or seventh grade become conscious of particular signs of maturation, such as breast development (Rierdan and Koff, 1980). As adolescents mature, they turn their attention to other body features: ankles, hips, or thighs too fat; protruding buttocks or stomach; nose too long, pointed, wide, or pug; chin pointed, sunken, or double; eyes bulgy, sunken, too big, the wrong shape, or crossed; teeth crooked, decayed, or missing; face homely, scarred, pimply, or mole spotted (Collins and LaGanza, 1982).

One study showed the importance of individual body characteristics in self-ratings of physical attractiveness by female and male college students (Lerner and Karabeneck, 1974). The mean age of females was 19.5 years and of males 20.4 years. These ratings, given in table 5-1, show that both females and males felt that general appearance, face, facial complexion, weight distribution, body build, and teeth were important to physical attractiveness. Females also emphasized eyes, shape of legs, hips, waist, and chest. Males were not as concerned about these features but placed more

TABLE 5-1

Mean importance of selected body characteristics for own physical attractiveness for males and females.

BODY CHARACTERISTICS	FEMALE'S OWN IMPORTANCE (N = 114)	MALE'S OWN IMPORTANCE (N = 70)
General appearance	1.3	1.5
Face	1.4	1.5
Facial complexion	1.6	1.8
Distribution of weight	1.7	2.0
Body build	1.7	1.9
Teeth	1.9	2.0
Eyes	1.9	2.4
Shape of legs	2.2	2.8
Hips	2.2	2.8
Hair texture	2.3	2.3
Waist	2.3	2.4
Chest	2.4	2.6
Nose	2.4	2.4
Mouth	2.4	2.4
Profile	2.5	2.3
Thighs	2.5	2.9
Height	2.9	2.7
Chin	3.1	2.8
Arms	3.1	3.0
Hair color	3.2	3.2
Neck	3.2	2.8
Width of shoulders	3.4	2.9
Ears	3.9	3.5
Ankles	4.1	4.2

Note: Respondents ranked characteristics on a scale of 1 to 5, from very important to very unimportant, respectively.

From: Lerner, R. M. and Karabeneck, S. A. (1974). "Physical Attractiveness, Body Attitudes, and Self-Concept in Late Adolescents," *Journal of Youth and Adolescence*, 3:307–316. Used by permission.

emphasis on profile, height, neck, and shoulder width. Males and females were moderately but equally concerned about hair texture, nose, and mouth. Both were least concerned about ankles, ears, hair color, and arms. It is evident that these evaluations reflect cultural stereotypes of attractiveness.

The ideal masculine body image consists of being tall, having dark hair, broad shoulders and chest, big muscles, a slim waist, and well-proportioned arms and legs (Feinman and Gill, 1978). Some adolescent boys, however, at least early in their development, look skinny, uncoordinated, out of proportion, and weak. Late developers are still short and childlike. Others are wide, fat, and dumpy, some with protruding breasts. Boys who deviate from the norm may be given nick-

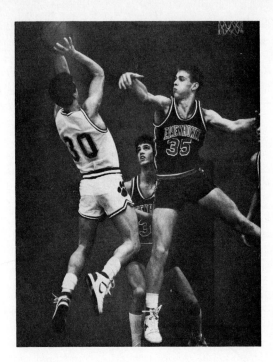

A man with the ideal masculine body image is tall and has dark hair, broad shoulders and chest, big muscles, a slim waist, and well-proportioned arms and legs. (Robert Harbison)

names: "slim," "beany," "broomstick," "Crisco," or "fatso." The boy with the weak-looking build may spend hours working out on barbells or in the school gym to try to improve his build. The fat adolescent who is not able to diet successfully may withdraw from normal social contacts with girls and show marked symptoms of emotional maladjustment. So much emphasis is put on having an athletic build that the boy who is not able to conform feels extremely self-conscious and isolated.

WEIGHT

Obesity

Many adolescents worry about being overweight (Steele, 1980). Ten to 15 percent of all adolescents are truly **obese,** girls more than boys (Storz, 1982; U.S. Dept. of Commerce, 1985). Being overweight not only represents a future health hazard—obesity is related to cardiovascular disease, hypertension, joint disease, and gynecological disorders—but also affects the adolescent's social relationships, self-esteem, ego identity development, and emotional adjustment (Shestowsky, 1983; Stein, 1987). Furthermore, if an obese teenager has a history of a weight problem and does not reduce, the odds are twenty-eight to one that she or he will become and remain an obese adult (Brownell, 1982).

    The *causes of obesity are not a simple matter.* Krieshok and Karpowitz (1988) divide the causes into two major categories: (1) *physiological contributors*, and (2) *psychological contributors*. Physiological contributors may also be divided into three categories as follows:

obese

External Variables   These may be regulated to some extent by the person. *They include food type and variety* and *activity level*. Obese adolescents do not necessarily eat more food, overall, but they prefer foods that are calorically dense and highly flavored (Drewnowski, 1983). They eat large quantities of high-calorie foods (Keesey and Pawley, 1986). Furthermore, their physiological responses tend to encourage this consumption and do not become inhibited after the food is consumed. Specifically, *after eating meals high in carbohydrates or sugars, their insulin levels are elevated, which increases hunger and food consumption.* In fact, just the sight and smell of foods can elevate the insulin level in obese people (Rodin, 1982).

metabolism   *Activity level is another external variable related to excess fat accumulation.* If exercise is moderate, the appetite is reduced somewhat, **metabolism** increases, and fat accumulation is decreased. If the activity level is low, fat accumulates because metabolism declines. Obese people have been found to be less active than people of normal weight. However, if exercise is too strenuous, the appetite increases so that the loss of fat is not great. The body has compensating mechanisms that relate to activity levels.

Internal Variables   Internal variables are also physiological variables that contribute to obesity. *These are genetically controlled and cannot be changed by the person* (except perhaps through surgery). There are differing opinions as to the strength of the genetic component (Edelman, 1980). One suggestion is that endomorphs tend to have longer intestines than do ectomorphs, require more food before satiation, and allow more calories to be absorbed. This argument is substantiated by the fact that surgically shortening the intestinal length can increase weight loss (Powers, 1980).

Mediated Variables   *These variables are those over which the individual may have some regulation but not complete control.* One such variable is the fat cells in the body. Everyone has fat cells, but overweight people have unusually large cells or more cells than do people of normal weight. Food type, variety, activity level, and genetic variables all affect the development of fat cells, but the cells are more likely to be increased in number if excess weight is gained before the age of 12. This is why *eating habits developed before adolescence are important determinants of fat deposition on the body during adolescence* (Krieshok and Karpowitz, 1988). Also, people who have elevated numbers of fat cells may be limited in the amount of excess fat they are able to lose permanently.

Numerous psychological factors are also important contributors to obesity. Eating is a greater positive reinforcement for obese people because they find it to be a more pleasurable activity than do people of normal weight. Jacobs and Wagnor (1984) found that the reinforcement values of spending time with friends and family were higher for obese people than for people of normal weight. *For other people, eating is a negative reinforcement of disturbed emotions,* that is, it can eliminate anxiety, depression, and upset. Oral activity becomes a means of finding security and release from tension.

For still other people, eating becomes a means of punishment. They have poor self-esteem or hate themselves. Weight gain becomes a way of reinforcing their own negative self-conceptions and proving they are right in feeling that way. Obese adolescents, already feeling ineffective, suffer further damage to their self-esteem through the ridicule to which they are often subjected (Sobal, 1984). Becoming more inactive and withdrawn, they may turn to eating as a form of comfort.

The important question is how best to help obese adolescents to lose weight. *Psychotherapy* has been found to be successful in a number of situations (Meer, 1984). But one report of the use of a *group approach* to help significantly overweight girls showed mixed results (Zakus, 1979). Ten girls aged 12 to 18 with an average weight of 231 pounds, started the program. Five dropped out in the initial sessions and had an average net gain of 8 pounds over a six-month period. Of the five who stayed in the program for six months, three each lost an average of over 8 pounds, but each of the other two gained an average of over 7 pounds. Like most other people on diets, all five both gained and lost weight during the six-month period. It is significant that this intense behavior modification program, which developed consciousness of eating habits, tried to change them, and helped with weight reduction diets, failed to produce better results. This effort illustrates how difficult it is to modify eating behavior well established by adoles-

HIGHLIGHT   Family Factors and Obesity

The beginnings of obesity may be found in the early relationships between parents and children (Brone and Fisher, 1988). The childhoods of many obese adolescents are characterized by intense parental involvement, overprotectiveness, and rigidity (Hertzler, 1981). Overprotectiveness involves an unusually high concern for the child's welfare. For example, in clinical interviews parents frequently speak for their obese children or correct them when they attempt to speak for themselves. One father would not put his obese daughter on a diet because he would not permit her to be deprived of anything (Brone and Fisher, 1988). One important manifestation of overprotectiveness is overfeeding. Furthermore, parents often show a hypocondriacal concern for the child's health. Outside interests and friends are often seen as threats to the parent-child relationship. Parental frustrations and disappointments in their lives often underlie the intense parental involvements in the lives of obese adolescents. Obese adolescents are often from lower socioeconomic status families. Parents try to compensate by seeing that the child stays healthy and close to the family. Many obese adolescents emerge from childhood handicapped by feelings of ineffectiveness, dependency, and lack of direction.

Some of these adolescents rebel against their parents to try to increase separation from them. While the obese child appears healthy and well cared for, the obese adolescent is a source of embarrassment to parents, who now urge him or her to reduce. One way the obese adolescent asserts independence is by rejecting the parents' pleas to reduce and by eating as a show of defiance (Brone and Fisher, 1988).

There seems to be some evidence that addictive eating is more common in adolescents whose parents are themselves addicted to alcohol, drugs, gambling, or overeating. Whether this is inherited or learned behavior is uncertain. (Marston, et al., 1988)

cence. According to Brownell (1982), if a cure for obesity is defined as a reduction to ideal weight and maintenance of that weight for 5 years, a person is more likely to recover from most forms of cancer than from obesity. Certainly a better approach is for parents to *develop moderate eating habits in young children* so they will less likely be faced with unacceptable obesity in adolescence.

One method that has been devised for overweight adolescents is to send them to a residential *weight management camp* (Southam et al., 1984). Such a camp in Tacoma, Washington, emphasizes three aspects: (1) nutrition education, (2) behavior modeling, and (3) physical activity. Participants came only for five days, but follow-up studies of them six months after camp revealed permanent weight loss, leading the researchers to conclude that this was a useful approach to adolescent weight management therapy (Brandt, Maschhoff, and Chandler, 1980).

The most successful approaches to treating obesity recognize that it is a multicausal problem. Comprehensive examinations are necessary to elicit genetic, metabolic, environmental, familial, and emotional factors. After reasons for obesity are diagnosed, proper medical and dietary treatments are instituted. If eating becomes an effort to relieve anxiety, *therapy* may be needed to deal with the basic emotional causes.

Underweight

Underweight adolescents have the opposite problem: they are burning up more calories than they are consuming. Males particularly worry about being too skinny or "not having a good build." In one study of 568 adolescent males, over half were dissatisfied with their body, and 71 percent reported eating to gain weight (Fleischer and Read, 1982).

Underweight adolescents need to conserve energy by spending more hours in bed and omitting strenuous exercise to increase the consumption of fattening foods and to overcome a poor appetite.

NUTRITION

Digestion

One of the things adults notice most about adolescents is that they are constantly eating. During the period of rapid growth, the adolescent needs greater quantities of food to take care of bodily requirements. The stomach increases in size and capacity in order to be able to digest these increased amounts of food. Research shows that the caloric requirement for girls may increase on the average by 25 percent from ages ten to fifteen and then decrease slightly and level off. The caloric requirement for boys may increase on the average by 90 percent from ages ten to nineteen. Figure 5-1 shows the increase. No wonder the adolescent boy finds it almost impossible to get enough to eat (Holt, 1972).

Importance of Nutrition

Development of proper eating habits during adolescence is extremely important to individual health. Attainment of maximum height, strength, and physical well-being depends upon the individual's eating enough body-building foods. Bone, muscle, nerve, and other tissue growth requires good nutrition. Nutritional defi-

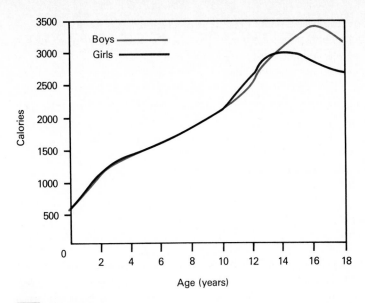

FIGURE 5-1

Daily caloric requirements for both sexes from birth to eighteen years.
Redrawn from Holt, E. L. Jr. (1972). "Energy Requirements." In H. L. Barnett and A. H. Einhorn, (Eds.), *Pediatrics*, 15th ed., p. 130. By permission of Appleton-Century-Crofts.

ciencies are related to physical and mental retardation, reduced stamina, lower resistance to infection, premenstrual tension in girls, and emotional instability.

Considerable attention has been given to the importance of good nutrition to pregnant teenage girls. Pregnancy during those years, when the adolescent mother's body is still in the formative stage, creates added physiological stress for the young girl. Her body makes increased nutritional requirements both for the growth of her body and for the development and subsequent feeding of her baby. Because many of these girls become pregnant out of wedlock, get very little or no prenatal care in the early stages of pregnancy, and show a depressed emotional state before and during pregnancy, they are poor obstetrical risks; their babies may be born prematurely, have congenital defects, or lack the necessary nutrients to survive during the first days and months of life. Furthermore, these young mothers may be prone to such complications of pregnancy as toxemia (the presence of toxic substances in the blood) or eclampsia (convulsions).

Deficiencies

Most studies of nutrition during adolescence show that many adolescents have inadequate diets (U.S. Departments of Agriculture and HHS, 1985). Deficiencies may be summarized as follows:

1. Insufficient calcium—due primarily to an inadequate intake of milk.
2. Insufficient iron—especially true for girls.

3. Inadequate protein—usually true only of girls.
4. Insufficient vitamins, especially A and C—due primarily to lack of enough fresh vegetables and fruit in the diet.
5. Insufficient thiamine and riboflavin.

Adolescent girls have nutritional deficiencies more often than boys. Several factors contribute to this deficit: girls eat less and so are less likely to get the necessary nutrients; they diet more often, depriving themselves of necessary nutrients; and the additional need for some nutrients because of menstruation or pregnancy imposes special problems.

Why do so many adolescents, both boys and girls, have inadequate diets (Lindholm, Touliatos, and Wenberg, 1984)? The reasons may be summarized as follows:

They skip breakfast because of lack of time in the morning, because they would rather sleep late, and for other reasons.

Snacks, which make up about one-fourth of the daily intake of food, *do not compensate for meals missed* because the snacks are primarily fats, carbohydrates, and sugars or because the intake from snacks is not sufficient to make up for the food missed.

Small quantities of foods are eaten, especially of fruits, vegetables, milk, cheese, and meat. Girls usually need more eggs and whole grain cereal than they eat. Also, girls who are dieting often develop nutritional deficiencies because of a low intake of food.

Inadequate knowledge of nutrition influences the development of poor nutrition practices. Many times high school boys and girls know so little about nutrition that they cannot select a well-balanced meal in a cafeteria. Many adolescents need to reduce dietary fat and sugar (Read, Harveywebster, and Usinger-Lesquereux, 1988).

Social pressures may cause poor eating habits. Adolescents who adopt bizarre eating habits often reflect the ideas of their social or cultural group. Some ethnic groups are notorious for their poor nutritional habits, regardless of the amount of money available to buy food (Walter, 1977).

Troubled family relationships and personal adjustments seem to accompany poor eating habits. Adolescents from broken or troubled homes may not have parents at home to cook for them or to see that they get an adequate diet. Those with emotional problems may have nervous stomachs, ulcers, or more complex reasons for not eating properly.

The family is poor and cannot afford to buy proper food. Altogether about 13 percent of U.S. families are below the poverty level (U.S. Dept. of Commerce, 1987).

ACNE

Skin Gland Development

At the onset of puberty, due to actions and reactions of the hormones of the body, the glands of the skin increase their activity. Three kinds of skin glands can cause problems for the adolescent:

1. *Merocrine* sweat glands, distributed over most of the skin surfaces of the body.
2. *Apocrine* sweat glands, located in the armpits, mammary, genital, and anal regions.
3. *Sebaceous* glands, oil-producing glands of the skin.

HIGHLIGHT   Health Concerns of Adolescents

So far, attention has been given in this chapter to adolescents' concern about body image, their self-consciousness about individual body characteristics, their preoccupation with developing and maintaining a good build, developing physical attractiveness, controlling weight, and dealing with individual problems such as acne. However, these discussions leave untouched the broader subject of overall health concerns of adolescents.

Sobal (1987) studied the health concerns of 278 seventh- and eighth-grade students in an urban junior high school. The students were from a working-class neighborhood; about three-fourths were white. Their reported health was: excellent (34 percent), good (50 percent) and fair or poor (16 percent). Ten percent said their rarely thought about their health; 55 percent did sometimes, and 35 percent did often. Table 5-2 shows the results in order of decreasing concern.

The ten issues about which there was the highest level of concern were dental problems, getting along with friends, nutrition, sex, vitamins, getting along with adults, acne, sport injuries, sleep, and headaches. Girls were significantly more concerned with eleven more issues than boys: menstruation, pregnancy, birth control, being overweight, dieting, child abuse, stomach pain, nervousness, depression, acne, and headaches. Boys reported more concern for two areas: sports injuries and sex. The topics most frequently reported for class presentation and discussion were sex, and, to a lesser extent, drugs (including both drinking and smoking as well as illicit drugs). Walker et al. (1982) found that concern about topics related to sexuality and childbirth increased in the higher grades.

TABLE 5-2

Young adolescents' health concerns.

TOPIC	MEDIAN CONCERN
Dental Problems	1.50
Getting Along with Friends	1.53
Nutrition	1.64
Sex	1.77
Vitamins	1.78
Getting Along with Adults	1.85
Acne	1.94
Sports Injuries	1.94
Sleep	1.96
Headaches	2.02
Child Abuse	2.12
Automobile Accidents	2.21
Tiredness	2.22
Stomach Pains	2.23
Health Services	2.26
Depression	2.34
Nervousness	2.39
Overweight	2.43
Drinking	2.57
Dieting	2.59
Pregnancy	2.60
Venereal Disease	2.61
Frequent Coughing	2.62
Suicide	2.63
Drugs	2.65
Underweight	2.67
Menstruation	2.69
Smoking	2.74
Birth Control	2.76
Homosexuality	2.82

Concern Level: 1—very, 2—somewhat, 3—no concern

From: Sobal, J. (1987). "Health Concerns of Adolescents." *Adolescence*, 22, 739–750.

During the adolescent years, the merocrine and apocrine sweat glands secrete a fatty substance with a pronounced odor that becomes more noticeable, causing body odor. The sebaceous glands develop at a greater speed than the skin ducts through which they discharge their skin oils. As a result the ducts may become plugged and turn black as the oil oxidizes and dries upon exposure to the air, creating a blackhead. This in turn may become infected, causing a pimple or ***acne*** to form.

acne

■ Treatment

For less severe cases, treatment from the beginning will prevent acne from becoming serious, either physically or psychologically. Adolescents need to keep their skin scrupulously clean. Some keep their skin very clean yet still have problems. Sometimes adolescents are restricted from eating certain foods, especially chocolate and fatty foods, but the role of these foods in triggering acne is not proved, and the results of dietary restrictions are often uncertain. It is known, however, that victims of acne have receptors in their cells that accept the male androgens, which in turn stimulate the activity of the sebaceous glands. Some doctors counteract this activity by prescribing oral contraceptives containing female estrogens. However, such pills work on only some patients, and undesirable side effects have made physicians more cautious ("Clean Skin," 1979).

Acne may be aggravated by tension and emotional upset that activate the skin glands. This is one reason why emotional upset may bring on acne or why a tense adolescent may be more susceptible to acne than a calm one. In all cases, the adolescent should receive concerned, prompt treatment.

EARLY AND LATE MATURATION

The effect of early or late physical maturation on both the psychological and social characteristics and adjustments of boys and girls has been the subject of

Adolescents are concerned about physical attractiveness, and they are often self-conscious about individual body characteristics. Many youths spend a part of their adolescence wearing braces to correct dental problems. (© Frank Siteman)

intensive investigation. The results of these studies are important in understanding adolescents who differ from the norm in either the timing or the rate of their development (Collins and Propert, 1983). (See figure 5-2.)

Early-maturing Boys

Early-maturing boys are large for their age, stronger, more muscular, and better coordinated than late-maturing boys, so they enjoy a considerable athletic advantage. They are better able to excel in football, basketball, swimming, track, tennis, soccer, and other competitive sports. They enjoy considerable social advantages in relation to their peers. (Blyth, Bulcroft, and Simmons, 1981.) Their superior build and athletic skills enhance their social prestige and position. They participate more frequently in extracurricular activities in high school (Pomerantz, 1979). They are often chosen for leadership roles; their peers tend to give them greater social recognition by appointing them to school offices, committee chairmanships, and mentioning them in the school newspaper. They tend to show more interest in girls and to be popular with them because of superior looks and more sophisticated social interests and skills. Early sexual maturation thrusts them into heterosexual relationships at an early age.

Adults, too, tend to favor early-maturing boys. Adults tend to rate them as more physically attractive, more masculine, better groomed, and more relaxed than late-maturing boys (Hamachek, 1976). Even more important, adults accept and treat them as more mature, able persons. The boys look older; the community therefore gives earlier recognition to their desires to assume adult roles and responsibilities (Peskin, 1972). As a result they are given privileges reserved for older people.

This attitude of adults has some disadvantages as well as advantages. Adults tend to expect more of them and expect adult behavior and responsibilities. Early-maturing boys have less time to enjoy the freedom that comes with childhood. One adolescent boy remarked:

> I was tall and well developed by the time I was 13 years of age. People always thought I was 5 or 6 years older than I really was. Consequently, they criticized me or made fun of me if I acted up or fooled around. "Don't be a kid, act your age," they used to tell me. My Dad expected me to help out around the place. I had to go to work when I was only 15—I lied about my age to get the job. I never seemed to have time to have fun like the rest of the kids my age (author's counseling notes).

Peskin (1972) has suggested other drawbacks to early maturation. The boy has a shorter time in which to adjust to the hormonal and physiological changes of adolescence. Thus, there may be greater initial anxiety at the time of pubertal onset. After the shock of initial adjustments, however, early-maturing boys manifest more favorable personality characteristics. They appear to be more poised, relaxed, good-natured, unaffected, and more likely to be admired by peers than are their later-maturing counterparts (Clausen, 1975).

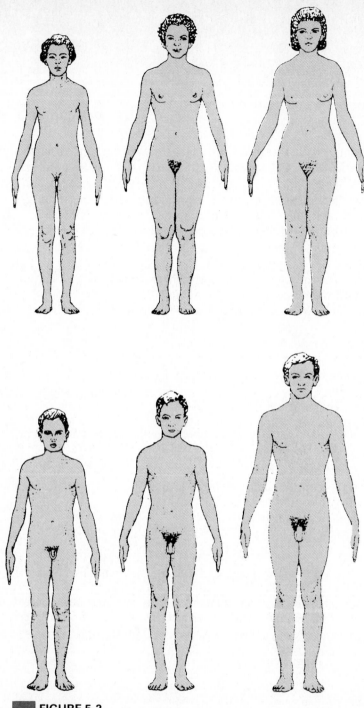

FIGURE 5-2

Variations in pubescent development. All three girls are 12¾ years and all three boys are 14¾ years of age but in different stages of puberty.

Adapted from Tanner, J. M. (September 1973). *Scientific American*, p. 38. Copyright © 1973 by *Scientific American*, Inc. All rights reserved.

Late-maturing Boys

Late-maturing boys suffer socially induced inferiority because of their delayed growth and development (Apter et al., 1981; Peskin, 1972). A boy who has not reached puberty at age fifteen may be eight inches shorter and thirty pounds lighter than his early-maturing male friends. Accompanying this size difference are marked differences in body build, strength, motor performance and coordination, and reaction time. Because physical size and motor coordination play such an important role in social acceptance, late maturers develop negative self-perceptions and self-concepts. They have been characterized as less attractive physically, less well groomed, less popular, more affected, more restless, bossy, and rebellious against parents and as having feelings of inadequacy, rejection, and dependency. They often become self-conscious. Some withdraw because of their social rejection (Dreyfus, 1976).

As evident in the case of Stephen, late maturers sometimes overcompensate by becoming overly dependent on others or overly eager for status and attention. At other times they try to make up for their inadequacies by belittling, attacking, or ridiculing others or by using attention-getting devices. A typical example is the

---

HIGHLIGHT   Late Maturation

In the following example, a fifteen-year-old boy, Stephen, adjusted to his late maturation by overconformity to rules on the one hand and by efforts to excel verbally and academically on the other hand. In relation to his parents he was dependent, undercontrolled, rebellious, and childish.

Stephen at fifteen was slight of build and had not as yet experienced any secondary sexual changes, such as body hair development, voice change, and the like. Always a good student, his application to his studies was far in excess of what was required and bordered on obsessional perfectionism. Indeed he had many features of the obsessive compulsive in his character structure, which had developed and continued from latency. He was punctilious, tidy, compliant, and fearful of authority. His strict regard for the rules to which he adhered with almost a legalistic fanaticism made him a questionable as-

set in games with his peers. As would be expected, he veered away from athletic pursuits and found success and pleasure in such activities as the debating team. All his aggressiveness and competitiveness focused on verbal, intellectual pursuits and he delighted in fault-finding and one-upping both peers and teachers. But at home, he let his guard down, as it were, and was given to temper outbursts, demanding, whining behavior, and fierce rivalry with his brother, four years younger. . . . Stephen was thus still a latency child at fifteen, with no apparent heterosexual interests; his sexuality was limited to the crude locker room vulgarity more characteristic of the eleven-year-old.

Shapiro, S. H. (1973). "Vicissitudes of Adolescence." In S. L. Cope (Ed.), *Behavior Pathology of Childhood and Adolescence* (New York: Basic Books), p. 95.

loud, daring show-off with a chip on his shoulder, ready to fight at the least provocation. The effects of these early negative social attitudes may persist into adulthood, long after physical differences and their social importance have disappeared (*Youth*, 1974). It has been found that late-maturing boys delay adult psychological commitments such as marriage and are less secure in their vocational status because they earn less (Peskin, 1972). In extreme cases of physical retardation caused by physiological factors, androgens are sometimes administered to hasten puberty, but social retardation may continue long afterward (Lewis et al., 1977).

Early-maturing Girls

Early maturation in girls tends to have a negative effect during their elementary school years. A girl who is already physically mature in fifth or sixth grade is at some disadvantage because she is out of phase with the majority of her classmates. She is taller, more developed sexually, and tends to feel awkward and self-conscious because she is different. For this reason she enjoys less prestige at this age than do her prepubertal friends.

By junior high school, however, the early-maturing girl comes into her own socially. She begins to look more like a grown-up woman, is envied by other girls for her adult looks and clothes, begins to attract the attention of older boys (which she likes), and starts dating earlier than normal. This creates some problems for her, however. Parents begin to worry because of her precocious heterosexual interests and may strive to curtail her social desires and activities. The girl may find herself emotionally unequipped to deal with sophisticated social activities and with sexual enticements. (Udry and Cliquet, 1982) This may create stress for her, so that this period of adjustment may be one of anxiety and upset. There is evidence also that the early-maturing girls do not do as well in school when they are in sixth and seventh grades (Blyth, Bulcroft, and Simmons, 1981). Perhaps this is because they focus much of their attention on social concerns. Overall, however, by the time early-maturing girls have reached seventeen years of age, they have more positive self-concepts, score higher on total adjustment and family adjustment, and enjoy better personal relations than do later maturers (Hamachek, 1976), although the net positive effect of early maturation does not seem to be as pronounced for girls as for boys.

Late-maturing Girls

Late-maturing girls are at a distinct social disadvantage in junior high school and high school (Apter et al., 1981). They look like "little girls" and resent being treated as such. They are largely bypassed and overlooked in invitations to boy-girl parties and social events. One study of adolescent girls in New York City showed that those who experienced menarche at ages fourteen to eighteen were especially late daters (Presser, 1978). As a consequence, late-maturing girls may be envious of their friends who are better developed. They are generally on a par with normal-maturing boys and so have much in common with them as friends. However, they avoid large, mixed groups of boys and girls, and their activities reflect the interests of those of younger age groups with whom they spend their time. One advantage is that late-maturing girls do not experience the sharp criticism of parents and other adults as do girls who develop early. The chief disadvantage seems to be the temporary loss of social status because of their relative physical immaturity.

SUMMARY

Adolescents are concerned about body image: physical attractiveness, body type, concepts of the ideal, body weight, and timing of their own development in relation to what is considered normal. Adolescents who are physically attractive are treated in more positive ways, develop more positive self-perceptions and personalities, and are more popular and better adjusted socially.

Three body types have been identified: ectomorph, mesomorph, and endomorph. Mesomorphs with medium builds are preferred in both boys and girls. Those who are tall and skinny (ectomorphs) or short and fat (endomorphs) are viewed more negatively.

Adolescents are concerned about individual body characteristics: general appearance, face and complexion, weight and body build, and teeth. Females are also concerned about the shape of their lags, breasts, and waist and about their eyes. Males worry about height, shoulders, profile, and neck. Males and females are equally concerned about hair texture, nose, and mouth and are less concerned about ankles, ears, hair color, and arms. Those who are deviant may become self-conscious.

Adolescents worry too about their weight. Obesity is not caused necessarily by overeating but by eating high-calorie foods and by underactivity. More calories are ingested than burned up. The most successful approach to treating obesity is a multifaceted one that considers it a multicausal problem. Underweight adolescents need to conserve energy and to increase their consumption of fattening foods.

Nutrition is extremely important to individual health. Adolescents may suffer a variety of deficiencies: calcium, iron, protein, vitamins A and C, and thiamine and riboflavin. There are a number of reasons for deficiencies: adolescents skip breakfast, snacks of junk food do not make up for meals missed, small quantities of food are eaten, inadequate knowledge of nutrition results in poor food selection, social pressures and troubled family relationships result in poor eating habits, or the family cannot afford to buy good food.

Adolescents worry too about body odor and acne caused by the increased secretion of skin glands during puberty. Prompt attention and treatment of acne may prevent it from becoming severe.

Young adolescents have a wide variety of health concerns. The top ten concerns according to one study are dental problems, getting along with friends, nutrition, sex, vitamins, getting along with adults, acne, sports injuries, sleep, and headaches. Girls were significantly more concerned with eleven more issues than boys: menstruation, pregnancy, birth control, being overweight, dieting, child abuse, stomach pain, nervousness, depression, acne, and headaches. Boys reported more concern for two areas: sports injuries and sex. Older adolescents would evidence greater concern about topics related to sexuality and childbirth.

The timing of physical maturation is important. Some adolescents mature earlier or later than average, with a differential effect. Early-maturing boys enjoy athletic, social, and community advantages. There may be greater anxiety because of sudden pubertal changes, at least for a while, and more pressure to act older than their age. In general, however, early maturation for boys is an advantage. Late-maturing boys suffer socially induced inferiority, which may carry over into adulthood.

Girls who mature in elementary school tend to feel awkward and self-conscious because they are different. By junior high school, however, they begin to be envied by their peers for their adult look. Early maturity results in precocious heterosexual interests, which may worry parents. Overall, however, by seventeen, these girls have more positive self-concepts, are better adjusted, and enjoy better personal relations than late maturers. Late-maturing girls are at a distinct social disadvantage. They look like "little girls" and resent being treated as such and are envious of their friends who have matured. These social advantages are temporary and may be overcome when maturation takes place.

DISCUSSION QUESTIONS

1. Do you agree that there is a great deal of emphasis on physical attractiveness during adolescence? Why? Why not?
2. What characteristics do you consider most important to physical attractiveness? Which body features are most important? What can the adolescent do who is not especially attractive?
3. Have you ever been overweight or underweight? What has helped you?
4. Do you eat breakfast? Lunch? Why or why not?
5. What do nutritionists consider to be a balanced diet?
6. What helps most in the prevention and/or treatment of acne?
7. Did you mature earlier or later than your classmates? How did you feel? How did it affect you? What happened? What did you do?

BIBLIOGRAPHY

Adams, G. R. (1980). "Social Psychology of Beauty: Effects of Age, Height, and Weight on Self-Reported Personality Traits and Social Behavior." *Journal of Social Psychology*, 112, 287–293.

Apter, A., Galatzer, A., Beth-Halachmi, N., and Laron, Z. (December, 1981). "Self-Image in Adolescents with Delayed Puberty and Growth Retardation." *Journal of Youth and Adolescence*, 10, 501–505.

Blyth, D. A., Bulcroft, R., and Simmons, R. G. (August, 1981). *The Impact of Puberty on Adolescents: A Longitudinal Study.* Paper presented at the annual meeting of the American Psychological Association, Los Angeles.

Bozzi, V. (1985). "Body Talk." *Psychology Today*, 19, 20.

Brandt, G., Maschhoff, T., and Chandler, N. S. (Winter, 1980). "A Residential Camp Experience as an Approach to Adolescent Weight Management." *Adolescence*, 15, 807–822.

Brenner, D., and Hinsdale, G. (Winter, 1978). "Body Build Stereotypes and Self-Identification in Three Age Groups of Females." *Adolescence*, 13, 551–561.

Brone, R. J., and Fisher, C. B. (1988). "Determinants of Adolescent Obesity: A Comparison With Anorexia Nervosa." *Adolescence*, 23, 155–169.

Brownell, K. D. (1982). "Obesity: Understanding and Treating A Serious, Prevalent, and Refractory Disorder." *Journal of Consulting and Clinical Psychology*, 50, 820–840.

Cash, T. F., and Janda, L. H. (December, 1984). "The Eye of the Beholder." *Psychology Today*, 18, 46–52.

Clark, Marguerite. (1966). "Health Problems of Adolescents." PTA Magazine, 60, 4–7, 33–34.

Clausen, J. A. (1975). "The Social Meaning of Differential Physical and Sexual Maturation." In Adolescence in the Life Cycle. Edited by S. E. Dragastin and G. H. Elder, Jr. New York: John Wiley and Sons.

"Clear Skin: Possible Help for Severe Acne." Time (February 26, 1979), p. 59.

Collins, J. D. (June, 1981). "Self-Recognition of the Body and Its Parts during Late Adolescence." Journal of Youth and Adolescence," 10, 243–254.

Collins, J. D., and LaGanza, S. (August, 1982). "Self-Recognition of the Face: A Study of Adolescent Narcissism." Journal of Youth and Adolescence, 11, 317–328.

Collins, J. D., and Propert, D. S. (Winter, 1983). "A Developmental Study of Body Recognition in Adolescent Girls." Adolescence, 18, 767–774.

Drewnowski, A. (1983). "Cognitive Structure in Obesity Dieting." In Obesity. Edited by M.R.C. Greenwood, pp. 87–101. New York: Churchill Livingstone.

Dreyfus, E. A. (1976). Adolescence: Theory and Experience. Columbus, Ohio: Charles E. Merrill Publishing Co.

Edelman, B. (1980). "Human Obesity: Determinants and Correlates of Overnutrition: An Annotated Bibliography." Catalog of Selected Documents in Psychology, 10, 9.

Eveleth, P. (September, 1978). "Difference between Populations in Body Shape of Children and Adolescents." American Journal of Physical Anthropology, 49, 373–381.

Feingold, A. (1982). "Do Taller Men Have Prettier Girlfriends?" Psychological Reports, 50, 810.

Feinman, S., and Gill, G. W. (June, 1978). "Sex Differences in Physical Attractiveness Preferences." Journal of Social Psychology, 105, 43–52.

Fleischer, B., and Read, M. (Winter, 1982). "Food Supplement Usage by Adolescent Males." Adolescence, 17, 831–845.

Gilbert, D. G., and Hagen, R. L. (1980). "Taste in Underweight, Overweight, and Normal-Weight Subjects Before, During, and After Sucrose Ingestion." Addictive Behaviors, 5, 137–142.

Grant, C. L., and Fodor, I. G. (1986). "Adolescent Attitudes Toward Body Image and Anorexic Behavior." Adolescence, 21, 269–281.

Hamachek, D. E. (1976). "Development and Dynamics of the Self." In Understanding Adolescence. 3d ed. Edited by J. F. Adams. Boston, Mass.: Allyn and Bacon.

Hertzler, A. A. (1981). "Obesity-Impact of the Family." Journal of the American Dietetic Association, 79, 525–530.

Holt, E. L. (1972). "Energy Requirements." In Pediatrics, 15th ed. Edited by H. L. Barnett and A. H. Einhorn. New York: Appleton-Century-Crofts.

Jacobs, S. B., and Wagner, M. K. (1984). "Obese and Nonobese Individuals: Behavioral and Personality Characteristics." Addictive Behaviors, 9, 223–226.

Jaquish, G. A., and Savins-Williams, R. C. (December, 1981). "Biological and Ecological Factors in the Expression of Adolescent Self-Esteem." Journal of Youth and Adolescence, 10, 473–485.

Katchadourian, H. (1977). The Biology of Adolescence. San Francisco: W. H. Freeman.

Keesey, R. E., and Pawley, T. L. (1986). "The Regulation of Body Weight." Annual Review of Psychology, 37, 109–133.

Krieshok, S. I., and Karpowitz, D. H. (1988). "A Review of Selected Literature on Obesity and Guidelines for Treatment." Journal of Counseling and Development, 66, 326–330.

Lerner, R. M., and Karabeneck, S. A. (1974). "Physical Attractiveness, Body Attitudes, and Self-Concept in Late Adolescents." Journal of Youth and Adolescence, 3, 307–316.

———. (Fall, 1976). "Physical Attractiveness, Physical Effectiveness, and Self-Concept in Late Adolescents." Adolescence, 11, 313–326.

Lewis, V. G., et al. (Spring, 1977). "Idiopathic Pubertal Delay beyond Age Fifteen: Psychologic Study of Twelve Boys." Adolescence, 12, 1–11.

Lindholm, B. W., Touliatos, J., and Wenberg, M. F. (Summer, 1984). "Predicting Changes in Nutrition Knowledge and Dietary Quality in Ten- to Thirteen-Year-Olds Following a Nutrition Education Program." Adolescence, 19, 367–375.

Lundholm, J. K., and Littrell, J. M. (1981). "Desire for Thinness among High School Cheerleaders: Relationship to Disordered Eating and Weight Control Behavior." Adolescence, 21, 573–579.

Marston, A. R., Jacobs, D. F., Singer, R. D., Widaman, K. F., and Little, T. D. (1988). "Characteristics of Adolescents at Risk for Compulsive Overeating on a Brief Screening Test." Adolescence, 89, 59–65.

Meer, J. (March, 1984). "Psychotherapy for Obesity." Psychology Today, 18, 10, 11.

Moore, D., and Schultz, N. R. (1983). "Loneliness at Adolescence: Correlates, Attributions, and Coping." *Journal of Youth and Adolescence*, 12, 95–100.

Ogundari, J. T. (Spring, 1985). "Somatic Deviations in Adolescence: Reactions and Adjustments." *Adolescence*, 20, 179–183.

Padin, M. A., Lerner, R. M., and Spiro, A., III (Summer, 1981). "Stability of Body Attitudes and Self-Esteem in Late Adolescents." *Adolescence*, 16, 371–384.

Peskin, H. (1972). "Pubertal Onset and Ego Functioning." In *The Adolescent: Physical Development, Sexuality and Pregnancy.* Edited by J. Kestenberg et al. New York: MSS Information Co.

Pomerantz, S. C. (March, 1979). "Sex Differences in Relative Importance of Self-Esteem, Physical Self-Satisfaction, and Identity in Predicting Adolescent Satisfaction." *Journal of Youth and Adolescence*, 8, 51–61.

Powers, P. S. (1980). *Obesity: The Regulation of Weight.* Baltimore: Williams and Wilkins.

Presser, H. B. (Summer, 1978). "Age at Menarche, Socio-Sexual Behavior, and Fertility." *Social Biology*, 25, 94–101.

Read, M. H., Harveywebster, M., and Usinger-Lesquereux, J. (1988). "Adolescent Compliance with Dietary Guidelines: Health and Education Implications." *Adolescence*, 23, 567–575.

Reis, H. T., Nezlek, J., and Wheeler, L. (1980). "Physical Attractiveness and Social Interaction." *Journal of Personality and Social Psychology*, 38, 604–617.

Rierdan, M., and Koff, E. (August, 1980). "Representation of the Female Body by Early and Late Adolescent Girls." *Journal of Youth and Adolescence*, 9, 339–346.

Rodin, J. (1982). Obesity: Why the Losing Battle? In *Psychological Aspects of Obesity: A Handbook.* Edited by B. B. Wolman, pp. 30–87. New York: Van Nostrand Reinhold.

Shapiro, S. H. (1973). "Vicissitudes of Adolescence." In *Behavior Pathology of Childhood and Adolescence.* Edited by S. L. Cope. New York: Basic Books.

Shea, J. A., and Adams, G. R. (1984). "Correlates of Romantic Attachment: A Path Analysis Study." *Journal of Youth and Adolescence,*, 13, 27–44.

Shestowsky, B. J. (Fall, 1983). "Ego Identity Development and Obesity in Adolescent Girls." *Adolescence*, 18, 551–559.

Sobal, J. (1984). "Group Dieting, the Stigma of Obesity, and Overweight Adolescents: Contributions of Natalie Allon to the Sociology of Obesity." *Marriage and Family Review*, 7, 9–20.

_____ . (1987). "Health Concerns of Young Adolescents." *Adolescence*, 87, 739–750.

Southam, M. A., Kirkley, B. G., Murchison, A., and Berkowitz, R. I. (Winter, 1984). "A Summer Day Camp Approach to Adolescent Weight Loss." *Adolescence*, 19, 855–868.

Steele, C. I. (1974). "Obese Adolescent Girls: Some Diagnostic and Treatment Considerations." *Adolescence*, 9, 81–96.

_____ . (Winter, 1980). "Weight Loss among Teenage Girls: An Adolescent Crisis." *Adolescence*, 15, 823–829.

Stein, R. F. (1987). "Comparison of Self-Concept of Nonobese and Obese University Junior Female Nursing Students." *Adolescence*, 22, 77–90.

Stewart, H. S. (Fall, 1982). "Body Type, Personality, Temperament, and Psychotherapeutic Treatment of Female Adolescents." *Adolescence*, 17, 621–626.

Storz, N. S. (Fall, 1982). "Body Image of Obese and Adolescent Girls in a High School and Clinical Setting." *Adolescence*, 17, 667–672.

Tanner, J. M. (1962). *Growth at Adolescence.* Springfield, Ill.: Charles C. Thomas.

_____ . (1970). "Physical Growth." In *Carmichael's Manual of Child Psychology.* Vol. 1. 3d ed. Edited by P. H. Mussen. New York: John Wiley and Sons.

Treaster, J. B. (November 15, 1971). "Yale versus Those Mushy Vegetables." *New York Times.*

Tucker, L. A. (1982). "Relationship Between Perceived Gonatotype of Body Cathexis of College Males." *Psychology Reports*, 50, 983–989.

_____ . (1983). "Muscular Strength and Mental Health." *Journal of Personality and Social Psychology*, 45, 1355–1360.

Udry, J. R., and Cliquet, R. L. (1982). "A Cross-Cultural Examination of the Relationship Between Ages at Menarche, Marriage, and First Birth." *Demography*, 19, 53–63.

United States Department of Agriculture and United States Department of Health and Human Services (1985). *Dietary Guidelines for Americans.* Home and Garden Bulletin, No. 232. Washington, D. C.: U. S. Government Printing Office.

U.S. Department of Commerce. Bureau of the Census. (1987). *Statistical Abstract of the United States,*

1987. Washington, D.C.: U.S. Government Printing Office.

Walker, D. K., Cross, A. W., Heyman, P. W., Ruck-Ross, H., Benson, P., and Tuthill, J.W.G. (1982). "Comparisons Between Inner City and Private School Adolescents' Perceptions of Health Problems." *Journal of Adolescent Health Care*, 3, 82–90.

Walter, J. P. (Fall, 1977). "Some Reflections on the Economics of Nutrition: Deprived Urban Black and Mexican American Youth." *American Economist*, 21, 30–34.

Young, H. B. (1971). "The Physiology of Adolescence." In *Modern Perspectives in Adolescent Psychiatry*. Edited by J. G. Howells. New York: Brunner/Mazel.

Youth: Transition to Adulthood. (1974). Report of the Panel on Youth of the President's Science Advisory Committee. Chicago: University of Chicago Press.

Zakus, G., et al. (1979). " A Group Behavior Modification Approach to Adolescent Obesity." *Adolescence*, 14, 481–490.

CHAPTER

6

Cognitive Growth and Change

COGNITIVE DEVELOPMENT

■ Cognition

cognition   **Cognition** is the act or process of knowing. The emphasis is not on the process by which information is acquired but on the mental activity or thinking involved in understanding. Figure 6-1 presents an image of cognition. In this view, S represents all stimuli or observable effects that the adolescent experiences. R represents the adolescent's responses to these events. C is the thinking and mental activity that occurs between stimuli and response. In this view, cognition is all the unobservable events in the mind—all the processes, activities, and units. The study of cognitive development, then, is the study of how these mental processes change with age.

■ Jean Piaget

Jean Paul Piaget (1896–1980) was a Swiss developmental psychologist who became interested in the growth of human cognitive capacities. He began his work in Alfred Binet's Paris laboratory where modern intelligence tests originated. Piaget disagreed with Binet's insistence that intelligence is fixed and innate and began to explore higher-level thought processes (Piaget and Inhelder, 1969). He became more interested in how children reached conclusions than in whether their answers were correct. Instead of asking questions and scoring them right or wrong, Piaget questioned children to find the logic behind their answers. Through painstaking observation of his own, as well as other, children, he began to construct his theory of cognitive development (see figure 6-1) (Piaget, 1950, 1967, 1971, 1972).

PIAGET'S STAGES OF DEVELOPMENT

■ The Four Stages

assimilation   Piaget theorized that children pass through a series of stages of thought from infancy to adolescence. Biological pressure to adapt to the environment (**assimilation** and **accommodation**) and to reorganize thinking moves the individual
accommodation   through the different stages of thought. Piaget divides cognitive development into four major periods. (Furth, 1970):

■ FIGURE 6-1

An image of cognition.   S = stimulus; R = response;
C = cognition or mental activity.

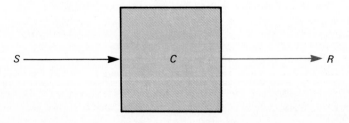

1. *The sensorimotor stage*—from birth to about two years.
2. *The preoperational stage*—from about two to seven years.
3. *The concrete operational stage*—from about seven to eleven or twelve years.
4. *The formal operational stage*—from eleven or twelve years on.

Berzonsky (1978) provides one of the best descriptions of Piaget's four stages:

> According to Piaget's theory, thought is internalized action. One initially acts overtly, i.e., one walks to the sink to get a drink of water. When one is thinking, however, the behavior is carried out covertly in one's mind, thought is thus internalized action. True directed thinking for Piaget is known as operations and involves internalized action that is reversible; i.e., one can mentally cancel out actions that have actually occurred. The type of operation that an individual is capable of using is the basis for naming the four stages. Sensorimotor operations are those carried out in action, not mentally. Preoperations deal with the internalization process; they are rigid rather than reversible. Concrete operations are internal actions which can be reversed but they involve actual behavior. Formal operations are not restricted to actual transformations of reality, they deal with abstractions which are independent of reality. (p. 279)

Sensorimotor Stage

During the **sensorimotor stage,** learning is related to the mastery of sensory-motor sequences (Furth, 1969). The infant moves from a self-centered, body-centered world to an object-centered world as the senses of vision, touch, taste, hearing, and smell bring him or her into contact with things with various properties and relationships to other objects. The child becomes intrigued with such simple

sensorimotor stage

During Piaget's sensorimotor stage, children under two years old become intrigued with simple motor activities such as picking up objects. (Teri Stratford)

motor activities as picking up objects, falling backward on a pillow, and blowing. Thinking, if any, occurs as a stimulus-response connection with the physical world without mediation, although the latter part of this period marks a transition to symbolic play, imitation, and representation of objects. Elkind (1967) labels the principal cognitive task during this period the *conquest of the object.*

Preoperational Stage

preoperational stage

The **preoperational stage** is the period when language is acquired so that children can deal with their world by manipulating symbols that represent the environment, as well as through motor activity and direct interactions with the environment. Symbolic play, or *internalized imitation*, emerges. When the imitations become internalized as what Piaget calls *images*, they become the first true *signifiers*, as opposed to the *significates*, or the objects or events being imitated. Perhaps the most important developments of this period are the increasing use of words as signifiers of things that are imitated and increasing differentiation of the signifiers from the significates (Phillips, 1969). Elkind (1967) labels the principal preoperational task the *conquest of the symbol.*

transductive reasoning

During this period there is evidence of **transductive reasoning** rather than **inductive** or **deductive reasoning.** Transductive reasoning occurs when the child proceeds from particular to particular, without generalization, rather than from the particular to the general (inductive) or from the general to the particular (deductive). For example, the dog Fido jumps on you because he has, and Brownie will jump on you because he is frisky like Fido, but Blackie will not jump on you because he is too big (when in fact he may). A error in judgment is made because the general concept that dogs jump on you is never developed.

inductive reasoning

deductive reasoning

syncretism

At this stage children sometimes make errors of **syncretism,** trying to link ideas that are not always related. Mother had a baby last time she went to the hospital, so next time she goes to the hospital, it is mistakenly expected she will bring home another baby. Children also make startling errors because their thinking is not *reversible* (it cannot go back to the beginning, to the point of origin). For example, if children are shown two plasticene balls of equal size and are asked: "Are they the same size, or does one have more plasticene in it than the other?" they reply: "They are the same." But if, while they are watching, one ball is rolled into a sausage shape, and they are asked the same question, they reply that one (usually the sausage) has more plasticene than the other (Phillips, 1969).

Preoperational thinking is also *egocentric*; that is, children have difficulty understanding why someone else cannot see something in the same way they do. They get upset, for example, when they cannot convince their mother not to wash their dirty rag doll. They gain security from it, and that is the important thing to them, whereas to their mother the important thing is that the doll is dirty. Children are also egocentric in their attitudes about other things (Ginsburg and Opper, 1969). Space and time are focused on them: when they walk, the moon follows them. Gradually, however, children learn to conceive of a time and spatial world existing independently of themselves and, through social interaction, to take into account the viewpoints of others. Social feedback is extremely important

a   b

FIGURE 6-2

Understanding the principle of conservation of volume.   (a) The child agrees that glasses A and B have the same amount of water. (b) The water from B is poured into the dish. The child is unable to understand that glass A and the dish still have the same amount of water, because the dish appears broader even though it is shallower. The child is unable to retain one aspect (the amount) when another aspect changes (the height of the water column and the width of the column).

in developing the capacity to think about their own thinking, without which logic is impossible.

Related to all the preceding characteristics is *centering*. It refers to children's tendency to focus attention on one detail and their inability to shift attention to other aspects of a situation (Muuss, 1988). For example, they may conclude there is more water in a shallow dish than in a glass because the dish is wider, even though they have already seen all the water poured from the glass into the dish (see figure 6-2). They ignore the greater height of the glass and the demonstration of pouring. As a result of their inability to maintain more than one relationship in their thinking at a time, children make errors of judgment, give inadequate or inconsistent explanations, show a lack of logical sequence in their arguments, and a lack of comprehension of constants (for example, if they have a brother, they need to realize their brother also has a brother). There is evidence of thinking but still an absence of operational thinking.

Concrete Operational Stage

During the **concrete operational stage,** children show a greater capacity for logical reasoning though still at a very concrete level. One of the reasons they can think more logically is that they are able to arrange objects into *hierarchical classifications* and comprehend *class inclusion relationships* (the inclusion of objects in different

concrete operational stage

Children exhibit a greater capacity for logical reasoning during Piaget's concrete operational stage, which occurs from about two to seven years of age.
(© The Christian Science Monitor/Neal Menschel)

levels of the hierarchy at the same time). This gives children the ability to understand the relations of the parts to the whole, the whole to the parts, and the parts to the parts. Suppose children are given a randomly organized array of blue and red squares and black and white circles. If they understand inclusion relationships, they discover there are two major collections (squares and circles) and two subtypes of each (blue versus red squares and black versus white circles). There is a hierarchy whose higher level is defined by shape and whose lower level is defined by color. This enables them to say that all squares are either blue or red, that there are more squares than blue squares, that there are more squares than red squares, that if you take away the red squares, the blue ones are left, and so on (Ginsburg and Opper, 1969).

Concrete operational children are capable also of *serialization*, serial ordering. In arranging animals, such as dogs and cats, into a hierarchy of classes, they may arrange dogs and cats into separate classes, and then dogs into further subdivisions such as bulldogs and setters or into subdivisions according to color or size. They learn that different objects may be grouped by size, by alphabetical order, or by age or that an object may simultaneously belong to more than one class. A child may be a boy, a fourth grader, an athlete, and a redhead, all at the same time. They learn that some relationships are *symmetrical* or *reciprocal*—two brothers are brothers to each other. In dealing with numbers, children learn that different combinations of numbers make the same total and that *substitutions* may be made with the same result. In dealing with liquids and solids, they learn that a change in shape does not necessarily change their volume or mass; the amount is conserved.

Piaget calls this stage the *concrete operations stage* of cognitive development because it involves concrete elements (objects, relations, or dimensions) and operations (such as addition or subtraction) and rules, or *properties*, that describe the way the operations may be performed. Elkind (1967) calls the major cognitive task of this period *mastering classes, relations*, and *quantities*.

Muuss (1988)* summarizes four concrete operations the child is able to perform:

1. *Combinativity.* Two or more classes can be combined into one larger, more comprehensive class. For example, all men and all women equals all adults. . . . A is larger than B and B is larger than C can be combined into a new statement that A is larger than C. . . .
2. *Reversibility.* Every operation has an opposite operation that reverses it. Supra-classes can be taken apart, so that the effect of combining subclasses is reversed. All adults except all women equal all men. . . .
3. *Associativity.* The child whose operations have become associative can reach a goal in various ways . . . but the results obtained . . . remain the same. For example, (3 plus 6) plus 4 equals 13, and 6 plus (3 plus 4) equals 13.
4. *Identity or nullifiability.* An operation that is combined with its opposite becomes nullified. Illustrations . . . are: give 3 and take away 3 results in null (p. 185).

Conservation refers to the recognition that properties of things such as weight or volume are not altered by changing their container or shape. Conservation tasks involve some manipulation of the shape of matter that does not alter the mass or volume of the matter (Piaget and Inhelder, 1969). A typical conservation problem is represented by the balls of clay in figure 6-3. In this example, the child is asked to confirm that A and B are the same size. Then B1 is changed to B2, then to B3, then to B4. The child is asked to compare A with B2, then with B3, and with B4, each time stating whether A and B are still the same. Children in the preoperational stage are guided by the shapes they see. Children in the concrete operational stage preserve a recognition of the equality between A and B that transforms their physical shape.

It is important to remember that the child's thinking is still linked to empirical reality (Piaget, 1967). Inhelder and Piaget (1958) write: "Concrete thought remains essentially attached to empirical reality. . . . Therefore, it attains no more than a concept of 'what is possible,' which is a simple (and not very great) extension of the empirical situation" (p. 250). Children have made some progress toward extending their thoughts from the actual toward the potential (Elkind, 1970), but the starting point must still be the real because concrete operational children can reason only about those things with which they have had direct, personal experience. When children have to start with any hypothetical or contrary-to-fact proposition, they have difficulty. Elkind (1967) also points out that one of the difficulties at this

* From Muuss, R. E. (1988). *Theories of Adolescence,* 5th ed. Copyright © McGraw Hill Publishing Company. Used by permission.

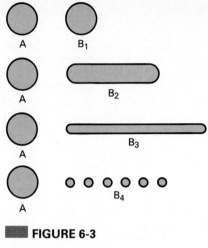

FIGURE 6-3

Conservation of mass.

stage is that the child can deal with only two classes, relations, or quantitative dimensions at the same time. When more variables are present, the child flounders. This ability to consider more than two variables at once is achieved only during the formal operations stage that follows.

One example illustrating combinatorial logic and the capacity to deal with problems in which many factors operate at the same time is the following. There are four differently colored poker chips: red (R), blue (B), yellow (Y), and green (G). The problem: arrange them in as many different color combinations as possible. The answer—there are sixteen color combinations, as follows: R;B;Y;G; RB;RY;RG;BY;BG;YG;RBY;RBG;BYG;RYG;RBYG; and none. Most adolescents can easily form all of these combinations; children cannot. It is in this sense that the combinatorial reasoning of the adolescent goes beyond the simpler syllogistic reasoning of the child (Elkind, 1970).

Formal Operational Stage

formal operational stage

The last stage of cognitive development, the ***formal operational stage,*** begins during early adolescence. Piaget subdivides the stage of formal operations further into substages III-A, almost full formal function (11 or 12 to 14 or 15 years), and III-B, full formal function (14 or 15 years and up). The division of the adolescent period at the age of 14 or 15 implies another restructuring and a disequilibrium, which then leads to a higher level of equilibrium and intellectual structure during late adolescence. The division III-A—the earlier substage, corresponding to early adolescence—appears to be a preparatory stage in which adolescents may make correct discoveries and handle certain formal operations, but the approach is still crude. They are not yet able to provide systematic and rigorous proof of their assertions. By the time adolescents reach substage III-B, they have become capable of formulating more elegant generalizations and of advancing more inclusive laws. Most of all, they are now able to provide spontaneously more systematic proof for their assertions, since they understand the importance of method of thought (Muuss, 1988).

The attainment of formal operations is not an all-or-nothing proposition. Between the age of 11 or 12 and 14 or 15, considerable modification, systemization, and formalization of thought processes can be observed. The complexity of the problems that the individual can handle increases substantially during these years, and reaches an equilibrium after substage III-B has been attained (Muuss, 1988).*

Some adolescents and adults never reach this formal operational stage because of limited intelligence or cultural deprivation. Elkind (1967) calls this final stage the *conquest of thought*. During this stage, the thinking of the adolescent begins to differ radically from that of the child (Barenboim, 1977; Piaget, 1972). The child has developed concrete operations and carried them out in classes, relations, or numbers, but their structure has never gone beyond the elementary level of logical "groupings" or additive and multiplicative numerical groups. He or she has never integrated them into a single, total system found in formal logic. Adolescents, however, are able to superimpose propositional logic on the logic of classes and relations. In other words, formal operations adolescents are able, through *inductive reasoning*, to systematize their ideas and deal critically with their own thinking to be able to construct theories about it. Furthermore, they can test these theories logically and scientifically, considering several variables, and are able to discover truth, scientifically, through *deductive reasoning* (Inhelder and Piaget, 1958). In this sense, adolescents are able to assume the role of scientists because they have the capacity to construct and test theories (Okun and Sasfy, 1977).

The difference between the way children approach problems and the logical, systematic approach of adolescents is given in the following example:

> E. A. Peel . . . asked children what they thought about the following event: "Only brave pilots are allowed to fly over high mountains. A fighter pilot flying over the Alps collided with an aerial cableway and cut a main cable, causing some cars to fall to the glacier below. Several people were killed." A child at the concrete-operational level answered: "I think the pilot was not very good at flying." A formal-operational child responded: "He was either not informed of the mountain railway on his route or he was flying too low. Also his flying compass may have been affected by something before or after take-off, thus setting him off course causing collision with the cable."
>
> The concrete-operational child assumes that if there was a collision the pilot was a bad pilot; the formal-operational child considers all the possibilities that might have caused the collision. The concrete-operational child adopts the hypothesis that seems most probable or likely to him. The formal-operational child constructs all possibilities and checks them out one by one. (Kohlberg and Gilligan, 1971, pp. 1061, 1062)

One of the experiments Piaget conducted, which led to discovering the strategies adolescents use in solving problems, involved a pendulum (Furth, 1970). The selected subjects were shown a pendulum suspended by a string (see figure 6-4). The problem was to discover what factors would affect the oscillatory speed

---

* From Muuss, R. E. (1988). *Theories of Adolescence*, 5th ed. Copyright © McGraw Hill Publishing Company. Used by permission.

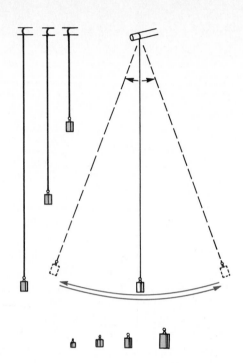

▩ FIGURE 6-4

The pendulum problem. The pendulum problem utilizes a simple apparatus consisting of a string, which can be shortened or lengthened, and a set of varying weights. The other variables that at first might be considered relevant are the height of the release point and the force of the push given by the subject.

From *The Growth of Logical Thinking from Childhood to Adolescence,* by Bärbel Inhelder and Jean Piaget, translated by Anne Parsons and Stanley Milgram. Copyright © 1958 by Basic Books, Inc. Reproduced by permission of Basic Books, Inc., Publishers.

of the pendulum. The subjects were to investigate four possible effects: changing the length of the pendulum, changing its weight, releasing the pendulum from various heights, or starting the pendulum with various degrees of force. The subjects were allowed to solve the problem in any way they chose.

The adolescents showed three basic characteristics in their problem-solving behavior. *First,* they planned their investigations systematically. They began to test all possible causes for variation in the pendulum swings: long or short string, light or heavy weight, high or low heights, and various degrees of force of push. *Second,* they recorded the outcomes accurately and with little bias under the different experimental conditions. *Third,* they were able to draw logical conclusions.

For example, they observed that height of drop and force had no effect upon oscillatory speed. Believing that pendulum weight or length of string might be involved, they tried different combinations of weight with different combinations of string length, only to find out that whatever the weight, the oscillation speed remained the same. They discovered, however, that changing the string length did alter the oscillation speed. They were able to conclude that pendulum length alone determined the speed of oscillation. Since this original experiment, the methods and result have been replicated by other researchers (Mecke and Mecke, 1971).

Younger subjects given the same problem may come up with the right answer by trial and error but fail to use systematic and scientific procedures or to be able to give a logical explanation of the solution. Children tend to form conclusions that seem warranted by the facts. But often these conclusions are premature and false because the child has not considered all of the important facts and is not able to reason logically about them. Even when presented with contrary evidence, the child tends to hold tenaciously to the initial hypothesis and to try to make the circumstances fit these preconceived notions.

> In summary, three interrelated characteristics of adolescent thought have emerged. These are: the ability to derive a proportion from two or more variables or a complex relationship; the ability to suggest mentally the possible effect of one or more variables upon another when a certain relationship is suspected among variables; and the capacity to combine and separate variables in a hypo-thetical-deductive framework ("if this is so, this will happen") so that a reasonable possibility is recognized before the test is made in reality. The fundamental prop-erty of adolescent thought is this reversible maneuvering between reality and possibility. (Gallagher and Noppe, 1976, p. 202)

One characteristic of adolescents' thinking that these ideas suggest is an ability to be *flexible*. They can be quite versatile in their thoughts and in dealing with problems. They can devise many interpretations of an observed outcome. Because they can even anticipate many possibilities prior to an actual event, they are not surprised by unusual outcomes. They are not stuck with their preconcep-tions. In contrast, younger children are confused by atypical results inconsistent with their simple perceptions of events.

It has already been suggested that the preoperational child begins to utilize symbols. But *the formal operational adolescent now begins to utilize a second symbol system: a set of symbols for symbol*. For example, metaphorical speech or algebraic symbols are symbols of other words or numerical symbols. The capacity to symbolize symbols makes the adolescent's thought much more flexible than the child's. Words can now carry double or triple meanings. Cartoons can represent a com-plete story that would otherwise have to be explained in words. It is no accident that algebra is not taught to elementary school children or that children have difficulty understanding political cartoons or religious symbols until approxi-mately junior high age (Elkind, 1970).

Another important difference between concrete operational children and for-mal operations adolescents is that the latter are able to orient themselves toward what is abstract and not immediately present. *They are able to escape the concrete present and think about the abstract and the possible*. This facility enables them to project themselves into the future, to distinguish present reality from possibility, and to think about what might be (Bart, 1983). Not only do adolescents have the capacity to accept and understand what is given, but they also have the ability to conceive of what might be possible, of what might occur (Ross, 1976). Because they can construct ideas, they have the ability to elaborate on what they receive, to gener-ate new or different ideas and thoughts. They become inventive, imaginative, and original in their thinking, and "possibility dominates reality." "The adolescent is the person who commits himself to possibilities . . . who begins to build 'systems' or 'theories' in the largest sense of the term" (Baker, 1982; Inhelder and Piaget,

During Piaget's formal operational stage, which begins during early adolescence and becomes firmly established in some people by age fifteen, the adolescent is able to use the scientific method to test theories. (Laima Druskis)

1958). This ability to project themselves into the future has many important consequences for their lives.

In summary, formal thinking, according to Piaget, involves four major aspects: *introspection* (thinking about thought), *abstract thinking* (going beyond the real to what is possible), *logical thinking* (being able to consider all important facts and ideas and to form correct conclusions, such as the ability to determine cause and effect), and *hypothetical reasoning* (formulating hypotheses and examining the evidence for them, considering numerous variables).

EFFECTS OF ADOLESCENT THOUGHT ON PERSONALITY AND BEHAVIOR

Idealistic Rebellion

Piaget begins his discussion of the relationship of adolescent thought to personality and behavior by stating that adolescence is that age at which the individual starts to assume adult roles (Inhelder and Piaget, 1958). Adolescents begin to discard their childhood inferiority and subordination to adults and to consider themselves as their equals and to judge them, with complete reciprocity, on the same plane as themselves. Because they want to be adults, they are motivated to take their places in the adult social framework, partly by participating in the ideas, ideals, and ideologies of adult society through the medium of a number of verbal symbols to which they were indifferent as children. As they become oriented to the adult world, their powers of reflective thinking enable them to evaluate what they learn (Schmidt and Davison, 1983). They become much more capable of moral reasoning (Steinberg et al., 1981). Furthermore, their ability to distinguish the possible from the real enables them to discern not only what the adult world is but what it might be like, especially under ideal circumstances. *This ability of adolescents to grasp what is and what might be makes them idealistic rebels* (White, 1980). They compare the possible with the actual, discover that the actual is less than ideal, and become critical observers of things as they are and usually ultra-critical of adults as well.

For a while, some adolescents develop the equivalent of a messianic complex. In all modesty, they attribute to themselves essential roles in the salvation of humanity. They may make a pact with God, promising to serve Him without return but planning to play a decisive role in the cause they espouse (Piaget, 1967). They see themselves in a major effort to reform the world, usually in verbal discussions, but, for some, in group movements. Some adolescents get caught up in political idealism and become preoccupied with the utopian reconstruction of society. By late adolescence, their attention shifts from egocentrism to a new-found soci-ocentrism (Enright, Shukla, and Lapsley, 1980).

At the same time that adolescents become political idealists, they also be-come champions of the underdog. Shapiro (1973) feels that it is adolescents' own inner turmoil that accounts for their empathic capacities for the suffering of others. By virtue of their own insecure psychological positions, they can easily identify with the weak, the poor, the oppressed, the victims of selfish society. Thus, social injustices that they perceive mirror their own internal, individual struggles. Elkind (1967) feels that young adolescents rebel primarily on a verbal level, doing little to work for humanitarian causes they espouse. Only later in adolescence do young people begin to tie their ideal to appropriate actions and to be more understanding, tolerant, and helpful.

Hypocrisy

Because of the discrepancy between what they say and what they do, adolescents are sometimes accused of hypocrisy. Elkind (1978) gives two examples to illustrate this tendency. First, his son complains at great length about his brother's going into his room and taking his things. He berates his father for not punishing the culprit; yet the same boy feels no compunction about going into his father's study, using his typewriter and calculator, and playing rock music on his father's stereo without asking. Second, a group of young people were involved in a "Walk for Water" drive, in which sponsors were paying them for each mile walked. The money was for testing the water of Lake Ontario and for pollution control. Elkind describes how pleased he was that these youths were not as valueless and materialistic as they were sometimes described to be. Yet the next day, a drive along the route the youths had walked revealed a roadside littered with fast food wrappers and soft drink and beer cans. City workers had been hired to clean up the mess. The question was: Did the cost of cleaning up amount to more money than was collected? And weren't these adolescents hypocritical? On the one hand, they objected to pollution, yet they were among the chief offenders in defacing their environment (Elkind, 1978).

The behavior of these adolescents was hypocritical to the extent that it re-vealed a discrepancy between idealism and behavior. But this assumes that they had the capacity to relate general theory to specific practice, which young adolescents are not necessarily able to do. Early adolescents have the capacity to formulate general principles such as "Thou shalt not pollute" but lack the experience to see the application of these general rules to specific practice. This is due to intellectual immaturity rather than a defect of character. Youths believe that if they can conceive and express high moral principles, they have attained them, and that nothing concrete need be done. This attitude confuses and upsets adults, who insist that ideals have to be worked for and cannot be attained instantly. This attitude is in turn considered cynical and hypocritical by youths (Elkind, 1978).

The ability of adolescents to think about themselves, their own thoughts, and society also leads to another manifestation of hypocrisy; pretending to be what they are not (Mitchell, 1980). They are expected to like school but rarely do. They are expected to be open and honest but are chastised when they are. They are expected to conform to parental viewpoints and beliefs even when they do not agree with them. They are expected not to be hurt or angry but really are. They are expected not to engage in behavior that will hurt or disappoint parents so they do not dare talk to them or talk to them about important things. They are expected to be other than what they are, to pretend to be what they are not. They are pressured not to be, not to feel, not to desire. They are expected to deny self and so behave hypocritically. And their newly achieved capacity to envision what should be enables them to go beyond their real selves and to pretend to be what others expect them to be.

Lack of Creativity

One would expect that adolescents who are capable of logical reasoning processes would also be creative. Torrance (1974) defines creativity as the

---

HIGHLIGHT   Cognitive Development and Sexual Behavior

More adolescents are becoming sexually active at an earlier age. One serious concern about this sexual activity is the possibility that many adolescents are functioning at a cognitive level that renders them unable to practice most forms of birth control effectively. The different forms of birth control demand: (1) acceptance of one's sexuality, (2) acknowledgment that one is sexually active, (3) anticipation in the present, and (4) the ability to view potential future sexual encounters realistically. While knowledge of human reproduction and birth control is an important part of adolescent education, sex educators might bear in mind that this knowledge probably will not be utilized by the adolescent who is functioning at the concrete operational stage of cognitive development. When parents, sex educators, physicians, and Planned Parenthood workers become aware that information alone may not be sufficient for some adolescents to effectively practice birth control, improved methods for controlling the epidemic of teenage pregnancies may be implemented (Pestrak and Martin, 1985).

"process of becoming sensitive to the problems, deficiencies, gaps in knowledge, missing elements, disharmonies, and so on: identifying the difficulty; searching for solutions, making guesses, or formulating hypotheses about the deficiencies; testing and retesting these hypotheses and possibly modifying and retesting them; and finally communicating the results" (p. 8). The adolescent becomes capable of doing these things.

But available investigations of the relationship of adolescent thinking processes to creative behavior suggest a negative relationship: adolescents become *less* creative, not *more* so (Wolf, 1981). The reason is *not* because they are less capable of being creative. They have a greater potential than before. But *in actuality they are less creative because of the pressures on them to conform—from both their peers and society in general.* The price they pay for acceptance is conformity. As a result, they squelch their individuality and begin to dress, act, and think like others in groups to which they desire to belong. One study emphasized that adolescents who rate highest in self-trust (who believe in themselves) are more willing to risk doing things that are imaginative and creative (Earl, 1987).

Pseudostupidity

Elkind (1978) points out that young adolescents also often demonstrate what he calls *pseudostupidity*, the tendency to approach problems at much too complex a level and fail, not because the tasks are difficult but because they are too simple. For example, adolescents go shopping to find a sock, shoe, or book but look in the least obvious places. Or they try to solve a problem by holding a number of variables in mind at the same time but lack the capacity to assign priorities and to decide which choice is more appropriate. In other words, the ability to perform formal operations gives them the capacity to consider alternatives, but this newfound capacity is not completely under control. Thus, adolescents appear stupid because they are in fact bright but not yet experienced.

Egocentrism

Another effect of adolescents' intellectual transformation is their development of a new form of egocentrism (Adams and Jones, 1982; Enright et al., 1979; Enright et al., 1980; Hudson and Gray, 1986; deRosenroll, 1987). As *adolescents develop the capacity to think about their own thoughts, they become acutely aware of themselves, their person, and ideas. As a result they become egocentric, self-conscious, and introspective.* They become so concerned about themselves that they may conclude that others are equally obsessed with their appearance and behavior. "It is this belief that others are preoccupied with his appearance and behavior that constitutes the egocentrism of the adolescent" (Elkind, 1967, p. 1029). As a result adolescents feel they are "on stage" much of the time, so that much of their energy is spent "reacting to an *imaginary audience.*" Elkind (1967) writes:

> And, since the audience is of his own construction and privy to his own knowledge of himself, it knows just what to look for in the way of cosmetic and behavioral sensitivities. The adolescent's wish for privacy and his reluctance to reveal himself may, to some extent, be a reaction to the feeling of being under the constant critical scrutiny of other people. (p. 1030)

The need to react to an imaginary audience helps account for the extreme self-consciousness of adolescents. Whether in the lunchroom or on the bus going home, youth feel that they are the center of attention. Sometimes groups of adolescents react to this audience by loud and provocative behavior because they believe everyone is watching them.

Elkind (1967) also discusses what he terms personal fable, adolescents' beliefs in the uniqueness of their own experiences. Because of their imaginary audiences and their beliefs that they are important to so many people, they come to regard themselves as special and unique. This may be why so many adolescents believe that unwanted pregnancies happen only to others, never to them.

Egocentrism and self-consciousness have other manifestations. On the one hand, adolescents believe everyone is looking; on the other hand, they feel totally alone, unique in a vast, uncaring universe. To be always on stage, scrutinized but rarely understood, imposes a terrific emotional strain. As a result, youths become critical and sarcastic in their relations with others, partly as a defense against their own feelings of inferiority and as a way of making themselves look good (Elkind, 1971). They employ numerous psychological mechanisms to protect their frail egos. Those with low self-esteem tend to present a false front to others and to mask their true feelings by fabricating an image (Elliot, 1982; Hauck and Loughead, 1985). The intellectualization and new-found ascetism of college students has been explained as just such a defense mechanism.

Whereas adolescents are often self-centered, they are frequently self-admiring too. Their boorishness, loudness, and faddish dress reflect what they feel others admire. The boy who stands in front of the mirror for two hours combing his hair is probably imagining the swooning reactions he will produce in his girl.

Egocentrism may also be linked to adolescents' desires for social reform and to their efforts to assume adult roles (White, 1980). They try not only to adapt their egos to the social environment but also to adjust the environment to their egos. They begin to think how they might transform society. Inhelder and Piaget (1958) write:

> The adolescent goes through a phase in which he attributes an unlimited power to his own thoughts so that the dream of a glorious future or of transforming the world through Ideas (even if this idealism takes a materialistic form) seems to be not only fantasy but also an effective action which in itself modifies the empirical world. This is obviously a form of cognitive egocentrism. (p. 345)

Self-Concept

The capacity to think about themselves is also necessary in the process of developing self-concept and identity (Okun and Sasfy, 1977). In doing this, adolescents have to formulate a number of postulates about themselves, such as "I am physically attractive" or "I'm smart in school" or "I'm popular." These postulates are based upon a number of specifics, such as "I'm attractive because I have pretty hair, a nice figure, or the boys notice me." Because of formal operational thinking, they are able to entertain a number of simultaneous ideas and to test each one by, for example, asking a friend: "What do you think of my hair?" or "Do you think I have ugly hair?" Gradually they begin to sort out what they feel is truth from error about themselves and to formulate total concepts of self.

HIGHLIGHT   Self-Consciousness under Pressure

In a cleverly designed experiment, the performances of children, adolescents, and adults in operating video games were measured when they did not know they were being observed and when an experimenter stood watching over their shoulder during the performance. While watching, the experimenter pointedly exhorted subjects to try to obtain the highest score they possibly could, reminding them they would have only one chance.

Children under 12 years generally improved under audience pressure; adolescents from 14 to 19 years showed substantial drops in performance; and adults aged 20 or older showed moderate drops in performance. This experiment suggests that self-consciousness is low in children, highest in adolescence, and intermediate or variable thereafter. (Tice, Buder, and Baumeister, 1985).

Decentering and a Life Plan

The process of adoption of adult roles, which is directly related to cognitive development, does not stop with egocentrism. The adolescent conceives of fantastic projects that are like a sophisticated game of compensatory functions whose goals are self-assertion, imitation of adult models, and participation in circles that are actually closed. Adolescents follow paths that satisfy them for a time but are soon abandoned as adolescents develop more cognitive objectivity and perspective. In other words, they begin to cure themselves of their idealistic crises and to return to the reality that is the beginning of adulthood. Piaget and Inhelder (1958) go on to emphasize that *"the focal point of the decentering process is the entrance into the occupational world or the beginning of serious professional training. The adolescent becomes an adult when he undertakes a real job. It is then that he is transformed from an idealistic reformer into an achiever"* (p. 346).

Piaget also refers to the importance of adolescent work in the community as a facilitator of human growth. He states that work helps the adolescent meet the storm and stress of that period. Work experience also stimulates the development of social understanding and socially competent behavior (Steinberg et al., 1981). True integration into society comes when the adolescent reformer attempts to put his ideas to work (Miller, 1978). In this process, the ego is gradually decentered as the personality develops and begins to affirm a life plan and adopt a social role.

CRITIQUE OF PIAGET'S FORMAL OPERATIONAL STAGE

Age and Percentages

Since Piaget formulated his concept of a formal operational stage of cognitive development, investigators have been examining various components of the formulation. One question concerns the age at which formal operational thought replaces the concrete operational stage. Piaget (1972) himself advanced the possibility that in some circumstances, the appearance of formal operations may be delayed to fifteen to twenty years of age and "that perhaps in extremely disadvantageous conditions, such a type of thought will never really take shape" (p. 7). Piaget (1971) acknowledged that social environment can accelerate or delay the onset of formal operations. It has been found that in fact fewer economically deprived adolescents achieve formal thought than do their more privileged counterparts and that there is a complete absence of formal operations among the mentally retarded (Gaylord-Ross, 1975). Ross (1974) has suggested that the absolute percentage of adolescents demonstrating formal operational thinking has usually been below 50 percent, and that when a larger proportion (around 60 percent) have shown formal thinking, they have been drawn from "gifted" samples or from older, more academic, college students.

It is important for adults, especially parents and teachers, to realize that *not all same-aged adolescents are at the same stage of development.* Many have not yet achieved formal operations. These youths cannot yet understand reasoning that is above their level of comprehension; to ask them to make decisions among numerous alternatives or variables that cannot be grasped simultaneously is to ask them to do the impossible. A very few youths may make the transition to formal operations by age ten or eleven, but only about 40 percent have progressed beyond concrete operations by high school graduation (Bauman, 1978).

Test Criteria

The measured percentages of people reaching formal operational thinking depend partially upon which criteria of formal thinking are used and the level of the tests employed. Piaget distinguishes between an easy level (III-A) and a more advanced level (III-B). One researcher (Tomlinson-Keasey, 1972), using Piaget's III-A level to measure the percentage of females achieving formal operational thinking, demonstrated that 32 percent of eleven-year-old girls, 67 percent of college women, and 54 percent of adult females had reached that level. But when the more advanced III-B criteria were used in measurements, the percentages were 4 percent for girls, 23 percent for college students, and 17 percent for adults (Tomlinson-Keasey, 1972, p. 364). In reviewing the research, Arlin (1975) and Kuhn (1979) observe that only approximately 50 percent of the adult population actually attain the full stage of formal thinking (III-B). Kuhn (1979) suggests that the formal operations stage, quite in contrast to the preceding childhood stages of Piaget's theory, may never be attained by a significant proportion of the general adolescent population. Piaget (1980) readily admits that the subjects of his study were "from the better schools in Geneva" and that his conclusions were based on a "privileged population." In spite of evidence critical of his assumptions, he maintains that "all normal individuals are capable of reaching the level of formal operation" (Piaget, 1980, p. 75) as long as the environment provides the necessary cognitive stimulation. Although not all adolescents or adults reach the formal level, there is still a significant increase in the use of formal operational thinking during adolescence, especially between ages eleven and fifteen (Ross, 1974).

Beyond Formal Operations

Investigations of the Piagetian stage of formal operations suggest that progressive changes in thought structures may extend beyond the level of formal operations. The implication is that cognitive growth is continuous; there is no end point beyond which new structures may appear. Researchers continue to seek these new structures (Arlin, 1975; Arlin, 1977; Commons, Richards, and Kuhn, 1982).

Although the results of investigations are still tentative, there is some evidence that a fifth stage of development can be differentiated. It has been labeled a **problem-finding stage** (Arlin, 1975). This new stage characterizes creative thought, the envisioning of new questions, and the discovery of new heuristics in thought. *The new stage represents an ability to discover problems not yet delineated, to formulate these problems, or to raise general questions from ill-defined problems.*

problem-finding stage

Not all subjects in the problem-solving stage should be characterized as having reached the problem-finding stage. Arlin (1975) in her research with college seniors found that all subjects high in problem finding had reached formal operational thinking, but not all subjects who had reached formal thinking were high in problem finding. This fact demonstrates that *sequencing was evident: formal operations had to be accomplished before persons could move on to the next stage.*

Maturation and Intelligence

maturation

To what extent does the **maturation** of the nervous system play a role in cognitive development? It is certain that maturation plays a part: the nervous system must be sufficiently developed for any real thought to take place. This is one reason why a greater percentage of older adolescents evidence formal thought than do younger adolescents (Ross, 1976).

In order to determine the relationship among maturation, intelligence, and cognition, Webb (1974) tested very bright (IQs of 160 and above) six- to eleven-year-old children to ascertain their levels of thinking. All subjects performed the concrete operational tasks easily, indicating that they were skilled in thinking at their developmental stage, but only four males, aged ten and older, solved the formal thought problems, indicating that regardless of high intelligence, a degree of maturation interacting with experience was necessary for movement into the next stage of cognitive development.

Other research helps clarify further the relationship among development, intelligence, and cognition. Other things being equal, individuals of high IQ are more likely to develop formal thought sooner than those of low IQ, but it is the interaction of age and intelligence that contributes to cognitive ability (Cloutier and Goldschmid, 1976). Thus, the research emphasizes that *cognitive development is influenced both by the maturation of the nervous system (age) and by the level of intelligence.* Not all adolescents reach formal operations, but if they do reach it, not all do so at the same age, and not all reach it to the same level for all tasks.

Culture and Environment

Cross-cultural studies in which task results are compared across different cultures and environments have shown that formal thought is more dependent upon social experience than is sensorimotor or concrete operational thought (Carlson, 1973). The attainment of the first three Piagetian stages appears to be more or less universal, but full attainment of formal thinking, even in college students and adults, is far from guaranteed. Adolescents from various cultural backgrounds show considerable variability in abstract reasoning abilities. Some cultures offer more opportunities to adolescents to develop abstract thinking than others do by providing a rich verbal environment and experiences that facilitate growth by exposure to problem-solving situations. Cultures that provide stimulating environments facilitate the acquisition of cognitive skills necessary to deal with the abstract world. Piaget has cited research to indicate, for example, that children on Martinique are slower than children in Montreal to develop cognitively (Miller, 1978).

Social institutions such as the family and school accelerate or retard the development of formal operations. Parents who encourage exchanges of thoughts, ideational explorations, academic excellence, and the attainment of ambitious educational and occupational goals are fostering cognitive growth. Schools that encourage students to acquire abstract reasoning and develop problem-solving skills enhance cognitive development.

Underdeveloped societies do not encourage advanced levels of cognitive development. One reason may be that in simple cultures, there is not as great a need for formal thought (Dasen, 1972; Dulit, 1972). The degree of urbanization (Youniss and Dean, 1974), literacy, and the amount of education (Carlson, 1973) also relate to formal thought development. Because formal thought relies heavily upon verbal factors, a lack of linguistic skills will result in poorer performance in solving formal thought problems (Gallagher and Noppe, 1976). However, a lack of linguistic skills does not imply an inability to solve problems as much as it implies a lack of ability to perform well on a particular cognitive test. Similarly, understanding language does not guarantee high-level thinking, even though formal thought is enhanced by verbal interchange (Furth, 1970).

HIGHLIGHT   Gender Differences in Formal Operations

Piaget was concerned with fundamental questions of sequence and orderliness of cognitive changes and not with the variables that have always been of concern to the educational and developmental psychologist: individual differences, sex, socioeconomic level, IQ, reading level, and so forth. Piaget's theory has stimulated considerable research into sex differences on ability to solve Piagetian problems, especially on spatial processing tasks (Jamison and Signorella, 1980; Liben, 1978;

Liben and Goldbeck, 1980; and Ray, Georgiou, and Ravizza, 1979). From childhood into early adulthood, males perform consistently better than females on Piagetian-type horizontal and vertical spatial tasks (judging the position of liquid in a tilted container and judging the position of plumb lines in an oblique context). Liben and Goldbeck (1980) conclude that sex differences persist (Plake, Kaplan, and Steinbrunn, 1986).

Aptitude

It has been found, also, *that different people have different aptitudes for solving different types of problems.* For example, boys do significantly better than girls in solving conservation of volume tasks (Elkind, 1975; Hobbs, 1973; Tomlinson-Keasey, 1972). This must be interpreted as a matter of differential socialization and application of mental abilities, not as evidence of a difference in ability to do formal thinking. Girls, on the other hand, score much higher on tests of creative thinking (Milgram, 1978; Ross, 1976). Formal thinking, then, is not applied with equal facility to all types of tasks. A particular student may be able to apply formal reasoning to a science task, another to a problem with semantic content, or to one involving the processing of personal information (Berzonsky, 1978). Students who have studied the sciences may do exceptionally well on some of the Piagetian formal thought tasks. (The pendulum experiment is commonly employed in physics classes.) Gallagher and Noppe (1976) write:

> According to Piaget, a lawyer may be formally operational with respect to law, whereas carpenters, mechanics, or locksmiths can reason deductively about aspects of their particular trades. With this hypothesis in mind, it is possible that the persons most able to exhibit logical-mathematical reasoning while completing traditional tasks designed by Inhelder and Piaget are individuals associated with the sciences. Unfortunately, at present, there are few tasks devised to tap formal thought in specific content area. (p. 209)

Piaget does admit to differentiation in cognitive aptitude with increasing age, depending on interest, motivation, and environmental stimulation, so that some adolescents may show their operational skills in logic, mathematics, or physics, while others may show it in literature, linguistics, or artistic endeavor, and still others in practical skills such as are performed by the carpenter, the locksmith, or the mechanic. However, in spite of this concern, it is important to keep in mind that Piaget's theory has been studied, tested, and developed in the adolescent age range primarily with content material that came from science and mathematics. *Piaget has shown little concern with the question of how formal operations might manifest themselves in artistic and literary endeavors* (Muuss, 1988). Gallagher (1978) has expanded the investigation of formal thought research to include analogy and metaphor. Gardner even suggests that formal operations might actually interfere with artistic development:

> Formal operations may even at times serve to hinder artistic development, since the tendency to focus on underlying content, to abstract meaning, to be sensitive to the explicit demands of a task, to proceed in a systematic exhaustive manner, and, above all, to translate problems and questions into logical-propositional terms may all militate against the sensitivity to detail and nuance and the faithfulness to the particular properties of object and medium that are so vital for the artist (Gardner, 1973, p. 308).

Assuming that formal operations are manifested within the context of a particular aptitude, to get accurate measurement it will be necessary first to isolate the superior aptitude of each individual and then to present a formal task congruent with that aptitude. So far, no such individualized approach has been accomplished (Ross, 1974).

Motivation and Response

Caution should be exercised in using the results of formal operations tests in predicting the scholastic behavior of adolescents. Test models describe what adolescents are capable of doing intellectually but not necessarily what they will do in a specific situation. Fatigue, boredom, or other factors affecting motivation may prevent adolescents from displaying full cognitive performance in any given situation. Also, Piaget's models are qualitative, not quantitative, measurements. They are used to describe thought problems and do not necessarily duplicate or predict in depth the performance of adolescents.

Role of School and Education

The development of abstract thinking and formal operations problem solving is encouraged in a number of ways (Danner and Day, 1977). Experimental or problematic situations can be presented that allow students opportunities to observe, analyze possibilities, and draw inferences about perceived relationships. Teachers who use authoritative approaches rather than social interchange stifle real thinking. Discussion groups, debates, question periods, problem-solving sessions, and science experiments are approaches that encourage the development of formal thinking and problem-solving abilities. Teachers need to be prepared to handle group discussions and stimulate interchange and feedback. Teachers must also be willing to give explicit help and encouragement and allow the necessary time for reasoning capacities to develop. Some students develop such abilities at a relatively slow pace (Arons, 1978). Piaget (1972) sets forth two goals of education that incorporate this philosophy:

> The principal goal of education is to create men who are capable of doing new things, not simply of repeating what other generations have done—men who are creative, inventive, and discoverers. The second goal of education is to form minds which can be critical, can verify, and not accept everything they are offered. . . . We need pupils who are active, who learn early to find out by themselves, partly by their own spontaneous activity and partly through material we set up for them; who learn early to tell what is verifiable and what is simply the first idea to come to them. (p. 5)

According to Elkind (1970), several general principles of education are implicit in Piaget's image of the child. The child's mind is not an empty slate. On the contrary, the child has a host of ideas about the natural and physical world, but they differ from those of adults and are expressed in a different linguistic mode. The first prerequisite for educating children is to develop effective modes of communication with them.

The second concept of education important for children is the need to aid them in the modification of their existing knowledge, in addition to helping them learn new material. Chil-

The development of abstract thinking and formal operations problem solving is encouraged in school by discussion groups, debates, question periods, problem-solving sessions, and science experiments. (© The Christian Science Monitor/ R. Norman Matheny)

dren are always unlearning, relearning, and acquiring new knowledge. They come to school with their own ideas of space, time, causality, quantity, and number. The purpose of education is to broaden incomplete knowledge.

Third, children are by nature knowing creatures, and the desire to know is part of their makeup. *Education need not concern itself with instilling a zest for knowledge; rather, it needs to ensure that it does not dull their eagerness by overly rigid curricula that disrupt the child's own rhythm and pace of learning.* The best teacher is dedicated to the growth of both pupils and self, is curious to learn, is willing to try new things, to evaluate and be critical, and tries to instill similar values in the pupils.

SUMMARY

Cognition is the act or process of knowing, with the emphasis on the mental activity involved in understanding.

Jean Piaget became interested in exploring thought processes and discovering how children reach conclusions. He theorized that children pass through four stages of thought from infancy to adolescence: the sensorimotor stage, the preoperational stage, the concrete operational stage, and the formal operational stage. When adolescents reach the formal operational stage, they become capable of introspection (thinking about thought); abstract thinking (going beyond the real to what is possible); logical thinking (being able to consider all important facts and ideas and to form correct conclusions); and hypothetical reasoning (formulating hypotheses and examining the evidence for them, considering numerous variables).

The ability to do formal operational thinking has several effects on adolescent personality and behavior. Adolescents become egocentric and introspective and acutely aware of themselves as they begin to discard childhood subordination and inferiority. The more they think about themselves, the more they formulate an adult identity and self-concept. By late adolescence, their attention shifts from egocentrism to sociocentrism, and they become idealistic rebels because of their ability to distinguish the possible from the real. They are sometimes accused of hypocrisy, however, because their behavior does not always match their idealism. They have the capacity to become creative but become less so because of a need to conform. If they approach problems at too complex a level, they may be accused of pseudostupidity. As they become more mature, they give up some of their egocentrism and youthful idealism and attempt to put their ideas to work as they formulate a life plan. Some investigators suggest a fifth, problem-finding stage.

Several comments must be made about Piaget's formal operational stage. Not all adolescents are at the same stage of development. Some never reach formal operational thinking. The percentage who do depends upon the test criteria established. Maturation and intelligence both play a prominent part in development. Culture, environment, and education also influence the development of formal thinking. Such personal factors as gender, aptitude, and motivation influence Piagetian-type test results. The school can play an important role by encouraging questions, discussion, and the free exchange of ideas, by emphasizing logical thinking, and by using experimental and problem-solving approaches to teaching. The best teacher is dedicated to the growth of both pupils and self, is curious to learn, is willing to try new things, to evaluate and be critical, and tries to instill similar values in the pupils.

DISCUSSION QUESTIONS

1. Describe the characteristics of formal operational thinking.
2. What evidence do you have that adolescents are egocentric? According to Piaget, why are they that way?
3. Do adolescents think logically? Why or why not?
4. How does the idealism of adolescents compare with that of adults?
5. What does it mean to move from egocentrism to sociocentrism?
6. According to Piaget, does maturation or environment have more influence on the development of formal operational thinking?

7. What evidence is there that adolescents are hypocritical?
8. Are modern schools stimulating formal operational thinking? In what ways are they? In what ways are they not?
9. Comment on the statement: "Many adolescents are functioning at a cognitive level that renders them unable to practice most forms of birth control effectively."
10. What factors prevent adolescents from being more creative?
11. Are there significant gender differences in formal operational abilities? Explain.

BIBLIOGRAPHY

Adams, G. R., and Jones, R. M. (February, 1982). "Adolescent Egocentrism: Exploration into Possible Contributions of Parent-Child Relations." *Journal of Youth and Adolescence*, 11, 25–31.

Arlin, P. K. (1975). "Cognitive Development in Adulthood: A Fifth Stage?" *Developmental Psychology*, 11, 602–606.

————. (1977). "Piagetian Operations in Problem Finding." *Developmental Psychology*, 13, 297–298.

Arons, A. B. (Fall, 1978). "Reasoning Modes and Processes Arising in Secondary and College Level Study of Natural Science, Humanities, and the Social Sciences." *Andover Review*, 5, 3–8.

Baker, C. D. (June, 1982). "The Adolescent as Theorist: An Interpretative View." *Journal of Youth and Adolescence*, 11, 167–181.

Barenboim, C. (December, 1977). "Developmental Changes in the Interpersonal Cognitive System from Middle Childhood to Adolescence." *Child Development*, 48, 1467–1474.

Bart, W. M. (Winter, 1983). "Adolescent Thinking and the Quality of Life." *Adolescence*, 18, 875–888.

Bauman, R. P. (Spring, 1978). "Teaching for Cognitive Development." *Andover Review*, 83–98.

Berzonsky, M. D. (Summer, 1978). "Formal Reasoning in Adolescence: An Alternative View." *Adolescence*, 13, 279–290.

Carlson, J. S. (1973). "Crosscultural Piagetian Studies: What Can They Tell Us?" Paper presented at the biennial meeting of the International Society for the Study of Behavioral Development. Ann Arbor, Mich.

Cloutier, R., and Goldschmid, M. L. (December, 1976). "Individual Differences in the Development of Formal Reasoning." *Child Development*, 47, 1097–1102.

Commons, M. L., Richards, F. A., and Kuhn, D. (1982). "Systematic and Metasystematic Reasoning: A Case for Levels of Reasoning Beyond Piaget's Stage of Formal Operations." *Child Development*, 53, 1058–1069.

Danner, F. W., and Day, M. C. (December, 1977). "Eliciting Formal Operations." *Child Development*, 48, 1600–1606.

Dasen, P. (1972). "Cross-Cultural Piagetian Research: A Summary." *Journal of Cross-Cultural Psychology*, 3, 23–39.

deRosenroll, D. A. (1987). "Creativity and Self-Trust: A Field of Study." *Adolescence*, 22, 419–432.

Dulit, E. (1972). "Adolescent Thinking à la Piaget: The Formal Stage." *Journal of Youth and Adolescence*, 1, 281–301.

Earl, W. L. (1987). "Creativity and Self-Thrust: A Field of Study." *Adolescence*, 22, 419–432.

Elkind, D. (1967). "Egocentrism in Adolescence." *Child Development*, 38, 1025–1034.

————. (1970). *Children and Adolescents: Interpretive Essays on Jean Piaget*. New York: Oxford University Press.

————. (1975). "Recent Research on Cognitive Development in Adolescence." In *Adolescence in the Life Cycle*. Edited by S. E. Dragastin and G. H. Elder, Jr. New York: John Wiley and Sons.

————. (Spring, 1978). "Understanding the Young Adolescent." *Adolescence*, 13, 127–134.

Elliot, G. C. (1982). "Self-Esteem and Self-Presentation among the Young as a Function of Age and Gender." *Journal of Youth and Adolescence*, 11, 135–153.

Enright, R. D.; Lapsley, D. K.; and Shukla, D. G. (Winter, 1979). "Adolescent Egocentrism in Early and Late Adolescence." *Adolescence*, 14, 687–695.

Enright, R. D., Shukla, D. G., and Lapsley, D. K. (April, 1980). "Adolescent Egocentrism—Sociocentrism and Self-Consciousness." *Journal of Youth and Adolescence*, 9, 101–116.

Furth, H. G. (1969). *Piaget and Knowledge*. Englewood Cliffs, N.J.: Prentice-Hall.

————. (1970). "On Language and Knowing in Piaget's Developmental Theory." *Human Development*, 13, 241–257.

————. (1970). *Piaget for Teachers*. Englewood Cliffs, N.J.: Prentice-Hall.

Gallagher, J. M. (1978). "The Future of Formal Thought Research: The Study of Analogy and Metaphor." In *Topics in Cognitive Development: Language and Operational Thought*. Vol. 2. Edited by B. Z. Presseisen, D. Goldstein, and M. Appel. New York: Plenum Press.

Gallagher, J. M., and Noppe, I. C. (1976). "Cognitive Development and Learning." In *Understanding Adolescence*. 3d ed. Edited by J. F. Adams. Boston, Mass.: Allyn and Bacon.

Gardner, H. (1973). *The Arts and Human Development*. New York: John Wiley and Sons.

Gaylord-Ross, R. J. (1975). "Paired-Associate Learning and Formal Thinking in Adolescence." *Journal of Youth and Adolescence*, 4, 375–382.

Germain, R. B. (1985). "Beyond the Internal-External Continuum: The Development of Formal Operational Reasoning about Control of Reenforcements." *Adolescence*, 20, 939–947.

Ginsburg, H., and Opper, S. (1969). *Piaget's Theory of Intellectual Development: An Introduction*. Englewood Cliffs, N.J.: Prentice-Hall.

Hauck, W. E., and Loughead, M. (1985). "Adolescent Self-Monitoring." *Adolescence*, 20, 567–574.

Hobbs, E. D. (1973). "Adolescents' Concepts of Physical Quantity." *Developmental Psychology*, 9, 431.

Hudson, L. M., and Gray, W. M. (1986). "Formal Operations, the Imaginary Audience and the Personal Fable." *Adolescence*, 84, 751–765.

Inhelder, B., and Piaget, J. (1958). *The Growth of Logical Thinking from Childhood to Adolescence*. New York: Basic Books.

Jamison, W., and Signorella, M. L. (1980). "Sex-Typing and Spatial Ability: The Association between Masculinity and Success on Piaget's Water-Level Task." *Sex Roles*, 6, 345–353.

Kohlberg, L., and Gilligan, C. (Fall, 1971). "The Adolescent as a Philosopher: The Discovery of the Self in a Postconventional World." *Daedalus*, 1051–1086.

Kuhn, D. (1979). "The Significance of Piaget's Formal Operations Stage in Education." *Journal of Education*, 161, 34–50.

Leadbeater, B. J., and Dionne, J. (Spring, 1981). "The Adolescent's Use of Formal Operational Thinking in Solving Problems Related to Identity Resolution." *Adolescence*, 16, 111–121.

Liben, L. S. (1978). "Performance on Piagetian Spatial Tasks as a Function of Sex, Field Dependence, and Training." *Merrill-Palmer Quarterly*, 24, 97–110.

Liben, L. S., and Goldbeck, S. L. (1980). "Sex Differences in Performance on Piagetian Spatial Tasks: Differences in Competence or Performance?" *Child Development*, 51, 594–597.

Mecke, G., and Mecke, V. (1971). "The Development of Formal Thought as Shown by Explanation of the Oscillations of a Pendulum: A Replication Study." *Adolescence*, 6, 219–228.

Milgram, R. M. (June, 1978). "Quantity and Quality of Creative Thinking in Children and Adolescents." *Child Development*, 49, 385–388.

Miller, J. P. (Summer, 1978). "Piaget, Kohlberg, and Erikson: Developmental Implications for Secondary Education." *Adolescence*, 13, 237–250.

Mitchell, J. (Fall, 1980). "Adolescent Hypocrisy." *Adolescence*, 15, 731–736.

Muuss, R. E. (1988). *Theories of Adolescence*. 5th ed. New York: McGraw Hill.

Okun, M. A., and Sasfy, J. H. (Fall, 1977). "Adolescence, the Self-Concept, and Formal Operations." *Adolescence*, 12, 373–379.

Pestrak, V. A., and Martin, D. (1985). "Cognitive Development and Aspects of Adolescent Sexuality." *Adolescence*, 22, 981–987.

Phillips, J. J., Jr. (1969). *The Origin of Intellect: Piaget's Theory*. San Francisco: W. H. Freeman and Co.

Piaget, J. (1950). *The Psychology of Intelligence*. London: Routledge and Kegan Paul.

———. (1967). *Six Psychological Studies*. Translated by A. Tenzer and D. Elkind. New York: Random House.

———. (1971). "The Theory of Stages in Cognitive Development." In *Measurement and Piaget*. Edited by D. R. Green. New York: McGraw-Hill.

———. (1972). "Intellectual Evolution from Adolescence to Adulthood." *Human Development*, 15, 1012.

———. (1980). "Intellectual Evolution from Adolescence to Adulthood." In *Adolescent Behavior and Society: A Body of Readings*, 3rd ed. Edited by R. E. Muuss. New York: Random House.

Piaget, J., and Inhelder, B. (1969). *The Psychology of the Child*. New York: Basic Books.

———. (Winter, 1976). "The Development of Formal Thinking and Creativity in Adolescence." *Adolescence*, 11, 609–617.

Plake, B. S., Kaplan, B. J., and Steinbrunn, J. (1986). "Sex Role Orientation, Level of Cognitive Development, and Mathematics Performance in Late Adolescence." *Adolescence*, 83, 607–613.

Ray, W. J., Georgiou, S., and Ravizza, R. (1979). "Spatial Abilities, Sex Differences, and Lateral Eye Movements." *Developmental Psychology*, 15, 455–457.

Ross, R. J. (1974). "The Empirical Status of the Formal Operations." *Adolescence*, 9, 413–420.

Schmidt, J. A., and Davison, M. L. (May, 1983). "Helping Students Think." *Personnel and Guidance Journal*, 61, 563–569.

Shapiro, S. H. (1973). "Vicissitudes of Adolescence." In *Behavior Pathology of Childhood and Adolescence*. Edited by S. L. Copel. New York: Basic Books.

Steinberg, L. D., Greenberger, E., Jacobi, M., and Garduque, L. (April, 1981). "Early Work Experience: A Partial Antidote for Adolescent Egocentrism." *Journal of Youth and Adolescence*, 10, 141–157.

Tice, D. M., Buder, J., and Baumeister, R. F. (1985). "Development of Self-Consciousness: At What Age Does Audience Pressure Disrupt Performance?" *Adolescence*, 20, 301–305.

Tomlinson-Keasey, C. (1972). "Formal Operations in Females from Eleven to Fifty-four Years of Age." *Developmental Psychology*, 6, 364.

Torrance, E. P. (1974). *Torrance Tests of Creative Thinking Norms—Technical Manual*. Lexington, Mass.: Personnel Press.

Webb, R. A. (1974). "Concrete and Formal Operations in Very Bright 6- to 11-Year-Olds." *Human Development*, 17, 292–300.

White, K. M. (Spring, 1980). "Problems and Characteristics of College Students." *Adolescence*, 15, 23–41.

Wolf, F. M. (Summer, 1981). "On Why Adolescent Formal Operators May Not Be Critical Thinkers." *Adolescence*, 16, 345–348.

Youniss, J., and Dean, A. (1974). "Judgment and Imaging Aspects of Operations: A Piagetian Study with Korean and Costa Rican Children." *Child Development*, 45, 1020–1031.

CHAPTER

7

Intelligence and Information Processing

There are three basic approaches to understanding cognition during adolescence. One is the P*iagetian approach*, discussed in the last chapter, which emphasizes the qualitative changes in the way adolescents think. A second is the *psychometric approach*, which measures quantitative changes. This chapter begins with this approach, emphasizing the meaning of intelligence according to various measures and discussing the numerous changes that take place as people mature.

The third view is the *information-processing approach*, which examines the progressive steps, actions, and operations that take place when the adolescent receives, perceives, remembers, thinks about, and utilizes information. This view is also presented in this chapter as a way of understanding why and how adolescents think in more advanced ways than when they were children and what abilities are developed when they become more efficient problem solvers.

INTELLIGENCE

 ## Meaning

Intelligence has almost as many definitions as experts who try to measure it (Ellison, 1984). Some definitions describe it as an innate capacity to learn, think, reason, understand, and solve problems. Other definitions focus on mental abilities that are developed, almost without biological limit. Various types of mental abilities have been described. Sternberg (1985) and his colleagues at Yale University arranged abilities into the following three major groupings in describing intelligence:

Componential Intelligence   Componential intelligence includes general learning and comprehension abilities, such as good vocabulary, high reading comprehension, ability to do test items such as analogies, syllogism, and series, and ability to think critically. This is the traditional concept of intelligence as measured on tests.

Experiential Intelligence   Experiential intelligence includes ability to select, encode, compare, and combine information in meaningful ways to create new insights, theories, and ideas.

Contextual Intelligence   Contextual intelligence includes adaptive behavior in the real world, such as the ability to size up situations, achieve goals, and solve practical problems (Sternberg and Wagner, 1986).

In an effort to include the influence of both heredity and environment in the development of intelligence, Cattell (1963) described two dimensions of intelligence: *crystallized* and *fluid*. **Crystallized intelligence** includes knowledge and skills measured by tests of vocabulary, general information, and reading comprehension. It arises out of experience and represents the extent of acculturation and education. **Fluid intelligence** is a person's ability to think and reason abstractly as measured by reasoning tests, such as figural analogies and figural classifications. It involves the processes of perceiving relationships, deducing correlates, reason-

crystallized intelligence

fluid intelligence

ing inductively, abstracting, forming concepts, and solving problems as measured by tasks with figural, symbolic, and semantic content. Fluid intelligence has a hereditary base in neurophysiological structures; therefore it is not influenced as much as crystallized intelligence by intensive education and acculturation.

HIGHLIGHT   Seven Frames of Mind

Howard Gardner, an associate professor at the Boston University School of Medicine, objects to assessing intelligence in only two dimensions: *linguistic* and *logical-mathematical abilities*. His concept also includes the following dimensions:

Spatial intelligence: The ability to form spatial images and to find one's way around in an environment. The sailors in the Caroline Islands of Micronesia navigate among hundreds of islands using only the stars and their bodily feelings. Intelligence testers in Micronesia would have to come up with an entirely different list of intelligences and testing methods.

Musical intelligence: The ability to perceive and create pitch and rhythmic patterns. There are individuals who are otherwise classified as mentally retarded who can play a song on a piano after hearing it once. A talented jazz trombonist may not be able to read a newspaper.

Body-kinesthetic intelligence: The gift of fine motor movement, as seen in a surgeon or dancer.

Interpersonal intelligence: Involves understanding others, how they feel, what motivates them, and how they interact. Certain people interact well with others because of their empathetic understanding; others, such as politicians, are highly skilled at understanding others and manipulating them.

Intrapersonal intelligence: Centers on the individual's ability to know himself or herself and to develop a sense of identity.

Gardner insists that people have to develop completely different concepts of who is bright and how to measure brightness. He says:

Five hundred years ago in the West, a tester would have emphasized linguistic memory because printed books weren't readily available. Five hundred years from now, when computers are carrying out all reasoning, there may be no need for logical-mathematical thinking and again the list of desirable intelligences would shift. What I object to is this: Decisions made about 80 years ago in France by Alfred Binet, who was interested in predicting who would fail in school, and later by a few Army testers in the United States during World War I, now exercise a tyrannical hold on who is labeled as bright or not bright. These labels affect both people's conceptions of themselves and the life options available to them.

Gardner's concept is unique because he claims independent existences for different intelligences in the human neural system. He would like to stop measuring people according to some unitary dimension called "intelligence." Instead he would like to think in terms of different intellectual strengths.

From: Ellison, J. (June, 1984). "The Seven Frames of Mind," *Psychology Today*, 18, 21–26.

Measurement

One of the most widely used measures of intelligence is the Wechsler Adult Intelligence Scale (WAIS), which may be used on people sixteen years old and older (Wechsler, 1955). Younger adolescents are usually given the Wechsler Intelligence Scale for Children (WISC-R). The WAIS divides intelligence into two components: verbal skills and performance/manipulation skills. Six subtests comprise the verbal component: Information, Comprehension, Arithmetic, Similarities, Digit Span, and Vocabulary. Five tests—Digit Symbol, Picture Completion, Block Design, Picture Arrangement, and Object Assembly—comprise the performance scores.

Intelligence Quotient

*intelligence
quotient* (IQ)

The so-called **IQ (*intelligence quotient*)** originally referred to a score on the Stanford-Binet intelligence test, obtained by applying a formula no longer used. The use of the abbreviation IQ has been retained by psychologists and educators as a convenient way of referring to a score on an intelligence test. In the Wechsler Intelligence Scales and the 1972 revision of the Stanford-Binet, scores are converted into IQ by referring to tables in the test manuals (Holroyd and Bickley, 1976; Terman and Merrill, 1973).

Changes with Age

It used to be a truism that IQ remained constant. Now it is recognized that *the IQ of an individual may vary considerably during his or her lifetime*: it may rise or fall depending on the intellectual environment in which the person is placed. Pinneau (1961) reanalyzed the data from the Berkeley Growth Study and converted all the scores to deviation IQs. He found that children tested at five years and at subsequent ages up to seventeen years showed median changes from 6 to 12 points, with the range of individual changes from 0 to 40 points. The direction of the change is not always predictable, at least for individuals. In general, predictability of test scores varies with the length of the interval between tests and with the age at the initial test. Test-retest correlations decrease as the interval between tests increases.

In summary, although most adolescents do not show gross changes in relative IQ placement, some do, so an *IQ measurement should not be interpreted as a fixed attribute but rather as a score on a test at a particular time*. The score may change as a result of a number of influences, creating the need for retesting over a period of years to make current judgments of the IQ of some people.

Any attempts to measure changes also depend on the tests used, when and how they are employed, and what they purport to measure. Figure 7-1 shows the curves on eleven Wechsler subtests (Bayley, 1968). It must be emphasized that the results obtained from the Berkeley Growth Study were longitudinal measurements, which tend to minimize intellectual decline (the less-able subjects drop out and are not available for testing). Cross-sectional measurements tend to maximize decline (older subjects are less educated). Both methods of measurement, however, show that verbal scores remain the most stable and performance

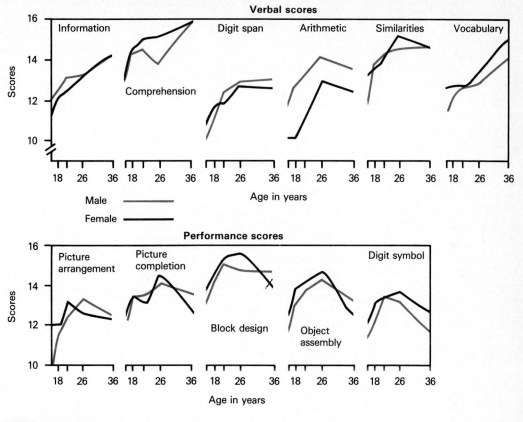

FIGURE 7-1

Curves of mean scores for adolescents and young adults on the eleven Wechsler subtests, Berkeley Growth Study.

From: Bayley, N. (1968). "Behavioral Correlates of Mental Growth: Birth to Thirty-Six Years," *American Psychologist*, 23: 1–17. Copyright 1968 by the American Psychological Association. Reprinted by permission of the publisher and author.

scores decline the most. Figure 7-2 shows the cross-sectional scores on the verbal and performance portions of the WAIS as a function of age (Wechsler, 1955).

These findings were further delineated by Horn and Cattell (1967), who felt that data for fluid and crystallized intelligence scores should be separated. They found that *fluid intelligence declined after age fourteen* and that the sharpest decline came in early adulthood. The decline in fluid intelligence was evidenced by poorer performance on tests requiring abstract thinking, inductive reasoning, relational thinking, and short-term memory and on tests requiring figural classification, analogy, and the completion of logical series. Horn and Cattell also reported that at least *twenty studies, both cross-sectional and longitudinal, showed increases in crystallized intelligence throughout adulthood.* They reasoned that learning through experience and acculturation continues for many years. Therefore intelligence, defined as knowl-

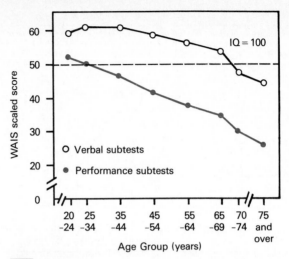

■ **FIGURE 7-2**

Scales scores on the verbal and performance portion of the WAIS as a function of age.

Adapted and reproduced by permission from the manual for the *Wechsler Adult Intelligence Scale*. Copyright © 1955 by The Psychological Corporation. Reproduced by permission. All rights reserved.

edge, increases until at least age sixty. When the scores on the tests for both fluid and crystallized intelligence were combined, however, the composite intelligence score remained substantially the same or increased slightly from age fourteen to sixty.

Schaie (1978) did not accept Horn's arguments as valid since the data were based on cross-sectional studies. He believed the *apparent decline in fluid intelligence was due to generational differences.* Older subjects were more poorly educated and had less exposure to intellectual stimulation and fewer opportunities to grow during their lifetime than did the younger subjects. The increase in crystallized intelligence could be expected since a greater number and variety of life experiences would increase their knowledge over many years.

Taken together, these findings show that the measurement of intelligence is a complex undertaking and that it is difficult to sort out age-related differences from other causes.

Factors Influencing Test Results

One of the reasons for variations in IQ and other measures of intelligence is that it is sometimes difficult to get valid test results. Results vary not only because intelligence may vary but also because of factors influencing test scores (Hubble and Groff, 1982). One of the most important influences is the presence of *anxiety* in the subjects tested. Anxious youths do not do as well on tests as those evidencing greater emotional security. A prime example is that of a ten-year-old in the Boston school system who would not answer test questions and whose record subsequently contained this entry: "The child's IQ is so low she is not testable." After a young psychologist talked with the child, she was tested and achieved an IQ score of 115 ("Aptitude Test Scores," 1979).

Motivation also has a marked influence on test results (Sewell et al., 1982). An otherwise bright student, poorly motivated to do well on a test, will not measure up to his or her capacity. Furthermore, the tests are not free of *cultural bias*. Tests to measure IQ were originally designed to measure "innate" general intelligence apart from environmental influences. But research over a long period has shown that *sociocultural factors* play a significant role in the outcome of the tests (Carmines and Baxter, 1986). Children reared in stimulus-rich environments may show enduring superiority in intelligence capacities, whereas those reared under intellectually sterile conditions may become retarded in relation to what they would otherwise be capable of doing (Scarr and Weinberg, 1978). Furthermore, the test language, illustrations, examples, and abstractions are middle class and thus are designed to measure intelligence according to middle-class standards. Many adolescents from low socioeconomic status families grow up in a nonverbal world or a world where words used are so different that understanding middle-class expressions on an intelligence test is difficult. Adolescents do poorly not because they are less intelligent but because they do not comprehend language foreign to their backgrounds and experiences. Those from minority groups who are also from lower socioeconomic families are handicapped (Roberts and DeBlossie, 1983). Native American adolescents and others from rural areas who have been raised in an environment free from considerations of time do poorly on tests with a time limit. When allowed to do the test at their own rate, they score much higher.

Efforts to develop culturally unbiased tests have been very frustrating. The general approach has been to use language familiar to the particular minorities for which the test is designed. But the major problem with the tests so far developed is how to evaluate their accuracy. Most have been measured against IQ scores, which continue to reflect a cultural bias (Rice, 1979a).

A more promising approach is known as SOMPA (System of Multicultural Pluralistic Assessment), which consists of the Wechsler IQ test, an interview in which the examiner learns the child's health history, a "sociocultural inventory" of the family's background, and an "adaptive-behavior inventory" of the child that evaluates the child's nonacademic performance in school, at home, and in the neighborhood. A complete medical exam evaluates the child's physical condition, manual dexterity, motor skill, and visual and auditory ability. The final score on SOMPA is obtained not only from the IQ test but also through the other inventories. Thus, a child who receives 68 on the Wechsler may earn an *adjusted* IQ of 89 when scores on the sociocultural and the adaptive-behavior inventories are taken into account (Rice, 1979a). Thus, SOMPA measures potential rather than current ability.

Importance of IQ

One of the most important considerations is that IQ *scores alone are not predictive of occupational or personal success* (Trotter, 1986). A follow-up of fifty-two superintelligent men from a study begun in 1921 at Stanford University by Lewis Terman revealed

One way to understand information processing in humans is to compare it to the actions of a computer. (Robert Harbison)

some interesting results (Hagan, 1983). Sixty years after the initial study began, the men with the highest IQs could scarcely be distinguished from the general population in relation to marriage, family, and domestic relations. In terms of achievement, the majority had received advanced degrees and were successful, yet some were not, and those with IQs of 150 were just as successful as those with IQs of 180. IQ is at best only a crude predictor of achievement. It taps only a few facets of intelligence and prerequisites for success.

Dangers of Labeling

One must be particularly cautious about interpreting test scores and labeling an individual "superior," "average," or "dull" on the basis of intelligence test scores, even over a period of time (Mehrens and Lehmann, 1985). This caution applies especially to black and Mexican-American children. Not only do the tests not accurately measure the learning ability of these children, but the testers may be incompetent to interpret test results, ignorant of anxieties experienced by children having language problems, and insensitive to the cultural backgrounds of minority children. Yet in some communities IQ scores determine whether children are put into classes for the mentally retarded. Once these individuals are labeled "slow" or "mentally retarded," the social stigma may remain with them all their lives (Calhoun, 1978).

Labels also have a way of becoming self-fulfilling prophecies because youths tend to try to live up to what is expected of them. The central theme of a classic book, *Pygmalion in the Classroom*, is that "one person's expectation for another person's behavior can quite unwittingly become a more accurate prediction simply for its having been made" (Rosenthal and Jacobson, 1968). As an example, the authors present findings from a study in which 20 percent of the children in a classroom were randomly selected and their teachers told they would show marked academic growth during the school year. Eight months later, this group was found to have achieved much more than other children in the class even though there was no factual reason for this improvement, because the group had been selected at random. The important element was that once the teachers expected the children to show significant gains, they did so. The prophecy of high achievement became self-fulfilling when interested people related to the students as though the achievement level had already been reached.

SCHOLASTIC APTITUDE

SAT

One of the most widely used tests in the United States is the Scholastic Aptitude Test (SAT). It is an important test because it is used by a majority of colleges as one basis for admission (Franco, 1983). Over 1 million high school seniors took the test in 1988. The combined verbal and math scores often determine eligibility not only for admission but also for scholarships and financial aid. The Educational Testing Service (ETS), which produces the SAT, claims that in combination with high school records, the SATs have proved to be better predictors of students' first-year performance in college than any other measurement. Nevertheless, the rumblings and protests against the use or misuse of the test grow louder (Rice, 1979b; Robinson, 1983).

Objections to the test arise from the claim that it measures basic abilities acquired over a student's lifetime and is thus immune to last-minute cramming and "coach-proof." But a study by the Federal Trade Commission's Bureau of Consumer Protection showed that special coaching can improve SAT scores by an average of 25 points out of the possible 800 (Rice, 1979b). More than eighty coaching schools in one nationwide chain tutored 30,000 students in a recent year, in ten-week courses, and improved scores on the average by 25 points. The schools claim that in individual cases they can improve scores up to 100 points. Recently, the author talked to a lawyer who had wanted to raise his verbal score on the SAT for admission to law school before applying. He studied a vocabulary of 5,000 most-used words and was able to raise his verbal score by 60 points.

The basic question is: If coaching can raise a student's score, should the test be relied on as a basic measure of scholastic aptitude? And should admission to college depend partly on a skill gained by those who can afford a coaching course? In all fairness, the College Entrance Examination Board has long issued warnings against making admissions decisions on the basis of the SAT score alone. The ETS itself has said that an individual's score can vary plus or minus 30 to 35 points, a spread of 60 to 70 points. For these reasons some of the best schools rely equally or more on student essays, interviews, and other admission procedures (Chance, 1988). Even high marks from school may be questioned, for they vary greatly from school to school, and the standards for good grades have been declining since the late 1960s. The number of students with A averages has increased so rapidly that there are now as many straight A students as there are those with C averages.

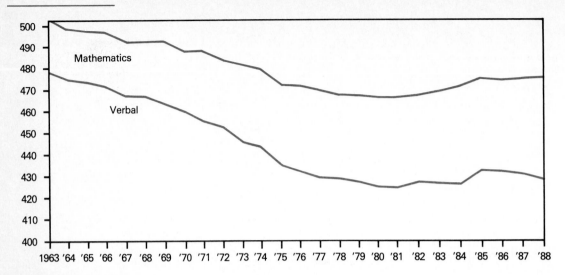

■ FIGURE 7-3

Scholastic aptitude test average scores.

■ Test Scores

The SAT score averages for college-bound seniors dropped until 1980, after which they increased until 1985. Since 1985, math scores have held steady, and verbal scores have declined. Figure 7-3 shows score averages from 1963 through 1988. Declining scores led to increased criticism of the schools for relaxing teaching and learning standards and for not teaching the basics. That average scores on achievement tests also declined was objective evidence that students were not learning as much. Part of the blame for the drop was laid to changes and problems in the family, increased television viewing, and such problems as turbulence in national affairs (Zuckerman, 1985). Males continue to score somewhat higher than females, especially on math scores, probably reflecting differences in cultural conditioning (Denno, 1982). Seventh- and eighth-grade girls may view intellectual achievement more positively than boys, but by the time they are college seniors, girls begin to view achievement as a more masculine pursuit, and their scores drop in relation to boys (Mills, 1981).

INFORMATION PROCESSING

■ Meaning

In chapter 6, we discussed the qualitative changes that take place in the way adolescents think. This *Piagetian approach* to cognitive development tells about the development of logical thinking and its implications as represented by adolescent thought and behavior. In the first section of this chapter, we discussed the *psychometric view* of intelligence as represented by a variety of mental abilities and as measured by "intelligence" tests.

HIGHLIGHT   The ACT Assessment Program

The ACT Assessment Program (American College Testing Program, 1986) is the second most widely used college admissions test, administered to more than a million students each year. The ACT Assessment Program consists of three parts: (a) the Academic Tests, (b) the Student Profile Section (SPS), and (c) the ACT Interest Inventory. The Academic Tests are English Usage Tests, Mathematics Usage Tests, Social Studies Reading Tests, and the Natural Sciences Reading Test. The Student Profile Section is a 192-item inventory of demographics, high school activities and accomplishments, and academic and extracurricular plans for college. The UNIACT is a survey of students' vocational preferences based on Holland's typology.

The ACT Academic Tests yield standard scores of 1 to 36 that are averaged to create the ACT Composite. The mean composite score in 1985 was 18.2 (Kifer, 1985). SPS has been shown to be valid, with follow-up studies showing a 69% to 70% match between students' choices of major on the SPS and actual choices at the end of the freshman year (Laing, Valiga, and Eberly, 1986).

But neither of these views of cognition really describes the *process* by which information is transmitted. *The information-processing approach to cognition emphasizes the progressive steps, actions, and operations that take place when the adolescent receives, perceives, remembers, thinks about, and utilizes information.* Studying the development of information-processing abilities provides additional insight into the growth of cognitive abilities during adolescence.

One way of understanding information processing in humans is to compare it to the actions of a computer (Klahr and Wallace, 1975). Information is coded and fed into a computer in an organized way, where it is stored in the memory banks. When any of that information is required, the computer is asked to produce it. The machine searches for the relevant information and reproduces or prints out the items requested.

Information processing by adolescents is basically similar but far more sophisticated. The adolescent receives information, organizes it, stores it, retrieves it, thinks about it, and combines it in such a way as to answer questions, solve problems, and make decisions. The most elaborate computer used in creating *artificial intelligence* cannot match the capacity of the human mind and nervous system in the input and output of information. Each new generation of computers is more advanced than the last. Similarly, as each year passes, the adolescent's ability to process information increases, due partly to the continued development of the brain and nervous system but mostly to learning experience and practice that improve mental abilities and strategies (Sigel and Cocking, 1977).

Steps in Information Processing

Information processing can be divided into a series of logical steps, illustrated in figure 7-4. The diagram shows information flowing in one direction only from the

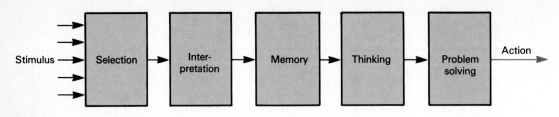

FIGURE 7-4

Steps in information processing.

time a stimulus is received until an action is begun. The general flow is in this direction, but there may be some flow backward as well as forward. For example, an adolescent may receive and select some information and take it in and out of memory to think about it over a long period of time before making a decision and instituting action. Nevertheless, the flowchart helps in understanding the total process. Let us look at the steps in more detail.

Stimuli

Every person is constantly bombarded with stimuli: audible, visual, and tactile. As you walk down the street, you are exposed to sounds, sights, and even physical contact when someone bumps into you or touches you. Your senses are your *receptors*, your contacts with the world outside yourself. Through them, you receive all information.

Selection

You do not really hear, see, or feel all the stimuli you are exposed to, primarily because you cannot focus attention on everything at once, and you may not be interested in much of what is happening. You may dimly hear a horn honking, but you may not notice the color and make of the car from which the sound is emitted or care about who is doing the honking. But if you hear someone call your name, your attention is directed immediately to the source, and you see that the person calling your name is your next-door neighbor, a good friend, driving her blue car, which you have seen many times before. Your friend pulls over, you walk over to talk, and your attention is directed to the conversation rather than the hundreds of other sights and sounds around you. Thus, the information you receive is sorted out through your own selection. You are interested in some happenings but not others, so you are motivated to direct your attention to that which you are interested in (Hamilton, 1983).

Interpretation

Once received through selective attention, the information is not just photo-copied before it is stored in your mind. You interpreted it according to your perception of it. Two people can witness the same happening but perceive it differently. A friend makes a critical remark; one adolescent takes it personally and is insulted and the other not at all. Thus, you make judgments about everything to which you are exposed, partly according to your past experiences. The adolescent girl brought up by an alcoholic father may perceive her boyfriend as drunk when he has one beer. Another girl may not consider him inebriated at all. Thus, we interpret information differently according to our perception of it. Adolescents, as well as adults, may sometimes make faulty judgments because of inaccurate perception or insufficient information. Thus, there is often the need to make additional inquiry, to gain further information, or to check one's perception with facts to make sure the perception is accurate.

Memory

Information that is useful must be remembered long enough to undergo additional processing. The process of remembering involves a series of steps. The most widely accepted model is a three-stage one by Murdock (1974): **sensory storage, short-term storage,** and **long-term storage.** Information is seen as passing from one compartment to another, with decreasing amounts passed on at any one time to the next stage. Figure 7-5 illustrates the three-stage model of memory. Information is held only briefly (as little as a fraction of a second) before the image begins to decay and/or is blocked out by other incoming sensory information. Information that has not already faded from the sensory store is *read out* to the short-term store. Because of the limited capacity of the short-term store, information to be held longer must be further rehearsed and transferred to the relatively permanent long-term store. For all practical purposes, long-term storage capacity is infinite. In the process of retrieval, stored information is obtained by searching, finding, and remembering, either through recall or recognition. Memory efficiency depends on all three of these processes and is usually at a maximum during adolescence and young adulthood.

Information received by the senses is held briefly in one of several specific sensory stores. Auditory information is held in an *auditory sensory store* and visual information in a visual sensory store. The auditory sensory store is referred to as

sensory storage

short-term storage

long-term storage

FIGURE 7-5

Three-stage model of memory.

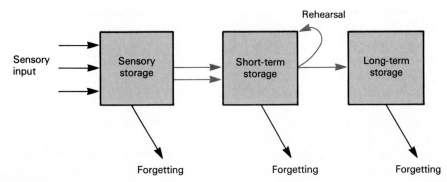

HIGHLIGHT   Three Measures of Remembering

Psychologists have outlined three ways of measuring memory: the *recall, recognition,* and *relearning* methods. In the recall method, you are asked to remember something without being given any cues. Whom did George Bush defeat for the presidency of the United States in 1988? You are either able to recall the information or not.

In the recognition method, you are asked to select among alternatives that are listed. These alternatives are your cues to help you remember. The following example illustrates this method:

In 1988 George Bush defeated _____ for the presidency of the United States.

a. Ronald Reagan
b. Michael Dukakis
c. Jesse Jackson

You recognize and check the correct answer/B.

When you can neither recall nor recognize the correct answer, it may still be possible to measure whether you have any memory of something by recording the amount of time you need to relearn something and comparing it with the time you needed to learn the material originally. If relearning takes less time than the original learning, some memory trace is still present.

echoic memory, the *visual sensory store* as *iconic memory*. Other sensory stores include those for *tactile information* and for *smell*. Research evidence indicates that the *ability to retrieve information from the sensory store does not change much as children and adolescents mature* (Steingold, 1973; Wickens, 1974).

There is some confusion about the difference between short-term and long-term memory. One helpful distinction was given by Waugh and Norman (1965). They used the terms **primary memory** and **secondary memory.** Primary memory, considered synonymous with short-term memory, involves information still being rehearsed and focused on in one's conscious mind. Secondary memory, or long-term memory, is characterized by how deeply the information has been processed, not by how long the information has been held. Deep processing, in which perceived information has been passed into layers of memory below the conscious level, constitutes secondary memory. For example, when a subject memorizes a word list, the words under immediate consideration are at the primary or short-term memory stage. Words already looked at, memorized, and tucked away are at the secondary or long-term memory level, though they were learned only a short time before. Specific words recalled several days or months later are recalled from secondary memory. Secondary memory can last for thirty seconds or for years. These two layers of memory are used synonymously in this discussion with short-term and long-term memory, though some secondary memory stores may be recalled after relatively short time intervals.

In measuring primary or short-term memory, the subject is presented a short string of digits, letters, or words and then tested for the total that can be recalled

primary memory

secondary memory

immediately. When measured in this way, *primary memory span is remarkably similar across a wide spectrum of ages,* leading to the conclusion that *short-term memory also changes very little during adolescence* (Kail, 1979).

The most significant changes in memory storage occur in long-term ability or in the capacity to shift information from short- to long-term storage. *Adolescents are more efficient at deep processing and show superior ability in long-term memory.* Interestingly enough, subjects of all ages (twenty to seventy-nine) can best remember sociohistoric events that occurred when the subjects were fifteen to twenty-five years old, indicating that these are the most impressionable years as far as memory is concerned (Botwinick and Storandt, 1974).

Improving Memory Ability

Many factors influence memory ability. *Mental repetition* or *rehearsal* of information improves retention. A grocery list or telephone number that is repeated can be held for relatively long periods of time. If not rehearsed, it is soon lost.

But simply repeating information is not a satisfactory way of remembering everything. Some people can repeat their social security number over and over again and still not be able to recall it on demand. Various *mnemonic techniques* (memory techniques) may be employed. *Organizing material* into meaningful units is one such technique. This process called *chunking* enables a person to remember the material as a meaningful unit rather than its individual parts. For example, if you are presented with the letters NOTGNIHSAW, you would have difficulty remembering them, but when combined into the word WASHINGTON, recalling them is easy. A good student reading this chapter will try to remember the outline and major sections rather than just focusing on details without regard for the whole.

Arranging material in a *logical order,* such as alphabetically, is another aid to memory. Material that is presented in *one category* (for example, animals) is easier to remember than miscellaneous information that is not easily grouped (Kail, 1979). Material that is *meaningful and familiar* and in which the adolescent is interested is easier to remember than nonsense syllables. For example, an adolescent knowledgeable about music and interested in it may remember a long list of composers of songs, a task an indifferent adolescent would find burdensome.

Anything is easier to remember if *cues are provided.* For example, an adolescent girl is asked to remember the name of a math teacher she had in sixth grade. She does not remember so is given the following cues: the teacher is male, six feet tall, has brown eyes and hair, is of medium build, and speaks with a southern accent. This description may enable the student to visualize the teacher and to remember his name.

Information may be *coded* so that it may be associated with something familiar. This technique is used to remember notes on the music staff. (See figure 7-6.) The letters FACE refer to the notes between the lines. The letters EGBDF are the first letters of the words in the phrase: "Every Good Boy Does Fine." The letters represent the notes on the lines. Codes may be visual, such as a color code, with each color representing something different. A map, with its symbols, is a good illustration of a visual representation of roads, cities, railroads, rivers, highways,

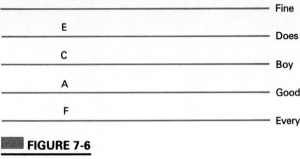

FIGURE 7-6

Codes to remember notes of a music staff.

and so forth. A code may also be audible, such as the ringing of a timer bell to remind you to turn the burner off on a stove.

Another way to remember material is by *visualizing position or place*. The technique, called the *method of loci*, visualizes information, objects, or persons in particular locations. Thus, if you need to remember the objects of furniture in a room, you can visualize the room and each part of it, and you will be able to recall many of the things in it. Some students remember textbook information by visualizing the location of the material on the page.

Thinking

Information processing also involves *thinking* about something after it has been *retrieved* from memory stores. Once facts are obtained, the relations between them and to other important information are noted so that inferences may be drawn and conclusions formulated. Actually, adolescents can be taught to think rationally, be critical of the first ideas that pop into their heads, examine evidence, and sort out the facts to discover truth from error (Barron, 1985).

Problem Solving

One of the end results of information processing is *problem solving*. This begins with *problem finding*: determining the problem so that one can determine what needs to be done. The second step is *to evaluate the elements of the problem* to decide what information and tasks one has to work with. This step usually requires insightful reorganization and thinking about various facets of the problem. The third step is *to generate a list of solutions and to evaluate them ahead of time* by trying to foresee the effects or consequences each solution will produce, so that one way may be chosen.

Let us suppose that you lock your keys in your car. The problem is how to open the door. You remember that your other keys are at home. But all the doors at home are locked and every window is closed. The nearest locksmith is miles away. You know that the car door lock-release button is visible through the window above the solid panel of your door. You remember you are due at work in half an hour.

After thinking about the problem, you come up with a list of possible solutions:

Have your car towed to an auto dealer to have the door opened.
Leave the car and take a cab to work and worry about the problem later.
Walk or get a ride home to pick up your other keys.
Call your roommate and request that the keys be brought to you.
Break the window to release the lock button.
Borrow a coat hanger from the corner dry cleaner to stick through the edge of the window to release the button.

In evaluating the various solutions, you decide to try the coat hanger first. You do, and it works.

One of the differences between adolescents and children in problem-solving ability is the nature of adolescents' information processing (Keating and Bobbitt, 1978). *Adolescents are better able to remember more information, consider all possible relationships, think about them logically, and generate and evaluate different variables and solutions ahead of time before deciding on a solution and course of action.* Children usually do not get sufficient information, remember enough of it, think about it logically enough, or consider all possible relations before arriving at solutions. Their information-processing ability is limited in relation to that of adolescents (Sternberg and Nigro, 1980; Sternberg and Rifkin, 1979).

In perspective, the information-processing approach brings us closer to understanding *why* and *how* adolescents think in more advanced ways than when they were children. Such an approach sheds light on what abilities are developed when individual adolescents become more efficient problem solvers.

SUMMARY

Intelligence has been defined and described in many ways. Sternberg groups it into three categories: verbal intelligence, problem-solving ability, and practical intelligence. Cattell describes two dimensions: crystallized and fluid intelligence. In addition to linguistic and logical-mathematical abilities, Gardner includes five other facets of intelligence: spatial, musical, body-kinesthetic, interpersonal, and intrapersonal intelligence. Gardner feels we should stop measuring people according to one unitary dimension and instead think in terms of various intellectual strengths.

One approach to understanding adolescent cognition is the psychometric approach. Various tests have been used to measure "intelligence." One of the most common is the Wechsler Adult Intelligence Scale (WAIS), which may be used on people sixteen years old and older. (There is also a Wechsler scale for children.) Scores are divided into two major components: verbal skills and performance/manipulation skills. IQ refers to a score originally derived from the Stanford-Binet intelligence test. It used to be thought that IQ remained constant throughout one's lifetime. Now it is known that scores may vary considerably and are only a score on a test taken at a particular time and evaluated according to preestablished criteria.

Scores may vary according to how and what is measured. Cross-sectional measurements tend to maximize decline, whereas longitudinal measurements minimize it. Scores on verbal portions of the WAIS remain the most stable as people age; performance scores decline the most. Similarly, fluid intelligence scores may show some decline (especially when measured cross-sectionally), but crystallized intelligence scores may increase, however they are measured.

A number of factors may influence test results. Anxiety influences the scores negatively. The degree of motivation is important, as are sociocultural factors. Tests are usually not free of cultural biases and are not as valid when used with minorities of low socioeconomic status. Furthermore, scores such as IQ cannot be used alone as predictive of either occupational or personal success, so it is dangerous to label people as "average" or "dull" on the basis of intelligence test scores alone.

One of the most widely used tests is the SAT. The test is supposed to be a basic measure of scholastic aptitude, but coaching can improve scores considerably, and thus the test reflects learning as well as basic aptitude. Average scores of college-bound seniors declined steadily from 1969 until 1980, increased until 1985, with math scores holding steady and verbal scores declining since then.

Another way of understanding adolescent cognition is through the information-processing approach, which describes the way information is transmitted. The process may be divided into a series of logical steps: selecting information from sensory stimuli, interpreting it, remembering it, thinking about it, and using it in solving problems and making decisions. Once information is received, selected, and interpreted, it is put in a series of memory storages: sensory storage, short-term storage, and long-term storage. Information in the sensory store begins to decay in a fraction of a second; that which is not faded is read out to the short-term store. Information to be held for a period of time must be further rehearsed before it is transferred to the relatively permanent long-term store. Stored information is retrieved as needed by searching, finding, and remembering. The capacity for sensory storage and short-term storage does not change much during adolescence. Adolescents are, however, more efficient than children at deep processing and show superior ability in long-term memory.

There are three measures of remembering: recall, recognition, and relearning. Recall is more difficult than recognition because no cues are given. If relearning is accomplished more speedily than original learning, some memory trace for the information has remained.

A number of factors improve memory ability: mental recognition and rehearsal, organizing material into meaningful units (chunking), arranging material in logical order or into categories, presenting material that is meaningful and familiar, and providing cues or codes so that what is to be remembered is associated with something familiar. Another way to remember is by visualizing position or place (the method of loci).

Information processing also involves thinking and problem solving. The steps employed in problem solving are problem finding, evaluating the elements of the problem, and generating a list of solutions, which can be evaluated and from which a right one may be selected.

The information-processing approach sheds light on why and how adolescents think in advanced ways and what abilities are developed when they become more efficient problem solvers.

DISCUSSION QUESTIONS

1. How would you describe an intelligent person? What factors distinguish a person who is intelligent from one who is not?

2. Have you ever known someone who was a genius in some ways and very "dumb" in others? Describe the person.

3. Are parents generally smarter than adolescents? Explain.

4. Do you think all students should be given intelligence tests and told the test results? Why or why not? Should parents and teachers know the scores?

5. Have you ever taken so-called IQ tests at different times, only to discover that your scores changed? Why did they? Explain.

6. What is the difference between cross-sectional and longitudinal measurements? Why do cross-sectional measurements accentuate intellectual decline and longitudinal measurements minimize it?

7. What do you think of the SAT? Should it be used as a basis for admission to college? Why or why not? What criteria would you use for selection?

8. In what ways is the human mind similar and dissimilar to a computer?

9. Selective attention means each person notices something different depending on interest and motivation. What sort of things do you notice and remember most easily?

10. Are you more attracted by audible, visual, or tactile stimuli?

11. When you are studying for an exam, what techniques do you use to help you remember?

12. When you are faced with problems, what techniques do you find most helpful in making decisions or arriving at solutions?

BIBLIOGRAPHY

American College Testing Program. (1986). *The ACT Assessment Program*. Iowa City, IA.: American College Testing Program.

"Aptitude-Test Scores: Grumbling Gets Louder." (May 14, 1979). *U.S. News & World Report*. pp. 76ff.

Barron, F. (1985). *Rationality and Intelligence*. Cambridge, England: Cambridge University Press.

Bayley, N. (1968). "Behavioral Correlates of Mental Growth: Birth to Thirty-six Years." *American Psychologist*, 23, 1–17.

Botwinick, J., and Storandt, M. (1974). *Memory Related Functions and Age*. Springfield, Ill.: Charles C. Thomas.

Calhoun, G. (Spring, 1978). "New Trends in Special Education." *Adolescence*, 13, 55–58.

Carmines, E. G., and Baxter, D. J. (1986). "Race, Intelligence, and Political Efficacy among School Children." *Adolescence*, 22, 437–442.

Cattell, R. B. (1963). "Theory of Fluid and Crystallized Intelligence: A Critical Experiment." *Journal of Educational Psychology*, 54, 1–22.

———. (1971). *Abilities: Their Structure, Growth and Action*. Boston: Houghton Mifflin.

Chance, P. (1988). "Testing Education." *Psychology Today*, 22, 20–21.

College Entrance Examination Board. (1979). *National College-Bound Seniors*. Princeton, N.J.

Denno, D. (Winter, 1982). "Sex Differences in Cognition: A Review and Critique of the Longitudinal Evidence." *Adolescence*, 17, 779–788.

Ellison, J. (June, 1984). "The Seven Frames of Mind." *Psychology Today*, 18, 21–26.

Franco, J. N. (January, 1983). "Aptitude Tests: Can We Predict Their Future?" *Personnel and Guidance Journal*, 61, 263, 264.

Hagan, P. (May, 1983). "Does 180 Mean Supergenius?" *Psychology Today*, 17, 18.

Hamilton, J. A. (October, 1983). "Development of Interest and Enjoyment in Adolescence. Part I. Attentional Capacities." *Journal of Youth and Adolescence*, 12, 355–362.

Holroyd, R. G., and Bickley, J. (1976). "Comparison of the 1960 and 1972 Revisions of the Stanford-Binet LM." *Journal of Youth and Adolescence*, 5, 101–104.

Horn, J. L., and Cattell, R. B. (1967). "Age Differences in Fluid and Crystallized Intelligence." *Acta Psychologica*, 26, 107–129.

Hubble, L. M., and Groff, M. G. (December, 1982). "WISC-R Verbal Performance IQ Discrepancies among Quay-Classified Adolescent Male Delinquents." *Journal of Youth and Adolescence*, 11, 503–508.

Kail, R. V. (1979). *Memory Development in Children*. San Francisco: Freeman.

Keating, D., and Bobbitt, B. (1978). "Individual and Developmental Differences in Cognitive Processing Components of Ability." *Child Development*, 49, 155–167.

Kerr, B. A., and Colangelo, N. (1988). "The College Plans of Academically Talented Students." *Journal of Counseling and Development*, 67, 42–48.

Kifer, E. (1985). "Review of the ACT Assessment Program." In *Ninth Mental Measurement Yearbook*, edited by J. V. Mitchell, pp. 31–45. Lincoln: Buros Mental Measurement Institute, University of Nebraska Press.

Klahr, D., and Wallace, J. G. (1975). *Cognitive Development: An Information-Processing View*. Hillsdale, N.J.: Erlbaum.

Laing, J., Valiga, M., and Eberly, C. (1986). "Predicting College Freshmen Major Choices from ACT Assessment Program Data." *College and University*, 61, 198–205.

Mehrens, W. A., and Lehmann, I. J. (January, 1985). "Testing the Test. Interpreting Test Scores to Clients: What Score Should You Use?" *Journal of Counseling and Development*, 5, 317–320.

Mills, C. J. (April, 1981). "Sex Roles, Personality, and Intellectual Abilities in Adolescents." *Journal of Youth and Adolescence*, 10, 85–112.

Murdock, B. B., Jr. (1974). *Human Memory: Theory and Data*. Potomac, Md.: Lawrence Erlbaum Associates.

Pinneau, S. R. (1961). "Changes in Intelligence Quotient." Boston: Houghton Mifflin.

Rice, B. (September, 1979a). "Brave New World of Intelligence Testing." *Psychology Today*, 27ff.

———. (September, 1979b). "The SAT Controversy: When an Aptitude Is Coachable." *Psychology Today*, 30ff.

Roberts, E., and DeBlossie, R. R. (Winter, 1983). "Test Bias and the Culturally Different Early Adolescent." *Adolescence*, 18, 837–843.

Robinson, S. E. (January, 1983). "Nader versus ETS: Who Should We Believe?" *Personnel and Guidance Journal*, 61, 260–262.

Rosenthal, R., and Jacobson, L. (1968). *Pygmalion in the Classroom: Teacher Expectation and Pupil's Intellectual Development*. New York: Holt, Rinehart and Winston.

Scarr, S., and Weinberg, R. A. (October, 1978). "The Influence of 'Family Background' on Intellectual Attainment." *American Sociological Review*, 43, 674–692.

Schaie, K. W. (September, 1978). "External Validity in the Assessment of Intellectual Development in Adulthood." *Journal of Gerontology*, 33, 695–701.

Sewell, T.; Farley, F. H.; Manni, J.; and Hunt, P. (Fall, 1982). "Motivation, Social Reinforcement, and Intelligence as Predictors of Academic Achievement in Black Adolescents." *Adolescence*, 17, 647–656.

Sigel, I. E., and Cocking, R. R. (1977). *Cognitive Development from Childhood to Adolescence: A Constructive Perspective*. New York: Holt, Rinehart, and Winston.

Steingold, K. (1973). "Developmental Differences in Intake and Storage of Visual Information." *Journal of Experimental Child Psychology*, 16, 1–11.

Sternberg, R. J. (Spring, 1981). "The Nature of Intelligence." *New York University Education Quarterly*, 12, 10–17.

Sternberg, R. J. (1985). *Beyond IQ*. Cambridge, England: Cambridge University Press.

Sternberg, R., and Nigro, G. (1980). "Developmental Strategies in the Solution of Verbal Analogies." *Child Development*, 51, 27–38.

Sternberg, R., and Rifkin, B. (1979). "The Development of Analogical Reasoning Processes." *Journal of Experimental Child Psychology*, 27, 195–232.

Sternberg, R. J., and Wagner, R. K., eds. (1986). *Practical Intelligence: Nature and Origins of Competence in the Everyday World*. Cambridge, England: Cambridge University Press.

Terman, L. M., and Merrill, M. A. (1973). *Stanford-Binet Intelligence Scale: Manual for the Third Revision: 1972 Norms Edition*. Boston: Houghton Mifflin.

Trotter, R. J. (1986). "Three Heads Are Better Than One." *Psychology Today*, 20, 56–62.

Waugh, N. C., and Norman, D. A. (1965). "Primary Memory." *Psychological Review*, 72, 89–104.

Wechsler, D. (1955). *Manual for the Wechsler Adult Intelligence Scale*. New York: Psychological Corporation.

Wickens, C. D. (1974). "Limits of Human Information Processing: A Developmental Study." *Psychological Bulletin*, 81, 739–755.

Zuckerman, D. (January, 1985). "Too Many Sibs Put Our Nation at Risk?" *Psychology Today*, 19, 5, 10.

CHAPTER

8

Self-Concept and Self-Esteem

Perhaps no other aspect of adolescent psychology has received more attention over the years than the subjects of self-concept and self-esteem (Stefanko, 1984). As early as 1890, William James (1890) devoted a whole chapter to the self in *The Principles of Psychology.* Carl Rogers (1961) made a 1947 address before the American Psychological Association on self-concept, as did Hilgard in 1949. The subject continues to receive more attention than probably any other topic in adolescent psychology.

This chapter will consider and discuss the meanings of self-concept and self-esteem and their importance and relationship to mental health, interpersonal competence and social adjustments, school progress, vocational aspirations, and delinquency. The development of a positive self-concept will be emphasized along with its relationship to maternal and paternal identification, parental interest and concern, broken homes, socioeconomic status, race and nationality, birth order, and physical appearance. The chapter concludes by considering the relative stability of self-concept during adolescence—that is, whether the adolescent's self-conception changes.

MEANING AND EXPLANATION

Self-Concept

self

self-concept

The **self** has been defined as that part of one's personality of which one is aware. **Self-concept** may be defined as conscious, cognitive perception and evaluation by individuals of themselves; it is their thoughts and opinions about themselves. It has been called the individual's "self-hypothesized identity." Erikson (1968) refers to it as the individual's "ego identity," or the individual's self-perceived, consistent individuality. It begins with an awareness of uniqueness, an awareness that individuals are distinct, separate from others, people in their own right. The first awareness was described by a young adolescent girl: "I was sitting in the taxi with my mother when I suddenly realized, it dawned on me, that I am I and she is she." The first step in the development of a self-concept is the recognition that one is a distinct, separate individual.

Self-concept also implies a developing awareness of *who* and *what* one is (Hodgson and Fischer, 1978). It describes what individuals see when they look at themselves, in terms of their self-perceived physical characteristics, personality skills, traits, roles, and social statuses. It might be described as the system of attitudes they have about themselves. It is their ego identity or personal identity, which is the sum total of their self-definitions or self-images (Adams, 1977; Chassin and Young, 1981).

Self-concept is often described as a global entity: how people feel about themselves in general. But it has also been described as made up of multiple self-conceptions, with concepts developed in relation to different roles (Griffin, Chassin, and Young, 1981). Thus, a person may rate himself or herself as a son or daughter, student or athlete, friend, and so forth. These conceptions of different aspects of the self may differ, which helps to explain how behavior varies in different roles.

Numerous writers have emphasized that a development of the sense of self is not possible until adolescents reach a formal operations stage of cognitive development (Adams, 1977; Enright and Deist, 1979; Manaster et al., 1977; Okum and Sasfy, 1977). This stage enables them to think about themselves, to become self-conscious, to become introspective. Adolescents gather evidence that helps them evaluate themselves: Am I competent? Am I attractive to the opposite sex? Am I intelligent? Am I friendly? From this evidence they form postulates about themselves and check out their feelings and opinions through further experiences and relationships. They compare themselves with their own ideals and those of others:

> Through experience (often painful . . .) the adolescent gradually becomes more specific and realistic in his self-theory; he draws parameters for his self-theory to avoid unnecessary disillusionment and to insure optimal functioning. . . . We can view adolescence not only as physical emergence, but as a unique type of cognitive emergence embracing the important function of the construction of a viable self-theory. (Okum and Sasfy, 1977, p. 378)

Whether individuals have an accurate self-concept is significant. All people are six different selves: the people they are, the people they think they are, the people others think they are, the people they think others think they are, the people they want to become, and the people they think others want them to become. Self-concepts may or may not be close approximations of reality, and the self-concepts are always in the process of becoming, particularly during childhood, when they are undergoing the maximum change. A number of years ago, in *Becoming: Basic Considerations for a Psychology of Personality*, Gordon W. Allport (1950) emphasized that personality is less a finished product than a transitive process: it has some stable features, but at the same time it is undergoing change. Allport coined the word **proprium,** which he defined as "all aspects of personality that   *proprium* make for inward unity." This is the self or ego that has a core of personal identity that is developing in time.

Ruth Strang (1957) has outlined four basic dimensions of the self. First, there is the *overall, basic self-concept*, which is the adolescent's view of his or her personality and "perceptions of his abilities and his status and roles in the outer world" (p. 68).

Second, there are the *individual's temporary or transitory self-concepts*. These ideas of self are influenced by the mood of the moment or by a recent or continuing experience. A recent low grade on an examination may leave a temporary feeling of being stupid; a critical remark from parents may produce a temporary feeling of deflated self-worth.

Third, there are the adolescents' *social selves*, the selves that they think others see, which influence in turn how they see themselves. If they have the impression that others think they are stupid or socially unacceptable, they tend to think of themselves in these negative ways. Their perceptions of others' feelings color their views of themselves (Street, 1988). Identity comes partly from an involvement of the self with others, in intimacy, love, group participation, cooperation, and competition. It evolves through social interactions, encompassing both continuity of self and identification with something beyond the self. William Carlyle (1970) states: "Show me the man who is your friend and I will know what your ideal of manhood is—and what kind of man you wish to be."

Part of self-concept is the sense of social status, the position in which individuals place themselves in the social system in the present or the future. For example, adolescents from low socioeconomic status groups who see themselves as not belonging there but as members of a higher socioeconomic class are molding new identities because of their higher aspirations.

ideal self   Fourth, there is the **ideal self**, the kind of people adolescents would like to be. Their aspirations may be realistic, too low, or too high. Ideal selves that are too low impede accomplishment; those that are too high may lead to frustration and self-deprecation. Realistic self-concepts lead to self-acceptance, mental health, and accomplishment of realistic goals.

Self-Esteem

Having built concepts of themselves, adolescents must deal with the esteem with which they view themselves. When they perceive themselves, what value do they place on the selves they perceive? Does this appraisal lead to self-acceptance and *self-esteem*   approval, to a feeling of self-worth? If so, then they have enough **self-esteem** to accept and live with themselves. If people are to have self-esteem, there must be a correspondence between their concepts of self and their self-ideals.

With the onset of puberty, most young people begin to make a thorough assessment of themselves, comparing not only their body parts but also their motor skills, intellectual abilities, talents, and social skills with those of their peers and their ideals or heroes. It is not surprising that this critical self-appraisal is accompanied by self-conscious behavior that makes adolescents vulnerable to embarrassment. As a consequence, throughout adolescence, they are preoccupied with attempting to reconcile their selves as they perceive them with their ideal selves (Handel, 1980). By late adolescence, they may have managed to sort themselves out—to determine what they can most effectively be and to integrate their goals into their ideal selves.

Carl Rogers (1961) was one of the most important contemporary theorists in the development of a theoretical and practical structure of self-ideals. Rogers pictures the end point of personality development as a basic congruence between the phenomenal field and experience and the conceptual structure of the self—a situation that results in freedom from internal conflict and anxiety. What individuals discover they are and what they perceive themselves to be and want to be begin to merge, and they are therefore able to accept themselves, be themselves, and live as themselves without conflict. Their self-perception and relationships with others bring self-acceptance and self-esteem. Psychological maladjustment occurs when there is a divergence between the selves they are being in relationship to others and the selves they perceive that they are or want to be.

IMPORTANCE OF AN ADEQUATE SELF-CONCEPT AND SELF-ESTEEM

Mental Health

Self-esteem has been called the "survival of the soul"; it is the ingredient that gives dignity to human existence. It grows out of human interaction in which the self is considered important to someone. The ego grows through small accomplishments, praise, and success.

Individuals whose identities are weak or whose self-esteem has never sufficiently developed manifest a number of symptoms of emotional ill health (Brennan and O Loideain, 1980; Koenig, 1988). They may evidence psychosomatic symptoms of anxiety. Low self-esteem has also been found to be a factor in drug abuse (Reardon and Griffing, 1983) and in unwed pregnancy (Black and deBlassie, 1985; Blinn, 1987; Horn and Rudolph, 1987; Patten, 1981). In fact, unwed pregnancy is often an effort on the part of young women to enhance their self-esteem (Streetman, 1987).

Sometimes the adolescent with a weak identity and low self-esteem tries to develop a false front or facade with which to face the world (Elliott, 1982). The facade is a compensating mechanism; its aim is to overcome the feeling of worthlessness by convincing others that one is worthy: "I try to put on an act to impress people." But putting on an act is a strain. To act confident, friendly, and cheerful when one feels the opposite is a constant struggle. The anxiety that one might make a false step and let the guard slip creates considerable tension.

Another reason for anxiety is that *the person with low self-esteem shows a shifting and unstable identity.* Adolescents with low self-esteem are overly vulnerable to criticism, rejection, or any other evidence in their daily lives that testifies to their inadequacy, incompetence, or worthlessness. They may be deeply disturbed when laughed at, scolded, blamed, or when others have a poor opinion of them. The more vulnerable they feel themselves to be, the higher are their anxiety levels. Such adolescents report: "Criticism hurts me terribly" or "I can't stand to have anyone laugh at me or blame me when something goes wrong." As a result they feel awkward and uneasy in social situations and avoid embarrassment whenever they can.

Interpersonal Competence and Social Adjustments

Those with poor self-concepts are often rejected by other people. *Acceptance of others and acceptance by others, especially by best friends, are related to self-concept scores,* with highest acceptance in a group with moderate self-concept scores and lowest in a group with low self-concept scores. "Acceptance of self is positively and significantly correlated with acceptance of, and by, others." Thus, "there is a close relationship between self-acceptance and social adjustment." One of the signs of possible disturbance during adolescence is an inability to establish friendships or to meet new people ("An Expert Tells," 1978).

Poor social adjustment, which is related to low self-concept and self-esteem, manifests itself in a number of ways. Adolescents with low self-esteem tend to be outstanding in their social invisibility. (See chapter 12.) They are not noticed or selected as leaders, and they do not participate as often in class, club, or social activities. They do not stand up for their own rights or express their opinions on matters that concern them. These adolescents more often develop feelings of isolation and are more often afflicted with pangs of loneliness. One man writes: "I used to be so shy that I first went out with a woman at 21. Words cannot express how excruciatingly, how desperately lonely I was in those days" (Zimbardo, 1978, p. 18). Shy people often feel awkward and tense in social situations, which makes it more difficult for them to communicate with others. (Ishiyama, 1984). Because they want to be liked, they are more easily influenced and led and usually let others make decisions because they lack the necessary self-confidence. One person commented: "I believe now that one of my ways of coping with shyness was to go to great lengths to be pleasing, even to the point of being submissive in thought and action" (Zimbardo, 1978, p. 18). Those who submit unwillingly to others are less likely to like them and to have faith in them. If adolescents have a fundamental contempt for themselves, they will hate and despise others, but if they trust and respect themselves, they also will trust and respect others as members of the human race.

Progress in School

An increasing amount of evidence supports the theory that *there is a correlation between self-concept and achievement in school* (Bell and Ward, 1980). Successful students feel more sense of personal worth and somewhat better about themselves. In general, the higher are the grade averages, the more likely the student is to have a high level of self-acceptance. Strathe and Hash (1979) write: "A significant relationship among such things as academic achievement, school satisfaction, and self-esteem has been reported for individuals at all grade levels from primary grades through college" (p. 185). The authors point out that there are "significant and positive correlations between self-concept and performance in the academic role" and that studies of school dropouts show that low aspirations, accomplishments, and self-esteem were already present or predictable by the start of the tenth grade. One reason is that students who have confidence in themselves have the courage to try and are motivated to live up to what they believe about themselves. Students who have negative attitudes about themselves impose limitations on their own achievement. They feel they "can't do it anyhow" or are "not smart enough."

This relationship between negative self-concept and school achievement begins early. Unfavorable views of self may already be established before children enter first grade. These children start out in school with a feeling they are not going to do well, and as a result, they do not.

Boys from minority groups are less likely to develop a positive self-concept from high achievement because of the attitudes of the group toward good grades.

The attitudes of significant others—mothers, fathers, grandparents, older siblings, special friends, teachers, or school counselors—can have an important influence on students' academic self-concepts. In one study, 40 percent of black high school seniors ranked above average in their academic self-concepts, and 54 percent of the remaining students ranked average (Johnsen and Medley, 1978). These high self-concepts were the result of the positive attitudes and support other important persons showed toward these students. The students in this sample felt that others had confidence in their academic abilities, so they had confidence in themselves.

Vocational Aspirations

The desire and expectation to get ahead vocationally also depend on self-esteem. Women who have both a career and marriage tend to have higher self-esteem than those who have become homemakers. Boys who aspire to upward mobility also show a strong sense of self-esteem, whereas downwardly mobile boys more often wish for changes in self that are so extensive that they indicate self-rejection. Both those with low and high self-esteem consider it important to get ahead, but those with low self-esteem are less likely to expect they will succeed. They are more likely to say, "I would like to get ahead in life, but I don't think I will ever get ahead as far as I would like." They less often think they possess those qualities essential for success.

There is a difference also in the types of positions desired by low and high self-esteem adolescents. In general, those with low self-esteem want to avoid both positions in which they will be forced to exercise leadership and jobs in which others dominate them; they want to be neither power wielders nor power subjects. Avoiding leadership or supervision by others is a way of avoiding criticism or judgment.

Delinquency

There is a close relationship between delinquency and self-concept. Delinquent youths tend to show lower self-esteem than do nondelinquent youths (Lund and Salary, 1980). Their delinquency may be overcompensation for their inadequate self-concepts (Bynner, O'Malley, and Bachman, 1981). One theory is that they have low self-esteem and so adopt deviant patterns of behavior to reduce self-rejecting feelings. In other words, if their behavior begins to match their low opinions of themselves, they decrease their own self-derogation and rejection (Kaplan, 1978). They seek to restore their self-respect by aligning themselves with deviant groups that accord them the approval denied by the rest of society (Rosenberg and Rosenberg, 1978). Thus, an adequate self-concept protects the adolescent from delinquency; those who see themselves as "good people" or "nondelinquents" have developed an inner containment against becoming delinquent. One effective form of treatment of delinquent youths is to place them in group homes where they can model appropriate behavior of house parents and build self-confidence necessary for changing undesirable behavior. As self-esteem improves, so does their behavior (Krueger and Hansen, 1987).

DEVELOPMENT OF A POSITIVE SELF-CONCEPT

Maternal Relationship and Identification

A number of factors contribute to the development of a positive self-concept and high self-esteem (Openshaw, Thomas, and Rollins, 1983). *The quality of parent-adolescent relationships is clearly an important factor in adolescent self-esteem* (Demo, Small, and Savin-Williams, 1987; Gecas and Schwalbe, 1986; Hoelter and Harper, 1987). Late adolescent girls who feel close to their mothers tend to see themselves as confident, wise, reasonable, and self-controlled. Those who feel distant from their mothers tend to perceive themselves in negative terms: as rebellious, impulsive, touchy, and tactless. These findings indicate that the degree of maternal identification influences self-concept (Offer, Ostrov, and Howard, 1982). Both males and females who identify closely with a parental model strive to be like the model in such a way that blending of self with the qualities of the model brings about a

HIGHLIGHT   The Self's Development

As shown in figure 8-1, the beginnings of the self occur through four primary input channels: *auditory cues, physical sensations, body image cues,* and *personal memories.* These input channels provide the emotional medium that allows the self to grow (Hamachek, 1985). Self-awareness develops when young children begin to recognize the distinction between self and not-self, between their bodies and the remainder of their visible environment. When personal experience widens and intellectual functioning expands, the self differentiates further as one gains increased ability both to understand the outside world more fully (to be the "knower" or "doer") and to see oneself as an object in the outside world (to be the "known"). The self-as-object involves attributes that are physical (how one looks), social (how one relates), emotional (how one feels), and intellectual (how one thinks). These attributes interact with that aspect of the self that comes to know through its perceiving, performing, thinking, and remembering functions.

The component of the self that is the knower constitutes the "I" or the "agent of experience," and that dimension of the self that is the known constitutes the "me" or "the content of experience."

The interactive combination of these attributes and functions leads to the development of two core ingredients of the self, namely, self-concept (ideas about oneself) and self-esteem (feelings and evaluations about oneself). Self-concept can be more specifically differentiated into the perceived self (the way people see themselves) and into the "real" self (the way a person really is, as measured more objectively through tests or clinical assessments) and the "ideal" self (the way a person would like to be). Out of all this emerges personality, which, depending on who is describing it, can be either the sum total of (a) one's own internal self-perceptions, or (b) another person's external perceptions of that individual (Hamachek, 1985, pp. 138, 139).

---

real likeness but not an identity. Erikson (1968) felt that overidentification with parents cuts off a "budding identity" by stifling the ego. However, children with inadequate parental identification will also have poor ego identity. Research indicates that ego identity of girls is weak with poor maternal identification and weak again with overidentification that borders on the pathological. A moderate degree of identification seems to be the healthiest.

The mothers with whom adolescent girls identify vary greatly. Mothers who believe in sex-role equality, whose concepts of ideal daughters are those who are independent, self-sufficient, and free of external control, are likely to have daughters who develop positive self-images by believing in the same principles. These are the girls who grow to be politically and socially gregarious and who value personal autonomy and humanitarianism.

Paternal Relationship and Identification

Fathers are important, too, in a girl's development. Warm, rewarding father-daughter relationships play a vital role in helping a girl to value her femininity and to move toward a positive acceptance of herself as a woman. The adolescent

FIGURE 8-1

Schematic overview of the self's development.

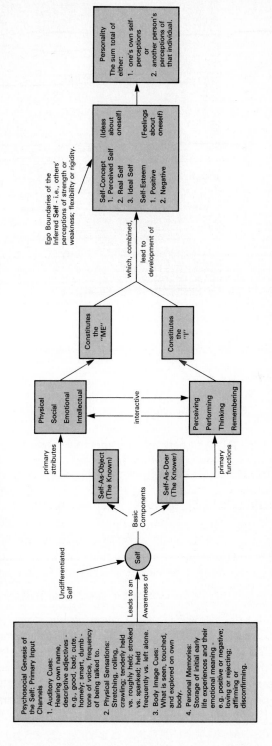

From: Hamachek, D. E. (1985). "The Self's Development and Ego Growth: Conceptual Analysis and Implications for Counselors." *Journal of Counseling and Development*, *64*, 136–142. Copyright © 1985 American Association of Counseling and Development. Reprinted by permission.

The quality of parent-adolescent relationships is clearly an important factor contributing to the development of a positive self-concept and high self-esteem. (Robert Harbison)

girl who values and loves her father and whose father values and loves her invariably seems more comfortable with her own femaleness and with her relationship to men. As a result she is able to make easier and more satisfactory heterosexual adjustments. The same is true for the adolescent boy. If he identifies with his father but shares mutually warm feelings with his mother, his relationships with women are more likely to be comfortable and pleasant.

Middle-class fathers are considerably more likely than working-class fathers to be supportive of their sons, although only somewhat more likely to be supportive of their daughters. As a result middle-class boys tend to have a higher self-esteem than those from working-class families, for adolescents who have a close relationship with their fathers are considerably more likely to have high self-esteem and a stable self-image than are those who describe these relationships as distant. Other data supports the well-known psychoanalytic theory that boys' positive relationships with their fathers and girls' relationships with their mothers are more crucial to adequate self-concept than is membership in a social class.

Parental Interest, Concern, and Discipline

A key factor in determining whether parents have a positive effect in helping their adolescents build a healthy ego identity is the warmth, concern, and interest they show them. Parents who care and show interest are more likely to have adolescents who have high self-esteem. Furthermore, high self-esteem adolescents have parents who are democratic but also less permissive than those of low self-esteem adolescents. Their parents are strict but consistent, and they demand high standards, although they are also flexible enough to allow deviations from rules under special circum-

HIGHLIGHT   Self-Esteem and Symbolic Interaction

Symbolic interaction emphasizes that a child's self-esteem is a function of the parents' reflected appraisal of the child's worth. Parents who are supportive, warm, and nurturing and who show approval and other positive sentiments confirm in the adolescent's mind that his or her parents accept him or her as a competent, effective, and worthwhile individual. Thus parental support is related positively to the adolescent's self-esteem

The type of parental control attempts also influences self-esteem. There are two types of control: *induction* and *coercion*. Induction is the attempt to point out to the adolescent the consequences of behavior. Parents utilizing induction will attempt to avoid a direct contest of wills and seek to induce voluntary behavior in the adolescent. Induction transmits to the adolescent a recognition of ability to evaluate the consequences of behavior and to make a decision based on the evaluation. The adolescent emerges with more confidence in the choices made and in the ability to make those choices. Thus, self-esteem is enhanced.

Coercion involving parental control attempts utilizing physical strength or social status to elicit desired behavior. It utilizes punishment, which is negatively related to self-esteem.

Figure 8-2 illustrates the symbolic interaction model and its influence on the child's self-esteem.

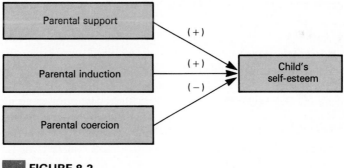

FIGURE 8-2

Symbolic interaction.

From: Openshaw, D. K., Thomas, D. L., and Rollins, B. C. (Summer, 1983). "Socialization and Adolescent Self-Esteem: Symbolic Interaction and Social Learning Explanations," *Adolescence*, 70, 317–329.

stances (Graybill, 1978). There seems to be a combination of warmth and firm discipline. The relationship with parents appears to be characterized by good communication, strong identification and ties of affection (Peterson and Kellam, 1977). Low self-esteem adolescents have parents who are often inconsistent in expectations and discipline. Sometimes the parents are too restrictive or critical and rejective of their children. For example, adolescents who feel unduly pressured to achieve and succeed in school also are likely to have low self-esteem and to feel they are incapable of reaching the goals set for them by their families (Eskilson et al., 1986). Certainly adolescents who are physically abused by parents develop a low self-esteem. (Hjorth, 1982).

Broken Families

What happens to the self-esteem of the growing child when a family is broken by divorce? It depends on a number of factors. The mother's age at the time of the marital rupture is important. If the mother is very young, the negative effect on the child is much greater than if the mother is older, because the younger mother is less able to cope with the upset of divorce. The effect also depends on the child's age at the time of the marital rupture. Young children are more adversely affected than are older children. Remarriage also influences self-esteem. Parish and Dostal (1980) found that children from remarried families evaluated them-selves more positively than children from divorced but not remarried families. However, children who did not get along with their stepfathers tended to be more disturbed than children whose mothers did not remarry. Students whose mothers were relatively young when they were widowed were less likely to have high self-esteem. These students were not poorly adjusted but tended to be in the inter-mediate category. Children from intact families tended to evaluate themselves the most positive of all (Parish and Taylor, 1979).

Other research gives variable results. One study of high school female seniors showed that two-thirds of those who were high in ego identity (identity achievers) came from homes broken by either divorce or death (St. Clair and Day, 1979). These findings indicate that broken homes do not necessarily have the adverse effects on adolescents that are sometimes supposed. Another study of third-, sixth-, and eighth-grade children from intact, single-parent, and reconstituted families found no significant differences in self-concept scores of children from these different types of homes (Raschke and Raschke, 1979). Self-concept scores were significantly lower, however, for children who reported higher levels of family conflict, regardless of family type. It is the quality and harmony of interpersonal relationships that are the important factors, not the type of family structure alone. Parish and Parish (1983) studied self-concepts of fifth- through eighth-graders and found the same results: *whether a child came from an intact, reconstituted, or divorced family was not as important as whether the existing family was happy or unhappy.* When children perceive conflict between parents or between themselves and their parents, lower self-esteem can be expected (Cooper, Holman, and Braithwaite, 1983). Amato (1986) found lower self-esteem among adolescents from conflicting families and from those where the parent-adolescent relationship was poor. How-ever, one of the significant findings is that *loss of self-esteem when parents divorce is usually temporary.* Amato (1988) found no significant association between adult self-esteem and having experienced parental divorce or death as a child.

Socioeconomic Status

The effects of socioeconomic status (SES) on self-esteem are variable. Generally, lower SES students have lower self-esteem than higher SES students. However, in their study of eleventh-grade students from three high schools in North Carolina,

Richman, Clark, and Brown (1985) found that the higher SES females had lower self-esteem than middle or low SES females. Higher SES females felt under great pressure to excel in academics, physical attractiveness, social activities, and so on. Perceived failure in any one of these areas led to loss of self-esteem and feelings of inadequacy. Lower SES males and females were more used to failure, so it was not as traumatic for them as for high SES females.

Socioeconomic status of the parents, by itself, is not enough to produce low self-esteem children. Lower-class, low-income families produce high self-esteem children if the parents' self-esteem is high. This parental self-esteem depends in turn on the prestige of the nationality or religious group or on the self-acceptance of the members within the group. The best example is that of Jewish adolescents, who, though they come from a religious group that is a minority in American society, nevertheless have far greater self-esteem than do Catholics or Protestants, probably because of the high self-esteem of the Jewish parents and the generally adequate parent-child relationship, measured by the degree of interest Jewish parents show in their children.

Race and Nationality

The influence of dissonance on self-esteem is also felt among mixed racial groups. In general *when black adolescents attend white schools, they evidence a lower self-esteem than when attending predominantly black schools.* Black students in segregated schools have higher self-esteem than black students in integrated schools. The desegregated school may have certain advantages, but enhancing self-esteem is not one of them. Recent findings suggest that with the increase of racial pride brought about by the civil rights and black consciousness movements, self-esteem among blacks has risen. Rust and McCraw (1984) found that among a public high school sample of black and white adolescents from Tennessee, the black students had significantly higher levels of self-esteem than did the white students. Richman, Clark, and Brown (1985) found this same thing in North Carolina.

Overall there is some evidence that black youths have higher self-esteem when not exposed to white prejudices. When surrounded primarily by black people with similar physical appearance, social class standing, family background, and school performance, they rate themselves much higher in self-esteem than when surrounded by white people. (Simmons et al., 1978).

Like those of any other race, some black adolescents have high self-esteem, others low. One study found that black early adolescents who had established close friendships and achieved some degree of intimacy felt good about themselves and had high self-concepts. This finding emphasizes an important factor in self-esteem. Psychosocial adjustments are all important to adolescents in developing high self-concepts. *Those who have trouble gaining group acceptance and maintaining close friendships also show signs of low self-concepts* (Paul and Fischer, 1980).

Some efforts have been made to do cross-cultural comparisons of adolescents. Comparisons of Indian, American, Australian, and Irish adolescents showed that American youths had higher self-concepts and self-esteem than did the others, with Australian, Indian, and Irish adolescents following in order of declining ego strength (Agrawal, 1978). When American, Irish, and Israeli youths were compared, Americans ranked highest, with Irish and Israeli youths lower but similar to each other (Offer et al., 1977). However, *the development of an adequate self-image depends on a strong and stable sense of ethnic identity and the degree of social pride and support form one's cultural group* (Rosenthal, Moore, and Taylor, 1983).

Birth Order

There is little correlation between the child's birth order in the family and self-esteem (Gecas and Pasley, 1983). An only child, however, is more likely to have higher self-esteem than those with siblings. Also, those who are the first of their gender to be born in their family seem to have some advantage. Thus, a first-born boy in a family of all daughters enjoys high self-esteem, as does a first-born girl in a family of all sons (West, Jones, and McConahay, 1981). However, there are too many other variables—spacing of children, total number in the family, parent-child interactions, and so forth— to assume that birth order alone is a key to understanding self-concept (Steelman, 1985).

Physical Handicaps

As might be expected, *adolescents with physical handicaps or negative body images have more difficulty developing positive self-concepts and self-esteem than do those who are physically more average* (Landon et al., 1980). The importance of physical attractiveness and body image has been discussed in chapter 5. It is certain that the degree of physical attractiveness and acceptance of one's physical self are influential factors in the development of a total self-concept (Padin, Lerner, and Spiro, 1981; Pomerantz, 1979). One study showed that adolescents who thought themselves "too short" or "too heavy" showed not only lower self-concepts but also lower self-actualization, indicating that the fulfillment of their innermost potential may be greatly inhibited by their negative sense of self-worth (Hogan and McWilliams, 1978).

HIGHLIGHT   Bibliotherapy

Bibliotherapy involves using assigned reading to enhance self-perception. It is based on the belief that persons are affected by what they read. It involves assigning adolescents literature relevant to their personal problems and needs. The readers are given an opportunity to share experiences vicariously with specific characters in the stories. For example, stories about blacks that hold them in high esteem will help improve the self-esteem of black adolescents reading the stories. Stories that emphasize virtues, accomplishments, and positive images of racial or ethnic minorities enable children of these groups to feel good about themselves and their identities (Calhoun, 1987).

CHANGES OR STABILITY IN SELF-CONCEPT

To what extent does self-concept change during adolescence? *Overall, self-concept gradually stabilizes.* (Chiam, 1987; Ellis and Davis, 1982; Schiff and Koopman, 1978). A ten-year longitudinal study of adolescents, beginning in grades 5 and 6 and continuing until they were out of high school, showed only a slight increase in self-concept. For the majority of youth, those who had a negative self-concept when entering adolescence entered adulthood with the same negative feelings (Barnes and Farrier, 1985).

Adolescents are extremely sensitive, however, to important events and changes in their lives (Balk, 1983). One study found a lowered self-concept of high school juniors after they and their families had moved a long distance to another town (Kroger, 1980). Adolescents who have been getting along well but who get involved with the wrong crowd and begin to adopt deviant behavior may show less self-respect and an increase in their own self-derogation (Kaplan, 1977).

One study showed that self-esteem was lowest at around twelve years of age (Protinsky and Farrier, 1980). The researchers raised the question: what important factors were responsible for the sharp decline in a positive self-image? By applying careful statistical controls, they showed that the onset of puberty itself was not the determining factor, for twelve-year-olds in junior high school had lower self-esteem, higher self-consciousness, and greater instability of self-image than did twelve-year-olds in elementary school. When differences in race, socioeconomic class, or marks in school were considered, none of these variables was found to be determinative. The general findings held true for black students as well as white students, middle-class as well as working-class respondents, and for students with high as well as low grades. Nor was age itself significant. There was virtually no difference between the self-image ratings of eleven- and twelve-year-olds in the sixth grade or between twelve- and thirteen-year-olds in the seventh grade. The one factor that was determinative was whether the student had entered junior high school. *The move from a protected elementary school, where a child had few teachers and one set of classmates, to a much larger, more impersonal junior high, where teachers, classmates, and even classrooms were constantly shifting, was disturbing to the self-image.* In addition, the students moved from a relatively safe elementary school environment to a more hostile junior high school in which males, particularly, were much more likely to experience victimization such as being harassed or beaten up (Blyth et al., 1978). This study clearly illustrates that self-image can be affected, at least for a while, by disturbing events.

Educators can take into account the effect of different schools on self-concepts (Tierno, 1983), and put pupils who are having difficulties into alternative schools to try to change the pupils' attitudes, behavior, and self-concepts. Transferring pupils to different schools is particularly effective with junior high school pupils but less effective at the senior high level (Strathe and Hash, 1979).

This also means, however, that self-image and self-esteem can be improved by helpful events. Summer camp experiences have been found to be helpful in improving the self-concepts of young adolescents (Flynn and Beasley, 1980).

Stake, DeVille, and Pennell (1983) and Waksman (1984a, 1984b) report good results with what they call *assertion training* of secondary and college-level students who are timid and withdrawn and incapable of dealing with other students, teachers, and relatives. Through role playing and behavioral rehearsal, youths are taught to maintain eye contact, how to talk to others, to greet them, to ask questions, to refuse some requests, and to express their feelings. By so doing, they are able to overcome their reputations of nonassertiveness and to change others' opinions of them. Rotherarm and Armstrong (1980) also reported significant increases in assertiveness of ninth- and twelfth-grade girls after ten weeks of assertion training. Wehr and Kaufman (1987) report improved assertiveness of ninth-grade boys and girls after only four hours of training.

In summary, the concept of the self is not completely solidified by adolescence, although recognizable trends and traits persist. With increasing age, these recognizable traits become more stable. However, self-concepts are subject to change under the influence of powerful forces. Assisting the adolescent who has a negative identity to find a mature and positive image of self is a major undertaking, but it can be done in some cases. It is certain that the change is easier during adolescence than in adulthood.

SUMMARY

Self-concept is the conscious, cognitive perception and evaluation by individuals of themselves. It is their ego identity: it defines who and what they are. It is made up of numerous components: their basic self-perception, their temporary, changing, transitory views of themselves, their social self, and their ideal self.

What value do they place on the selves they perceive? This appraisal is their self-esteem and is vitally important for a number of reasons. The level of self-esteem influences mental health, interpersonal competence and social adjustments, progress in school, and vocational aspirations and is even related to whether adolescents align themselves with deviant groups.

How is a positive self-concept developed? The beginning of the self occurs through four primary input channels: auditory cues, physical sensations, body image cues, and personal memories. These input channels provide the emotional medium that allows the self to grow. The self grows further as personal experience widens, and the self comes to know its attributes: physical, social, emotional, and intellectual. The self also comes to know its perceiving, performing, thinking, and remembering functions. The contributions of these attributes and functions leads to the development of self-concept and self-esteem.

The adolescent's maternal and paternal relationships are important, since the parents are role models with which the adolescent identifies. A healthy ego identity is developed through warm concern and interest on the part of parents. Parents who are supportive and nurturing and show approval develop positive self-esteem in their adolescents. Similarly, parents who seek to stimulate positive, voluntary behavior help adolescents to gain confidence over their ability to make wise choices and so enhance self-esteem.

Whether a family is intact, reconstituted, or divorced is not as important in developing positive self-esteem as whether the existing family is happy or unhappy. In general, adolescents from lower socioeconomic status families have lower self-esteem than those from higher status families, but much depends on parental self-esteem, which is passed on to children. Race and nationality are not as important as having a strong sense of ethnic identity and social pride in one's cultural heritage. Similarly, birth order shows little correlation with self-esteem. The degree of physical attractiveness and especially the acceptance of one's physical self influence the development of a total self-concept. Self-concept usually stabilizes during adolescence. It may be influenced temporarily by events but overall changes little as individuals grow to young adulthood.

DISCUSSION QUESTIONS

Class members might be asked to think about themselves when they were adolescents and to apply the following questions to themselves.

1. How did you feel about yourself? Did you like yourself? Why or why not?
2. If you were to describe yourself when you were an adolescent, what would you say?
3. In what ways did your concept of yourself differ from your ideal of what you wanted to be like?
4. Have your feelings about yourself changed much as you have become older? Why or why not?
5. What did your teachers think you were like? Were they accurate in their evaluations?
6. How did your parents feel about you? How did their views affect your feelings about yourself?
7. How did your friends feel about you? What do you believe they thought you were like? Were they right?
8. What events in your life have most influenced how you feel about yourself?
9. Describe the socioeconomic level of your family. How did the work that your father and/or your mother did influence your self-image and the attitudes and opinions of others toward you?
10. Are your parents divorced, separated, remarried? Have these factors influenced your self-esteem? In what ways?

BIBLIOGRAPHY

Adams, G. R. (Summer, 1977). "Personal Identity Formation: A Synthesis of Cognitive and Ego Psychology." *Adolescence*, 12, 151–164.

Agrawal, P. (March, 1978). "A Cross-Cultural Study of Self-Image: Indian, American, Australian, and Irish Adolescents." *Journal of Youth and Adolescence*, 7, 107–116.

Allport, Gordon, W. (1950). *Becoming: Basic Considerations for a Psychology of Personality*. New Haven, Conn.: Yale University Press.

Amato, P. R. (1986). "Marital Conflict, the Parent-Child Relationship, and Child Self-Esteem." *Family Relations*, 35, 403–410.

———. (1988). "Long-Term Implication of Parental Divorce for Adult Self-Concept." *Journal of Family Issues*, 9, 201–213.

Balk, D. (April, 1983). "Adolescents' Grief Reactions and Self-Concept Perceptions following Sibling Death: A Study of 33 Teenagers." *Journal of Youth and Adolescence*, 12, 137–161.

Barnes, M. E., and Farrier, S. C. (Spring, 1985). "A Longitudinal Study of the Self-Concept of Low-Income Youth." *Adolescence*, 20, 199–205.

Bell, C., and Ward, G. R. (Winter, 1980). "An Investigation of the Relationship between Dimensions of Self Concept (DOSC) and Achievement in Mathematics." *Adolescence*, 15, 895–901.

Black, C., and DeBlassie, R. R. (1985). "Adolescent Pregnancy: Contributing Factors, Consequences, Treatment, and Plausible Solutions." *Adolescence*, 20, 281–290.

Blinn, L. M. (1987). "Phototherapeutic Intervention to Improve Self-Concept and Prevent Repeat Pregnancies Among Adolescents." *Family Relations*, 36, 252–257.

Blyth, D. A., et al. (July, 1978). "The Transition into Early Adolescence: A Longitudinal Comparison of Youth in Two Educational Contexts." *Sociology of Education*, 51, 149–162.

Brennan, T. G., and O Loideain, D. S. (February, 1980). "A Comparison of Normal and Disturbed Adolescent Offer Self-Image Questionnaire Responses in an Irish Cultural Setting." *Journal of Youth and Adolescence*, 9, 11–18.

Bynner, J. M., O'Malley, P. M., and Bachman, J. G. (December, 1981). "Self-Esteem and Delinquency Revisited." *Journal of Youth and Adolescence*, 10, 407–441.

Calhoun, G. (1987). "Enhancing Self-Perception Through Bibliotherapy." *Adolescence*, 88, 929–943.

Campbell, M. M., et al. (December, 1977). "Psychological Adjustment of Adolescents with Myelodysplasia." *Journal of Youth and Adolescence*, 6, 397–407.

Carlyle, W. (1970). *You're My Friend So I Brought You This Book.* Edited by John Marvin. New York: Random House.

Chassin, L. C., and Young, R. D. (Fall, 1981). "Salient Self-Conceptions in Normal and Deviant Adolescents." *Adolescence*, 16, 613–620.

Chiam, H. (1987). "Changes in Self-Concept During Adolescence." *Adolescence*, 85, 69–76.

Cooper, J. E.; Holman, J.; and Braithwaite, V. A. (February, 1983). "Self-Esteem and Family Cohesion: The Child's Perspective and Adjustment." *Journal of Marriage and the Family*, 45, 153–159.

Demo, D. H., Small, S. A., and Savin-Williams, R. C. (1987). "Family Relations and the Self-Esteem of Adolescents and Their Parents." *Journal of Marriage and the Family*, 49, 705–715.

Elliott, G. C. (April, 1982). "Self-Esteem and Self-Presentation among the Young as a Function of Age and Gender." *Journal of Youth and Adolescence*, 11, 135–153.

Ellis, D. W., and Davis, L. T. (Fall, 1982). "The Development of Self-Concept Boundaries across the Adolescent Years." *Adolescence*, 17, 695–710.

Enright, R. D., and Deist, S. H. (Spring, 1979). "Social Perspective Taking as a Component of Identity Formation." *Adolescence*, 14, 185–189.

Erikson, E. H. (1968). *Identity: Youth and Crisis.* New York: Norton.

Eskilson, A., Wiley, M. G., Muehlbauer, G., and Dodder, L. (1986). "Parental Pressure, Self-Esteem and Adolescent Reported Deviance: Bending the Twig Too Far." *Adolescence*, 83, 501–515.

"An Expert Tells How to Cope with Shyness." (9 October 1978), *U.S. News & World Report*, pp. 58–60.

Flynn, T. M., and Beasley, J. (Winter, 1980). "An Experimental Study of the Effects of Competition on the Self-Concept." *Adolescence*, 15, 799–806.

Gecas, V., and Pasley, K. (December, 1983). "Birth Order and Self-Concept in Adolescence." *Journal of Youth and Adolescence*, 12, 521–533.

Gecas, V., and Schwalbe, M. L. (1986). "Parental Behavior and Adolescent Self-Esteem." *Journal of Marriage and the Family*, 48, 37–46.

Graybill, D. (September, 1978). "Relationship of Maternal Child-Rearing Behaviors to Children's Self-Esteem." *Journal of Psychology*, 100, 45–47.

Griffin, N., Chassin, L., and Young, R. D. (Spring, 1981). "Measurement of Global Self-Concept versus Multiple Role-Specific Self-Concepts in Adolescents." *Adolescence*, 16, 49–56.

Hamachek, D. E. (1985). "The Self's Development and Ego Growth: Conceptual Analysis and Implications for Counselors." *Journal of Counseling and Development*, 64, 136–142.

Handel, A. (December, 1980). "Perceived Change of Self among Adolescents." *Journal of Youth and Adolescence*, 9, 507–519.

Hilgard, E. R. (1949). "Human Motives and the Concept of Self." *American Psychologist*, 4, 374–382.

Hjorth, C. W. (April, 1982). "The Self-Image of Physically Abused Adolescents." *Journal of Youth and Adolescence*, 11, 71–76.

Hodgson, J. W., and Fischer, J. L. (December, 1978). "Sex Differences in Identity and Intimacy Development in College Youth." *Journal of Youth and Adolescence*, 7, 371–392.

Hoelter, J., and Harper, L. (1987). "Structural and Interpersonal Family Influences on Adolescent Self-Conception." *Journal of Marriage and the Family*, 49, 129–139.

Hogan, H. W., and McWilliams, J. M. (September, 1978). "Factors Related to Self-Actualization." *Journal of Psychology*, 100, 117–122.

Horn, M. E., and Rudolph, L. B. (1987). "An Investigation of Verbal Inter-Action, Knowledge of Sexual Behavior and Self-Concept in Adolescent Mothers." *Adolescence*, 87, 591–598.

Ishiyama, F. I. (Winter, 1984). "Shyness: Anxious Social Sensitivity and Self-Isolating Tendency." *Adolescence*, 19, 903–911.

James, William. (1890). *The Principles of Psychology*. New York: Holt.

Johnsen, K. P., and Medley, M. L. (September, 1978). "Academic Self-Concept among Black High School Seniors: An Examination of Perceived Agreement with Selected Others." *Phylon*, 39, 264–274.

Kaplan, H. B. (March, 1977). "Increase in Self-Rejection and Continuing/Discontinued Deviant Response." *Journal of Youth and Adolescence*, 6, 77–87.

———. (September, 1978). "Deviant Behavior and Self-Enhancement in Adolescence." *Journal of Youth and Adolescence*, 7, 253–277.

Koenig, L. J. (1988). "Self-Image of Emotionally Disturbed Adolescents." *Journal of Abnormal Child Psychology*, 16, 111–126.

Kroger, J. A. (Winter, 1980). "Residential Mobility and Self Concept in Adolescence." *Adolescence*, 15, 967–977.

Krueger, R., and Hansen, J. C. (1987). "Self-Concept Changes During Youth-Home Placement of Adolescents." *Adolescence*, 86, 385–392.

Landon, G., Rosenfeld, R., Northcraft, G., and Lewiston, N. (December, 1980). "Self-Image of Adolescents with Cystic Fibrosis." *Journal of Youth and Adolescence*, 9, 521–528.

Lund, N. L., and Salary, H. M. (Spring, 1980). "Measured Self-Concept in Adjudicated Juvenile Offenders." *Adolescence*, 15, 65–74.

Manaster, G. J., et al. (Winter, 1977). "The Ideal Self and Cognitive Development in Adolescence." *Adolescence*, 12, 547–558.

Nye, F. I. (1957). "Child Adjustment in Broken and in Unhappy Unbroken Homes." *Marriage and Family Living*, 19, 356–361.

Offer, D., et al. (September, 1977). "The Self-Image of Adolescents: A Study of Four Cultures." *Journal of Youth and Adolescence*, 6, 265–280.

Offer, D., Ostrov, E., and Howard, K. I. (August, 1982). "Family Perceptions of Adolescent Self-Image." *Journal of Youth and Adolescence*, 11, 281–291.

Okum, M. A., and Sasfy, J. H. (Fall, 1977). "Adolescence; the Self-Concept, and Formal Operations." *Adolescence*, 12, 373–379.

Openshaw, D. K., Thomas, D. L., and Rollins, B. C. (Summer, 1983). "Socialization and Adolescent Self-Esteem: Symbolic Interaction and Social Learning Explanations." *Adolescence*, 18, 317–329.

Padin, M. A., Lerner, R. M., and Spiro, A., III. (Summer, 1981). "Stability of Body Attitudes and Self-Esteem in Late Adolescents." *Adolescence*, 16, 271–384.

Parish, J. G., and Parish, T. S. (Fall, 1983). "Children's Self-Concepts as Related to Family Structure and Family Concept." *Adolescence*, 18, 649–658.

Parish, T. S., and Dostal, J. W. (August, 1980). "Evaluations of Self and Parent Figures by Children from Intact, Divorced, and Reconstituted Families." *Journal of Youth and Adolescence*, 9, 347–351.

Parish, T. S., and Taylor, J. C. (December, 1979). "The Impact of Divorce and Subsequent Father Absence on Children's and Adolescents' Self-Concepts." *Journal of Youth and Adolescence*, 8, 427–432.

Patten, M. A. (Winter, 1981). "Self Concept and Self Esteem: Factors in Adolescent Pregnancy." *Adolescence*, 16, 765–778.

Paul, M. J., and Fischer, J. L. (April, 1980). "Correlates of Self-Concept among Black Early Adolescents." *Journal of Youth and Adolescence*, 9, 163–173.

Petersen, A. C., and Kellam, S. G. (September, 1977). "Measurement of the Psychological Well-Being of Adolescents: The Psychometric Properties and Assessment Procedures of the How I Feel." *Journal of Youth and Adolescence*, 6, 229–247.

Pomerantz, S. C. (March, 1979). "Sex Differences in the Relative Importance of Self-Esteem, Physical Self-Satisfaction, and Identity in Predicting Adolescent Satisfaction." *Journal of Youth and Adolescence*, 8, 51–61.

Protinsky, H., and Farrier, S. (Winter, 1980). "Self-Image Changes in Pre-Adolescents and Adolescents." *Adolescence*, 15, 887–893.

Raschke, H. J., and Raschke, V. J. (May, 1979). "Family Conflict and Children's Self-Concepts: A Comparison of Intact and Single-Parent Families." *Journal of Marriage and the Family*, 41, 367–374.

Reardon, B., and Griffing, P. (Spring, 1983). "Factors Related to the Self-Concept of Institutionalized, White, Male, Adolescent Drug Abusers." *Adolescence*, 18, 29–41.

Richman, C. L., Clark, M. L., and Brown, K. P. (1985). "General and Specific Self-Esteem in Late Adolescent Students: Race × Gender × SES Effects." *Adolescence*, 20, 555–566.

Rogers, C. R. (1961). *On Becoming a Person: A Therapist's View of Psychotherapy.* Boston: Houghton Mifflin.

Rosenberg, F. R., and Rosenberg, M. (September, 1978). "Self-Esteem and Delinquency," *Journal of Youth and Adolescence*, 7, 279–291.

Rosenberg, M., and Simmons, R. G. (1972). "Black and White Self-Esteem: The Urban School Child." American Sociological Association Monograph Series. Washington, D.C.

Rosenthal, D. A., Moore, S. M., and Taylor, M. J. (April, 1983). "Ethnicity and Adjustment: A Study of the Self-Image of Anglo-, Greek-, and Italian-Australian Working Class Adolescents." *Journal of Youth and Adolescence*, 12, 117–135.

Rotherarm, M. J., and Armstrong, M. (Summer, 1980). "Assertiveness Training with High School Students." *Adolescence*, 15, 267–276.

Rust, J. O., and McCraw, A. (Summer, 1984). "Influence of Masculinity-Femininity on Adolescent Self-Esteem and Peer Acceptance." *Adolescence*, 19, 357–366.

St. Clair, S., and Day, H. D. (September, 1979). "Ego Identity Status and Values among High School Females," *Journal of Youth and Adolescence*, 8, 317–326.

Schiff, E., and Koopman, E. J. (March, 1978). "The Relationship of Women's Sex-Role Identity to Self-Esteem and Ego Development." *Journal of Psychology*, 98, 299–305.

Simmons, R. G., et al. (October, 1978). "Self-Esteem and Achievement of Black and White Adolescents." *Social Problems*, 26, 86–96.

Stake, J. E., DeVille, C. J., and Pennell, C. L. (October, 1983). "The Effects of Assertive Training on the Performance Self-Esteem of Adolescent Girls." *Journal of Youth and Adolescence*, 12, 435–442.

Steelman, L. C. (February, 1985). "The Social and Academic Consequences of Birth Order: Real, Artifactual, or Both?" *Journal of Marriage and the Family*, 47, 117–124.

Stefanko, M., (Spring, 1984). "Trends in Adolescent Research: A Review of Articles Published in Adolescence—1976–1981." *Adolescence*, 19, 1–14.

Strang, R. (1957). "The Adolescent Views Himself. New York: McGraw-Hill.

Strathe, M., and Hash, V. (Spring, 1979). "The Effect of an Alternative School in Adolescent Self-Esteem." *Adolescence*, 14, 185–189.

Street, S. (1988). "Feedback and Self-Concept in High School Students." *Adolescence*, 23, 449–456.

Streetman, L. G. (1987). "Contrasts in Self-Esteem of Unwed Teenage Mothers." *Adolescence*, 23, 459–464.

Tierno, M. J. (Fall, 1983). "Responding to Self-Concept Disturbance among Early Adolescents: A Psychosocial View for Educators." *Adolescence*, 18, 577–584.

Waksman, S. A. (Spring, 1984a). "Assertion Training with Adolescents." *Adolescence*, 73, 123–130.

——— . (Summer, 1984b). "A Controlled Evaluation of Assertion Training with Adolescents." *Adolescence*, 19, 277–282.

Wehr, S. H., and Kaufman, M. E. (1987). "The Effects of Assertive Training on Performance in Highly Anxious Adolescents." *Adolescence*, 85, 195–205.

West, C. K., Jones, P. A., and McConahay, G. (Fall, 1981). "Who Does What to the Adolescent in the High School: Relationships among Resulting Affect and Self-Concept and Achievement." *Adolescence*, 16, 657–661.

Zimbardo, P. G. (June, 1978). "Misunderstanding Shyness: The Counterattack." *Psychology Today*, 17ff.

CHAPTER
9

Emotional Disorders

A wide variety of human emotions—joy, love, affection, fear, anxiety, anger, and hostility—are found in various degrees in all people. From one point of view, the only factors distinguishing so-called normal from abnormal emotions are the degree and frequency with which these feelings are inhibited or expressed. It is common to be anxious under some circumstances, but when anxiety becomes constant and all-consuming, completely dominating a person's life, it is not usual or healthy. Most people can express love and affection; when a person cannot, the condition must be considered atypical of the usual emotional response. Similarly, all people feel some anger and hostility, but when these become so intense that they result in the destruction of self or others, they become problem behavior.

This chapter is concerned with some selected emotional disturbances found in adolescents:

Mood disorders: The discussion will focus on depression.
Anxiety disorders: Three types of illnesses under this category will be discussed: *generalized anxiety disorder, obsessive-compulsive disorder,* and *phobic disorders.*
Disorders of impulse control: Special attention will be given to *pyromania,* the compulsion to set fires.
Psychological factors affecting physical condition.
Somatoform disorders: Special attention will be given to *conversion disorder* (hysterical neurosis, conversion type).
Eating disorders: Two major types of illnesses will be discussed: *anorexia nervosa* and *bulimia.*
Schizophrenic disorders: Various manifestations in adolescents will be discussed.

DEPRESSION

▇ Characteristics

depression **Depression** *is characterized by feelings of sadness, despair, melancholia, listlessness, and a reduction of mental activity and physical drive* (Stehouwer, Bultsma, and Blackford, 1985). The depression may be caused by biological factors including genetic predisposition. It may be accompanied by one or more physical complaints such as gastrointestinal disturbances, with the person preoccupied with hypochondriasis. Depressed adolescents may complain frequently of fatigue, being excessively tired upon wakening in the morning after an adequate amount of sleep. They may describe feelings of emptiness, isolation, and alienation. They usually show deficits in social and cognitive functioning (Altmann and Gotlib, 1988; Deal and Williams, 1988; Slotkin, et al., 1988) and in their self-image (Koenig, 1988). They often complain of difficulty in concentrating in school. In fact, bright students who fail are frequently suffering from anxiety and/or depression, with these two frequently found together (Strauss, et al., 1987). If they try to improve, without result, they may spend long hours going to the movies, watching television, or just wasting time. Depressed adolescents may show suicidal tendencies and in some cases actually attempt suicide. Some succeed.

Acute Depression

Emery (1983) describes different syndromes of depression in adolescents. The first is *acute depression*, meaning serious but the course is reversible. Adolescents may complain of boredom and social isolation and actually spend less time interacting with peers, siblings, and parents. They may cry easily and daydream a lot (Siegel and Griffin, 1983). The episode usually lasts a fairly short time. It may be brought on by physical illness or problems, trouble with the law, trouble at school or with drugs, loss of intimate relationships, or inadequate family relationships.

Chronic Depression

Chronic depression is more severe. The adolescent has usually experienced repeated rejection, severe emotional trauma, or a loss of love, either of a family member or a friend. He or she is weary of the world and often not able to perform ordinary tasks. The depressed mood may be evident for years and be accompanied by psychotic features and melancholia (loss of pleasure in almost everything).

Masked Depression

Masked depression is more difficult to recognize. The adolescent is depressed but in an effort to escape or deny depression may become overactive and engage in various types of acting-out behavior. Sexual promiscuity, especially in females, is often a disguised attempt to avoid feelings of depression and loneliness. Continually dating, going out, and engaging in a constant round of social activities may be an attempt to escape depression. Other adolescents abuse drugs or are in trouble with the law. Restlessness and anger are frequently present (Maag, Rutherford, and Parks, 1988).

ANXIETY DISORDERS

Generalized Anxiety Disorder

Anxiety as an alerting response to internal or external dangers is not an illness. But when the anxiety becomes so pervasive and tenacious that it interferes with continued functioning of the personality, it is a neurotic illness. Neurotic anxiety is far more severe than most people experience, but it can be felt in even the most routine circumstances. Adolescents suffering from **generalized anxiety disorder** tend to make an enormous catastrophe out of the smallest mishap and believe that the perceived catastrophe exists. People in this state cannot see the facts in the situation; therefore it is impossible to reason them out of their feelings. Such internal anxiety may be accompanied by feelings of inferiority, sleep disturbances, nervousness, shaking and trembling, sweating, tearfulness, somatic complaints such as respiratory or digestive disturbances, dizziness, or an increase in psychomotor activity to try to escape or cover up the fear. It may also manifest itself in behavior disturbances.

generalized anxiety disorder

John, a boy of sixteen who had made straight A's in grade ten and D's and E's in grade eleven, was referred to a psychiatrist because he missed 120 class periods in one semester. He said, "I know my parents want me to do well and last year that was enough, but now I hassle with them all the time; particularly my mother. I want to go into a profession, but this worries me; and I can't get my head together enough to do any work." (Miller, 1974, p. 345)

In this case, John lost two teachers that he especially liked when he started grade 11. He neither knew nor liked any of the new teachers to whom he was assigned. Because he was insecure anyhow, this episode was enough to stimulate intense anxiety, which he tried to get away from by skipping school.

Obsessive-Compulsive Disorder

obsessive-compulsive disorder

Obsessive-compulsive disorder is an anxiety state characterized by obsessive thoughts or overwhelming urges to engage in repetitive behavior. Obsessions and compulsions often develop from traumatic experiences that may have been only partly suppressed. Children try to forget about a disturbance by engaging in some type of distracting behavior. For example, to relieve tension, they go outdoors and concentrate on stepping on each crack in the sidewalk. The traumatic experience passes, but thereafter, each time they feel tense, they experience a compulsion to step on the cracks of the sidewalks. They have long since forgotten the incident, but the compulsion remains.

Obsessions may include obsessive thoughts or rituals. One girl forced her family to shower outside in the freezing cold to avoid contamination of the house. Another youngster forced his mother to spend hours rubbing "imaginary" dirt off door knobs, while another forced his father to start every car journey from the beginning each time their car was overtaken from the left!

Obsessional ideas are often dramatic and bizarre. A 13-year-old girl had an image of the Holy Being's penis that constantly intruded her mind. When her male therapist attempted a thought-stopping technique to alleviate the obsession, she then became obsessed with the image of the therapist's penis! Another felt that his eyes were being "destroyed" and had to touch them continuously. Many of these adolescents are so perfectionistic that they cannot do their school work for fear of making mistakes (Apter and Tyano, 1988, p. 187).

Phobic Disorders

phobia

A **phobia** is an excessive, uncontrolled fear that usually develops during childhood through exposure to severe, traumatic episodes that children subsequently repress in memory. The episode passes, but the phobia remains. A phobia may develop out of reaction to fear or guilt. The *Diagnostic and Statistical Manual of Mental Disorders* III-R (American Psychiatric Association, 1987) divides phobias into three categories: (1) *simple phobias*, (2) *social phobias*, and (3) *agoraphobia*. Simple phobias, or anxiety states, include *musophobia*, fear of dirt or contamination, which may result in excessive cleanliness or constant and repeated washing. It may have originated because of fear and guilt. For example, adolescents who feel guilty about masturbation and therefore

HIGHLIGHT   Types of Phobias

NAME	OBJECT OR SITUATION FEARED
Acrophobia	Heights
Agoraphobia	Open places
Algophobia	Pain
Anthophobia	Flowers
Astraphobia	Storms, thunder, lightning
Cardiophobia	Heart attack
Claustrophobia	Enclosed spaces or confinement
Cyberphobia	Computers
Decidophobia	Making decisions
Ergophobia	Work
Gephydrophobia	Crossing bridges
Hematophobia	Blood
Hydrophobia	Water
Iatrophobia	Doctors
Lalophobia	Public speaking
Monophobia	Being alone
Mysophobia	Contamination or germs
Nyctophobia	Darkness
Ochlophobia	Crowds
Ombrophobia	Rain
Pathophobia	Disease
Peccatophobia	Sinning
Phobophobia	Fear
Photophobia	Light
Pyrophobia	Fire
Syphilophobia	Syphilis
Taphophobia	Being buried alive
Thanatophobia	Death
Toxophobia	Being poisoned
Trichophobia	Hair
Xenophobia	Strangers
Zoophobia	Animals (usually a specific kind)

wash their hands whenever they have the urge are symbolically eliminating the desire or the effect. Other simple phobias are *acrophobia* (fear of high places) and *claustrophobia* (fear of closed places).

Social phobias are characterized by extreme fears of social interactions, particularly those with strangers and those where the person might be evaluated negatively, such as on a job interview or a first date. Because this kind of phobia limits social interaction, it disrupts an individual's life. One such fear is *homilopho-bia* (fear that other people may find something wrong with one's appearance, attire, or demeanor).

Agoraphobia is the most handicapping of all phobias. It means literally "fear of open spaces" and involves an intense fear of leaving one's home or other familiar places. In extreme cases, the adolescent is bound to his or her home, never daring to leave. In other cases, the adolescent will leave home but refuses to venture to selected public places.

DISORDERS OF IMPULSE CONTROL

disorders of impulse control

Disorders of impulse control take many forms. The urge to steal (*kleptomania*) is one example. One common and serious compulsion is *pyromania*, the urge to set fires. It is serious because arson is a criminal offense, yet many thousands of such fires are set each year.

> Joan S. was a sophomore in college at the time she began to set fires in her dorm. The first fire was set in a room down the hall, the second—a week later—was set in a room across from hers. By this time, fire insurance personnel were deeply involved in investigating to see who was starting the fires. The next day Joan set fire to her own room, after carefully removing some of her best clothes from her closet. A lie detector test administered routinely to all dorm residents pointed to Joan as the culprit. She didn't know why she set the fires, was sorry that she did, and was referred to a psychiatrist for diagnosis and treatment (Author's counseling notes).

Not all adolescents who set fires are pyromaniacs. Some do it out of boredom and the need for excitement. These youths are likely to torch objects and structures that appear safe to burn. They do not want to hurt anyone (Wooden, 1985). Setting hay fields or empty buildings on fire in these instances becomes a means of generating excitement. True pyromaniacs, however, act compulsively, and sometimes impulsively, out of neurotic need. They usually have a history of fire starting from the time they were youngsters. Most have sexual conflicts or problems they are trying to resolve. Others suffer from acute anxiety, rejection, or conflict with parents. Some are psychotic. Others set fires as a means of attracting attention because of feelings of rejection or inferiority. Setting a fire becomes a means of being destroyed or of destroying. It is an act of momentary awesome power for an individual who feels impotent, helpless, or victimized. An act of arson renders others trapped or helpless (Bartholomew, 1987). Those who set fires to their own houses usually do so out of anger, resentment, or hostility toward parents or siblings who have withheld love or attention or who have mistreated or misunderstood them. Although they have no desire really to injure anyone, their actions are nevertheless deep-seated expressions of negative emotions. Often the adolescent puts the fire out himself or herself, calls the fire station, or is the one who "discovers" the fire. Many adolescent fire starters take out their hostility on school property. School-related fires accounted for 14 percent of fires in one study (Wooden, 1985).

PSYCHOLOGICAL FACTORS AFFECTING PHYSICAL CONDITION

Psychological factors affecting physical condition are also called psychosomatic reactions. A number of psychosomatic disorders come from persistent upset, fear, or rage, though the emotional condition is not labeled as a particular neurosis or psychosis. Asthma, hay fever, eczema, ulcers, headaches, and many other physical difficulties sometimes have an emotional origin (Choquet and Menke, 1987).

psychological factors affecting physical condition

The American Psychological Association has classified ten types of psychosomatic reactions according to the organs or systems of the body affected (Lambert et al., 1972, p. 148):

1. *Skin reactions:* Some types of eczema, acne, hives.
2. *Musculoskeletal reactions:* Backache, arthritis, rheumatism (due to functional causes).
3. *Respiratory reactions:* Asthma, hay fever, bronchitis.
4. *Cardiovascular reactions:* High blood pressure, migraine headaches, palpitation of the heart.
5. *Blood and lymphatic reactions.*
6. *Gastrointestinal reactions:* Ulcers, colitis, constipation, hyperacidity.
7. *Genitourinary reactions:* Menstrual disturbances, painful urination, vaginal contractions.
8. *Endocrine reactions:* Glandular disturbances, obesity, hyperthyroidism.
9. *Nervous system reactions:* Anxiety, fatigue, convulsions.
10. *Sense organ reactions:* Quite varied.

SOMATOFORM DISORDERS

Somatoform disorders *are those in which the individual experiences symptoms of physical health problems that have psychological rather than physical causes. One such disorder is* **conversion disorder,** in which anxiety or upset becomes so severe that it results in physical symptoms such as temporary blindness or paralysis. The illness is usually the result of one or more emotionally charged life situations with which the person finds difficulty coping. The unconscious conflict produces malfunctioning of one of the special senses or of the voluntary nervous system, such as temporary blindness or paralysis.

somatoform disorders

conversion disorder

A 13-year-old black girl was evaluated by pediatrics for lower extremity weakness and for "strange spells." The girl's spells had occurred about five times over a 4-year period. She described the spells as numbness of left side of body, difficulty in breathing, shaking of her body, and brief loss of consciousness. She also had auditory and visual hallucinations of dead family members who had advised her to be "good."

Her family history was tragic: the mother had died after the girl was born, 4 siblings had been burned to death, the father had died of a heart attack one year before, and the grandmother had died of cancer 6 months before. The girl was living with her great aunt at the time she was being evaluated. The girl's first spell occurred after the fire that killed her siblings, with recurrences taking place at times of tragedy or when she thought about the deaths of her family. (Simonds, 1975, p. 176)

EATING DISORDERS

Anorexia Nervosa

anorexia nervosa

Anorexia nervosa *is a life-threatening emotional disorder characterized by an obsession with food and weight* (Gilbert and DeBlassie, 1984). It is sometimes referred to as the "starvation sickness" or "dieter's disease." The major symptoms are a constant preoccupation with food and dieting, body image disturbances (Mallick, Whipple, and Huerta, 1987; Muuss, 1985), excess weight loss (15 percent or more of body weight), amenorrhea (cessation of menstrual period), hyperactivity (excessive exercise), extreme moodiness, social isolation, and strong feelings of insecurity, inadequacy, helplessness, depression, and loneliness (American Psychiatric Association, 1987). It is associated with numerous medical conditions: slow heart beat, cardiac arrest (a frequent cause of death), low blood pressure, dehydration, hypothermia, electrolyte abnormalities, metabolic changes, constipation, and abdominal distress. The anorexic feels cold, even in warm weather. The body grows fine silky hair to conserve body heat. A potassium deficiency may cause malfunction of the kidneys (Muuss, 1985).

Once the illness has progressed, anorexics become thin and emaciated in appearance. Treichel (1982) also found brain abnormalities coupled with impaired mental performance and lessened reaction time and perceptual speed due to malnutrition.

Between 5 and 10 percent of anorexics die because of medical problems associated with malnutrition. Their obsession with dieting is combined with a compulsion to exercise, which leads to social isolation and withdrawal from family and friends. Hunger and fatigue are usually denied, and any attempt to interfere with the regime is angrily resisted. Anorexics are very hard to treat (Grant and Fodor, 1984).

Anorexia is rare among males (Svec, 1987). Ninety-five percent of anorexics are females, usually between ages twelve to eighteen. The disorder has become more common and now affects about 1 percent of adolescent females. It has been showing up lately among all economic classes and wider age groups. Some believe that more than half a million people are anorexic (Seligman and Zaborsky, 1983). This is due partly to intense pressure in the culture to be thin. The current generation has developed an intense dislike of body fat. Anorexics seem to be perfectionists and are especially weight sensitive (Van den Broucke and Vandereyken, 1986). Davis, Best, and Hawkings (1981) found that dieting concern appeared as early as the fourth grade and was related to a negative physical self-image, particularly in girls. Subjects who were more obese were the most concerned with weight and dieting and reported more dissatisfaction with their physical appearance. At each age level, girls expressed more dieting concern and revealed more negative self-images than boys since femininity was associated with slimness (Grant and Fodor, 1984).

Anorexia nervosa is a life-threatening emotional disorder that is characterized by an obsession with food and weight. (© Susan Rosenberg/ Photo Researchers, Inc.)

The fact that anorexia nervosa appears at puberty after the development of sexual characteristics suggests that sexual conflict is a central issue in the illness (Romeo, 1984). Apparently anxiety develops over feminine physiological changes. The girl's developing body symbolically demands coming to terms with her female sexual identification. She has the task of integrating her new body image with her concept of female sexual roles. If she cannot accept her female sexual identity, she seeks to repress her development and regresses physically to a stage of prepubertal development. In fact, this is what happens. She distorts her body image through extreme weight loss and takes on a slim, masculine appearance. She may become severely emaciated in appearance, removing all outward signs of her secondary sex characteristics. In addition, she stops menstruation (Jenkins, 1987). These efforts represent a desperate attempt to halt her sexual development. Instead of progressing forward through adolescence, she follows a pathological deviation and regresses to a prepubertal stage of development (Romeo, 1984).

Piazza, Rollins, and Lewis (1983) have emphasized that anorexics have a pervasive sense of inadequacy and distorted body images that often lead to depression. They have low self-esteem reflecting negative attitudes about physical attractiveness (Baird and Sights, 1986; Grant and Fodor, 1986). Hooker and Convisser (1983) explain that they tend to separate their bodies from their person: "I see my body as something that drags along behind me." This split into a mind-body dichotomy is so complete that they literally do not know how they look.

They rarely look at themselves and even when forced to rarely perceive their body image accurately. They view their bodies with disgust, which is a projection of how they actually feel about themselves.

Anorexics often have disturbed relationships with their parents (Eisele, Hertsgaard, and Light, 1986). The families are often rigid and overprotective with a hypochondriacal concern for the child's health (Brone and Fisher, 1988). Often a power struggle develops between the adolescent girl and her parents, particularly with her mother (Goldstein, 1981; Levin et al., 1983, p. 54). This desire to guide and control becomes more evident as parental concern grows. The more the parents try to change the pattern, the more intense the power struggle becomes. The adolescent girl puts up a desperate fight against feeling enslaved and exploited and against not being permitted to feel competent to lead a life of her own. In this struggle for identity and a sense of inadequacy, she will not accept anything that parents or others have to offer and would rather starve to death than continue a life of accommodation. At the same time, anorexics are unsure of themselves, are self-critical, and are concerned that no one knows or cares what they are really like, so they experience loneliness in spite of the best efforts of family and friends (Gilbert and DeBlassie, 1984).

There are various forms of treatment for anorexia nervosa. Medical treatment monitors the physical condition of the anorexic and tries to get her weight back in the safe range. Behavior modification uses rewards and deprivation, contingent on eating behavior and weight gain. It may be successful in achieving weight gain but does not come to grips with more severe psychological problems. Family therapy seeks to solve underlying family interaction problems and to improve relationships with the anorexic. Individual psychodynamic approaches strive to help the individual resolve her emotional conflicts. Probably the most effective treatment combines medical and psychological approaches. The goals are to eliminate the anorexic symptoms and to enable the patient to feel and act like an independent person who likes herself, is confident about her capabilities, and is in control of her life. Accomplishing these goals may require long-term therapy (Gilbert and DeBlassie, 1984).

Bulimia

bulimia   **Bulimia** is a *binge-purge syndrome*. The name comes from the Greek *bous limos*, which means "ox hunger" (Ieit, 1985). It was first identified by Marlene Boskind-Lodale (1978). The first cases of bulimia that appeared in the literature were in connection with anorexia nervosa (Casper, 1983). Some clinicians diagnosed bulimia as a subgroup of anorexia (Garfinkel, Moldofsky, and Gardner, 1980). However, since binge eating occurred in both obese and normal weight individuals, bulimia was designated a separate eating disorder (American Psychiatric Association, 1987).

Bulimia is characterized by a compulsive and rapid consumption of large quantities of high calorie food in a short period of time. One study of the frequency and duration of binging episodes among bulimic clients in an outpatient setting revealed an average of 13.7 hours spent in binge eating each week, with a range of 15 minutes to 8 hours for each episode (Mitchell, Pyle, and Eckert, 1981). Binging and purging may occur many times daily. Caloric consumption ranged

HIGHLIGHT　Five Theories about Causes of Anorexia

Social theory. Anorexics are brainwashed by a culture that emphasizes being slim so they become obsessed with foods and diets.

Psychosexual theory. The anorexic is unwilling to accept her role as a woman and her feminine sexuality. She fears sexual intimacy so she uses the disorder to delay or regress her psychosexual development.

Family systems theory. The anorexic comes from a superficially good family that is overprotective, rigid, and poor problem solvers who avoid conflict. This interferes with the adolescent's identity formation.

Biological theory. A disturbance in the hypothalamus triggers anorexic behavior.

Psychobiologic regression hypothesis. Once body weight drops below a critical level because of inadequate diet, neuroendocrine functions are impaired, which reverses the developmental changes of puberty. The girl regresses to a prepubertal stage of development (Muuss, 1985, pp. 526, 527).

from 1,200 to 11,500 calories per episode, with carbohydrates as the primary food. Many clients reported losing the ability to perceive a sense of fullness. Episodes took place secretly, usually in the afternoon or evening and some at night. Induced vomiting was the usual aftermath of the binge-eating episodes. Other bulimics used laxatives, diuretics, enemas, amphetamines, compulsive exercising or fasting to offset the huge food intake (Leclair and Berkowitz, 1983).

The bulimic feels driven to consume food and, because of a concern about body size, to purge afterward. Binges usually follow periods of stress and are accompanied by anxiety, depressed mood, and self-deprecating thoughts during and after the episode (Ieit, 1985). The most usual victims are college-age females, or those in the early 20s (Lachenmeyer and Muni-Brander, 1988), although the pattern is becoming more common in high school females (Johnson et al., 1984; Van Thorre and Vogel, 1985). Females of any racial or ethnic group may become bulimic. Males occasionally become bulimic (Folkenberg, 1984). Bulimics consider their behavior abnormal and are embarrassed by it. As a result, they become socially isolated, though they may long for companionship (Leclair and Berkowitz, 1983).

Bulimics have been described as having higher than normal impulsivity (Pyle, Mitchell, and Eckert, 1981). They are sometimes kleptomaniacs, commonly stealing food (Van Thorre and Vogel, 1985). They frequently have strong moral beliefs and are anxious, depressed, and with low self-esteem (Baird and Sights, 1986, Brouwers, 1988). They wish to be perfect yet have a poor self-image, negative self-worth, are shy, and lack assertiveness (Holleran, Pascale, and Fraley, 1988). They are often preoccupied with fear of rejection in sexual relationships and with not being attractive enough to please a man (Van Thorre and Vogel, 1985). They have traditional and exaggerated concepts of femininity that describe the ideal woman

HIGHLIGHT   A Student's Binge-Purge Behavior

The first vomiting period perpetuated itself into a five-year-long habit in which I had daily planned and unplanned binges and self-induced vomiting sessions up to four times daily. I frequently vomited each of the day's three meals as well as my afternoon "snack" of three or four hamburgers, four to five enormous bowls of ice cream, dozens of cookies, bags of various potato chips, packs of Swiss cheese, two large helpings of french fries, at least two milkshakes, and to top it off, an apple or banana followed by two or more pints of cold milk to help me vomit more easily.

During the night, I sneaked back into the kitchen in the dark so I would not risk awakening any family member by turning on a light. . . . Every night I wished that I could, like everyone else, eat one apple as a midnight snack and then stop. However, every night I failed, but continuously succeeded in consuming countless bowls of various cereals, ice cream sundaes, peanut butter and jelly sandwiches,

bananas, potato chips, Triscuits, peanuts, Oreos, orange juice and chocolate chip cookies. Then I tiptoed to the bathroom to empty myself. Sometimes the food did not come up as quickly as I wanted; so, in panic, I rammed my fingers wildly down my throat, occasionally making it bleed from cutting it with my fingernails. Sometimes I would spend two hours in the bathroom trying to vomit, yet there were other nights when the food came up in less than three minutes. I always felt immensely relieved and temporarily peaceful after I had thrown up. There was a symbolic sense of emptying out the anxiety, loneliness and depression inside of me, as well as a sense of rebellion to hurt my body, to throw up on the people who hurt me, so to speak (Muuss, 1986, p. 261).

From: Muuss, R. E. (1986). "Adolescent Eating Disorder: Bulimia." *Adolescence*, 22: 257–267.

as accommodating, passive, and dependent. Although many bulimic women are successful in careers, this apparent competence is deceptive. Their need for dependency is not expressed in obvious ways. They appear competent and perfectionistic, but their overriding motivation is the desire for approval (Leclair and Berkowitz, 1983). Because of unrealistic standards and the drive for perfection, pressure builds up, which is relieved through lapses of control during binge-purge episodes. This is followed by feelings of shame and guilt, which contribute to the sense of low self-esteem and depression (Pyle, Mitchell, and Eckert, 1981). They are often difficult to treat because they resist seeking help or they sabotage treatment.

The family situations of bulimics are similar to those of anorexics. Many of the families demonstrate the characteristics of enmeshment, overprotectiveness, perfectionism, and rigidity. They place a great deal of emphasis on attractiveness, physical fitness, achievement, and success (Roberto, 1986). The families may be isolated, conscious of appearance, and attentive to the special meaning of food and eating. The family is likely to be overtly conflictual (Schwartz, 1987), hostile, controlling, and neglectful (Humphrey and Stern, 1988). Like substance-abuse families, members seem to have trouble controlling impulses and appetite.

SCHIZOPHRENIC DISORDERS

One way of adjusting to disturbing situations is to withdraw, retreat, or escape from them. Sometimes the withdrawal is harmless and helpful: college students drop a course they do not need in which they are doing poorly. At other times adolescents find life and circumstances so unpleasant and unbearable that they withdraw completely into an imaginary world of their own making or choosing. In its extreme form, such withdrawal becomes one of the most common psychoses of adolescence: **schizophrenia.** The high-risk for the onset of the illness begins at seventeen years (Holzman and Grinker, 1974).

schizophrenia

There are various degrees of withdrawal between dropping a course and schizophrenia, in which the withdrawal is only partial but nevertheless effective in providing temporary relief. Adolescents withdraw by isolating themselves from social groups or through alcohol, drugs, or sleep. They withdraw by dropping out of school, or they seek to escape through athletics, an overactive social life, staying away from home, or promiscuous sex. Becoming preoccupied with school work to the exclusion of any close friendships or leisure-time activities is a form of escape.

Many schizophrenics present a family history of such disorders. This may be due to a genetic predisposition to schizophrenia. Gottesman and Schields (1982) found that when one of a set of identical twins has schizophrenia the risk of both twins having it was 46 percent, whereas the risk for fraternal twins was only 14 percent. In addition to genetic factors, there is a biochemical cause of schizophrenia. Schizophrenics seem to be particularly sensitive to the action of *dopamine*, which is a neurochemical transmitter that speeds nerve transmission. In schizophrenics, the rapid speed of transmission between neurons or nerve cells causes incoherent, bizarre behavior. Administering drugs called *phenothiazines* inhibits the effect of dopamine on nerve transmission and is one of the most effective treatments for the illness (Uhr, Stahl, and Berger, 1984).

One environmental cause of schizophrenia in adolescents is rejection at home while growing up. Typically the children grow up in families where the father is a weak figure. Many times the children have been unplanned and unwanted. Studies of characteristics of adolescents who become schizophrenic reveal that they tend to be social isolates; they show less social interest in others, group activities, or athletics. They evidence a high degree of social incompetence, exhibit few leadership skills, and are submissive, anxious, dependent, and careless. Thus, they could be characterized as shut-in, withdrawn personality types. Many show deviant antisocial behavior such as aggression and incorrigibility (Silverton, Harrington, and Mednick, 1987).

Schizophrenic adolescents also evidence excessive dependency on parents and on staff and hospital personnel during treatment. In early childhood many have had some infectious illnesses, more physical handicaps, a greater number of eating and sleeping disturbances, slower motor development and physical coordination, and delayed development of speech. During early childhood, also, their social isolation is evident. They achieve less in school and in their jobs as adults than one would expect on the basis of their intellectual levels (Grinker and Holzman, 1973; Weiner, 1980).

Some of these adolescents have rejecting parents, though the manifestations of rejection vary. Some parents are hostile; others are overprotective. Some are perfectionists. The effect of the hostile perfectionist on the adolescent is damaging. Such a parent is cold, hard, severe, rigid, domineering, and ambitious.

There are various manifestations of schizophrenia. The *disorganized type* often acts silly, laughs or smiles without provocation, shows fleeting hallucinations and fantastic delusions that have little meaning, or engages in symbolic, repetitive motions. The *catatonic type* manifests disturbance of motor function (Lidz, 1974). He or she may remain muscularly rigid in one position or refuse to talk, fearful that any movement may have devastating consequences on the world (Lidz, 1974). In an overexcited phase, this type may destroy property or injure others. The *paranoid type* evidences delusions of grandeur or of persecution and may have upsetting hallucinations. This type may believe he or she is Jesus Christ or an agent of the CIA whose mission is to save the president from assassination. They may believe "someone" is out to kill them. Their hallucinations often include bizarre, terrifying perceptive experiences.

SUMMARY

This chapter has discussed some selected emotional disturbances found in adolescents. One of these is depression. Acute depression is usually temporary; chronic depression is more severe. Masked depression is difficult to recognize since the adolescent hides it through acting-out behavior.

Anxiety states discussed here include generalized anxiety disorder, where anxiety is out of proportion to any factors associated with it. Anxiety can also be expressed through various manifestations of obsessive-compulsive behavior. Phobic disorders are anxiety states characterized by excessive, uncontrolled fear of particular objects or situations. Simple phobias include fear of animals or dirt. Social phobias involve extreme fear of social situations. Agoraphobia is the most handicapping of all phobias since the person is afraid to leave home or other familiar places.

Psychological factors affecting physical condition are also called psychosomatic reactions.

Somatoform disorders are those in which the individual has physical health problems that have a psychological rather than a physical cause. One example is conversion disorder in which anxiety becomes so severe that it leads to physical symptoms such as blindness, paralysis, or other physical disability.

Eating disorders have become common in recent years because of an overemphasis in our culture on slimness and a hatred of being fat. Anorexia nervosa is a life-threatening emotional disorder, primarily in females, characterized by an obsession with food and weight. Its symptoms are a constant preoccupation with dieting, extreme weight loss, amenorrhea, hyperactivity, social isolation, and strong feelings of inadequacy, helplessness, or loneliness.

Bulimia is a binge-purge syndrome in which the victim consumes large quantities of high calorie food and then vomits or uses laxatives, enemas, amphetamines, or fasting to offset the huge food intake. Those suffering from bulimia are impulsive perfectionists, with an overwhelming desire for approval. When emotional pressure builds up, they seek to release it during binge-purge episodes.

Schizophrenia is an extreme, psychotic withdrawal characterized by hallucinations and delusions. The disorganized type evidences symbolic, repetitive motions and behavior, fleeting hallucinations, and fantastic delusions. The catatonic type is a disturbance of motor function. Symptoms of the paranoid type include delusions of grandeur or of persecution.

DISCUSSION QUESTIONS

1. What are the differences among acute, chronic, and masked depression? What causes depression?
2. Have you known anyone suffering from generalized anxiety disorder? What was the person like?
3. Describe manifestations of obsessive-compulsive behavior.
4. Do you know anyone with a phobia or phobias? Describe the person. Have you known anyone suffering from agoraphobia? What methods of treatment are used to cure phobias?
5. Why do kleptomaniacs steal? Why do pyromaniacs set fires? Should those suffering from these disorders be prosecuted as criminals? Why or why not?
6. What are some examples of psychosomatic reactions?
7. Describe a typical conversion disorder.
8. Have you known anyone with anorexia nervosa or bulimia? Describe them and their symptoms. What should parents do if they suspect their adolescent girl is suffering from one of these disorders?
9. Do you think the emphasis on slimness in our culture is good or bad? What should be done about the emphasis?
10. What are some of the suspected causes of schizophrenia? Have you ever known a person who became a schizophrenic? Describe the person.

BIBLIOGRAPHY

Albert, N., and Beck. A. T. (1975). "Incidence of Depression in Early Adolescence: A Preliminary Study." *Journal of Youth and Adolescence,* 4, 301–307.

Altmann, E. O., and Gotlib, I. H. (1988). "The Social Behavior of Depressed Children: An Observational Study." *Journal of Abnormal Child Psychology,* 16, 29–44.

American Psychiatric Association. (1987). *Diagnostic and Statistical Manual of Mental Disorders.* 3d ed., Washington, D.C.: American Psychiatric Association.

Apter, A., and Tyano, S. (1988). "Obsessive-Compulsive Disorders in Adolescence." *Journal of Adolescence,* 11, 183–194.

Baird, P., and Sights, J. R. (1986). "Low Self-Esteem as a Treatment Issue in the Psychotherapy of Anorexia and Bulimia." *Journal of Counseling and Development,* 64, 449–451.

Bartholomew, K. L. (1987). "Reasons for Teenage Boys Setting Fires." *Medical Aspects of Human Sexuality,* 21, 83.

Boskind-Lodale, M. (1978). "The Definition and Treatment of Bulimorexia: The Gorging/Purging Syndrome of Young Women." Ph.D. dissertation, Cornell University.

Brone, R. J., and Fisher, C. B. (1988). "Determinants of Adolescent Obesity: A Comparison with Anorexia Nervosa." *Adolescence,* 23, 155–169.

Brouwers, M. (1988). "Depressive Thought Content among Female College Students with Bulimia." *Journal of Counseling and Development,* 66, 425–428.

Casper, R. (1983). "On the Emergence of Bulimia Nervosa as a Syndrome: A Historical View." *International Journal of Eating Disorders,* 2, 3–17.

Choquet, M., and Menke, H. (1987). "Development of Self-Perceived Risk Behavior and Psychosomatic

Symptoms in Adolescents: A Longitudinal Approach." *Journal of Adolescence*, 10, 291–308.

Davis, S. W., Best, D. L., and Hawkings, R. C. II. (1981). "Sex Stereotypes, Weight, and Body Image in Childhood and Adolescence." Mimeographed paper.

Deal, S. L., and Williams, J. E. (1988). "Cognitive Distortions As Mediators Between Life Stress and Depression in Adolescents." *Adolescence*, 90, 477–490.

Eisele, J., Hertsgaard, D., and Light, H. K. (1986). "Factors Related to Eating Disorders in Young Adolescent Girls." *Adolescence*, 82, 283–290.

Emery, P. E. (Summer, 1983). "Adolescent Depression and Suicide." *Adolescence*, 18, 245–258.

Folkenberg, J. (March, 1984). "Bulimia: Not for Women Only." *Psychology Today*, 18, 10.

Garfinkel, P. G., Moldofsky, H., and Gardner, D. M. (1980). "The Heterogeneity of Anorexia Nervosa: Bulimia as a Subgroup." *Archives of General Psychiatry*, 37, 1036–1040.

Gilbert, E. H., and DeBlassie, R. R. (Winter, 1984). "Anorexia Nervosa: Adolescent Starvation by Choice." *Adolescence*, 19, 839–846.

Goldstein, M. J. (October, 1981). "Family Factors Associated with Schizophrenia and Anorexia Nervosa." *Journal of Youth and Adolescence*, 10, 385–405.

Gottesman, I. I., and Schields, J. (1982). *The Schizophrenic Puzzle*. New York: Cambridge University Press.

Grant, C. L., and Fodor, I. G. (April, 1984). "Body Image and Eating Disorders: A New Role for School Psychologists in Screening and Prevention." Mimeographed paper. New York University, School of Education, Health, Nursing, and Arts Profession.

————. (1986). "Adolescent Attitudes Toward Body Image and Anorexic Behavior." *Adolescence*, 82, 269–281.

Grinker, R. R., and Holzman, P. S. (1973). "Schizophrenic Pathology in Young Adults: A Clinical Study." *Archives of General Psychiatry*, 28, 168–175.

Holleran, P. R., Pascale, J., and Fraley, J. (1988). "Personality Correlates of College-Age Bulmics." *Journal of Counseling and Development*, 66, 378–381.

Holzman, P. S., and Grinker, R. R., Sr. (1974). "Schizophrenia in Adolescence. *Journal of Youth and Adolescence*, 3, 267–279.

Hooker, D., and Convisser, E. (December, 1983). "Women's Eating Problems: An Analysis of a Coping Mechanism." *Personnel and Guidance Journal*, 62, 236–239.

Humphrey, L. L., and Stern, S. (1988). "Object Relations and the Family System in Bulimia: A Theoretical Integration. *Journal of Marital and Family Therapy*, 14, 337–350.

Ieit, D. (February, 1985). "Anxiety, Depression, and Self-Esteem in Bulimia: The Role of the School Psychologist." Paper presented at the annual meeting of the Eastern Educational Research Association, Virginia Beach, Virginia.

Jenkins, M. E. (1987). "An Outcome Study of Anorexia Nervosa in an Adolescent Unit." *Journal of Adolescence*, 10, 71–81.

Johnson, C., Lewis, C., Love, S., Lewis, L., and Stuckey, M. (February, 1984). "Incidence and Correlates of Bulimic Behavior in a Female High School Population." *Journal of Youth and Adolescence*, 13, 15–26.

Koenig, L. J. (1988). "Self-Image of Emotionally Disturbed Adolescents." *Journal of Abnormal Child Psychology*, 16, 111–126.

Lachenmeyer, J. R., and Muni-Brander, P. (1988). "Eating Disorders in a Nonclinical Adolescent Population: Implications for Treatment." *Adolescence*, 23, 303–312.

Lambert, B. G., et al. (1972) *Adolescence: Transition from Childhood to Maturity*. Monterey, Calif.: Brooks/Cole Publishing Co.

Larson, R., and Johnson, C. (December, 1981). "Anorexia Nervosa in the Context of Daily Experience." *Journal of Youth and Adolescence*, 10, 455–471.

Leclair, N., and Berkowitz, B. (February, 1983). "Counseling Concerns for the Individual with Bulimia." *The Personnel and Guidance Journal*, 61, 352–355.

Levin, E., Adelson, S., Buchalter, G., and Bilcher, L. (February 21, 1983). "Karen Carpenter." *People*.

Lidz, T. (1974). "Schizophrenia Thinking." *Journal of Youth and Adolescence*, 3, 95–98.

Maag, J. W., Rutherford, R. B., and Parks, B. T. (1988). "Secondary School Professionals' Ability to Identify Depression in Adolescents." *Adolescence*, 23, 73–82.

Mallick, M. J., Whipple, T. W., and Huerta, E. (1987). "Behavioral and Psychological Traits of Weight-Conscious Teenagers: A Comparison of Eating-Disordered Patients and High- and Low-Risk Groups." *Adolescence*, 85, 157–168.

Miller, D. (1974). *Adolescence: Psychology, Psychopathology, and Psychotherapy*. New York: Jason Aronson.

Mitchell, J. E., Pyle, R. L., and Eckert, E. D. (1981). "Frequency and Duration of Binge-Eating Episodes in Patients with Bulimia." *American Journal of Psychiatry*, 138, 835, 836.

Muuss, R. E. (1985). "Adolescent Eating Disorder: Anorexia Nervosa." *Adolescence*, 20, 525–536.

_____ . (1986). "Adolescent Eating Disorder: Bulimia." *Adolescence*, 22, 257–267.

Piazza, E., Rollins, N., and Lewis, F. S. (Summer, 1983). "Measuring Severity and Change in Anorexia Nervosa." *Adolescence*, 18, 293–305.

Pyle, R. L., Mitchell, J. E., and Eckert, E. D. (1981). "Bulimia: A Report of 34 Cases." *Journal of Clinical Psychiatry*, 42, 60–64.

Roberto, L. G. (1986). "Bulimia: The Transgenerational View." *Journal of Marital and Family Therapy*, 12, 231–240.

Romeo, F. F. (Fall, 1984). "Adolescence, Sexual Conflict, and Anorexia Nervosa." *Adolescence*, 19, 551–555.

Schwartz, R. C. (1987). "Working with 'Internal' and 'External' Families in the Treatment of Bulimia." *Family Relations*, 36, 242–245.

Seligman, J., and Zabarsky, M. (March 7, 1983). "A Deadly Feast and Famine." *Newsweek*.

Seligman, L. (June, 1983). "An Introduction to the New DSM-III." *Personnel and Guidance Journal*, 61, 601–605.

Siegel, L. J., and Griffin, N. J. (Winter, 1983). "Adolescents' Concepts of Depression among Their Peers." *Adolescence*, 18, 965–973.

Silverton, L., Harrington, M. E., and Mednick, S. A. (1987). "Motor Impairment and Antisocial Behavior in Adolescent Males at High Risk for Schizophrenia." *Journal of Abnormal Child Psychology*, 16, 177–186.

Simonds, J. F. (1975). "Hallucinations in Nonpsychotic Children and Adolescents." *Journal of Youth and Adolescence*, 4, 171–182.

Slotkin, J., Forehand, R., Fauber, R., McCombs, A., and Long, N. (1988). "Parent-Completed and Adolescent-Completed CDIs: Relationship to Adolescent Social and Cognitive Functioning." *Journal of Abnormal Child Psychology*, 16, 207–217.

Stehouwer, R. S., Bultsma, C. A., and Blackford, I. T. (1985). "Developmental Differences in Depression: Cognitive-Perceptual Distortion in Adolescent Versus Adult Female Depressives." *Adolescence*, 20, 291–299.

Strauss, C. C., Last, C. G., Hersen, M., and Kazdin, A. E. (1987). "Association between Anxiety and Depression in Children and Adolescents with Anxiety Disorders." *Journal of Abnormal Child Psychology*, 16, 57–68.

Strober, M. (August, 1981). "Comparative Analysis of Personality Organization in Juvenile Anorexia Nervosa." *Journal of Youth and Adolescence*, 10, 285–295.

Svec, H. (1987). "Anorexia Nervosa: A Misdiagnosis of the Adolescent Male." *Adolescence*, 87, 617–623.

Treichel, J. (1982). "Anorexia Nervosa: A Brain Shrinker?" *Science News*, 122, 122–123.

Uhr, S., Stahl, S. M., and Berger, P. A. (1984). "Unmasking Schizophrenia." VA *Practitioner*, 1, 42–53.

Van den Broucke, S., and Vandereycken, W. (1986). "Risk Factors for the Development of Eating Disorders in Adolescent Exchange Students: An Exploratory Study." *Journal of Adolescence*, 9, 145–150.

Van Thorre, M. D., and Vogel, F. X. (Spring, 1985). "The Presence of Bulimia in High School Females." *Adolescence*, 20, 45–51.

Weiner, I. B. (1980). "Psychopathology in Adolescence," In *Handbook of Adolescent Psychology*. Edited by J. Adelson. New York: John Wiley and Sons.

Wooden, W. S. (January, 1985). "The Flames of Youth." *Psychology Today*, 19, 22–28.

CHAPTER
10

Adolescent Alienation

Emotional disturbance in adolescents does not always manifest itself in emotional illness. Instead of turning inward, the adolescent may turn outward, expressing pent-up emotions through various forms of acting-out behavior: truancy from school, running away from home, aggressive, explosive behavior, sexual promiscuity, vandalism, theft, assault, rape, even the destruction of one's own life or that of another.

For the most part, emotionally disturbed adolescents feel alienated from friends, family, and school. They are out of the mainstream of adolescent and adult society. Their actions are an expression of feelings of alienation, which they have found difficult to deal with in socially approved ways (Calabrese, 1987).

This chapter discusses three manifestations of disturbed, acting-out behavior: *running away, suicide,* and *juvenile delinquency.*

RUNNING AWAY

Incidence

Surveys indicate that over 700,000 youths, ages ten to seventeen, leave home annually without adult consent, at least for overnight. Almost 60 percent of these youths are females, many of whom are assisted by boyfriends who may provide some financial and psychological support for their behavior (Adams and Munro, 1979). An analysis of the youths served under the National Runaway Youth Program across the United States reveals the following profile of youths served (U.S. Dept. of HHS, 1980):

> Sex: female (59.4%)
> Age: 16 years (25%)
> Race/ethnic origin: white (74%)
> Living situation past three years: home with parents or legal guardians (82.4%)
> Juvenile justice system involvement: no involvement (59.4%)
> Reasons for seeking services: poor communication with parent figures (51.8%)
> Parent participation: one or both parents (51.9%)
> Length of stay: less than 14 days (84.1%)
> Disposition: home with parents or legal guardian (30.4%)

These youths come from a variety of home backgrounds and social classes, indicating that the problem is not always one of simple situational causation (Adams and Munro, 1979).

Psychological Profiles

Historically, running away has been defined as a behavioral manifestation of psychopathology, so that the American Psychiatric Association has endorsed the "runaway reaction" as a specific disorder. Numerous investigations describe the runaway as insecure, depressed, unhappy, and impulsive (Benalcazar, 1982), with emotional problems, low self-esteem, and an unmanageable personal life. Unfortunately, the research does not

Emotional disturbance in adolescence does not always manifest itself in emotional illness. The adolescent may express his or her pent up emotions by running away from home. (© Frank Siteman)

always sort out whether these characteristics are antecedents to or consequences of running away (Adams and Munro, 1979).

Counterliterature rejects the psychopathology explanation for all youths and suggests that many have normal IQs, positive self-concepts, and are not particularly psychopathic, depressed, or emotionally disturbed. There does seem to be sufficient evidence to say that *causal factors suggest a complex interaction among family factors (conflict), school stress (academic difficulties), and interpersonal communication as causal agents.* Runaways often have strong egos, resent being "put down," are impulsive, and show poor judgment. Unable to control their environment (whether at home, at school, or in the community) or to communicate with or relate to adults, they cannot tolerate sustained, close, interpersonal relationships, so they leave (Adams and Munro, 1979). If runaways stay away, the negative effects, such as curtailment of schooling, may be long lasting, seriously limiting the adolescent's employment chances and future possibilities. Running away may compound their problems. Many turn to drugs, crime, prostitution, or other illegal activities. Now AIDS is an ever-present threat to those who exchange sex for money or gifts (Hersch, 1988).

Environmental Causes

Of all the background factors that relate to running away, *a poor home environment is the central reason for leaving home.* Typically runaways report conflict with parents, alienation from them, differences in values from parents, the need for independence, rejection and hostile control, lack of warmth, affection, and parental support, plus problematic marital relationships with much internal conflict and family disorganization (Loeb, Burke, and Boglarsky, 1986). Runaway girls view their parents as more controlling and punitive of their behavior in the home, whereas many runaway boys report minimal family control and supervision, which leads to outside forces, such as peers, becoming causal agents in running away. Thus, low levels of control of boys especially allows them opportunities to leave. Many parents of runaways are so absorbed with their own problems that they have little time to consider their child. Such youths report they are not wanted at home (Johnson and Carter, 1980). For others, running away is a culmination of a whole series of conflicts or problems. One boy commented:

> I wasn't about to sit around there and be yelled at and messed with. I didn't do nothing that bad. My mother said she was going to court with me so what was I supposed to do? She just kept yelling, and yelling about court. What was I gonna say? I don't want to go to no court. (Palenski and Launer, 1987, p. 353).

A study of thirty male and female adolescent runaways representing various ages, family structures, and ethnic groups emphasized problems with parents as a major reason for running away. Table 10–1 shows the replies when these adolescents were asked: "What are some of the reasons for your leaving home?" When the parents were asked why their adolescents left home, they replied that their children did not want to listen to authority, were afraid of being punished, did not want a curfew, or wanted to be free; or they left home because of boyfriends,

TABLE 10–1

Runaways' reasons for leaving home.

REASON	NUMBER OF RUNAWAYS INDICATING REASON
Arguments with parents	7
Doesn't like stepfather	1
Doesn't like mother and father	1
Father raped me	1
Don't want a curfew	1
Father beat me when I was drinking	1
Mother beat me	1
Mother punishes me severely	1
Don't like it at home	1
Nobody understands me	1
No freedom	1
Fighting with siblings	4
Parents don't like boyfriend	1
Fighting with mother over boyfriend	1
To go with boyfriend	2
School problems	5

From: Spillane-Grieco, E. (Spring 1984). "Characteristics of a Helpful Relationship: A Study of Empathetic Understanding and Positive Appeal between Runaways and Their Parents," *Adolescence*, 19: 63–75.

arguments over friends, or problems at school. Fourteen parents said they did not know why their adolescents left home (Spillane-Grieco, 1984).

Adams, Gullotta, and Clancy (1985) made a distinction between *adolescent runaways* and **throwaways.** Runaways left home because of personal family conflict, alienation, and poor social relations. Throwaways had been encouraged or asked to leave home. Throwaways, more often than runaways, reported that their parents did not get along with one another, said unpleasant things about them, called them names, and frequently punished and beat them.

throwaway

Pressures, difficulties, and failures at school also contribute to running away. Children who are slow learners, left back to repeat grades, or ostracized by school personnel seek to escape the school environment that hostilely rejects them (Johnson and Carter, 1980).

Typologies

All runaways, however, are not alike, so there have been numerous efforts to classify them according to type and motive. The simplest classification is to divide them into two groups: the *running from* and the *running to* (Roberts, 1982). The running from adolescents could not tolerate their home situation or one or both parents. The running to adolescents were pleasure seekers, running to places or people providing a wide variety of activities. Some enjoyed running away and liked the friends they met on the way. They usually did not return until picked up by the police.

In their discussion of ungovernable and incorrigible girls, Greene and Esselstyn (1972) outline three distinct types of runaway girls: the *rootless*, the *anxious*, and the *terrified*. The **rootless runaway** was a pleasure seeker who sought immediate gratification. She dropped out of school, quit a series of jobs, used drugs, and became sexually active. She was lavishly praised by parents, but they never set limits on her. When the family began to get frightened and started to set limits, the girl rebelled and ran away again when the family imposed a curfew or rule.

rootless runaway

anxious runaway

The **anxious runaway** came from a multiproblem family and often had to do household chores, care for younger siblings, and worry about finances. If her father was at home, he might have drunk excessively and been physically and verbally abusive, so she left temporarily, usually for a few hours or overnight, seeking someone to talk to, often a friend's mother. The **terrified runaway** fled from her father's or stepfather's sexual advances toward her. She would invite friends to stay with her when she was home or stayed away as often as she could to avoid being alone with her sexually abusive father (Greene and Esselstyn, 1972).

terrified runaway

One of the most helpful classifications is by Roberts (1982) who arranged runaways along a parent-youth conflict continuum. Figure 10–1 illustrates the categories. The 0–1 category included youths who wanted to travel but whose parents arranged a compromise so that the youth would not strike out alone. *Runaway explorers* wanted to travel for adventure and to assert their independence. They informed their parents where they had gone, usually by note, and then left without permission. If not picked up by the police, they generally returned home

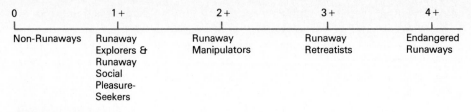

0	1+	2+	3+	4+
Non-Runaways	Runaway Explorers & Runaway Social Pleasure- Seekers	Runaway Manipulators	Runaway Retreatists	Endangered Runaways

FIGURE 10–1

Formulation of the degree of parent-youth conflict continuum.

Roberts, A. R. (Summer, 1982). "Adolescent Runaways in Suburbia: A New Typology," *Adolescence,* 17: 379–396.

on their own. *Social pleasure seekers* usually had conflict with parents over what they felt was a major issue: dating a certain boy, an early curfew, or grounding that prevented them from attending an important event. They sneaked out of the house to engage in the forbidden activity and either sneaked back in or stayed in a friend's house overnight, usually telephoning the parents the next morning to ask to come home.

Runaway manipulators usually had more serious ongoing conflict with parents over home chores, choice of friends, and so forth, so they tried to manipulate parents by running away and tried to force them to return on the runaway's own terms.

Runaway retreatists experienced even more conflict and tension at home, with frequent yelling, hitting, or throwing objects. The homes might be broken; the majority of adolescents had one or more school problems and retreated into drugs or getting drunk daily prior to running away.

Endangered runaways left to escape recurring physical and/or sexual abuse inflicted on them by parents or stepparents, often while in a drunken state. These youths often used drugs like amphetamines, acid, cocaine, or mescaline and had drinking problems themselves. Usually a beating or threat of another one precipitated running away (Roberts, 1972). Physical and/or sexual abuse of both males and females is often a reason for running away (Janus, Burgess, and McCormack, 1987).

It is quite obvious that not all runaways are the same or leave home for the same reasons. There are, however, clusters of situational and personal variables that appear repeatedly in their case histories. One study in Hawaii found that children from single-parent families had less chance of becoming chronic runaways than those from intact families (Matthews and Ilon, 1980). The reason was that there was much more quarreling in the two-parent families, which the child felt powerless to prevent and from which escape seemed the only solution.

Help

Since 1978, the National Runaway Youth Program within the U.S. Youth Development Bureau has promoted assistance to youths, who are vulnerable to exploitation and to dangerous encounters. Aid is now offered nationwide. The program also funds the National Toll-Free Communication System to enable youths to contact their families and/or centers where they can get help. Most of the individual programs throughout the country have developed multiple-service components to meet various needs of young people. Other community social service agencies and juvenile justice/law enforcement systems use their services (U.S. Dept. of HHS, 1980).

SUICIDE

Frequency

The incidence of suicide among children, especially among those under age thirteen, is rare. It is rare because children are still dependent on love objects for gratification; they have not yet completed the process of identification within themselves; thus, the thought of turning hostility toward themselves is too painful and frightening. Only as children find more self-identity can they be independent enough to commit suicide.

The suicide mortality rate increases with advancing age, reaching a peak in males over 85 years of age and in females at ages 45 to 54 (U.S. Bureau of Census, 1987). Figure 10-2 shows the trends. The rate per 100,000 among males aged 15 to 24 is 19.4; among females aged 15 to 24 the suicide rate is 4.3. The suicide rate in the 15 to 24 year age group has tripled over the last 30 years (Hepworth, Farley,

FIGURE 10–2

Suicide mortality, by sex and age groups, 1983.

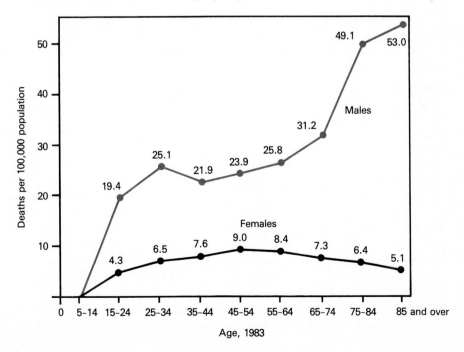

and Griffiths, 1986). The suicide rate among college students varies considerably from school to school. The rate is extraordinarily high at a few schools like Harvard and Yale, indicating there may be elements in some college environments conducive to suicide ("College Suicides," 1980).

Only a small percentage of attempted suicides succeed. Estimates of the ratio of suicide attempts to fatalities vary from as high as 120:1 in children to 5:1 in adults. About 5,000 young people between 15 and 24 years of age successfully commit suicide each year (The Suicide Prevention Center, 1984). Females attempt suicide much more frequently than do males, but many more males than females are successful in completing the suicide. One of the reasons males more often succeed is that they frequently use more violent means—hanging, jumping from heights, shooting, or stabbing themselves—whereas females more often use passive and less dangerous methods, such as taking pills. Females more often make multiple threats but less often really want to kill themselves or actually do it.

Causes and Motives

What are the causes of adolescents seeking to take their own lives? What are their motives? There is a variety of contributing factors (Greuling and DeBlassie, 1980).

Suicidal adolescents tend to come from disturbed family backgrounds (Wright, 1985). There may have been much conflict between the parents and between the parents and children, considerable family violence, or the parents may have manifested negative, rejecting attitudes toward the children (Wade, 1987). There may have been frequent unemployment and economic stress in the home, early parental physical or emotional deprivation, the absence or loss of one or both parents, or illness or abandonment by the father.

Other studies relate adolescent suicide with frequent parental absence because of unemployment (Stack, 1985). *As a consequence, there is often an absence of any warm, parental figure with whom to identify and a sense of emotional and social isolation.* Suicide attempters often state that they do not feel close to any adult. They often have trouble communicating with significant others around them (Stivers, 1988). There is no one to turn to when they need to talk to someone.

The background of social isolation makes these adolescents particularly vulnerable to a loss of love object, which may trigger the suicide attempt. The loss of a parent in childhood makes any subsequent loss of a family member, mate, boyfriend, or girlfriend particularly hard (Neiger and Hopkins, 1988). Depression may follow recent life stresses (Friedrich, Rearms, and Cochran, 1982).

One frequent component of suicidal tendencies is depression (Cosand, Bourque, and Kraus, 1982). This depression may follow the loss of the love object and is characterized by mourning, crying spells, dejected mood, withdrawal of interest in the world, the inhibition of activities, lack of motivation in performing tasks, and a painful dejection (Hafen and Frandsen, 1986). Psychosomatic symptoms such as appetite loss, sleep disturbance, increased fatigability, or decreased sexual interest may appear. Sometimes the depression may not be readily apparent; the individual may try to cover it up with overactivity, preoccupation with trivia, or acting-out behavior such as delinquency, use of drugs, or sexual promiscuity.

Although only a small percentage of attempted suicides succeed, the suicide rate in the fifteen- to twenty-four-year-old age group has tripled in the past thirty years. (AP/Wide World Photos)

The risk of suicide among adolescents is increased with alcohol and drug abuse. Under the influence of drugs or alcohol, adolescents are more likely to act on impulse (Sommer, 1984). Or, adolescents sometimes overdose and kill themselves without intending to do so (Gispert, et al., 1985).

Stress may also stimulate suicidal attempts (Peck, 1987). Part of this stress may originate in poor home conditions that produce terrible strains (McAnarney, 1979). The stress may also arise from current situations: the pressure of completing school work and getting acceptable grades, the indecision of vocational choice, the pressure to find social acceptance, conflict over sexual intimacy (especially without close emotional involvement), and the feeling of inadequacy as pressure mounts.

Lack of investment in the future is characteristic of suicidal adolescents. They are more likely to view their futures with feelings of hopelessness, without real plans or expectations. They usually see only the discomfort and pain of the present situation.

Some suicidal adolescents have been categorized as immature personalities with poor impulse control. The combination of impulsiveness and resurgent sexual and aggressive drives, coupled with poor ego development, is illustrated in the following case:

Bob . . . was preoccupied with pleasure seeking, he had little supervision, and would be passively defiant and withdrawn when interrupted. Since age four he had been hospitalized at least once a year with head and body injuries, four of which resulted from being hit by cars. When a teacher reprimanded him for taking liberties with a girl, he hung himself with his belt in the cloakroom where the teacher had sent him. "I was sore at the teacher because of my report card the day before," he said. (Yacoubian and Lourie, 1973, p. 155)

Other suicidal adolescents have been shown to be highly suggestible in following the directions or examples of others (Robbins, 1983). This factor of suggestibility has been borne out by studies of adolescent "suicide epidemics." Residents of Clear Lake City, Texas, home of the astronauts and the Johnson Space Center, were shocked by a wave of suicides of six teenagers within a two-month period. Plano, Texas, had eight youth suicides within fifteen months after a high school student asphyxiated himself. The affluent counties north of New York City were shaken by a string of twelve deaths (Doan and Peterson, 1984). When one suicide occurs, it brings others to the surface who are vulnerable. Small groups of adolescents have even banded together to form a suicide subculture (Lester, 1987). Suicidal adolescents are likely to have a history of suicide within the family and close friends who have killed themselves.

Suicide may be a direct result of mental illness (Cosand, Bourque, and Kraus, 1982). Some adolescents experience hallucinations telling them to kill themselves. Others threaten suicide, in part, because of anticipated guilt occasioned by voices directing them toward external aggression.

Guilt and/or anger and hostility are important emotional components of suicide. The adolescents may be in the terminal stages of a romance. Girls may believe they are pregnant. Their suicide attempts are efforts to punish either themselves or their boyfriends. Guilt and shame over an out-of-wedlock pregnancy can be powerful motivating factors in suicides.

in such cases, suicide becomes an act of aggression, expressed inwardly at the self, in contrast to homicide, an act of aggression expressed outwardly. The pregnant girl, for example, could try to get even with her boyfriend by killing herself (suicide) to make the boy feel sorry or by killing him directly (homicide). D. Miller (1974) writes: "Of all the aggressive acts of which people are capable, suicide is [sometimes] one of the most aggressive; it is a hostile act directed at loved ones, at society, as well as at the self. The survivors are always left wondering how they failed" (p. 305).

Suicide is a cry for help to get attention or sympathy or an attempt to manipulate other people. Attempted suicide is not an effort to die but rather a communication to others in an effort to improve one's life. As a matter of fact, desired changes in the life situation as a result of attempted suicide may be accomplished. However, many suicidal gestures for help misfire and lead to death (Walker and Mehr, 1983).

Contrary to common opinion, suicide attempts in a great majority of cases are considered in advance and weighed rationally against other alternatives. The attempter may have tried other means: rebellion, running away from home, lying, stealing, or other attention-getting devices. Having tried these methods and failed, the person turns to suicide attempts. Most adolescents who attempt suicide talk about it first (Pfeffer, 1987; Shafi, 1988). If others are alerted in time, if they pay attention to these developments and take them seriously enough to try to remedy the situation, a death may be prevented (Fujimura, Weis, and Cochran, 1985).

HIGHLIGHT   Suicidal Risks

One of the ways of preventing suicide is to recognize symptoms in those who become suicide prone (Gispert, 1987). Some eighty school professionals were asked to list the most important indicators of suicidal risk in students. The professionals listed the following indicators:

Indicator	SCHOOL PROFESSIONALS REPORTING INDICATOR	
	Number	Percentage
Depression (sadness, despair, eating problems, indifference, sleeping problems)	56	70
Verbal or written cues (Verbal or written cues include comments about committing suicide, acknowledgment of the problem, requests for help, or indications of depressive, morbid, or suicidal themes in art, written work, or conversation.)	48	60
Social isolation, withdrawal (absence of peer support)	45	56
Academic problems (low grades, truancy, lateness)	27	34
Self-destructive behavior (suicide attempts, self-mutilation, restlessness, proneness to accidents)	27	34
Drugs, alcohol	27	34
Other school problems	26	33
Acting out (running away, delinquency, pregnancy, sexual permissiveness)	25	31
Physical appearance (poor grooming, deterioration of dress)	17	21
Agitation	16	20
Somatic complaints	11	14

In addition to the above, other writers list the following (Allen, 1987; McGuire, 1983):

Preoccupation with themes of death
Giving away prized possessions or
    making a will
Recent suicide of a friend or relative
Recent disappointment or loss

Grob, M. C., Klein, A. A., and Eisen, S. V. (April, 1983). "The Role of the School Professional in Identifying and Managing Adolescent Suicide Behavior," *Journal of Youth and Adolescence*, 12: 162–173.

JUVENILE DELINQUENCY

▨ Definitions

juvenile delinquent

The term *juvenile delinquency* refers to the violation of the law by a juvenile, in most states anyone under eighteen years of age. The legal term **juvenile delinquent** was established for young lawbreakers to avoid the disgrace and stigma of being classified in legal records as criminals and to separate under-age people and treat them differently from adult criminals. Most are tried in juvenile courts where the intent is to rehabilitate them.

A young person may be labeled a delinquent for breaking any of a number of laws, ranging from murder or armed robbery to running away from home or truancy from school. Because laws are inconsistent, a particular action may be labeled delinquent in one community but not in another. Furthermore, law enforcement officials differ in the method and extent of enforcement. In some communities, the police may only talk to adolescents who are accused of minor crimes; in others the police refer youths to their parents; in still others, they may arrest them and refer them to juvenile court. As with adults, many crimes adolescents commit are never discovered or, if discovered, are not reported or prosecuted. Most statistics therefore understate the extent of juvenile crime.

▨ Incidence

Statistics on juvenile delinquency include either the numbers of *persons* arrested, the number of *court cases* handled, or the number of *offenses* committed. Obviously, one adolescent may commit more than one offense, but not all cases are taken to court. During the period 1970–1985, the number of serious crimes committed by those under 18 rose slightly (table 10–2), but the total percentages of those under 18 who were arrested declined (figure 10–3). This is partly due to the decline of juveniles in the population (U.S. Bureau of the Census, 1987).

▨ **TABLE 10–2**

Changes in serious crimes and all other crimes committed by persons under age eighteen, 1970, 1980, and 1985.

TYPE OF CRIME	1970	1980	CHANGE	1985	CHANGE SINCE 1980
Serious crime[a]	523,677	750,800	43%	654,500	− 13%
All other crime	920,454	848,500	− 8	1,110,440	+ 31%
Total	1,444,131	1,599,300	8	1,764,940	10%

[a]Larceny, burglary, motor vehicle theft, robbery, aggravated assault, forcible rape, murder and nonnegligent manslaughter, or arson.

From: U.S. Bureau of the Census, Department of Commerce (1987). *Statistical Abstract of the United States, 1987* (Washington, D.C.: U.S. Government Printing Office, table 279.

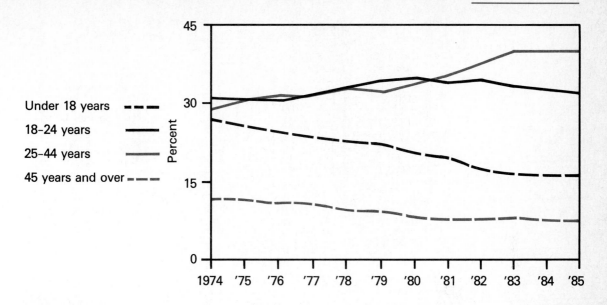

Under 18 years — — —

18–24 years ▬▬▬

25–44 years ▬▬▬

45 years and over ▬ — ▬

FIGURE 10–3

Persons arrested: percentage by age, 1974–1985.

From: U.S. Bureau of the Census, Department of Commerce (1987). *Statistical Abstract of the United States*, 1987, (Washington, D.C.: U.S. Government Printing Office), p. 163.

Of all persons arrested in 1985, 17 percent were juveniles—under age 18; an additional 32 percent were aged 18 to 24. Figure 10.4 shows the percentages. This means that 49 percent of all arrests during 1985 were of people under age 25. As seen in figure 10.5, the incidence of delinquency among males under age 18 is three and one-half times that among females of the same age (U.S. Bureau of the Census, 1987).

The Census Bureau groups eight crimes together as "serious crimes"—larceny, burglary, motor vehicle theft, robbery, aggravated assault, forcible rape, murder and nonnegligent manslaughter, and arson—and gives totals for them. Table 10.2 shows that from 1970 to 1980, arrests for this group of crimes increased dramatically: 43 percent for those under 18. From 1980 to 1985, however, the number of serious crimes committed by those under age 18 declined by 13 percent (due partly to a decline in population of this age group). The number of arrests for other types of crimes continued to increase despite a declining proportion of that age group (U.S. Bureau of the Census, 1987).

Causes of Delinquency

Concern about the problem of delinquency has motivated considerable investigation and research efforts to try to find its causes. In general, the causes may be grouped into three major categories: *sociological factors* include influential elements

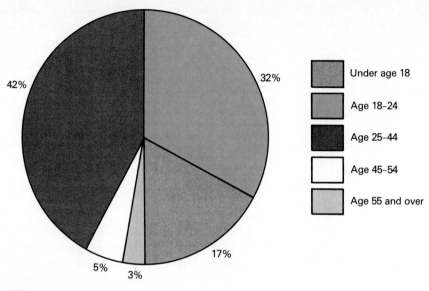

42%   32%

17%

5%   3%

Under age 18

Age 18–24

Age 25–44

Age 45–54

Age 55 and over

FIGURE 10–4

Age distribution of all people arrested, 1985.

From: U.S. Bureau of the Census, Department of Commerce (1987). *Statistical Abstract of the United States, 1987.* (Washington, D.C.: U.S. Government Printing Office, table 279).

FIGURE 10–5

People arrested, by sex and age, 1985.

From: U.S. Bureau of the Census, Department of Commerce (1987). *Statistical Abstract of the United States, 1987.* (Washington, D.C.: U.S. Government Printing Office).

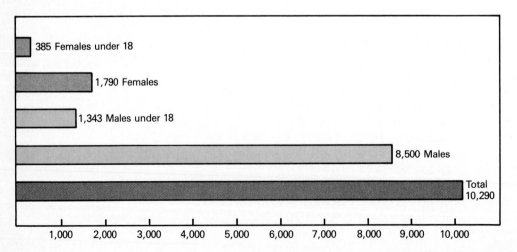

385 Females under 18

1,790 Females

1,343 Males under 18

8,500 Males

Total
10,290

1,000   2,000   3,000   4,000   5,000   6,000   7,000   8,000   9,000   10,000

in society and culture; *psychological factors* include the influences of interpersonal relationships and personality components; *biological factors* include the effects of organic and physical elements.

Sociological Factors in Delinquency   The most important sociological factors that have been investigated in relation to juvenile delinquency are the following:

Socioeconomic status and class
Affluence, hedonism, and cultural values
Violence in our culture and in the media
Alcohol or drug usage
Peer group involvement and influences
Neighborhood and community influences
Social and cultural change, disorganization, and unrest
School performance
Family background

Socioeconomic status and class have been found to be less important in relation to juvenile delinquency than was once thought (Tolan, 1988). Traditionally delinquency was thought to be a by-product of poverty and low socioeconomic status. For both males and females, delinquency is more common among youths who have fewer educational and occupational opportunities and become frustrated with the circumstances of their lives (Weller and Luchterhand, 1983).

Studies show, however, that juvenile delinquency is becoming more evenly distributed through all socioeconomic status levels. In fact there is as great an incidence of some forms of delinquency among adolescents of the middle class as among those of other classes. Tygart (1988) found, for example, that high socioeconomic status (SES) youths were more likely to be involved in school vandalism than low SES youths. The big difference is that middle-class adolescents who commit delinquent offenses are less often arrested and charged with them than are their lower-class counterparts. The son or daughter from a well-to-do family is let off with a warning, while those from poorer families are arrested and punished.

Affluence and hedonistic values and life-styles among modern youths are conducive to delinquent patterns of behavior. Today's youths, especially those of the middle class, have access to cars, alcoholic beverages, drugs, and pocket money. They are involved in a whirl of social activities: dating, dances, sports events, partying, rock concerts, driving around, parking, and hanging out at their favorite meeting places. Their interests and attitudes lend themselves to late hours, getting into mischief, and involvement in vandalism or delinquent acts just for kicks (Riemer, 1981; Wasson, 1980). Thus, delinquency among contemporary adolescents is partly a by-product of participation in the legitimate youth culture.

There is some evidence also that violent youths have been influenced by the *violence they see in our culture and in the media*. May (1986) found that youths who behave in a violent manner give more selective attention to violent cues. In other words, they imitate what they have seen and heard. (See chapter 18.)

The Guardian Angels provide an alternative for adolescents who want to resist some of the more negative influences of their peer group. (Robert Harbison)

Efforts have been made to determine to what extent delinquency is related to *alcohol or drug usage* among adolescents. Dawkins and Dawkins (1983) found that drinking was strongly associated with serious delinquency for both blacks and whites, especially when other factors were present, such as previous arrests, association with criminals or drug users, or heroin use by the adolescent. Stuck and Glassner (1985) emphasize the strong correlation between drug usage and criminal activity.

Peer group involvement becomes a significant influence in delinquency. Adolescents become delinquent because they are socialized into it, particularly by peers (Covington, 1982; Mitchell and Dodder, 1980; Zober, 1981). Adolescents who have a high degree of peer orientation are also more likely to have a high level of delinquency involvement. Bowker, Gross, and Klein (1980) found that a girl's relationships with girlfriends were more important in determining gang membership and seriousness of delinquency than any other factor.

Various *neighborhood and community influences* are also important. Most larger communities can identify areas in which delinquency rates are higher than in other neighborhoods. Not all adolescents growing up in these areas become delinquent, but a larger than average percentage do because of the influence and pressures of the cultural milieu in which they live.

Today's adolescents are also living in a period of *rapid cultural change, disorganization, and unrest*, which tends to increase delinquency rates. (See chapter 1.) Values that once were commonly accepted are now questioned. Social institutions such as the family that once offered security and protection may exert an upsetting influence instead. The specter of social, economic, and political unrest stimulates anxieties and rebellion.

School performance is an important factor in delinquency (Grande, 1988). Dunham and Alpert (1987) studied school dropout behavior of 137 juvenile delinquents and found 14 factors that yielded a high level of prediction of whether they would drop out of school or not, such as misbehavior in school, disliking school, the negative influence of peers with respect to dropping out and getting in trouble, and a weak relationship with parents. A lack of school success—poor grades, classroom misconduct, and an inability to adjust to the school program and to get along with administrators, teachers, and parents—are associated with delinquency. Youths who do not conform to expectations in the academic setting are soon labeled as troublemakers. The negative attitudes of school personnel stimulate additional misbehavior. Absenteeism increases, as do hedonistic activities such as alcohol and drug use. These activities in turn prevent students who become "high" in school from performing academically.

Family background has an important influence on adolescent development and adjustment and hence on social conduct (Anolik, 1981; Fisher, 1980; Kroupa, 1988; Madden and Harbin, 1983; Streit, 1981). Broken homes and strained family relationships have been associated with delinquent behavior (Anolik, 1980). Lack of family cohesion and troubled family relationships are particularly important correlates of delinquency (Tolan, 1988).

Psychological Factors in Delinquency   Broken homes can be a contributing factor to delinquency. But broken homes in and of themselves are no worse than, and sometimes not as detrimental as, intact but unhappy, disturbed family relationships. Usually studies of delinquency compare the rates for adolescents from broken homes with those from intact homes, many of which are fairly happy. However, if comparisons are made between adolescents from broken homes with adolescents from intact but unhappy homes, the results are fairly similar. Overall, *family environment is a much more important factor in delinquency than is family structure* (LeFlore, 1988).

Adolescents' relationships with their parents are particularly important. Overall, both males and females are closer to their mothers than to their fathers, but closeness to a father is a better predictor of delinquent behavior, especially among males (Johnson, 1987). Also, parental behavior patterns influence the behavior of children in the family. Thus, Johnson and O'Leary (1987) found that parents who were most hostile toward one another and who had conduct-disordered (CD) girls were most likely to perceive their children's behavior as problematic. Also, the children modeled their behavior after their hostile parents.

There have been efforts also to determine whether certain *personality factors* predispose the adolescent to delinquency (Bernstein, 1981; Thornton, 1982). Is there such a thing as a criminal type? No one personality type can be associated with delinquency, but it is known that those who become delinquent are more likely to be socially assertive, defiant, ambivalent to authority, resentful, hostile, suspicious, destructive, impulsive, and lacking in self-control (Curtis, Feczko, and Marohn, 1979; Serok and Blum, 1982; Thompson and Dodder, 1986). Some consistently exhibit a low self-esteem or negative self-image. Others keep their self-esteem only through denial of their problems and by failure to admit the incongruency between their behavior and their perceptions of self (Zieman and Benson, 1983). Such adolescents become adept at denial. They deny they have a problem, refuse to accept responsibility for their actions, and continually blame other persons or circumstances for getting them in trouble (Mitchell and Dodder, 1983). In some cases, delinquency is a symptom of deeper neuroses, an outgrowth of fears, anxieties, or hostilities. Walsh and Beyer (1987) found that the most important cause was love deprivation while growing up. In other instances delinquency occurs in basically emotionally healthy adolescents who have been handled incorrectly, misdirected, misled, or suffered temporary traumatic experiences. In some cases, delinquency is the result of poor socialization that results in the adolescents' not developing proper impulse controls (Eisikovits and Sagi, 1982; Stefanko, 1984). Thus, the psychodynamics of delinquents' behavior are different, though the results of that behavior lead to similar trouble (Hoffman, 1984).

Biological Factors in Delinquency   Most delinquency has environmental causes, but in some cases organic or biological factors may be directly or indirectly influential. It has been found, for example, that some juvenile delinquents show evidence of a *maturational lag in the development of the frontal lobe system of the brain*, which can result in neurophysiological dysfunction and delinquent behavior (Voorhees, 1981). It is not that the cognitive function is impaired; rather, the juveniles cannot act on the basis of the knowledge they have.

Other researchers have emphasized the role of biological influences in delinquency (Anolik, 1983). Mednick and Christiansen (1977) have shown that the *autonomic nervous system (ANS) in criminals recovers more slowly from environmental stimulation* as compared to noncriminals. This slow recovery time reduces the ability to alter their behavior through punishment; thus, the individual is not as motivated to inhibit unwanted behavior.

It is true that certain personality characteristics, such as *temperament*, are genetically influenced, so that a child may have a predisposition to behave poorly. If the parents do not know how to cope, psychological disturbance may result (Schwarz, 1979).

Sheppard (1974) believes that at least 25 percent of delinquency can be blamed on *organic causes*. He cites the case of a 15-year-old girl who was suffering from too much insulin in her blood, keeping her blood sugar count too low. She was restless, jumpy, fidgety, and unable to think or act rationally. Proper medication and diet corrected the difficulty. Sheppard cites other examples of delinquency due to a hearing impairment, hyperactivity from hyperthyroidism, or abnormal brain wave patterns. Other research indicates a definite relationship between selected health problems such as vision, hearing, speech, and neurological difficulties. Causes can even originate in prenatal and perinatal complications (Penner, 1982).

Juvenile Street Gangs

Adolescent gang members are primarily male (Bowker, Gross, and Klein, 1980). They join street gangs for a number of reasons: companionship, protection, excitement, and heterosexual contacts (Friedman et al., 1975). One factor that predisposes youths to gang membership is poor family relationships. If emotional and social needs of adolescents are not met through interpersonal relationships in the family, youths turn to the gang to fulfill status needs that would otherwise go unmet. Friedman et al.'s (1975) study of street gangs in Philadelphia showed that gang members had poor mother-son relationships, and of the over 60 percent who had fathers or father substitutes at home, large numbers reported shouting at, cursing, or striking their fathers. Parental defiance was the most important correlate of gang membership.

Gang members are forced to commit illegal acts, especially violent ones, that many would never do if acting on their own. Street gangs hold nearly absolute control over the behavior of individuals. Table 10–3 compares street gang members and nonmembers in Philadelphia in terms of gang coercion to commit antisocial and illegal acts. As can be seen, gangs forced both members and nonmembers to engage in antisocial and illegal acts, but significantly more gang members than nonmembers were forced to cause trouble in the neighborhood,

TABLE 10–3

Percentage of gang coercion of street gang members and nonmembers to commit antisocial and illegal acts.

ITEM	GANG	NONGANG
Stay out all night long	17%	16%
Cause trouble in neighborhood	21	13
Call police names	22	14
Get drunk	32	16
Bother grownups	15	10
Fight	44	21
Get a weapon or hide a weapon	29	12
Stab someone or injure someone with a weapon	22	10
Shoot at someone	25	9
Take heroin, scag, or smack	7	8
Have sex with a girl	38	14
Have sex with other guys	4	3
Steal	27	13
Fight at school	38	18
Skip homework	25	9
Take pot, grass, reefers, hash, or marijuana	20	15
Stay away from school	24	13
"Shake down" other guys	24	33
Take speed or methedrine	7	6
Break up parties	26	9
Destroy public property	20	12
Mark or spray paint on walls	30	15

From: Friedman, C. J., et al. (1976). "Juvenile Street Gangs: The Victimization of Youth," *Adolescence*, 11: 527–533. Used by permission.

verbally abuse police, get drunk, fight, get or hide a weapon, stab or injure some-one with a weapon, shoot at someone with a gun, steal, fight at school, skip homework, stay away from school, break up parties, destroy public property, and mark or spray paint on walls (Friedman et al., 1976). The violent nature of these gangs is revealed in the fact that 44 percent of members were forced to fight, 22 percent were forced to stab or injure someone, and 25 percent were forced to shoot at someone. Thus, the gangs held life-and-death power over others and were a direct challenge to the authority of the family, community, police, the school, and the individual (Miller, 1975).

The Juvenile Justice System

The statutes and customs of each state determine the process for handling juve-nile delinquents. Although this process varies from state to state, each system consists of four separate entities: the police, the juvenile court, the correctional system, and private community programs.

The Police   The first contact any adolescent has with the juvenile justice system is the local police department. Charged with maintaining and enforcing the law, the police perform the function of screening cases that may go before the court. When offenses are discovered, the police may take any one of several actions: (1) ignore the offenses; (2) let the juvenile go with a warning; (3) report the problem to parents; (4) refer the case to the school, a welfare agency, clinic, counseling or guidance center, or family society; (5) take the juvenile into custody for questioning, to be held or reprimanded by a juvenile officer; or (6) after investigation, arrest the juvenile and turn the matter over to a juvenile court. If arrested and waiting trial, the juvenile may be released with or without bail or kept in a special detention center awaiting disposition of his or her case. If special juvenile facilities are not available, juvenile offenders are sometimes kept in jail with adult offenders.

One problem is that in the beginning of the process, the matter is left entirely to police discretion. They must enforce the law, but they do so differentially. An individual officer may arrest adolescents who come from the wrong section of town or have the wrong color skin or wild hair, but may let other adolescents go who come from well-to-do-families or are neatly dressed. Many officers enjoy harassing anyone who is an adolescent or a "punk type" kid. Some officers are far harder on juveniles than are other officers. Also, parents who are able to afford lawyers ensure that their youths will be treated more fairly before the law. One of the reasons adolescents become bitter toward the police is because of unfair and differential treatment or harassment (Moretz, 1980).

Some communities hire juvenile officers who are specialists in dealing with youths. Such officers go far beyond law enforcement functions and strive to assist adolescents and their families in solving problems. Some large cities have sep-arate juvenile bureaus with five basic functions:

1. The discovery of delinquents, potential delinquents, and conditions contrib-uting to delinquency.

2. The investigation of cases of juveniles who are delinquents or involved as accessories by association with adult criminals.
3. The protection of juveniles.
4. The disposition of juvenile cases.
5. The prevention of juvenile delinquency.

Police in many communities now go far beyond law enforcement, from sponsoring boys' clubs to offering drug education programs or safety education in local schools.

The Juvenile Court   As a last resort, the juvenile court is asked to make the disposition of a case. But procedures vary from state to state. How "parental" should the judge be? Cases are often dealt with informally in private hearings. The "trial" consists of private talks in the judge's chambers. But without any formal trial, what happens in such cases depends completely on the inclinations of the judge. Plea bargaining between lawyers is common, so that in this instance, the attorneys decide the case.

The best juvenile court systems hire judges with special qualifications for juvenile court work, who understand not only the law but also child psychology and social problems. A variety of medical, psychological, and social services are available along with adequate foster family and institutional care and recreational services and facilities. A qualified probation staff with limited case loads and plans for constructive efforts works under state supervision. Detention of juveniles is kept at a minimum—if possible, outside of jails and police stations. An adequate record system is maintained and safeguarded against indiscriminate public inspection (Dreyfus, 1976).

The best juvenile court systems hire judges with special qualifications for juvenile court work. These judges understand not only the law but also child psychology and social problems.
(H. Armstrong Roberts)

The Correctional System   The majority of juvenile offenders brought to court, especially those charged for the first time, are placed on probation, given suspended sentences, and/or ordered to get help from the proper medical, psychological, or social service agency or personnel. The purpose of the court is not just to punish but also to ensure proper treatment and rehabilitation of the delinquent. Thus, the judge often must make quick decisions regarding the best treatment.

The backbone of the correctional procedure is the *probation system*, whereby the juvenile is placed under the care of a probation officer to whom she or he must report and who strives to regulate and guide his or her conduct. For the system to work, however, the delinquent has to have a clear understanding of probation requirements and of the punishments for violating probation. Stumphauzer (1976) tells of one teenaged child molester who understood that while on probation he was "to stay out of trouble" and "mind his grandmother" or he "would get into more trouble." But when asked which behaviors were permitted, which were not, and what "minding his grandmother" meant, he did not know. He was not even sure what would happen if he molested another child. Only after consultation was it made clear that if he molested another child he would be taken out of his home and placed in juvenile hall. He also was given some *positive* behaviors to perform (be in by 9:00 P.M. on week nights), which would be rewarded (being able to stay out until 11:00 P.M. on one weekend night) if he obeyed. Probation based entirely on threat of punishment is poor rehabilitation. Programs that focus on positive behavior and positive reinforcement are more helpful. Studies show that juvenile offenders placed on probation have lower rearrest rates and generally better records than those detained in juvenile facilities (Dreyfus, 1976).

Most juvenile correction systems include *detention centers* (Rettig, 1980). Most of these are reception and diagnostic centers where juveniles are placed under temporary restraint awaiting a hearing, or if hearings have already been held, they are placed in the center for further diagnosis and evaluation before more permanent action is taken. About one-third of adolescents in detention centers are not even delinquents (U.S. Bureau of the Census, 1987). They are juveniles in need of supervision (JINS) who are wards of the court because their parents cannot, will not, or should not care for them. Some of the parents are ill or deceased; others have neglected, rejected, or abused them to the point where they have been taken out of the home. Others are youths who have run away from home. Many are awaiting disposition by the court. Critics charge that detention centers are no place for juveniles. They are often overcrowded. Sexual psychopaths and narcotics peddlers are detained with juveniles arrested for curfew violations. At best, the centers are a bad influence.

The correctional system also includes *training schools, ranches, forestry camps*, and *farms*. About three-fourths of the juveniles in public custody are held in these types of facilities. (These do not include the juveniles in jail, in privately operated facilities, foster homes, facilities exclusively for drug abusers, homes for dependent or neglected children, or federal correctional facilities.) Most authorities feel that in their traditional forms, such training schools and correctional institutions do not correct or rehabilitate (Stumphauzer, 1976). While youths are being punished, "rehabilitated," or "corrected," they are exposed to hundreds of other delinquents who spend their time running their own behavior modification program to shape additional antisocial and delinquent behavior. The influence is therefore negative, not positive. The system has been improved greatly by what has been called *token economy*, which places the emphasis on a "twenty-four-hour positive learning environment." In this system, students earn points for good behavior, with points convertible to money that can be used to purchase goods or privileges. Money can be spent for room rental, fines for misconduct, in the commissary or snack bar, or for recreation. Students earn points for academic accomplishments and school work, for proper social behavior, for doing chores or other jobs, or for social development. Under this system, they make great gains in academic achievement, on-the-job training, or eliminating assaultive, disruptive, and antisocial behavior.

One of the criticisms of correctional institutions for youthful offenders is that once the juveniles are released to the community, they often come under the same influences and face some of the same problems that were responsible for their getting into trouble in the first place. One suggestion has been to use *halfway houses* and *group homes* where youths could live, going from there to school or to work. This way, some control can be maintained until they have learned self-direction (Stumphauzer, 1976). Halfway houses and group homes are also used in lieu of other types of facilities, especially for runaways or dislocated adolescents or for emotionally or socially troubled youths. Youths are given food, shelter, and clothing as needed, opportunities for recreation, transportation to and from school or other activities, occupational therapy and vocational guidance, on-the-job training opportunities, and individual and group counseling. Referrals are also made to help adolescents get proper treatment and services. One of the most important needs is to prepare youths for employment after discharge (Weissman, 1985).

Sending adolescents to *prison* is the worst way to rehabilitate them. A percentage of inmates of a prison population are sociopaths who prefer antisocial behavior, have no regard for the interests of others, show little or no remorse, are untreatable, and for whom prison may be justified. They are in contrast to adolescents who are put in prison for relatively minor offenses. In spite of this, the average sentences of juveniles are greater than for adults who have committed the same crimes (Rich, 1982). Juvenile offenders tend to be passive, dependent youths who are easily bullied, try to maintain friendships with others, and then get into trouble trying to model their behavior after the group's expectations. They have had no adequate adult male models with whom they could have had significant relationships. They are often school dropouts, unemployed, and without plans for the future. Left with no reasonable course of action, they engage in random activities with the wrong gang that eventually get them into trouble with the law. Once they have a prison record, their chances of finding a useful life are jeopardized.

When sent to prison, they learn that guards are arbitrary and unfair in the way they mete out punishment. One prisoner may be denied the privilege of one movie for a given offense, while another may be placed in solitary for ten days. They learn that fear, bribery, cheating, and sadism are ways of dealing with problems. When they compare their lot to that of the guards, they notice the complete lack of work activity of the guards and conclude it does not pay to work. In addition, many timid souls are harassed and bullied by fellow prisoners who may use them in any number of ways, including for homosexual activities. If adolescents were not antagonistic toward authority and the system upon arrival in prison, they soon become so. They grow to hate the prison and vow never to return—not by becoming law abiding but by never again being caught. Prison provides a model of criminal behavior, unleashes the revenge of society, guards, and prisoners on other prisoners, and stimulates each inmate to want to get out to seek his own vengeance. The result is that two-thirds to three-fourths of those committed to prison are repeaters.

Counseling and therapy both individually and in groups are important parts of any comprehensive program of treatment and correction of juvenile offenders. Individual therapy on a one-to-one basis is time-consuming, with too few professionals and too many delinquents, but is effective in some instances (Stumphauzer, 1976). Some therapists feel that group therapy reaches a juvenile sooner than individual therapy because the delinquent feels less anxious and defensive in the group situation. Group therapy is sometimes offered to both juvenile offenders and their parents, when it becomes similar to other types of family therapy. Work with parents is especially important in correcting family situations that contribute to the delinquency in the first place (Roberts, 1982).

Critique of the Juvenile Justice System   *The worst criticism of the juvenile justice system is that it does not work.* The present trend to try juveniles as adults has not helped (Boucher, 1983). Neither juvenile nor adult crime has been reduced as a result of the juvenile court system, nor has the system reduced the rate of recidivism. Almost all critiques of the system point out the lack of coordination and definition in the system, the defective delivery of services, the confusion of roles and responsibilities of the judges, social workers, police, counsel, community agencies, and the system's failure to protect either the child or society. As long as the emphasis is on punishing the juvenile offender, treatment and rehabilitation will be neglected (Wolff, 1987).

Knowledge of the Law   A neglected area of investigation has been the extent to which ignorance of the law has been a factor in juveniles' getting into trouble or, once in trouble, of not getting full protection under the law. The assumption has always been that ignorance of the law is no excuse, but it is still a reason why some teenagers get arrested and are not able to utilize their legally permitted rights. An investigation of the knowledge of the law of sophomore, junior, and senior students in six classes in a high school in a small industrial city in Oregon revealed widespread ignorance of the law (Saunders, 1981). The students could answer correctly fewer than half the questions. In general, the students were most familiar with motor vehicle laws and less acquainted with laws relating to the family or the rights of minors to medical care. They were least acquainted with procedural rights (when arrested, rights of bail, custody, appeal, and so forth). The author concludes that lack of knowledge may prompt teenagers to acquiesce in the face of legal intimidation and fail to seek legal help. Blacks unfamiliar with open housing regulations, for example, would be unlikely to try to settle except in segregated areas. Or juveniles without knowledge of their medical rights would fail to seek diagnosis and treatment for something like venereal disease. Lack of knowledge is often responsible for failure to seek many kinds of help available. Sametz (1981) suggests that all children in the public schools should be taught public law, definitions of crimes, their own rights, and the roles of professionals within the criminal justice system.

Private, Community Programs   Private, community programs established to treat delinquency have taken many forms. Communities have established both resident and outpatient centers (Fairchild and Wright, 1984), drug abuse centers, rap centers, coffee houses, youth centers, boys' or girls' clubs, big brother or big sister programs (Seide, 1982), youth employment agencies, and psychoeducational programs (Carpenter and Sugrue, 1984). The success of the program indicates that youths and their families can best be served by institutions and agencies cooperating in planning and executing programs.

Prevention

Any effort to curb delinquency needs to focus on prevention. This means identifying children (such as hyperactive ones) who may be predisposed to getting in trouble. It may mean focusing on their family life and relationships and assisting parents in learning more effective parenting skills. It may mean putting antisocial youths into groups of prosocial peers, such as day camps, where their behavior is influenced positively. It may mean targeting young children in preschool settings before problems arise. It may mean assisting older children with learning disabilities before they become behavior problems. Hurley (1985) writes: "A partial list of the proposed links to crime include television viewing, poor nutrition, eyesight problems, teenage unemployment, teenage employment, too little punishment, too much punishment, high IQ, low IQ, allergies and fluorescent lighting" (p. 68). To root out the various links to crime and to correct these causes will take great commitment in the years ahead.

SUMMARY

Alienated adolescents feel estranged from family, friends, and school. They turn away from the mainstream of youth and adult society and express their feelings through various types of acting out behavior. This chapter discusses three manifestations of alienation: running away, suicide, and juvenile delinquency.

Adolescents run away from home for a number of reasons, most important of which is conflict in the family. Pressures and difficulties at school also contribute to running away. Runaways have been classified in various ways. "Running from" adolescents have not been able to tolerate their home or school situation. Some seek to escape a multiproblem family. Some flee from physical or sexual abuse. "Running to" adolescents are pleasure seekers, running to other places or people to seek thrills and adventure.

Adolescents commit suicide for a variety of reasons: disturbed family situations, emotional and social isolation, loss of a love object, depression, stress, immaturity, poor impulse control, suggestion and example of others, mental illness, guilt, anger, or hostility, or as a cry for help. Adults ought to be alert to signs and symptoms that the adolescent is suicide prone.

Juvenile delinquency is the violation of the law by anyone under legal age. From 1970 to 1985, the number of those under eighteen who were arrested rose slightly, but the total percentages who were arrested who were under 18 declined, due partly to a decline of juveniles in the population. Still, 49 percent of all arrests in 1985 were of people under age 25. Arrests among males were over three and one-half times that among females of the same age.

The causes of delinquency may be grouped into three major categories: sociological, psychological, and biological. Sociological factors include family background, socioeconomic status, educational and occupational opportunities, affluence and hedonistic life-styles, alcohol or drug usage, peer group pressures, neighborhood and community influences, rapid cultural change and conflicting values, and school performance.

Psychological factors include relationships with parents, personality factors such as low self-esteem, or deeper neuroses.

Biological factors include deficiencies in the development of the frontal lobe of the brain, retardation in autonomic nervous system responses, chromosomal aberrations, inheritance of certain troublesome temperaments, or various other organic causes such as abnormal blood sugar level; hearing, vision, or speech impairment; hyperthyroidism; or abnormal brain wave patterns or other neurological difficulties.

Adolescents often organize themselves into juvenile gangs for protection, companionship, excitement, or heterosexual contacts. Such gangs are a problem if they force members and some nonmembers to engage in antisocial and illegal acts that they would not do if acting on their own. In such cases, the only way to deal with delinquency is to dismantle or redirect the criminal activities of the group.

The juvenile justice system consists of the police, the juvenile court, and the correctional system (including the probation system, detention centers, training schools, ranches, forestry camps, farms, halfway houses, group homes, treatment centers, and prisons). The worst criticism of the juvenile justice system is that it does not work.

Various private and community programs are also offered: resident and outpatient treatment centers, drug abuse centers, rap centers, coffee houses, youth centers, boys' or girls' clubs, big brother or big sister programs, youth employment agencies, and psychoeducational programs.

Any effort to curb delinquency ought to focus on prevention.

DISCUSSION QUESTIONS

1. Have you known an adolescent who ran away from home? What were the circumstances?
2. Should runaways be forced to return home? When? When not?
3. What can or should be done to help parents of runaways?
4. Have you known an adolescent who committed suicide? What were the reasons?

5. Do you think that some rock music and performers influence some adolescents to commit suicide? Explain.

6. How do you explain that greater percentages of white adolescents than black adolescents commit suicide?

7. What are the major symptoms of suicidal tendencies? What should you do if you realize someone is manifesting these symptoms?

8. How do you account for the fact that the percentages of those who are arrested who are under eighteen are decreasing?

9. Why do far greater numbers of males than females become delinquent? What sociological, psychological, and biological factors may be exerting an influence?

10. What should parents do if their adolescent is running around with a group whose members are known to be delinquent?

11. Why do some adolescents brought up in crime-prone neighborhoods not become delinquent?

12. What is the role of the school in preventing delinquency?

13. How do relationships with parents affect delinquency?

14. How do biological factors affect delinquency?

15. When you were growing up, were there any delinquent juvenile gangs in your area? Describe them.

16. What is your opinion of the juvenile justice system? How could it be improved? What do you think is needed to be able to reform known offenders? Have you known a juvenile offender who was sent to a training school or correctional institution who became a productive, law-abiding citizen? What factors made the difference?

17. How can juvenile delinquency be prevented?

BIBLIOGRAPHY

Adams, G. R., Gullotta, T., and Clancy, M. A. (1985). "Homeless Adolescents: A Descriptive Study of Similarities and Differences Between Runaways and Throwaways." *Adolescence*, 22, 715–724.

Adams, G. R., and Munro, G. (September, 1979). "Portrait of the North American Runaway: A Critical Review." *Journal of Youth and Adolescence*, 8, 359–373.

Allen, B. P. (1987). "Youth Suicide." *Adolescence*, 22, 271–290.

Anolik, S. A. (Winter, 1980). "The Family Perceptions of Delinquents, High School Students, and Freshman College Students." *Adolescence*, 15, 903–911.

———. (December, 1981). "Imaginary Audience Behavior and Perceptions of Parents among Delinquent and Nondelinquent Adolescents." *Journal of Youth and Adolescence*, 10, 443–454.

———. (Fall, 1983). "Family Influences upon Delinquency: Biosocial and Psychosocial Perspectives." *Adolescence*, 18, 489–498.

Benalcazar, B. (Fall, 1982). "Study of Fifteen Runaway Patients." *Adolescence*, 17, 553–566.

Benda, B. B. (1987). "Predicting Juvenile Recidivism; New Method, Old Problems." *Adolescence*, 22, 691–704.

Bernstein, R. M. (Fall, 1981). "The Relationship between Dimensions of Delinquency and Developments of Self and Peer Perception." *Adolescence*, 16, 543–556.

Boucher, C. R. (Spring—Summer, 1983). "A Child Development Perspective on the Criminal Responsibilities of Juveniles." *New York University Education Quarterly*, 14, 7–13.

Bowker, L. H., Gross, H. S., and Klein, M. W. (Fall, 1980). "Female Participation in Delinquent Gang Activities." *Adolescence*, 15, 509–519.

Bowker, L. H., and Klein, M. W. (Winter, 1983). "The Etiology of Female Juvenile Delinquency and Gang Membership: A Test of Psychological and Social Structural Explanations." *Adolescence*, 18, 739–751.

Bynner, J. M., O'Malley, P. M., and Bachman, J. G. (December, 1981). "Self-Esteem and Delinquency Revisited." *Journal of Youth and Adolescence*, 10, 407–441.

Calabrese, R. L. (1987). "Adolescence: A Growth Period Conducive to Alienation." *Adolescence*, 22, 929–938.

Carpenter, P., and Sugrue, D. P. (Spring, 1984). "Psychoeducation in an Outpatient Setting—Designing a Heterogeneous Format for a Heterogeneous Population of Juvenile Delinquents." *Adolescence*, 19, 113–122.

"College Suicides: Exaggerated by Half." (August, 1980). *Psychology Today*, p. 81.

Cosand, B. J., Bourque, L. B., and Kraus, J. F. (Winter, 1982). "Suicide among Adolescents in Sacramento County, California, 1950–1979." *Adolescence*, 17, 917–930.

Covington, J. (August, 1982). "Adolescent Deviation and Age." *Journal of Youth and Adolescence*, 11, 329–344.

Curtis, G., Feczko, M. D., and Marohn, R. C. (December, 1979). "Rorschach Differences in Normal and Delinquent White Male Adolescents: A Discriminant Function Analysis." *Journal of Youth and Adolescence*, 8, 379–392.

Dawkins, R. L., and Dawkins, M. P. (Winter, 1983). "Alcohol Use and Delinquency among Black, White, and Hispanic Adolescent Offenders." *Adolescence*, 18, 799–809.

Doan, M., and Peterson, S. (November 12, 1984). "As 'Cluster Suicides' Take Toll of Teenagers." *U.S. News & World Report*, pp. 49, 50.

Dreyfus, E. A. (1976). *Adolescence: Theory and Experience*. Columbus, Ohio: Charles E. Merrill Publishing Co.

Dunham, R. G., and Alpert, G. P. (1987). "Keeping Juvenile Delinquents in School: A Prediction Model." *Adolescence*, 22, 45–57.

Eisikovits, Z., and Sagi, A. (June, 1982). "Moral Development and Discipline Encounter in Delinquent and Nondelinquent Adolescents." *Journal of Youth and Adolescence*, 11, 217–230.

Emery, P. E. (Summer, 1983). "Adolescent Depression and Suicide." *Adolescence*, 18, 245–258.

Fairchild, H. H., and Wright, C. (Summer, 1984). "A Social-Ecological Assessment and Feedback-Intervention of an Adolescent Treatment Agency." *Adolescence*, 19, 263–275.

Fischer, J. L. (October, 1980). "Reciprocity, Agreement, and Family Style in Family Systems with a Disturbed and Nondisturbed Adolescent." *Journal of Youth and Adolescence*, 9, 391–406.

Friedman, C. J., et al. (1975). "A Profile of Juvenile Street Gang Members." *Adolescence*, 10, 563–607.

––––––. (1976). "Juvenile Gangs: The Victimization of Youth." *Adolescence*, 11, 527–533.

Friedrich, W., Rearms, R., and Jacobs, J. (October, 1982). "Depression and Suicidal Ideation in Early Adolescents." *Journal of Youth and Adolescence*, 11, 403–407.

Fujimura, L. E., Weis, D. M., and Cochran, J. R. (June, 1985). "Suicide: Dynamics and Implications for Counseling." *Journal of Counseling and Development*, 63, 612–615.

Gispert, M. (1987). "Preventing Teenage Suicide." *Medical Aspects of Human Sexuality*, 21, 16.

Gispert, M., Wheeler, K., Marsh, L., and Davis, M. S. (1985). "Suicidal Adolescents: Factors in Evaluation." *Adolescence*, 20, 753–762.

Grande, C. G. (1988). "Delinquency: The Learning Disabled Students' Reaction to Academic School Failure." *Adolescence*, 23, 209–219.

Greene, N. B., and Esselstyn, T. C. (1972). "The Beyond Control Girl." *Juvenile Justice*, 23, 13–19.

Greuling, J. W., and DeBlassie, R. R. (Fall, 1980). "Adolescent Suicide." *Adolescence*, 59, 589–601.

Grob, M. C., Klein, A. A., and Eisen, S. V. (April, 1983). "The Role of the High School Professional in Identifying and Managing Adolescent Suicidal Behavior." *Journal of Youth and Adolescence*, 12, 163–173.

Hafen, B. Q., and Frandsen, K. J. (1986). *Youth Suicide: Depression and Loneliness*. Provo, UT.: Behavioral Health Associates.

Hepworth, D. H., Farley, O. W., and Griffiths, J. C. (February, 1986). "Research Capsule." *Social Research Institute Newsletter*. Salt Lake City, UT.: Graduate School of Social Work.

Hersch, P. (1988). "Coming of Age on City Streets." *Psychology Today*, 22, 28–37.

Hoffman, V. J. (Spring, 1984). "The Relationship of Psychology to Delinquency: A Comprehensive Approach." *Adolescence*, 19, 55–61.

Hurley, D. (March, 1985). "Arresting Delinquency." *Psychology Today*, 19, 62–68.

Janus, M., Burgess, A. W., and McCormack, A. (1987). "Histories of Sexual Abuse in Adolescent Male Runaways." *Adolescence*, 22, 405–417.

Johnson, P. L., and O'Leary, K. D. (1987). "Parental Behavior Patterns and Conduct Disorders in Girls." *Journal of Abnormal Child Psychology*, 15, 573–581.

Johnson, R. E. (1987). "Mother's Versus Father's Roles in Causing Delinquency." *Adolescence*, 22, 305–315.

Johnson, R., and Carter, M. M. (Summer, 1980). "Flight of the Young: Why Children Run Away from Their Homes." *Adolescence*, 15, 483–489.

Kreider, D. G., and Motto, J. A. (1970). "Parent-Child Role Reversal and Suicidal States in Adolescence." *Adolescence*, 9, 365–370.

Kroupa, S. E. (1988). "Perceived Parental Acceptance

and Female Juvenile Delinquency." *Adolescence*, 23, 171–185.

LeFlore, L. (1988). "Delinquent Youths and Family." *Adolescence*, 23, 629–642.

Lester, D. (1987). "A Subcultural Theory of Teenage Suicide." *Adolescence*, 22, 317–320.

Loeb, R. C., Burke, T. A., and Boglarsky, C. A. (1986). "A Large Scale Comparison of Perspectives on Parenting Between Teenage Runaways and Non-runaways." *Adolescence*, 21, 921–930.

McAnarney, E. R. (Winter, 1979). "Adolescent and Young Adult Suicide in the United States—A Reflection of Societal Unrest." *Adolescence*, 14, 765–774.

McGuire, D. (1983). "Teenage Suicide: A Search for Sense." *International Journal of Offender Therapy and Comparative Criminology*, 27, 211–217.

Madden, D. J., and Harbin, H. T. (July, 1983). "Family Structures of Assaultive Adolescents." *Journal of Marital and Family Therapy*, 9, 311–316.

Matthews, L. J., and Ilon, L. (July, 1980). "Becoming a Chronic Runaway: The Effects of Race and Family in Hawaii." *Family Relations*, 29, 404–409.

May, J. M. (1986). "Cognitive Processes and Violent Behavior in Young People." *Journal of Adolescence*, 9, 17–27.

Mednick, S. S., and Christiansen, K. O. (1977). *Biosocial Bases of Criminal Behavior.* New York: Gardner Press.

Miller, D. (1974). *Adolescence: Psychology, Psychopathology, and Psychotherapy.* New York: Jason Aronson.

Mitchell, J., and Dodder, R. A. (June, 1980). "An Examination of Types of Delinquency through Path Analysis." *Journal of Youth and Adolescence*, 9, 239–248.

———. (August, 1983). "Types of Neutralization and Types of Delinquency." *Journal of Youth and Adolescence*, 12, 307–318.

Moretz, W. J. (Summer, 1980). "Male-Female Comparisons of Attitudes toward the Justice System among Senior High School Students." *Adolescence*, 15, 257–266.

Neiger, B. L., and Hopkins, R. W. (1988). "Adolescent Suicide: Character Traits of High-Risk Teenagers." *Adolescence*, 23, 469–475.

Palenski, J. E., and Launer, H. M. (1987). "The 'Process' of Running Away: A Redefinition." *Adolescence*, 22, 347–362.

Parrott, C. A., and Strongman, K. T. (Summer, 1984). "Locus of Control and Delinquency." *Adolescence*, 19, 459–471.

Peck, D. L. (1987). "Social-Psychological Correlates of Adolescent and Youthful Suicide." *Adolescence*, 22, 863–878.

Penner, M. J. (Summer, 1982). "The Role of Selected Health Problems in the Causation of Juvenile Delinquency." *Adolescence*, 17, 347–368.

Pfeffer, C. (1987). "Suicidal Children Announce Their Self-Destructive Intentions." *Medical Aspects of Human Sexuality*, 21, 14.

Rettig, R. P. (Summer, 1980). "Considering the Use and Usefulness of Juvenile Detention: Operationalizing Social Theory." *Adolescence*, 15, 443–459.

Rich, Philip. (Spring, 1982). "The Juvenile Justice System and Its Treatment of the Juvenile: An Overview." *Adolescence*, 17, 141–152.

Riemer, J. W. (Spring, 1981). "Deviance as Fun." *Adolescence*, 16, 39–43.

Roberts, A. R. (Summer, 1982). "Adolescent Runaways in Suburbia: A New Typology." *Adolescence*, 17, 379–396.

Roberts, R. (January, 1982). "Treating Conduct-Disordered Adolescents and Young Adults by Working with the Parents." *Journal of Marital and Family Therapy*, 8, 15–28.

Robbins, D. (1983). "A Cluster of Adolescent Suicide Attempts: Is Suicide Contagious?" *Journal of Adolescent Health Care*, 3, 253–255.

Sametz, L. (Spring, 1981). "The Educator's Role in the Juvenile Justice System." *Adolescence*, 16, 101–109.

Saunders, L. E. (Fall, 1981). "Ignorance of the Law among Teenagers: Is It a Barrier to the Exertion of Their Rights as Citizens?" *Adolescence*, 16, 711–726.

Schwarz, J. C. (1979). "Childhood Origins of Psychopathology." *American Psychologist*, 34, 879–885.

Seide, F. W. (Spring, 1982). "Big Sisters: An Experimental Evaluation." *Adolescence*, 17, 117–128.

Serok, S., and Blum, A. (Summer, 1982). "Rule-Violating Behavior of Delinquent and Nondelinquent Youth in Games." *Adolescence*, 17, 457–464.

Shafi, M. (1988). "Suicidal Children." *Medical Aspects of Human Sexuality*, 22, 63.

Sheppard, B. J. (1974). "Making the Case for Behavior as an Expression of Physiological Condition." In *Youth in Trouble.* Edited by B. L. Kratonile. San Rafael, CA.: Academic Therapy Publications.

Simonds, J. F. (1975). "Hallucinations in Nonpsychotic Children and Adolescent." *Journal of Youth and Adolescence*, 4, 171–182.

Sommer, B. (1984). "The Troubled Teen: Suicide, Drug

Use, and Running Away." *Women's Health*, 9, 117–141.

Spillane-Grieco, E. (Spring, 1984). "Characteristics of a Helpful Relationship: A Study of Empathetic Understanding and Positive Regard between Runaways and Their Parents." *Adolescence*, 19, 63–75.

Stack, S. (May, 1985). "The Effect of Domestic/Religious Individualism in Suicide, 1954–1978." *Journal of Marriage and the Family*, 47, 431–447.

Stefanko, M. (Spring, 1984). "Trends in Adolescent Research: A Review of Articles Published in Adolescence—1976–1981." *Adolescence*, 19, 1–14.

Stivers, C. (1988). "Parent-Adolescent Communication and Its Relationship to Adolescent Depression and Suicide Proneness." *Adolescence*, 23, 291–295.

Streit, F. (Summer, 1981). "Differences among Youthful Criminal Offenders Based on Their Perceptions of Parental Behavior." *Adolescence*, 16, 409–413.

Strober, M. (August, 1981). "A Comparative Analysis of Personality Organization in Juvenile Anorexia Nervosa." *Journal of Youth and Adolescence*, 10, 285–295.

Stuck, M. F., and Glassner, B. (1985). "The Transition from Drug Use and Crime to Noninvolvement: A Case Study." *Adolescence*, 20, 669–679.

Stumphauzer, J. S. (1976). "Modifying Delinquent Behavior: Beginnings and Current Practices." *Adolescence*, 11, 13–28.

The Suicide Prevention Center. (1984). *Suicide Statistics*. Los Angeles, CA.

Thompson, W. E., and Dodder, R. A. (1986). "Containment Theory and Juvenile Delinquency: A Reevaluation Through Factor Analysis." *Adolescence*, 21, 365–376.

Thornton, W. E. (Winter, 1982). "Gender Traits and Delinquency Involvement of Boys and Girls." *Adolescence*, 17, 749–768.

Tolan, P. (1988). "Socioeconomic, Family, and Social Stress Correlates of Adolescent Antisocial and Delinquent Behavior." *Journal of Abnormal Child Psychology*, 16, 317–331.

Tygart, C. (1988). "Public School Vandalism: Toward a Synthesis of Theories and Transition to Paradigm Analysis." *Adolescence*, 23, 187–200.

U.S. Bureau of the Census. Department of Commerce (1987). *Statistical Abstract of the United States, 1987.*

Washington, D.C.: U.S. Government Printing Office.

U.S. Department of Health and Human Services. Office of Human Development (August, 1980). *Status of Children, Youth, and Families (1979)*. DHHS Publication No. (OHDS) 80–30274.

Voorhees, J. (Spring, 1981). "Neuropsychological Differences between Juvenile Delinquents and Functional Adolescents: A Preliminary Study." *Adolescence*, 16, 57–66.

Wade, N. L. (1987). "Suicide as a Resolution of Separation—Individuation Among Adolescent Girls." *Adolescence*, 22, 169–177.

Walker, B. A., and Mehr, M. (Summer, 1983). "Adolescent Suicide—A Family Crisis: A Model for Effective Intervention by Family Therapists." *Adolescence*, 70, 285–292.

Walsh, A., and Beyer, J. A. (1987). "Violent Crime, Sociopathy, and Love Deprivation among Adolescent Delinquents." *Adolescence*, 22, 705–717.

Wasson, A. S. (Fall, 1980). "Stimulus-Seeking, Perceived School Environment and School Misbehavior." *Adolescence*, 15, 603–608.

Weiner, F. (1970). *Psychological Disturbance in Adolescence*. New York: John Wiley and Sons.

Weissman, S. (April, 1985). "Preparing Incarcerated Youth for Employment." *Journal of Counseling and Development*, 63, 524–525.

Weller, L., and Luchterhand, E. (Spring, 1983). "Family Relationships of 'Problem' and 'Promising' Youth." *Adolescence*, 18, 93–100.

Wolff, S. (1987). "Antisocial Conduct: Whose Concern?" *Journal of Adolescence*, 10, 105–118.

Wright, L. S. (1985). "Suicidal Thoughts and Their Relationship to Family Stress and Personal Problems Among High School Seniors and College Undergraduates." *Adolescence*, 20, 575–580.

Yacoubian, J. H., and Lourie, R. S. (1973). "Suicide and Attempted Suicide in Children and Adolescents." In *Pathology of Childhood and Adolescence*. Edited by S. L. Copel, New York: Basic Books.

Zieman, G. L., and Benson, G. P. (December, 1983). "Delinquency: The Role of Self-Esteem and Social Values." *Journal of Youth and Adolescence*, 12, 489–500.

Zober, E. (Summer, 1981). "The Socialization of Adolescents into Juvenile Delinquency." *Adolescence*, 16, 321–330.

CHAPTER
11

Substance Abuse, Addiction, and Dependency

This chapter focuses on three selected health problems of adolescents: *drug abuse, smoking,* and *excessive drinking.* These three problems have been selected because of their frequency and their importance in the lives of adolescents. Drug abuse is considered by some the greatest social health problem relating to youths (Thorne and DeBlassie, 1985). The purpose of this section is to take a look at the total problem and to ask and try to answer a number of questions. Which drugs are most commonly abused? Has the abuse of drugs been overestimated? Who is using drugs and for what reasons? Why do adolescents try drugs? Where? With whom? Why do many adolescents not try or use them? Large numbers of youths also smoke tobacco, though the medical profession is now strongly allied against its use. What can be done to prevent adolescents from starting? Drinking also becomes a problem for society as well as for the individual when it is excessive. This chapter also focuses on alcohol as the drug of preference among adolescents.

DRUG ABUSE

Physical Addiction and Psychological Dependency

By definition, a drug is a substance used as a medicine. As such, some drugs are used by virtually everyone. Aspirin is a very effective drug, but even aspirin is lethal if taken in excess. Drug abuse, therefore, is the use of a drug for other than a medicinal purpose or in improper quantities or administration. The problem is drug abuse, not drug use.

physical addiction or physical dependency

psychological dependency

There is also a distinction between **physical addiction, or physical dependency,** and **psychological dependency.** An addictive drug is one that is physically habit forming because the body builds up a physical need for the drug, so that its sudden denial results in withdrawal symptoms. Psychological dependency is the development of a persistent, sometimes overpowering psychological need for a drug, resulting in a compulsion to take it. A well-established habit of psychological dependency may be more difficult to overcome than one involving physical dependency, especially if people become so deeply involved with a drug that they cannot function without it. Physical dependency on heroin, for example, may be broken, but individuals go back to it because of psychological dependency on it. It is a mistake, therefore, to assume that the only dangerous drugs are those that are physically addictive.

The drugs most commonly abused may be grouped into a number of categories: *narcotics, stimulants, depressants, hallucinogens, marijuana,* and *inhalants. Alcohol* and *nicotine* are also drugs. Because they are more widely used than any of the others, they will be discussed in separate sections of this chapter.

Narcotics

Narcotics include *opium* and its derivatives such as *morphine, heroin,* and *codeine.* Opium is a dark, gummy substance extracted from the juice of unripe seed pods of the opium poppy. Opium is usually taken orally or sniffed—that is, it is heated and its vapor inhaled. *Morphine,* the chief active ingredient in opium, is extracted as a bitter, white powder with no odor. Each grain of opium contains about one-tenth of a grain of morphine. Morphine is used medicinally to relieve extreme pain because of its depressant effect on the central nervous system. Addicts refer to it as "M" or "monkey." It may be sniffed, but the powder is usually mixed with water and injected under the skin with a hypodermic needle ("skin popping"). For maximum effect, it is injected directly into a vein ("mainlined") (O'Brien and Cohen, 1984).

Heroin ("H," "horse," or "Harry") is produced from morphine by a simple chemical process. Like its relative, it is a white, odorless powder. If dirty needles or ingredients are used, the result may be blood poisoning or serious infections, such as AIDS or hepatitis, a leading cause of death among addicts. Heroin is the most widely used opiate but is more addictive than morphine because it is stronger. Traditionally more hard-core heroin addicts come from the ghettos of large cities than from any other area. A large percentage of all heroin addicts came from New York alone. If California, Illinois, and New Jersey are added, these four states contain 78 percent of the heroin addicts in the United States. Street supplies are diluted ("cut") with milk sugar to squeeze out maximum profits. Heroin is also often diluted with bitter-tasting quinine to make it impossible for addicts to gauge the heroin concentration by tasting the mixture. Pure quinine injected in sufficient quantity may be a leading cause of the deaths that are attributed to a heroin overdose. Addicts often die, also, if they shoot heroin while under the influence of alcohol or barbiturates, for the combination of drugs has a double depressive effect (O'Brien and Cohen, 1984). In all likelihood this is what happened to comedian John Belushi.

Codeine is also a morphine derivative. Often used in cough syrups or to relieve mild body aches, it has the same but milder analgesic properties as other narcotics. *Paregoric* a liquid preparation containing an extract of opium, is used medicinally to counteract diarrhea and abdominal pain. Codeine and paregoric are often used by young people who think they are not addictive. Actually they can be.

The synthetic opiates, *Demerol* (meperidine) and *Dolophine* (methadone), were created as chemical substitutes for the natural opiates and are used in medicine as pain relievers. They are addictive and restricted by law to medical use.

The consequences of morphine and heroin use are severe. They are the most physically addictive of all drugs. Users quickly develop tolerance and physical dependence and must therefore gradually increase the dosage. They quickly develop a psychological dependence as well. Because dependence becomes total and heroin is expensive (addicts spend several hundred dollars daily) many users turn to crime or prostitution to support their habit. Without the drug, withdrawal symptoms begin to appear. The first symptoms are running eyes and nose, yawning, sweating, dilation of the pupils of the eye, and appearance of goose pimples on the skin (from which the expression "cold turkey" originated). Within twenty-four hours addicts develop leg, back, and abdominal cramps, violent muscle spasms, vomiting, and diarrhea. The expression "kicking the habit" developed as a result of the muscle spasms during withdrawal. Bodily functions such as respiration, blood pressure, temperature, and metabolism, which have been depressed, now become hyperactive. These symptoms gradually diminish over a period of a week or more. Females who have babies while addicted deliver infants who are addicts or who are born dead from drug poisoning.

Addiction may have other effects. Addicts usually lose their appetite for food, with consequent extreme weight loss and severe malnutrition. They neglect their health, suffer chronic fatigue, and are in a general devitalized condition. Sexual interest and activity decline; most marriages end in separation or divorce. They become accident prone—fall frequently, drown, or may set themselves on fire if they drop off to sleep while smoking. They lose the willpower to carry on daily functions and pay little attention to their appearance. Ambition, purpose, pride, and honesty disappear. Their whole life centers on getting the next "fix."

Because the prognosis for curing heroin addiction is so discouraging, methadone is now given as a substitute drug through medically recognized methadone maintenance programs. The drug blocks the hunger for heroin and the effects of it, with the result that the majority of addicts no longer have a constant desire to obtain heroin. Studies show outstanding success with methadone maintenance. The majority of patients who are regularly given medically prescribed doses of methadone become productive citizens, returning to work or school and evidencing arrest-free behavior (O'Brien and Cohen, 1984).

Stimulants

Cocaine ("coke," or "snow") is extracted from the leaves of the South American coca plant and is available as an odorless, fluffy, white powder. It is mistakenly classified as a narcotic and is therefore subject to the same penalties as opiates, but it is a stimulant rather than a depressant to the central nervous system. Even though it is expensive, it is widely used in the youth drug culture, as well as among more affluent groups (U.S. Bureau of the Census, 1988).

The drug depresses the appetite and increases alertness. It is not effective when taken orally, so users sniff or inject it intravenously into the bloodstream. The newest form, "crack," is smoked and is one of the most difficult drug habits to break. Aside from financial depletion, the main undesirable effects are nervousness, irritability, and restlessness from overstimulation, sometimes extending to mild paranoia; physical exhaustion and mental confusion from insomnia; loss of weight; fatigue or depression when "coming down"; and various afflictions of the nasal mucous membranes and cartilage. Taking large doses can lead to a severe psychosis while the person is still on the drug. Large doses can produce headache, cold sweat, rapid and weak pulse, hyperventilation, nausea, vertigo, tremors and convulsions, unconsciousness, and even death (Grinspoon and Bakalar, 1977). Psychological dependence is severe; withdrawal is characterized by a profound depression for which cocaine itself appears to be the only remedy. The compulsion to resume cocaine is strong; once established, the habit is difficult to break. One of the most famous addicts was Sigmund Freud who escalated his use well into the twentieth century (Herbert, 1984).

Amphetamines are stimulants and include such drugs as benzedrine, dexedrine, diphetamine, and methedrine ("speed"). They are used medically for treating obesity, mild depression, fatigue, and other conditions. The drugs are usually taken orally in the form of tablets or capsules. Because they are stimulants, they increase alertness, elevate mood, and produce a feeling of well-being. Large doses may produce a temporary rise in blood pressure, palpitations, headache, dizziness, sweating, diarrhea, pallor and dilation of the pupils, vasomotor disturbances, agitation, confusion, apprehension, or delirium. Regular amphetamine users do not develop physical dependence, for withdrawal does not produce abstinence symptoms, but users soon develop an intense psychological need to continue taking the drug and require larger doses as tolerance develops. Mental depression and fatigue are experienced after the drug has been withdrawn, so psychic dependence develops quickly because the "high" is so enticing and the "low" so depressing. Patients usually need to be treated in mental hospitals, especially those who inject the drugs into their veins. Some users end up swallowing whole handfuls of tablets instead of only one or two. The outcome of this or injecting the drugs intravenously is an amphetamine psychosis (O'Brien and Cohen, 1984).

One of the amphetamines, *methedrine* ("speed"), is particularly dangerous because it is commonly injected under the skin or directly into a vein, often causing rupturing of the blood vessels and death. Other hazards are infections such as tetanus, AIDS, syphilis, malaria, or hepatitis from dirty needles. The heavy user displays a potential for violence, paranoia, physical depletion, or bizarre behavior. Suicides are frequent during the periods of deep depression following withdrawal.

Depressants

Barbiturates are depressants that decrease the activity of the central nervous system, usually producing sedation, intoxication, and sleep. They include drugs commonly used in sleeping pills, such as *Quaalude*, *Nembutal*, *Seconal*, *Tuinal*, *Amytal*, or *phenobarbital*. Some of these drugs—Nembutal, Tuinal, and Seconal, for example—are short acting, meaning the effects set in sooner and wear off sooner. Others, such as phenobarbital, are long acting. Barbiturates are widely prescribed medicinally for insomnia, nervousness, or epilepsy. When taken as directed, in small doses, there is no evidence that the long-acting barbiturates are addictive. There is a greater chance of addiction with the short-acting drugs. All barbiturates are dangerous when abused because they develop total addiction: both physical and psychological dependence. Dosages must be increased as tolerance develops; an overdose may cause death.

Barbiturate users exhibit slurred speech, staggering gait, and sluggish reactions. They may be easily moved to tears or laughter, are emotionally erratic, and are frequently irritable and antagonistic. They are prone to stumble and drop objects and are often bruised or have cigarette burns.

When the abuser has become physically dependent, withdrawal symptoms become severe in about twenty-four hours. Increasing nervousness, headache, anxiety, muscle twitching, tremor, weakness, insomnia, nausea, and a sudden drop of blood pressure occur. Convulsions that can be fatal are an ever-present danger with barbiturate withdrawal. Delirium and hallucinations may develop. When barbiturates are taken in combination with alcohol or narcotics, the sedative effect is multiplied and can result in coma or death.

Tranquilizers such as *Miltown*, *Equanil*, *Placidyl*, *Librium*, and *Valium* are similar to barbiturates in their effects, for they too act upon the central nervous system. The hazards of Valium are supplied to physicians by the manufacturer, Roche Laboratories. The product information supplied reads in part:

> Warnings: . . . patients receiving . . . Valium (diazepam) should be cautioned against engaging in hazardous occupations requiring complete mental alertness such as operating machinery or driving a motor vehicle. . . .
>
> Since Valium (diazepam) has a central nervous system depressant effect, patients should be advised against the simultaneous ingestion of alcohol and other central nervous system depressant drugs. . . .
>
> *Physical and Psychological Dependence*: Withdrawal symptoms (similar in character to those noted with barbiturates and alcohol) have occurred following abrupt discontinuance of diazepam (convulsions, tremor, abdominal and muscle cramps, vomiting and sweating). . . . Particularly addiction-prone individuals (such as drug addicts or alcoholics) should be under careful surveillance when receiving diazepam (Valium package insert, 1988).

In short, these products, when abused, have the same dangers as barbiturates. Drugs like Valium and Librium have been called the "opium of the masses," particularly because one-half of the most common drugs abused may be classified as tranquilizers, barbiturates, or analgesics (Clayton, 1979). *Analgesics* such as *Darvon* are pain killers.

Other common depressants used sometimes, but not as often abused, include bromides and sleep remedies such as Nytol. When used in excess, however, they produce psychological dependence.

Hallucinogens

Hallucinogens, or psychedelic drugs, include a broad range of substances that act on the central nervous system to alter perception and the state of consciousness. The best known psychedelic drug is LSD (lysergic acid diethylamide), a synthetic drug that must be prepared in a laboratory. Other hallucinogens include *peyote* and *mescaline* (derived from the peyote cactus plant), *psilocybin* (derived from a species of mushrooms), and four synthetics, PCP (phencyclidine), STP (also known as DOM—dimethoxymethylamphetamine), DMT (dimethyl tryptomine), and MDA (methylene dioxyamphetamine). DMT may also be prepared from natural plants that grow in the West Indies and parts of South America. STP and MDA share some of the same characteristics of the amphetamines. It is estimated that in 1985, approximately 12 percent of young adults 18 to 25 years of age had used hallucinogens at some time (U.S. Bureau of the Census, Statistical Abstract of the U.S., 1988).

Each compound has users who claim unique effects from using a particular drug. In general, the drugs produce unpredictable results, including distortions of color, sound, time, and speed. A numbing of the senses in which colors are "heard" and sounds are "seen" is common. Some people experience "bad trips" that are intensely frightening and characterized by panic, terror, and psychosis. In one study of young, middle-class male users, a majority of those who experienced a "bad trip" reported the feeling that "no one anywhere could help," that they were "no longer able to control their perceptions," or that they were afraid they had "destroyed part of themselves with the drug" (Rubinow and Cancro, 1977, p. 8). Users have been driven to suicide, violence, or murder or have been permanently hospitalized as psychotic.

LSD, or "acid," must be viewed with extreme suspicion because the drug is so powerful, its strengths are often unknown, and its effects are so unpredictable. A dose of only 50 to 200 micrograms (no larger than a pinpoint) may take the user on a "trip" for eight to sixteen hours. Hallucinations and other psychotic reactions sometimes occur days or months after the last dose, indicating possible brain damage. Infants born of mothers who have taken LSD during pregnancy have shown abnormalities of chromosomal structure. But whether LSD causes pathological chromosomal deviations and genetic defects in users is not definitely known (O'Brien and Cohen, 1984). Users develop psychological but not physical dependence.

Peyote and mescaline are milder hallucinogens than LSD (Picou, Wells, and Miranne, 1980), as is psilocybin. Peyote has been used for years by Navajo Indians, members of the Native American church, as part of their religion. DMT is a shorter-acting hallucinogen whose effects may come and go within the space of two hours, after a sudden and harsh onset. STP appeared in the early spring of 1967. Doses of more than three milligrams can cause hallucinations lasting eight to ten hours. It is said to be 200 times more powerful than mescaline but only one-tenth as potent as LSD. PCP seems to be one of the hallucinogens that is used increasingly. PCP users tend to be more antisocial, hostile, and violent than nonusers. PCP causes hostility, paranoid symptoms, and prolonged psychotic or depressive states in many users. Its use is related to violent actions including violence against self (suicide) (Simonds and Kashani, 1979).

Sharp and Graeven (1981) made a study of 200 PCP users in northern California and found the following results.

> Heavy chronic . . . use of PCP had a profoundly destructive impact upon a wide range of experiences and events in their lives. The impact affected the subjects' ability to perform adequately at school or work, their relationships with parents and with lovers or spouses, their physical and mental health, and their involvement with the criminal justice system . . . These findings suggest that PCP use impedes many of the developmental tasks and processes of adolescence and young adulthood. (P. 496)

Marijuana

Marijuana (cannabis) is made from the dried leaves of the wild hemp plant. The plant is hardy and useful: it thrives in virtually every country of the world and produces a strong fiber for making cloth, canvas, and rope. The oil serves as a fast-drying paint base. For these reasons, U.S. farmers grew cannabis, and as late as World War II the federal government licensed production of cannabis in the South and the West. Federal law now forbids growing marijuana, but illegal production has skyrocketed in the United States in recent years.

The principal acting ingredient in cannabis is the chemical delta-9-THC, which will be referred to here as simply **THC.** The THC content of cannabis varies   **THC** depending upon the variety. In 1975 the THC content of "street" marijuana rarely exceeded 1 percent. In recent years new varieties have been produced, commonly containing THC content higher than 5 percent (U.S. Dept. of HHS, June 1980). These have more noticeable effects on users than did weaker strains. The THC content also varies with the part of the plant utilized. There is very little THC in the stem, roots, or seeds; the flowers and leaves contain more. *Ganja*, which comes from the flower tops and small leaves, ranges from 4 to 8 percent in THC content. *Hashish*, derived from the resin extracted from unfertilized female flowers, may have a THC content of 12 percent. *Hashish oil*, a concentration of resin, has been found to have a THC content as high as 28 percent, with typical samples containing 15 to 20 percent (U.S. Dept. of HHS, June 1980).

This variability in the THC content of different varieties of plants, and in the different parts and preparations made from them, has made it difficult for scientists to determine physical effects and psychological effects of marijuana use. Studies often yield conflicting results because of a lack of standardized procedures. What do research studies show concerning marijuana?

Tolerance to cannabis, diminished response to a given repeated drug dose, has now been well substantiated. Users are able to ingest ever larger quantities without disruptive effects (National Institute on Drug Abuse, 1980).

Physical dependency, as indicated by withdrawal symptoms, does not occur in ordinary users ingesting small or weak amounts. However, withdrawal symptoms can occur following discontinuance of high-dose chronic administration of THC. These symptoms include irritability, restlessness, decreased appetite, sleep disturbance, sweating, tremor, nausea, vomiting, and diarrhea. It should be emphasized that these symptoms occur only after unusually high doses of orally administered THC under research-like conditions. Psychological dependency may develop over a period of time and may make it difficult for chronic users to break the marijuana habit (National Institute on Drug Abuse, 1980).

An increase in heart rate and reddening of the eyes are the most consistently reported physiological effects of marijuana. The heart rate increase is closely related to dosage. Marijuana use decreases exercise tolerance of those with heart disease; therefore, use by those with cardiovascular deficiencies appears unwise. However, the drug produces only minimal changes in heart function of young, healthy, subjects.

Clinical studies are beginning to point to various harmful effects of marijuana on the lungs and as a cause of lung cancer. The smoke contains far stronger tars and irritants than do regular cigarettes; one "joint" is the equivalent of smoking four cigarettes of tobacco, so heavy usage over a long period may harm the lungs. The tar from marijuana is tumor producing when applied to the skin of test animals. Following exposure to marijuana smoke, the lung's defense systems against bacterial invasion have been shown to be impaired (U.S. Dept. of HHS, June 1980).

Because marijuana is an intoxicant, it impairs memory and concentration. It interferes with a wide range of intellectual tasks in a manner that impairs classroom learning among student users (Hendin et al., 1981). Adolescents with good to excellent academic records who become heavy marijuana users begin to have difficulty in completing assignments, paying attention, or remembering and using what they read or hear in class. Some find it increasingly difficult to read aloud or speak in class and generally stop participating in the learning process. As a group, heavy users appear to be extremely tense, restless, and loud in class. When not being disruptive, they are often inattentive, lost in daydreams or mindless staring, and frequently "nod off." They cut classes regularly, with little if any regard for the consequences of their actions (U.S. Dept. of HHS, Sept, 1981).

Marijuana also alters time and space sense, impairs vision, and retards reaction time and performance abilities in manipulative and coordination tasks. The more complex is the task and the more acute is the intoxication, the greater is the degree of disruption (U.S. Dept. of HHS, June 1980). Drivers believe they are doing a good job of keeping in the correct lane when in fact they are weaving. One low-dose street joint can result in a significant decrease in driving skill; a strong dose of two joints may result in reduced performance for five to six hours. Therefore, driving under the influence of marijuana is hazardous; the degree of hazard is related to the degree of intoxication. The simultaneous use of alcohol and marijuana is more dangerous than that of either substance alone.

Evidence is accumulating that chromosomal and genetic damage may be possible by heavy marijuana use (National Institute on Drug Abuse, 1980). So far, however, the evidence is conclusive only in laboratory mice. When average to heavy doses of marijuana were given to male mice, several results became evident. Males had more trouble making the females pregnant. If pregnancy occurred, more fetuses died before and after birth. If the sons survived and grew up, they were less fertile than normal. An examination of the chromosomes of both fathers and sons revealed abnormal chromosomes and birth defects even in the third generation (Dalterio, 1984). These researchers were convinced that marijuana damages the chromosomes and that these effects can be passed to succeeding generations.

Research has also suggested that heavy marijuana use may impair reproductive functioning in humans (U.S. Dept. of HHS, June 1980). Chronic cannabis use is associated with reduced levels of the male hormone, testosterone, in the bloodstream, which in turn may reduce potency and sexual drive and diminish sperm count and motility. It is also associated with possible interference with fertility in females. These preliminary findings may have greater significance for the marginally fertile (National Institute on Drug Abuse, 1980). Because the effects of marijuana on pregnant women and human fetuses have not been sufficiently established, most doctors strongly advise against smoking marijuana during pregnancy (Nahas, 1979). Other questions of possible marijuana effects continue to be unresolved. Evidence concerning an effect on the body's principal defense against disease, the immune response, remains contradictory (U.S. Dept. of HHS, June 1980).

The long-term effects of chronic cannabis usage on behavior are only partially known. It is certain, however, that the overall effect depends on the level and length of usage. Prolonged cannabis psychosis has been reported in Eastern literature under conditions of unusually heavy use. There is evidence that marijuana users may have more difficulty in deciding career goals and may more often drop out of college to reassess their goals ("Drug Pushers," 1979; Picou, 1980). There is some evidence that marijuana administration coupled with monetary reward for work performance results in a decline in productivity with heavier marijuana consumption.

Research is also revealing some positive and therapeutic uses of marijuana. The usefulness of cannabis in treating glaucoma by reducing internal eye pressures has been confirmed. The use of THC in reducing nausea and vomiting of cancer patients receiving chemotherapy shows unusual promise. In all likelihood, a small pharmaceutical company will soon be granted a license to produce an oral pill containing THC to treat nausea in cancer patients (Bridgwater, 1984). Because THC dilates pulmonary air passages, its usefulness in treating asthmatics has been demonstrated (Tashkin et al., 1975). Marijuana is a lung irritant, however, so use of aerosolized THC seems prudent. In the years ahead, more important questions in relation to marijuana use will be answered.

Inhalants

The solvent fumes from nail polish remover, plastic glue, gasoline, cleaning fluids, paint thinner, and other hydrocarbons are sniffed to give an intoxicating effect. Impairment of orientation, memory, intellectual functions, and judgment are frequent, together with blurring of vision, ringing ears, slurred speech, headache, dullness, dizziness, dilated pupils, and staggering, followed by drowsiness, stupor, and even unconsciousness. Upon recovery, the individual usually does not recall what happened during the period of intoxication. Use of inhalants may cause permanent damage and impairment of the brain tissue function (acute brain syndrome). The subject may die suddenly of asphyxia, become addicted, or develop inhalation psychosis (Schneider, 1980). Accidental deaths while intoxicated from glue sniffing include suffocation from a plastic bag over the head and falls from high places. Reports of damage to the kidneys, liver, heart, blood, and nervous system from sniffing glue with a toluene base remain a possibility. Use of inhalants is a serious matter and should be discouraged whenever possible (Chitwood, Wells, and Russe, 1981).

Patterns and Intensity of Use

Five patterns of drug use may be identified:

Experimental use is defined as the short-term, nonpatterned trial of one or more drugs, with a maximum frequency of ten times per drug. It is motivated primarily by curiosity or by a desire to experience new feelings. Users in this category feel they are in control of their lives, rarely use any drug on a daily basis, and tend not to use drugs to escape the pressure of personal problems.

Social-recreational use occurs in social settings among friends or acquaintances who desire to share an experience. Social and recreational use tends to vary in frequency, intensity, and duration but not to escalate in either frequency or intensity to patterns of uncontrolled use. Users typically do not use addictive drugs like heroin; they are therefore able to exercise control over their behavior.

Circumstantial-situational use is motivated by the desire to achieve a known and anticipated effect. This would include the student who takes stimulants to stay

HIGHLIGHT   Use of Steroids by Athletes

Since several competitors were disqualified from the last Olympics because of the illegal use of **anabolic steroids,** attention has focused on the use of these drugs by athletes of all ages. Fuller and LaFountain (1987) interviewed 50 athletes who admitted to steroid use. The athletes ranged in age from 15 to 45 years with an average age of 19. No systematic differences between high school and college-level athletes were found. The athletes included weight lifters, football players, wrestlers, body builders, and track stars. These athletes justified use of the drugs because of the need to be competitive.

> We should be allowed to take them because all those other countries take them . . . the women too.
> You have no choice if you want to compete in the big time (Fuller and LaFountain, 1987, p. 971).

There is no question that steroids increase muscle mass, strength, and performance and reduce fat deposits and fluid retention by the body. They also increase hostility and aggression. Users gain an intense killer instinct. However, the same hostility results in fights and arguments with others, increased sexual aggression, and beating up girlfriends or boyfriends when frustrated.

The most serious harm comes to various parts of the body. The athlete can suffer damage to the heart, liver, reproductive system, and stomach as a result of taking anabolic steroids. Heart attacks, sterility, ulcers, and liver tumors are common in addition to psychological and emotional instability.

Many athletes are not concerned because they don't realize the harm, or they choose to deny the potential health problems.

> You can abuse anything. Even aspirin. I don't think there is any proven test that steroids really do hurt you (p. 972).

Other athletes place their performance above all health considerations.

> It gives me a chance to achieve for myself and I do all I can to make my body stronger . . . If my coach says steroids will make me stronger I will use them (p. 974).

It appears that many athletes of the 1980s are not heeding the warnings about the dangers of steroid use.

---

awake or the person who takes sedatives to relieve tension and go to sleep. Paton and Kandel (1978) identify four psychological conditions that lead to illicit drug use by adolescents: a depressed mood, normlessness (not having definite values, opinions, or rules to live by), social isolation, and low self-esteem. The greatest danger from this type of use is that the person will become accustomed to drug use to solve problems and ultimately escalate to intensified use.

Intensified drug use is generally a long-term pattern of using drugs at least once daily to achieve relief from a persistent problem or stressful situation. Drug use becomes a customary activity of daily life, with people ordinarily remaining socially and economically integrated in the life of the community. Some change in functioning may occur depending on the frequency, intensity, and amount of use.

Compulsive drug use is use at both high frequency and high intensity of relatively long duration, producing physiological or psychological dependence, with discontinuance resulting in physiological discomfort or psychological stress. Motivation to continue comes from the physical or psychological comfort or relief obtained by using the drug. Users in this category include not only the street "junkie" or skid-row alcoholic but also the opiate-dependent physician, the barbiturate-dependent housewife, or the alcohol-dependent businessman.

All research studies show that the most frequently used drugs in the United States are alcohol, tobacco, and marijuana, in that order. Table 11–1 shows the percentage of youths, aged twelve to seventeen using various types of drugs in 1979, 1982, and 1985 (U.S. Bureau of the Census, Statistical Abstract of the United States, 1988). These figures indicate a decline in current use (past month) of hallucinogens, tranquilizers, and analgesics. Current use of marijuana, inhalants, cocaine, stimulants, sedatives, alcohol, and cigarettes continued to increase from 1982 to 1985.

Youths are trying drugs at increasingly younger ages. It is not unusual for children 8 to 10 years old to use drugs. An elementary school official in Washington, D.C., complained that he had not been able to keep one third-grader from smoking marijuana every day at recess. Threats of expulsion did not help because the child insisted he could not break the habit. He did refuse to share his cigarettes with classmates because, he said, "the habit is dangerous" ("Drug Pushers," 1979). One longitudinal study in the San Francisco area showed that socially precocious females were more likely to become involved with drugs earlier than were males, although for both boys and girls, the transition to junior high school played an important role in initiating drug use (Keyes and Block, 1984).

▉ TABLE 11–1

Percentage of youth, ages 12–17, using drugs

DRUG	EVER USED			PAST MONTH		
	1979	1982	1985	1979	1982	1985
Marijuana	30.9	26.7	23.7	16.7	11.5	12.3
Inhalants	9.8	NA	9.1	2.0	NA	3.6
Hallucinogens	7.1	5.2	3.2	2.2	1.4	1.1
Cocaine	5.4	6.5	5.2	1.4	1.6	1.8
Heroin	.5	<.5	<.5	<.5	<.5	<.5
Stimulants	3.4	6.7	5.5	1.2	1.3	1.8
Sedatives	3.2	5.8	4.0	1.1	.9	1.1
Tranquilizers	4.1	4.9	4.8	.6	.7	.6
Analgesics	3.2	4.2	5.9	.6	2.6	1.9
Alcohol	70.3	65.2	55.9	37.2	26.9	31.5
Cigarettes	54.1	49.5	45.3	12.1	14.7	15.6

From: U.S. Bureau of the Census (1988). *Statistical Abstract of the United States*, 1988 (Washington, D. C.: U.S. Government Printing Office).

A nationwide sample of high school seniors showed the following lifetime illicit usage figures (in percentages) of the classes of 1984 and 1987 (Bell and Battjes, 1985; Drug Usage . . . , 1988):

	1984	1987
Used alcohol	92.6	92.2
Used cigarettes	69.7	67.2
Used marijuana	54.9	50.2
Used stimulants (not under doctor's orders)	27.9	21.6
Used tranquilizers (not under doctor's orders)	12.4	10.7
Used other sedatives	13.3	8.7
Used hallucinogens	13.3	10.6
Used cocaine	16.1	15.2
Used inhalants	19.0	18.6
Used opiates (other than heroin) (not under doctor's orders)	9.7	9.2
Used heroin	1.3	1.2

When compared to the drug use of high school seniors in 1984, the 1987 figures represent a decline since 1984 in the use of the following drugs (Bell and Battjes, 1985; Drug Usage . . . , 1988):

Hallucinogens, 20 percent decline
Tranquilizers, 14 percent decline
Marijuana, 9 percent decline
Other sedatives, 35 percent decline
Cigarettes, 4 percent decline
Other opiates, 5 percent decline
Stimulants, 23 percent decline
Cocaine, 6 percent decline
Inhalants, 2 percent decline
Heroin, 8 percent decline

Sedatives, stimulants, and hallucinogens fell much out of favor, but the decline in use of tranquilizers, marijuana, inhalants, cigarettes, cocaine, heroin and other opiates was also noteworthy. *No drugs increased in lifetime use by high school seniors from 1984 to 1987.* Figures 11–1 and 11–2 show the trends from 1980 to 1987.

Why Drugs Are First Used

Why do adolescents first use drugs? *The overwhelming majority try drugs out of curiosity, to see what they are like* (Levine and Kozak, 1979). Apparently this is a strong motive for trying a drug. Adolescents have heard what different drugs do and decide to try them. For example, the hallucinogens are supposed to release a store of elaborate, rich, and colorful fantasies; marijuana will reduce ego controls and provide an experience of intoxication. If adolescents are more attracted by the promises of a drug than repelled by its potential harm, they may be led to experiment.

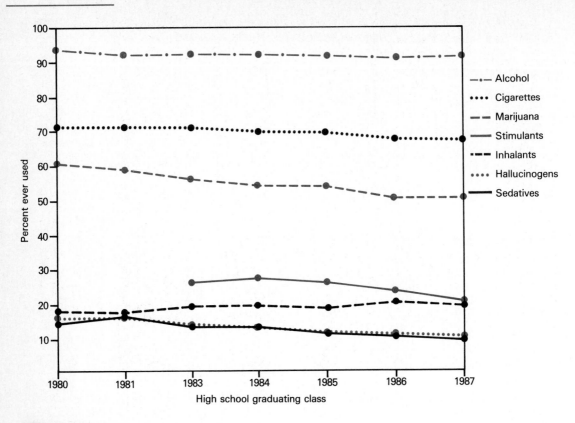

FIGURE 11–1

Lifetime drug usage among graduating seniors, U.S., by year.

Statistics from: *Drug Abuse: America's High School Students,* 1988 (Rockville, MD.: National Institute on Drug Abuse).

Another reason for trying drugs is fun or sensual pleasure. Users are seeking an exciting experience. Adolescents are growing up in a fun-oriented culture that emphasizes the need and value of having a good time. If smoking grass is fun, this becomes a strong motive for its use (Lowney, 1984).

Another aspect of having fun is to experience sensual pleasure. This pleasure may be sexual, and many adolescents feel that pot makes the exploration of sex less inhibited and more delightful. The pleasure motive may be in seeking an increased sensitivity of touch or taste. A marijuana party also may involve a period where everyone "gets the hungries" and explores as wide a variety of taste delights as is available.

Another strong motive for trying drugs is the social pressure to be like friends or to be part of a social group (Chitwood, Wells, and Russe, 1981; Glynn, 1981; Huba and Bentler, 1980; Levine and Kozak, 1979). Whether friends use drugs or not is one of the most significant factors in determining adolescent drug usage (Hundleby and Mercer, 1987). Adolescents say: "Many of my friends tried it and I didn't want to

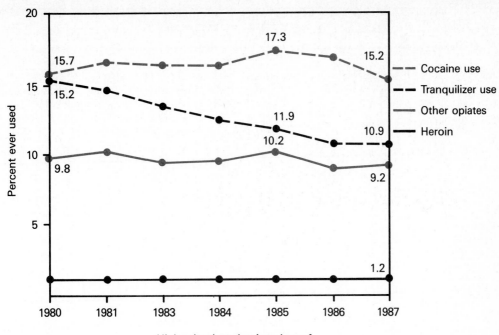

FIGURE 11–2

Lifetime drug usage among graduating seniors, U.S., by year.

Statistics from: *Drug Abuse:America's High School Students*, 1988. (Rockville, MD.: National Institute on Drug Abuse).

be different," or "Everybody is doing it," or "My friends urged me to try it, and I didn't want them to think I was chicken." This motive is especially strong among immature adolescents who are seeking to belong to a crowd or gang. Some youths gain recognition by being far more daring than others, by taking chances that others will not take. In this case, the pressure is to go beyond what others are doing to show them how much more grown-up they are.

One important motive for trying drugs is to relieve tensions, anxieties, pressures, to escape from problems, or to be able to deal with or face them. Students say:

"I needed to get away from the problems that were bugging me."
"I felt tired and depressed and needed a lift."
"I had to stay awake to study for exams."
"When I'm on grass, I have more self-confidence and can do anything."

Those who use drugs as an escape from tension, anxiety, problems, or reality or to make up for personal inadequacies are likely to become entwined in a drug habit. These are the emotionally immature who are insecure, passive, dependent persons, who find life frustrating and anxiety provoking, who tend to withdraw

HIGHLIGHT   Polydrug Users and Abusers

A survey among 433 high school seniors was conducted in the fall of 1982 in two central Texas communities (Wright, 1988). The purpose of the survey was to determine the percentages that were *polydrug users** or *abusers***. The following percentages of non-users, users, and abusers responded in the affirmative to each of the following statements:

STATEMENTS	POLYDRUG		
	Non-user %	User %	Abuser %
I have seriously considered a suicide attempt within the last month.	4.5	10.0	27.3
I have engaged in delinquent behavior which resulted in a loss or destruction of property valued at more than $50.	14.5	26.7	55.5
Most or all of my friends smoke pot.	5.1	30.0	66.6
If something feels good, I usually do it and don't worry about the consequences.	20.5	50.0	63.6
I try to play as much as possible and work as little as possible.	21.4	53.3	45.5
I consider myself to be an agnostic or atheist (both were defined).	5.3	6.7	22.7
I usually go to church weekly.	44.9	20.0	18.2
I usually drink more than six alcoholic drinks when I drink.	17.7	31.0	68.2
I smoked my first joint (marijuana) before I was 14.	10.4	33.4	81.8
I had my first alcoholic drink before I was 12.	30.0	46.7	81.8
If one of my friends had a serious drug problem I would probably not tell any adult.	43.2	76.7	71.4

The major reasons given for using a variety of drugs was to seek relief or for pleasure.

* *Polydrug users.* Those who use one or more mood-altering drugs (i.e., alcohol, cocaine, stimulants, or downers) in addition to marijuana on a regular (weekly) basis.
** *Polydrug abusers.* (a) Those who use one or more of the mood-altering substances investigated on a regular basis in addition to using marijuana on a daily basis, or (b) those who use one or more of these mood-altering drugs on a daily basis in addition to using marijuana on a weekly basis.

From: Wright, L. S. "High School Polydrug Users and Abusers." *Adolescence*, 80: 853–861.

from active involvement as much as possible, or who lean on others, or drugs, for help.

There are those users whose primary motive for trying a drug is to gain self-awareness, increased awareness of others, or more religious insight or to become more creative. The sense of increased awareness or greater creativity may be more imagined than real, but the person believes that the drug provides the awareness. There is the appeal that the drug has the potential to create a mystical experience, to give crucial insights into personality or emotional problems or a new vision of life in terms of loving relationships. This is an especially strong motive for using the psychedelics.

Compulsive Drug Use

The reasons for adolescents' first using drugs and for continuing to use them are sometimes different (Capuzzi and Lecoq, 1983). *Those who continue to use nonaddictive drugs as a means of trying to solve emotional problems become psychologically dependent upon the drugs* (Ginsberg and Greenley, 1978). Drugs become a means of finding security, comfort, or relief. When individuals become psychologically dependent upon drugs that are also physiologically addicting—drugs such as alcohol, barbiturates, and heroin—dependence is secondarily reinforced by the desire to avoid the pain and distress of physical withdrawal.

The need to use drugs excessively originates within the families in which children grow up (Huba and Bentler, 1980; Rees and Wilborn, 1983). Drug abusers are not as close to their parents and are more likely to have negative adolescent-parental relationships and a low degree of supportive interaction with them than are nonusers (Tudor, Petersen, and Elifson, 1980; Wright, 1982). Adolescents who use drugs regularly are more likely to have parents who drink excessively and/or use other psychotropic drugs (McDermott, 1984). They are more likely to come from broken homes or not to live with both parents (Johnson, Shontz, and Locke, 1984; Stern, Northman, and Van Slyck, 1984). Chronic users find family relationships rewarding and meaningful less often, experience parental deprivation more often, and are more dissatisfied with parents (Hundleby and Mercer, 1987). Their parents less often use praise, encouragement, and helpful counsel and less often set limits on their behavior (Coombs and Landsverk, 1988). Vicary and Lerner (1986) found that parental conflict in child-rearing practices, inconsistent discipline, restrictive discipline, and maternal rejection were all associated with marijuana and alcohol use in older adolescents. Parental physical and sexual abuse also may lead to self derogation and to drug use (Dembo et al., 1987).

A study of public secondary school students from eighteen high schools in New York State revealed the following correlations. Students who started to use illicit drugs:

Lacked closeness to parents.
Had parents who used authoritarian control in discipline.
Had parents who used hard liquor and psychoactive drugs.
Lacked intimate ties with a best friend.
Had a history of marijuana use.
Exhibited signs of depression.
Were more often involved in delinquency than nonusers (Kandel et al., 1978).

Another study of the family relationships of adolescent drug users in comparison to nonusers revealed that the families of users:

More often treated the adolescent as a scapegoat for family problems.
Showed inferior ability in arriving at decisions.
Evidenced fewer positive communications among members.
Allowed less freedom for open expression of opinions.
Were less cooperative with one another (Gantman, 1978).

Overall, the family relationships of adolescents who abused drugs were similar to those of adolescents who were emotionally disturbed.

The net effect of these types of family situations is to create personality problems that cause individuals to be more likely to turn to drugs. Numerous other studies correlate drug addiction and dependency with disturbed family relationships (Shaver, 1983).

TOBACCO AND SMOKING

Incidence

Over half of all junior high school students and two-thirds of all senior high school students have smoked cigarettes. About one-third of senior high school students are regular smokers. More than one-half of all youths who smoke have their first cigarette before the age of twelve (Bell and Battjes, 1985; Johnston, O'Malley, and Bachman, 1985; Schneider, 1980). The incidence of cigarette smoking increases with age and reaches a peak of not quite one-half of the population in the 26 to 34 age bracket who are current smokers (Miller, 1983). Overall, there are almost as many female as male youths who smoke. In some places, female adolescent smokers outnumber male smokers (Welte and Barnes, 1987). In the past several years, there has been a slight decline in the incidence of cigarette smoking among youths. Figure 11–1 shows the trends for high school seniors.

Why Adolescents Start Smoking

Most youths are aware of the dangers of smoking. If so, why do they start and continue to smoke? Typical answers include:

"Because the rest of my crowd smokes."
"It makes me look big."
"To feel sophisticated."
"I was curious."
"Because I was tense and nervous."
"Because I enjoy smoking."
"Because I wasn't supposed to."

Fundamentally, these reasons are in accord with sociological and psychological explanations. *Adolescents are brainwashed from the early years of childhood by the huge advertising industry.* Cigarette smoking is identified with masculinity, independence, nature, athletic prowess, beauty, youth, intelligence, sex appeal, sociability, wealth, and the good life. Every conceivable gimmick and scheme has been used by the advertising industry to encourage smoking. The appeal is always to the

HIGHLIGHT   Families of Drug Abusers

One of the best summaries of the relationship between family factors and drug abuse was given by Jurich and colleagues. They identify some family factors that have an impact on drug use:

Lack of family closeness
Isolation of adolescent from family
Lack of closeness with parents
Little parental support
Lack of love
Need for recognition, trust, love not filled
Parental rejection, hostility

Conflict
Marital conflict
Husband irresponsible
Unhappy home
Wife unhappy
Disharmony in family
Children as pawns in marital discord
High degree of stress, trauma

Scapegoating
Parents use adolescent as scapegoat for inadequacy

Role model
Parents inadequate role models
Parents are drug users
Parents serve as models of drug abuse

Divorce, family break up
Broken home

One or both parents absent much of time
Father absence especially harmful
Single-parent home

Discipline
Parents show lack of coping skills
Inconsistent discipline
Discipline too autocratic or laissez-faire

Hypocritical morality
Double standard of behavior: one for selves, another for adolescents
Denial of problems with self and of parental faults

Psychological crutches
Parents lack confidence in coping with life, so use drugs as psychological crutch
Adolescents do not learn coping skills from parents so follow parental model of coping by using drugs, alcohol

Communication gap
Lack of ability to communicate
Parents do not understand
Parents do not press communication for fear of hearing anything negative
Cries for help not heard

Jurich, A. P., Polson, C. J., Jurich, J. A., and Bates, R. A. (Spring, 1985). "Family Factors in the Lives of Drug Users and Abusers." *Adolescence,* 20, 143–159.

emotions and to the desire for acceptability, popularity, datability, and sexual allure. The sultry woman's voice, the society setting, the back-to-nature promises, the tattooed hairy hands: all promise rewards the teenager seeks.

Youths are also imitating their parents and other adults who smoke (Cooreman and Perdrizet, 1980; Goodstadt, Lawson, and Langford, 1982). There is little hope of changing teenage smoking habits unless the habits of parents and older (perhaps adult) siblings are changed. One of the primary reasons so many adolescents

Most youths are aware of the dangers of smoking, so why do they start and continue to smoke? Explanations include exposure to advertising, imitation of parents and other adults, peer group pressure, and needs for status and self-esteem. (© Frank Siteman)

smoke is that they see adults smoking; they are striving to imitate adult behavior and find peer approval.

Some adolescents start smoking because of peer group pressure (Sarvela and McClendon, 1983). This is apparent in the early years of adolescence, and it is particularly true of males who start to smoke as a social coping mechanism (Urberg and Robbins, 1981). Those who are the first to exhibit adult habits are admired; those who do not smoke are "chicken"; those who have not learned to inhale are missing all the fun. Adoption of the smoking habit starts as an act of conformity to peers as well as to parents and advertisers.

Early smoking may be linked also to self-esteem and status needs of some youths. Often adolescents who smoke do so as a compensatory device because they have fallen behind their age equals in school, because they do not participate in extracurricular activities, or because they have other ego needs they are trying to satisfy. Girls often start to smoke as a sign of rebellion and autonomy (Urberg and Robbins, 1981). Children of lower-class parents often begin smoking earlier than children of middle-class parents, primarily to gain social status.

Why Adolescents Continue Smoking

Once they begin to smoke, youths continue for the same reasons that adults do:

Relief of tension. Heavy smokers tend to be overly tense and restless people.

Development of an unconscious habit. A reflex action develops that is hard to break: the action of reaching for a cigarette.

Association with sociability and pleasure. Smokers associate the activity with after-dinner coffee, conversation, a social gathering, or pleasant surroundings.

Compulsion for oral activity. This oral hypothesis states that smoking is an attempt to regain the passive pleasure of infantile nursing.

Physical addiction to nicotine. Numerous studies now support the conclusion that smokers not only become psychologically dependent on smoking but also physically addicted. This finding is based on several facts. First, the body develops a physical craving for nicotine that can be alleviated by injecting nicotine or by increasing the nicotine content of cigarettes smoked.

Second, only about 2 percent of smokers are able to use cigarettes intermittently or occasionally. The typical pattern of nicotine use is not only daily but hourly. According to Russell (1971):

> The level of nicotine in the brain is crucial. . . . It is probable that nicotine is present in the brain . . . within a minute or two of beginning to smoke, but by 20–30 minutes after completing the cigarette most of this nicotine has left the brain for other organs. This is just about the period when the dependent smoker needs another cigarette. The smoking pattern of the dependent smoker who inhales a cigarette every 30 minutes of his waking life (a pack and a half per day) is such as to insure the maintenance of a high level of nicotine in his brain. (p. 8)

Third, withdrawal of nicotine produces nervousness, drowsiness, anxiety, lightheadedness, headaches, energy loss, fatigue, constipation or diarrhea, insomnia, dizziness, sweating, cramps, tremor, and palpitations.

Fourth, smokers become tolerant of nicotine. Youthful smokers can tolerate only a few puffs. Gradually they can tolerate one, then two, then three or more cigarettes. If they exceed their tolerance level, they show signs of acute anxiety. As tolerance levels rise, smokers may reach levels that would have been disastrous earlier in their smoking career (Russell, 1971).

Fifth, when the supply of cigarettes is curtailed, smokers evidence unreasonable, antisocial behavior similar to that of heroin addicts. When the tobacco ration for men in Germany was cut to two packs per month after World War II, it was noted that

> the majority of habitual smokers preferred to do without food even under extreme conditions of nutrition rather than to forgo tobacco. Thus, when food rations in prisoner-of-war camps were down to 900–1,000 calories, smokers were still willing to barter their food rations for tobacco. Of 300 German civilians questioned, 256 had obtained tobacco at the black market. . . . In disregard of considerations of personal dignity, conventional decorum, and esthetic-hygienic feelings, cigarette butts were picked up out of the street dirt by people who . . . would in other circumstances have felt disgust at such contact. Smokers also condescended to beg for tobacco, but not for other things. . . .
>
> 80 percent of those questioned declared that it felt worse to do without nicotine than without alcohol. (Brill and Christie, 1974)

Sixth, follow-up studies of smokers who have quit show a high relapse rate. At the end of forty-eight months, more than 80 percent of those who had successfully stopped smoking were smoking again (Hunt and Matazarro, 1970). This percentage does not include those who entered smoking clinics but were not able to stop smoking.

The conclusion is that cigarette smoking is a highly addictive habit that is difficult to break. Once started, it is not a habit that the majority of smokers can break by an effort of the will. So-called "smokeless cigarettes" have been offered as a possible substitute for regular cigarettes, but manufacture has been discontinued because of lack of consumer acceptance. This is probably fortunate since the substance is associated with increased oral cancer. Other long-term health risks are unknown (Dignan et al., 1986).

Keeping Adolescents from Starting

The best answer is to keep adolescents from starting in the first place. A number of studies have been conducted to determine the most effective way to keep adolescents from starting to smoke and to help more of them to stop once they have started (Perry et al., 1983). Some of the most important suggestions include the following proposals:

Antismoking education should avoid extreme scare tactics that attempt to frighten adolescents into stopping. It is all right to point to the facts, such as the relationship between smoking and lung cancer, respiratory illnesses, and cardiovascular disease, or the dangers of smoking during pregnancy or while taking oral contraceptives (Greenwood, 1979). Moderate anxiety can be especially useful in preventing adolescents from starting. But extreme scare tactics lead adolescents to deny that smoking will cause physical harm and to reject the teachings of the person who is trying to scare them. Research shows that teachers who are against smoking are more effective in antismoking education than are teachers who are neutral (Thompson, 1978). Teachers need to take a stand but not use extremely negative approaches, especially those that exaggerate.

The primary appeal should be positive. The program should appeal to adolescents' vanity, their pride, their belief in themselves, and their sense of achievement. They should be encouraged to establish control over their own behavior, and not to blame others for their own habit (Sheppard, Wright, and Goodstadt, 1985). Appealing to their desire to maintain physical fitness has been proved to be an effective preventative (Tucker, 1984).

Adolescents should be told all the facts as honestly as possible. A program should avoid half-truths and make every effort to avoid creating a credibility gap (Lotecka and Lassleben, 1981). Even when adolescents have the facts about the hazards of smoking, some start or continue to smoke anyway because of the tendency to feel: "Lung cancer or other illnesses won't happen to me" (Shor and Williams, 1978, 1979; Thompson, 1978). Presenting factual information on the hazards does not often change behavior, but it usually has considerable influence on knowledge and attitudes.

Efforts should enlist the help of student leaders and of students themselves (Erickson and Newman, 1984; Perry et al., 1980). An antismoking campaign at Central High School in Great Falls, Montana, was sponsored by the students' cancer club. When the campaign ended, the whole cultural climate of the high school had changed from prosmoking to antismoking, and most of the students had pledged not to smoke. A research study at the University of New Hampshire showed that non-

smokers suffered negative physiological and psychological symptoms from tobacco smoke pollution in public places, which suggests that schools have a
responsibility to limit smoking (Shor and Williams, 1978, 1979). However, even
students who do not smoke feel that their friends who do ought to have a place
provided by the school, primarily because they feel the decision to smoke is a
personal one to be regulated by the individual, not by the school.

A program should begin early, when the child is young, and continue periodically over a
span of years. A recurring program is more effective than a single mass exposure. Ten percent
of children in the United States are regular smokers by age twelve. Education laws
in New York State require that antismoking education be started after grade eight.
This is too late. Fourth or fifth grade is a better time to begin.

Students should be helped to discover and analyze their own inner, hidden, emotional, or
social reasons for smoking and to deal with these problems so that the smoking crutch
will not be needed.

No one teaching method can be considered best (Hansen and Evans, 1982). A comparison of didactic approaches, group discussion, psychological persuasion, and
a combination of all three showed that the didactic approach was most successful in changing behavior, the combination approach was best at improving
knowledge, and psychological persuasion had the most effect on attitudes
(Thompson, 1978).

Antismoking education programs have been largely unsuccessful in changing
smoking behavior among adolescents who already smoke. The percentage who
now smoke is similar to the number in 1970. But if antismoking education can be
given in elementary grades before students start smoking, the program can be
effective in reducing the number who begin.

ALCOHOL AND EXCESSIVE DRINKING
Incidence

Studies of junior high, senior high, and college students reveal that a substantial
proportion of adolescents drink. Findings from 1985 indicate that 56 percent of
youths aged 12 to 17 and 93 percent aged 18 to 25 have had a drink (U.S. Bureau
of the Census, 1988). The proportion of youths who have ever used alcohol increases each grade level to 92 percent for twelfth-grade youths. Given that drinking is common in the United States, it is no surprise that a vast majority of
adolescents have been introduced to alcohol.

It is not drinking as such but frequent drinking of large quantities that creates
problems (Hughes and Dodder, 1983). In a nationwide sampling of students in
grades seven through twelve, one of three said that alcohol was the "most serious
social problem at my school" (Solarzano, 1984). Alcohol is also a major factor in
crime (Dawkins and Dawkins, 1983). More than 50 percent of all arrests are for
public drunkenness or driving under the influence. Alcohol is involved in half of
all homicides. It is a major factor in child abuse and family violence. The majority
of pedestrians who are injured by cars have been drinking at the time of the
accident. One can only guess the percentage of adolescents who have been drink-

In a nationwide sampling of students in grades seven through twelve, one in three said that alcohol was the "most serious social problem at my school." Organizations such as Students Against Driving Drunk (S.A.D.D.) have evolved to deal with some of the problems associated with drinking. (© Frank Siteman)

ing when unwed pregnancy occurs. And alcohol abuse during pregnancy causes over 200,000 premature deaths a year (U.S. Dept. of HEW, 1980). Alcohol abuse continues to be the major drug abuse problem.

There is some indication, however, that drinking and heavy drinking among adolescents are on the decline. Figure 11–3 shows the trends in drinking habits of high school seniors. The decline, though modest, is encouraging.

Beer is the preferred beverage among boys of all ages, regardless of the frequency with which they drink, and among girls of all ages who drink once a week or more. Older girls who drink only once a month or more or once a year or more prefer distilled spirits to beer. The social contexts in which adolescents drink are subject to legal restrictions. Youths drink before they can legally buy alcoholic beverages or patronize licensed premises. Most who begin to drink do so at home under parental supervision. Much of this drinking occurs on holidays and other special occasions. As youths grow older, they tend to drink more often outside the home, until the most likely drinking places are those where adults are not present.

The prevalence of drinking among junior high and senior high youths has motivated many states to reexamine their laws regulating legal drinking ages. After the Vietnam War, many states lowered the drinking age to eighteen. The argument was: "If they're old enough to fight, they're old enough to vote and to drink" ("The Drinking Age," 1979). But authorities complained that giving eigh-

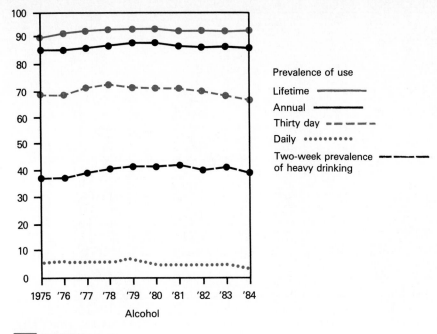

Prevalence of use

Lifetime ————

Annual ————

Thirty day — — — —

Daily •••••••••

Two-week prevalence — —— —
of heavy drinking

Alcohol

▨ FIGURE 11–3

Trends in lifetime, annual, and thirty-day prevalence of alcohol, high school seniors.

Johnston, L. D., O'Malley, P. M., and Bachman, J. G. (1985). *Use of Licit and Illicit Drugs by America's High School Students, 1975–1984* (Rockville, Md.: National Institute on Drug Abuse), p. 54.

teen-year-olds the right to purchase alcoholic beverages also made them available to their younger friends in junior and senior high school—the seniors purchased it for them. As a result many states that lowered the drinking age have raised it again to age twenty or twenty-one (Newman, 1987).

It is clear that alcohol is the drug of choice for adolescents and young adults, just as it has been for decades. The frequency of regular drinking typically increases for men and women after graduation from high school, so that among those in the 18 to 25 year age group, 72 percent report they are current users of alcohol (past month) (U.S. Bureau of the Census, 1988). (See figure 11–4 for age trends.) As can be seen in the figure, more men than women are frequent users, and more whites than blacks are frequent users.

Correlations with Drinking ▨

There are wide variations in drinking habits among different ethnic groups (Adler and Kandel, 1982). Some groups, such as Italian-Americans and Jews, exhibit drinking habits that are well integrated into their culture. The vast majority drink, but these groups have the lowest rates of alcoholism of any other groups in the United States, primarily because of the patterns of their drinking. Italian-Americans have

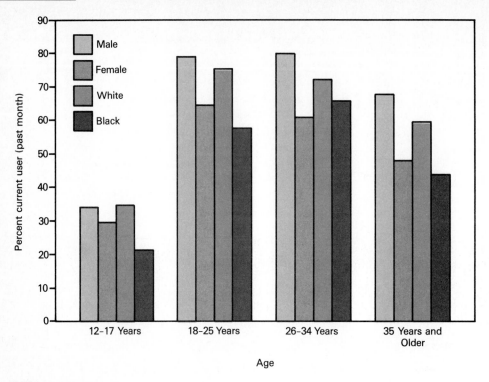

FIGURE 11–4

Current users of alcohol, by age, sex, and race, 1985.

Statistics from: U.S. Bureau of the Census (1988). *Statistical Abstract of the United States*, 108th edition (Washington, D.C.: U.S. Government Printing Office), p. 112.

strong sanctions against drunkenness, and the whole family usually drinks wine with meals. As a consequence, they have few alcohol-related problems, although second and later generations begin to show higher rates of heavy drinking.

In contrast to these patterns, Irish-Americans have more problem drinkers than do other Americans of the same social class. They often deliberately seek to get drunk, often drink distilled spirits rather than wine, and often take five or six drinks on a single occasion. Consequently they have high rates of alcoholism, and their adolescents follow their example.

Drinking patterns among adolescents generally follow the adult models in their communities (Glynn, 1981). Parents who drink or who sanction drinking are more likely to have adolescents who drink; parents who do not drink or who disapprove of drinking are more likely to have youths who do not. Parents who are modest to heavy drinkers are more likely to have adolescents who are moderate to heavy drinkers (Barnes, Farrell and Cairns, 1986). Furthermore, *chronic alcoholism is more likely to run in families.* About one-third of any sample of alcoholics will have had at least one parent who was an alcoholic (Cotton, 1979). Children who are exposed to drinking by their parents, however, do not necessarily grow up to be problem drinkers. The highest rates of alcoholism among adolescents are found in groups that are under pressure to refrain from drinking until age 21 or in families, such as the Irish, who themselves have high rates of alcoholism.

Drinking is also related to religious affiliation and church attendance. Jews have the lowest proportion of abstainers among the three major religions and the lowest proportion of heavy drinkers ("The Jewish Recipe," 1982). Catholics and liberal Protestants have a relatively high proportion of drinkers and heavy drinkers. Conservative Protestants have the largest proportion of abstainers and the lowest proportion of heavy drinkers. In a longitudinal study of drinker status in adolescence, one group of investigators reported that religiousness and frequency of church attendance were strongly related to abstinence (Jessor and Jessor, 1973). In other studies, problem drinkers among youths score lower than nonproblem drinkers on an index of religious participation.

There are a number of other significant correlations with drinking:

1. The highest proportion of abstainers (62 percent) in the general population is found among people with less than an eighth-grade *education*. The proportion of heavier drinkers increases fairly steadily, from 6 percent of those with grammar school education to 15 percent of college graduates (Harris and Associates, 1974).
2. Proportionately more people on the lower *socioeconomic levels* are abstainers than are those on the upper levels. Both moderate and heavier drinking increases as social class rises (Harris and Associates, 1974). Alcohol use among adolescents is highest when fathers are professionals or managers.
3. Youths from rural areas and small towns are more likely to be abstainers than are adolescents from cities and suburbs. *The largest proportions of heavy drinkers live in urban and suburban areas*; the smallest proportion of heavy drinkers live in rural communities and small towns (Gibbons et al., 1986).
4. The incidence of deviant drinking among *juvenile delinquents* is decidedly higher than in the general adolescent populations, suggesting that overdrinking is but one class of antisocial behavior among those who are maladjusted and who have the potential for getting into trouble (Farrow and French, 1986). Those who are the heaviest drinkers are those who are also most often involved in such crimes as shoplifting, breaking and entering, and auto theft (Dawkins and Dawkins, 1983).
5. There is a positive correlation between *heavy television viewing* and alcohol consumption. Although cause and effect cannot be inferred, it is plausible that adolescents are taught subtly by television that alcohol is good, healthy, and harmless (Tucker, 1985). Certainly much youthful drinking is portrayed on television programs (DeFoe and Breed, 1988).

Why Adolescents Drink

Adolescents drink for a number of reasons. Drinking is a widespread adult custom, so drinking by adolescents reflects their perception of the attitudes and behavior of adults in our society (Halebsky, 1987). *Adolescents use alcohol as an integral part of adult role playing*, as a rite of passage into the adult community (Barnes, 1981).

Youths drink also because of *peer group pressure and the need for peer identification,* sociability, and friendship (Johnson, 1986; Sarvela and McClendon, 1983). Drinking becomes a social custom of a particular group; therefore the adolescent who wants to be a part of the group drinks too (Fondacaro and Heller, 1983). One way of avoiding drinking is associating with peers who, themselves, do not drink (Brown and Stetson, 1988). In general, fewer percentages of blacks than whites of all ages are current drinkers (U.S. Dept. of HHS, 1980). Far fewer percentages of Mexican-American college-age females drink than do Anglo college-age females, although there are few differences in the drinking habits of Mexican-American and Anglo-American college males (Trotter, 1982).

Another major reason why some youths drink is *as a means of rebellion,* indicated especially in studies of adolescents who are problem drinkers (Glynn, 1981). Such youths evidence signs of rebellion and alienation from adults and adult institutions. In other words, their drinking is antinormative, indicative of their estrangement from family and community. This is why adolescents who are excessive drinkers are also more likely to commit delinquent acts.

One study of personality characteristics of alcohol-abusing adolescents found them to have negative feelings about themselves, to be irresponsible, immature, impulsive, dogmatic, defensive, undependable, self-centered, distrustful, and nonconformist (Mayer, 1988).

Not all adolescents who get drunk become problem drinkers (Finn and Brown, 1981). *Problem drinkers start to drink in excess for psychological rather than social reasons. Heavy, escapist drinking is symptomatic of serious personality problems.* Such youths do not get along at home or at school; they receive more failing grades, are more delinquency prone, participate less often in extracurricular activities, spend more nights out away from home, and are not as close to their parents. Only a small percentage of youths are problem drinkers, but they are already evidencing the psychological imbalance that prompts them to rebel or to seek escape through alcohol.

SUMMARY

This chapter focuses on three selected health problems of adolescents: drug abuse, smoking, and excessive drinking. A distinction needs to be made between drug addiction and psychological dependency. Some drugs are physically habit forming, meaning the body builds up a physical need for the drug. Psychological dependency is the development of an overpowering psychological need for a drug. Both physical addiction and psychological dependency are hard to break.

Abused drugs (in addition to alcohol and tobacco) may be grouped into a number of categories. The categories include the following drugs:

Narcotics—opium, morphine, heroin, codeine, and synthetic opiates (meperidine and methadone)

Stimulants—cocaine, amphetamines (benzedrine, dexedrine, diphetamine, and methedrine)

HIGHLIGHT   Alcohol Abuse and Alcoholism

Alcohol abuse is the use of alcohol to a degree that causes physical damage, impairs physical, social, intellectual, or occupational functioning, or results in behavior harmful to others. One does not have to be an alcoholic to have problems with alcohol. The person who drinks only once a month but drives while intoxicated and has an accident is an alcohol abuser. So is a man who gets drunk and beats up his children.

Alcoholism is dependence on alcohol: drinking compulsively and excessively, leading to functional impairment. Some alcoholics drink large amounts daily. Others drink heavily only on weekends. Others may go through long periods of sobriety interspersed with binges of daily heavy drinking lasting for weeks or months. Or heavy drinking may be limited to periods of stress, associated with periods of anxiety or strain.

Warning Signals

The following are some of the warning signals that a drinking problem is developing:

> You drink more than you used to and tend to gulp your drinks.
> You try to have a few extra drinks before or after drinking with others.
> You have begun to drink alone.
> You are noticeably drunk on important occasions.

You drink the "morning after" to overcome the effects of previous drinking.
You drink to relieve feelings of boredom, depression, anxiety, or inadequacy.
You have begun to drink at certain times, to get through difficult situations, or when you have problems.
You have weekend drinking bouts and Monday hangovers.
You are beginning to lose control of your drinking; you drink more than you planned and get drunk when you did not want to.
You promise to drink less but do not.
You often regret what you have said or done while drinking.
You are beginning to feel guilty about your drinking.
You are sensitive when others mention your drinking.
You have begun to deny your drinking or lie about it.
You have memory blackouts or pass out while drinking.
Your drinking is affecting your relationship with friends or family.
You have lost time at work or school due to drinking.
You begin to stay away from people who do not drink.

Depressants—barbiturates (Quaalude, Nembutal, Seconal, Tuinal, Amytal, or phenobarbital), tranquilizers (Miltown, Equanil, Placidyl, Librium, and Valium), and analgesics (Darvon)
Hallucinogens—LSD, peyote, mescaline, psilocybin, PCP, STP, DMT, and MDA
Marijuana—in various forms (the plant cannabis, ganja, hashish, hashish oil)
Inhalants—nail polish remover, plastic glue, gasoline, cleaning fluids, paint thinner, and other hydrocarbons.

The most frequently abused drugs in the United States are alcohol, tobacco, and marijuana, in that order. Current use of hallucinogens, tranquilizers, marijuana, and analgesics among youths ages 12 to 17 has begun to decline. Abuse of inhalants, cocaine, stimulants, sedatives, alcohol, and cigarettes by that age group is increasing. Alcohol continues to be the drug of choice of all age groups.

Adolescents begin to use drugs for a number of reasons: out of curiosity, for fun and sensual pleasure, because of social pressure to be like friends, to relieve tensions, anxiety, and pressures, to escape from problems, and to try to gain increased awareness, insight, and creativity. Those who continue to use drugs may build up a physical addiction and/or psychological dependency. Chronic abusers often have troubled family relationships and personal problems and turn to drugs to lessen pain and conflict and as a substitute for meaningful human relationships.

Over half of all junior high school and two-thirds of senior high school students have smoked cigarettes. The incidence of smoking increases with age and reaches a peak of almost half the population in the 26 to 34 age bracket. Adolescents are influenced to start by cigarette advertising, by the model of adults who smoke, by peer group pressure, and by their own need for status. Some smoke as an expression of rebellion and autonomy and a desire to be grown up. Once they start, they continue to smoke to relieve tension because it becomes an unconscious habit, in association with sociability, because of compulsion for oral activity, and because of a physical addiction to nicotine. The best solution is to keep adolescents from starting in the first place by antismoking education.

Substantial proportions of adolescents drink; by the senior grade of high school, 92 percent have. Frequent drinking of large quantities is a major factor in crime, homicides, traffic accidents, child abuse and family violence, pedestrian injuries, unwed pregnancy, and premature deaths of babies. Drinking patterns among adolescents generally follow the adult models in their communities. Chronic alcoholism is likely to run in families. The amount of drinking is also related to religiosity, education, and socioeconomic level and is a factor in juvenile delinquency.

Alcohol abuse is the use of alcohol to a degree that causes physical damage, and impairs physical, social, intellectual, or occupational functioning. Alcoholism is compulsive, alcohol dependence: excessive drinking, leading to functional impairment. Only a small percentage of youths are problem drinkers, but they are already evidencing the psychological imbalance that prompts them to rebel or seek escape through alcohol.

DISCUSSION QUESTIONS

1. Was drug abuse a problem in the high school you attended? Explain. What drugs were most commonly used? Was drug abuse limited to any particular type of student? What type of family background did abusers come from? What effect did drug abuse have on the lives of these adolescents?

2. Did your high school offer drug education? What type of program? With what effect? What approaches should be taken to combat drug abuse among adolescents?

3. What should parents do if they discover their adolescent is using: marijuana? narcotics? LSD? speed? cocaine? inhalants?

4. Discuss the current situation of drug abuse in college: its effects, consequences, and what, if anything, should be done about it.

5. Would you be willing to relate your experience with a particular drug? If you were able to break the habit, how did you do it?

6. Do you smoke regularly? How old were you when you started? Why do you smoke? Have you ever tried to stop? With what effect?

7. Discuss ways and means of how to quit smoking, such as attending smoking clinics or joining antismoking campaigns. What way works the best?

8. Discuss drinking patterns that you know exist among adolescents and the effects and consequences in the lives of these youths.

9. Do you know any adolescents who are alcohol abusers or alcoholics? Discuss their situations.

10. What should an adolescent do who has a problem with alcohol? What should parents do?

BIBLIOGRAPHY

Adler, I., and Kandel, D. B. (April, 1982). "A Cross-Cultural Comparison of Sociopsychological Factors in Alcohol Use among Adolescents in Israel, France, and the United States." *Journal of Youth and Adolescence*, 11, 89–113.

Barnes, G. M. (Spring, 1981). "Drinking among Adolescents: A Subcultural Phenomenon or a Model of Adult Behaviors." *Adolescence*, 16, 211–229.

Barnes, G. M., Farrell, M. P., and Cairns, A. (1986). "Parental Socialization Factors and Adolescent Drinking Behavior." *Journal of Marriage and the Family*, 48, 27–36.

Bell, C. S., and Battjes, R. (1985). *Prevention Research: Deterring Drug Abuse among Children and Adolescents*. NIDA Research Monograph 63. Rockville, Md.: National Institute on Drug Abuse.

Bokos, P. J., Lipscomb, S. T., and Schwartzman, J. (June, 1984). "Macrosystemic Approaches to Drug Treatment." *Personnel and Guidance Journal*, 62, 583, 584.

Bridgwater, C. A. (January 1984). "Marketing Marijuana." *Psychology Today*, 18, 77.

Brill, H. Q., and Christie, R. L. (1974). "Marihuana Use and Psychosocial Adaptation: Follow-up Study of a Collegiate Population." *Archives of General Psychiatry*, 31, 713–719.

Brown, S. A., and Stetson, B. A. (1988). "Coping with Drinking Pressures: Adolescent Versus Parent Perspectives." *Adolescence*, 23, 297–301.

Capuzzi, D., and Lecoq, L. L. (December, 1983). "Social and Personal Determinants of Adolescent Use and Abuse of Alcohol and Marijuana." *Personnel and Guidance Journal*, 62, 199–205.

Chitwood, D. D., Wells, K. S., and Russe, B. R. (Winter, 1981). "Medical and Treatment Definitions of Drug Use: The Case of the Adolescent User." *Adolescence*, 16, 817–830.

Clayton, R. R. (August, 1979). "The Family and Federal Drug Abuse Policies Programs: Toward Making the Invisible Family Visible." *Journal of Marriage and the Family*, 41, 637–647.

Coombs, R. H., and Landsverk, J. (1988). "Parenting Styles and Substance Use during Childhood and Adolescence." *Journal of Marriage and the Family*, 50, 473–482.

Cooreman, J., and Perdrizet, S. (Fall, 1980). "Smoking in Teenagers. Some Psychological Aspects." *Adolescence*, 15, 581–588.

Cotton, N. S. (January, 1979). "The Familial Incidence of Alcoholism." *Journal of Studies on Alcohol*, 40, 89–116.

Dalterio. S. L. (November, 1984). "Marijuana and the Unborn." *Listen*, 37, 8–11.

Dawkins, R. L., and Dawkins, M. P. (Winter, 1983). "Alcohol Use and Delinquency among Black, White, and Hispanic Adolescent Offenders." *Adolescence*, 18, 799–809.

DeFoe, J. R., and Breed, W. (1988). "Youth and Alcohol in Television Stories with Suggestions to the Industry for Alternative Portrayals." *Adolescence*, 23, 533–550.

Dembo, R., Dertke, M., LaVoie, L., Borders, S., Washburn, M., and Schmeidler, J. (1987). "Physical Abuse, Sexual Victimization and Illicit Drug Use: A Structural Analysis among High Risk Adolescents." *Journal of Adolescence*, 10, 13–33.

Dignan, M., Block, G., Steckler, A., Howard, C., and Cosby, M. (1986). "Locus of Control and Smokeless Tobacco Use among Adolescents." *Adolescence*, 82, 377–381.

"The Drinking Age." (January 13, 1979). *Economist*, p. 39.

"Drug Abuse: America's High School Students." (1988). National Institute on Drug Abuse/University of Michigan Institute for Social Research.

"Drug Pushers Go for Even Younger Prey." (August 13, 1979). U.S. News & World Report, p. 31.

Erickson, L., and Newman, I. M. (January, 1984). "Developing Support for Alcohol and Drug Education: A Case Study of a Counselor's Role." *Personnel and Guidance Journal*, 62, 289–291.

Farrow, J. A., and French, J. (1986). "The Drug Abuse-Delinquency Connection Revisited." *Adolescence*, 21, 951–960.

Finn, P., and Brown, J. (February, 1981). "Risks Entailed in Teenage Intoxication as Perceived by Junior and Senior High School Students." *Journal of Youth and Adolescence*, 10, 61–76.

Fondacaro, M. R., and Heller, K. (August, 1983). "Social Support Factors and Drinking among College Student Males." *Journal of Youth and Adolescence*, 12, 385–399.

Fuller, J. R., and LaFountain, M. J. (1987). "Performance-Enhancing Drugs in Sport: A Different Form of Drug Abuse." *Adolescence*, 22, 969–976.

Gantman, C. A. (December, 1978). "Family Interaction Patterns among Families with Normal, Disturbed, and Drug-Abusing Adolescents." *Journal of Youth and Adolescence*, 7, 429–440.

Gibbons, S., Wylie, M. L., Echterling, L., and French, J. (1986). "Patterns of Alcohol Use among Rural and Small-Town Adolescents." *Adolescence*, 84, 887–900.

Ginsberg, I. J., and Greenley, J. R. (March, 1978). "Competing Theories of Marijuana Use: A Longitudinal Study." *Journal of Health and Social Behavior*, 19, 22–34.

Glynn, T. J. (October, 1981). "From Family to Peer: A Review of Transitions of Influence among Drug-Using Youth." *Journal of Youth and Adolescence*, 10, 363–383.

Goodstadt, M. C., Lawson, S. L., and Langford, E. R. (Winter, 1982). "Role-Models Regarding Smoking and Fitness: A Survey of Youth Agencies in Ontario." *Adolescence*, 17, 931–938.

Greenwood, S. G. (June, 1979). "Warning: Cigarette Smoking Is Dangerous to Reproductive Health." *Family Planning Perspectives*, 11, 168–172.

Grinspoon, L., and Bakalar, J. B. (March, 1977). "A Kick from Cocaine." *Psychology Today*, 41ff.

Gullotta, T., and Adams, G. R. (October, 1982). "Substance Abuse Minimization: Conceptualizing Prevention in Adolescent and Youth Programs." *Journal of Youth and Adolescence*, 11, 409–424.

Halebsky, M. A. (1987). "Adolescent Alcohol and Substance Abuse: Parent and Peer Effects." *Adolescence*, 22, 961–967.

Hansen, W. B., and Evans, R. L. (Spring, 1982). "Feedback versus Information Concerning Carbon Monoxide as an Early Intervention Strategy in Adolescent Smoking." *Adolescence*, 17, 89–98.

Harber, R. A. (March, 1983). "The Family Dance around Drug Abuse." *Personnel and Guidance Journal*, 61, 428–431.

Harris. L., and Associates, Inc. (1974). *Public Awareness of the National Institute on Alcohol Abuse and Alcoholism Advertising Campaign and Public Attitudes Toward Drinking and Alcohol Abuse.* Reports prepared for the National Institute on Alcohol Abuse and Alcoholism. Phase Four Report and Overall Summary.

Hendin, H., Pollinger, A., Ulman, R., and Carr, A. C. (September, 1981). *Adolescent Marijuana Abusers and Their Families.* NIDA Research Monograph 40. Rockville, Md.: National Institute on Drug Abuse.

Herbert, W. (April, 1984). "Freud under Fire." *Psychology Today*, 18, 10–12.

Huba, G. J., and Bentler, P. M. (October, 1980). "The Role of Peers and Adult Models for Drug Taking at Different Stages in Adolescence." *Journal of Youth and Adolescence*, 9, 449–465.

Hughes, S. P., and Dodder, R. A. (February, 1983). "Alcohol-Related Problems and Collegiate Drinking Patterns." *Journal of Youth and Adolescence*, 12, 65–76.

Hundleby, J. D., and Mercer, G. W. (1987). "Family and Friends as Social Environments and Their Relationship to Young Adolescents' Use of Alcohol, and Marijuana." *Journal of Marriage and the Family*, 49, 151–164.

Hunt, W. A., and Matazarro, J. D. (1970). "Habit Mechanisms in Smoking." In *Learning Mechanisms in Smoking.* Edited by W. A. Hunt. Chicago: Aldine.

Jessor, R., and Jessor, S. L. (1973). *Problem Drinking in Youth: Personality, Social, and Behavioral Antecedents* and Correlates. Institute of Behavioral Science Publication No. 144, Boulder, Colo.: University of Colorado.

"The Jewish Recipe for Moderate Drinking." (March 15, 1981). Psychology Today, pp. 78–80.

Johnson, G. M., Shontz, F. C., and Locke, T. P. (Summer, 1984). "Relationships between Adolescent Drug Use and Parental Drug Behavior." Adolescence, 19, 295–299.

Johnson, K. A. (1986). "Informal Control Networks and Adolescent Orientation toward Alcohol Use." Adolescence, 21, 767–784.

Johnston, L. D., O'Malley, P. M., and Bachman, J. G. (1985). Use of Licit and Illicit Drugs by America's High School Students, 1975–1984. Rockville, Md.: National Institute on Drug Abuse.

Jurich, A. P., Polson, C. J., Jurich, J. A., and Bates, R. A. (Spring, 1985). "Family Factors in the Lives of Drug Users and Abusers." Adolescence, 20, 143–159.

Kandel, D. B., et al. (March, 1978). "Antecedents of Adolescent Initiation into Stages of Drug Use: A Developmental Analysis." Journal of Youth and Adolescence, 7, 13–40.

Keyes, S., and Block, J. (February, 1984). "Prevalence and Patterns of Substance Use among Early Adolescents." Journal of Youth and Adolescence, 13, 1–13.

Levine, E. M., and Kozak, C. (March, 1979). "Drug and Alcohol Use, Delinquency, and Vandalism among Upper Middle Class Pre- and Post-Adolescents." Journal of Youth and Adolescence, 8, 91–101.

Lotecka, L., and Lassleben, M. (Fall, 1981). "The High School 'Smoker': A Field Study of Cigarette-Related Cognitions and Social Perceptions." Adolescence, 16, 513–526.

Lowney, J. (Winter, 1984). "Correspondence between Attitudes and Drinking and Drug Behavior: Youth Subculture over Time." Adolescence, 19, 875–892.

McDermott, D. (Spring, 1984). "The Relationship of Parental Drug Use and Parents' Attitude Concerning Adolescent Drug Use to Adolescent Drug Use." Adolescence 19, 89–97.

Mayer, J. E. (1988). "The Personality Characteristics of Adolescents Who Use and Misuse Alcohol." Adolescence, 23, 383–404.

Meyer, R. E. (1975). "Psychiatric Consequences of Marihuana Use: The State of the Evidence." In Marihuana and Health Hazards: Methodological Issues in Current Marihuana Research. Edited by J. R. Tinklenberg. New York: Academic Press.

Miller, J. D. (1983). National Survey on Drug Abuse: Main Findings 1982. DHHS Publication No. (ADM) 83–1263. Rockville, Md.: National Institute on Drug Abuse.

Nahas, G. G. (1979). Keep Off the Grass. New York: Reader's Digest Press.

National Institute on Drug Abuse (1980). Review of the Evidence on Effects of Marijuana Use. Washington, D. C.: U.S. Government Printing Office.

Newman, J. (1987). "Psychological Effects on College Students of Raising the Drinking Age." Adolescence, 22, 503–510.

O'Brien, R., and Cohen, S. (1984). The Encyclopedia of Drug Abuse. New York: Facts on File.

Paton, S. M., and Kandel, D. B. (Summer, 1978). "Psychological Factors and Adolescent Illicit Drug Use: Ethnicity and Sex Differences." Adolescence, 13, 187–200.

Perry, C. L., Killen, J., Slinkard, L. A., and McAlister, A. L. (Summer, 1980). "Peer Teaching and Smoking Prevention among Junior High Students." Adolescence, 15, 277–281.

Perry, C. L., Telch, M. J., Killen, J., Burke, A., and Maccoby, N. (Fall, 1983). "High School Smoking Prevention: The Relative Efficacy of Varied Treatments and Instructions." Adolescence, 18, 561–566.

Picou, J. S., Wells, R. H., and Miranne, A. C. (Fall, 1980). "Marijuana Use, Occupational Success Values and Materialistic Orientations of University Students: A Research Note." Adolescence, 15, 829–834.

"Pot Smokers Risk Cancer Study Says" (February 11, 1988). Portland, ME.: Portland Press Herald.

Rees, C. D., and Wilborn, B. L. (February, 1983). "Correlates of Drug Abuse in Adolescents: A Comparison of Families of Drug Abusers with Families of Nondrug Abusers." Journal of Youth and Adolescence, 12, 55–63.

Rubinow, D. R., and Cancro, R. (March, 1977). "The Bad Trip: An Epidemiological Survey of Youthful Hallucinogen Use." Journal of Youth and Adolescence, 6, 1–9.

Russell, M. A. H. (1971). "Cigarette Smoking: Natural History of a Dependence Disorder." British Journal of Medical Psychology, 44, 9.

Sarvela, P. D., and McClendon, E. J. (August, 1983). "Correlates of Early Adolescent Peer and Personal Substance Use in Rural Northern Michigan." *Journal of Youth and Adolescence*, 12, 319–332.

Schneider, S. (Spring, 1980). "An Analysis of Drug/Poison Inhalation." *Adolescence*, 15, 191–193.

Sharp, J. G., and Graeven, D. B. (December, 1981). "The Social, Behavioral, and Health Effects of Phencyclidine (PCP) Use." *Journal of Youth and Adolescence*, 10, 487–499.

Shaver, P. (May, 1983). "Down at College." *Psychology Today*, 17, 16.

Sheppard, M. A., Wright, D., and Goodstadt, M. S. (1985). "Peer Pressure and Drug Use—Exploding the Myth." *Adolescence*, 20, 949–958.

Shor, R. E., and Williams, D. C. (November, 1978). "Normative Beliefs about Tobacco Smoking on Campus in Relation to an Exposition of the Viewpoint of the Nonsmoker's Rights Movement." *Journal of Psychology*, 100, 261–274.

_____ . (1979). "Reported Physiological and Psychological Symptoms of Tobacco Smoke Pollution in Nonsmoking and Smoking College Students." *Journal of Psychology*, 101, 203–218.

Simonds, J. F., and Kashani, J. (Winter, 1979). "Phencyclidine Use in Delinquent Males Committed to a Training School." *Adolescence* 14, 721–725.

Solorzano, L. (August 27, 1984). "Student Think Schools are Making the Grade." *U.S. News & World Report*, pp. 49–51.

Stern, M., Northman, J. E., and Van Slyck, M. R. (Summer, 1984). "Father Absence and Adolescent 'Problem Behaviors': Alcohol Consumption, Drug Use, and Sexual Activity." *Adolescence*, 19, 301–312.

Svobodny, L. A. (Winter, 1982). "Biographical, Self-Concept, and Educational Factors among Chemically Dependent Adolescents." *Adolescence*, 17, 847–853.

Tashkin, D. P., et al. (1975). "Effects of Smoked Marijuana in Experimentally Induced Asthma." *American Review of Respiratory Disease*, 112, 377–386.

Thompson, E. L. (March, 1978). "Smoking Education Programs 1960–1976." *American Journal of Public Health*, 68, 250–257.

Thorne, C. R., and DeBlassie, R. R. (1985). "Adolescent Substance Abuse." *Adolescence*, 20, 335–247.

Trotter, R. T. (Summer, 1982). "Ethical and Sexual Patterns of Alcohol Use: Anglo and Mexican-American College Students." *Adolescence*, 17, 305–325.

Tucker, L. A. (Summer, 1984). "Cigarette Smoking Intentions and Physical Fitness: A Multivariate Study of High School Males." *Adolescence*, 19, 313–321.

_____ . (1985). "Television's Role Regarding Alcohol Use among Teenagers." *Adolescence*, 20, 591–598.

Tudor, C. G.; Petersen, D. M.; and Elifson, K. W. (Winter, 1980). "An Examination of the Relationship between Peer and Parental Influences and Adolescent Drug Use." *Adolescence*, 15, 783–795.

U.S. Bureau of the Census, Department of Commerce. (1988). *Statistical Abstract of the United States, 1988*. Washington, D. C.: U.S. Government Printing Office.

_____ . (1980). *National Institute on Alcohol Abuse and Alcoholism*. 7th Annual Report. Rockville, Md.: National Institute on Alcohol Abuse and Alcoholism.

_____ . (June 1980). *Marijuana Research Findings: 1980*. Rockville, Md.: National Institute on Drug Abuse.

_____ . (September 1981). *Adolescent Marijuana Abusers and Their Families*. Rockville, Md.: National Institute on Drug Abuse.

Urberg, D., and Robbins, R. L. (October, 1981). "Adolescents' Perceptions of the Costs and Benefits Associated with Cigarette Smoking. Sex Differences and Peer Influence." *Journal of Youth and Adolescence*, 10, 353–361.

Valium Package Insert (1988). Roche Laboratories.

Vicary, J. R., and Lerner, J. V. (1986). "Parental Attributes and Adolescent Drug Use." *Journal of Adolescence*, 9, 115–122.

Welte, J. W., and Barnes, G. M. (1987). "Youthful Smoking: Patterns and Relationships of Alcohol and Other Drug Use." *Journal of Adolescence*, 10, 327–340.

West, J. D., Hosie, T. W., and Zarski, J. J. (1987). "Family Dynamics and Substance Abuse: A Preliminary Study." *Journal of Counseling and Development*, 65, 487–490.

Wright, L. S. (Summer, 1982). "Parental Permission to Date and Its Relationship to Drug Use and Suicidal Thoughts among Adolescents." *Adolescence*, 17, 409–418.

_____ . (1985). "High School Polydrug Users and Abusers." *Adolescence*, 80, 853–861.

CHAPTER
12

Adolescent Society, Culture, and Subculture

adolescent
society

adolescent
culture

A careful sociological analysis of adolescents as an identifiable segment of the population ought to make a distinction between adolescent society and adolescent culture. **Adolescent society** refers to the structural arrangements of subgroups within an adolescent social system. It refers to the organized network of relationships and association among adolescents. **Adolescent culture** is the sum of the ways of living of adolescents; it refers to the body of norms, values, attitudes, and practices recognized and shared by members of the adolescent society as appropriate guides to action. Adolescent society refers to the interrelationships of adolescents within their social systems; their culture describes the way they think, behave, and live.

This chapter is concerned with both adolescent society and with adolescent culture. It focuses on formal and informal adolescent societies but especially on the formal in-school groups and subsystems. Factors that influence the adolescent's social position in a formal group are outlined and discussed, along with the subculture that exists at the high school and college levels. The chapter concludes with a discussion of two important material aspects of adolescent culture—clothing and automobiles—and two nonmaterial aspects of adolescent culture—music and language.

CULTURE AND SOCIETY

Adolescent society is not one single, comprehensive, monolithic structure that includes all young people. There are usually numerous adolescent societies with wide variations among various age groups, socioeconomic levels, and ethnic or national backgrounds. Furthermore, adolescent societies are only vaguely structured. They exist without any formal, written codification and without traditions of organizational patterns. Individuals move into and out of each system within a few short years, contributing to structural instability. Each local group of adolescents is provincial, with few ties beyond school membership and the local gang and clique. Although there are nationwide youth organizations, fan clubs, or competitive athletic events, most adolescent societies are primarily local, variably replicated in community after community.

The same cautions should be applied to adolescent culture. One cannot speak of U.S. adolescent culture as though it were a body of beliefs, values, and practices uniformly espoused by all youths throughout the country. Just as there are regional, ethnic, and class versions of the national adult culture, so there are variations in expression of adolescent culture among differing segments of the population. Adolescent culture is not homogeneous; the popular image of adolescent culture usually refers to urban, middle-class youth. Actually there may be important deviations from this pattern. A more accurate description would convey that there are numerous versions of teenage culture expressed by various segments of American youth who share some common elements of a general middle-class youth culture but who participate selectively and in varying degrees in the activities of the organized adolescent society.

But before adolescent society or culture can be analyzed, an important question needs to be answered: Are adolescent society and culture unique and different from those of the adult world?

THE ADOLESCENT SUBCULTURE

According to one point of view, **adolescent subculture** emphasizes conformity in the peer group and values that are contrary to adult values (Gallagher, 1979). This subculture exists primarily in the high school, where it constitutes a small society, one that has most of its important interactions within itself, and maintains only a few threads of connection with the outside adult society. This happens because children are set apart in schools, where they take on more and more extracurricular activities for longer periods of training. Segregated from the adult world, they develop subcultures with their own language, styles, and, most important, value systems that may differ from those of adults. As a result the adolescent lives in a segregated society and establishes a subculture that meets with peer, but not adult, approval.

adolescent subculture

An opposite point of view is that adolescents reflect adult values, beliefs, and practices—the theory of an adolescent subculture, segregated and different from adult culture, is a myth. This view is substantiated by a number of studies. One study of 6,000 adolescents from 10 different nations revealed that for the most part adolescents were not alienated from their parents. Today's youth had great respect for parents (Atkinson, 1988). Two other researchers compared parent versus adolescent political views over an eight-year period and found that the generations were moving closer together rather than apart (Jennings and Niemi, 1978). One investigator found that where there was conflict between generations, it usually centered on mundane, day-to-day issues such as noisiness, tidiness, punctuality, and living under the same roof rather than on fundamental values such as honesty, perseverance, and concern for others (Coleman et al., 1977).

From this point of view, the cultural norms shared by teenagers in the United States are not very different from those shared by adult Americans. (Were it otherwise, the indoctrinational efforts of parents, teachers, preachers, and others would constitute a pretty sorry record; and the theory of learning by imitation would be totally—instead of only partially—discredited.)

A False Dichotomy

The more studies that are conducted and the more closely these are analyzed, however, the more evident it becomes that adolescents choose to follow neither parents nor friends exclusively (Duncan, 1978; Niemi et al., 1978). One explanation is that in many instances, parents and friends are quite alike, so the peer group serves to reinforce rather than violate parental values. Adolescents tend to choose friends who are like themselves; thus there may be "considerable overlap between the values of parents and peers because of commonalities in their backgrounds— social, economic, religious, educational, even geographic" (Cosner and Larson, 1980).

Also, there are considerable differences among adolescents depending upon their age and year in school, sex, socioeconomic status, and educational level. The younger adolescents are, the more likely they are to conform to parental values and mores and less likely to be influenced by peers. A study of 272 nine-, ten-, and eleven-year-old boys and girls attending school in a large metropolitan area of the Southeast revealed a very high degree of conformity to parents

(Thompson, 1985). The subjects were asked to indicate who was most likely to be influential on a variety of issues: parents, peers, or a best friend. Table 12–1 shows the results. As can be seen, there were only four items on which parental opinions was not the major influence: choice of TV program to watch (8), choice of music (9), choice of reading material (10), and preference of sports (15). At the age of these adolescents, parents exerted the primary influence even on such matters as clothes and food. On those items in which there were significant sex differences, females were more parent oriented than males. However, peer influence increased for both sexes as the children got older.

Girls aged 12 to 15 have been found to be significantly more parent oriented than peer oriented with younger girls giving mothers first place, fathers second, and friends third (Niles, 1979). With increasing age, however, peer influence increases and parental influence declines. At the college level, freshmen show less disagreement with parents on certain social problems than do juniors or seniors. Apparently increasing age and education widens the gap between parents and adolescents (Sebald and White, 1980). College itself seems to have a liberalizing effect on students. It has also been found that adolescents with the highest IQs are more likely to be peer oriented than those with less intelligence (Niles, 1979).

Sex is also a significant variable in the degree of parent-peer orientation. Males tend to show more disagreement with parents than do females, but females

▨ TABLE 12-1

Parent-peer influence on a variety of issues.*

ITEMS	PARENT	PEER	BEST FRIEND
1. Choice of clothes worn at school	72.2%	25.9%	1.9%
2. Which clothes to buy	75.3%	14.4%	10.3%
3. How late to stay out	95.9%	3.0%	1.1%
4. Whether to attend party	85.3%	8.5%	6.2%
5. Food preferences	93.4%	5.1%	1.5%
6. How money is spent	69.4%	14 %	16.6%
7. How free time is spent	54.2%	29.2%	16.6%
8. Which TV programs to watch	49.2%	29.5%	21.4%
9. Choice of music	30 %	44.4%	25.6%
10. Choice of reading material	33.5%	38.9%	27.6%
11. Manners of speech	70.9%	14 %	15.1%
12. Standards of conduct	83 %	13.7%	3.3%
13. Church attendance	92.4%	4.4%	3.2%
14. Opinions of people	70.6%	26.8%	2.6%
15. Preference of sports	46 %	31.6%	22.4%
16. Counsel of personal problems	70.6%	7.3%	22.1%
17. Hair style	54 %	44.5%	1.5%
18. Choice of clubs	57 %	27.6%	15.4%

*Percentages of responses to categories parent, peer, and best friend by item.
From: Thompson, D. N. (1985). "Parent-Peer Compliance in a Group of Preadolescent Youth." *Adolescence*, 20: 501–508.

who do disagree with parents tend to do so at younger ages, reflecting the earlier maturational age of the females (Eitzen and Brouillette, 1979).

There are also socioeconomic status differences in parent-peer orientation. In general, upper-class adolescents are more closely supervised by parents and show less behavioral autonomy than lower-strata adolescents. Low socio-economic status adolescents are more likely to drop out of school to seek employment; they achieve earlier financial independence and are less subject to parental influence and control than their middle-class counterparts (Fasick, 1984).

Whether adolescents are more parent or peer oriented will depend partially on the degree of emotional closeness between parents and their youths; that is, on the *affect* relationship. Youths who have a close emotional attachment to parents will more likely be parent oriented than will adolescents who are hostile toward parents or who reject them. To put it another way, the quality of adolescent-adult interaction is inversely related to peer-group involvement (Eitzen and Brouillette, 1979; Hanks and Eckland, 1978). Other research has revealed that individual adolescents differ markedly in their parent and peer orientations.

Distinctive Social Relationships and Culture

It is nevertheless useful to recognize as distinctive a system of social relationships in which adolescents engage, not in the sense that it is the only world to which they are responsive but in the sense that it is a society over which adults exercise only partial control. Most modern teenagers are *both* typically confused adolescents in the adult world and relatively self-assured and status-conscious members of their peer groups—depending on the set of interactions being analyzed.

These same conclusions might be reached with respect to other aspects of adolescent culture. Adolescents reflect many adult values and norms, but certain aspects of their lives are distinguishable from American adult culture because in these areas adolescents can exercise some control and make their own decisions. Such matters as styles of dress, tastes in music, language, popular movie and recording stars, use of the automobile, dating customs and practices, and behavior at youth hangouts or at sporting events are properly adolescent subcultural, for they may even sometimes run counter to adult preferences (Brown, 1982). It is therefore proper and possible to point to certain aspects of adolescent culture that are identifiable as separate because they are developed and practiced predominantly by adolescents, sometimes in contradiction to adult norms. Furthermore, the further along adolescents are in school, the more likely they are to listen to peers rather than to parents in matters pertaining to social judgments. Figure 12–1 shows the frequency with which adolescents mentioned parents, other adults, and peers as competent referents in matters pertaining to making social judgments (Young and Ferguson, 1979).

Two especially notable areas of adolescent-adult disagreement are drugs and sexual behavior (Brown, 1982; Glynn, 1981; Huba and Bentler, 1980; Shah and Zelnik, 1981). The primary reason adolescents and adults disagree in these matters is that cultural change has been so rapid and so great that youthful behavior *is* different from adult values. Take the attitude toward the smoking of marijuana, for example. In 1985 only 27 percent of adults aged 26 and over had ever used

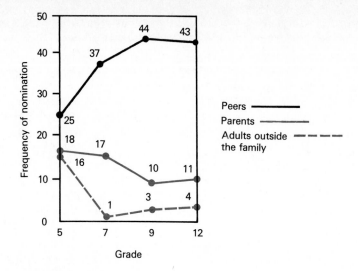

FIGURE 12-1

Frequency of reference group nominations for social items, as a function of grade level.

From: Young, W., and Ferguson, L. R. (June, 1979). "Developmental Changes through Adolescence in the Spontaneous Nominations of Reference Groups as a Function of Decision Content," *Journal of Youth and Adolescence*, 8: 239–252. Used by permission.

marijuana, in contrast to 64 percent of youths aged 18 to 25 (U.S. Bureau of the Census, 1988). This wide difference between adolescent and adult behavior indicates that youthful marijuana smoking is subcultural. Furthermore, those adolescents who are the most peer oriented are most likely to be users; those who are most parent oriented are less likely to use it.

Similarly, several attitude surveys have revealed that the sexual attitudes of adolescents are more liberal than those of adults (Thornton and Camburn, 1987). An attitude survey among 916 families in the Detroit area revealed that 65 percent of 18-year-old daughters and 77 percent of 18-year-old sons expressed approval of premarital sex for young people, but only 32 percent of the mothers approved (Thornton and Camburn, 1987). These youthful attitudes, therefore, may be regarded as subcultural. However, even though the study revealed that differences in attitudes existed, the mothers did exert some influence. Adolescents whose mothers were fundamentalist Protestants and those whose mothers attended church regularly were significantly less likely than others to approve of premarital sexual intercourse.

Differences between parental and adolescent sexual attitudes vary somewhat according to age group and sex. Fisher and Hall (1988) found that middle and late adolescents were more liberal in their sexual attitudes than early adolescents and also more liberal than their parents. Early adolescents more likely reflected the sexual values of their parents. Males were also more liberal than females. Other studies have revealed that adolescents are more likely to incorporate the sexual values of their parents into their own value system if there has been at least a moderate amount of parent-child dialogue about sex (Fisher, 1988).

Thus, whether a youthful subculture exists depends on what areas of concern one is examining. Overall, youth culture reflects adult culture. In specific areas, however, youth culture is a distinct subculture. Also, the more rapid the social change, the more likely that youth's views become different from those of their parents. In this sense, certain aspects of adolescent life become subcultural—at least for a while.

ADOLESCENT SOCIETIES

Like adult social structures, adolescent societies may be divided into two groups: formal and informal.

Formal Societies

Formal adolescent societies include primarily groups of in-school youths. Linkages with peers are determined by whether adolescents are enrolled in school, which school they are enrolled in, and which student organizations they join. They are identified with their particular school, team, and teachers. There are also out-of-school church or youth groups, but for the most part only in-school youths participate in these activities also. Therefore, any formal, well-defined social system to which adolescents belong is invariably related to in-school youth.

Informal Societies

Informal adolescent societies generally describe those loosely structured groups of out-of-school youth who get together socially but who have little opportunity to participate in a formally structured network of social relationships. These youth are too scattered and too involved in trying to find their places in adult society to be characterized as a separate adolescent society. One exception might be the adolescent street gang, which may exist as a subsociety all its own.

This does not mean that all adolescents who remain in school are actively participating members of the organized adolescent society. Some adolescents remain in school but are really excluded from school life. Those who finally drop out of school have poor attendance records and rarely hold school office or have been active in school affairs. There are some who are socially outside "the society," though they may still be physically in it.

Age-Grade Societies

Adolescent societies are not only in-school but also ***age-grade societies*** (Montemayor and VanKomen, 1980). Adolescents are identified with a certain grade or class in school. This identification allows them to take certain courses, participate in certain school-sponsored activities (for which being a freshman or a senior is a prerequisite for eligibility), or give or attend parent-permitted parties (for one's classmates). Freshmen compete with sophomores in sports or other events. Class membership is important in influencing friendship associations. Among pairs of

age-grade societies

friends, the one item that two members have in common far more often than any other—including religion, father's occupation, father's education, common leisure interests, grades in school, and others—is class in school.

Social Class and Status

Evidence continues to mount that an individual's ready acceptance by and active involvement in adolescent society are influenced by socioeconomic background. (See chapters 2 and 13.) Social leadership scores of children in middle-class schools are higher than those of children in working-class schools, and the average scores for aggressive and withdrawn maladjustment are lower in middle-class than in working-class schools. Higher social class students far more often attend athletic events, dances, plays, and musical activities than those from the lower classes. Furthermore, youths who identify themselves with organized youth groups such as Boy Scouts, Girl Scouts, and church youth fellowship groups are preponderantly from middle-class rather than lower-class homes.

This does not mean that every individual from low socioeconomic status families is a social reject. Chapter 8 emphasizes that the youngster who has been given high self-esteem, even though from a poor home, will adjust more easily than another poor youngster with low esteem. Nevertheless, students whose fathers are college graduates (one clue to middle-class status) are far more likely than students whose fathers have only grade school education to be identified as members of the leading crowd, to be chosen as friends, and to be viewed as people whom one would "like to be like."

IN-SCHOOL SUBSYSTEMS

subsystems   In-school adolescent societies also may be divided into distinct **subsystems** in which adolescents participate and in which they are assigned status positions. Furthermore, a particular student may be simultaneously involved in more than one of three distinct subsystems.

The Formal, Academic Subsystem

The student is involved in a formal, academic subsystem shaped by the school administration, faculty, curriculum, textbooks, classrooms, grades, rules, and regulations. Students in this group are concerned with intellectual pursuits, attaining knowledge, achievement, and making the honor roll. In this system, seniors outrank freshmen, and the honor roll student outranks the D student, but the degree varies from school to school. In some schools good students are rejected socially, especially if they also manifest undesirable personality traits; other students may refer to them as "grinds," "nerds," "geeks," or "losers." In recent years, however, students have become more and more aware of the emphasis on academic achievement in high schools and have been more willing to be identified with those getting good grades. The "bookworm" is a social isolate who is still scorned. The very bright student who gets A's without studying is admired and envied, especially if she or he also participates in extracurricular and athletic activities. Whether getting good grades has a positive value will depend on the social group of which a student is part. One reason for underachievement is negative peer pressure against studies (Newman, 1976).

The Semiformal, Activities Subsystem

The student may be involved in a semiformal, activities subsystem, which includes all sponsored organizations and activities such as athletics, drama, and departmental clubs (Grabe, 1981). There may be dozens of independent formal school organizations that may be subdivided further into subgroups, ranging from varsity basketball to the knitting club. Each group has a prestige ranking in the eyes of the students, which conveys a certain status rating to its members. Each group has specific offices, with the result that the individual's status is determined partly by which of these offices he or she holds. The amount of prestige that any position bestows depends on its rank within each respective group and the prestige standing of the group in relation to all other groups (Newman and Newman, 1987).

Educators are not completely in agreement about the value of extracurricular activities and organizations in preparing students for adult life (Cuccia, 1981). Students who participate in extracurricular high school activities have been found to be those most involved in adult voluntary organizations and most politically active fifteen years after graduation (Hanks and Eckland, 1978). Many high school athletes have career ambitions to become professional athletes, but fewer than 2 percent of those participating in high school sports will become professional athletes (Lee, 1983). Certainly participation in athletics is one contribution to social acceptability in the average high school (Williams, 1983).

One in-school adolescent society is the semiformal activities subsystem which includes all sponsored organizations and activities. (Ken Karp)

As students go through college, those who are able to make athletic teams begin to reap tangible benefits. Not only do they enjoy financial benefits and a superior social status while in college, but they are also more socially mobile and achieve superior economic levels and business success when they get out. An investigation of adult males who had played football at Notre Dame revealed that "first team football players experienced greater income mobility in later life than second team and reserve players, and first team ballplayers were over-represented as top ranking executives in their companies. (Thirty-four percent were top executives.) This success was achieved despite the fact that fewer ball-players earned graduate degrees than did other students (Sack and Thiel, 1979).

Friendship Subsystem

The student may be involved in an informal network of friendship subsystems that operate primarily within the boundaries of the school world. Friendship choices are directed overwhelmingly to other students in the same school, and the majority of these choices are directed to members of the same grade and sex group.

Of the three subsystems, membership in the informal friendship system is most important in the eyes of other students. This is the only subsystem unencumbered by adult sponsorship. This is the adolescent's world, and the status an individual enjoys in this world is of major importance. Status in the academic and activities subsystems is coveted but primarily for the prestige, acceptance, and standing it gives one within the network of informal peer groupings.

Students attach prestige rankings to being a member of one clique rather than another. Various descriptive titles convey the general reputation, central values, and activities shared by the group, such as the "leading crowd," "athletic crowd," "dirty dozen," "sexy six," and "beer drinkers." The adolescent's general social status within the student body appears to be a function of his or her combined rankings within each of the several subsystems. Furthermore, a student who scores high or low in one system is likely to hold a similar position within the others, but because the important system from the student's viewpoint is the informal one, it is more determinative of behavior than the other two.

Some friendship groups may be in active, open rebellion against the school's educational and social activities. Those in these groups reject the rules of the school system and flaunt authority. Cohen (1979) subdivides this group into *greasers* and *hippies*. The greasers are interested in cars, drinking, and fights and emphasize hedonism, toughness, and an early adoption of adult privileges usually denied adolescents. The hippies are also in rebellion, rejecting the legitimacy of the adult world and serious planning or preparation for adulthood.

COLLEGIATE SUBCULTURES

Classifications

Classifications of collegiate subcultures have been made in order to reach a better understanding of the college student's world. Four separate classifications may be identified.

The *collegiate subculture* is the college world of football, Greek letter societies (sororities and fraternities), cars, drinking, dates, and card parties, with courses and professors in the background. Students in this subculture are not hostile to college but avoid its academic demands, preferring to turn college into a country club. It is a characteristically middle- and upper-middle-class group, for it requires money and leisure to pursue the strenuous schedule of social activities.

The *vocational subculture* prevails in urban colleges and universities attended by children of lower-middle-class families. Many of these students are married and putting themselves through school. They buy their education somewhat as one buys groceries since they are customers in a diploma market. The symbol of their subculture is the student placement office. There is some indication that an increasing number of middle- and upper-middle-class students are becoming interested in the vocational aspects of college, for they are attending college as a means of professional advancement and preparation.

The *academic subculture* has learning, knowledge, and ideas as central values. Members of this group are seriously involved in their course work beyond the minimum required for passing and graduation, and they identify with their college and its faculty.

The *nonconformist subculture* includes the intellectual, radical, alienated, bohemian student. This is a more difficult group to identify because it is essentially nonconformist and includes a wide variety of types of students. It may include the radical protester; the scholarly, intellectual, but social rebel; the deviant but peaceful isolate. When students' intellectual, political, social, and cultural norms are at odds with their teachers, parents, and school, they form their own nonconformist cultures.

Changes

College culture has changed drastically in the years since World War II. After World War II, returning veterans dismissed the previously dominant collegiate subculture as childish and worked to make college a stepping-stone to better jobs and careers. Following the Soviet Union's launching of Sputnik in 1957, the need for highly trained U.S. scientists, technicians, and scholars shifted emphasis to the academic subculture. During the 1960s, civil rights, war, ecology, and other social concerns became of major interest, with many students participating in what adults characterized as the nonconformist, radical subculture. Today the trend is toward a vocational emphasis. Rapidly rising tuition costs have stimulated students to want to get their money's worth, with the result that most seem more serious about their education and careers than the campus radicals of the late 1960s. Since 1971 there has been a steady decline in political liberalism. There are fewer causes and fewer rebels, leaving students freer to concentrate on their own lives and on personal fulfillment.

MATERIAL CONCERNS OF ADOLESCENT CULTURE

Another way to understand adolescent culture is to examine the material artifacts that youths buy or make and use in their daily lives. Two groups—adolescent clothing and automobiles—have been selected for discussion because they are so important in the adolescent's life.

Clothing

One of the most noticeable aspects of adolescent culture is the adolescent's preoccupation with clothing, hair styles, and grooming. (See also chapter 5.) Adults, reflecting on this preoccupation, accuse adolescents of being rebellious nonconformists or, at the other extreme, of being superficial in their values. Sociologists and social psychologists point out that neither accusation is true. Adolescents are conformists, especially when it comes to clothing and appearance within their own peer groups. And rather than showing superficiality because of their concern about appearance, they are actually evidencing both their need to find and express their own individual identity and their need to belong to a social group.

Clothing is an important means by which individual adolescents discover and express their identities (Dienstfrey, 1982). As adolescent boys and girls search for self-images with which they can be comfortable, they are preoccupied with experimentation with their appearance. Clothing and appearance are expressions of themselves as they strive to control their impressions on others. Clothing is a visual means of communicating to others the kind of role a person wishes to play in life. Adolescents applying for jobs, for example, endeavor to communicate by the clothes they wear the kind of people they are and the type of job they expect to obtain. One study showed that adolescents preferred designer jeans to those not so labeled (Lennon, 1986). In selecting the more expensive jeans, they were portraying an image about themselves.

Appearance also plays an important role in social interaction, for it provides a means of identification. If a boy dresses like a tough delinquent, he is likely to be treated as a delinquent. Clothing enables one adolescent to discover the social identity of another person and to pattern his or her behavior and responses according to what is expected. As human beings within a society develop social selves, dress and adornment are intimately linked to their interacting with one another.

Clothing is one means by which adolescents express their dependence-independence conflicts or their conformity-individuality conflicts. Clothing can be a medium of rebellion against the adult world. Adolescents who are hostile or rebellious toward their parents may express their antipathy by wearing clothes or hair styles they know their parents dislike. The more fuss the parents make, the more determined adolescents are to stick to their own styles. Nonacceptable clothing styles, deliberately chosen by adolescents, mirror their rebellion against authority. However, the dominant motives in selecting the styles are the desire to be recognized by others as superior or the desire to depend on and be like others (Koester and May, 1985). Adolescents who buy clothes to show independence (from parents especially) wear clothes that will give them recognition or acceptance in their own peer groups.

In recent years, clothing and hair styles have been used by some youths as an expression of rebellion against particular mores and values in adult society.

Adult puritanical culture emphasized that "cleanliness is next to godliness"; therefore, some teenagers express their rejection of what they perceive as a hypocritical, materialistic, godless culture by choosing to remain unclean and unkempt. Youths of the 1960s chose various symbols of a youth culture that was predominantly antiwar and antiestablishment. Ban-the-bomb symbols; beads, flowers, and headbands; fringed leather, Indian-style jackets; granny dresses; moccasins or sandals; beards and wild hair were an expression of independence, dissatisfaction with the status quo, and the determination of these youths to show solidarity against the onslaughts of adult criticism and attack. Such clothing symbolized their rejection of middle-class philosophy and values. Students of the 1980s who adopt punk-rock styles are expressing the same rebellion against middle-class society and conformity to their own peer groups (Gold, 1987). Clothing remains a basic expression of personality, life-style, and political philosophy.

For adolescents, the most important function of clothing is to assure their identity and sense of belonging with peer groups (Horowitz, 1982). A number of studies have shown the relationship between adolescents' appearance and their social acceptance. Those who are defined by their peers as fashionable dressers have high status; well-dressed but not fashionable students occupy the middle ground; poorly dressed students have low status (Hinton and Margerum, 1984). Consciously or not, other students look down on those not dressed correctly.

Adolescents who are satisfied with the way they look also have a more acceptable self-concept and make a more adequate personal adjustment (Kness, 1983). Preoccupations with clothing and appearance are not superficial or unimportant to youths who are concerned about peer-group acceptance. They must either conform or be rejected.

The Automobile

Another material aspect of adolescent culture is the automobile. The automobile has become important in the life of the adolescent for a number of different reasons.

The automobile is a status symbol. Eitzen (1975) reports that when boys are asked what impresses girls the most, they rank being an athlete first, followed by being in the leading crowd, followed by having a nice car. Owning or having access to a car adds to one's prestige in the eyes of the crowd.

The type of car one owns or drives is important, and the status attached to various types of changes over the years. Not long ago, to drive the family car—especially if it was a new, large, and expensive one—added greatly to prestige. Later the big car was out, and the small, fast, expensive sports car was in. Now college students who cannot afford expensive sports cars are turning to compacts, primarily because of the lower price. For the majority of youths, owning a car is still one of the most coveted symbols of status.

The automobile is a means of freedom and mobility. A car allows adolescents the opportunity to get away from home and drive to the neighboring town, to the big city, or to Florida during the spring break from school. It provides adolescents with a home away from home. If particularly devoted to it, they may spend hours

The automobile has become important in the life of the adolescent, serving as a status symbol, a means of freedom and mobility, a symbol of power and masculinity or glamor and sexuality, or a hobby. (© Frank Siteman)

in it each day, eating at drive-in restaurants, watching movies at drive-ins, talking with the gang, or making love.

The automobile is a symbol of power and masculinity. Even the names convey the message: Cougar, Mustang, Thunderbird. The tachometer gives a measure of the adolescent's daring and speed. The insecure boy especially finds that the automobile becomes a means of controlling an enormous amount of power and of gaining for himself a feeling of strength and virility. The more power in the engine, the louder the muffler, the more the tires will scream, the faster the car will go, and the more daringly the boy drives it, the more manly he feels. Some boys become exhibitionists, primarily to impress girls.

For a number of youths an automobile has become a hobby. Many adolescent boys share a love for power and speed. Drag strip or stock car races are opportunities to compete in socially sanctioned ways to see who can build the fastest engine or soup up an old car. Such races provide opportunities for boys to prove themselves as men and as expert mechanics.

The automobile has become a symbol of glamour and sexuality, of romantic conquest and acceptability. Madison Avenue has been quick to use not only snob appeal but also sex appeal. Advertisements imply that any man who drives a certain car will automatically fill it with beautiful women or that any girl who drives up in a certain car with plush upholstery will be considered as glamorous and beautiful as the model in the ad. The sensuous beauty in a low-cut evening gown caresses her automobile in such a fashion as to make every male watcher identify with the car—if he only had that car, maybe she would caress him too. The automobile has also become a favorite lovers' retreat. It allows for mobility, a fair degree of privacy,

HIGHLIGHT   The Automobile and Social Activity

The availability of an automobile has significant influence on the daily life of the adolescent. Schlecter and Gump interviewed adolescents to determine the differences that access to a car made. They classified three groups of adolescent males:

Unrestricted drivers: Drove without any parental limitations.
Limited drivers: Drove with parental limitations.
Nondrivers: Either did not have a license or drove infrequently.

The unrestricted drivers explored by going from one friend's home to another and then "cruised" to a number of spots to "see what was happening." They went to more different settings, more frequently beyond their own neighborhood, and spent more time with friends, especially girlfriends or boyfriends. Certainly driving helped these adolescents to achieve new and more solid relationships with peers of both sexes.

The limited drivers who drove with parental permission and limitations often used the car for specific social activities, to go to work, or to drive other family members. Driving with parental consent gave them a degree of independence and autonomy, so they were less childlike in relationships to the adult world than nondrivers.

Nondrivers were severely restricted in social activities. Their activities usually consisted of spending a limited amount of time at friends' homes or activities in outdoor settings. They spent significantly less time with friends than did the driving group. As one subject declared: "A teenager without a license is just not a teenager."

The researchers concluded by suggesting that driving seemed to have a positive influence on adolescents' social responsibility, freedom from parental controls, and engagement in work behavior.

Schlecter, T. M., and Gump, P. V. (Spring, 1983). "Car Availability and the Daily Life of the Teenage Male," Adolescence, 18, 101–113.

and even some degree of comfort and warmth, something that the local lovers' lane cannot offer in the middle of winter.

For some, the automobile has become a means of expressing hostility and anger. Psychiatrists have hypothesized that driving a powerful automobile provides an outlet for expression of frustration and hostility. Immature people who jump into their cars when frustrated and angry and go careening down the highway are unintentionally using the automobile as a convenient weapon to kill, maim, mutilate, or destroy. It has been widely publicized that hostile and explosive mental attitudes are major causes of injuries and deaths from automobiles and that the accident-prone driver rebels against authority. The way adolescents use cars and the attitudes with which they drive are indications and tests of their emotional maturity. One investigator has pointed to the fact that some disturbed adolescents use the automobile as a means of committing suicide or murder and that after such a suicide is publicized, the number of similar auto fatalities increases by almost one-third (Phillips, 1979). Apparently the behavior of young automobile drivers is affected by the processes of suggestion and modeling.

NONMATERIAL ASPECTS OF ADOLESCENT CULTURE

Music

Music is an important part of adolescent culture. Popular music has taken many forms: pop, rhythm, blues, folk, country western, jazz, and rock. The most common themes are ballads of love. Bobby Brown sings about sweet little *Roni* who gives a special kind of love that makes him feel good (Baby Face, 1988). The Judds implore *Give Me a Little Love*. A man can buy a girl a diamond ring, take her on a plane to a foreign land, and buy her fancy clothes, but these things are not what matters. Every girl wants love and a man to make her feel important (Kennedy, 1988). The song *Money* explains that money can fly us to paradise and buy expensive things, but it is not able to give a kiss or walk in the rain (Oshin, 1988).

The love that is portrayed in modern music is usually an ultra-romantic, inevitable love. Debbie Gibson explains to her lover that she's *Lost in Your Eyes*. She is in love and she becomes weak when he looks at her. She realized it the first time she saw him (Gibson, 1988). Rod Stewart reveals the powerlessness and the pain of unrequited love in the song *My Heart Can't Tell You No*. He complains that it is torture when the person you love is in love with someone else. He tries hard, but when he looks at her his heart breaks. He tells her he cannot see her anymore (Climie and Morgan, 1988).

Music is an important part of adolescent culture; youths spend much of their time listening to music. (Robert Harbison)

Sometimes the songs are sensual. This is evident in the song *You Got It (The Right Stuff)* sung by The New Kids on the Block. The first "time" was great and he has fallen in love by the third time. He likes everything she does, and all he wants is her (Starr, 1988).

Some of the songs deal with the problem of marriage and family living. In the country song *Hold Me*, Emmylou Harris tells about her husband who tried to leave her after a misunderstanding. He left one morning, but turned his car around at the edge of town and headed home. He asks his wife to hold him and tell him tomorrow will be different (Oshin, 1988).

Fast Car is about a girl whose father is an alcoholic and whose mother has left home. She quits school, lives in a shelter, and works in a market as a check-out girl. She tells her boyfriend she wants to go away in his fast car. They will find a better life (Chapman, 1988).

Barbara Mandrell tells about her *Child Support*. She's divorced and her ex-husband's child support payments are months late. However, her child brings her great joy and she leans on him for support (Schuyler, 1987).

Some songs reflect a particular outlook on life. The Grammy Award winner for the 1988 song of the year admonishes *Don't Worry, Be Happy*. Bobby McFerrin tells us simply: there is trouble in every life—don't worry, be happy. Worrying makes the problems double (McFerrin, 1988).

Some of the songs are a commentary on the problems of youth. The song *Runaway Go Home* by the Gatlin Brothers tells the story of a beauty queen who ran away from her Minnesota home at age seventeen and became a prostitute. A potential john is waiting for her, and she must go with him to earn some money. The singer implores her to run to the telephone and call home (Gatlin, 1985).

In the song *Papa Don't Preach*, Madonna admits that her father had warned her about a man, and now she is in trouble. She has decided to keep her baby because she is in love. She tells her father not to preach to her (Elliot, 1986).

Some songs deal with social problems. White Lion sings about *When the Children Cry*. Little children are told that they were born into an evil world. Man has corrupted much of it, but the children must try to rebuild the world. There is hope when the children sing (Bratta and Tramp, 1987, 1989).

A number of songs reflect the drug problem. In the song *Sugar Free*, the singer tell his friend he is glad he is not like him. His friend spends all of his money on drugs and wants to be high all of the time (Gray, 1986).

The most controversial music today is some hard rock, or *heavy metal* (defined as loud and hedonistic), which is direct and candid in its sensuality, emotionalism, or chagrin. Lyrics show stark realism and shocking sophistication. The group W.A.S.P. ("We Are Sexually Perverted") sings a song by the title *Fuck like a Beast*. *Darling Nicki* is a heavy breather filled with four-letter words, sung by Prince, and is about a girl in a hotel lobby masturbating with a magazine.

Other songs deal with violence, death, and suicide. A tune by Blue Oyster Cult is about a suicide pact between young lovers. Mental health experts are concerned about the suicide and homicide rate among adolescents and worry about songs that urge youth to squeeze the trigger.

Heavy metal groups try to outdo one another in being as different as possible. Groups like Twisted Sister emphasize a very weird appearance, featuring unusual makeup and tattered clothing. Other groups like W.A.S.P. try to make their music as violent, sexy, and crude as possible.

The group Motley Crue is known as one of the most outrageous bands of the 1980s. Songs like *Use It or Lose It* exemplify their stick-it-in society's face attitude.

Rock groups are under criticism not only because of what they sing but because of what they do. W.A.S.P.'s Blackie Lawless appears on stage with "blood" streaming down his face and chest. On stage, mayhem runs throughout the entire show as feathers fly and chunks of raw meat are tossed into the crowd. Dee Snider of Twisted Sister admits that "our goal always has been to be totally outrageous, to do things that everyone's parents would see and just want to run out of the room. . . . The makeup, the clothes have always been designed for maximum shock value" ("Dee and the Boys Lead Shock Rock Attack," 1986, p. 59).

Alice Cooper probably led the trend toward mayhem on stage. He himself has been "hanged," "guillotined," "electrocuted," and attacked by black widow spiders. He frequently splashes "blood" on fans in the first few rows. His shocking antics have included "biting" the head off of a live bird or bat. In his 1988 European tour, he was forbidden by German authorities from 1) dismembering or attacking baby dolls with a sword, 2) chopping off a female mannequin's legs with an ax, and 3) pretending to disembowel a pregnant woman and remove babies from within her (Alice Cooper: Banned in Germany, 1989)

One result of recent trends has been the formation of adult groups opposed to "rockporn." A number of wives of government officials have formed the Parents' Music Resource Center (PMRC). They, PTA groups, and others are trying to get the Recording Industry of America and the National Association of Broadcasters not to record or air controversial songs or videos and to establish a rating system similar to the one used for movies. Some recording companies have already given orders to identify albums and cassettes that possess a blatant, explicit lyric content. Some stations are shying away from airing controversial music.

One compelling argument for the controversy is that it is impossible to listen to rock music for days, months, and years without being affected by it. One adolescent girl writes:

> I have a 14-year-old brother who listens to AC/DC, Motley Crue, WASP and probably every other gross group there is. I have never heard such vulgar stuff in my life. His entire room is covered with posters. You walk in there and all you see is *tongues* sticking out, or *blood*—it is sickening. I think such things should be outlawed. (Darlene, 1986, p. 27)

Youth counters by saying that many times they do not pay attention to the lyrics; they only like the beat of the music. Nevertheless, evidence is accumulating that the trend toward more and more sex and violence is having an effect on some people. (See chapter 18 on moral development.)

HIGHLIGHT   Parents Say Singer's Lyrics Prompted Son's Suicide

The parents of a teen-ager who shot himself to death 14 months ago have filed suit against singer Ozzy Osbourne, contending their son was influenced by song lyrics about suicide.

John Daniel McCollum, 19, allegedly was listening to an Osbourne album titled "Speak to the Devil" when he shot himself Oct. 27, 1984, with his father's .22-caliber pistol. Two of the album's songs, "Suicide Solution" and "Paranoid," refer to suicide.

"It is my opinion those songs had a direct correlation in John's death," attorney Thomas Anderson said at a news conference Monday.

The lawsuit, filed in Superior Court last October on behalf of Jack McCollum and Geraldine Lugenbuehl of Indio, contends the young man followed the lyrics of "Suicide Solution," which say, "Where to hide, suicide is the way out. Don't you know what it's really about?"

A line from "Paranoid" says: "Can you help me? Oh, shoot out my brains, oh yeah."

Osbourne and CBS Records, which also is named in the suit, should have known that the lyrics would be heard by and would influence people "vulnerable to the ideas, suggestions and emotions" of rock music, the suit contends.

The suit seeks unspecified general and punitive damages.

Anderson said Osbourne and CBS were sued "to teach them a lesson. It is our hope that this case—as a result of applying California law—will make parents aware of what's in these records."

Osbourne, formerly with the group Black Sabbath, would not comment on the suit, said a spokesman at Jensen Communications who refused to give his name.

CBS Records Group would have no comment because the matter was in the courts, spokesman Robert Altshuler in New York said Monday.

Jack McCollum told reporters his son was drinking the night he died.

"But I don't believe he had a problem with alcohol," he said.

Portland (Maine) *Press Herald*, January 15, 1986, p. 15.

Language

The other aspect of the nonmaterial culture of adolescents that will be discussed is language. The special language of a particular group or social class is referred to by linguists as **argot**. Each group in society has its own argot, including professional groups like lawyers or doctors but also other groups: youth in general or deviant groups such as drug addicts or delinquents. Each of these groups develops a language of its own that is meaningful to its members (Tobias, 1980).

argot

The meanings of slang expressions change quite rapidly, and there are variations from one section of the country to the other, even from one school to another in the same city. It is, therefore, difficult to discuss word meanings. The following is intended only as a representative sample of slang expressions of youths in Portland, Maine (Hoose, 1987).

Barfo—gross, disgusting.

Coyote ugly—someone whose appearance you don't like, just like a dog.

Gnarly—really cool, weird, strange, funky, awesome.

Headbangers—heavy metal fans.

Mongo—really big, cool.

Posers—showoffs, people who pretend to be other than they are.

Radical or Rad—really good, awesome, different, cool, far out.

Skids—low-lifes, losers, bums.

Space shot—an airhead or bubblehead, goony.

Thrasher—a skateboarder, something that's funny, wild.

Beat—stupid, ridiculous, out of date, a drag.

Horedog—someone you like, a friend.

Power—to study.

Powerdrill—to study intensely.

Scooping—when a girl dates a lot of guys or when a girl goes out to pick someone up.

Yeewdogie—an admiring expression, often used by guys to compliment a girl's appearance.

Trendles or trendites—teenyboppers, those who dress faddishly.

Wastoids—druggies, delinquents, losers.

There are at least three major functions of adolescent argot:

Argot is a shorthand device designed to save elaborate explanation and time. To say *cool* is much simpler than to go into a lengthy explanation of one's reactions or feelings. The word makes a concept clear for the teenager by summing up complex and recurrent phenomena in one word.

Argot is coined to make possible a more precise reference to certain observations or experiences than the ordinary adult vocabulary would allow. To use the word *gut* for an easy course or *rap* for a discussion is to impart specific meaning to adolescent experience.

Adolescent argot also is used as a reinforcer and maintainer of group solidarity. Adolescents who speak the language of the group reflect a desire to be part of the group; they reflect the feelings, attitudes, and culture of the group; and they show they are in the group. Just as the background, breeding, and social status of Englishmen is associated with their language and the accent with which they speak, so adolescents' group identifications are judged and reflected by whether they speak a particular language. Their language reflects who and what they are and with what group they are identified.

SUMMARY

Adolescent society refers to the organized networks of associations among adolescents. Adolescent culture is the sum of the ways of living of adolescents. There are wide variations in adolescent societies and culture among various groups.

Some adults feel that adolescents have their own subculture and others that adolescent culture is a reflection of adult culture. Actually both are true: certain aspects of adolescent culture (such as sexual behavior and use of marijuana) are subcultural because they run counter to adult culture. In general, however, much of adolescent culture reflects adult values, depending on parent-versus-peer orientation.

Adolescent societies may be divided into formal (primarily in-school) and informal (out-of-school) groups. Most in-school groups are also age-grade, that is, identified with a particular age and grade in school. Active involvement in formal adolescent society is more prevalent among high socioeconomic status youths.

In-school subsystems may be divided into three groups: the formal, academic subsystem; the semiformal, activities subsystem; and the friendship subsystem. Of the three, membership in the friendship subsystem is the most important in the eyes of students.

Collegiate subcultures may be divided into four classifications: collegiate subculture, vocational subculture, academic subculture, and nonconformist subculture. College culture today has a vocational and materialistic emphasis, plus a social one.

To understand adolescent society, one must understand the material artifacts and the nonmaterial aspects that make up the lives of youths. Clothing is one of the most noticeable aspects of adolescent culture. It is an important means by which adolescents discover and express their identities; it expresses their dependence-independence conflict with adults; it may even express a life-style and political philosophy and ensures the adolescent's identity and sense of belonging with peer groups.

The automobile is another important material part of adolescent culture. It is a status symbol, a means of freedom and mobility, a symbol of power and independence, a hobby, a symbol of glamour and sexuality. Ready access to an automobile has a great influence on the adolescent's daily life, social activity, freedom, and work behavior.

Music is an important nonmaterial aspect of adolescent culture. Popular music takes many forms: pop, rhythm, blues, folk music, country western, jazz, and rock. The most common themes of ballads relate to love. Some songs deal with the problems of marriage and family living. Various songs reflect different outlooks on life: some positive, others cynical. Some of the songs relate to the problems of youth: premarital pregnancy and others. Other music deals with social problems: war or drugs.

Hard rock and heavy metal groups have come under fire for their explicit lyrics relating to sex, murder and suicide. These groups are also criticized for the bloody, shocking, deafening antics they create on stage. Numerous adult groups have been formed to discourage rockporn and bring some control over the situation. The argument is that such music has a harmful effect on youth, especially on disturbed youngsters who might be pushed over the edge to commit suicide or otherwise follow the suggestions of the rock music and musicians. Some youth counter by saying they are not affected by the lyrics but like the music because of its beat.

The special language of a particular group is called *argot*. Adolescents use their own argot to save elaborate explanation, to make precise referral to certain observations or experiences, and as a reinforcer and maintainer of group solidarity. To be part of a particular group means one has to speak their language.

DISCUSSION QUESTIONS

1. Is adolescent society subcultural?
2. The studies cited in this chapter present the life and values of high school youths with their emphasis on athletics, clubs, organizations, clothes, and cars as quite superficial. Are adolescents more serious minded than these studies indicate? Are they less superficial, more concerned with world problems, ecology, and academics?
3. Adolescents from low socioeconomic status families seem to be at a disadvantage. They are described as seldom seen in organizations, as nonjoiners, as nonparticipants in extracurricular activities. They are followers rather than leaders and usually are not among the most popular students in school. Is this true? What was the situation in your high school?
4. Is clothing as important to adolescents as this chapter claims?
5. Do you and your parents agree or disagree on important values?
6. Is there a generation gap? Is it fact or fiction?
7. Is college alienating youths from their parents and from the rest of society?
8. Do parents or peers exert the greatest influence on the lives of youths?
9. Do extracurricular activities contribute to adolescent development? Explain.
10. Is there much snobbishness and socioeconomic class discrimination in high school?
11. What factors determine popularity and prestige in high school?
12. What is your opinion of college fraternities and sororities?
13. What is your opinion of punk-rock clothing and hair styles?
14. Should high school students be allowed to own cars?
15. Do you feel that some rock music has a negative influence on adolescents' behavior? Explain.

BIBLIOGRAPHY

"Alice Cooper: Banned in Germany." (May, 1988). *Metal Maniacs*, 33, 22, 35.

Atkinson, R. (1988). "Respectful, Dutiful Teenagers." *Psychology Today*, 22, 22–26.

Bratta, V., and Tramp, M. (1987, 1989). *When The Children Cry*. Vavoom Music, Inc. (ASCAP).

Brown, B. B. (April, 1982). "The Extent and Effects of Peer Pressure among High School Students: A Retrospective Analysis." *Journal of Youth and Adolescence*, 11, 121–133.

Chapman, T. (1988). *Fast Car*. April Music/Purple Rabbit Music.

Climie, S., and Morgan, D. (1988). *My Heart Can't Tell You No*. Rare Blue Music Inc. (ASCAP)/Little Shop of Morgansons (BMI).

Cohen, J. (Fall, 1979). "High School Subcultures and the Adult World." *Adolescence*, 14, 491–502.

Coleman, J., et al. (1977). "Adolescents and Their Parents: A Study of Attitudes." *Journal of Genetic Psychology*, 130, 239–245.

Cosner, T. L., and Larson, G. L. (Spring, 1980). "Social Fabric Theory and the Youth Culture." *Adolescence*, 15, 99–104.

Cuccia, N. J. (Winter, 1981). "Sociopolitical Attitude Differences between School Activity Participants and Nonparticipants." *Adolescence*, 16, 871–879.

Darlene (1986). "Mail Boy." *Rock Scene*, no. 8.

"Dee and the Boys Lead Shock Rock Attack." (Spring, 1986). *Hit Parader*, 59.

Dienstfrey, H. (December, 1982). "Clothes Power." *Psychology Today*, 68ff.

Duncan, D. F. (Spring, 1978). "Measuring the Generation Gap: Attitudes toward Parents and Other Adults." *Adolescence*, 13, 77–81.

Eitzen, D. S. (1975). "Athletics in the Status System of Male Adolescents: A Replication of Coleman's *The Adolescent Society*." *Adolescence*, 10, 267–276.

Eitzen, D. S., and Brouillette, J. R. (Spring, 1979). "The Politicization of College Students." *Adolescence*, 14, 123–134.

Elliot, B. (1986). *Papa Don't Preach*. Elliot/Jackobson Music Pub. Co. (ASCAP)

Face, B. (1988). *Roni*. Hiptrip/Kear MUSIC.

Fasick, F. A. (Spring, 1984). "Parents, Peers, Youth Culture and Autonomy in Adolescence." *Adolescence*, 19, 143–147.

Fisher, T. D. (1988). "The Relationship between Parent-Child Communication about Sexuality and College Students' Sexual Behavior and Attitudes as a Function of Parental Proximity." *Journal of Sex Research*, 24, 305–311.

Fisher, T. D., and Hall, R. G. (1988). "A Scale for Comparison of the Sexual Attitudes of Adolescents and Their Parents." *The Journal of Sex Research*, 24, 90–100.

Gallagher, B. J. (Fall, 1979). "Attitude Differences across Three Generations: Class and Sex Components." *Adolescence*, 14, 503–516.

Gatlin, L. (1985). *Runaway Go Home*. Larry Gatlin Music.

Gibson, D. (1988). *Lost in Your Eyes*. Creative Block Music Ltd/Deborah Ann's Music (ASCAP).

Glynn, T. J. (October, 1981). "From Family to Peer: A Review of Transitions of Influence among Drug-Using Youth." *Journal of Youth and Adolescence*, 10, 363–383.

Gold, B. D. (1987). "Self-Image of Punk Rock and Non-punk Rock Juvenile Delinquents." *Adolescence*, 87, 535–544.

Grabe, M. (Spring, 1981). "School Size and the Importance of School Activities." *Adolescence*, 16, 21–31.

Gray, P. (1986). *Sugar Free*. MCA Music Australia PTY., Limited.

Hanks, M., and Eckland, B. K. (Summer, 1978). "Adult Voluntary Associations and Adolescent Socialization." *Sociological Quarterly*, 19, 481–490.

Hinton, K., and Margerum, B. J. (Summer, 1984). "Adolescent Attitudes and Values Concerning Used Clothing." *Adolescence*, 19, 397–402.

Horowitz, T. (Fall, 1982). "Excitement vs. Economy: Fashion and Youth Culture in Britain." *Adolescence*, 17, 627–636.

Hoose, S. (August 30, 1987). "Teen Lingo Puts Dweebs to the Test." Portland, ME.: *Maine Sunday Telegram*.

Huba, G. J., and Bentler, P. M. (October, 1980). "The Role of Peer and Adult Models for Drug Taking at Different Stages in Adolescence." *Journal of Youth and Adolescence*, 9, 449–465.

Jennings, M., and Niemi, R. (March, 1978). "Continuity and Change in Political Orientations: A Longitudinal Study of Two Generations." *Journal of Youth and Adolescence*, 7, 1–11.

Kennedy, P. (1988). *Give Me a Little Love*. Rondor Music (London) Ltd. (PRS).

Kness, D. (1983). "Clothing Deprivation Feelings of Three Adolescent Ethnic Groups." *Adolescence*, 18, 659–674.

Koester, A. W., and May, J. K. (1985). "Profiles of Adolescents' Clothing Practices: Purchase, Daily Selection, and Care." *Adolescence*, 20, 97–113.

Lee, C. C. (May, 1983). "An Investigation of the Athletic Career Expectations of High School Student Athletes." *The Personnel and Guidance Journal*, 61, 544–547.

Lennon, S. J. (1986). "Adolescent Attitudes Toward Designer Jeans: Further Evidence." *Adolescence*, 21, 475–482.

McFerrin, B. (1988). *Don't Worry, Be Happy*. Prob Noblem Music (BMI).

Montemayor, R., and VanKomen, R. (October, 1980). "Age Segregation of Adolescents In and Out of School." *Journal of Youth and Adolescence*, 9, 371–381.

Newman, B. M., and Newman, P. R. (1987). "The Impact of High School on Social Development." *Adolescence*, 22, 525–534.

Newman, P. R. (Fall, 1976). "Social Settings and Their Significance for Adolescent Development." *Adolescence*, 11, 405–418.

Niemi, R. G., et al. (Winter, 1978). "The Similarity of Political Values of Parents and College-Age Youths." *Public Opinion Quarterly*, 42, 503–520.

Niles, F. S. (Fall, 1979). "The Adolescent Girls' Perceptions of Parents and Peers." *Adolescence*, 14, 591–597.

Oshin, K. T. (1988). *Hold Me*. Wooden Wonder Music.

———. (1988). *Money*. Wooden Wonder Music.

"Parents Say Singer's Lyrics Prompted Son's Suicide." (January 15, 1986). *Portland (Maine) Press Herald*.

Phillips, D. P. (March, 1979). "Suicide, Motor Vehicle Fatalities, and the Mass Media: Evidence toward a Theory of Suggestion." *American Journal of Sociology*, 84, 1150–1174.

Sack, A. L., and Thiel, R. (January, 1979). "College Football and Social Mobility: A Case Study of Notre Dame Football Players." *Sociology of Education*, 52, 60–66.

Schuyler, T. (1987). *Child Support*. Screen Gems—EMI Music, Inc.

Sebald, H., and White, B. (Winter, 1980). "Teenagers' Divided Reference Groups: Uneven Alignment with Parents and Peers." *Adolescence*, 15, 979 -984.

Shah, F., and Zelnik, M. (May, 1981). "Parent and Peer Influence on Sexual Behavior, Contraceptive Use, and Pregnancy Experience of Young Women." *Journal of Marriage and the Family*, 43, 339–348.

Starr, M. (1988). *You Got It (The Right Stuff)*. SBK April Music Inc./Maurice Starr Music.

Thompson, D. N. (1985). "Parent-Peer Compliance in a Group of Preadolescent Youths." *Adolescence*, 20, 501–508.

Thorton, A., and Camburn, D. (1987). "The Influence of the Family on Premarital Sexual Attitudes and Behavior." *Demography*, 24, 323.

Tobias, J. J. (Spring, 1980). "A Glossary of Affluent Suburban Juvenile Slanguage." *Adolescence*, 15, 227–230.

U.S. Bureau of the Census. Department of Commerce. (1988). *Statistical Abstract of the United States, 1988*. Washington, D.C.: U.S. Government Printing Office.

Williams, E. G. (Spring, 1983). "Adolescent Loneliness." *Adolescence*, 18, 51–66.

Wonder, S. (1984). *Don't Drive Drunk*. Jobete Music Inc. and Black Bull Music, Inc.

Young, J. W., and Ferguson, L. R. (June, 1979). "Developmental Changes through Adolescence in the Spontaneous Nominations of Reference Groups as a Function of Decision Content." *Journal of Youth and Adolescence*, 8, 239–252.

CHAPTER
13

Social Development, Relationships, and Dating

The developmental tasks of adolescence that relate only to social development and relationships should include at least six important needs of youths:

1. The need to establish caring, meaningful, satisfying relationships with individuals.
2. The need to broaden childhood friendships by getting acquainted with new people of differing backgrounds, experiences, and ideas.
3. The need to find acceptance, belonging, recognition, and status in social groups.
4. The need to pass from the homosocial interests and playmates of middle childhood to heterosocial concerns and friendships.
5. The need to learn about, adopt, and practice dating patterns and skills that contribute to personal and social development, intelligent mate selection, and successful marriage.
6. The need to find an acceptable masculine or feminine sex role and to learn sex-appropriate behavior.

The content of this chapter has been selected primarily with these social needs of the adolescent in mind. Discussion of masculine-feminine sex roles and appropriate sexual values and behavior is reserved for chapters 14 and 15.

COMPANIONSHIP

Need for Friends

The need for close friends becomes crucial during adolescence (Yarcheski and Mahon, 1984). Up to this time, children's dependence on peers has been rather loosely structured. They have sought out playmates of their own ages with whom they share common interests or activities. They have engaged them in friendly competition and won or lost some measure of their respect and loyalty, but emotional involvement with them has not been intense. Children have not depended primarily on one another for emotional satisfaction. They have looked to their parents for fulfillment of their emotional needs and have sought their praise, love, and tenderness. Only if they have been unloved, rejected, and adversely criticized by parents will they have turned to friends or parent substitutes for emotional fulfillment. During adolescence, the picture changes. Sexual maturation brings new feelings, the need for emotional fulfillment and for emotional independence and emancipation from parents. Adolescents now turn to their peers to find the support formerly provided by their families (Sebald, 1986).

Adolescents' first needs are for relationships with others with whom they can share common interests. As they grow older, they desire a closer, caring relationship that involves sharing mature affection, problems, and their most personal thoughts. They need close friends who stand beside them and for them in an understanding, caring way. Friends share more than secrets or plans; they share feelings and help each other resolve personal problems and interpersonal conflicts (Werebe, 1987). As one boy said: "He is my best friend. We can tell each other things we can't tell anyone else; we understand each other's feelings. We can help each other when we are needed" (Selman and Selman, 1979, p. 72).

One of the reasons friendships are crucial is that adolescents are insecure and anxious about themselves (Goswick and Jones, 1982). They lack personality definition and secure identities. Consequently they gather friends around them from whom they gain strength and who help establish the boundaries for their selves. From them they learn the necessary personal and social skills and societal definitions that help them to become part of the larger adult world. They become emotionally bound to others who share their vulnerabilities and their deepest selves. They become comrades in a hostile world.

One of the greatest problems of adolescents is the problem of loneliness (Williams, 1983). One adolescent girl commented: "I'm really lonely. My mom and dad both work, so are not home a lot. My brother is six years older than I am, so we don't have too much in common. If it weren't for some friends, I wouldn't have anyone to talk to." Adolescents describe their loneliness as emptiness, isolation, and boredom (Moore and Schultz, 1983). Males seem to have a greater problem with loneliness than adolescent females, probably because it is more difficult for males to express their feelings (Avery, 1982).

For the most part, also, youth are lonelier than older people (Medora and Woodward, 1986). A survey by *Psychology Today* found that 79 percent of those under age 18 said they felt lonely "sometimes" or "often." Only 37 percent of those over age 55 said they felt this way (Parlee, 1979).

Part of loneliness is situational; it is socially conditioned because youth culture emphasizes that if you are alone on Friday night, you will be miserable, so adolescents end up feeling that way (Meer, 1985). Various research studies at the University of Nebraska have revealed that the loneliest group of students was low-income, single, adolescent mothers (Medora and Woodward, 1986).

Sometimes loneliness occurs even with others around because it is difficult to communicate or get close. One adolescent expressed this in a poem:

A void of nothingness
Is where I sit
I cannot come into your life
Nor can you into mine
And so we sit in a room
Empty of all but ourselves
And because we cannot or will not
Touch each other's minds
We cannot escape into ourselves
Or into each other.*

* Caren Williams, "Do Not Enter, Do Not Exit." *High Grade*, Student Publication, Humanities Department, Colorado School of Mines, Golden, Colorado, Spring 1980, p. 3, quoted in E. G. Williams, "Adolescent Loneliness." *Adolescence* 18 (Spring 1983): 51–66.

HIGHLIGHT   Factors Contributing to Adolescent Loneliness

Mijuskovic (1986) has summarized a number of factors that contribute to adolescent loneliness.

1. Sense of separation and alienation from parents.*
2. Broken families.
3. New cognitive abilities leading to an awareness of self.
4. Increasing sense of freedom that is frightening.
5. The search for self-identity.
6. The struggle for meaningful goals.
7. Marginal status of adolescents in society.
8. Fierce competitive individualism leading to feelings of failure and rejection.
9. Excessive expectation of popularity.
10. A low self-esteem and strong feelings of self-pity, pessimism regarding being liked and accepted by others.
11. Apathy and aimlessness, low educational and occupational aspirations leading to a cycle of failure and withdrawal.
12. Severe individual shyness and self-consciousness.

---

* Other research has revealed that a lack of positive parental involvement in the life of the child contributes to the loneliness of the offspring (Lobdell and Perlman, 1986).

Early Adolescent Friendships

The need for companionship causes young adolescents to pair off: to choose a best friend or chum or two, almost always of the same sex in the beginning. The adolescent will spend long hours conversing with this friend on the telephone, will attend school, club, and athletic events with him or her, and strive to dress alike, look alike, and act alike. Usually this best friend is from a similar socioeconomic, racial, and home background, from the same neighborhood, school, and school grade, of the same age, and with numerous interests, values, and friends in common. Best friends usually get along well if they are well selected because they are similar and thus compatible. Successful friendships, like successful marriages, are based on each person meeting the needs of the other. If best friends meet each other's needs, the bonds of friendship may be drawn tightly.

These early adolescent friendships are intense, emotional, and sometimes stormy if needs are not met (Yarcheski and Mahon, 1984). Adolescents may have made a bad choice. Instead of their best friends meeting their needs, they stimulate frustration and anger. The more intense and narcissistic are the emotions that drove adolescents to seek companionship, the more likely it is that sustained friendships will be tenuous, difficult, and tempestuous. Once thwarted, immature, rejected, unstable adolescents react with excessive emotion, which may disrupt their friendships temporarily or permanently.

Friendships during early adolescence are unstable. There is usually an increase in friendship fluctuations accompanying the onset of pubescence (at about age 13 for girls and age 14 for boys), followed by a decline in friendship fluctua-

The need of young adolescents for companionship causes them to choose a best friend, usually of the same sex. (Robert Harbison)

tions. After 18 years of age, friendship fluctuations increase because students leave home for college, jobs, the armed services, or marriage.

Broadening Early Friendships

When young adolescents leave the confines of their neighborhood elementary schools and transfer to district or consolidated junior high schools, they are immediately exposed to much broader and more heterogeneous friendships. They now have an opportunity to meet youths from other neighborhoods, social classes, and different ethnic and national origins. These youths may act, dress, speak, and think differently from those they have known before. *One social task at this stage of development is to broaden their acquaintances,* to learn how to relate to and get along with many different types of people. During this early period, adolescents want many friends (Monks and Ferguson, 1983). Usually there is an increase in the number of friends during early adolescence (until about age 15). After that, adolescents become more discriminating, and the number of reported friendships decreases (LaGaipa, 1979). Two studies of 1,300 seventh to twelfth graders in three Midwestern U.S. communities revealed that younger adolescents generally favored crowd membership, but the importance of crowd affiliation declined with age. Figure 13-1 shows the trend (Brown, Eicher, and Petrie, 1986).

GROUP ACCEPTANCE AND POPULARITY

As the number of acquaintances broadens, adolescents become increasingly aware of their need to belong to a group. They want to be liked by their peers; therefore, by midadolescence the goal toward which they strive is acceptance by members of a clique or crowd they strongly admire. At this stage they are sensitive to criticism or to others' negative reactions to them. They are concerned about what people think because

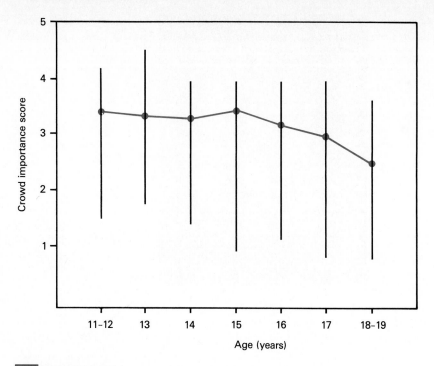

FIGURE 13-1

Age differences in the importance of crowd affiliation.

Adapted from: Brown, B. B., Eicher, S. A., and Petrie, S. (1986). "The Importance of Peer Group ("Crowd") Affiliation in Adolescence." *Journal of Adolescence*, 9: 73– 96. Used with permission.

their concepts of who they are and their degree of self-worth are partly a reflection of the opinions of others.

The following questions are typically asked by adolescents in the seventh, eighth, or ninth grades who are worried about their social positions.

How should a boy who is very shy go about overcoming the problem?

How can you get other kids to like you?

How can you become more sociable?

Why do you feel left out when you're around a group of friends that don't even know you're there?

What do you do when a person hates you?

Why are some kids so popular and others not? How can you get popular?

If you're a dud like me, how can you become graceful?

Conformity

Best friends are chosen partly on the basis of homogamy: the choice of someone like oneself (Finney, 1979). One researcher found that adolescents choose their friends so as to maximize the congruency (similarity) within the friendship pair (Kandel,

1978). If there is a state of imbalance such that the friend's attitude or behavior is incongruent, the adolescent will either break off the friendship and seek another friend or keep the friend and modify her or his own behavior.

Cliques and groups operate in the same way. Each group takes on a personality of its own: members are characterized according to dress and appearance, scholastic standing, extracurricular participation, social skills, socioeconomic status, reputation, and personality qualifications. (See chapter 12.) One way the individual has of being part of a particular group is to be like other members of the group. This may include using special slang, wearing a certain type of pin, hair ribbon, or different-colored socks on each foot. When a fad is in fashion, every person in the group adopts it. Those who are different are excluded. In one study of 200 high school students from two large suburban high schools, the students listed conformity (in activity, argot, attitude, dress, and interest) as one of the most important requirements for popularity (Sebald, 1981).

Of course, conformity can be a helpful, positive social influence or a negative one, depending on the group and its values. The adolescent boy who wants to belong to a juvenile gang of delinquents and has to pull off a robbery to do so is obviously conforming but to a peer code that may get him in trouble.

Conformity needs also depend on adolescents' family adjustments. Youths with a good family adjustment who are fond of their parents have less need to conform to peer demands, at least in some areas, so that when confronted with decisions, parental rather than peer opinions are accepted. The significant point is that total adjustment to parents influences the degree to which adolescents conform to parents versus peers.

Socioeconomic status also correlates with adolescent conformity. Higher-status adolescents conform more than ones from low socioeconomic status families. They more often like school, plan to continue their education, attend church, and make higher-level vocational choices. (See chapter 14.)

Adolescent females show a greater degree of conformity than do adolescent males. This means that members of girls' groups are more concerned with harmonious relations, social approval and acceptance, and living up to peer expectations than are members of boys' groups. In one study of peer pressure among high school students, this pressure was a more dominant and influential feature of life for girls than for boys. The pressures reported by females were much more intense than for males (Brown, 1982). However, for girls, the pressure was to be active in organizations and to maintain a "nice girl" image. For boys, the pressure was to be a "macho" athlete, to use drugs or alcohol, and to become sexually involved. The differences in expectations were part of the reason that males were found to be relatively insensitive to their sexual partners.

Achievement

Another way of finding group acceptance and approval is through achievement: in sports, club membership, recreational activities, or academic subjects. But the recognition and acceptance the individual achieves depends on the status accorded the activity by the peer group. Research indicates consistently that high school athletes are awarded higher social status (by several criteria of interpersonal popularity) than are scholars but that athlete-scholars are the most popular of all, suggesting some positive status given to both academic and athletic achievements. Because of the negative status awarded some activities, participation or achievement in these activities is a handicap to the adolescent seeking wider social acceptance.

Participation

Joining in-school clubs and participating in a variety of out-of-school social activities are other ways the adolescent has of finding social acceptance. The most popular students are the joiners, usually in multiple activities in schools but also as members of out-of-school, community-sponsored youth groups and as participants in every conceivable type of social and recreational activity among friends. The group life of adolescents has been characterized as herd life. The herd assembles at the local hangout for refreshments and small talk; the herd goes joyriding in the car, to a movie or a dance, or to hear a rock group. The herd may go on a hayride, skiing, or to the seashore. The herd may hang out at the local shopping mall (Anthony, 1985). To be part of the social scene, one has to join and be with the herd.

Efforts have been made to determine the criteria for popularity among adolescents. Older studies (Eitzen, 1975) indicated the importance of participating in athletics, of being in the leading crowd, and of being a leader in activities. Is there less emphasis now on sports and more on academics in the United States' high schools? Are adolescents today less concerned about being in the leading crowd? The overall answer is that the criteria for popularity have not changed. When boys were asked what are the most important criteria for popularity with other boys and with other girls, *the boys ranked being in athletics first, being in the leading crowd second, and being a leader in activities third, followed by having high grades, and coming from the right family last* (Bozzi, 1986). When girls were asked the same question, *girls placed being in the leading crowd first, being a leader in activities second, being a cheerleader third, having high grades fourth, and coming from the right family last* (Bozzi, 1986). Athletics was still selected as the most important criterion for popularity for boys and being in the leading crowd as the most important criterion for popularity for girls.

It is evident that participation in athletics is the most important criterion for social popularity of boys. However, the question arises regarding the contribution of athletics to the popularity and social status of girls. With athletics for women becoming more popular, does this increase their social status in relation to their friends?

Research by Williams and White (1983) indicated that female athletes received the lowest social status ratings. In another study, 222 high school students from a small Midwestern high school were surveyed to discover the importance of gender role in status determination (Kane, 1988). Males were asked which female athlete they would most like to date. Figure 13-2 shows that males would most like to date those female athletes whom they felt engaged in sports appropriate for their sex. Tennis was the overwhelming first choice as the most sex-appropriate sport for females. Basketball was the highest sex-inappropriate sport chosen.

These results indicate that *males preferred females who evidenced traditional notions of feminine behavior, who engaged in "lady-like" sports activities.* Interestingly, females showed the same preferences in choosing other girls as best friends.

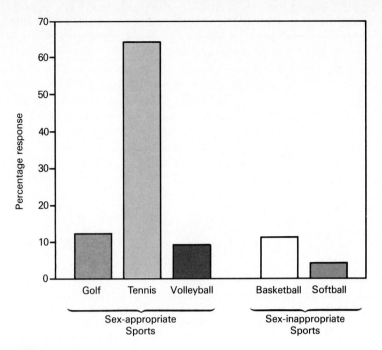

FIGURE 13-2

Percentage of male subjects who chose to date female athletes by sex-appropriate/sex-inappropriate sport typology.

From: Kane, M. J. (1988). "The Female Athletic Role as a Status Determinant within the Social System of High School Adolescents." *Adolescence*, 23: 253–264.

Personality and Social Skills

Personal qualities and social skills are important criteria for popularity and have been found to be very important in gaining social acceptance (Meyers and Nelson, 1986). *Considerable evidence shows that personal qualities are the most important factors in popularity.* A study of 204 adolescents in the seventh, ninth, and twelfth grade revealed that interpersonal factors were more important in friendship bonds than either achievement or physical characteristics. This was true of adolescents at all grade levels (Tedesco and Gaier, 1988). *Interpersonal factors* included character traits, personality, intimacy, and social conduct. *Achievement factors* included academic qualities and athletic prowess. *Physical characteristics* included physical appearance and material things such as money or autos. The older they became, the more adolescents emphasized interpersonal factors and de-emphasized achievement and physical characteristics in friendship bonds. Other research also emphasizes the importance of personal qualities as a criterion of popularity.

Thus, *one of the principal ways adolescents find group acceptance is by developing and exhibiting personal qualities that others admire and by learning social skills that ensure accept-*

ance. Table 13-1 gives a summary of personality traits youths like or dislike in one another. The summary is a composite of a number of studies (Hansen and Hicks, 1980; Kemper and Bologh, 1980; Sebald, 1981).

In general, popular youths are accepted because of their personal appearance, sociability, and character. They are neat, well-groomed, good-looking youths who are friendly, happy, fun loving, outgoing, and energetic, have developed a high degree of social skills (Adams, 1983), and like to participate in many activities with others. They may be sexually experienced but are not promiscuous (Newcomer, Udry, and Cameron, 1983). They have a good reputation and exhibit qualities of moral character that people admire. They are usually those with high self-esteem and positive self-concepts.

Shyness

In a survey among tenth-grade boys and girls in a secondary school in Victoria, British Columbia, about one-half of the students rated themselves as "moderately shy" or "quite shy" (Ishiyama, 1984). Shyness usually increases during early adolescence because of increased self-awareness, the development of heterosexual interests, and the desire to be part of a social group (Hauck, Martens, and Wetzel, 1986). Shyness in social situations has been referred to as ***social-evaluative anxiety*** (Warren et al., 1984). The person is anxious about being the center of attention, making mistakes in front of others, behaving, being expected to say something, or being compared with others. Shyness stems from a fear of negative evaluation of self by others, a desire for social approval, low self-esteem, and a fear of rejection (Connolly, et al., 1987). It may have its origins in childhood, in such problems as being teased, criticized, ridiculed, and compared with siblings. It may arise out of self-consciousness about appearance, weight, height, or some deficit. Gilmartin (1985) found that shy men often grew up in disharmonious, verbally abusive families. They tended to be social isolates, growing up as only children without support from kin.

social-evaluative anxiety

In extreme form, the shy adolescent may manifest physiological reactions to shyness: blushing, butterflies in one's stomach, fast pulse, bodily shaking, heart palpitation, and nervous sweating. Shy persons may become fidgety or nervous, avoid eye contact, stammer or stutter, or speak inaudibly. They may feel that their problems are unique. They may have overlooked the possibility that others are equally shy but do not appear so. As a consequence, they attribute the cause of shyness to their own personalities; they lower their own self-confidence and avoid social situations, which reinforces their negative experience and expectations. They may experience considerable suffering over many years. Therapeutic intervention may help them to break this cycle and restore their self-confidence (Ishiyama, 1984).

Deviance

Until now, little has been said about achieving group acceptance through deviant behavior; that is, behavior different from that of the majority of youths (largely middle class) but considered acceptable in a particular group that itself deviates from the norms. Whereas overtly aggressive, hostile behavior may be unaccepta-

TABLE 13-1

Personality traits liked or disliked.

LIKED	DISLIKED
Personal Appearance	*Personal Appearance*
Good-looking	Homely, unattractive
Feminine, nice figure (girls)	Boyish figure, or too fat or skinny (girls)
Masculine, good build (boys)	Sissy, skinny, fat (boys)
Neat, clean, well groomed	Sloppy, dirty, unkempt
Appropriate clothes	Clothes out of style, don't fit, not appropriate, dirty
	Greaser (boys)
	Physical handicap
Social Behavior	*Social Behavior*
Outgoing, friendly, gets along with others	Shy, timid, withdrawn, quiet
Active, energetic	Lethargic, listless, passive
Participant in activities	Nonjoiner, recluse
Social skills: good manners, conversationalist, courteous, poised, natural, tactful, can dance, play many games, sports	Loud, boisterous, ill-mannered, disrespectful, braggart, show-off, not "cool," giggles, rude, crude, tongue-tied, doesn't know how to do or play anything
Lots of fun, good sport	Real drip, poor sport
Acts age, mature	Childish, immature
Good reputation	Bad reputation
Being cool	
Conforming	
Personal Qualities of Character	*Personal Qualities of Character*
Kind, sympathetic, understanding	Cruel, hostile, disinterested
Cooperative, gets along well, even tempered, stable	Quarrelsome, bully, bad-tempered, domineering, sorehead
Unselfish, generous, helpful, considerate	Inconsiderate, selfish, stingy
Cheerful, optimistic, happy, pleasant	Pessimistic, complaining person
Responsible, dependable	Irresponsible, not reliable
Honest, truthful, fair, straightforward	Liar, cheat, unfair
Good sense of humor	Can't take a joke, no sense of humor
High ideals	Dirty minded
Self-confident, self-accepting but modest	Conceited, vain
Good sense, intelligent	

ble in society as a whole, it may be required in a ghetto gang as a condition of membership. Or what might be considered a bad reputation in the local high school (fighter, troublemaker, uncooperative, antisocial, sexually promiscuous, delinquent) might be a good reputation among a group of delinquents. One study of 12- to 16-year-old boys who were overaggressive and bullies toward younger, weaker youths showed that the bullies enjoyed average popularity among other boys (Olweus, 1977); those who were the targets of aggression were far less popular than the bullies. These findings illustrate that standards of group behavior vary with different groups so that popularity depends not so much on a fixed standard as on group conformity.

Two writers have suggested that sometimes peer groups are formed because of hostility to family authority and a desire to rebel against it. When this happens, the peer groups may become delinquent gangs, hostile to all established authority yet supportive of the particular deviancy accepted by the group (Bensman and Liliesfield, 1979).

HETEROSOCIALITY

Psychosocial Development

One of the most important social goals of midadolescence is to achieve heterosociality. In the process of psychosocial development, children pass through three stages.

autosociality **Autosociality**—the early preschool period of development in which the child's chief pleasure and satisfaction is himself or herself. This is most typical of the 2-year-old who wants to be in the company of others but who plays alongside them, not with them. The adolescent who is still a loner, who does not have any friends, is still in this preschool period of development.

homosociality **Homosociality**—the primary school period of development in which the child's chief pleasure and satisfaction are in being with others of the same sex (not for sexual purposes but for friendship and companionship). Every normal child passes through this important stage of forming same-sex friendships. But adolescents who never get to know or feel comfortable with the opposite sex remain at this stage of psychosocial development.

heterosociality **Heterosociality**—the adolescent and adult stage of development in which the individual's pleasure and friendships are found with those of both sexes.

Getting acquainted and feeling at ease with the opposite sex is a painful process for some youths. Here are some typical questions that worry the adolescent becoming attracted to new relationships:

> How do you go about talking to a girl?
> What can you do if you're chicken to ask a girl on a date?
> How can you attract the opposite sex?
> Does a girl wait for a boy to actually say he likes her? . . . [my] trouble is that I feel I don't hit it off exactly right with them, I'm more a friend than a boy.
> Why are we so self-conscious when we meet new boys?

Should you worry if you don't have dates right away?

How can you get a boy to notice you and like you?

Why is it that boys shy away from being introduced?

With sexual maturity comes a biological-emotional awareness of the opposite sex, a decline in hostile attitudes, and the beginning of emotional responses. The girl who was looked upon before as a sissy, giggly, pain-in-the-neck kid now takes on a new allure. On the one hand, the now-maturing male is fascinated and mystified by this young woman; on the other hand, he is awed, terrified, and bewildered. No wonder he ends up asking: "How do you go about talking to a girl?"

The boy's first effort is to tease by engaging in some sort of physical contact: swipe her books, pull her hair, hit her with a snowball. Her response is often a culturally conditioned, predictable one: scream, run (either away or after him), and pretend to be upset. The boy is not very good at talking to girls, but he knows how to roughhouse, so he uses this time-honored method of making his first emotionally charged heterosocial contacts.

Gradually these initial contacts take on a more sophisticated form. Teasing is now kid stuff. To be "cool"—confident, poised, unemotional, a good conversationalist, comfortable and mannerly in social situations—is the order of the day. The group boy-girl relationships change into paired relationships, and these deepen into affectionate friendships and romance as the two sexes discover each other. Table 13-2 lists the usual stages of psychosocial development (Selman and Selman, 1979).

Overall the average age for choosing opposite-sex companionship has been declining, probably because of earlier sexual maturity and changing social customs. A boyfriend-girlfriend relationship at early ages may not be reciprocal, and the object of affection may not be aware of the love affair. (The author once knew a preadolescent boy who sold his girlfriend to another boy for 100 baseball cards, but the girl was never aware of the fact that she had been a girlfriend in the first

TABLE 13-2

Ages and stages in psychosocial development.

AGE	STAGES
Infancy	Autosocial: Boy and girl interested only in themselves.
About ages 2–7	Seek companionship of other children regardless of sex.
About ages 8–12	Homosocial: Children prefer to play with others of the same sex; some antagonism between sexes.
Ages 13–14	Girls and boys become interested in one another (heterosocial) with girls' interests developing first.
Ages 15–16	Some boys and girls pair off.
Ages 17–18	Majority of adolescents are dating; some, particularly girls, marry.

place.) With advancing age, however, expected and actual reciprocity begin to converge.

Adolescent Love and Crushes

Along with the development of real or imagined reciprocal relationships comes the experience of "being in love." One survey indicated that love-prone people fell in love for the first time at the average age of 14 (Rubenstein, 1983). Falling in love serves as a positive need in the lives of most people. If the love is reciprocated it is associated with fulfillment and ecstasy (Hatfield and Sprecher, 1986). College dating couples who report they are in love are also the ones who report the greatest happiness. Young adolescents may have an intense crush on someone they really do not know and fantasize romantic encounters with this person. The fewer actual romantic contacts, the more likely they are to develop an intense emotional crush and to fantasize the involvement. Often a crush is on an older person. It may even be a crush on an older person of the same sex. Therefore, imagining oneself in love with someone of the opposite sex serves a useful purpose: it motivates adolescents to seek heterosocial companionship. Finally, the desire for cross-sex companionship motivates them to the next big step: going out on a date.

Intense love can also be risky business. Success sparks delight and failure invites despair. Unrequited love is associated with emptiness and anxiety. Loss of love can be a devastating experience for the adolescent (Hatfield and Sprecher, 1986).

DATING

Sociologists have been careful to emphasize that dating in American culture is not always equivalent to courtship, at least in the early and middle years of

HIGHLIGHT   Questions Junior High Adolescents Ask about Social Development and Relationships

The following questions illustrate some of the concerns of junior high adolescents (grades seven, eight, nine) about social development and relationships:

How can I get over being shy in groups?
Do you have to follow everybody else to be popular?
How can you get others to like you?
What do boys look for in a girl?

At what age can you begin dating?
Should seventh-graders be allowed to go to school dances?
What do you do if you're scared to ask a girl to go on a date?
Why shouldn't a girl call a boy if she wants to?

From written questions submitted to the author by adolescents in family life education classes.

adolescence. If dating is not courtship, what are the primary purposes of dating in the eyes of adolescents (McCabe, 1984; Roscoe, Diana, and Brooks, 1987)?

Purposes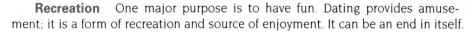

Recreation   One major purpose is to have fun. Dating provides amusement; it is a form of recreation and source of enjoyment. It can be an end in itself.

Companionship without the Responsibility of Marriage   Wanting to be with the opposite sex is a strong motive for dating. Wanting the friendship, acceptance, affection, and love of the opposite sex is a normal part of growing up.

Status Grading, Sorting, and Achievement   Youths of higher socioeconomic levels date more frequently than do lower-class youths, and they use dating partly to achieve, prove, or maintain status. Membership in certain cliques is associated with the status-seeking aspects of dating. However, the most recent research emphasizes a significant decline in dating as a means of gaining or proving status (Gordon, 1981). There are still significant prestige dimensions to cross-sex socializing, but this is not a major motive for dating.

Socialization   Dating is a means of personal and social growth. It is a way of learning to know, understand, and get along with many different types of people. Through dating, youths learn cooperation, consideration, responsibility, numerous social skills and matters of etiquette, and techniques for interacting with other people.

Sexual Experimentation or Satisfaction   Studies have shown that dating has become more sex oriented as more adolescents have sexual intercourse. Whether dating is used to have sex or sex develops out of dating depends on the attitudes, feelings, motives, and values of the boy and girl. Most research, however, indicates that men want sexual intimacy in a relationship sooner than women, with the discrepancy a source of potential conflict (Knox and Wilson, 1981; McCabe and Collins, 1979).

Mate Sorting and Selection   Whether this is a conscious motive or not, it is eventually what happens, especially among older youths with prior dating experience. The longer a couple dates, the less they tend to overidealize each other and the greater are their chances of knowing each other. Also, dating provides an opportunity for two people to become a pair. If the boy and girl are similar in personality characteristics, they are more likely to develop a compatible relationship than if they are dissimilar in physical attractiveness and psychological and social characteristics (Till and Freedman, 1978). Whether dating results in the selection of the most compatible pairs will depend on the total experience. Not all dating patterns result in wise mate selection, especially if dating partners are chosen on the basis of superficial traits (Cote and Koval, 1983). Also, some dating partners develop selfish, competitive, inconsistent, or other undesirable habits during dating that are not at all good preparation for kind and cooperative marriage relationships (Laner, 1986). In this case, dating is negative preparation for marriage.

Achieving Intimacy   One survey of undergraduates at the University of Arizona found that one-third (37 percent of the men, 25 percent of the women) were "somewhat anxious" or "very anxious" about dating (Timnick, 1982). A similar survey at the University of Indiana found that one-half the subjects (54 percent of the men and 42 percent of the women) rated dating situations as difficult (Timnick, 1982). The development of intimacy is the primary psychosocial task of the young adult. By *intimacy* is meant the development of openness, sharing, mutual trust, respect, affection, and loyalty, so that a relationship with the opposite sex can be characterized as close, enduring, and involving love and commitment (Roscoe, Kennedy, and Pope, 1987).

The capacity to develop intimacy varies from person to person. Research emphasizes that males form the closest friendships with females, since they feel less anxiety with women and less competition with them than with males (Peretti, 1980). Usually, females find it easier than males to talk intimately (Fischer, 1981; Nitzberg, 1980). One study of college students showed significant differences in the level of intimate disclosure. The level of freshman males to males was low; of freshman males to females and senior males to males, moderate; and of senior males to females and females of either age to friends of either sex, high (Klos and Loomis, 1978). Another study of college dating couples showed that women were more likely to be high disclosures than men (Rubin et al., 1980). Also, those with egalitarian sex-role attitudes and who were strongly in love disclosed more than those with traditional sex-role attitudes or who were not as much in love.

Some adolescents establish only superficial relationships with friends. Others remain isolated, withdrawn, and self-preoccupied, never developing close peer relationships. Others are self-aware, sensitive individuals who communicate openly and deeply with friends. They are sensitive to the innermost thoughts and feelings of their partner and are willing through self-disclosure to share personal information, private thoughts, and feelings. Therefore, heterosocial relationships vary greatly in the depth of communication and intensity of feelings in the relationship. Dating can provide the opportunity for close relationships, but whether real intimacy develops varies with individuals and with different pairs. It also depends on the degree of closeness in the families in which adolescents grow up. Adolescents who grow up in close families are more likely to be able to develop close, reciprocal relationships with friends (Bell, Cornwell, and Bell, 1988). However, dating can remain quite superficial. Under such conditions, it is not as helpful a means of mate selection or marriage preparation as it otherwise might be.

One helpful description of intimacy development was made by Orlofsky, who studied the intimacy statuses of junior and senior males at the State University of New York at Buffalo. Orlofsky divided the men into five groups (Orlofsky and Ginsburg, 1981):

Isolates withdraw from social situations and lack personal relationships with peers except for a few casual acquaintances. They participate in few extracurricular activities, are not very popular, and do not begin to date until two or more years later than students in other statuses. They rationalize by saying they prefer work and studies, which does not give them much time for interpersonal involvement.

Pseudointimates enter into somewhat premature, security-motivated heterosexual love relationships that lack closeness and depth and are without much shared feeling.

Stereotyped relationships are relationships with either male or female friends that are characterized by superficiality and by a low degree of personal communication and closeness. Relationships with girls are either formal and stiff or are characterized by sexual conquest. In neither case is the girl treated as a whole person. Like isolates, they begin dating late, but they maintain and enjoy relationships.

Preintimates have not entered into an enduring love relationship, are ambivalent about commitment, and try to develop "pure" love relationships devoid of ties and obligations. Given time and maturity, they may form intimate relationships.

Intimates form deep relationships with male and female friends and are involved in an enduring, committed love relationship with a girlfriend or wife.

Age Patterns for Dating

The median age at which youths begin dating has decreased by almost three years since World War I, primarily because of peer pressure to date earlier (Hennessee, 1983). Parents also exercise less control at earlier ages than they used to (Felson and Gottfredson, 1984). In 1924 the median age for girls beginning to date was 16 years. Today it is about 13 years. There is also some evidence that adolescents from nonintact families begin dating earlier than those from intact, happy families. Dating apparently meets emotional and social needs not fulfilled in their relationships with parents (Coleman, Ganong, Ellis, 1985).

Common Problems

A study of 227 women and 107 men in a random sample of students at East Carolina University sought to identify dating problems (Knox and Wilson, 1983). Table 13-3 shows the problems experienced by the women. *The most frequent problems expressed by the women were unwanted pressure to engage in sexual behavior, where to go and what to do on dates, communication, sexual misunderstandings, and money.* An example of sexual misunderstandings was leading a man on when the woman did not really want to have intercourse. Some of the women complained that the men wanted to move toward a sexual relationship too quickly.

The problems most frequently mentioned by the men (see table 13-4) *were communication, where to go and what to do on dates, shyness, money, and honesty/openness.* By honesty/

TABLE 13-3

Dating problems experienced by 227 university women.

PROBLEM	PERCENTAGE
Unwanted pressure to engage in sexual behavior	23
Places to go	22
Communication with date	20
Sexual misunderstandings	13
Money	9

Adapted from: Knox, D., and Wilson, K. (1983). "Dating Problems of University Students." *College Student Journal*, 17: 225–228.

TABLE 13-4

Dating problems experienced by 107 university men.

PROBLEM	PERCENTAGE
Communication with date	35
Place to date	23
Shyness	20
Money	17
Honesty/openness	8

Adapted from: Knox, D., and Wilson, K. (1983). "Dating Problems of University Students." *College Student Journal*, 17: 225–228.

openness the men meant how much to tell about themselves and how soon, and getting their partner to open up (Knox and Wilson, 1983).

The problem of communication was mentioned by both men and women. Some students become anxious and nervous when the conversation starts to drag. One senior commented: "After awhile you run out of small talk about weather and your classes. When the dialogue dies, it's awful."

Both college men and women look for honesty and openness in a relationship. Part of the problem is caused by the fact that both the man and woman strive to be on their best behavior. This involves a certain amount of pretense or *imaging*   play acting, called **imaging,** to present oneself in the best possible manner.

Going Steady

For many adults, particularly parents, going steady is equivalent to committing an unforgivable sin. As a result, steady dating probably receives more attention than any other aspect of dating, except perhaps sex and dating behavior. How widespread is going steady? Is it harmful or useful? Why do youths do it, often in spite of contrary pressures from their parents and leaders?

HIGHLIGHT   Questions Senior High Adolescents Ask about Dating

The following questions about dating have been asked by senior high school adolescents (grades ten, eleven, twelve):

Is it all right to date several boys at once?
How can you tell if you're really in love?
How should a girl refuse a date?
Will boys take you out if you're not willing to go all the way?
How can you break up without hurting the other person?

What do you do if your parents don't want you to go with your boyfriend because he's three years older (I'm fifteen; he's eighteen)?
What kind of boys do girls like best?

From written questions submitted to the author by adolescents in family life education classes.

Because one of the worries of parents is that youths will make premature commitments, they urge their offspring to date a large number of partners. Research indicates, however, that those who date the greatest number of partners also have the greatest number of different steady relationships; the larger is the number of casual partners, the greater are the chances of going steady with them. Because marital success is positively correlated with the number of friends of both sexes one has before marriage, youths ought to go with large numbers of partners though their chances of going steady with any one are greater. Steady dating for a long period can limit the number of dating partners, and a community that accepts steady dating as the norm for the group makes it harder for youths to avoid the pattern. In some cases they either have to go steady or not date.

Going steady has advantages and disadvantages. It is not often marriage oriented. The primary motive seems to be to enjoy the company of someone else. Steady dating also provides security for some adolescents. Apparently, they go steady because they need to, emotionally and socially. They try to find someone to love and be loved by, who understands and sympathizes. Steady dating meets a real need. Those who go steady are also those who have the highest self-esteem (Samet and Kelly, 1987).

The disadvantages are many. Some youths feel "it's a drag," that they have more fun with different people. One girl said, "Instead of going steady, I wound up staying home steady. Ted didn't take me out." Some youths are not mature enough emotionally to handle such an intimate relationship and the problems that arise. And breaking up leads to hurt feelings. One boy asked: "How can I ditch Kathy without hurting her feelings?" This is a frequent remark from youths who are involved but who do not know how to get uninvolved. The problem of jealousy often arises. Boys tend to be jealous over sexual issues; girls complain of lack of time and attention. The basic problem may be that neither person is ready for an intense, intimate relationship with one person over a long period of time. Most youths admit that steady dating becomes a license for increasing sexual intimacy. "You get to feeling married, and that's dangerous" is the way one adolescent expressed it. Others feel that going steady adds respectability to petting or even to intercourse and that this is an advantage rather than a disadvantage. Research indicates that those within a particular socioeconomic class who date the most frequently and who begin at the earliest ages are more likely to get married early as well; therefore, whenever steady dating pushes youths prematurely into early marriage, it is a serious disadvantage. (See chapter 17.)

SUMMARY

In their efforts to become mature adults, adolescents seek to break their dependency ties with parents and replace them with close, emotional attachments with friends with whom they can share common interests, find their identities, and overcome loneliness.

Initially, young adolescents pair off and choose a best friend or chum or two, usually of the same sex. These early friendships may be intense, emotional, and unstable if adolescents have made a poor choice of friends. Gradually friendships broaden to include youths from other neighborhoods and groups.

Adolescents also want group acceptance and popularity. They find this through several means: by conforming to group standards, through achievement, by participation in activities, and by developing desirable personality qualities and social skills.

Some adolescents have trouble because they are shy. Others seek to belong to deviant groups and are excluded from more conservative groups.

A major step is to achieve heterosociality, to broaden friendships to include both sexes. Boy-girl relationships slowly evolve. Young adolescents may develop intense love affairs or crushes; sometimes the relationships are only fantasized with someone they scarcely know, but the desire for cross-sex companionship motivates them to want to date.

Dating is not equivalent to courtship. It does, however, fulfill some important functions: as a means of recreation (to have fun), to fulfill the need for companionship and intimacy; as a means of status grading, sorting, and achievement; as a means of personal and social growth; as an opportunity for sexual experimentation, satisfaction, or exploitation; and as a means of mate sorting and selection. The median age at which dating begins has decreased by almost three years since World War I.

The most common dating problems include unwanted sexual pressure, sexual misunderstandings, communication, honesty and openness, places to go, and money.

Going steady has advantages and disadvantages. It provides companionship, someone to love and be loved by, and security for some adolescents. It may, however, become boring instead of fun. Some youths are not mature enough emotionally for an intimate relationship. Problems of hurt feelings, jealousy, and sexual involvement develop. If steady dating pushes youths into early marriage, it is a distinct disadvantage.

DISCUSSION QUESTIONS

Discuss the questions that junior high and senior high adolescents ask (they are found in the Highlight sections in the chapter).

BIBLIOGRAPHY

Adams, G. R. (June, 1983). "Social Competence during Adolescence: Social Sensitivity, Locus of Control, Empathy, and Peer Popularity." *Journal of Youth and Adolescence*, 12, 203–211.

Anthony, K. H. (1985). "The Shopping Mall: A Teenage Hangout." *Adolescence*, 20, 307–312.

Avery, A. W. (December, 1982). "Escaping Loneliness in Adolescence: The Case for Androgyny." *Journal of Youth and Adolescence*, 11, 451–459.

Bell, L. G., Cornwell, C. S., and Bell, D. C. (1988). "Peer Relationships of Adolescent Daughters: A Reflection of Family Relationship Patterns." *Family Relations*, 37, 171–174.

Bensman, J., and Liliesfield, R. (October, 1979). "Friendship and Alienation." *Psychology Today*, 56ff.

Bozzi, V. (1986). "Gotta Ring, Gotta Car?" *Psychology Today*, 20, 3.

Brown, B. B. (April, 1982). "The Extent and Effects of Peer Pressure among High School Students: A Retrospective Analysis." *Journal of Youth and Adolescence*, 11, 121–133.

Brown, B. B., Eicher, S. A., and Petrie, S. (1986). "The Importance of Peer Group ("Crowd") Affiliation in Adolescence." *Journal of Adolescence*, 9, 73–96.

Chambliss, J., et al. (January, 1978). "Relationships between Self-Concept, Self-Esteem, Popularity, and Social Judgments of Junior High School Students." *Journal of Psychology*, 98, 91–98.

Coleman, M., Ganong, L. H., and Ellis, P. (1985). "Family Structure and Dating Behavior of Adolescents." *Adolescence*, 20, 537–543.

Connolly, J., White, D., Stevens, R., and Burstein, S. (1987). "Adolescents' Self-Reports of Social Activity: Assessment of Stability and Relations to Social Adjustment." *Journal of Adolescence*, 10, 83–95.

Cote, R. M., and Koval, J. E. (Fall, 1983). "Heterosexual Relationship Development: Is It Really a Sequential Process?" *Adolescence*, 18, 507–514.

Eitzen, D. S. (1975). "Athletics in the Status System of Male Adolescents: A Replication of Coleman's *The Adolescent Society*." *Adolescence*, 10, 267–276.

Felson, M., and Gottfredson, M. (August, 1984). "Social Indicators of Adolescent Activities near Peers and Parents." *Journal of Marriage and the Family*, 46, 709–714.

Finney, J. W. (September, 1979). "Friends' Interests: A Cluster-Analytic Study of College Student Peer Environments, Personality, and Behavior." *Journal of Youth and Adolescence*, 8, 299–315.

Fischer, J. L. (February, 1981). "Transitions in Relationship Style from Adolescence to Young Adulthood." *Journal of Youth and Adolescence*, 10, 11–23.

Gilmartin, B. G. (1985). "Some Family Antecedents of Severe Shyness." *Family Relations*, 34, 429–438.

Gordon, M. (February, 1981). "Was Waller Ever Right? The Rating and Dating Complex Reconsidered." *Journal of Marriage and the Family*, 43, 67–76.

Goswick, R. A., and Jones, W. H. (October, 1982). "Components of Loneliness during Adolescence." *Journal of Youth and Adolescence*, 11, 373–383.

Hansen, S. L., and Hicks, M. W. (Spring, 1980). "Sex Role Attitudes and Perceived Dating-Mating Choices of Youth." *Adolescence*, 15, 83–90.

Hatfield, E., and Sprecher, S. (1986). "Measuring Passionate Love in Intimate Relationships." *Journal of Adolescence*, 9, 383–410.

Hauck, W. E., Martens, M., and Wetzel, M. (1986). "Shyness, Group Dependence and Self-Concept: Attributes of the Imaginary Audience." *Adolescence*, 21, 529–534.

Hennessee, J. A. (May, 1983). "'Monkey See, Monkey Do' Dating." *Psychology Today*, 17, 74.

Ishiyama, F. I. (Winter, 1984). "Shyness: Anxious Social Sensitivity and Self-Isolating Tendency." *Adolescence*, 19, 903–911.

Kandel, D. B. (September, 1978). "Homophily, Selection, and Socialization in Adolescent Friendships." *American Journal of Sociology*, 84, 427–436.

Kane, M. J. (1988). "The Female Athletic Role as a Status Determinant within the Social System of High School Adolescents." *Adolescence*, 23, 253–264.

Kemper, T. D., and Bologh, R. W. (February, 1980). "The Ideal Love Object: Structural and Family Sources." *Journal of Youth and Adolescence*, 9, 33–48.

Klos, D. S., and Loomis, D. F. (June, 1978). "A Rating Scale of Intimate Disclosure between Late Adolescents and Their Friends." *Psychological Reports*, 42, 815–820.

Knox, D., and Wilson, K. (April, 1981). "Dating Behaviors of University Students." *Family Relations*, 30, 255–258.

———. (1983). "Dating Problems of University Students." *College Student Journal*, 17, 225–228.

LaGaipa, J. J. (1979). "A Developmental Study of the Meaning of Friendship in Adolescence." *Journal of Adolescence*, 2, 201–213.

Laner, M. R. (1986). "Competition in Courtship." *Family Relations*, 35, 275–279.

Lobdell, J., and Perlman, D. (1986). "The Intergenerational Transmission of Loneliness: A Study of College Females and Their Parents." *Journal of Marriage and the Family*, 48, 589–595.

McCabe, M. P. (Spring, 1984). "Toward a Theory of Adolescent Dating." *Adolescence*, 19, 159–170.

McCabe, M. P., and Collins, J. K. (December, 1979). "Sex Role and Dating Orientation." *Journal of Youth and Adolescence*, 8, 407–425.

Medora, N., and Woodward, J. C. (1986). "Loneliness among Adolescent College Students at a Midwestern University." *Adolescence*, 21, 391–402.

Meer, J. (July, 1985). "Loneliness." *Psychology Today*, 19, 28–33.

Meyers, J. E., and Nelson, W. M. III. (1986). "Cognitive Strategies and Expectations as Components of Social Competence in Young Adolescents." *Adolescence*, 21, 291–303.

Mijuskovic, B. (1986). "Loneliness: Counseling Adolescents." *Adolescence*, 21, 941–950.

Monks, F. J., and Ferguson, T. J. (February, 1983). "Gifted Adolescents: An Analysis of Their Psychosocial Development." *Journal of Youth and Adolescence*, 12, 1–18.

Moore, D., and Schultz, N. R. (April, 1983). "Loneliness at Adolescence: Correlates, Attributions, and Coping." *Journal of Youth and Adolescence*, 12, 95–100.

Newcomer, S. F., Udry, J. R., and Cameron, F. (Fall, 1983). "Adolescent Sexual Behavior and Popularity." *Adolescence*, 18, 515–522.

Nitzberg, M. (Winter, 1980). "Development of Likert Scale to Measure Salience of Need for Interpersonal Relationships with Parents and Friends." *Adolescence*, 15, 871–877.

Olweus, D. (December, 1977). "Aggression and Peer Acceptance in Adolescent Boys: Two Short-Term Longitudinal Studies of Ratings." *Child Development*, 48, 1301–1313.

Orlofsky, J. L., and Ginsburg, S. D. (Spring, 1981). "Intimacy Status: Relationship to Affect Cognition." *Adolescence*, 16, 91–99.

Parlee, M. B. (October, 1979). "The Friendship Bond." *Psychology Today*, 43ff.

Peretta, P. O. (Fall, 1980). "Perceived Primary Group Criteria in the Relational Network of Closest Friendships." *Adolescence*, 15, 555–565.

Roscoe, B., Diana, M. S., and Brooks, R. H. II. (1987). "Early, Middle, and Later Adolescents' Views on Dating and Factors Influencing Partner Selection." *Adolescence*, 22, 59–68.

Roscoe, B., Kennedy, D., and Pope, R. (1987). "Adolescents' Views of Intimacy: Distinguishing Intimate from Nonintimate Relationships." *Adolescence*, 87, 511–516.

Rubenstein, C. (July, 1983). "The Modern Art of Courtly Love." *Psychology Today*, 17, 40–49.

Rubin, Z., Hill, C. T., Peplau, L. A., and Dunkel-Schetter, C. (May, 1980). "Self-Disclosure in Dating Couples: Sex Roles and the Ethic of Openness." *Journal of Marriage and the Family*, 42, 305–317.

Samet, N., and Kelly, E. W. (1987). "The Relationship of Steady Dating to Self-Esteem and Sex-Role Identity among Adolescents." *Adolescence*, 22, 231–245.

Sebald, H. (Spring, 1981). "Adolescents' Concept of Popularity and Unpopularity, Comparing 1960 with 1976." *Adolescence*, 16, 187–193.

———. (1986). "Adolescents' Shifting Orientation toward Parents and Peers: A Curvilinear Trend over Recent Decades." *Journal of Marriage and the Family*, 48, 5–13.

Selman, R. L., and Selman, A. P. (October, 1979). "Children's Ideas about Friendships: A New Theory." *Psychology Today*, 71ff.

Tedesco, L. A., and Gaier, E. L. (1988). "Friendship Bonds in Adolescence." *Adolescence*, 89, 127–136.

Till, A., and Freedman, E. M. (June, 1978). "Complementarity versus Similarity of Traits Operating in the Choice of Marriage and Dating Partners." *Journal of Social Psychology*, 105, 147–148.

Timnick, L. (August, 1982). "How You Can Learn to Be Likable, Confident, Socially Successful for Only the Cost of Your Present Education." *Psychology Today*, 42ff.

Warren, R., Good, G., and Velten, E. (Fall, 1984). "Measurement of Social-Evaluative Anxiety in Junior High School Students." *Adolescence*, 19, 643–648.

Werebe, M. J. G. (1987). "Friendship and Dating Relationships among French Adolescents." *Journal of Adolescence*, 10, 269–289.

Williams, E. G. (Spring, 1983). "Adolescent Loneliness." *Adolescence*, 18, 51–66.

Williams, J. W., and White, K. A. (1983). "Adolescent Status Systems for Males and Females at Three Age Levels." *Adolescence*, 18, 381–389.

Yarcheski, A., and Mahon, N. E. (Winter, 1984). "Chumship Relationships, Altruistic Behavior, and Loneliness in Early Adolescents." *Adolescence*, 19, 913–924.

CHAPTER

14

Gender Identity and Sex Roles

gender

gender identity

gender role or sex role

One of the most important considerations in any discussion of adolescent sexuality is the concept of gender identity and sex roles. ***Gender*** refers to one's sex. ***Gender identity*** is the individual's internal sense or perception of being male or female. ***Gender role or sex role*** is the outward expression of maleness or femaleness in social settings. This chapter begins with a discussion of biological determinants of gender, and then goes on to discuss environmental influences. Theories of sex-role development are explained and changing concepts of masculinity and femininity examined along with the trend toward androgyny. Finally, the meaning and development of homosexuality are discussed, along with the adjustments homosexuals face.

BIOLOGICAL BASIS OF GENDER

Genetic Bases

Klinefelter's syndrome

Turner's syndrome

Biological gender is genetically and hormonally determined (Goleman, 1978). This biological influence is well known. The fetus becomes a male or female depending on whether it has XY or XX sex chromosomes and on the balance between the male and female sex hormones in the bloodstream. Occasionally nature makes a mistake: the male gets an extra X (female) chromosome (labeled XXY, ***Klinefelter's syndrome***), so a "man" is produced with a distinctly feminine appearance and with small testicles that are incapable of producing sperm (McCary and McCary, 1982). Sometimes a female is born with one of the X chromosomes missing (labeled XO, ***Turner's syndrome***), so that her external sex organs are poorly developed and infantile in size and her ovaries are missing. To what extent, then, can she be labeled a woman? Genetically she is only part woman. Until about six weeks of development, it is not possible to tell whether the growing fetus will be a boy or girl, for they have identical equipment prior to this time.

Hormonal Influences

hermaphroditism

pseudo-hermaphroditism

Hermaphroditism is the condition in which an individual has the gonads of both sexes (has both testes and ovaries). True hermaphroditism is rare, with only about one hundred cases reported worldwide (McCary and McCary, 1982). ***Pseudohermaphroditism*** is much more common, occurring in about 1 out of every 1,000 infants. In this disorder, the male may have rudimentary testes, but his external genitals are not fully developed or are feminine in appearance. This condition is caused by an inability to respond to male hormones as the male child develops. The female hermaphrodite has ovaries, though usually incompletely developed, but her external genitals and other bodily characteristics are male to a greater or lesser degree. This condition results from an excess of male hormones in her bloodstream as she develops into womanhood.

Hormones have a definite influence on physical characteristics. Male hormones can be administered to a woman, encouraging the growth of the beard, body hair, the clitoris, and the development of masculine muscles, build, and strength. Similarly, female hormones can be administered to a man, encouraging breast development and other female traits. Physical femaleness or maleness is thus somewhat tenuous and may be partially altered.

Hormones alter physical characteristics, but do they influence sex-typed behavior (Parlee, 1978)? If human females are exposed to excessive androgenic influences prior to birth, they become more tomboyish, more physically vigorous, and more assertive than other females. They prefer boys rather than girls as playmates and choose strenuous activities over the relatively docile play of most prepubertal girls. Similarly, adolescent boys born to mothers who receive estrogen and progesterone during pregnancy tend to exhibit less assertiveness and physical activity and may be rated lower in general masculine-typed behavior (Zussman, Zussman, and Dalton, 1975). *The studies suggest that changes in prenatal hormonal levels in humans may have marked effects on gender-role behavior; after birth, however, hormonal changes usually accentuate or minimize certain masculine-feminine characteristics already evident.*

Studies have shown, however, a direct relationship between the role of production of testosterone and measures of aggression and hostility among normal adult males (Persky, Smith, and Basu, 1971). Interestingly, this relationship did not hold true for men over thirty years of age. This means that some of the variance in adolescent behavior and some of the turbulence of this period may be accounted for by the effect of the rapid increase in the secretion of testosterone at puberty.

ENVIRONMENTAL INFLUENCES ON GENDER IDENTITY AND ROLES

Masculinity and Femininity

Biological influence is only part of the picture; environment also plays an important role. Certain qualities of maleness are defined and become "masculine," not only because of heredity but also in the way society prescribes that a male ought to be a man. Society prescribes how a male ought to look and behave, what type of personality he ought to have, and the roles he should perform. Similarly, a female is created not only by genetic conception but also by those psychosocial forces that mold and influence her personality. **Masculinity** and **femininity** refer to those qualities of personality characteristic of man or woman. When one speaks of a masculine man, that person is expressing a value judgment based on an assessment of the personality and behavior characteristics of the male according to culturally defined standards of "maleness." Similarly, a feminine woman is labeled according to culturally determined criteria for "femaleness." In this sense, the development of masculinity or femininity is education in human sexuality; in what it means to be a man or woman or in what it means to be sexual, within the context of the culture in which one lives.

masculinity

femininity

Concepts of masculinity and femininity have undergone considerable changes in the United States. In the days of George Washington, a "true man," especially a gentleman, could wear hose, a powdered wig, and a lace shirt without being considered unmanly; today he would be considered quite feminine. Thus, the judgments made about masculinity or the extent of "manliness" are subjective judgments based on the accepted standards of "maleness" as defined by the culture. These standards vary from culture to culture or with different periods of history in the same society.

A woman is labeled "feminine" acording to culturally determined criteria for "femaleness." (Robert Harbison)

Theories of Sex-Role Development

Because environment plays such an important role in the establishment of the criteria for masculinity and femininity and in development of maleness or femaleness, it is important to understand how this development takes place. Three major theories explain how sex-role behavior is learned: cognitive developmental theory, social learning theory, and parental identification theory.

Cognitive Developmental Theory

The cognitive developmental theory suggests that sex-role identity has its beginning in the gender cognitively assigned to the child at birth and subsequently accepted by him or her while growing up. At the time of birth, gender assignment is made largely on the basis of genital examination. The child from that point on is considered a boy or a girl. If genital abnormalities are present, this gender assignment may prove to be erroneous if it is not in agreement with the sex chromosomes and gonads that are present. However, even if it is erroneous, Money and Ehrhardt (1972) have pointed out that sex identification usually follows the sex in which the child is reared. This is true despite ambiguities in physical sexual characteristics. If a hermaphrodite is assigned one sex at birth, he or she will grow up to be that sex even though it may later be discovered that the original assessment was wrong. If sex reassignment is to be successful, it should be done before age 18 months. A child given sex reassignment after 18 months of age may never differentiate the new gender identity sufficiently to accept it completely.

The cognitive assignment of gender influences everything that happens thereafter (Marcus and Overton, 1978). Kohlberg (1966), the chief exponent of this view, emphasized that the child's self-categorization (as a boy or girl) is the basic organizer of the sex-role attitudes that develop. The child who recognizes that he is a male begins to value maleness and to act consistently with gender expectations. He begins to structure his own experience according to his accepted gender and to act out appropriate sex roles. He reflects sex-role differences if he fantasizes himself as a daddy with a wife and children, just as a girl does who pretends she is a grown-up woman with breasts, lipstick, a job, and children to take care of. Sex differentiation takes place gradually as children learn to be male or female according to culturally established sex-role expectations and their interpretations of them.

It is important to emphasize that according to this theory, girls do not become girls because they identify with or model themselves after their mothers; they model themselves after their mothers because they have realized that they are girls. They preferentially value their own sex and are motivated to appropriate sex-role behavior.

Social Learning Theory

The social learning theorists reason differently. In their view, *a child learns sex-typed behavior the same way he or she learns any other type of behavior: through a combination of reward and punishment, indoctrination, observation of others, and modeling.* From the beginning, boys and girls are socialized differently. Boys are expected to be more active, hostile, and aggressive. They are expected to fight when teased and to stand up to bullies. When they act according to expectations, they are praised; when they refuse to fight, they are criticized for being "sissies." Girls are condemned or punished for being too boisterous or aggressive and are rewarded when they are polite and submissive (Williams, 1988). As a consequence, boys and girls grow up manifesting different behaviors.

Traditional sex roles and concepts are taught in many ways as the child grows up (Brinkerhoff and MacKie, 1985; Brody and Steelman, 1985; Roopnarine, 1986). Giving children gender-specific toys may have considerable influence on vocational choices. Such toys influence boys to be scientists, astronauts, or football players and girls to be nurses, teachers, or stewardesses (Kacerguis and Adams, 1979). Publishers have made an effort to remove sexual stereotypes and prejudices. In spite of some progress, an analysis of 113 recently published books for children and adolescents revealed that males were portrayed as active and more likely to give than to receive help, while females were portrayed as passive and more likely to receive than give help. The stereotype of the dependent female was reflected in the female characters (White, 1986).

Without realizing it, many teachers still develop traditional masculine-feminine stereotypical behavior in school. Studies of teachers' relationships with boys and girls reveal that teachers encourage boys to be more assertive in the classroom (Sadker and Sadker, 1985). When the teacher asks questions, the boys call out comments without raising their hands, literally grabbing the teacher's attention. Most girls sit patiently with their hands raised, but if a girl calls out, the teacher reprimands her: "In this class, we don't shout out answers; we raise our hands." The message is subtle but powerful: boys should be assertive academically; girls should be quiet.

Much has been done also to try to change school courses and programs that promote sex-typed roles. Traditionally physical education courses for boys emphasized contact sports and competition; those for girls promoted grace, agility, and poise. Home economics was offered only to girls; shop and auto mechanics only to boys. Guidance counselors urged girls to become secretaries and nurses, boys to become business managers and doctors. Females were usually prepared for marriage and parenthood, boys for a vocation. Gradually these emphases are being eliminated, so that both males and females are free to choose the programs they want.

Social learning theory thus emphasizes that boys develop "maleness" and girls "femaleness" through exposure to scores of influences—parents, peers, school, the mass media—that indoctrinate them in what it means to be a man or a woman in the culture in which they are brought up (Aneshensel and Rosen, 1980). They are further encouraged to accept the so-called appropriate sex identity by being rewarded for one kind of behavior and punished for another (Flake-Hobson, Skeen, and Robinson, 1980). Thus, sex-role concepts and stereotypes of a particular culture become self-fulfilling prophecies (Snyder, 1982). Those who lived up to societal expectations are accepted as normal; those who do not conform are criticized and pressured to comply. Society ostracizes nonconformers and forces them to seek those with similar concepts or identities.

Parental Identification Theory

identification   Children also find appropriate sex roles through a process of **identification,** especially with parents. *Parental identification is the process by which the child adopts and internalizes parental values, attitudes, behavioral traits, and personality characteristics.* This theory is sometimes discussed as one form of social learning; in other instances, it is considered psychoanalytic theory. It is listed separately here as parental identification to emphasize the importance of parents' influence in sex-role learning. When applied to sex-role development, parental identification theory suggests that children develop sex-role concepts, attitudes, values, characteristics, and behavior by identifying with their parents, especially with the parent of the same sex (Hock and Curry, 1983). Identification begins immediately after birth because of the child's early dependency on parents. This dependency in turn normally leads to a close emotional attachment. Sex-role learning takes place almost unconsciously and indirectly in this close parent-child relationship. Children may learn that some mothers are soft, warm, and gentle, that they are affectionate, nurturing, and sensitive. Others may learn that fathers are muscular, sometimes rough or loud, or not as involved in day-by-day child care. However, it may happen that children learn that their mothers are rough or loud and not as involved in day-by-day child care and that their fathers are warm, gentle, affectionate, nurturing, and sensitive. But the important point is that children listen and observe that each parent behaves, speaks, dresses, and acts differently in relation to the other parent, to other children, or to people outside the family. Thus, *children learn what a mother, a wife, a father, a husband, a woman, or a man is through example and through daily contacts and associations.*

Parental identification is the process by which the child adopts and internalizes parental values, attitudes, behavioral traits, and personality characteristics. (Robert Harbison)

Of course, *the extent to which identification takes place depends on the amount of time parents spend with their children and the intimacy and intensity of the contact.* Parents have a greater influence when they have a good marital adjustment and there is mutual love, respect, and support (Klein and Shulman, 1981; McDonald, 1980). Usually, young boys and girls identify more closely with the mother than with the father, primarily because they are more often with their mother (Acock et al., 1982). As a result, young boys often show more similarity to their mothers than to their fathers. This is one explanation of why males are often more anxious than females regarding their sex-role identification (Currant et al., 1979). On the one hand, they are more severely punished for being "sissies" than girls for being masculine, and, on the other hand, they have more difficulty breaking away from feminine influences and finding suitable male role models (Coates, 1987). When the father is absent from the home, the male child has the greater difficulty because of the lack of masculine influence. However, studies show that *the effect of father presence depends partially upon the personality of the father himself.* If fathers are nurturing and involved in raising their children, the children can learn that men can be warm and supportive. The father's involvement may be beneficial not because it will support traditional male roles but because it will help break them down (Rosen and Aneshensel, 1978).

The sex-role concepts the child learns depend not only on the intensity of parental relationships, but also on the patterns of role models exemplified (Hansen and Darling, 1985; Lamke and Filsinger, 1983). Daughters of rural mothers, especially those with large families, learn more traditional feminine roles than daughters from urban families where the mother is able to spend more time outside the family (Hertsgaard and

Light, 1984). High-status parents exert more influence than low-status ones, and the parent with more education is able to exert more influence (Acock, Barker, and Bengtson, 1982; Lueptow, 1980). A girl who closely identifies with a masculine mother becomes only weakly identified with a typically feminine personality (Smith and Self, 1980). One brought up by a mother with nontraditional sex-role attitudes will get a less stereotyped concept of femininity than one whose mother holds conservative concepts (Weeks, Wise, and Duncan, 1984). One study of adolescents of employed mothers showed that the adolescents had more liberal sex-role orientation and attitudes toward the division of household tasks than adolescents of homemaker mothers (Gardner and LaBrecque, 1986). Another study of adolescents from dual-career families showed less traditional sex-role attitudes relative to adolescents from single-earner families (Stephan and Corder, 1985). Sons whose mothers are employed also grow up with a different attitude toward working wives and mothers than those whose mothers are not employed (Powell and Steelman, 1982). Similarly, a boy brought up by a father who represents

HIGHLIGHT   Different Concepts of Gender

The concept of gender has biological and psychological components (Holden, 1988). The following list includes both aspects:

Biological Components of Gender

Gonadal gender: Whether one has ovaries (female) or testes (male). The true hermaphrodite would have both sets of gonads.

Chromosomal gender: Whether one has XX (female) or XY (male) chromosomes. The only sure way to determine if one is a biological male or female is to examine chromosomes.

External genital gender: Whether one has a clitoris, labia, and vaginal opening (female) or penis and scrotum (male).

Hormonal gender: Whether one has a preponderance of estrogen and progesterone (female) or androgens and testosterone (male).

Other internal accessory organs and gender: Whether there is a uterus and vagina (female) or prostate and seminal vesicles (male).

Psychological Components of Gender

Assigned gender: The gender assigned a child at the time of birth and the gender in which a child is reared. Babies with incomplete or abnormal genital development may be assigned the wrong gender, one that does not agree with chromosomal gender.

Perceived gender: The gender other persons believe the individual to be, based on appearance, clothing, personality, and behavior. This perception sometimes does not agree with biological fact.

Gender identity: The person's private, internal sense of maleness or femaleness, which is expressed in personality and behavior.

Social gender: Maleness or femaleness as defined by a particular society or culture and the extent to which the person fits the stereotypes.

Erotic attraction and gender: The sex to which the person is erotically attracted.

Gender roles: The sex roles one performs in everyday life.

traditional ideas of masculinity and the role of the husband and father in the family will likely develop quite different concepts from one brought up by an egalitarian parent. As a result, sex-role concepts are perpetuated from one generation to the next. They can be gradually changed, however, if each generation is able to analyze existing concepts in order to discard outmoded ideas and roles and to adopt improved ones.

CHANGING CONCEPTS OF MASCULINITY
Traditional Concepts

Traditionally, masculinity has implied some specific characteristics: aggressiveness, dominance, strength, daring, courage, forcefulness, ruggedness, adventurousness, independence, confidence, and lack of emotion (David and Brannon, 1976). Man's aggressiveness, strength, and courage were needed in warfare, hunting, and protecting his family from harm. His dominance was expected in his relationships with his wife and children. His aggressiveness, forcefulness, and confidence were expected in business; adventurousness, daring, ruggedness, and bravery were traits needed in exploring the unknown or in facing new challenges. And in times of crisis or even in close associations with others, man was expected to be unexpressive and unemotional.

Although men needed many of these traits in primitive societies or on the frontier, where they were required to protect and provide with their bare hands or with primitive weapons, some of these traits are not necessary today. Some measure of aggressiveness may help in business or in furthering oneself and one's ideas in relationship to others, but the overaggressive male gets into trouble with friends, family, society, or the law. An earth full of aggressive males results in world wars and destruction. Thus, aggressiveness tends to be more and more outmoded in the contemporary United States. Cooperation is needed for economic, social, and physical survival.

The Inexpressive Male

One of the unfortunate components of traditional masculinity has been the insistence that U.S. *males not show emotions.* Italian, French, Russian, or Spanish males embrace and kiss one another and their sons, or even weep, but not English males or males in the United States. They were never to express affection toward other men to avoid all suspicion of homosexuality (Tognoli, 1980). Anglo-American males were cautioned not to show affection, grief, disappointment, appreciation of beauty, or even joy, else they would appear unmanly.

The Cowboy Type   Balswick and Peek (1971) call the inexpressive male "a tragedy of American society." They identify two types of inexpressive males. They call one the *cowboy type*: the two-fisted, strong, silent, 100 percent American he-man. He is rough and tough, does not talk much, and above all never shows any tenderness or affection toward women. He likes them but is embarrassed by them and seldom kisses them. To do so would betray his manhood. He treats them with respect but roughly and without affection. As Manville (1969) suggests:

The on-screen John Wayne doesn't feel comfortable around women. He does like them sometimes. But at the right time, and in the right place—which he chooses. And always with his car/horse parked directly outside, in/on which he will ride away to his important business back in Marlboro country.

This inexpressiveness and reserve of men toward women has been labeled the "cowboy syndrome." The cowboy loved his horse and was intrigued by a girlfriend but usually chose the horse. The stereotype of today's rough adolescent male is of a he-man who loves his motorcycle, is "turned on" by his girlfriend, but who, if he is a real man, hesitates to express tender feelings toward his girl; paradoxically, such expression would conflict with his image of maleness. So when he hops on his bike and speeds away, he and his pals leave the women behind.

The Playboy Type   The other type of inexpressive male described by Balswick and Peek (1971) is the *playboy type*. His is the James Bond image, the Don Juan with dozens of sexy girlfriends, all of whom he makes love to but with whom he is never to get emotionally involved. He wants a "playgirl" to sleep with in a nonfeeling way, and his measure of masculinity is judged by the degree to which he can make conquests without getting caught. (If he gets married, he is finished!) This type of male is incapable of showing deep, tender emotion; women and sex are purchasable commodities. Such a male would have difficulty in establishing a close, companionable, affectionate relationship with any woman. It is this type of male to whom women are objecting: "We don't want to be treated as sex objects."

The modern adolescent boy has been thoroughly indoctrinated in the cowboy syndrome and the playboy philosophy. Both concepts have had a marked effect on his personality and his sexual behavior: he has learned to gauge his masculinity partly by his sexual prowess with women, by his ability to seduce, arouse, and satisfy numerous sexual partners without emotional involvement.

Finding an adequate self-concept and a satisfactory male image is a particular problem for the black adolescent male or for the white male adolescent from a low socioeconomic status group, especially in a father-absent home. One way such males have traditionally proved their masculinity is through the sexual exploitation of women.

Traditional concepts of masculinity are changing, especially among middle-class, better-educated youths. Many men no longer feel threatened by doing "women's" chores in the home or even by open expression of feeling. Some are learning to care for small children (Melson and Fogel, 1988). Elements of traditional concepts remain, however: the middle- and upper-class male likes to think of himself as a playboy, the lower-class male as a rough, tough he-man. Both feel threatened by changing concepts of femininity with which they are confronted. Many men are still troubled by commitment and intimacy (Freudenberger, 1987). What men have not realized is that healthy, nonexploitative relationships with women would not only free women from sex-role typing but would eliminate the necessity for males to try constantly to prove their manhood (Pleck, 1981). The result would be doubly liberating.

CHANGING CONCEPTS OF FEMININITY
The Passive Female

Traditionally, females have been depicted as passive, dependent, quiet, meek, gentle, warm and affectionate, kind, sentimental, soft hearted, and sensitive (Hall and Black, 1979). They have also been supposed to be more emotional and excitable, fickle, and frivolous than males. Numerous societies consider them man's inferior physically, intellectually, and socially. Most women are weaker in terms of physical strength and muscle power, but they are often healthier, live longer, have fewer illnesses, and lack numerous sex-linked defects of the male such as color blindness, baldness, and hemophilia (bleeding disease).

Women and Work

Women have been given an inferior status in U.S. society (Fabes, 1983). Table 14-1 shows that in the United States, men continue to be paid higher wages than women. Data in table 14-2 show that one of the reasons for women's lower wages is not only discrimination but also the continued dominance of higher-paid professions by men. A comparison of the 1972, 1980, 1983, and 1985 figures, however, indicates that male dominance is slowly declining.

A number of factors influence these earnings differentials. Men have higher-status jobs than women. Men more often aspire to higher positions than women (Corder and Stephan, 1984). A greater percentage of men than women graduate from college and go on to earn higher degrees. Men have about twice as much work experience as women of comparable age. If all these factors are adjusted statistically so that women are assumed to have the same occupational status, education, working hours full time, and work experience as men, the income level of women is still only 64 percent of the male income level. The conclusion is inescapable: the primary reason for the lower income of women is discrimination; women are not receiving equal pay for equal work. Nationally, a female college graduate averages only slightly more income than a male with an elementary

TABLE 14-1

Median annual income of year-round, full-time workers, by sex and age, 1984.

AGE GROUP	MALE	FEMALE
All ages	$24,004	$15,422
14–19	8,886	8,509
20–24	13,043	11,435
25–34	21,607	15,896
35–44	27,610	17,137

From: U.S. Bureau of the Census, Department of Commerce, *Statistical Abstract of the United States*, 1987 (Washington, D.C.: U.S. Government Printing Office, 1987), p. 441.

TABLE 14-2

Percentage of males in various professions, 1972, 1980, 1983, 1985.

PROFESSION	1972	1980	1983	1985
Engineers	99.2	96.0	94.2	93.3
Lawyers and judges	96.2	87.2	84.2	81.8
Physicians and surgeons	90.7	87.1	84.2	82.8
College teachers	72.0	66.1	63.7	64.8
Authors, artists, entertainers, and athletes	68.3	60.7	57.3	55.5
Social workers	44.9	36.7	35.7	33.3
Teachers (except college and university)	30.0	29.2	29.1	27.0
Librarians, archivists, and curators	18.4	18.6	15.6	15.3
Nurses	2.4	3.5	4.2	4.9

From: U.S. Bureau of the Census, Department of Commerce, *Statistical Abstract of the United States,*
1987 (Washington, D.C.: U.S. Government Printing Office, 1987), p. 385.

school education. Such sex discrimination is obviously unjust. Women are taught
and pressured to assume an inferior position (Hughes and Gove, 1981).

There have been some changes in these traditional female concepts, however. Women are
insisting on full employment rights and equality and on relieving them of the
burden of child care by getting society and husbands to provide help. *The concept
of the ideal female image and role is being changed slowly* by a shift in occupational roles
and redefining of responsibilities in the family (Keyes and Coleman, 1983). There
seems to be a gradual shift toward egalitarian sex roles (Winters and Frankel,
1984).

Personality traits that are considered desirable are also changing. Assertiveness training
has helped many women stand up for themselves and their own rights (Stake,
DeVille, and Pennell, 1983). The ideal woman today is physically strong (she may
even work out on weight-lifting equipment to build up her muscles). She may
seek equal participation with men in a wide variety of organized sports (Nixon,
Maresca, and Silverman, 1979). She is intelligent, assertive, independent, and self-
actualizing, fully in charge of her own life without having to be totally dependent
on a husband. But at the same time she has kept traditional traits that have been
her most positive assets: emotional warmth, sensitivity, kindness, and affection.

ANDROGYNY

Description

androgyny

What seems to be emerging is a gradual mixing of male and female traits and
roles to produce **androgyny** (male and female in one). Androgynous persons are
not sex typed with respect to roles (although they are distinctly male or female
in gender). They match their behavior to the situation rather than being limited
by what is culturally defined as male or female. An androgynous male feels
comfortable cuddling and caring for a young boy; an androgynous female feels
comfortable pumping gas and changing oil in her car. Androgyny expands the

range of human behavior, allowing individuals to cope effectively in a variety of situations (Flake-Hobson, Skeen, and Robinson, 1980).

Advantages

This mixing of roles is advantageous to both sexes. Traditional men have lacked sensitivity and emotional warmth and so encountered difficulty in forming close attachments and friendships. They saw danger in intimacy, afraid of a smothering relationship, or rejection and hurt. Women saw danger in isolation, independence, and achievement, afraid of being set apart by success, being ridiculed, or being left alone. Men's aggressiveness led to conflict and violence. Women's passive submission led to exploitation (Gilligan, 1982). Both sexes were restricted in their behavior and relationship by narrow and constricting sex-typed roles.

In recent years, a number of studies have asked: "Can a man or woman possess androgynous traits and be psychologically healthy and well adjusted?" This is an important question since, historically, psychologists taught that mental health depended on a clear-cut separation between male and female roles (Cook, 1985). An analysis of the relationship between sex-role orientation and self-esteem of 106 high school seniors revealed that masculinity was predictive of high self-esteem in females and femininity was predictive of high self-esteem and good social relations in males (Lamke, 1982). One study of 956 students in ninth to twelfth grade found no relationship between ego identity and masculinity and femininity during adolescence (Lamke and Peyton, 1988). Other studies reveal that androgynous individuals have better social relationships and superior adjustments than any other adolescents (Avery, 1982; Wells, 1980). Undifferentiated adolescents (neither masculine, nor feminine, nor androgynous) have the poorest adjustments. A study of the relationship of sex roles to physical and psychological health of 180 men and women with an average age of 18.3 revealed that androgynous individuals always showed a more favorable adjustment (Small, Teagno, and Selz, 1980). They possessed adaptive capabilities and resources such as effective coping techniques, emotional integration, communication skills, and a well-defined self-concept with a high level of ego strength and integration.

Development

How and when is androgyny developed? *Adolescents who score low in traditional sex typing and high in socialization show a pattern of androgynous identification, or modeling of a parental pair in which neither the father nor the mother exemplifies the typical sex-role stereotypes.* Instead, both parents provide models for their children of competence, tolerance, consideration of others, and sharing of responsibilities (White, 1980). As a result, the children identify with the characteristics of both parents.

Two different studies of young adolescents showed that girls were more androgynous than boys early in their development (Mills, 1981; Nicholson and Antill, 1981). In seventh and eighth grades, girls viewed intellectual achievement more positively than same-age boys. Only later were girls socialized into a more feminine role that viewed achievement as a "masculine" pursuit. Boys appeared to be more sex typed, so that intellectual pursuits were not part of the male role until later. Thus, *society tended to encourage a more androgynous sex role for boys as they got older but reinforced a more traditionally defined feminine sex role as the girls aged.* Nicholson and Antill (1981) describe the result: the number of problems reported by females remained at a high level as they got older, primarily because of pressures to conform to a feminine sex-role identity. But since the sex-role demands on boys declined as they got older, they reported fewer problems.

Adolescent Ideals

Analysis of male-female traits that junior high adolescents consider ideal showed that they regarded many feminine traits as socially desirable (Rust and Lloyd, 1982). There was also considerable support for mixing masculine-feminine traits (Curry and Hock, 1981). Both sexes felt that possessing altruistic understanding, gentleness, gratitude, kindness, and sharing emotional expression were descriptive of the ideal male. Turning to the ratings of the ideal female, the females stressed assertiveness, having competence and confidence as well as showing stereotypical altruistic understanding and emotional expression. This pattern suggests that cultural changes in ideal traits are having a significant impact on the ideals of adolescents (Currant et al., 1979).

HOMOSEXUALITY

Meaning

homosexuality

heterosexuality

Homosexuality *refers to sexual orientation in which one develops sexual interest in those of the same biological sex.* Kinsey was one of the first social scientists to emphasize that there are degrees of **heterosexuality** and homosexuality. He developed a six-point scale of sexual behavior, shown in figure 14-1 (Weinberg and Williams, 1974). He found that some persons have a mixture of homosexuality and heterosexuality so are bisexual. Some of these persons live a typical heterosexual life with their mates and children and yet enjoy homosexual sex on the side.

Homosexuality does not describe physical appearance, sex roles, or personality. Some homosexual men are masculine in appearance and actions; some are outstanding athletes. Some lesbian women are feminine in appearance and behavior. Nor can one tell by behavioral characteristics that they are homosexual. They may play stereotyped sex roles in society and in their families. Others exhibit

FIGURE 14-1

Kinsey's continuum of heterosexuality-homosexuality.

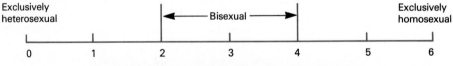

1   Predominantly heterosexual, only incidentally homosexual
2   More heterosexual than homosexual
3   Equally heterosexual and homosexual
4   More homosexual than heterosexual
5   Predominantly homosexual, only incidentally heterosexual

some of the physical and personality characteristics of the opposite sex and assume opposite-sex roles.

Different types of persons are homosexuals. Some are poorly adjusted or even psychotic (as are some heterosexuals); others are psychologically well adjusted. Most are creative, contributing members of society. Homosexuality is considered deviant in our culture but is not so regarded in some other cultures.

"For a mental condition to be considered a psychiatric disorder," a decision of the American Psychiatric Association read, "it should regularly cause emotional distress or regularly be associated with generalized impairment of social functioning; homosexuality doesn't meet these criteria" (McCary and McCary, 1982, p. 457). However, in the 1980 edition of the *Diagnostic and Statistical Manual of Mental Disorders* (DSM-III), the APA included a new category of mental illness called **ego-dystonic homosexuality** in which homosexuality is unacceptable to the individual involved. Thus, if a sustained pattern of homosexual arousal is an unwanted source of distress, and the person desires instead a heterosexual orientation, he or she has a psychological problem and it is recognized as such.

ego-dystonic homosexuality

Causes*

Considerable research has been done to find out what causes homosexuality. The research falls into three major categories: biological theories, psychoanalytic theories, and social learning theories.

Biological Theories   One theory is that homosexuality is inherited. Generally speaking, the genetic theory of homosexuality has been discarded today. Behavior as complicated as this cannot be explained that easily.

Another biological theory relates the levels of male and female hormones in the body to homosexuality. But baseline hormonal levels of homosexuals and heterosexuals are only slightly dissimilar. However, in one study (Medical First, 1984), a single injection of *Premarin*, an estrogen preparation, was given to 12 heterosexual women, 17 heterosexual males, and 14 homosexual males. The estrogen suppressed testosterone levels in both groups of men, but not in the women. However, 72 and 96 hours later, the homosexuals had significantly lower levels of testosterone than the heterosexuals. Apparently, the homosexuals were more influenced by the female hormone estrogen. Their bodies had less ability to recover from its influence and regain normal testosterone levels than did the heterosexual males. "This is the first study in this country clearly suggesting and presenting evidence of biological differences between homosexuals and heterosexuals as a group," said Dr. Brian Gladue, the chief researcher (Medical First, 1984).

One implication is that our bodies respond differently to changes in hormonal levels. These levels, in turn, may have differential effects on development and behavior. Part of sexual differentiation takes place in the *hypothalamus* of the brain (Kimura, 1985).

---

* Part of the research in this section has been taken from Rice, F. P. (1989). *Human Sexuality* Copyright © 1989 by Wm. C. Brown Publishers. Reprinted by permission.

Before birth, prenatal hormones can influence the brain so that a baby is born with a predisposition to develop behavior associated with the opposite sex (Ellis and Ames, 1987; Money, 1987).

Psychoanalytic Theories   Traditionally, homosexuality was thought to be caused by problems in parent-child relationships in the family. The troubled relationships were thought to cause problems in identifying with the parent of the same sex. However, a study of 322 gay men and women from different sections of the country revealed that two-thirds perceived their relationships with their fathers as extremely satisfactory or satisfactory; three-fourths perceived their relationships with their mothers as extremely satisfactory or satisfactory (Robinson, Skeen, Flake-Hobson, and Herman, 1982). Sixty-four percent felt that they were always loved by their mothers, but only 36 percent felt that they were always loved by their fathers. Only 4 percent never or hardly ever felt loved by their mother, and 11 percent did not feel loved by their father.

In summary, it can be said with certainty that negative family relationships may be significant factors in the background of some male and female homosexuals, but certainly not in all. *There is not sufficient evidence to assert that parental relationships might be the primary cause of homosexuality.*

Social Learning Theories   Behaviorists would emphasize that homosexuality is simply the result of learning. According to behavioral theories, psychological conditioning through reinforcement or punishment of early sexual thoughts, feelings, and behavior is what influences sexual preference. Thus, a person may lean toward homosexuality if he or she has unpleasant, heterosexual experiences and rewarding same-sex experiences. A girl who is raped, or whose first attempts at heterosexual intercourse are quite painful, might turn to homosexuality (Grundlach, 1977). Parents who wanted a boy and who dress their girl in boys' clothing and encourage masculine interests and behavior might be encouraging lesbianism. As a matter of fact, children who exhibit atypical gender-role behavior and show opposite-sex interests (for example, boys who avoid sports like baseball and football but enjoy activities like playing house or jacks) are more likely to become homosexual (Money and Russo, 1979).

The behaviorist view explains why some people change their sexual orientation from heterosexual to homosexual and back again. A person in an unhappy heterosexual marriage may turn to a friend of the same sex for comfort. A positive sexual relationship may develop from this friendship. If that relationship sours, the person may enter into another heterosexual partnership (Masters and Johnson, 1979).

In another study, 686 homosexual men, 293 homosexual women, 337 heterosexual men, and 140 heterosexual women were interviewed intensively for three to five hours (Bell, Weinberg, and Hammersmith, 1981). The researchers strove to gain data that would uncover the causes of homosexuality. They then analyzed the data statistically through "path analysis" to establish cause and effect. *They could not find solid support for psychoanalytical, social learning, or various sociological theories, so they came to the conclusion that homosexuality must have a biological basis.*

The conclusion is that we do not know for certain the causes of homosexuality. There are a number of plausible causative factors, but no single factor emerges as a consistent reason. Perhaps one explanation may be that many different types of homosexuals exist. They are not a homogeneous group, so what contributes to one person's homosexuality may not contribute to another's (Robinson and Dalton, 1986). The tendency in some persons seems to be there from childhood. In most cases, the children of homosexuals do not grow up to be homosexuals, indicating that modeling and imitation alone cannot account for persons becoming homosexuals (Miller, 1979; Norton, 1987). Most homosexuals do not choose their sexual preference. In fact, many deny it and fight against it for years, since they are afraid of public and personal recrimination.

Adjustments

After years of denial, some homosexuals accept their preferences, establish close friendships with their own sex, and are much happier and psychologically better adjusted because of it. The unhappiest persons are those who are never able to accept their condition and lead separated, secretive life-styles, seeking anonymous sexual encounters in public restrooms or other places. They are often isolated, lonely, unhappy people—terribly afraid of rejection—even by other homosexuals (Harry, 1979). Lesbians are usually better able than male homosexuals to establish close

---

HIGHLIGHT   Homosexual Life-Styles

Not all homosexuals are alike or live alike any more than do heterosexuals. Bell and Weinberg studied 979 homosexual men and women and found that about 75 percent of them could be assigned to one of the following categories based on established statistical criteria:

Close-coupled homosexuals had a close relationship with one partner, regarded themselves as "happily married," had few problems, and appeared to be the best adjusted of the group.

Open-coupled homosexuals lived in a stable relationship with one person but had many outside sexual partners. This is most prevalent among males.

Functional homosexuals were not coupled, had a high number of sexual partners, and little interest in settling down. They tended to be young with a high degree of sexual interest.

Dysfunctional homosexuals were not coupled, had a large number of sexual partners, were very active sexually, but had major problems with their sexual performance, and often had serious emotional and social problems and were sexually dissatisfied with their way of life.

Asexual homosexuals were loners, either by choice or because they could not find a partner, were closet homosexuals, seldom interacting with other homosexual men, and tended to be less exclusively homosexual.

Bell, A. P., and Weinberg, M. S. (1978). *Homosexuality: A Study of Diversity Among Men and Women* (New York: Simon and Schuster).

friendships, since society is more tolerant of women living and being seen together.

SUMMARY

Gender is one's sex: male or female. Gender identity is the individual's internal perception of being male or female. Gender role is the outward expression of maleness or femaleness in social settings.

The biological basis of gender includes both heredity and hormonal influences. Both affect physical characteristics. Hormones usually accentuate or minimize certain masculine-feminine traits already in evidence.

Environmental influences are a major determinant of gender identity and roles. Concepts of masculinity and femininity vary from culture to culture and have undergone changes in the United States.

There are three major theories of sex-role development. Cognitive developmental theory suggests that sex-role identity has its beginnings in the gender cognitively assigned to the child at birth and subsequently accepted by him or her while growing up. Thus, girls model themselves after their mothers because they realize they are females.

Social learning theory says that children learn sex-typed behavior through a combination of rewards and punishments, indoctrination, observation of others, and modeling. Boys and girls learn sex-typed behavior as defined by their culture and as taught and exemplified by significant others.

Parental identification theory says that children learn appropriate sex roles by identifying with parents and internalizing parental values, attitudes, traits, and personality characteristics. The extent to which identification takes place depends on the time parents spend with their children and the intensity of the contact. The sex-role concepts also depend on the patterns of role models exemplified.

One of the disadvantages of traditional concepts of masculinity in the United States has been the insistence that males not express emotions. This restriction prevents men from establishing close, affectionate relationships with others. Both the "cowboy type" and "playboy type" of men are taught that it is unmanly to express tender feelings toward women.

Traditional concepts of females as being passive, meek, and dependent have kept them from accomplishment in their own right. Women still are paid only 62 percent as much as men for the same work, education, and experience.

Traditional concepts are changing, however. Men are becoming more expressive and women more independent and assertive. What is emerging is a gradual mixing of male and female traits and roles to produce androgyny, which has advantages for both sexes.

Homosexuality refers to sexual orientation. It does not describe physical appearance, sex roles, or personality. There are differing degrees of heterosexuality and homosexuality in everyone. There are three groups of theories about the causes of homosexuality: biological, psychoanalytical, and social learning theories. The causes are not completely understood. Homosexuality can be functional or dysfunctional; it can involve close relationships or social isolation, depending on how the individual perceives, accepts, and/or adjusts to the situation and the attitudes of others toward them.

DISCUSSION QUESTIONS

1. Have you ever known a hermaphrodite or pseudohermaphrodite? Describe the person and situation.
2. What happens if a woman is given male hormones? If a man is given female hormones? What are steroids? Should athletes be given them? What effect do they have on men, on women?
3. How do people learn sex-typed behavior according to:
   a. Cognitive developmental theory?
   b. Social learning theory?
   c. Parental identification theory?
4. Should young boys be allowed to play with toys traditionally for girls, such as dolls, baby carriages, housekeeping toys, and dishes? Explain.
5. Should young girls be allowed to play traditional boys' games, such as football, baseball, basketball, and hockey? Explain.
6. Should boys and girls be taught traditional sex-typed roles and behavior? Explain.
7. What is the effect on boys and girls of being reared in a father-absent home?
8. What is the effect on boys and girls of being reared in a family where the mother works full time outside the home?
9. According to feminists, what changes should be made in relation to women's rights and roles? What do women want and seek today? In what ways do traditional concepts of femininity work against the well-being of women? Should women become more masculine? Explain.
10. What changes should be made in traditional concepts of masculinity? Explain. Will men become too "sissy" if taught to be more emotional?
11. What do you think of the concept of androgyny? What are the advantages and disadvantages of mixing male-female roles?
12. Will equality result in identical personalities and gender roles?
13. What causes homosexuality? What is the evidence that it is biologically determined? Psychologically determined? Explain.

BIBLIOGRAPHY

Acock, A. C., Barker, D., and Bengtson, V. L. (May, 1982). "Mother's Employment and Parent-Youth Similarity." *Journal of Marriage and the Family,* 44, 441–455.

Aneshensel, C. C., and Rosen, B. C. (February, 1980). "Domestic Roles and Sex Differences in Occupational Expectations." *Journal of Marriage and the Family,* 42, 121–131.

Avery, A. W. (December, 1982). "Escaping Loneliness in Adolescence: The Case for Androgyny." *Journal of Youth and Adolescence,* 11, 451–459.

Balswick, J. O., and Peek, C. W. (1971). "The Inexpressive Male: A Tragedy of American Society." *Family Coordinator,* 20, 363–368.

Bell, A. P., and Weinberg, M. S. (1978). *Homosexualities: A Study of Diversity Among Men and Women.* New York: Simon and Schuster.

Bell, A. P., Weinberg, M. S., and Hammersmith, K. S. (1981). *Sexual Preference—Its Development in Men and Women.* Bloomington, IN.: Indiana University Press.

Brinkerhoff, M. B., and MacKie, M. (May, 1985). "Religion and Gender: A Comparison of Canadian and American Student Attitudes." *Journal of Marriage and the Family,* 47, 415–429.

Brody, C. J., and Steelman, L. C. (May, 1985). "Sibling Structure and Parental Sex-Typing of Children's Household Tasks." *Journal of Marriage and the Family,* 47, 265–273.

Coates, S. (1987). "Extreme Femininity in Boys." *Medical Aspects of Human Sexuality*, 21, 104–110.

Cook, E. P. (May, 1985). "Androgyny: A Goal for Counseling." *Journal of Counseling and Development*, 63, 567–571.

Corder, J., and Stephan, C. W. (May, 1984). "'Females' Combination of Work and Family Roles: Adolescents' Aspirations." *Journal of Marriage and the Family*, 46, 391–402.

Currant, E. F., et al. (March, 1979). "Sex-Role Stereotyping and Assertive Behavior." *Journal of Psychology*, 101, 223–228.

Curry, J. F., and Hock, R.A. (Winter, 1981). "Sex Differences in Sex Role Ideals in Early Adolescence." *Adolescence*, 16, 779–789.

David, D. S., and Brannon, R., eds. (1976). *The Forty-Nine Percent Majority: The Male Sex Role*. Reading, Mass.: Addison-Wesley.

Ellis, L., and Ames, M. A. (1987). "Neurohormonal Functioning and Sexual Orientation: A Theory of Homosexuality–Heterosexuality." *Psychological Bulletin*, 101, 233–258.

Fabes, R. A. (Fall, 1983). "Adolescents' Judgments of the Opposite Sex." *Adolescence*, 18, 535–540.

Flake-Hobson, C., Skeen, P., and Robinson, B. E. (April, 1980). "Review of Theories and Research Concerning Sex-Role Development and Androgyny with Suggestions for Teachers." *Family Relations*, 29, 155–162.

Freudenberger, H. J. (1987). "Today's Troubled Men." *Psychology Today*, 21, 46–49.

Gardner, K. E., and LaBrecque, S. V. (1986). "Effects of Maternal Employment on Sex-Role Orientation of Adolescents." *Adolescence*, 21, 875–885.

Gilligan, C. (June, 1982). "Why Should a Woman Be More Like a Man?" *Psychology Today*, 68ff.

Goffman, E. (August, 1977). "Genderisms." *Psychology Today*, 60–63.

Goleman, D. (November, 1978). "Special Abilities of the Sexes: Do They Begin in the Brain?" *Psychology Today*, 48ff.

Grundlach, R. (1977). "Sexual Molestation and Rape Reported by Homosexual and Heterosexual Women." *Journal of Homosexuality*, 2, 367–384.

Hall, J. R., and Black, J. D. (February, 1979). "Assertiveness, Aggressiveness, and Attitudes toward Feminism." *Journal of Social Psychology*, 107, 57–62.

Hansen, S. L., and Darling, C. A. (Spring, 1985). "Attitudes of Adolescents toward Division of Labor in the Home." *Adolescence*, 20, 61–72.

Harry, J. (October, 1979). "The Marital Liaisons of Gay Men." *Family Coordinator*, 28, 622–629.

Hertsgaard, D., and Light, H. (Winter, 1984). "Junior High Girls' Attitudes toward the Rights and the Roles of Women." *Adolescence*, 19, 847–853.

Hock, R. A., and Curry, J. F. (December, 1983). "Sex Role Identification of Normal Adolescent Males and Females as Related to School Achievement." *Journal of Youth and Adolescence*, 12, 461–470.

Holden, C. (1988). "Doctor of Sexology." *Psychology Today*, 22, 45–48.

Hotelling, K., and Forrest, L. (1985). "Gilligan's Theory of Sex-Role Development: A Perspective for Counseling." *Journal of Counseling and Development*, 64, 183–186.

Hughes, M., and Gove, W. R. (October, 1981). "Playing Dumb." *Psychology Today*, 74ff.

Kacerguis, M. A., and Adams, G. R. (July, 1979). "Implication of Sex Typed Child Rearing Practices, Toys, and Mass Media in Restricting Occupational Choices of Women." *Family Coordinator*, 369–375.

Keyes, A., and Coleman, J. (December, 1983). "Sex-Role Conflicts and Personal Adjustment: A Study of British Adolescents." *Journal of Youth and Adolescence*, 12, 443–459.

Kimura, D. (1985). "Male Brain, Female Brain: The Hidden Difference." *Psychology Today*, 19, 50–58.

Klein, M. M., and Shulman, S. (Spring, 1981). "Adolescent Masculinity-Femininity in Relation to Parental Models of Masculinity-Femininity and Marital Adjustment." *Adolescence*, 16, 45–48.

Kohlberg, L. (1966). "A Cognitive-Developmental Analysis of Children's Sex Role Concepts and Attitudes." In *The Development of Sex Differences*. Edited by E. Maccoby. Palo Alto, Calif.: Stanford University Press.

Lamke, L. I. (June, 1982). "Adjustment and Sex-Role Orientation in Adolescence." *Journal of Youth and Adolescence*, 11, 247–259.

Lamke, L. K., and Filsinger, E. E. (Summer, 1983). "Parental Antecedents of Sex Role Orientation." *Adolescence*, 18, 429–432.

Lamke, L. K., and Peyton, K. B. (1988). "Adolescent Sex-Role Orientation and Ego Identity." *Journal of Adolescence*, 11, 205–215.

Lueptow, L. B. (February, 1980). "Social Structure, Social Change, and Parental Influence in Adolescent Sex-Role Socialization: 1964–1975." *Journal of Marriage and the Family*, 42, 93–103.

McCary, J. L., and McCary, S. P. (1982). *Human Sexuality.* 4th ed. New York: D. Van Nostrand Co.

McDonald, G. W. (May, 1980). "Parental Power and Adolescents' Parental Identification: A Reexamination." *Journal of Marriage and the Family*, 42, 289–296.

Manville, W. H. (1969). "The Locker Room Boys." *Cosmopolitan*, 166, 110–115.

Marcus, D. E., and Overton, W. F. (June, 1978). "The Development of Cognitive Gender Constancy and Sex Role Preferences." *Child Development*, 49, 434–444.

Masters, W. H., and Johnson, V. E. (1979). *Homosexuality in Perspective.* Boston: Little, Brown.

"Medical First: Physical Link Found in Homosexuality" (September, 1984). Portland, ME.: *Portland Press Herald.*

Melson, G. F., and Fogel, A. (1988). "Learning To Care." *Psychology Today*, 22, 39–45.

Miller, B. C. (October, 1979). "Gay Fathers and Their Children." *Family Coordinator*, 28, 533–552.

Miller, M. M., and Reeves, B. (Winter, 1976). "Dramatic TV Content and Children's Sex-Role Stereotypes." *Journal of Broadcasting*, 20, 35–50.

Mills, C. J. (April, 1981). "Sex Roles, Personality, and Intellectual Abilities in Adolescents." *Journal of Youth and Adolescence*, 10, 85–112.

Money, J. (1987). "Sin, Sickness, or Status? Homosexual Gender Identity and Psychoneuroendocrinology." *American Psychologist*, 42, 384–399.

Money, J., and Ehrhardt, A. A. (1972). *Man and Woman, Boy and Girl.* Baltimore, Md.: Johns Hopkins University Press.

Money, J., and Russo, A. J. (1979). "Homosexual Outcome of Gender Identity Role in Childhood: Longitudinal Follow-up." *Journal of Pediatric Psychology*, 4, 29–41.

Nicholson, S. I., and Antill, J. K. (August, 1981). "Personal Problems of Adolescents and Their Relationship to Peer Acceptance and Sex-Role Identity." *Journal of Youth and Adolescence*, 10, 309–325.

Nixon, H. L., Maresca, P. J., and Silverman, M. A. (Winter, 1979). "Sex Differences in College Students' Acceptance of Females in Sport." *Adolescence*, 14, 755–764.

Norton, J. (1987). "Sexual Orientation in Children of Gay/Lesbian Parents." *Medical Aspects of Human Sexuality*, 21, 83–86.

Parlee, M. B. (November, 1978). "The Sexes under Scrutiny: From Old Biases to New Theories." *Psychology Today*, 62ff.

Persky, H., Smith, K. D., and Basu, G. K. (1971). "Relation of Psychologic Measures of Aggression and Hostility to Testosterone Production in Man." *Psychosomatic Medicine*, 33, 265–277.

Pleck, J. H. (September, 1981). "Prisoners of Manliness." *Psychology Today*, 69ff.

Powell, B., and Steelman, L. C. (May, 1982). "Testing an Underlisted Comparison: Maternal Effects on Sons' and Daughters' Attitudes toward Women in the Labor Force." *Journal of Marriage and the Family*, 44, 441–455.

Robinson, B. E., Skeen, P., Flake-Hobson, C., and Herman, M. (1982). "Gay Men's and Women's Perceptions of Early Family Life and Their Relationships with Parents." *Family Relations*, 31, 79–83.

Robinson, L. H., and Dalton, R. (1986). "Homosexuality in Adolescence." *Medical Aspects of Human Sexuality*, 20, 106–114.

Roopnarine, J. L. (January, 1986). "Mothers' and Fathers' Behaviors toward the Toy Play of Their Infant Sons and Daughters." *Sex Roles: A Journal of Research*, 14, 59.

Rosen, B. C., and Aneshensel, C. C. (September, 1978). "Sex Differences in Educational-Occupational Expectation Process." *Social Forces*, 57, 164–186.

Rust, J. O., and Lloyd, M. W. (Spring, 1982). "Sex-Role Attitudes and Preferences of Junior High School Age Adolescents." *Adolescence*, 17, 37–43.

Sadker, M., and Sadker, M. (March, 1985). "Sexism in the Schoolroom of the 80s." *Psychology Today*, 19, 54–57.

Small, A., Teagno, L., and Selz, K. (August, 1980). "The Relationship of Sex Role to Physical and Psychological Health." *Journal of Youth and Adolescence*, 9, 305–314.

Smith, M. D., and Self, G. D. (February, 1980). "The Congruence between Mothers' and Daughters' Sex-Role Attitudes: A Research Note." *Journal of Marriage and the Family*, 42, 105–109.

Snyder, M. (July, 1982). "Self-Fulfilling Stereotypes." *Psychology Today*, 60ff.

Stake, J. E., DeVille, C. J., and Pennell, C. L. (October, 1983). "The Effects of Assertive Training on the Performance Self-Esteem of Adolescent Girls." *Journal of Youth and Adolescence*, 12, 435–442.

Stephan, C. W., and Corder, J. (1985). "The Effects of Dual-Career Families on Adolescents' Sex-Role Attitudes, Work and Family Plans, and Choices of Important Items." *Journal of Marriage and the Family*, 47, 921–929.

Tognoli, J. (July, 1980). "Male Friendships and Intimacy across the Life Span." *Family Relations*, 29, 273–279.

U.S. Bureau of the Census. Department of Commerce. (1987). *Statistical Abstract of the United States*, 1987. Washington, D.C.: U.S. Government Printing Office.

Weeks, M. O., Wise, G. W., and Duncan, C. (Fall, 1984). "The Relationship between Sex-Role Attitudes and Career Orientations of High School Females and Their Mothers." *Adolescence*, 19, 595–607.

Weinberg, M. S., and Williams, C. J. (1974). *Male Homosexuals*. New York: Oxford University Press.

Wells, K. (February, 1980). "Gender-Role Identity and Psychological Adjustment in Adolescence." *Journal of Youth and Adolescence*, 9, 59–73.

White, K. M. (Spring, 1980). "Problems and Characteristics of College Students." *Adolescence*, 15, 23–41.

White, H. (1986). "Damsels in Distress: Dependency Themes in Fiction for Children and Adolescents." *Adolescence*, 82, 251–256.

Williams, K. (1988). "Parents Reinforce Feminine Role in Girls." *Medical Aspects of Human Sexuality*, 22, 106–107.

Winters, A. S., and Frankel, J. (Summer, 1984). "Women's Work Roles as Perceived by Lower Status White and Black Female Adolescents." *Adolescence*, 19, 403–415.

Zussman, J. U., Zussman, P. P., and Dalton, K. K. (April, 1975). *Postpubertal Effect of Prenatal Administration of Progesterone*. Paper presented at the Society for Research in Child Development dinner.

CHAPTER

15

Sexual Values, Behavior, and Education

The onset of puberty is accompanied by an increasing interest in sex. At first this interest is self-centered, focusing on the adolescent's bodily changes and observable happenings. Most adolescents spend a lot of time looking in the mirror or examining body parts in detail. This early concern is also centered on developing an acceptable body image rather than on erotic sensations or expression.

Gradually young adolescents become interested not only in their own development but also in that of others. More and more questions arise concerning development, changes, and sexual characteristics of the opposite sex. Adolescents also become fascinated with basic facts about human reproduction. Both boys and girls also slowly become aware of their own developing sexual feelings and drives and how these are aroused and expressed. Most adolescents begin some experimentation: touching themselves, playing with their genitals, exploring holes and crevices. Often by accident they experience orgasm through self-manipulation. Interest in sex as erotic feeling and expression increases. Adolescents begin to compare their ideas with those of others and spend a lot of time talking about sex, telling jokes, using sex slang, and exchanging sex-oriented literature. Adults are sometimes shocked at the language and jokes. Many parents have been horrified at finding "dirty" books hidden under the mattress. But these activities are motivated by a desire to understand human sexuality; they are a means of understanding, expressing, and gaining control over their sexual feelings.

Gradually also adolescents become more interested in sexual experimentation with others. Part of this is motivated by curiosity; part by a desire for sexual stimulation and release; part by a need for love, affection, intimacy, and acceptance from another person. In some adolescents, the need for emotional fulfillment and reassurance is a stronger motive for sexual participation than is physical fulfillment. Along with experimentation, however, comes concern over their own behavior.

Much has been written about a sexual revolution. This revolution has not been without its benefits. Most adolescents are far more open and honest about sex and have little hesitancy in talking about it. This attitude should contribute to more satisfying sex in marriage.

The "new morality" has also included some changes in sexual attitudes and behavior. The most recent research documents the increasing sexual permissiveness of youths, especially of females, and the fact that society now is pluralistic as far as sexual morality is concerned. We now tolerate and accept not one standard of sexual behavior but many. In general, adolescents now accept an individual ethic—the fact that all people must decide on their own standards for themselves (Marin, 1983).

These changes have not been without problems. Along with increased promiscuity has come a rise in venereal disease, illegitimacy, therapeutic abortions, and unwed pregnancy. The reason for the rise is that although adolescents have become more sexually active, a majority still are not regularly and responsibly using effective means of birth control.

Today's adolescents, along with those of past generations, are confronted with the task of making sexual decisions. Youths today have the same sexual drives and urges that other generations have had, but the difference is that these urges are being constantly stimulated and the guidelines for their control or expression are less clearly defined. Despite the sex literature, many adolescents are still uninformed or misinformed about their sexuality, resulting in the need for positive programs of sex education to counteract the half-truths and distortions and to help adolescents wade through a jungle of moral confusion (Parcel and Luttmann, 1981).

CHANGING ATTITUDES AND BEHAVIOR

Premarital Sexual Behavior

For a number of years, researchers indicated that the real revolution in sexual attitudes and behavior had occurred in the 1920s and had remained fairly constant since that time. In the late 1960s and early 1970s, however, researchers began to notice significant changes in attitudes and behavior (Bell and Coughey, 1980; Diepold and Young, 1979). Studies indicated a rapid rise in the percentage of youths engaging in heavy petting and premarital sexual intercourse.

The most recent survey of premarital sexual behavior of adolescent females 15 to 19 years of age is the National Survey of Family Growth (NSFG) conducted in 1982 (Hofferth, Kahn, and Baldwin, 1987). (See figure 15-1.)

The survey is significant because figures are calculated for the years 1971, 1976, 1979, and 1982. A trend toward an increase in premarital sexual intercourse during this period is evident. The proportion of U.S. teenage women who had premarital sexual intercourse rose from 32 percent in 1971 to 39 percent in 1976, 43 percent in 1979, and 45 percent in 1982. Virtually all growth in the incidence of **coitus** between 1979 and 1982 was accounted for by the growth in sexual activity among never-married white adolescent females. The rate among black adolescent females declined.

coitus

It is evident from figure 15-2 that premarital sexual activity has increased with age also. In 1982, 19 percent of 15-year-old girls had had premarital sexual intercourse. That percentage increased to 73 percent by age 19. A representative sample of never-married American women 20 to 24 years of age revealed that 80 percent had had sexual involvement (Tanfer and Horn, 1985). A greater percentage of black women (88 percent) had had intercourse than had white women (78 percent).

A 1979 survey also measured the percentage of men aged 17 to 21 who ever had intercourse before marriage. By 20 years of age, 81 percent of the men had had sexual intercourse. The percentage of men having premarital coitus continued somewhat greater than for women of comparable age. The rate for black men was greater than for white men. The average age at which the men first had intercourse was 15.7 years (Zelnik and Shah, 1983).

Correlates

Significant correlates with premarital sexual behavior are (Clayton and Bokemeier, 1980; Singh, 1980):

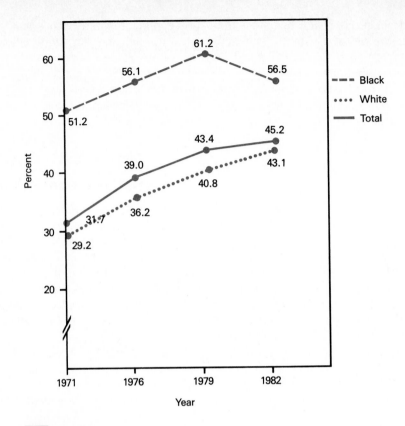

■ FIGURE 15-1

15 to 19-year-old females who ever had premarital intercourse, by year.

Statistics from: Hofferth, S. L., Kahn, J. R., and Baldwin, W. (1987). "Premarital Sexual Activity among U.S. Teenage Women Over the Past Three Decades." *Family Planning Perspectives, 19: 46–53.*

Race: Other things being equal, blacks report a higher incidence of premarital coitus than whites (Houston, 1981; Juhasz and Sonnenshein-Schneider, 1987, Singh, 1980).

Religion: Religiosity and a lower level of sexual permissiveness go together (Fisher and Hall, 1988; Gunderson and McCary, 1980; Juhasz and Sonnenshein-Schneider, 1980; Medora and Woodward, 1982).

Young age at first intercourse: Those who are youngest at first intercourse tend to be more permissive subsequently than do those who report older ages at first intercourse (Dignan and Anspaugh, 1978).

Liberality: A high level of sexual and social liberalism is correlated with a high level of sexual permissiveness (Troiden and Jendrek, 1987).

Sexual attractiveness: Those who feel they are the most sexually and socially attractive report the highest levels of sexual permissiveness (Mac-

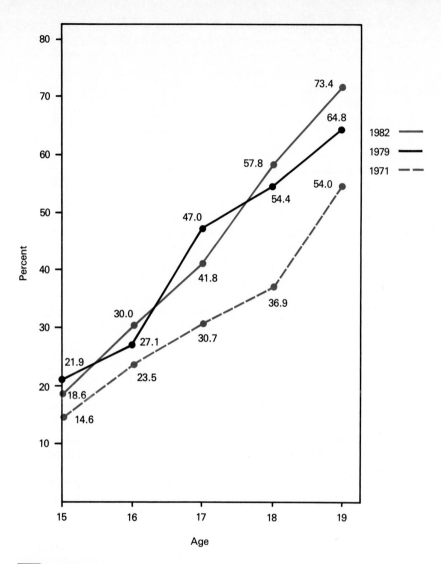

FIGURE 15-2

Females who ever had premarital sexual intercourse, by age, 1971, 1979, 1982.

Statistics from: Hofferth, S. L., Kahn, J. R., and Baldwin, W. (1987). "Premarital Sexual Activity among U.S. Teenage Women over the Past Three Decades." *Family Planning Perspectives,* 19: 46–53.

Corquodale and DeLamater, 1979; Murstein and Holden, 1979; Newcomer et al., 1983).

Parental standards and relationships: Parents who are most liberal in their views of premarital sexual intercourse are those most likely to have adolescents whose views are also liberal (Baker, Thalberg, and Morrison, 1988; Juhasz and Sonnensheim-Schneider, 1980; Thornton and Canburn, 1987).

Mothers' attitudes and standards of behavior when they were adolescents are especially influential in forming adolescent attitudes (Newcomer and Udry, 1984). One study showed that high school females whose mothers were employed outside the home had a greater tendency to engage in sex relations than did those whose mothers were not working. This was attributed to their greater independence and lack of supervision (Hansson et al., 1981). Parental strictness, discipline, and control show a curvilinear relationship to sexual attitudes and behavior. Sexual permissiveness is highest among adolescents who view their parents as not strict at all, lowest among parents who are moderately strict, and intermediate among those who perceive their parents to be very strict (Miller, et al., 1986).

Peer standards: Adolescents tend to form sexual standards close to peer standards (Juhasz, 1980; Shah and Zelnik, 1981). Furthermore, they are more likely to engage in sex when peers make involvement seem thrilling and exciting (Bauman and Udry, 1981; Billy and Udry, 1985).

Gender: Females tend to be less permissive than males, although this double standard is being eliminated slowly (Houston, 1981; Miller and Olson, 1988; Singh, 1980). Females do, however, place more emphasis on the quality of a relationship before intercourse takes place (Christopher and Cate, 1985).

Drug usage: Those who take drugs are more likely to have had premarital sexual intercourse than those who do not take drugs (Murstein and Holden, 1979).

Father absence: Girls particularly who grow up in a father-absent home are more likely to seek sexual relationships as a means of finding affection and social approval than are girls in father-present homes (Eberhardt and Schill, 1984; Newcomer and Udry, 1987; Stern, Northman, and Van Slyck, 1984).

Divorced and reconstituted families: Adolescents from divorced and reconstituted families report more sexual experience than those from intact families (Kinnaird and Gerrard, 1986).

Parents' education: Adolescents of parents with only a high school education or less are more likely to have experienced intercourse and more permissive attitudes than those with more education (Miller and Olson, 1988).

Changing Attitudes

There have been indications of changing attitudes toward premarital sexual permissiveness. Robinson and Jedlicka (1982) investigated the attitudes of college students at a large, southern state university toward the Judeo-Christian ethic as it relates to premarital sexual behavior. The researchers found a liberalization of student attitudes between 1965 and 1970 and an increasing conservatism since then. These results present an apparent contradiction. *While more students are engaging in sexual intercourse with increasing numbers of partners, at the same time they are more likely to view it as immoral and sinful.* This finding is in keeping with other research, which shows that not all those who indulge feel happy about it. A survey of 3,500 junior and senior high school students revealed that even among those who had intercourse, 25 percent of both sexes said they thought it was wrong (Zabin et al., 1984). Although in the minority, apparently some students are not able to accept their sexual behavior without negative feelings.

Recent national polls also indicate that there are an increasing number of older youths who say that premarital sexual intercourse is wrong. In 1985, 18 percent of 18- to 29-year olds opposed premarital intercourse, but in 1987, 27 percent were opposed (Gallup, 1987). The primary reason given for disapproval was because of moral or religious beliefs. The second most frequently cited reason for disapproval was the risk of sexually transmitted disease. Fear of AIDS was a key factor in the reversal of beliefs. The Gallup analysts concluded that the sexual revolution of the last quarter century may be coming to a halt and that the dramatic trend toward the acceptance of premarital intercourse has experienced a reversal in recent years.

Masturbation

The term **masturbation** refers to any type of self-stimulation that produces erotic arousal, whether or not arousal proceeds to orgasm. It is commonly practiced among both males and females in premarital, marital, and postmarital states. The reported incidence of masturbation varies somewhat among studies. A study of undergraduate students in a class on Human Relationships and Sexuality at the University of Northern Iowa revealed that 92 percent of the males and 64 percent of the females had masturbated (Story, 1982). A study of 18-year-olds revealed that over 90 percent of the males and at least 50 percent of the females masturbated (Diepold and Young, 1979).

masturbation

Practically all competent health, medical, and psychiatric authorities now say that masturbation is a normal part of growing up and does not have any harmful physical and mental effects, nor does it interfere with normal sexual adjustment in marriage. In fact, women who have never masturbated to orgasm before marriage have more difficulty reaching orgasm during coitus in the first year of marriage than do those who have masturbated to orgasm. Masturbation serves as a useful function in helping the individual to learn about his or her body, to learn how to respond sexually, and to develop sexual identity as well as to provide sexual release (Wagner, 1980). The only ill effect from masturbation comes not from the act itself but from guilt, fear, or anxiety when the adolescent believes the practice will do harm or create problems (Parcel and Luttmann, 1981). These negative emotions can do a great deal of harm. If numbers of youths continue to believe that masturbation is unhealthy or harmful but continue to practice it, anxiety eventually results.

Apparently old myths die hard. Many youths still believe that masturbation causes mental illness, idiocy, pimples, impotency, or other ills ascribed to it in the past. Much of the literature directed to adolescents or their adult leaders, teachers, or parents takes the viewpoint that masturbation is not harmful if it is not excessive. But what is excessive? An investigation by Haas (1979) revealed that two-thirds of the boys and half of the girls 16 to 19 years old masturbated once a week or more. There is no medical reason for limitation, and efforts to do so only shift the worry to what is too often. Masturbation should be considered excessive only in the same sense that reading or watching television can be excessive: the activities themselves are not bad, but when they become all-consuming they suggest the presence of problems that the individual is unable to handle. An adolescent who masturbates to the exclusion of normal friendships and social activities has a problem, not with masturbation, but in social relationships. The term *excessive* is vague, undefined, and subjective. Are adolescents who masturbate daily doing it to excess, especially if they seem to have made a happy emotional and social adjustment? As a general rule, it is probably best for parents to disregard evidence of masturbation in juveniles.

SEX AND ITS MEANING

Sex and Emotional Intimacy

With an increasing number of adolescents having sexual intercourse at younger ages, the question arises regarding the meaning attached to these relationships. Has the increase in premarital sexual intercourse been accompanied by emotional intimacy, development of loving feelings, and increasing commitment?

For years research has shown that the preferred standard for youth is permissiveness with affection. *However, there is a significant number of adolescents today who engage in coitus without affection or commitment.* Figure 15-3 shows the results of a survey among 237 (male and female) undergraduate students enrolled in 1986 at Illinois State University (Sprecher et al., 1988). The subjects ranged in age from 18 to 47 with a mean age of 20. All four undergraduate classes were represented. Ninety percent of the respondents were white, 8 percent black, and 2 percent other. Forty-nine percent were Catholic, 22% were Protestant, 3% Jewish, and the remainder were either another religion or no religion.

As indicated, 45 percent agreed that heavy petting was acceptable on a first date, 28 percent agreed that sexual intercourse was acceptable on a first date, and 22 percent found oral-genital sex acceptable on a first date. The comparable figures for casual dating showed that 61 percent approved of heavy petting, 41 percent approved of intercourse, and 28 percent approved of oral-genital sex while casually dating. The largest increase in acceptability for sexual behavior occurred between the casual and serious dating stages. Surprisingly, there were no significant differences according to gender, although there were differences according to age. The 16-year-olds were less sexually permissive than those 21 years of age.

Other research emphasizes gender as well as age differences in relation to coital activity (Earle and Perricone, 1986; McCabe, 1987). A survey among 929 students in 14 South Carolina colleges and universities during 1985 separated those who were early coital initiators (ECI—initial coitus at age 16 or younger) from late coital initiators (LCI—initial coitus from 17 to 20 years of age) (Faulkenberry, et al., 1987). Sixty-two percent of the male ECIs and 47 percent of the male LCIs had first intercourse with a casual acquaintance, unknown partner, or relative. This compares with 29 percent of the female ECIs and 16 percent of the female LCIs who had first intercourse with a casual acquaintance, unknown partner, or relative. Table 15-1 shows the results. These findings indicate that *far greater percentages of females than males had first coitus within the context of intimacy—with a steady or with an engaged partner.*

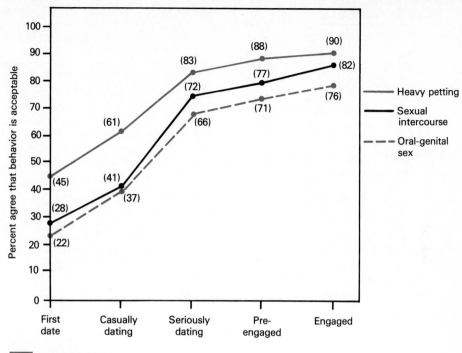

FIGURE 15-3

Acceptance of sexual activity by relationship stage.

From: Sprecher, S., McKinney, K., Walsh, R., and Anderson, C. (August 1988). "A Revision of the Reiss Premarital Sexual Permissiveness Scale." *Journal of Marriage and the Family*, 50: 821–828. Copyrighted 1988 by the National Council on Family Relations, 1910 West County Road B, Suite 147, St. Paul, Minnesota 55113. Reprinted by permission.

Sex and Satisfaction

Another way to examine the quality of present-day sexual practices is to examine the extent to which these relationships bring satisfaction and fulfillment to those involved. Darling and Davidson (1986) chose a sample of 328 never-married, sexually active male and female undergraduate students from a state university and examined their sexual behavior, attitudes, and concerns, as well as any changes they sought in their sex lives. Eighty-one percent of males but only 28 percent of females reported current satisfaction with their sexual experiences. The changes males desired centered on physical factors. Males desired more frequent intercourse, different positions for intercourse, more foreplay, oral-genital stimulation by their partner, their partner to use contraception rather than themselves, more frequent orgasms, a sex partner to be available on a more frequent basis, and more time before they had orgasm. They did mention an important social factor: the need for more verbal communication before and after sex.

TABLE 15-1

Percentage distribution of responses to questions concerning initial coital activity of ECIs and LCIs* by sex.

QUESTION AND RESPONSE	MALE		FEMALE	
	ECI (N = 95) %	LCI (N = 83) %	ECI (N = 80) %	LCI (N = 138) %
Question				
The first person with whom I engaged in sexual intercourse was				
Response				
Engaged partner	0	6	8	15
Steady boyfriend/girlfriend	38	47	64	70
Casual acquaintance	51	40	25	15
Unknown partner	6	7	1	1
Relative	5	0	3	0

* ECI = subjects having initial coitus at age 16 or younger; LCI = subjects having initial coitus from 17 to 20 years of age.

From: Faulkenberry, J. R., Vincent, M., James, A., and Johnson, W. (1987). "Coital Behaviors, Attitudes, and Knowledge of Students Who Experience Early Coitus." *Adolescence,* 22: 321–322.

Females also centered their attention on desired physical changes. They wanted more foreplay, more frequent orgasm, multiple orgasms, more time before male ejaculation, more frequent intercourse, different positions for intercourse, an available sex partner on a more frequent basis, stimulation of their nipples by their partner, and more time before orgasm by their partner. In addition to these physical factors, females mentioned the need for more verbal communication before and after sex and the need for more tenderness by their partner (see table 15-2) (Darling and Davidson, 1986).

The researchers comment:

The sexual concerns of these young men and women point to the apparent failure of the sexual revolution. While the incidence of various sexual behaviors would appear to have changed, *a further result has been a preoccupation with the race toward sexual intercourse and the achievement of orgasm. In the process, sexuality, affection, and intimacy have been sidetracked.* A further concern relating to our sexual "speedway" is that females feels pressured to achieve orgasm before they are ready . . . Females experience greater sexual enjoyment when they are involved in close interpersonal relationships with partners who are considerate of their emotional arousal and orgasmic needs (Darling and Davidson, 1986, pp. 416, 417).

■ TABLE 15-2

Desired changes in sexual lives of coitally active college students, by gender.

DESIRED CHANGE	PERCENT FEMALES	PERCENT MALES
More foreplay	43.8	39.1
More frequent orgasms	39.0	33.7
Ability to have multiple orgasms	34.3	35.9
More verbal communication after sex with partner	29.5	31.5
More time before male ejaculation	29.5	
More frequent intercourse	27.6	60.9
More verbal communication before sex with partner	21.9	30.4
Different positions for intercourse	20.0	46.7
Available sex partner/more frequent basis	19.-	32.6
More time before orgasm by partner	20.0	
More tenderness by partner	19.0	
Oral stimulation/nipples by partner	19.0	
Contraception by partner not self		35.9
Oral-genital stimulation by partner		37.0
More time before orgasm by self		29.3

Adapted from: Darling, C. A., and Davidson, J. K. (1986). "Coitally Active University Students: Sexual Behaviors, Concerns, and Challenges." *Adolescence*, 21: 403–419.

Sexual Pluralism and the Individual Ethic ■

Perhaps the only real answer to the question of meaning attached to present-day sexual practices is to recognize there are individual and social differences in sexual attitudes and behavior. We live in a **pluralistic society**: our society accepts not one but a number of standards of sexual behavior. There have been a number of efforts to categorize these standards. The work of Reis has been particularly noteworthy (Jurich, 1979; Reis, 1971). He outlined four standards of sexual permissiveness in our culture: *abstinence, double standard, permissiveness with affection*, and *permissiveness without affection*. But the present situation among adolescents would seem to require an expansion of Reis's categories to include the following:

pluralistic society

Abstinence
The double standard
Sex with affection, commitment, and responsibility
Sex with affection and commitment but without responsibility
Sex with affection and without commitment
Sex without affection
Sex with ulterior motives

The exact meaning of *abstinence* may vary depending on the point at which sexual activity ceases and abstaining begins. Some adolescents allow kissing only

HIGHLIGHT   The Exclusion of Intimacy

Some professionals feel that present-day teen-aged sexual relationships have no emotional meaning. Dr. W. Godfrey Cobliner of the Department of Gynecology/Obstetrics at the Albert Einstein School of Medicine, Bronx, New York, says that converging evidence from a variety of sources, including his own personal interviews, suggests that *sexual involvement is often sporadic, episodic, without commitment, and accompanied by a deliberate effort to suppress tender, romantic feelings and intimacy.* Cobliner has found an unmistakable disassociation from tenderness and love in the sexual involvement of some young people. The relationship between the sexes is goal directed and lacking in tenderness. The primary goal is a casual encounter of individual sexual gratification without shared intimacy. He says we have established a mode in which sex precedes the development of sentiment. Relationships with partners are expected to be unstable and transient.

One college male explains:

When I meet an attractive girl, I look for quick and easy pleasure. I make small talk, take her out to dinner—perhaps to a dance to make her come across. But they should not give too much warmth, should not become sentimental, and should not

cry. That would upset me. I stay cool. If any feelings well up in me, I check them at once. I am afraid of strong feelings of passion (Cobliner, 1988, p. 103).

A college-aged female explains:

As a woman, one has to be on guard if one has sex with a fellow one likes. One gets easily hurt if one gets involved. They make love to you, but then they leave. You never suspect it . . . You can get upset if you care for him. It takes you quite some time to recover . . . You can become the victim of your own strong feelings. I have to always be on guard. I have to curb my feelings (Cobliner, 1988, pp. 103, 104).

Cobliner indicates that the restraint of feelings leads to diminished sexual gratification and to a rise of two types of psychiatric disturbance—**depersonalization** and **derealization** (separation of the self from feelings). Sex, then, acts as a barrier and inhibitor of enduring attachment and a sense of continuity. Instead of promoting inner ease and well-being, the partners are perturbed and anxious to suppress the feelings of affection toward one another that accompany sexual union (Cobliner, 1988).

with affection; others kiss without affection. Kissing can be perfunctory, light kissing, heavy kissing, or French kissing. Some adolescents feel that necking is allowed (all forms of kissing and embracing) but disallow petting (body caresses below the neck). Others allow caressing of the female breasts but not of the genitals. Others engage in genital stimulation, even mutual masturbation to orgasm, but stop short of actual coitus. Some adolescents are technical virgins—meaning they never allow the penis to enter the vagina but engage in oral-genital, interfemoral stimulation (penis between the thighs), or other activity except intercourse itself.

The *double standard* refers to one standard of behavior for males, another for females. As will be seen in a later discussion, any differences in standards between males and females are slowly being eliminated (Bell and Coughey, 1980).

Some adolescents will engage in *sex only with affection, commitment, and responsibility*. They are in love; they are committed to each other and accept the responsibility and consequences of their actions. Responsibility in this case includes the use of dependable means of contraception to prevent unwanted pregnancies. In case of accidental pregnancy, they are willing to take full financial and other responsibility for whatever course of action they decide to pursue. But what does commitment mean? Interpretations vary. Some adolescents will have intercourse only if engaged, others only if they have an understanding to marry, others only if they are living together, others if they are committed to exclusive dating and going steady. "If you're in love and going steady, it's all right." But the distinguishing feature of this standard is that it includes love and responsibility as well as a defined degree of commitment.

Some adolescents want *sex with affection and commitment but without responsibility*. They are in love, have committed themselves to one another, usually on a temporary basis only, but assume no real responsibility for their actions. Because they do not show real concern and care for one another, one wonders how they define love. They show evidence of immature sexual behavior.

Sex with affection and without commitment has become the standard of many adolescents. They would not think of making love unless they really loved (liked) and felt affection for each other. They may or may not show responsibility in the practice of birth control but have made no promises or plans for the future. They are affectionate, are having intercourse, and that's it, at least for the time being.

Sex without affection characterizes people having sexual intercourse without emotional involvement, without the need for affection. They engage in sex for sex's sake because they like it, enjoy it, and do so without any strings attached. Some may be having sex for subconscious reasons and motives they do not recognize or understand. Some who practice this standard have already had sex with a large number of partners. Some of these people see nothing wrong with this and enjoy it. Others are promiscuous but feel conflict and guilt that they have difficulty controlling. Some people who have sex without affection are responsible in the use of contraceptives; others are irresponsible.

Sex with ulterior motives may include a number of different motives:

1. *To punish*—"She made me mad, so just for spite, I did it." In this case, sex becomes an expression of hostility, anger, or revenge. Some adolescents have sex and strive for pregnancy to get even with parents or to punish a former lover.
2. *To win or return favors*—to get gifts or as an exchange for a pleasant evening. "I spent fifteen dollars on you tonight; now what do I get?" "I can't thank you enough for the coat." This is really the prostitution of sex: giving sex as payment.

3. *To control behavior*—"If I sleep with you, will you marry me?" "Let's have a baby; then our parents will have to give us permission to marry."
4. *To build up the ego*—"Wait until the others find out whom I slept with last night." "I bet you five dollars I can score." "I'll show you who's irresistible."
5. *To exploit selfishly*—to use the other person for physical satisfaction without regard for that person's well-being or without regard for the consequences.

All these standards of behavior are being practiced in our culture. Most adolescents feel that what the other person does sexually is his or her own business; no one else has a right to interfere or judge. The only qualification they make is "as long as no one is hurt." Because intercourse involves two people, however, no ethic can be completely individualistic. At the very least it must take into account one's sex partner. One's actions may also affect many others: a child conceived out of wedlock, families and relatives, others in the community if one needs to turn to them for help or assistance. There is no such thing as behavior that does not affect someone else.

Not everyone who goes to bed with someone else does so out of love. Sex can mean "I love you," "I need you," "I don't care about you," or "I hate you and want to hurt you." Sex can therefore be either loving or hateful, helpful or harmful, satisfying or frustrating. The outcome will depend partially upon motives, meanings, and relationships, not just on whether one has it or does not. Sex is more than what one does; it expresses what one is and feels. Sex is not what you do but what you are. Morality is a question of how one human being deals with another human being, responsibility, or irresponsibility.

Sexual Aggression

One survey of 507 university men and 486 university women revealed that almost all (97.5% of the men and 93.5% of the women) had experienced unwanted sexual activity, such as kissing, petting, or intercourse (Muehlenhard and Cook, 1988). More men than women experienced unwanted intercourse. More women than men were likely to have engaged in unwanted kissing. The ten most important reasons given for engaging in unwanted sexual activity were: enticement by partners, altruism (desire to please partner), inexperience (desire to build experience), intoxication, reluctance (felt obligated, under pressure), peer pressure, sex-role concern (afraid of appearing unmasculine or unfeminine), threat to terminate the relationship, verbal coercion, or physical coercion. Whatever physical coercion existed was mostly of a nonviolent nature.

Another study of 275 undergraduate single women at Arizona State University revealed that over 50% of the participants reported being pressured into kissing, breast and genital manipulation, and oral contact with their partners' genitals (Christopher, 1988). The women rarely encountered either verbal threat of force or the use of physical force. The most common form of pressure was persistent physical attempts. The next most likely form of pressure was positive verbal statements that later proved to be untrue.

In other research, women report on their rejection strategies (Perper and Weis, 1987). These include: avoiding enticing behavior, avoiding intimate situations, ignoring sexual signals the man gives, using diversion and distraction, making excuses ("I have a big exam the next day."), saying "no," and physical rejection. Women also use delaying themes: "I'm not ready, wait. I need an emotional relationship." Women also threaten: "I'll not see you again if you don't stop." "I'll leave."

In another completely different type of study, university females reported on sexual offenses they had experienced since they were 14 years of age (Herold, Mantle, and Zemitis, 1979). Altogether, 84 *percent had experienced some type of sexual offense* Figure 15-4 shows the result.

CONTRACEPTIVES AND SEXUALLY TRANSMITTED DISEASES

Use of Contraceptives among Adolescents

With almost one-third of 16-year-old females and over two-thirds of 17-year-old females having premarital coitus, the rate of use of contraceptives becomes important (Zabin, 1981). What percentage of these young people are using some form of protection against pregnancy? Results from the 1979 Zelnik and Kantner (1980) study show that only 39 percent of 15- to 19-year-old unmarried girls *sometimes* used contraception; overall, only 34 percent of these teenage girls *always* used some method of contraception whenever they had intercourse; and 27 percent *never* used contraceptives. These figures indicate large numbers who are not

FIGURE 15-4

Percentage of females, age fourteen and over, experiencing sexual offenses.

From: Herold, E. S. et al. (Spring 1979). "A Study of Sexual Offenses against Females," *Adolescence* 14: 65–72. Used by permission.

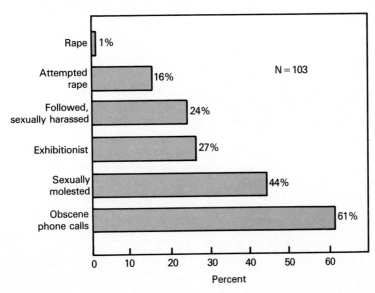

HIGHLIGHT   Date Rape

Date rape occurs on a voluntary, prearranged date, or after a woman meets a man on a social occasion and voluntarily goes with him (Koss, Gidyca, and Wisniewski, 1987). A survey of 282 university women revealed that 24 percent of their dates forcibly tried to have coitus. One-third of the coital attempts were successful. (Kanin and Parcell, 1977). Over half of the coital attempts were initiated without foreplay so these women certainly were not leading their dates on. One student wrote:

Charlie and I went parking after the movie. He asked me to get in the back seat with him, which I did, because I trusted him and felt safe with him. We necked and petted awhile and then he became violent. He ripped off my panties, pinned me down on the seat, and forced himself on me. I couldn't do anything about it. He had the nerve to ask me afterward if I enjoyed it (Student paper).

Men who rape women on a date are likely to have a history of repeated episodes of sexual aggression, where they use physical force to gain sexual ends. They are generally more aggressive than other men, and some are hostile to all women. Some exhibit symptoms of sexual sadism in which they experience arousal from a female's emotional distress (Heilbrun and Loftus, 1986). Greendlinger and Byrne (1987) found the likelihood of college men committing rape was correlated with their coercive fantasies, aggressive tendencies, and acceptance of the rape myth (that women like to be forced).

From Rice, F. P. (1989). *Human Sexuality.* Copyright © 1989 by Wm. C. Brown Publishers. Reprinted by permission.

protected against unwanted pregnancy. As a result, one out of every ten women aged 15 to 19 becomes pregnant each year in the United States (Trussell, 1988). Four out of five of these young women are unmarried. Among those who use contraceptives, the most popular method is the pill, followed by the condom (Beck and Davies, 1987). Withdrawal and rhythm, both relatively inefficient methods, are the next most commonly used methods. Only small percentages of adolescents use the diaphragm, sponge, IUD, or foam.

Why Contraceptives Are Not Used

The biggest problem is getting sexually active teenagers to use effective contraceptives in the first place. Even sexually active teenagers who say they do not want pregnancy often do not use contraceptives (Jones and Philliber, 1983). Users have to have a knowledge of methods, be willing to admit that they are sexually active, and be willing and able to obtain contraceptives as needed (McCary and McCary, 1982). Some students are misinformed about "safe" times and the likelihood of pregnancy. Many do not believe pregnancy will happen to them. One young man remarked about his girl: "She didn't look like the type" (Barret and Robinson, 1982, p. 350). There is a small percentage of unmarried adolescents who really want to get

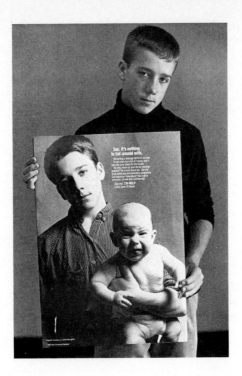

The biggest problem in preventing pregnancy is getting sexually active teenagers to use contraceptives. Male adolescents, as well as females, must be educated in the effective use of contraceptives. (© The Christian Science Monitor/Neal Menschel)

pregnant (Rogel et al., 1980). Some believe they are in love and that pregnancy will ensure marriage (Scott, 1983). Because some have moral objections to intercourse, they deny the consequences of pregnancy or romanticize about the thrills of maternity; or they hesitate to obtain help for fear of parental disapproval (Milan and Kilmann, 1987).

One study of 1,200 young women 12 to 19 years of age sought to find out why they delayed so long in going to the family planning clinic for birth control help (Zabin and Clark, 1981). Only 14 percent sought protection *before* first intercourse. Fifty percent were sexually active but not yet pregnant. The remaining 36 percent came to the clinic because they suspected pregnancy. Most of the sexually active delayed coming from three months to several years after first coitus. Only about half of the sexually active had used any method of contraception at last intercourse before coming to the clinic.

When asked why they delayed coming to the clinic, a variety of answers were given. Table 15-3 lists the most common answers in order of decreasing frequency. Several factors in this list and from other studies (Chamie et al., 1982; De Amicis et al., 1981; Herold, 1981; Herold and Goodwin, 1981; Urberg, 1982) stand out as particularly important. *One,* many of these adolescents showed anxieties and fears. They were afraid of parents or that birth control was dangerous or they were afraid of being examined (Lowe and Radius, 1987; Scott et al., 1988). Others did not get contraceptives because of fear or embarrassment about sex itself (Fisher, 1983). *Two,* they displayed widespread ignorance. They thought they had not had

▌ **TABLE 15-3**

Reasons for delaying going to the family planning clinic for birth control help.*

REASON	PERCENTAGE CITING CONTRIBUTING REASON
Just didn't get around to it	38.1
Afraid my family would find out if I came	31.0
Waiting for closer relationship with boyfriend	27.6
Thought birth control dangerous	26.5
Afraid to be examined	24.8
Thought it cost too much	18.5
Didn't think had sex often enough to get pregnant	16.5
Never thought of it	16.4
Didn't know where to get birth control help	15.3
Thought I had to be older to get birth control	13.1
Didn't expect to have sex	12.8
Thought I was too young to get pregnant	11.5
Thought birth control wrong	9.2
Partner opposed	8.4
Thought I wanted pregnancy	8.4
Thought birth control I was using was good enough	7.8
Forced to have sex	1.4
Sex with relative	0.7
Other	9.7

* Adapted, with permission, from Zabin, L. S., and Clark, S. D., Jr. (Sept.–Oct. 1981). "Why They Delay: A Study of Teenage Family Planning Clinic Patients," *Family Planning Perspectives*, 13: 205ff.

sex often enough to get pregnant, that they were too young, that birth control cost too much, that the method they were using was all right, that they had to be older to get help, or they did not know where to get help. *Three,* they showed a lack of maturity and responsibility. They had not got around to it or never thought of it so didn't plan for it (Gruber and Chambers, 1987). *Four,* they were ambivalent in their feelings (Levinson, 1986). They wanted to wait until they were closer to their boyfriend, they did not expect to have sex, they thought birth control was wrong, that their partner opposed it, or that they wanted pregnancy (Studer and Thornton, 1987). And *five,* a small number had delayed because sex had been forced upon them against their will, or they had been sexually abused by a relative.

The median delay of nine months for these women who did eventually get to a family planning clinic involved a period of prolonged risk of pregnancy. This of course did not include those who never got to a clinic at all, thereby increasing the risk, unless they went to a private physician. It is clear that *widespread education is needed no later than junior high school level if these youths are to avoid unwanted pregnancies* (Zabin and Clark, 1981; Zelnik and Kim, 1982).

HIGHLIGHT   Talking about Contraception

The Alan Guttmacher Institute sponsored a series of group discussions to investigate some possible reasons for poor contraceptive practices among teenagers. The following are comments of teenagers attending the discussion (M is the moderator and P the participant).

On lack of planning

M: Do you ever have sex without any method?

P: Sometimes. Sometimes I have no alternative.

P: When you're our age, you can't always say when you're going to have sex . . . because, you know. . . .

P: It just happens.

On taking a chance

P: There could be that casual guy you just met. You know it's going to be a big thing and you want to have sex with him, and you're not going to say, "Give me a few weeks. Let me get started on the pill" or "I'm going to run down to Planned Parenthood and get a diaphragm." . . . You take a chance.

On putting the responsibility on the girl

P: You really can't tell [whether or not the girl is on the pill]. Why bring it up? You know sooner or later. You can ask if you want to, and she can ask or tell you, but why do it? The girl is smart. I really don't think she would go through with it if she wasn't prepared. So, hey, I wouldn't say nothing.

M: So you are assuming that [if] she doesn't say anything, she is on something?

P: I don't care if she [is] or not. That's her problem.

On ambivalent feelings

P: If I did [use a contraceptive], then I'd have sex more. Then it would be too easy. The risk won't be there; the risk won't stop me.

M: Why do you need to stop? What's wrong with having sex?

P: I don't feel it's right. I haven't been raised that way.

On using withdrawal

P: You don't have to bother with putting on a rubber, bother with inserting foam, or taking a pill every day. It sounds like a cop-out, but you don't have to bother.

On confusion about the pill

P: She hears one thing, I hear something else. We don't travel in the same circles. She hears that she can't get pregnant for eight months after she goes off the pill. I hear I can't get pregnant 'til four months after I go off the pill. But I know someone who got pregnant a day after she stopped taking the pill.

On use of a condom

P: It's inconvenient, of course. The guys don't like them. [They say,] "It's unnatural, you know," [or] "I don't want to be cooped up," [or] "It's like having sex with a gym shoe."

Kisker, E. E. (March–April 1985). "Teenagers Talk about Sex, Pregnancy, and Contraception," *Family Planning Perspectives*, 17: 83–90. Reprinted with permission from *Family Planning Perspectives*.

Should Adolescents Have Contraceptives?

On June 9, 1977, the U.S. Supreme Court affirmed that no state could legally restrict the distribution of contraceptives to minors, that nonprescription devices could be dispensed by those other than registered pharmacists, and that such devices could be openly displayed and advertised (Beiswinger, 1979; *Carey*, 1977). The courts have also ruled that clinics do not have to notify parents before prescribing contraceptives for adolescents under age eighteen (Donovan, 1983). Whether adolescents should have access to contraceptives has been a controversial subject. Some adults are worried that the ready availability of contraceptives will increase promiscuity. Nevertheless, about 80 percent of adults agree that contraceptive information should be made available to everyone, including teenagers (Rinck, Rudolph, and Simkins, 1983). Evidence indicates that even if they do not have contraceptives, youths who are so inclined will have sexual intercourse anyhow. Most youths usually seek contraceptive help after they have already been having intercourse (Zelnik and Kantner, 1980). One study of black and Hispanic adolescents revealed a two-year time lapse between the age at first intercourse and the age at which they first visited the family planning clinic (Schwartz and Darabi, 1986). Many were afraid they were already pregnant when they went for help. Another study indicated that about one-third of the women being served in family planning clinics were in their teens (Furstenberg et al., 1983).

Making contraceptives available or unavailable therefore has almost no influence on whether youths have sex, but it may be a major determinant as to whether a particular girl gets pregnant ("New Insights," 1982). One of the major goals of sex education ought to be to provide education in contraception (Lincoln, 1984; Maslach and Kerr, 1983). Some who oppose sex education argue that they are afraid if teenagers "know too much," they will use their knowledge to "get into trouble." Evidence indicates, however, that sexual knowledge has no influence on sexual behavior (Lieberman, 1981). What really influences behavior are the values and morals accepted by individuals and the groups to which youths belong. The fact remains that since the Zelnick and Kantner (1980) study, contraceptives have become much more readily available to teenagers, but youths who have coitus use them only about half the time.

Sexually Transmitted Diseases

People of all ages (children, youth, and adults) may be exposed to sexually transmitted diseases (STDs) through sexual contact. At the present time, *Chlamydial infections* are the most common STDs (Judson, 1985). *Gonorrhea* is very common. Its incidence surpasses that of chicken pox, measles, mumps, and rubella combined (Silber, 1982). About one in every four cases of gonorrhea involves an adolescent. As many as one in thirty-five adolescents have *genital herpes* (Oppenheimer, 1982). Other STDs, such as *syphilis*, are also found among adolescents. Youth in the 20- to 24-year-old bracket are hardest hit by STDs, followed by 15- to 19-year olds (Carroll and Miller, 1982).

Authorities are becoming more concerned about the possibility of an AIDS epidemic among adolescents ("Kids and Contraceptives," 1987) because adolescents are sexually active and inconsistent contraceptive users. Many have unrealistic attitudes. They feel that "it won't happen to me," so they take unnecessary chances. In addition, about one-third of an adult male sample and one-fifth of an adult female sample reported having had homosexual experiences during adolescence (Petersen, et al., 1983). Furthermore, a small group of adolescents are intravenous drug users. *Adolescents who are most sexually active, who engage in homosexual contacts, and who are intravenous drug users comprise a high-risk group for contracting* AIDS; they can easily become infected and transmit the disease to others.

One of the problems is that the incubation period for AIDS may be from a few years to up to 10 years (Wallis, 1987). An adolescent can be exposed to the virus, carry it for years without knowing it, and not come down with the disease until after adolescence has passed. For this reason, not many cases are reported during adolescence itself.

UNWED PREGNANCY AND ABORTION

The net result of the increase in premarital sexual intercourse accompanied by a lack of efficient use of contraceptives has been an increase in the incidence of out-of-wedlock pregnancies, now estimated at 1 million each year among women 15 to 19 years of age. Of this number, 115,000 are miscarriages or stillbirths, 420,000 (42 percent) are induced abortions, and the remaining 465,000 babies are born alive. About 225,000 expectant mothers marry hastily before their babies are born, leaving 240,000 babies born out of wedlock in 1988 (Trussell, 1988).

Over 90 percent of teenage mothers decide to keep their babies. (Ulrike Welsch)

Over 90 percent of mothers decide to keep their babies (Alan Guttmacher, 1981). Some let their parents or other relatives adopt their babies, but the remainder want to raise their children themselves, assisted by whatever family or other help they can get. They have many motives for keeping their babies. One is to have someone to love. One mother said: "I planned on having this baby. She was no accident. I always wanted a baby so that I could have someone to care for. Now I can give her all the love that I never had myself." Another motive is to fulfill herself through her child.

From most points of view, unmarried motherhood of a young teenage girl is a tragedy (Kellam et al., 1982; Roosa, Fitzgerald, and Carlson, 1982). The single mother who decides to keep her baby may become entrapped in a self-destructive cycle consisting of failure to continue her education, repeated pregnancies, failure to establish a stable family life, and dependence on others for support (Rice, 1983). If she marries, the chances of her remaining married are only about one in five. Because few manage to complete their high school education, they are unable to get a good job to support themselves and their family and are likely to require welfare assistance for years (Dillard and Pol, 1982; Rice, 1983). Additional information on the adolescent mother may be found in chapter 17.

SEX KNOWLEDGE AND SEX EDUCATION

Adolescent Interests

One study of ninth-grade boys and girls from schools in the Boston area sought to discover the degree of interest in each of 112 topics listed on an interest checklist (Rubenstein, 1976). The topics covered a wide variety of subjects. The top thirteen topics are listed in table 15-4. Boys and girls selected twelve of the same topics, which is remarkable considering the total number on the list. Girls selected the topic "rape," which was not among the top thirteen topics on the boys' list and the boys selected "oral intercourse," which was not among the thirteen on the girls' list.

One surprising result was the adult level of concern of these fourteen-year-old adolescents. They were not interested in learning more about sexual anatomy, necking, petting, dating, masturbation, or menstruation. Their primary concerns were sexual intercourse, its consequences, and its context. Girls were interested in birth control; venereal disease; pregnancy, abortion; whether they would enjoy intercourse, fear it, or feel guilty; and whether it would be associated with love. Boys were more interested in the pleasure-punishment aspects of sex—enjoyment of sex, sexual intercourse, and oral-genital intercourse—although they too were interested in venereal disease, birth control, pregnancy, abortion, and in love, guilt, and fear as accompaniments of sex. Both boys and girls were interested in sex offenses and prostitution. These findings are in keeping with other studies that show students' interests are in intercourse, birth control, venereal disease, and pregnancy (McCormick, Folcik, and Izzo, 1985). Any sex education curriculum should take these interests into consideration.

TABLE 15-4

Top thirteen sexual topics of interest to ninth-grade boys and girls, in order of interest.

GIRLS	BOYS
Birth control	Venereal disease
Abortion	Enjoyment of sex
Birth control pill	Sexual intercourse
Venereal disease	Birth control
Pregnancy	Love
Love	Oral intercourse*
Fear of sex	Pregnancy
Guilt about sex	Abortion
Rape*	Guilt about sex
Enjoyment of sex	Birth control pill
Sexual intercourse	Fear of sex
Sex offenses	Sex offenses
Prostitution	Prostitution

* Not listed by the opposite sex among the top thirteen items.

From: Rubenstein, J. S. (Winter, 1976). "Young Adolescents' Sexual Interests," *Adolescence*, 11: 487–496. Used by permission.

Sources of Sex Information

Two hundred eighty-eight students from five public schools were surveyed to determine their sources of sexual information, their sexual knowledge, and sexual interests (Davis and Harris, 1982). The students ranged in age from eleven to eighteen and were in grades six through twelve. A little over one-third were Anglo, a little over one-third were Hispanic, and about one-fourth were Native American Navajo and Pueblo Indians. Sixty-four percent were female and 36 percent male. A little over one-half were from rural schools in small communities, and the remainder were from urban schools in large communities. Table 15-5 shows the percentages of students receiving information from different sources.

As predicted, *friends* were the most frequently cited source of sexual information followed by *schools*, *books and magazines*, and *parents*. The majority of students received a little information from *television and movies*, but less than 8 percent received any information from *church*. Surprisingly, *brothers and sisters* and *doctors and nurses* were named by only half the students as sources of information about sex. Females reported receiving more information about sex from their parents and less from movies than did males. Older students were likely to receive more information from friends and less from movies, indicating a greater freedom among older students to discuss sexual topics.

TABLE 15-5

Percentages of students receiving information from different sources.

SOURCE	A LOT	A LITTLE	NONE
Friends	43.5	47.4	9.1
School	36.0	47.7	16.3
Books/magazines	25.5	51.0	23.4
Parents	26.1	50.2	23.7
Movies	18.6	51.9	29.5
Television	9.8	55.8	34.4
Brothers/sisters	20.3	32.9	46.9
Doctors/nurses	15.1	33.8	51.1
Church	2.8	4.6	92.6
Other	15.2	16.6	68.3

From: Davis, S. M., and Harris, M. B. (Summer, 1982). "Sexual Knowledge, Sexual Interests, and Sources of Sexual Information of Rural and Urban Adolescents from Three Cultures," *Adolescence*, 17: 478.

Of the three ethnic groups, Anglo students appeared to be the most knowledgeable and the Native American Indians the least. Females indicated a greater knowledge of sexual facts and terms than did males and a greater degree of interest than males in a number of terms. Older subjects scored higher on tests of sexual knowledge, indicating that formal or informal sex education was taking place. They also were more interested in terms like *pregnancy* and *birth control*, reflecting their greater likelihood of having intercourse (Davis and Harris, 1982).

The Parents' Role

If, as some people maintain, the place of sex education is in the home, then parents are not doing a very good job. Fox and Inazu (1980) found that only about one-third of the 449 mothers in their study had talked with their 14- or 15-year-old daughters about intercourse or birth control. Not quite one-half had discussed menstruation and sexual maturity. Parents were not the best source of factual information about sex. Another study of over 500 adolescents and their mothers indicated that whatever parent-child communication about sex took place had no effect on the teenagers' subsequent sexual and contraceptive behavior (Newcomer and Udry, 1985). Not all studies agree with these findings, however. Most research reveals that parents are an important source of transmission of values and attitudes and do have an influence on adolescent attitudes and behavior, especially by way of example (Fisher, 1986; Shah and Zelnick, 1981). As far as providing formal sex education is concerned, however, many parents are deficient.

There are a number of reasons for this:

Some parents are too embarrassed to discuss the subject, or they deal with it in negative ways. Many parents have been brought up to feel that all sex is wrong and dirty and become intensely uncomfortable any time the subject is mentioned. Some have a pathological, irrational fear of sex, generated by years of repressive and negative teaching. If they do discuss sex, the messages they give their children are negative ones, which interfere with sexual satisfaction (Darling and Hicks, 1982). Some adolescents also feel embarrassed talking to their parents so do not discuss the subject with them (Fox and Inazu, 1980).

Parents have difficulty overcoming the incest barrier between themselves and their adolescents. That is, the taboo on parent-child sexual behavior may be so strong that any verbalization about sex in this relationship becomes almost symbolic incest. It has been found that even in families where there has been some communication about sex with young children, this communication drops as the children approach adolescence.

Some parents are uninformed and do not know how to explain to their children. One mother remarked, "I don't understand menstruation myself, so how can I explain it to my daughter?" But parents need more than background knowledge and subject matter; they also have to have practice in putting ideas together in words in ways meaningful to their children. The author has found that when parents are given sample questions that children ask, the parents learn by having to struggle to put the answer into words. After some practice, parents are able to explain easily.

Some parents are afraid that knowledge will lead to sexual experimentation; they do not tell their children because they want to keep them innocent. The old argument is: Keep them ignorant and they won't get into trouble (Roosa, 1983). In fact, the reverse is true: youths who are uninformed are more likely to get into trouble. There is no evidence to show that sexual knowledge per se leads to sexual experimentation. There is a lot of evidence to show that ignorance leads to trouble.

Other parents tell too little too late. Most parents are shocked to learn that the time to explain the basic physical facts about reproduction is *before* puberty. Most children ought to know about fertilization and how it takes place in humans by ages seven to nine. For some children, this is too late; they ask questions during the preschool period that demand a simple, honest explanation. The parent who says, "Wait until you are older" is running the risk of telling too little too late. The time to explain about menstruation is before the girl starts her menses, not after. As one boy said, "All the way through my childhood, whenever I asked questions about sex, my parents would say: 'Wait until you're older.' Now that I'm 18 and I ask them something, they remark, 'For Pete's sake, you're 18 years old, you ought to know that!'"

Some parents set a negative example at home. It is not just the words parents use that are important; it is also the lives they lead and the example they set (Strouse and Fabes, 1985). One adolescent remarked: "My parents never came out and actually told me the facts of life. . . . But indirectly they told me plenty. They made me feel that sex was dirty and something to be ashamed of or embarrassed about."

Parents can do a better job by becoming better informed, both to increase their own knowledge and to be more comfortable in talking about sexuality. Reading or attending classes in human sexuality will help parents tremendously. The schools can play an important role by teaching parents so they can do a better job of teaching their children (Alexander, 1984). Parents can also help start and support family life and sex education programs in the schools to supplement their own efforts.

Role of Public Schools

Nationwide surveys indicate that about 75 percent of parents favor sex education in the schools. (Richardson and Cranston, 1981). Because so many parents do an inadequate job and adolescents need more reliable sources of information than peers, the public schools have a responsibility. There are several reasons.

Family life and sex education are natural parts of numerous courses already offered to adolescents. Biology courses should cover the reproductive system when other bodily systems are discussed; not to do so is hypocritical. It is difficult to study sociology or social problems without including a study of the family as the basic social unit or of social problems such as illegitimacy, early marriage, or divorce. Health education usually includes such topics as menstrual hygiene, masturbation, acne, venereal disease, and body odor. Home economics deals with parent-teen relationships, preparation for marriage, and child care and development. Literature courses may stimulate discussion about youth in today's world, moral values, interpersonal relationships, or other topics properly belonging to family life and sex education. Discussions of sex or sex behavior are hard to avoid in a course in the modern novel or in poetry. Even the study of the Bible as literature contains a sexual aspect. Thus, if existing courses are taught honestly, family life and sex education will have a place in many of them.

Preparing youth for happy marriage and responsible parenthood is an important educational goal (Kirby and Scales, 1981). It is certain that having a happy marriage and being good parents are among the most important personal goals of the average parent. If the school does not prepare youth for this goal, as well as for a vocation, is it preparing them for living as well as for making a living?

The school is the only social institution that reaches all youth and therefore has a unique opportunity to reach youth who need family life and sex education the most (Dryfoos, 1984; Scales and Kirby, 1981). Some parents do an excellent job, but the majority of parents do not. Are their children to be deprived of proper information, attitudes, examples, and guidance? One would hope not. Other community youth-service organizations such as churches and scouts have a responsibility also, for family life and sex education of youth is a community responsibility. None of these groups reaches as many youths, especially those of low socioeconomic status, as does the school.

The school, as the professional educational institution, is or can be equipped to do a fine job. This does not mean that all teachers are qualified to teach or that the individual school already has the expertise and resources to develop a program, but it does mean that the school is able to train teachers (Schultz and Boyd, 1984), develop curricula, and provide the necessary resources once priorities and needs are established. (For more information on sex education in the schools, see: Arcus, 1986; Gunderson and McCary, 1980; Harriman, 1986; Kirby and Scales, 1981; Leigh, Loewen, and Lester, 1986; Marsman and Herold, 1986; Parcel and

Luttmann, 1981; Philliber and Tatum, 1982; Richardson and Cranston, 1981; Scales, 1981; and Silverstein and Buck, 1986.)

Availability in the Schools █

Numerous public opinion polls have shown that sex education in the schools has strong support. But to what extent are schools providing programs? A national study of sex education at all grade levels in large school districts (cities over 100,000 population) revealed that 67 percent of districts with elementary grades, 75 percent of those with junior high school grades, and 76 percent of those with senior high school grades provided some sex education to some portion of their students (Sonenstein and Pittman, 1984). Of those offering sex education, 61 percent of the districts offered sex education at all three levels. Of those elementary districts offering sex education, all said they integrated the material into other curriculum subjects, but 60 percent provided only five or fewer hours of instruction. Of those secondary districts offering sex education, 73 percent of junior high and 89 percent of senior high provided six or more hours of instruction. Of those offering sex education, 11 percent of junior high and 16 percent of senior high districts offered separate sex education courses. Of those with programs, over 40 percent made participation compulsory at all grade levels.

There is a difference, however, between offering sex education and comprehensive sex education. Table 15-6 indicates the total percentages of large city schools that include a particular topic in their sex education curriculum, by comprehensiveness of the program. Column 1 lists the proportions of large city school districts discussing the topics at any grade. More than one-half the districts discussed all the topics. Column 2 gives the percentage discussing each topic with 75 percent of the students enrolled. Using this criterion, 35 to 45 percent of the districts covered each topic.

The third column shows the percentage of districts that discuss each topic with 75 percent enrollment and for at least one class period. When this measure of comprehensiveness is used, only 6 to 37 percent of the districts discuss the topic. The fourth column shows the proportion of all districts discussing each topic, with 75 percent enrollment, for at least one class period, with the topics introduced before the ninth grade. Using this criterion, an average of 27 percent of districts cover topics in the physiological cluster, 18 percent cover interpersonal issues, 13 percent cover pregnancy avoidance, and only a few cover the most controversial topics. Thus, comprehensive discussions before the ninth grade are quite rare.

Over one-half the schools said that one of their major goals was to reduce teenage pregnancy and childbearing. Yet only 19 to 25 percent of districts offering in-depth sex education talked about family planning sources and contraceptives, and only 7 to 11 percent did so before ninth grade. About one-fourth of those districts offered in-depth discussion of intercourse and pregnancy possibilities, the consequences of pregnancy, and sexual decision making (Sonenstein and Pittman, 1984).

■ TABLE 15-6

Percentage of large city school districts that include a particular topic in their sex education curriculum, by comprehensiveness of program.

TOPIC	1 TOPIC DIS- CUSSED	2 75% ENROLL- MENT	3 IN-DEPTH DISCUS- SION	4 TOPIC INTRODUCED BEFORE NINTH GRADE
Physiological				
Changes at puberty	71.5	43.7	36.8	36.6
Physical differences	72.1	45.4	32.2	31.4
Sexually transmitted diseases	71.5	44.3	37.4	27.3
Responsibilities of parenthood	69.3	43.7	32.8	17.4
Pregnancy and childbirth	67.0	42.0	31.0	23.3
Interpersonal issues				
Love relationships and commitment	65.4	41.4	28.7	16.9
Sexual feelings and attraction	68.2	42.0	26.4	20.3
Consequences of teen pregnancy	66.4	40.8	27.0	18.6
Communication with opposite sex	63.1	40.8	23.6	18.0
Intercourse and pregnancy probability	65.4	41.4	25.3	21.5
Teen marriage	65.9	40.8	25.3	7.6
Personal values	63.1	39.7	28.7	19.8
Sexual decision making	64.2	41.4	26.4	18.6
Contraception and family planning				
Most likely time in cycle for pregnancy	65.9	40.8	19.0	14.0
Family planning sources	63.7	41.4	19.0	7.0
Communication with parents	62.0	37.9	19.0	16.3
Resistance to peer pressure for sex	64.8	40.8	23.6	18.6
Contraceptives	62.0	39.1	24.7	11.0
Media messages about sex	61.5	40.8	18.4	11.0
Controversial issues				
Rape and sexual abuse	63.7	41.4	18.4	8.7
Masturbation	56.4	37.9	5.7	1.7
Abortion	54.7	34.5	8.0	2.3
Gynecologic examination	58.1	35.1	7.5	2.3
Homosexuality	52.0	35.1	6.3	2.9

From: Sonenstein, F. L., and Pittman, K. J. (January–February, 1984). "The Availability of Sex Education in Large City School Districts," *Family Planning Perspectives*, 16: 19–25. Reprinted with permission from *Family Planning Perspectives*.

HIGHLIGHT   School Birth Control Clinics

Deeply disturbed by the rising tide of teenage pregnancies and the threat of AIDS, some high school administrators now offer contraceptive education programs and contraceptive services in birth control clinics right on the school premises. To many, the idea of a school-based clinic that deals with sex is shocking. Critics argue that to provide such services is condoning teenage sex, but proponents say that family planning programs in high schools are responses to desperate situations. A clinic was established in DuSable High School in Chicago because more than one-third of 1,000 female students in the school found themselves pregnant each year (Plummer, 1985).

The high rate of pregnancies resulted in a 50 percent dropout rate from school. One function of the clinic is to keep pregnant girls in school to continue their education. The DuSable High School clinic is just one of many school-based clinics that have been established across the country. Dozens of other cities have established similar programs. This approach is pragmatic. It is based on the realization that adolescents can at least be protected from unwanted pregnancy and from sexually transmitted disease even if they are not going to reduce their sexual activity (Zellman, 1982).

Other studies have revealed that formal sex instruction can have a positive influence on contraceptive knowledge and behavior (Dawson, 1986). Therefore, *contraception and the prevention of unwanted pregnancy ought to be among the most important topics discussed in planned programs.*

Another nationwide study of high schools showed that only about one-third offered separate courses in sex education. Of those four-year schools offering courses, only one-half did so beginning at ninth grade (Orr, 1982). Although significant gains have been made, too many schools offer too little, too late. One nationwide study indicated that large proportions of adolescents initiated coitus before they took a sex education course (Marsiglio and Mott, 1986).

SUMMARY

Premarital sexual attitudes and behavior have changed radically since the early 1970s. Those changes include an increase in premarital intercourse during adolescence, especially for women, a decrease in the age at first intercourse, and an increase in the number of those believing their own behavior is immoral or sinful.

Almost all adolescent males and over half of all females masturbate regularly. The practice is not harmful and should be considered normal.

With increasing numbers of adolescents having sexual intercourse at younger ages, the question arises regarding the meaning attached to these relationships. While the preferred standard of youth is permissiveness with affection, many engage in coitus without affection or commitment. Women are less likely to have sex without affection than men. There is some evidence that both men and women are preoccupied with the race toward sexual intercourse and achievement of orgasm, leaving affection and intimacy sidetracked.

However, not all adolescents have the same standards. Our society is pluralistic: it accepts not one but a number of different standards of sexual behavior. Those standards might be grouped into different categories: abstinence, double standard, sex with affection, commitment, and responsibility, sex with affection and commitment but without responsibility, sex with affection and without commitment, sex without affection, and sex with ulterior motives.

One of the problems adolescent boys and girls face is the pressure to engage in unwanted sexual activity. Date rape is not uncommon.

Only about one-third of 15- to 19-year-olds use contraception every time they have intercourse. There are various reasons why contraceptives are not used: fear and anxiety, ignorance, lack of maturity and responsibility, ambivalent feelings about sex, a desire to get pregnant, or rape. Ready availability of contraceptives does not increase promiscuity since, on the average, adolescents have been sexually active for nine months before going to a family planning center, but it does decrease unwanted pregnancy.

With so many adolescents being sexually active and not using reliable means of birth control, the number of premarital pregnancies among 15- to 19-year-olds has skyrocketed to over 1 million a year. Slightly over one-half are terminated by miscarriages, stillbirths, or therapeutic abortions. The remaining babies are born alive. About one-half of these mothers marry hastily before their babies are born, leaving 240,000 babies born out of wedlock each year.

Adolescents need sex education, with special focus on topics of concern to them—sexual intercourse, birth control, venereal disease, pregnancy, abortion— but also on love, guilt, and fear as accompaniments of sex. The following are the most frequently cited sources of sexual information, in order of decreasing frequency: friends, school, books and magazines, parents, movies, television, brothers/sisters, doctors/nurses, and church. Pornographic literature, especially that depicting violence, is considered harmful by some.

Parents are not doing a good job of sex education at home because they are too embarrassed, they have difficulty overcoming the incest barrier, they are uninformed, they are afraid knowledge leads to experimentation, they tell too little, too late, or they set a negative example at home.

The public schools have an important role, and the majority of parents support sex education in the schools. National studies of large school districts indicate that between 67 and 76 percent of districts offer some sex education to some portion of their students. Of those offering sex education, 61 percent offer it at all grade levels.

The programs in elementary school are usually integrated into other curriculum subjects, but 60 percent provide five or fewer hours of instruction. The higher the grade level, the more hours are offered and the more comprehensive the program becomes. Only a minority of junior and senior high districts offer separate sex education courses. Only about one-fourth of large city school districts offer comprehensive programs, discussing each topic, with 75 percent enrollment, for at least one class period, before the ninth grade level. Research of exemplary programs reveals that they accomplish their objectives.

Some schools have established birth control clinics in high school as one effective means of helping to combat teenage pregnancies.

DISCUSSION QUESTIONS

1. What changes have you seen in sexual attitudes and behavior since you were in high school?
2. Why don't more sexually active adolescents use effective contraceptives? What can be done to improve the situation?
3. What can be done to reduce the number of unwed pregnancies?
4. Should adolescents marry because of pregnancy? Why or why not?
5. What are the alternatives to abortion for teenage pregnancy? What do you think of them?
6. Comment on the statement: "Adolescents' primary source of sex information is their friends." How do you feel about this?
7. Did your parents tell you about sex when you were growing up? What did they tell you? How did they tell you?
8. What role could the school play in assisting parents? Why? Why doesn't the school do so?
9. Should sex education in the school be compulsory? For what grade levels? Who should teach it?
10. Did you have sex education in the schools in which you were brought up? Comment on the programs.

BIBLIOGRAPHY

Alan Guttmacher Institute. (1981). *Teenage Pregnancy.* New York: Alan Guttmacher Institute.

Alexander, S. J. (April, 1984). "Improving Sex Education Programs for Young Adolescents: Parents' Views." *Family Relations, 33,* 251–257.

Arcus, M. (1986). "Should Family Life Education Be Required for High School Students? An Examination of the Issues." *Family Relations, 35,* 347–356.

Baker, S. A., Thalberg, S. P., and Morrison, D. M. (1988). "Parents' Behavioral Norms as Predictors of Adolescent Sexual Activity and Contraceptive Use." *Adolescence, 23,* 265–282.

Barret, R. L., and Robinson, B. E. (July, 1982). "A Descriptive Study of Teenage Expectant Fathers." *Family Relations, 31,* 349–352.

Bauman, K. E., and Udry, J. R. (Fall, 1981). "Subjective Expected Utility and Adolescent Sexual Behavior." *Adolescence, 16,* 527–535.

Beck, J. G., and Davies, D. K. (1987). "Teen Contraception: A Review of Perspectives on Compliance." *Archives of Sexual Behavior, 16,* 337–368.

Beiswinger, G. L. (1979). "The High Court, Privacy, and Teenage Sexuality." *Family Coordinator, 28,* 191–198.

Bell, R. R., and Coughey, K. (July, 1980). "Premarital Sexual Experience among Coeds, 1958, 1968, and 1978." *Family Relations, 29,* 353–357.

Billy, J. O. G., and Udry, J. R. (Spring, 1985). "The Influence of Male and Female Best Friends on Adolescent Sexual Behavior." *Adolescence, 20,* 21–32.

Carey v. Population Services International (1977). 75–443.

Carroll, C., and Miller, D. (1982). *Health: The Science of Human Adaptation* (3rd ed). Dubuque, IA.: Wm. C. Brown.

Chamie, M., Eisman, S., Forrest, J. D., Orr, M. T., and Torres, A. (May–June 1982). "Factors Affecting Adolescents' Use of Family Planning Clinics." *Family Planning Perspectives 14,* 126ff.

Christensen, H. T., and Johnson, L. B. (1978). "Premarital Coitus and the Southern Black: A Comparative View." *Journal of Marriage and the Family, 40,* 721–732.

Christopher, F. S. (1988). "An Initial Investigation into a Continuum of Premarital Sexual Pressure." *The Journal of Sex Research, 25,* 255–266.

Christopher, F. S., and Cate, R. M. (April, 1985). "Anticipated Influences on Sexual Decision-Making for First Intercourse." *Family Relations, 34,* 265–270.

Clayton, R. R., and Bokemeier, J. L. (November, 1980). "Premarital Sex in the Seventies." *Journal of Marriage and the Family*, 42, 759–775.

Cobliner, W. G. (1988). "The Exclusion of Intimacy in the Sexuality of the Contemporary College-Age Population." *Adolescence*, 23, 99–113.

Darling, C. A., and Davidson, J. K. (1986). "Coitally Active University Students: Sexual Behaviors, Concerns, and Challenges." *Adolescence*, 22, 403–419.

Darling, C. A., and Hicks, M. W. (June, 1982). "Parental Influence on Adolescent Sexuality: Implications for Parents as Educators." *Journal of Youth and Adolescence*, 11, 231–244.

Davis, S. M., and Harris, M. B. (Summer, 1982). "Sexual Knowledge, Sexual Interests, and Sources of Sexual Information of Rural and Urban Adolescents from Three Cultures." *Adolescence*, 17, 471–492.

Dawson, D. A. (1986). "The Effects of Sex Education on Adolescent Behavior." *Family Planning Perspectives*, 18, 162–170.

DeAmicis, L. A., Klorman, R., Hess, D. W., and McAnarney, E. R. (Spring, 1981). "A Comparison of Unwed Pregnant Teenagers and Nulligravid Sexually Active Adolescents Seeking Contraception." *Adolescence*, 16, 11–20.

Diepold, J., Jr., and Young, R. D. (1979). "Empirical Studies of Adolescent Sexual Behavior: A Critical Review." *Adolescence*, 14, 45–64.

Dignan, M., and Anspaugh, D. (1978). "Permissiveness and Premarital Sexual Activity: Behavioral Correlates of Attitudinal Differences." *Adolescence*, 13, 703–711.

Dillard, K. D., and Pol, L. G. (April, 1982). "The Individual Economic Costs of Teenage Childbearing." *Family Relations*, 31, 249–259.

Donovan, P. (May–June 1983). "Challenging the Teenage Regulations: The Legal Battle." *Family Planning Perspectives*, 15, 126–130.

Dryfoos, J. G. (July–August 1984). "A New Strategy for Preventing Teenage Childbearing." *Family Planning Perspectives*, 16, 193–195.

Earle, J. R., and Perricone, P. J. (1986). "Premarital Sexuality: A Ten Year Study of Attitudes and Behavior in a Small University Campus." *The Journal of Sex Research*, 22, 304–310.

Eberhardt, C. A., and Schill, T. (Spring, 1984). "Differences in Sexual Attitudes and Likeliness of Sexual Behaviors of Black Lower-Socioeconomic Father-Present vs. Father-Absent Female Adolescents." *Adolescence*, 19, 99–105.

Faulkenberry, J. R., Vincent, M., James, A., and Johnson, W. (1987). "Coital Behaviors, Attitudes, and Knowledge of Students Who Experience Early Coitus." *Adolescence*, 22, 321–332.

Fisher, T. D. (1986). "Parent-Child Communication about Sex and Young Adolescents' Sexual Knowledge and Attitudes." *Adolescence*, 21, 517–527.

Fisher, T. D., and Hall, R. G. (1988). "A Scale for the Comparison of the Sexual Attitudes of Adolescents and Their Parents." *The Journal of Sex Research*, 24, 90–100.

Fisher, W. A. (March, 1983). "Why Teenagers Get Pregnant." *Psychology Today*, 17, 70, 71.

Fox, G. L., and Inazu, J. K. (July, 1980). "Mother-Daughter Communication about Sex." *Family Relations*, 29, 347–352.

Furstenberg, F. F., Jr., Shea, J., Allison, P., Herceg-Baron, R., and Webb, D. (September–October 1983). "Contraceptive Communication among Adolescents Attending Family Planning Clinics." *Family Planning Perspectives*, 15, 211–217.

Gallup, G. (1987). "More Today Than in 1985 Say Premarital Sex is Wrong." *The Gallup Report*, 263, 20.

Greendlinger, V., and Byrne, D. (1987). "Coercive Sexual Fantasies of College Men as Predictors of Self-Reported Likelihood of Rape and Overt Sexual Aggression." *The Journal of Sex Research*, 23, 1–11.

Gruber, E., and Chambers, C. V. (1987). "Cognitive Development and Adolescent Contraception: Integrating Theory and Practice." *Adolescence*, 22, 661–670.

Gunderson, M. P., and McCary, J. L. (1979). "Sexual Guilt and Religion." *Family Coordinator*, 28, 353–357.

————. (July, 1980). "Effects of Sex Education on Sex Information and Sexual Guilt, Attitudes, and Behaviors." *Family Relations*, 29, 375–379.

Haas, A. (1979). *Teenage Sexuality: A Survey of Teenage Sexual Behavior*. New York: Macmillan.

Hansson, R. O., O'Connor, M. E., Jones, W. H., and Blocker, T. J. (February, 1981). "Maternal Employment and Adolescent Sexual Behavior." *Journal of Youth and Adolescence*, 10, 55–60.

Harriman, L. C. (1986). "Teaching Traditional Versus Emerging Concepts in Family Life Education." *Family Relations*, 35, 581–586.

Heilbrun, A. B., Jr., and Loftus, M. P. (1986). "The Role of Sadism and Peer Pressure in the Sexual Aggression of Male College Students." *The Journal of Sex Research*, 22, 320–332.

Herold, E. S. (June, 1981). "Contraceptive Embarrassment and Contraceptive Behavior among Single Young Women." *Journal of Youth and Adolescence*, 10, 233–242.

Herold, E. S., and Goodwin, M. S. (April, 1981). "Premarital Sexual Guilt and Contraceptive Attitudes and Behavior." *Family Relations*, 30, 247–253.

Herold, E. S., et al. (1979). "A Study of Sexual Offenses against Females." *Adolescence*, 14, 65–72.

Hofferth, S., Kahn, J. R., and Baldwin, W. (1987). "Premarital Sexual Activity among U.S. Teenage Women over the Past Three Decades." *Family Planning Perspectives*, 19, 46–53.

Houston, L. N. (Summer, 1981). "Romanticism and Eroticism among Black and White College Students." *Adolescence*, 16, 263–272.

Jones, J. B., and Philliber, S. (June, 1983). "Sexually Active But Not Pregnant: A Comparison of Teens Who Risk and Teens Who Plan." *Journal of Youth and Adolescence*, 12, 235–251.

Judson, F. (1985). "Assessing the Number of Genital Chlamydial Infections in the United States." *Journal of Reproductive Medicine*, 30 (Supplement), 269–272.

Juhasz, A. M., and Sonnenshein-Schneider, M. (Winter, 1980). "Adolescent Sexual Decision-Making: Components and Skills." *Adolescence*, 15, 743–750.

———. (1987). "Adolescent Sexuality: Values, Morality, and Decision Making." *Adolescence*, 22, 579–590.

Jurich, A. P. (Winter, 1979). "Differential Determinants of Premarital Sexual Standards among College Students." *Adolescence*, 14, 797–810.

Kanin, E. J., and Parcell, S. R. (1977). "Sexual Aggression: A Second Look at the Offended Female." *Archives of Sexual Behavior*, 6, 67–76.

Kellam, S. G., Adams, R. G., Brown, O. H., Ensminger, M. E. (August, 1982). "The Long-Term Evaluation of the Family Structure of Teenage and Older Mothers." *Journal of Marriage and the Family*, 44, 539–554.

"Kids and Contraceptives," (February 16, 1987). *Newsweek*, pp. 54–65.

Kinnaird, K. L., and Gerrard, M. (1986). "Premarital Sexual Behavior and Attitudes toward Marriage and Divorce among Young Women as a Function of Their Mothers' Marital Status." *Journal of Marriage and the Family*, 48, 759–765.

Kirby, D., and Scales, P. (April, 1981). "An Analysis of State Guidelines for Sex Education Instruction in Public Schools." *Family Relations*, 30, 229–237.

Kisker, E. E. (March–April 1985). "Teenagers Talk about Sex, Pregnancy, and Contraception." *Family Planning Perspectives*, 17, 83–90.

Koss, M. P., Gidyca, C. A., and Wisniewski, N. (1987). "The Scope of Rape: Incidence and Prevalence of Sexual Aggression and Victimization in a National Sample of Higher Education Students." *Journal of Consulting and Clinical Psychology*, 55, 162–170.

Leigh, G. K., Loewen, I. R., and Lester, M. E. (1986). "Caveat Emptor: Values and Ethics in Family Life Education and Enrichment." *Family Relations*, 35, 573–580.

Levinson, R. A. (1986). "Contraceptive Self-Efficacy: A Perspective on Teenage Girls' Contraceptive Behavior." *The Journal of Sex Research*, 22, 347–369.

Lieberman, J. J. (Spring, 1981). "Locus of Control as Related to Birth Control Knowledge, Attitudes, and Practices." *Adolescence*, 16, 1–10.

Lincoln, R. (January–February 1984). "Too Many Teen Pregnancies." *Family Planning Perspectives*, 16, 4.

Lowe, C. S., and Radius, S. M. (1987). "Young Adults' Contraceptive Practices: An Investigation of Influences." *Adolescence*, 22, 291–304.

MacCorquodale, P. L. (February, 1984). "Gender Roles and Premarital Contraception." *Journal of Marriage and the Family*, 46, 57–63.

MacCorquodale, P., and DeLamater, J. (1979). "Self-Image and Premarital Sexuality." *Journal of Marriage and the Family*, 41, 327–339.

Marin, P. (July, 1983). "A Revolution's Broken Promises." *Psychology Today*, 17, 50–57.

Marsman, J. C., and Herold, E. S. (1986). "Attitudes Toward Sex Education and Values in Sex Education." *Family Relations*, 35, 357–361.

Maslach, G., and Kerr, G. B. (Summer, 1983). "Tailoring Sex Education Programs to Adolescents—A Strategy for the Primary Prevention of Unwanted Adolescent Pregnancies." *Adolescence*, 18, 449–456.

Marsiglio, W., and Mott, F. L. (1986). "The Impact of Sex Education on Sexual Activity, Contraceptive Use and Premarital Pregnancy among American Teenagers." *Family Planning Perspectives*, 18, 151–162.

McCabe, M. P. (1987). "Desired and Experienced Levels of Premarital Affection and Sexual Intercourse during Dating." *The Journal of Sex Research*, 23, 23–33.

McCormick, N., Folcik, J., and Izzo, A. (1985). "Sex Education Needs and Interests of High School Students in a Rural New York County." *Adolescence*, 22, 581–592.

Medora, N., and Woodward, J. C. (Spring, 1982). "Premarital Sexual Opinions of Undergraduate Students at a Midwestern University." *Adolescence*, 17, 213–224.

Milan, R. J., Jr., and Kilmann, P. R. (1987). "Interpersonal Factors in Premarital Contraception." *The Journal of Sex Research*, 23, 289–321.

Miller, B. C., McCoy, J. K., Olson, T. D., and Wallace, C. M. (1986). "Parental Discipline and Control Attempts in Relation to Adolescent Sexual Attitudes and Behavior." *Journal of Marriage and the Family*, 48, 503–512.

Miller, B. C., and Olson, T. D. (1988). "Sexual Attitudes and Behavior of High School Students in Relation to Background and Contextual Factors." *The Journal of Sex Research*, 24, 194–200.

Muehlenhard, C. L., and Cook, S. W. (1988). "Men's Self-Reports of Unwanted Sexual Activity." *The Joy of Sex Research*, 24, 58–72.

Murstein, B. I., and Holden, C. C. (Winter, 1979). "Sexual Behavior and Correlates among College Students." *Adolescence*, 14, 625–639.

Newcomer, S. F., and Udry, J. R. (May, 1984). "Mothers' Influence on the Sexual Behavior of Their Teenage Children." *Journal of Marriage and the Family*, 46, 477–485.

———. (July–August 1985). "Parent-Child Communication and Adolescent Sexual Behavior." *Family Planning Perspectives*, 17, 169–174.

———. (1987). "Parental Marital Status Effects on Adolescent Sexual Behavior." *Journal of Marriage and the Family*, 49, 235–240.

Newcomer, S. F., Udry, J. R., and Cameron, F. (Fall, 1983). "Adolescent Sexual Behavior and Popularity." *Adolescence*, 18, 515–522.

"New Insights into Teenage Pregnancy." (May–June 1982). *Family Planning Perspectives*, 14, 116ff.

Oppenheimer, M. (October, 1982). "What You Should Know about Herpes." *Seventeen*, pp. 154–155, 170.

Orr, M. T. (November–December 1982). "Sex Education and Contraceptive Education in U.S. Public High Schools." *Family Planning Perspectives*, 14, 304–313.

Parcel, G. S., and Luttmann, D. (January, 1981). "Evaluation of a Sex Education Course for Young Adolescents." *Family Relations*, 30, 55–60.

Perper, T., and Weis, D. L. (1987). "Proceptive and Rejective Strategies of U.S. and Canadian College Women." *The Journal of Sex Research*, 23, 455–480.

Petersen, J. R., Kretchner, A., Nellis, B., Lever, J., and Hertz, R. (March, 1983). "The Playboy Reader's Sex Survey, Part 2." *Playboy*, p. 90.

Philliber, S. G., and Tatum, M. L. (Summer, 1982). "Sex Education and the Double Standard in High School." *Adolescence*, 17, 272–283.

Plummer, W. (October 28, 1985). "A School's Rx for Sex." *People*, pp. 39–41.

Polit-O'Hara, D., and Kahn, J. R. (Spring, 1985). "Communication and Contraceptive Practices in Adolescent Couples." *Adolescence*, 20, 33–43.

Reis, I. L. (1971). *The Family System in America*. New York: Holt, Rinehart and Winston.

Rice, F. P. (1989). *Human Sexuality*. D'ubuque, IA.: Wm. C. Brown Co.

Richardson, J. G., and Cranston, J. E. (August, 1981). "Social Change, Parental Values, and the Salience of Sex Education." *Journal of Marriage and the Family*, 43, 547–558.

Rinck, C., Rudolph, J. A., and Simkins, L. (Winter, 1983). "A Survey of Attitudes Concerning Contraception and the Resolution of Teenage Pregnancy." *Adolescence*, 18, 923–929.

Robinson, I. E., and Jedlicka, D. (February, 1982). "Change in Sexual Attitudes and Behavior of College Students from 1965 to 1980: A Research Note." *Journal of Marriage and the Family*, 44, 237–240.

Rogel, M. J., Zuehlke, M. E., Petersen, A. C., Tobin-Richards, D. M., and Shelton, M. (December, 1980). "Contraceptive Behavior in Adolescence: A Decision-Making Perspective." *Journal of Youth and Adolescence*, 9, 491–506.

Roosa, M. W. (June, 1983). "A Comparative Study of Pregnant Teenagers' Parenting Attitudes and Knowledge of Sexuality and Child Development." *Journal of Youth and Adolescence*, 12, 213–223.

Roosa, M. W., Fitzgerald, H. E., and Carlson, N. A. (May, 1982). "A Comparison of Teenage and Older Mothers: A Systems Analysis." *Journal of Marriage and the Family*, 44, 367–377.

Rubenstein, J. S. (1976). "Young Adolescents' Sexual Interests." *Adolescence* 11, 487–496.

Scales, P. (October, 1981). "Sex Education in the '70s and '80s: Accomplishments, Obstacles and Emerging Issues." *Family Relations*, 30, 557–566.

Scales, P., and Kirby, D. (April, 1981). "A Review of Exemplary Sex Education Programs for Teenagers Offered by Nonschool Organizations." *Family Relations*, 30, 238–245.

Schultz, J. B., and Boyd, J. R. (October, 1984). "Sexuality Attitudes and Secondary Teachers." *Family Relations*, 33, 537–541.

Schwartz, D. B., and Darabi, K. F. (1986). "Motivations for Adolescents' First Visit to a Family Planning Clinic." *Adolescence*, 21, 535–545.

Scott, C. S., Shefman, L., Orr, L., Owen, R. G., and Fawcett, N. (1988). "Hispanic and Black American Adolescents' Beliefs Relating to Sexuality and Contraception." *Adolescence*, 23, 667–688.

Scott, J. W. (Winter, 1983). "Sentiments of Love and Aspiration for Marriage and Their Association with Teenage Sexual Activity and Pregnancy." *Adolescence*, 18, 889–897.

Shah, F., and Zelnik, M. (May, 1981). "Parent and Peer Influence on Sexual Behavior, Contraceptive Use, and Pregnancy Experience of Young Women." *Journal of Marriage and the Family*, 43, 339–348.

Silber, T. J. (May 1986). "Gonorrhea in Children and Adolescents." *Medical Aspects of Human Sexuality*, 16, 92H–92X.

Silverstein, C. D., and Buck, G. M. (1986). "Parental Preferences Regarding Sex Education Topics for Sixth Graders." *Adolescence*, 21, 971–980.

Singh, B. K. (May, 1980). "Trends in Attitudes toward Premarital Sexual Relations." *Journal of Marriage and the Family*, 42, 387–393.

Sonenstein, F. L., and Pittman, K. J. (January–February, 1984). "The Availability of Sex Education in Large School Districts." *Family Planning Perspectives*, 16, 19–25.

Sprecher, S., McKinney, K., Walsh, R., and Anderson, C. (1988). "A Revision of the Reiss Premarital Sexual Permissiveness Scale." *Journal of Marriage and the Family*, 50, 821–828.

Stern, M., Northman, J. E., and Van Slyck, M. R. (Summer, 1984). "Father Absence and Adolescent 'Problem Behaviors': Alcohol Consumption, Drug Use, and Sexual Activity." *Adolescence*, 19, 301–312.

Story, M. D. (Winter, 1982). "A Comparison of University Student Experience with Various Sexual Outlets in 1974 and 1980." *Adolescence*, 737–747.

Strouse, J., and Fabes, R. A. (1985). "Formal Versus Informal Sources of Sex Education: Competing Forces in the Sexual Socialization of Adolescents." *Adolescence*, 20, 251–263.

Studer, M., and Thornton, A. (1987). "Adolescent Religiosity and Contraceptive Usage." *Journal of Marriage and the Family*, 49, 117–128.

Tanfer, K., and Horn, M.C. (January–February, 1985). "Contraceptive Use, Pregnancy, and Fertility Patterns among Single American Women in Their 20s." *Family Planning Perspectives*, 17, 10–19.

Thompson, L., and Spanier, G. B. (1978). "Influence of Parents, Peers, and Partners on the Contraceptive Use of College Men and Women." *Journal of Marriage and the Family*, 40, 481–492.

Thornton, A., and Camburn, D. (1987). "The Influence of the Family on Premarital Sexual Attitudes and Behavior." *Demography*, 24, 323.

Troiden, R. R., and Jendrek, M. P. (1987). "Does Sexual Ideology Correlate with Level of Sexual Experience? Assessing the Construct Validity of SAS." *The Journal of Sex Research*, 23, 256–261.

Trussell, J. (1988). "Teenage Pregnancy in the United States." *Family Planning Perspectives*, 20, 262–272.

U.S. Bureau of the Census. Department of Commerce. (1987). *Statistical Abstract of the United States: 1987.* Washington, D.C.: U.S. Government Printing Office.

Urberg, K. A. (Fall, 1982). "A Theoretical Framework for Studying Adolescent Contraceptive Use." *Adolescence*, 17, 527–540.

Wagner, C. (Fall, 1980). "Sexuality of American Adolescents." *Adolescence*, 15, 567–580.

Wallis, C. (February 16, 1987). "You haven't heard anything yet." *Time*.

Zabin, L. S. (March–April, 1981). "The Impact of Early Use of Prescription Contraceptives on Reducing Premarital Teenage Pregnancies." *Family Planning Perspectives*, 13, 72ff.

Zabin, L. S., and Clark, S. D., Jr. (September–October, 1981). "Why They Delay: A Study of Teenage Family Planning Clinic Patients." *Family Planning Perspectives*, 13, 205ff.

Zabin, L. S., Hirsch, M. B., Smith, E. A., and Hardy, J. B. (July–August, 1984). "Adolescent Sexual Attitudes and Behavior: Are They Connected?" *Family Planning Perspectives*, 16, 181–185.

Zellman, G. L. (January–February, 1982). "Public School Programs for Adolescent Pregnancy and Parenthood: An Assessment." *Family Planning Perspectives*, 14, 15–21.

Zelnik, M., and Kantner, J. P. (September–October, 1980). "Sexual Activity, Contraceptive Use and Pregnancy among Metropolitan-Area Teenagers: 1971–1979." *Family Planning Perspectives*, 12, 230ff.

Zelnik, M., and Kim, Y. J. (May–June, 1982). "Sex Education and Its Association with Teenage Sexual Activity, Pregnancy, and Contraceptive Use." *Family Planning Perspectives*, 14, 117.

Zelnik, M., and Shah, F. K. (March–April, 1983). "First Intercourse among Young Americans." *Family Planning Perspectives*, 15, 64–70.

CHAPTER
16

Adolescents in Their Families

identity crisis   In some ways parents and adolescents are alike: both are experiencing an ***identity crisis*** relating to sexual life, roles, authority, emotional adjustment, and values. In other ways they are different, especially in their basic personalities and orientations to life. This chapter compares the identity crisis at middle age with a similar crisis at adolescence and then discusses some of the basic personality differences between parents and their adolescent children. I discuss some of the difficulties parents have with adolescents and what youths expect of their parents in the way of interest and help, communication, love and acceptance, trust, autonomy, discipline, home life, and parental example. Adolescent-sibling relationships and the relationships of youths with other relatives in the family are discussed. Finally, two special kinds of families are looked at: parent-absent families and reconstituted families.

MIDDLE AGE AND ADOLESCENT IDENTITY CRISES

Practically every book on youth emphasizes the period of adolescence as a time of identity crisis. (See chapter 8.) But it is important to emphasize also that middle age is a period of identity crisis for the adult. Adolescence arrives at a rather unhandy time for some parents. It comes at a time when middle-aged parents are asking: Who am I, what have I accomplished, where am I now, and what does the future hold for me? In some ways the psychosocial tasks of adolescence parallel those of middle age. (See chapter 3.)

■ Sexual Identity Crisis

Both parents and children are questioning their sexual identity during middle age and adolescence. The bodily changes at puberty require adolescents to readjust to their new sexuality. The reversal of these bodily changes for the female at menopause requires also that she readjust to her new, infertile ***sexual identity.*** As menstruation ceases and the childbearing years end, the woman may have difficulty accepting physical changes. Along with the loss of childbearing capacity may come a fear of decline in sexual attractiveness and responsiveness. If a woman tends to gain weight easily or if she has become careless about her personal appearance, she may have lost some of her appeal and may be especially sensitive when she sees her teenage daughter with her beautiful figure, skin, and hair, at the full bloom of her youth. It takes a mature mother not to be envious and a little bit frightened, both for herself and for her daughter. The mother may react by pushing her daughter into popularity and intimate relationships to relive her own life through that of her daughter, or she may react by sheltering, protecting, repressing her daughter, or denying her full womanhood out of anxiety and panic.

A father, too, has a crisis of sexual identity. He becomes sensitive about his growing paunch, increasing baldness, and gray hair. An example is the father who had a coronary attack while attempting to compete with his son in ten athletic contests. The father had finished eight events before he was rushed to the hospital. Some men fear loss of potency and physical charm. Some men start chasing other women; others encourage their teenage sons to do so. Still others become hostile, defensive, and resentful whenever their sons reach for manhood and want

sexual identity

increased contact with girls, an expanding social life, or adult sexual experiences. Some fathers become fearful for their daughters when they start going out with boys. The author knows of one father who thinks that every boy who takes out one of his daughters will seduce her. His fear may be a projection of his own guilt because of his own promiscuous sexual conduct when he was younger.

Crises of Roles

Both parents and adolescents start questioning their own roles in life. Adolescents have to face up to what they want out of life philosophically and vocationally. The father faces the fact that his life is half over and that he may not have accomplished nearly all he wanted to. He wonders where he is going from this point on, whether he should change jobs, and how he will find security for the future. The mother has to decide whether to continue her job or whether to go back to school to improve her job status. If she has been at home, she has to decide whether to take up a profession or how else to fulfill herself during the years after the children are launched. Her role of motherhood is about over, and she wonders what role she can best fulfill now.

This change in roles for parents and adolescents has some pitfalls. Will parents start pressuring their adolescents to assume roles they really wanted for themselves but never were able to fulfill? Will the adolescents be able to find fulfillment as independent adults, especially when the comfort and security of their homes seem so appealing? Or in their desire for independence, will they overreact, leave home and school prematurely, strike out on their own unprepared, and be unable to fulfill their own ambitions or dreams because they are too immature and unprepared to accomplish the task?

Authority Crisis

Parents and adolescents are simultaneously facing an **authority crisis.** Parents may resist losing authority. For years their children have depended on them for everything: their physical and emotional needs and guidance and advice. Now the adolescents strive for independence, for the right to govern their own lives and to make their own decisions. Parents have difficulties changing the pattern of child guidance that was developed over the years with a dependent child so that they can relate to their adolescents as growing adults (Pasley and Gecas, 1984). Parents who are most secure within themselves are best able to offer independence to their adolescents (Small, 1988).

authority crisis

Emotional Readjustment

Middle age and puberty demand drastic emotional readjustment. Adolescents strive to become individuals in their own right, a process called *individuation* (Anderson and Fleming, 1986; Fleming and Anderson, 1986). If the parents encourage dependency, their children cannot grow up; if they overreact and reject their adolescents, the adolescents are hurt and resentful and may be pushed into the arms of another boy or girl. The dependency-independency crisis must be solved in such a way that parent and child remain friends but now as adult to adult.

Reassessment of Values

Parents and adolescents are facing a conflict of values. Sometimes the conflict is between parental and adolescent values, but just as often the parents are experiencing value conflict within themselves, just as the adolescents are. The adults are aware of value changes around them that sometimes conflict with the traditional values with which they have grown up. They have lost some of the idealism of their own youth; usually they have become more cynical and realistic and less certain. At the same time, adolescents are also questioning the values with which they have grown up; they are getting acquainted with new and different friends, some of whom have completely different values than they do. Adolescents start rethinking their values: sometimes the new thoughts are shocking to parents, and never reassuring, because they remind the parents of their own confusion. The result is that adolescents make the adults feel even more uncertain. Adults may react with dogmatism and authoritarianism to convince both their adolescents and themselves that they are right. At other times they capitulate at the slightest challenge, leaving the adolescents insecure, with some loss of respect for their parents, but still groping through their own moral confusion.

Results of the Conflicts

What are some results of the identity crises parents and adolescents are facing? Generally confusion sets in, at least for a while. Families with adolescents can be described as living in a stage of transitional crisis characterized by confusion. The confusion usually continues until each generation resolves its own identity crisis.

Another result is that each generation is absorbed with its own problems and therefore tends to overlook, misinterpret, and misunderstand the problems of the other. Sometimes the feeling is expressed: "Don't bother me with your problems; I've got problems of my own." One of the chief complaints of both parents and youths about each other is: "They don't seem interested or try to understand my problems."

Mothers and fathers tend to underestimate the attitude divisions between themselves and their adolescents. Adolescents, on the other hand, tend to magnify such discrepancies, assuming them to be greater than they are. One study revealed a low level of agreement between parents and youth on how each perceived their relationship (Jessop, 1981).

If a permanent rift develops, parents and youths may never get back together or are able to do so only years later. Increasing numbers of youths are wandering around the country, some runaways, many voluntarily or otherwise cut off from all contact with their parents. Some of these are youths who have not been able to solve their own identity crisis and at the same time adjust to parents who are struggling with their own identities as well.

PARENT-ADOLESCENT PERSONALITY DIFFERENCES

Parent-adolescent misunderstanding arises also from the two different types of personalities of adults and youths. A comparison of two possible personality types is given in table 16-1. Although not all adults or youths fit the types described, enough are similar to make personality differences a major source of conflict.

▄ **TABLE 16-1**

Middle-aged adult and adolescent personalities.

MIDDLE-AGED ADULT GENERATION	ADOLESCENT GENERATION
1. Careful/experienced	1. Daring, adventurous, sometimes takes foolish chances
2. Holds to past, tendency to compare present with yesterday	2. Past irrelevant, lives in present
3. Realistic, sometimes skeptical about life, people	3. Idealistic, optimistic
4. Conservative in manners, morals, mores	4. Liberal, challenges traditional ideas, experiments with new customs
5. Generally contented, satisfied, accepts status quo	5. Critical with things as they are, desire to reform, change
6. Wants to stay youthful, fears age	6. Wants to be grown-up, but dislikes idea of ever being old

A careful look at table 16-1 reveals some significant differences between middle-aged parents and adolescent children. From a vantage point reached after many years of experience, parents feel that youths are crazy, reckless, and naive, too inexperienced even to recognize that they are foolish to take chances. Parents worry that their youths will have accidents, get hurt, or get in trouble with the law. Youths feel their parents are overly cautious and worry too much.

Parents who are middle aged tend to compare today's youths and life-styles with their own past. Parents often suffer from a perennial "cultural lag"—a situation that renders them helpless, relatively poorly informed, and places them against "experts" who have taken over a sizable proportion of the socialization process so that children and teenagers show a tendency to generalize the inefficiency of parents as instructors and have started to question their reliability as educators in general. In fact, there is some evidence that adolescents feel they have to socialize parents to bring them up to date on modern views (Peters, 1985).

Parents also become a little cynical about human character, somewhat disillusioned about trying to change the world and everybody in it; they realistically learn to accept some things as they are. Adolescents are still extremely idealistic and impatient with adults who are part of the establishment and accept and like things as they are. Adolescents want to reform the world overnight and become annoyed when their parents do not agree with their crusade. (See chapters 1 and 6.)

Adolescents also grow to be wary of adults, primarily because they feel most adults are too critical and will not understand them. Youths feel they have good ideas too and know more about some things than their parents do, and because they want to be grown-up, they may scoff at parental suggestions or ideas. Some youths become arrogant and contemptuous of adults, usually if they are insecure and envious of the adult's status. Adults react to criticism and rejection with anger and hurt.

Finally some aging adults become oversensitive about growing old or being considered aged. Because they hate to think of growing old, they focus more and more attention on staying young. If parents carry this insecurity to extremes in their dress and behavior, they succeed only in attracting the embarrassed shame and icy glares of their own teenagers and the amused ridicule of other youths as well.

Parents and youths view each other from prejudiced positions that do not help them to understand how to live with the other generation.

PARENT-ADOLESCENT CONFLICT

In spite of these personality differences, research indicates that parent-adolescent relationships are usually harmonious (Stefanko, 1984). When conflict occurs, the focus may be in any of five areas (Hall, 1987; Leslie, Huston and Johnson, 1986).

Social Life and Customs

Adolescents' social lives and the social customs they observe probably create more conflict with parents than any other area. The most common sources of friction are the following:

Choice of friends or dating partners.
How often they are allowed to go out, going out on school night, frequency of dating.
Where they are allowed to go, type of activity attended.
Curfew hours.
Age allowed to date, ride in cars, participate in certain events.
Going steady.
Choice of clothes, hair styles.

One of the most common complaints of parents is that the adolescent is never home and does not spend any time with the family (Felson and Gottfredson, 1984).

Responsibility

Parents become the most critical of adolescents who do not evidence enough responsibility. Parents expect adolescents to show responsibility in:

Performance of family chores (Grief, 1985; Light, Hertzgaard, and Martin, 1985; Sanik and Stafford, 1985).
Earning and spending money.
Care of personal belongings, clothes, and room.
Use of the family automobile.
Use of the telephone.
Doing work for others outside the home.
Use of family property or belongings: furniture, tools, supplies, equipment.

School

School performance, behavior at school, and adolescents' attitudes toward school receive much attention from parents. Specifically, the parent is concerned about adolescents':

Grades and level of performance (whether they are performing according to their potential).
Study habits and homework.
Regularity of attendance.
General attitude toward school studies and teachers.
Behavior in school.

Sometimes pressure on the adolescent to succeed in school is excessive, resulting in lowered self-esteem, deviant activity, and a feeling of failure in reaching goals set by families (Eskilson et al., 1986).

Family Relationships

Conflict arises over:

Immature behavior.
General attitude and level of respect shown to parents.
Quarreling with siblings.
Relationships with relatives, especially aged grandparents in the home.
Degree of orientation toward family or amount of autonomy from family (Jurich, Schumm and Bollman, 1987).

Values and Morals

Parents are concerned especially with:

Drinking, smoking, and use of drugs.
Language and speech.
Basic honesty.
Sexual behavior.
Obeying the law, staying out of trouble.
Going to church or Sunday school.

Variables Affecting Conflict

The focus of conflict in any one family will depend on a number of factors. The *age* of the adolescent is one factor. Girls are increasingly in conflict with their parents about boyfriends from age 12 on, with the peak years being 14 and 15. The same conflict for boys about girlfriends peaks at age 16.

The *sex* of the adolescent is another factor influencing conflict. Girls report a greater number of family problems than do boys, which is an indication of sex differences in the extent of difficulty. The sex of the parent is another factor influencing conflict. Most adolescents report more difficulties getting along with their fathers than with their mothers and that they are closer to their mothers (Cicirelli, 1980; Rubin, 1982). As a result their mothers exert more influence on them, even over educational goals (Smith, 1981).

The total *atmosphere within the home* influences conflict. Conflict of all types is more frequent in authoritarian homes than in democratic homes. In authoritarian homes, there is more conflict over spending money, friends, social life, activities outside the home, and home chores.

The *socioeconomic status* of the family influences the forms of conflict. Low socioeconomic status families are more often concerned about obedience, politeness, and respect, whereas middle-income families are more concerned with developing independence and initiative. Low socioeconomic status families may worry more about keeping children out of trouble at school; middle-class parents are more concerned about grades and achievement.

The *total environment* in which the child grows up will determine what parents worry about. An adolescent growing up in an area where there is high delinquency or considerable drug abuse will find parents more concerned with these problems.

Variations in parental reactions to adolescent behavior influence the extent and focus of conflict. Some parents show little concern about only a few specific problems. Others are greatly and generally dissatisfied with the behavior of their adolescents.

Family size has been found to be a significant variable, at least in middle-class families (Kidwell, 1981). The larger is the middle-class family, the greater is the degree of parent-youth conflict and the more often parents use physical force to control adolescents (Bell and Avery, 1985).

The variables influencing parent-adolescent conflict are almost countless, but the ones mentioned indicate how many factors may be involved. Not all parents and adolescents quarrel about the same things or to the same extent.

ADOLESCENT-PARENT EXPECTATIONS

What kind of parents do adolescents want and need? A compilation of research findings indicates that youths want and need parents who

> "Are interested in us and available to help us when needed."
> "Listen to us and try to understand us."
> "Talk with us, not at us."
> "Love and accept us as we are, faults and all."
> "Trust us and expect the best of us."
> "Treat us like grown-ups."
> "Discipline us fairly."
> "Are happy people with good dispositions and a sense of humor, who create a happy home."
> "Set a good example for us, and who will admit when they have made a mistake."

These qualities deserve closer examination (Williamson and Campbell, 1985).

Parental Interest and Help

One of the ways adolescents know their parents care about them is by the interest they show in them and by their willingness to stand beside them and help them as needed (Northman, 1985). One girl, a drum majorette, was bitter because her parents never came to a football or basketball game to see her perform. This same reaction is expressed by a high school basketball player:

> I'm the star player on the school basketball team, but never once has either parent come to see me play. They're either too busy or too tired or can't get a baby sitter for my younger sister. The crowds cheer for me, the girls hang around my locker, some kids even ask me for my autograph. But it doesn't mean much if the two most important people in my life don't care.

Adolescents want attention from their parents. They especially resent parents who are away from home too much. This is a special problem to adolescents whose mothers or fathers have positions of responsibility that require them to work long hours or be away from home a great deal (Gullotta et al., 1981; Jensen and Borges, 1986). Many youths are "latchkey" children who have to let themselves in the house after school because parents are not home.

Other parents overdo the companionship. Adolescents want to spend time with their own friends and do not want their parents to be pals. They need adult interest and help, not adults trying to act like adolescents.

The attention adolescents get from their parents depends partially on the birth order and spacing of the children. Middle-born adolescents feel cheated of parental attention and support and express a sense of being "pushed around" when it comes to the allocation and implementation of family rules and regulations (Kidwell, 1981). However, child spacing is important. Parents are more punitive and less supportive when their children are spaced too closely together.

Listening, Understanding, and Talking

One of the most frequent complaints of adolescents is that their parents do not listen to their ideas, accept their opinions as relevant, or try to understand their feelings and points of view. Adolescents want parents who will talk with them, not at them, in a sympathetic way.

> "We want parents we can take our troubles to and be sure they'll understand. Some parents won't listen or let their children explain. They should try to see things a little more from our point of view."
> "We wish our parents would lose an argument with us once and a while and listen to our side of problems."

Basically, adolescents are saying that they want sympathetic understanding, an attentive ear, and parents who indicate by their attitudes that they feel they have something worthwhile to say and therefore are willing to communicate with them. Research indicates that the respect parents show for adolescent opinions contributes greatly to the climate and happiness of the home.

Some parents feel threatened when their adolescent disagrees, does not accept their ideas, or tries to argue. Parents who refuse to talk and close the argument by saying "I don't want to discuss it; what I say goes" are closing the door to effective communication, just as are adolescents who get angry, stamp out of the room, refuse to discuss a matter reasonably, and go into their rooms to pout.

One key to harmonious parent-youth relationships is communication (Faw and Goldsmith, 1980). Some families spend little time together. If families are to talk, they have to be together long enough to do so; they also have to develop an openness between the generations. Many parents have no idea what their adolescents really think because they never give them a chance to explain (Thompson, Acock, and Clark, 1985).

Love and Acceptance

One of the important components of love is *acceptance*. One way love is shown is by knowing and then accepting adolescents exactly as they are, faults and all. There must be a determined effort by parents both to give affection and to achieve enough objectivity to see the child as a human being, entitled to human attributes. Adolescents do not want to feel that their parents expect them to be perfect before they will love them, nor can they thrive in an atmosphere of constant criticism and displeasure. Acceptance may also include *nurturance*, a parental attitude of warmth and helpful assistance toward the adolescent. *Rejection* is the opposite, reflecting indifference, nagging, or hostility. Adolescents may run away from homes where demonstration of love is lacking and affectional ties between parents and adolescents are weak; conflict intensifies to the point at which youths resort to flight. A high proportion of runaways report that they are not accepted at home by their parents. Adolescents who reject their parents do so as a defense against the hostility and rejection their parents have shown them.

The author once counseled a college girl whose course grades had fallen drastically. This girl had been a straight A student in high school and a superior student for the first few semesters of college. Then her grades plummeted. Subsequent conversation revealed that the girl's parents had always been perfectionists and overly critical. No matter what the girl did as a child her mother would say, "That's fine dear, but wouldn't it have been better if you had done this?" and would tell her what she should have done differently. No matter what the girl did, it was never good enough. The girl remarked, "I can never remember my parents being pleased about anything I did." Finally, the girl gave up trying since she could not please her parents anyway. It was at this point that her grades dropped.

Trust

Adolescents say:

"Why are our parents always so afraid we are going to do the wrong thing? Why can't they trust us more?"

"Our parents could trust us more than they often do. They should tell us what we need to know about dating without being old-fashioned. Then they should put us on our own and expect the best of us so we have something to live up to."

One of the most annoying evidences of distrust are parents' opening adolescents' mail, reading their diaries, or listening in on their telephone conversations. One girl complains:

> My mother is forever going through my room under the pretense of "cleaning." I don't like to have my desk straightened up (it's where I keep my diary) or my bureau rummaged through. . . . Don't you think a 16-year-old girl needs privacy?

Some parents seem to have more difficulty trusting their adolescents than others do. Such parents tend to project their own fears, anxieties, and guilts onto the adolescent. The most fearful parents are usually those who are the most insecure or who had personal difficulties themselves while growing up. The author has found, for example, that mothers who themselves have conceived or borne children out of wedlock are those most concerned about their own daughters' dating and sexual behavior. Most adolescents feel that parents should trust them completely unless they have given the adults reason for distrust.

Autonomy

One goal of every normal adolescent is to be accepted as an autonomous adult (Fasick, 1984). The research does indicate, however, that behavioral autonomy increases sharply during adolescence. It has been suggested in other sections of this book (see chapter 12 especially) that adolescents desire **autonomy** in some areas, such as clothing selection or choice of friends, but follow their parents' leads in other areas, such as formulating educational plans.

autonomy

Evidence indicates that the shift to emotional autonomy during adolescence is not as dramatic as the shift to behavioral autonomy. Adolescents want and need parents who will grant them autonomy in slowly increasing amounts as they learn to use it rather than all at once. Too much freedom too quickly granted may be interpreted as rejection. Youths want to be given the right to make choices, to exert their own independence, to argue with adults and to assume responsibility, but they do not want complete freedom. Those who have it worry about it because they realize they do not know how to use it.

The opposite extreme from rejection is continued domination and the encouragement of overdependency. Parents who have an unhappy marriage sometimes turn to their children for emotional satisfaction and develop too much dependency on them (Teyber, 1983). Parents who encourage dependency needs that become demanding and excessive, even into adulthood, are interfering with their child's ability to function as an effective adult. Some adolescents who have been dominated by their parents begin to accept and to prefer being dependent. The result is prolonged adolescence. Some adolescents, for example, may prefer to live with parents after marriage. Others who are overly dependent on parents never achieve mature heterosexual relationships, establish a vocational identity of their own choosing, or develop a positive self-image as separate, independent people. As in so many other affairs of life, a golden mean appears to be the optimum situation.

There seem to be some sex differences in the dependent-independent behavior of adolescents. Girls may be kept more dependent than boys in middle and late adolescence. There are also significant differences according to race and socioeconomic status. Black mothers and low-income mothers from rural areas tend to encourage the development of dependency in their daughters and to foster interdependence in the family. White mothers, and especially those of higher status, are more likely to encourage independence (Fu et al., 1984).

Discipline

What kinds of family discipline and control best meet adolescents' needs? *Overall, talking with adolescents is the most frequent disciplinary measure used and the one considered best for the age group* (deTurck and Miller, 1983; Smith, 1983). Fathers seem to exercise more authority over sons than do mothers, and mothers exercise more authority over daughters than do fathers (McKenry, Price-Boham, and O'Bryant, 1981). Parents with superior education and high religiosity tend to have greater power over adolescents than those with lower education and less religiosity (McDonald, 1979).

There are four basic patterns of family control: autocratic, authoritative but democratic, permissive, and erratic.

Autocratic—the parent makes any decisions relevant to the adolescent.
Authoritative, but democratic—decisions are made jointly by the parent and the adolescent.
Permissive—the adolescent has more influence in making decisions than does the parent.
Erratic—control is inconsistent, sometimes, authoritarian, sometimes democratic, sometimes permissive.

What effect does each method of control have on the adolescent (Enright et al., 1980; Harris and Howard, 1981)?

The usual effect of autocratic control is to produce a combination of rebellion and dependency (Balswick and Macrides, 1975). Adolescents are taught to be submissive, to obey, and to be dependent on their parents. They are expected to follow their parents' demands and decisions without question and not to try to make decisions themselves. They less often show initiative or autonomy as motivation for achievement, nor do they show adult independence. Adolescents in such environments usually are more hostile to their parents, often deeply resent their control and domination, and less often identify with them. When they succeed in challenging parental authority, youths may become rebellious, sometimes overtly aggressive and hostile, especially if the parents' discipline has been harsh and unfair and administered without much love and affection. Thus, the effects on children growing up in autocratic homes differ. The meeker ones are cowed; the stronger ones are rebellious. Both usually show some emotional disturbances and have problems. Those who rebel often leave home as soon as they can; some become delinquent.

Adolescents who grow up in homes where parents use harsh and physical punishment will model their aggressive behavior (Johnson and O'Leary, 1987). Family violence seems to beget more violence in and outside the home (Martin et al., 1987; Peek, Fischer, and Kidwell, 1985; Roscoe and Callahan, 1985). Neapolitan (1981) found that identification and communication with parents, usually thought to inhibit delinquent behavior, did not inhibit aggressive behavior in families where the father used harsh physical punishment. The more adolescents identified with a father who modeled aggressive behavior and the more quality interaction they had with a father who encouraged aggression, the more they took part in aggressive behavior themselves.

The other extreme is a permissive home, in which adolescents receive little guidance and direction, few restrictions from parents, and are expected to make decisions for themselves. The effects vary. If overindulged but not guided or properly socialized, pampered adolescents will be ill prepared to accept frustrations or responsibility or show proper regard for others with whom they associate. They often become domineering, self-centered, and selfish and get in trouble with those who will not pamper them the way their parents have. Without limits on their behavior, they feel insecure, disoriented, and uncertain. If they interpret the parents' lack of control as disinterest or rejection, adolescents blame them because they did not warn or guide them. Lax discipline, rejection, and lack of parental affection also have been associated with delinquency.

The authoritative but democratic home has the most positive effect upon adolescents (Balswick and Macrides, 1975; Kelly and Goodwin, 1983). Parents exercise authority but concern expresses itself through guidance. Parents also encourage individual responsibility, decision making, initiative, and autonomy. Adolescents are involved in making their own decisions while listening to and discussing the reasoned explanations of parents. Adolescents are encouraged to detach themselves gradually from their family. As a result the home atmosphere is likely to be one of respect, appreciation, warmth, and acceptance. This type of home, where there is warmth, fairness, and consistency of discipline, is associated with conforming, trouble-free nondelinquent behavior for both boys and girls.

Erratic, inconsistent parental control, like lack of control, has a negative effect on adolescents. Lacking clear, definite guidelines, they become confused and insecure. Such youths often evidence antisocial, delinquent behavior. They react by evidencing a great amount of rebellion against their parents.

Parental and Home Happiness

One of the most important influences upon the adolescent is the emotional climate of the family (Parish, Dostal, and Parish, 1981). Some families evidence a prevailing mood of gaiety, joy, optimism, and happiness. Other families reflect a climate of fear, depression, cynicism, and hostility, which as a negative effect on children (Forsstrom-Cohen and Rosenbaum, 1985). The happier the parents and the more positive the home climate, the more beneficial is the effect on the growing children. The best-adjusted children are those who grow up in happy homes where adolescents and parents spend pleasurable time together (McMillan and Hiltonsmith,

HIGHLIGHT   Parental Control Techniques

In his research on parental control techniques in 1,109 parent-adolescent encounters, Smith (1988) outlined seven methods of control.

1. *Power assertion*—physical punishment, deprivation, threats.
2. *Command*—imperative statements not accompanied by punishment or overt threat of punishment.
3. *Love withdrawal*—behavior that punishes or threatens to punish a child by means of temporary coldness or rejection.
4. *Self-oriented* **induction**—parents suggest possible gains or costs the child might experience as a result of a choice made.
5. *Other-oriented induction*—parents point to religion or ethical reasons, attraction to others, or personal obligations as reasons for a choice.
6. *Advice*—suggestion to the child how he/she may more efficiently, effectively, or easily accomplish what is desired by the parent.
7. *Relationship maintenance*—appeals to the child to maintain a positive orientation toward the parent.

The subjects of the study were 109 mothers and 88 fathers, predominantly middle-class, although of different income levels, in Columbia, S. Carolina. The relative frequency of parental control techniques were:

Command—34 percent of parent-adolescent encounters
Self-oriented induction—31 percent
Advice—14 percent
Relationship maintenance—10 percent
Power assertion—8 percent
Other-oriented induction—6 percent
Love withdrawal—1 percent

These findings are important because research generally indicates that parental explanations and reasoning (induction) are strongly associated with the child internalizing ethical and moral principles. Parents and adolescents who show mutual respect and exchange, and high regard for the needs of one another, who exchange ideas and information are those who are most successful at conflict resolution (McCombs, Forehand, and Smith, 1988). Use of physical punishment, deprivation and threats (power-assertive discipline) is associated with children's aggression, hostility, and delinquency. It impedes the development of emotional, social, and intellectual maturity (Portes, Dunham, and Williams, 1986).

1982). When the types of child-rearing practices are taken into account also, the effect is even more evident. Either very restrictive or very permissive child-rearing practices together with an unhappy marriage produce the most rebellion of all. There is also a tendency for parental happiness and rebellion to be more strongly related when the home is patriarchal. Numerous research studies emphasize the positive relationship of marital adjustment, family happiness, family solidarity, family cohesiveness, family cooperation, and nondelinquent behavior. In other words, the quality of the interpersonal relationship between the husband and wife and between the parent and child is crucial in its effect on the children (Burman, John, and Margolin, 1987).

Parental Example

Youths say they want parents who "practice what they preach," "set a good example for us to follow," "follow the same principles they try to teach us," and "make us proud of them." Adolescents want to feel proud of their parents, to feel they are the kind of people they can admire. Youths like adults who have a pleasant disposition, a good sense of humor, who do not get angry or upset all the time, who are fair, treat their children without favoritism, and who are truthful and honest as they want their teenagers to be. Youths object to adults who nag about things they themselves do all the time or who are hypocritical in their beliefs and actions. As one adolescent expressed it: "It's good to feel our parents have a religion they're sincerely trying to live right in the family and everywhere else. . . . It makes us feel we really belong and gives us something to build on."

Youths want to feel proud to be part of their families. In most communities, adolescents receive part of their identity from their family. Youths who like their family name, are proud of the neighborhood and house they live in, are proud of the work that their parents do and of the status of their parents in the community feel better about themselves. These adolescents are able to say proudly, "I am a Jones" or "I am a Levy."

RELATIONSHIPS WITH OTHER FAMILY MEMBERS

Adolescent-Sibling Relationships

Research efforts have concentrated on exploring parent-adolescent relationships in the family, but little information is available, and some of it is contradictory, on adolescent-sibling relationships. Yet the relationships between brothers and sisters are vitally important because they may have a lasting influence on development and on the individual's ultimate adult personality and roles. Sibling relationships are important in a number of ways (Blyth, Hill, and Thiel, 1982).

Older siblings are likely to serve as role models for younger brothers and sisters. Older youths represent sex-role models—masculine or feminine personalities or behavior—to younger siblings. They set a character and behavior example, representing through appearance, personality traits, and overall behavior the type of person they are. This has a strong influence on the development of younger brothers and sisters.

Older siblings often serve as surrogate parents, acting as caretakers, teachers, playmates and confidants. Pleasant relationships can contribute to younger children's sense of security, belonging, and acceptance. Hostile, rejecting relationships may create deep-seated feelings of anxiety, insecurity, resentment, or hostility. If older children feel they are displaced by younger siblings and lack attention and care formerly given to them, they may carry this feeling of displacement, jealousy, and competition into adulthood. If, however, older children feel useful, accepted, and admired because of the care they give younger children, this added appreciation and sense of usefulness contributes positively to their own sense of self-worth.

Many adolescents learn adult roles and responsibilities by having to care for younger brothers and sisters while growing up.

Siblings often provide companionship, friendship, and meet one another's needs for affection and meaningful relationships. They act as confidants for one another, are able to help one another when there are problems, and share many experiences (Cicirelli, 1980). Of course, the closer they are, the more likely also that conflict and tension will result, but this too has its positive aspects for it provides training opportunities in how to get along with others. Siblings of necessity have to learn to share, to consider one another's feelings and desires, and to deal with differences.

If siblings are six or more years apart in age, they tend to grow up like single children. If there is less than six years' difference, however, they are often a threat to each other's power and command over their parents, rivalry is more pronounced, and conflicts tend to be more severe. Relationships with siblings tend to be more frictional during early adolescence than later. As adolescents mature, they accept their siblings in a calmer, more rational manner, with the result that conflicting relationships subside and are replaced by friendlier, more cooperative ones.

Relationships with Relatives

Relationships with grandparents can have positive effects on adolescents. Baranowski (1982) discusses three of these.

First, a grandparent may be the key agent in restoring a sense of continuity in an adolescent's life, in linking the past to the present, and in transmitting knowledge of culture and family roots and thus having a positive impact on the adolescent's search for identity.

Second, grandparents may have a positive impact on parent-adolescent relations by conveying information about the parents to the adolescent. Adolescents also turn to grandparents as confidants and arbiters when they are in conflict with their parents.

Third, grandparents help adolescents understand aging and accept the aged. Adolescents who see their grandparents frequently, and have a good relationship with them, are more likely to have positive attitudes toward the elderly (Guptill, 1979).

During early adolescence, contact with older relatives may be frictional. Some grandparents assume an active role in the rearing and guidance of children in the family. Some interfere too much by nagging, ridiculing, or trying to control their grandchildren, often against the parents' wishes. Others take the adolescents' side against parents by pampering or overprotecting, thus undermining parental discipline. In either case, tension develops in the household, affecting all members negatively and stimulating adolescent rebellion and defiance. It is a rare grandparent who achieves the right degree of helping without interfering.

Gradually, as adolescents get older, they are able to accept grandparents and older relatives more graciously than before. Older relatives themselves usually are not as inclined to boss older adolescents as they are the younger adolescents. These two factors result in a gradual subsiding of tension between the generations.

Relationships with grandparents can have positive effects on adolescents by restoring a sense of continuity in the adolescent's life, offering an alternative confidant for adolescents in conflict with their parents, and helping the adolescent to understand aging. (© Frank Siteman)

PARENT-ABSENT FAMILIES
Incidence

Throughout this chapter the emphasis has been on parent-adolescent relationships in intact families: where the adolescent lives at home with both parents. This condition only exists in about three out of four families due to the high rate of divorce and separation. As can be seen in figure 16-1, 22 percent of all children aged 6 to 17 live with their mothers only, 3 percent with their father, and an additional 3 percent live apart from their parents. The figures are much higher for black children: 50 percent live with their mother only, 3 percent with their father, and 7 percent with neither parent. Of all teenagers, black and white, who live in one-parent families, about 91 percent live with their mother (Montemayor and Leigh, 1982) and therefore lack a father figure in the home (U.S. Dept. of Commerce, 1987).

Effect of Father Absence

What effect does father absence have on adolescents? The most important areas of investigation have included the following (Blechman, 1981; Edwards, 1987).

Relation to the development of masculinity-femininity
Association with delinquency
Impact on psychological health
Influences on school performance, achievement, and vocational aspirations
Attitudes toward self and parents

Let us discuss each of these in turn.

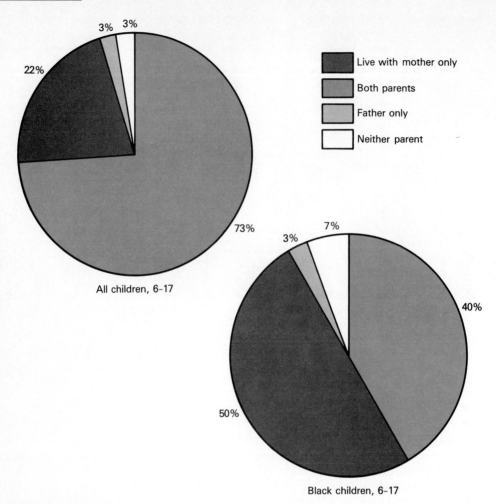

Live with mother only

Both parents

Father only

Neither parent

All children, 6–17

Black children, 6–17

FIGURE 16-1

Living status of children, six to seventeen years old.

From: U.S. Department of Commerce, Bureau of the Census (1987). *Statistical Abstract of the United States*, 1987. (Washington, D.C.: U.S. Government Printing Office), p. 48.

Development of Masculinity-Femininity

The common assumption has been that boys raised by their mothers and who therefore lack an effective father figure are more likely to score lower on measures of masculinity, to have unmasculine self-concepts and sex-role orientations, and to be more dependent, less aggressive, and less competent in peer relationships than those whose fathers are present (Rice, 1983). The younger a boy is when he is separated from his father and the longer is the separation, the more the boy will be affected in his early years. The older a boy gets, however, the early effects of father absence decrease.

The effect of father absence depends partially on whether boys have male surrogate models (Klyman, 1985). Father-absent boys with a father substitute such as an older male sibling are less affected than those without a father substitute. Male peers, especially older ones, may become important substitute models for paternally deprived boys. Young father-absent male children seek the attention of older males and are strongly motivated to imitate and please potential father figures.

The effect of father absence on daughters seems to be just the opposite. Daughters are affected less when young but more during adolescence (Rice, 1983). Their lack of meaningful male-female relationships in childhood can make it more difficult for them to relate to the opposite sex later on. Case studies of father-absent girls are often filled with details of problems concerning interactions with males. During adolescence, girls of divorced parents who live with their mothers may be inappropriately assertive, seductive, and sometimes sexually promiscuous (Eberhardt and Schill, 1984). These girls may have ambivalent feelings about men because of the negative memories they have of their fathers, and pursue men in inept and inappropriate ways. They begin dating early and are likely to engage in sexual intercourse at an early age. Girls whose fathers are dead may be excessively shy and uncomfortable around men, probably because they do not have as much experience being around men as did girls who grew up with males at home (Rice, 1983).

A study (Fleck et al., 1980) of 160 single female college students with psychologically absent fathers revealed that the women reported more attention seeking from males, more prosocial aggression, greater frequency and extent of heterosexual involvement—but also greater anxiety in dating than did women from father-present homes. Hepworth, Ryder, and Dreyer (1984) reported two major effects of parental loss on the formation of intimate relationships: avoidance of intimacy and accelerated courtship. Of course, just the opposite can occur when girls are brought up in a father-present home. If a girl overidentifies with a strong father figure, strong masculine identification can take place (Heilbrun, 1984).

Association with Delinquency

There seems to be a correlation between father absence and delinquency (Johnson, 1987). Adolescents from father-absent homes have a higher incidence of delinquency, but this does not mean that father absence causes delinquency. For one thing, children from father-absent families who get into trouble are more likely to be arrested and institutionalized when arrested than are those from intact families. Their mothers have fewer resources to fall back on when the children are in trouble. Furthermore, it may not be the family *type* (the one-parent family) but rather the family conflict that led to the disruption in the first place that causes the trouble. Levels of family conflict are better predictors of delinquency than family type (Blechman, 1982). We do know that adolescents who become delinquent are more likely to have had fathers who were cold, rejecting, punitive, neglectful, and mistrusting (Streit, 1981). (See chapter 10.) In these cases, having a father at home is a negative influence. Some adolescents get along better after their parents divorce (Bilge and Kaufman, 1983). Also, in groups such as low-income blacks, where father absence is common, factors other than father absence are more important as determinants of delinquency (Weller and Luchterhand, 1983).

Impact on Psychological Health

Is father absence a cause of psychological maladjustment, and is father presence necessary for mature mental health? These ideas have come under close scrutiny and have been subject to searching analysis (Bilge and Kaufman, 1983). For one thing, mothers who go through separation or divorce suffer a significant reduction or loss of income. Many live in poverty and are forced to raise their children in poor sections of town under adverse conditions. Problems develop with the children not because of father absence as such but as a by-product of poverty and low social status. Divorce or separation brings with it loss of environmental control. Mothers report being less able to discipline or influence their children after divorce, partly because the children are upset, partly because they put a lot of the blame for the absence of their father on the mother, partly because the mother feels guilty about the divorce and, in an effort to win their favor, is not as strict with them, and partly because the mother is working full time and therefore is not around to guide her children.

We know too that the greater is the mother's upset at the time of divorce or separation, the more the children will be upset. It is not father absence as such that does all the damage but the mother's mental state and her possible inability to cope and to meet the emotional needs of her children (Meijer and Himmelfarb, 1984). It is inevitable that the children will be affected. Much depends on the mother's family situation after divorce. Isaacs and Leon (1988) found that if a mother remains unmarried and shares residence with a new male partner, the result is problematic for the children involved, primarily because of the uncertainty of the future of the relationship.

It has been suggested too that the children's upset may have been a causal factor in the divorce rather than the other way around (Blechman, 1982). Temperamentally hard-to-handle children may also be a factor in marital breakup. Once divorce has taken place, these disturbed children are placed in the custody of their mothers and continue to exhibit psychological problems. Children who are easy to handle and who get along well with their fathers encourage their fathers to stay home; so though it appears that it is the intact family that has a more positive influence, in actual fact it is the best-adjusted children who have a positive influence on the marriage.

There seems to be some difference in the adjustment of sons and daughters. In a study of high school adolescents from disrupted families, male teenagers reported less conflict in their homes and a better self-image than did those from intact homes. With father gone, the son stepped in and assumed a "man-of-the-house" role, giving him a new status (Slater, Stewart, and Linn, 1983). The daughters, however, reported more conflict with their mothers after the father left. In this case, the females whose parents were still married had better self-concepts than those in disrupted families.

Children are as different as parents. Some children are better able to adjust to father absence than others. Research generally supports the finding that girls have fewer adjustment problems after divorce than do boys (Moore and Hotch, 1982).

There is a difference in affect also between father loss through divorce or separation and father loss because of death (Rozendal, 1983). Adolescents whose fathers have died are generally brought up in families that are warm and accepting. In contrast, those who have lost fathers through divorce generally have to deal with their own guilt and their parents' guilt and negative feelings of rejection of one another (Parish, 1980; Pichitino, 1983).

Influences on School Performance, Achievement, and Vocational Aspirations

A comparison of 559 youths in the seventh, eighth, and ninth grades showed that the children from the single-parent homes had the lowest grades and lowest occupational aspirations (Rosenthal and Hansen, 1980). Other research has suggested that parental divorce or separation delays cognitive development (Shinn, 1978) and such cognitive functioning as the development of moral judgment (Parish, 1980).

Here again, simple cause-effect relationships have not been clearly established. Certainly some adolescents are deeply upset by parental divorce or separation, so their grades in school suffer as a result—at least during a period of readjustment. But this does not happen to all. Usually some remain unaffected as far as scholastic achievement is concerned. Lower vocational aspirations and achievement are often a result of the changed financial status of the family (Amato, 1988; Mueller and Cooper, 1986; Saucier and Ambert, 1982). Blechman (1982) has suggested that a number of studies of children's academic performances are based on teacher evaluations and ratings, which reflect prejudices against those from one-parent families. When scrutinized, teachers' ratings do not agree with objective evaluations. Teachers based their judgments of children's performance not on their observation of the individual child but on their knowledge of the child's family background. "He comes from a broken home." "They're poor." "She has a record of running away from home." "He was picked up for drinking." Blechman suggests that teacher ratings should be avoided when objective estimates of school performance are desired.

Attitudes toward Self and Parents

One study in Canada indicated that adolescents from separated or divorced homes more often engaged in health-risk behavior (smoking, not fastening seat belts, and intemperate drinking) than those from intact families (Saucier and Ambert, 1983). Two major explanations were offered: (1) the health-risk behavior was an effort to improve self-esteem by adopting more daring attitudes or (2) the adolescents were less controlled by parents after parental breakup. This finding is in keeping with others that indicate that adolescents from father-absent homes have greater use and problems with alcohol, marijuana, and sexual activity than those from intact homes (Stern, Northman, and Van Slyck, 1984).

One of the problems of divorce is what it does to the adolescent's attitudes toward self and parent. Self-image seems to suffer, especially if adolescents blame themselves, feel guilty, or feel any social embarrassment because of what happens (Parish and Dostal, 1980; Parish and Taylor, 1979). Divorce is not the stigma it once was, but it is still a factor in social embarrassment.

Equally important is what it may do to the adolescent's feelings toward parents (Parish, 1981). Feelings may range from concern, or pity, to positive anger or hostility. The adolescent will often feel sorry for a mother who is left against her will but be very hostile toward one who asks her husband to leave. An adolescent may have a good relationship with his divorced mother until she remarries—then suddenly become very jealous and angry at her. Adolescents who blame their fathers for the breakup or who are deserted by them may grow angry and hostile toward them. Much depends on the reasons for the breakup and the adolescent's perception of it. This means that it is important for adolescents to understand the reasons. One college student remarked: "My mother called to say that she and dad were getting a divorce. I didn't even know they were having trouble." Parents often have a difficult time explaining years of increasing alienation or falling out of love or in love with someone else, but it is important to future parent-adolescent relationships that parents be honest and anxious to explain.

It is important also that parents emphasize that they are not divorcing or leaving their children, that they will continue to see them and care for them as before. Adolescents worry about how their needs will be met. These are real concerns with which parents must learn to cope.

HIGHLIGHT   Children and Parents in One-Parent, Stepparent, and Intact Families

A study of 399 children (192 primary and 207 secondary) in one-parent, steppparent, and intact families revealed the following relationship with fathers and stepfathers (Amato, 1987).

Compared with children in intact families, children in one-parent families reported less father support, less father control, less father punishment, more autonomy, more household responsibility, more conflict with siblings, and less family cohesion. Stepfathers were said to provide less support, control, and punishment than biological fathers in intact families, although stepfather involvement was positively associated with the number of years stepfamilies had been together.

RECONSTITUTED FAMILIES
Incidence

Over 80 percent of divorced men and 75 percent of divorced women eventually remarry. The high rate of divorce and remarriage means that about one in four marriages are now second marriages for one or both of the couple. In the next decade, close to one in three marriages may be second marriages. The median age of these remarriages is in the early or middle thirties, which means that the children are of elementary or preadolescent age (U.S. Dept. of Commerce, 1987).

Stepparents and Stepchildren

The probability of divorce in remarriages is slightly greater than in first marriages (Aquirre and Parr, 1982). *However, successful remarrieds state that second marriages are happier than first marriages* (Ganong and Coleman, 1984). This does not mean that remarriages are problem free. Finances are often a big problem (Fishman, 1983; Kargmen, 1983). *One of the biggest problems arises when there are children living at home* (Bridgwater, 1982; Lagoni and Cook, 1985). Adolescent stepchildren particularly have difficulty accepting their new stepfather or stepmother (Fine, 1986; Skeen, Covi, and Robinson, 1985). One reason is that they are jealous of the attention their own parent gives his or her mate (who is the stepparent) (Parish and Dostal, 1980). Another reason is that they feel their primary loyalty is toward their own parents and that the stepparent is an intruder (Lutz, 1983; Pink and Wampler, 1985). This was dramatically illustrated in the case of a new wife who was greeting her husband's older daughter for the first time. The woman was anxious to make a good impression. "I'm your new mother," she cooed. "The hell you are," replied the daughter and stamped out of the room (Bowerman and Irish, 1973). This case is not unusual. One of the typical reactions of a stepchild to a stepparent is rejection: "You're not my father," or "You're not my mother." This apparent rejection is hard for the stepparent to take and sometimes leads to a battle of will, a contest over authority, or resentment and bitterness. If children are infants when parents divorce and remarry, they usually grow up accepting the stepparent as a substitute mother or father (Papernow, 1984). Research indicates that adjustments with stepmothers and noncustodial biological mothers are more difficult than stepfather-child relationships (Sauer and Fine, 1988). Adjustments with stepfathers are usually easier than with stepmothers primarily because stepmothers play a more active role in relation to the children and spend more time with them than do stepfathers (Ambert, 1986; Clingempeel et al., 1984; Robinson, 1984). Stepdaughters especially have difficulties adjusting to stepmothers (Brand and Clingempeel, 1987). Also fairytales and folklore have developed the stereotype of the cruel stepmother, a myth hard to overcome (Fine, 1986). Problems are greater if the parent without custody tries to get a child to dislike the stepparent. If there are stepsiblings living together, trouble may also ensue if the natural parents show favoritism to their own children. If this happens, resentment and jealousy are likely to occur.

In contrast to these, other examples might be given to show satisfactory stepchild-stepparent relationships. One mother spoke of her husband's relationship with her child: "He's always referred to her as his daughter rather than his stepdaughter. He never made any issue of her being a stepchild. There are times when I think she is closer to him than she is to me. He is more her father than her real father ever was or is now" (Duberman, 1973, p. 285).

Relationships between stepsiblings also can be quite harmonious: "Our boys are the same age to the day. They are just like brothers. His son and my son are more alike than the two real brothers are. They all refer to each other as brothers; they are like one family" (Duberman, 1973, p. 286).

Out of eighty-eight couples who had remarried and had stepchildren, Duberman (1973) found that 64 percent of the families could be voted excellent as measured by a parent-child relationship score. In most families, however, working out problems and building good stepparent-stepchildren relationships takes time and effort (Mills, 1984; Crosbie-Burnett, 1984).

SUMMARY

The identity crisis adolescents face is more difficult if parents are experiencing a parallel crisis at the same time. Adolescents strive to come to terms with their newly developed sexuality; parents begin to fear the loss of theirs. Adolescents are working out their personal and vocational roles in life; parents are being forced to readjust their roles after the children are launched. Adolescents begin to challenge parental authority; parents hate to let go of it. Adolescents seek emotional emancipation from parents and fulfillment through peers; parents may seek emotional fulfillment through children and deeply resent peer competition. Adolescents are questioning adult values; many parents are also. Those parents who are not questioning values tend to hold more rigidly to those they have. These situations tend to put adolescents and parents in competition or opposition to one another. There can also be some basic personality differences between adolescents and parents: daring versus cautious, idealistic versus realistic, liberal versus conservative, critical versus satisfied, desirous of growing up versus desirous of staying young, and oriented to present versus oriented to past. These differences also create parent-adolescent conflict.

All parents have some difficulties with their adolescents. These problems usually are related to one or more of the following areas: social life, responsibility, school, attitudes and relationships in the family, or values and moral behavior. Adolescents want parents who show interest and concern, who will listen and talk to them and try to understand them and their problems, who love and accept them, who show they trust them, who are willing to grant autonomy and emotional independence, who discipline democratically and consistently, who strive to maintain a happy climate within the home, and who set a good example for them to follow.

Most parents are not as perfect as their adolescents would like them to be nor do most young people live up to all the expectations of parents. This results in some tension and conflict, especially during early adolescence, when both parents and youths are making their first adjustments to the identity crisis with which each is confronted. Gradually, however, conflict and tension subside if parents are willing to change their relationship with their children from a parent-dependent child orientation to an adult-growing adult relationship.

Most adolescents report close relationships with siblings in the family. These relationships are important. Older siblings often act as models and surrogate parents, fulfilling important emotional and social needs of younger brothers and sisters. Whenever sibling rivalry and jealousy exist, quarreling and resentment are common; therefore, it is important for all children to come to feel they are loved equally by the parents. Gradually, adolescents learn to get along with siblings as well as with other relatives who live with them in their family.

Because of the high rate of divorce, large numbers of adolescents live in one-parent families, most with their mothers. This situation may affect adolescents positively or negatively, depending on all the circumstances. And even in cases where adolescents have difficulties, one cannot say that father absence itself is the cause. Other factors accompanying the divorce, such as lower income and social status, social attitudes toward children from broken homes, the subsequent adjustment of the parents, and individual differences in children, are influential.

Most separated parents remarry, necessitating new adjustments among adolescents, stepsiblings, and stepparents. Most adolescents are able to adjust successfully and get along better in a reconstituted family than in their first family if the new environment is happy.

DISCUSSION QUESTIONS

1. When you were growing up, what were the major problems between you and your parents?
2. If you have an adolescent brother or sister living at home, what are the major sources of conflict between him or her and your parents?
3. Should adolescents be expected to obey their parents? Explain.
4. What do adolescents expect of parents? What kind of parents do they prefer?
5. Why don't adolescents listen to parents? Why do they feel they know it all?
6. What methods of discipline should parents use with adolescents?
7. What are the major sources of conflict between the adolescent and siblings?
8. Are your parents separated or divorced? How has their status affected you? What upset you the most? How did you feel about the situation?
9. What effect does father absence have on sons and on daughters?
10. Are your parents remarried? How do you get along with your stepparent? Explain. What are the major problems?

BIBLIOGRAPHY

Amato, P. R. (1987). "Family Processes in One-Parent, Stepparent, and Intact Families: The Child's Point of View." *Journal of Marriage and the Family,* 49, 327–337.

_____ . (1988). "Long-Term Implications of Parental Divorce for Adult Self-Concept." *Journal of Family Issues,* 9, 201–213.

Ambert, A. (1986). "Being a Stepparent: Live In and

Visiting Stepchildren." *Journal of Marriage and the Family*, 48, 795–804.

Anderson, S. A., and Fleming, W. M. (1986). "Late Adolescents' Home-Leaving Strategies: Predicting Ego Identity and College Adjustment." *Adolescence*, 21, 453–459.

Aquirre, B. E., and Parr, W. C. (1982). "Husband's Marriage Order and the Stability of First and Second Marriages of White and Black Women." *Journal of Marriage and the Family*, 44, 605–620.

Balswick, J. O., and Macrides, C. (1975). "Parental Stimulus for Adolescent Rebellion." *Adolescence*, 10, 253–266.

Baranowski, M. D. (Fall, 1984). "Grandparent-Adolescent Relations: Beyond the Nuclear Family." *Adolescence*, 17, 575–584.

Bell, N. J., and Avery, A. W. (May, 1985). "Family Structure and Parent-Adolescent Relationships: Does Family Structure Really Make a Difference?" *Journal of Marriage and Family Therapy*, 47, 503–508.

Bilge, B., and Kaufman, G. (January, 1983). "Children of Divorce and One-Parent Families: Cross-Cultural Perspectives." *Family Relations*, 32, 59–71.

Blechman, E. A. (February, 1982). "Are Children with One Parent at Psychological Risk? A Methodological Review." *Journal of Marriage and the Family*, 44, 179–195.

Blyth, D. A., Hill, J. P., and Thiel, K. S. (December, 1982). "Early Adolescents' Significant Others: Grade and Gender Differences in Perceived Relationships with Familial and Nonfamilial Adults and Young People." *Journal of Youth and Adolescence*, 11, 425–450.

Boss, P. G. (August, 1980). "The Relationship of Psychological Father Presence, Wife's Personal Qualities, and Wife/Family Dysfunction in Families of Missing Fathers." *Journal of Marriage and the Family*, 42, 541–549.

Bowerman, C. E., and Irish, D. P. (1973). "Some Relationships of Stepchildren to Their Parents." In *Love, Marriage, Family*. Edited by M. E. Lasswell and T. E. Lasswell, Glenview, Ill.: Scott, Foresman.

Brand, E., and Clingempeel, W. G. (1987). "Interdependencies of Marital and Stepparent-Stepchild Relationships and Children's Psychological Adjustment: Research Findings and Clinical Implications." *Family Relations*, 36, 140–145.

Bridgwater, C. A. (1982). "Second Marriages Fare Better with Childless Husbands." *Psychology Today*, 16, 18.

Burman, B., John, R. S., and Margolin, G. (1987). "Effects of Marital and Parent-Child Relations on Children's Adjustment." *Journal of Family Psychology*, 1, 91–108.

Circirelli, V. G. (February, 1980). "A Comparison of College Women's Feelings toward Their Siblings and Parents." *Journal of Marriage and the Family*, 78, 111–118.

Clingempeel, W. G., Brand, E., and Ievoli, R. (July, 1984). "Stepparent-Stepchild Relationships in Stepmother and Stepfather Families: A Multinational Study." *Family Relations*, 33, 465–473.

Cole, C., and Rodman, H. (1987). "When School-Age Children Are for Themselves: Issues for Family Life Educators and Parents." *Family Relations*, 36, 92–96.

Crosbie-Burnett, M. (July, 1984). "The Centrality of the Step Relationship: A Challenge to Family Theory and Practice." *Family Relations*, 33, 459–463.

deTurck, M. A., and Miller, G. R. (August, 1983). "Adolescent Perceptions of Parental Persuasive Message Strategies." *Journal of Marriage and the Family*, 34, 533–542.

Duberman, L. "Step-Kin Relationships." *Journal of Marriage and the Family*, 35, 283–292.

Eberhardt, C. A., and Schill, T. (Spring, 1984). "Differences in Sexual Attitudes and Likeliness of Sexual Behaviors of Black Lower-Socioeconomic Father-Present vs. Father-Absent Female Adolescents." *Adolescence*, 19, 99–105.

Edwards, J. N. (1987). "Changing Family Structure and Youthful Well-Being." *Journal of Family Issues*, 8, 355–372.

Enright, R. D., Lapsley, D. K., Drivas, A. E., and Fehr, L. A. (December, 1980). "Parental Influences on the Development of Adolescent Autonomy and Identity." *Journal of Youth and Adolescence*, 9, 529–545.

Eskilson, A., Wiley, M. G., Muehlbauer, G., and Dodder, L. (1986). "Parental Pressure, Self-Esteem and Adolescent Reported Deviance: Bending the Twig Too Far." *Adolescence*, 21, 501–515.

Fasick, F. A. (Spring, 1984). "Parents, Peers, Youth Culture and Autonomy in Adolescence." *Adolescence*, 19, 143–157.

Faw, T. T., and Goldsmith, D. F. (December, 1980). "Interpersonal Perceptions within Families Containing Behavior Problems with Adolescents." *Journal of Youth and Adolescence*, 9, 553–556.

Felson, M., and Gottfredson, M. (August, 1984). "Social Indicators of Adolescent Activities near Peers and Parents." *Journal of Marriage and the Family*, 46, 709–714.

Fine, M. (1986). "Perceptions of Stepparents: Variation in Stereotypes as a Function of Current Family Structure." *Journal of Marriage and the Family*, 48, 537–543.

Fishman, B. (July, 1983). "The Economic Behavior of Stepfamilies." *Family Relations*, 32, 359–366.

Fleck, J. R., Fuller, C. C., Malin, S. Z., Miller, D. H., and Acheson, K. R. (Winter, 1980). "Father Psychological Absence and Heterosexual Behavior, Personal Adjustment and Sex-Typing in Adolescent Girls." *Adolescence*, 15, 847–860.

Fleming, W. M., and Anderson, S. P. (1986). "Individuation from the Family of Origin and Personal Adjustment in Late Adolescence." *Journal of Marriage and the Family*, 3, 311–315.

Forsstrom-Cohen, B., and Rosenbaum, A. (May, 1985). "The Effects of Parental Marital Violence on Young Adults: An Exploratory Investigation." *Journal of Marriage and the Family*, 47, 467–472.

Fu, V. R., Hinkle, D. E., Shoffner, S., Martin, S., Carter, E., Clark, A., Culley, P., Disney, G., Ercanili, G., Glover, E., Kenney, M., Lewis, H., Moak, S., Stalling, S., and Wakefield, T. (Winter, 1984). "Maternal Dependency and Childrearing Attitudes among Mothers of Adolescent Females." *Adolescence*, 19, 795–804.

Ganong, L. H., and Coleman, M. (July, 1984). "The Effects of Remarriage on Children: A Review of the Empirical Literature." *Family Relations*, 33, 389–406.

Grady, K., Gersick, K. E., and Boratynski, M. (1985). "Preparing Parents for Teenagers: A Step in the Prevention of Adolescent Substance Abuse." *Family Relations*, 34, 541–549.

Grief, G. L. (1985). "Children and Housework in the Single Father Family." *Family Relations*, 34, 353–357.

Gullotta, T. P., Steven, S. J., Donohue, K. C., and Clark, V. S. (Fall, 1981). "Adolescents in Corporate Families." *Adolescence*, 16, 621–628.

Guptill, C. S. (November, 1979). "Youth's View of the Elderly." Paper presented at the 32d Annual Meeting of the Gerontological Society, Washington, D. C.

Hall, J. A. (1987). "Parent-Adolescent Conflict: An Empirical Review." *Adolescence*, 22, 767–789.

Harris, I. D., and Howard, K. I. (August, 1981). "Perceived Parental Authority: Reasonable and Unreasonable." *Journal of Youth and Adolescence*, 10, 273–284.

Helibrun, A. B. (October, 1984). "Identification with the Father and Peer Intimacy of the Daughter." *Family Relations*, 33, 597–605.

Hepworth, J., Ryder, R. G., and Dreyer, A. S. (January, 1984). "The Effects of Parental Loss on the Formation of Intimate Relationships." *Journal of Marital and Family Therapy*, 10, 73–82.

Isaacs, M. B., and Leon, G. H. (1988). "Remarriage and Its Alternatives Following Divorce: Mother and Child Adjustment." *Journal of Marriage and Family Therapy*, 14, 163–173.

Jensen, L., and Borges, M. (1986). "The Effect of Maternal Employment on Adolescent Daughters." *Adolescence*, 21, 659–666.

Jessop, D. J. (February, 1981). "Family Relationships as Viewed by Parents and Adolescents: A Specification." *Journal of Marriage and the Family*, 43, 95–106.

Johnson, P. L., and O'Leary, D. (1987). "Parental Behavior Patterns and Conduct Disorders in Girls." *Journal of Abnormal Child Psychology*, 15, 573–581.

Johnson, R. E. (1987). "Mothers' Versus Fathers' Role in Causing Delinquency." *Adolescence*, 22, 305–315.

Jurich, A. P., Schumm, W. R., and Bollman, S. R. (1987). "The Degree of Family Orientation Perceived by Mothers, Fathers, and Adolescents." *Adolescence*, 22, 119–128.

Kargman, M. W. (April, 1983). "Stepchild Support Obligations of Stepparents." *Family Relations*, 32, 231–238.

Kelly, C., and Goodwin, G. C. (Fall, 1983). "Adolescents' Perceptions of Three Styles of Parental Control." *Adolescence*, 18, 567–571.

Kidwell, J. S. (May, 1981). "Number of Siblings, Sibling Spacing, Sex, and Birth Order: Their Effects on Perceived Parent-Adolescent Relationships." *Journal of Marriage and the Family*, 43, 315–332.

Klyman, C. M. (1985). "Community Parental Surrogates and Their Role for the Adolescent." *Adolescence*, 20, 397–404.

Lagoni, L. S., and Cook, A. S. (1985). "Stepfamilies: A Content Analysis of the Popular Literature, 1961–1982." *Family Relations*, 34, 521–525.

Leslie, L. A., Huston, T. L., and Johnson, M. P. (1986). "Parental Reactions to Dating Relationships: Do They Make a Difference?" *Journal of Marriage and the Family*, 48, 57–66.

Light, H. K., Hertsgaard, D., and Martin, R. E. (1985). "Farm Children's Work in the Family." *Adolescence*, 20, 425–432.

Lutz, P. (July, 1983). "The Stepfamily: An Adolescent Perspective." *Family Relations*, 32, 367–375.

McCombs, A., Forehand, A., and Smith, K. (1988). "The Relationship between Maternal Problem-Solving Style and Adolescent Social Adjustment." *Journal of Family Psychology*, 2, 57–66.

McDonald, G. W. (November, 1979). "Determinants of Adolescent Perceptions of Maternal and Paternal Power in the Family." *Journal of Marriage and the Family*, 42, 752–770.

McKenry, P. C., Price-Boham, S., and O'Bryant, S. L. (October, 1981). "Adolescent Discipline: Different Family Members' Perception." *Journal of Youth and Adolescence*, 10, 327–337.

McMillan, D. W., and Hiltonsmith, R. W. (August, 1982). "Adolescents at Home: An Exploratory Study of the Relationship between Perception of Family Social Climate, General Well-Being and Actual Behavior in the Home Setting." *Journal of Youth and Adolescence*, 11, 301–315.

Martin, M. J., Schumm, W. R., Bugaighis, M. A., Jurich, A. P., and Bollman, S. R. (1987). "Family Violence and Adolescents' Perceptions of Outcomes of Family Conflict." *Journal of Marriage and the Family*, 49, 165–171.

Meijer, A., and Himmelfarb, S. (Spring, 1984). "Fatherless Adolescents' Feelings about Their Mothers—A Pilot Study." *Adolescence*, 19, 207–212.

Mills, D. M. (July, 1984). "A Model for Stepfamily Development." *Family Relations*, 365–380.

Montemayor, R., and Leigh, G. K. (October, 1982). "Parent-Absent Children: A Demographic Analysis of Children and Adolescents Living Apart from Their Parents." *Family Relations*, 31, 567–573.

Moore, D., and Hotch, D. F. (April, 1982). "Parent–Adolescent Separation: The Role of Parental Divorce." *Journal of Youth and Adolescence*, 11, 115–119.

Mueller, D. P., and Cooper, P. W. (1986). "Children of Single Parent Families: How They Fare as Young Adults." *Family Relations*, 35, 169–176.

Neapolitan, J. (Winter, 1981). "Parental Influences on Aggressive Behavior: A Social Learning Approach." *Adolescence*, 16, 831–840.

Northman, J. E. (1985). "The Emergence of an Appreciation for Help during Childhood and Adolescence." *Adolescence*, 20, 775–781.

Papernow, P. L. (July, 1984). "The Stepfamily Cycle: An Experimental Model of Stepfamily Development." *Family Relations*, 33, 355–363.

Parish, T. S. (Fall, 1980). "The Relationship between Factors Associated with Father Loss and Individual's Level of Moral Judgment." *Adolescence*, 15, 535–541.

_____ . (April, 1981). "Young Adults' Evaluations of Themselves and Their Parents as a Function of Family Structure and Disposition." *Journal of Youth and Adolescence*, 10, 173–178.

Parish, T. S., and Dostal, J. W. (August, 1980). "Evaluations of Self and Parent Figures by Children from Intact, Divorced, and Reconstituted Families." *Journal of Youth and Adolescence*, 9, 347–351.

Parish, T. S., Dostal, J. W., and Parish, J. G. (Spring, 1981). "Evaluations of Self and Parents as a Function of Intactness of Family and Family Happiness." *Adolescence*, 16, 203–210.

Parish, T. S., and Taylor, J. C. (December, 1979). "The Impact of Divorce and Subsequent Father Absence on Children's and Adolescents' Self-Concepts." *Journal of Youth and Adolescence*, 8, 427–432.

Pasley, K., and Gecas, V. (March, 1984). "Stresses and Satisfactions of the Parental Role." *Personnel and Guidance Journal*, 62, 400–404.

Peek, C. W., Fischer, J. L., and Kidwell, J. S. (1985). "Teenage Violence Toward Parents: A Neglected Dimension of Family Violence." *Journal of Marriage and the Family*, 47, 1051–1058.

Peters, J. F. (1985). "Adolescents as Socialization Agents to Parents." *Adolescence*, 20, 921–933.

Pichitino, J. P. (January, 1983). "Profile of the Single Father: A Thematic Integration of the Literature." *Personnel and Guidance Journal*, 61, 295–299.

Pink, J.E.T., and Wampler, K. S. (1985). "Problem Areas in Stepfamilies: Cohesion, Adaptability, and the Stepfather-Adolescent Relationship." *Family Relations*, 34, 327–335.

Portes, P. R., Dunham, R. M., and Williams, S. (1986). "Assessing Child-Rearing Style in Ecological Settings: Its Relation to Culture, Social Class, Early Age Intervention, and Scholastic Achievement." *Adolescence*, 21, 723–735.

Rice, F. P. (1983). *Contemporary Marriage*. Boston: Allyn and Bacon.

Robinson, B. E. (July, 1984). "The Contemporary American Stepfather." *Family Relations*, 33, 381–388.

Robinson, B. E., Rowland, B. H., and Coleman, M. (1986). "Taking Action for Latchkey Children and their Families." *Family Relations*, 35, 473–478.

Roscoe, B., and Callahan, J. E. (1985). "Adolescents' Self-Report of Violence in Families and Dating Relations." *Adolescence*, 20, 545–553.

Rosenthal, D., and Hansen, J. (October, 1980). "Comparison of Adolescents' Perceptions and Behaviors in Single- and Two-Parent Families." *Journal of Youth and Adolescence*, 9, 407–417.

Rozendal, F. G. (Winter, 1983). "Halos vs. Stigmas: Long-Term Effects of Parents' Death or Divorce on College Students' Concepts of the Family." *Adolescence*, 18, 947–955.

Rubin, Z. (June, 1982). "Fathers and Sons—The Search for Reunion." *Psychology Today*, 23ff.

Sanik, M. M., and Stafford, D. (Spring, 1985). "Adolescents' Contributions to Household Production: Male and Female Differences." *Adolescence*, 20, 207–215.

Saucier, J., and Ambert, A. (October, 1982). "Parental Marital Status and Adolescents' Optimism about Their Future." *Journal of Youth and Adolescence*, 11, 345–354.

Sauer, L. E., and Fine, M. A. (1988). "Parent-Child Relationships in Stepparent Families." *Journal of Family Psychology*, 1, 434–451.

Shinn, M. B. (1978). "Father Absence and Children's Cognitive Development." *Psychological Bulletin*, 85, 295–324.

Skeen, P., Covi, R. B., and Robinson, B. E. (1985). "Stepfamilies: A Review of the Literature with Suggestions for Practitioners." *Journal of Counseling and Development*, 64, 121–125.

Slater, E. J., Stewart, K. J., and Linn, M. W. (Winter, 1983). "The Effects of Family Disruption on Adolescent Males and Females." *Adolescence*, 18, 931–942.

Small, S. A. (1988). "Parental Self-Esteem and Its Relationship to Childrearing Practices, Parent-Adolescent Interaction, and Adolescent Behavior." *Journal of Marriage and the Family*, 50, 1063–1072.

Smith, T. E. (February, 1981). "Adolescent Agreement with Perceived Maternal and Paternal Educational Goals." *Journal of Marriage and the Family*, 43, 85–93.

———. (August, 1983). "Adolescent Reactions to Attempted Parental Control and Influence Techniques." *Journal of Marriage and the Family*, 45, 533–542.

Smith, T. E. (1988). "Parental Control Techniques." *Journal of Family Issues*, 2, 155–176.

Stefanko, M. (Spring, 1984). "Trends in Adolescent Research: A Review of Articles Published in Adolescence—1976–1981." *Adolescence*, 19, 1–14.

Stern, M., Northman, J.E., and Van Slyck, M. R. (Summer, 1984). "Father Absence and Adolescent 'Problem Behaviors': Alcohol Consumption, Drug Use and Sexual Activity." *Adolescence*, 19, 301–312.

Streit, F. (Summer, 1981). "Differences among Youthful Criminal Offenders Based on Their Perceptions of Parental Behavior." *Adolescence*, 16, 409–413.

Teyber, E. (July, 1983). "Effects of the Parental Coalition on Adolescent Emancipation from the Family." *Journal of Marital and Family Therapy*, 9, 305–310.

Thompson, L., Acock, A. C., and Clark, K. (1985). "Do Parents Know Their Children? The Ability of Mothers and Fathers to Gauge the Attitudes of Their Young Adult Children." *Family Relations*, 34, 315–320.

U.S. Department of Commerce, Bureau of the Census. (1987). *Statistical Abstract of the United States, 1987*. Washington, D. C.: U.S. Government Printing Office.

Weller, L., and Luchterhand, E. (Spring, 1983). "Family Relationships of 'Problem' and 'Promising' Youth." *Adolescence*, 18, 93–100.

Williamson, J. A., and Campbell, L. P. (1985). "Parents and Their Children Comment on Adolescence." *Adolescence*, 20, 745–748.

CHAPTER 17

Nonmarital Cohabitation and Adolescent Marriage

NONMARITAL COHABITATION

■ Definition and Incidence

unmarried
cohabitation

Unmarried cohabitation is now defined as two unrelated adults of the opposite sex sharing the same living quarters in which there is no other adult present (Spanier, 1983). According to this government definition, referred to as POSSLQ (Persons of Opposite Sex Sharing Living Quarters) (Davidson, 1983), there were 1,983,000 unmarried cohabiting couples in 1985 (U.S. Bureau of the Census, 1987), a 25 percent increase since 1980. Thirty-one percent of these couples had some children in the household under 15 years of age. A little over one-half had never been married; about one-third had been divorced; a few were married to someone else or widowed. Twenty-one percent of all the householders were under 25 years of age.

This latest definition eliminates groups of college students and others who live together in the same apartment for fun, convenience, and economy. It eliminates those who stay together on occasional weekends or while in Florida during the spring break. These temporary arrangements for convenience would not be considered *cohabitation* by some researchers because the term is more strictly applied to two persons of the opposite sex living together "under marriage-like conditions" (Rice, 1983). Studies of the incidence of cohabitation among college populations indicate that about 25 percent of students live with a dating partner at some point in their college career (Risman, et al., 1981; Tanfer, 1987). However, the rates vary depending upon the type of school, housing, parietal policies, sex composition, and ratio of the student body, as well as the researcher's sample and definition of cohabitation (Glick and Spanier, 1980). Of those who have cohabited, a great majority indicate that they would do so again (Newcomb, 1986).

■ Meanings Attached to Cohabitation

When couples decide to cohabit, the important question is, What meaning do they attach to the relationship? Do they consider themselves in love? Are they committed to one another in an exclusive relationship? Are they testing their relationship? Are they preparing for marriage? Are they engaged to be married? Do they consider themselves married? There are a wide variety of patterns and meanings associated with them, which may be grouped as follows:

Arrangements without commitment.
Intimate involvements with emotional commitment.
Living together as a prelude to marriage.
Living together as a trial marriage.
Living together as an alternative to marriage.

Arrangements without Commitment   Sometimes cohabitation arrangements are hastily or informally decided. After a weekend of fun and a short acquaintance, the fellow decides to move into his girl's apartment. He ends up staying the rest of the semester. Sometimes the arrangement is carefully worked out over a period of time as desirable for the couple. They just want to live, sleep, and have fun together. They are very good friends and lovers but want no permanent, intimate commitment. Their living together includes sharing expenses, doing the dishes and laundry, and sharing the other economic and material necessities that a married couple do, as well as sleeping together. This type of arrangement usually is of short duration. Either it develops into a greater commitment or the couple break up ("Cohabiting Young Women Plan to Get Married," 1987).

Intimate Involvements with Emotional Commitment   The majority of cohabiting college couples place themselves in this category (Macklin, 1980). Couples describe themselves as having a strong, affectionate relationship (Peterman, Ridley, and Anderson, 1974). Although some permit dating and sexual relationships outside the relationship, monogamy is the rule (Newcomb, 1986). Although there is a strong emotional commitment, there are no long-range plans for the future or for marriage. Such couples intend to continue the relationship indefinitely, but most involvements are of fairly short duration. Risman and colleagues' (1982) study of cohabitation in college found no statistically significant association between cohabitation and the type of relation that eventually evolved (i.e., whether the couple married or not). Cohabiting couples were not less likely to have married or more likely to have broken up by the end of the two-year study in comparison to couples that had not cohabited.

Living Together as a Prelude to Marriage   In this type of relationship, the couple have already committed themselves to legal marriage. They are engaged, formally or informally, but find no reason to live apart while they are waiting to be married or while they are making arrangements for their marriage. Many times, their living arrangements just develop over a time, without conscious intent. Here is one student's story:

> My boyfriend and I never really *decided* we were going to live together before marriage. It just happened. He would come over to my apartment weekends. It would be late, so I'd put him up for the night. Then several weekends he stayed the whole time; it was easier than driving all that distance back home. After a while, we got thinking: "Isn't this silly, why should we be separated, why can't he just move in with me?" So he did. Finally, he gave up his own place, because it was cheaper for us to maintain only one apartment. Six months later we got married. If someone would ask: "What made you decide to live together before marriage?" my answer would be: "I don't know. It just happened."

Under these circumstances there is never an intention that cohabitation will replace marriage or even be a trial period before marriage. It is just something the couple decide to do before they get married.

Living Together as a Trial Marriage   In this type of arrangement, the couple decide to live together to test their relationship: to discover if they are compatible and want to enter into legal marriage. This arrangement is "the little marriage before the big marriage that will last."

Living Together as an Alternative to Marriage   This arrangement has been called *companionate marriage, a covenant of intimacy,* or a *nonlegal voluntary association.* It is intended not as a prelude to marriage but as a substitute for it.

Changing Attitudes

The attitudes of society toward unmarital cohabitation have changed drastically in the past fifteen years. In the past, a woman who lived with a man without marriage was considered to be loose and immoral. Most landlords refused to rent to unmarried couples. Parents who found out their children were cohabiting out of wedlock threatened to disown them, withdrew financial support, forced them to withdraw from school, or put great pressure on them to get married. As a result, couples did not tell their parents about their arrangement and lived in fear that they would find out.

Today society has taken a more lenient attitude, and the social stigma of living together unmarried is diminishing as the custom becomes more accepted. Unmarrieds are, however, concentrated in urban areas where anonymity is easier to achieve. Criticism is more likely in small town, conservative, environments. Although the majority of parents have resigned themselves to their unmarried young adult children cohabiting, many still object to dependent children entering into such a relationship. Some parents object while their children are still in college; others are more permissive. A study of newly married couples who had cohabitated revealed that 80 percent of the women and 87 percent of the men reported that their parents were aware of their cohabiting, but only 56 percent of the women and 72 percent of the men had parental approval (Watson, 1983). Overall, however, society is more willing to ignore marital status. Unmarried couples are being accepted more readily and drawn more fully into the mainstream of society (Spanier, 1983). This in itself has eliminated part of the pressure to marry young and hastily.

Reactions to Cohabitation

Generally the majority of cohabiting couples report no regret at having cohabited. Among those who later married, Watson (1983) reported that only 9 percent of the women and 4 percent of the men expressed regrets. The proportion of dissatisfied couples is higher for those who do not marry. A few are devastated by relationships that do not work out. Some are very unhappy living together, experiencing much tension and frequent conflict. Yllo and Straus (1981) found a much higher rate of violence among cohabiting couples than among married couples, especially among the young.

Some individuals are hurt, either because the relationship did not work out or because they expected that it would result in marriage and it did not. Several studies have shown that men and women have somewhat different reasons for cohabitation. For many males cohabitation is no different from dating (Abernathy, 1981). Males most often cite their need for sexual gratification as the reason, whereas females state that marriage is their most important motive (Newcomb, 1979). When the relationship does not lead to marriage, some women feel used and exploited. The men expect them to pay half the expenses, do many of the household chores, and provide regular bed privileges without a commitment. As a result many cohabiting women develop negative views of marriage and of the role of husband. They begin to see themselves as a source of sex, not as a source of affection. Then there is always their anxiety about pregnancy, in spite of contraception. If pregnancy occurs, some say they would marry, yet marriage because of pregnancy is one of the worst possible motives in terms of subsequent chances for marital success. *All that can be said with certainty now is that cohabitation has been helpful to some and harmful to others.* The effect depends upon the individuals involved, on how they feel, and on what happens (Rice, 1983).

Still the majority of college students who have cohabited indicate positive feelings about the experience. Students report the experience as "pleasant," "successful," "highly productive." Many students indicate that it fostered personal growth and maturity, resulting in a deeper understanding of themselves or of what marriage requires (Newcomb, 1979; Rice, 1983). In comparison with noncohabiting couples in the Boston area, cohabiting men and women were more likely to report satisfaction with their relationship (Risman et al., 1981). Cohabiting men were more likely to say that having sexual intercourse with their partner was satisfying. Cohabiting couples reported seeing each other more often, having sexual intercourse more often, feeling greater love for each other, and disclosing more to their partner.

Adjustments

The author has talked to a number of couples who were living together out of wedlock. Some had a close emotional involvement without commitment to marriage of any kind; others intended their relationship to be a period of testing; others originally had no intention of marrying but saw their relationship as a substitute for legal marriage; others were waiting to get married and were living together in the meantime. Most seemed to have some problems.

One major category of problems relates to the emotional involvement and feelings of the individuals concerned (Trost, 1978). A minority complain about overinvolvement, feeling trapped, a loss of identity, the overpermissiveness of their partner, or the lack of opportunity to participate in activities with others. Without realizing it, these people became enmeshed in relationships for which they were not emotionally prepared. Once in, they did not know how to escape without hurt. Others report being exploited or used by another person who did not care about them. Jealousy of others' involvements is common. One major worry is concern and uncertainty about the future. This uncertainty pressures some into marriage, others into breaking off the relationship.

The other problems youths face while living together unmarried are similar to those of any other people sharing the same quarters. Arranging to do the housekeeping chores is a challenge to unmarried as well as married couples. One study of college couples who were cohabiting without being married showed that the women were still taking primary responsibility for performing most household tasks (Stafford et al., 1977). Traditional sex-role concepts and role specialization in the division of labor were quite evident among these couples. Far greater percentages of females than males reported cooking, dusting, dishwashing, vacuuming, doing laundry, scrubbing, feeding pets, and planning menus—traditionally feminine chores. Males reported major responsibility for cutting the lawn, washing the car, doing repairs, cleaning the garage, shoveling the snow—traditionally masculine chores. More males than females reported an equal sharing of traditionally feminine chores, indicating that men reported they helped with these tasks more often than women felt they did (Stafford et al., 1977). It is obvious that nonmarital cohabitation is not a cure-all for sex-role inequality. Some tasks are shared, but generally the female partners do women's work and the male partners men's work (as defined by traditional standards). This division leaves the women with most of the household duties regardless of whether they are going to school and are employed as well. A study of students from four colleges in the Boston area revealed that cohabiting men (in comparison with noncohabiting dating couples) were *not* more likely to say their relationship was egalitarian. Cohabiting women were more likely to report male dominance, and were more likely to see themselves at a power disadvantage (Risman et al., 1981).

The more studies that are done of cohabitation, the more evidence there is that the couples behave like ordinary married couples. Learning to know and understand each other's moods, temperaments, and personalities and adjusting to schedules, personal habits, and idiosyncrasies arise in unmarried relationships as well as in marriage unions. Many problems arise because couples are immature emotionally, socially, financially, and in other ways. They have to face most of the same problems that young married couples face as a result of their immaturities and insecurities. The majority of couples, however, report that their sex life is satisfying ("Cohabitation by the Unmarried," 1986). Cohabiting couples generally have intercourse more frequently and are more faithful contraceptive users than either married couples or unmarried noncohabitants (Bachrach, 1987).

Effect on Subsequent Marriage

One of the most important questions is what effect premarital cohabitation has on subsequent marital adjustment. One of the arguments used for cohabitation is that it weeds out incompatible couples, and it prepares people for more successful marriage. Is this true? No, according to several studies. Newcomb and Bentler (1980) conducted a longitudinal study examining the effects of premarital cohabitation on subsequent marital stability. After four years, they found no significant difference in marital stability between couples who had previously cohabited and those that did not. Moeller and Sherlock (1981) studied 139 recently married, college matriculating young adults and found that the marriages of previous cohabitants were more egalitarian and less husband-dominated, but there were no significant differences in the levels of conflict between the two groups. Similarly, Markowski and Johnston (1980) found some differences in temperament between those who had cohabited and those who had not, but they concluded that cohabitation "did not seem to greatly benefit nor harm the marriage relationship" (p. 125).

The results of studies seem to be affected partially by how long people have been married at the time of evaluation. Most research indicates that a period of disillusionment in relation to marriage occurs after the initial glow and excitement have worn off and couples have settled down to daily living. Presumably, the longer couples have lived together before marriage, the earlier in the relationship the period of disillusionment sets in. Thus, Watson (1983) found that compared with noncohabiting couples, cohabitants scored lower on *Spanier's Dyadic Adjustment Scale* during the first year of marriage (Spanier, 1976). The differences were reflected in lower scores on two subscales: Consensus (extent of agreement) and Satisfaction (with the relationship). Similarly, DeMaris and Leslie (1984) studied couples in the second year of marriage. Comparisons of married couples who had cohabited with those who had not found that cohabitants scored significantly lower in marital communication, consensus, and satisfaction. However, the researchers could not establish clear cause and effect: that cohabitation caused lower marital quality. There were too many other variables that might have influenced results (Meer, 1984).

In fact, Watson and DeMeo (1987) did a follow-up in the fourth year of their marriages of couples who had earlier taken part in the original studies of Watson and found that *the premarital relationships of the couples, whether of cohabitation or traditional courtship, did not appear to have had a long-term effect on marital adjustment of intact couples. After four years of marriage, marital adjustment was no longer affected by the living arrangement in the months leading up to marriage. Rather, the relationship the couple had subsequently built with one another was the important thing.* Until more representative data are available, we cannot conclude at this time that nonmarital cohabitation increases or decreases subsequent marital satisfaction and stability.

There are a number of important "ifs" to be answered before individual effects can be known. If after living together couples feel pushed into marriages for which they are not ready, the effect is detrimental. Studies at four colleges in the Boston area also revealed that cohabiting couples were no less likely to marry or no more likely to break up than noncohabiting couples who were dating. Cohabitation appeared to be part of the courtship process rather than a long-term alternative to marriage (Risman et al., 1981). However, those who were married by the end of the study reported a shorter interval between the time of first dating and the time they were married (22.8 months for cohabiting couples versus 35.8 months for noncohabiting couples). Those who had lived together before marriage had been under a great deal of pressure from parents either to marry or to end their cohabiting relationship. Cohabitation either speeded up their decision, or couples may have decided to live together only after they agreed to marry. Certainly, if cohabitation pushed couples into marriage when they were not ready, the result would be negative.

TRIAL MARRIAGE

Bertrand Russell on Trial Marriage ▪

The concept of a testing period before marriage is not new. It was first proposed by Judge Ben Lindsay (1927) in 1927. In *Marriage and Morals* (1929) Bertrand Russell (1961) approved of Lindsay's concept and asserted that marriage should not be final when there are no children, so that if the relationship proved sterile it could be easily dissolved. In outlining his view of a "new kind of marriage," Russell reiterated the views of Lindsay, who said there are three ways in which the new

HIGHLIGHT   Coed Dorms

The arrangement of men and women living in adjacent rooms represents what is, to adults, a departure from tradition. In a few instances men and women are allowed to share university apartments. But from a student's point of view, coed living is desirable because it is natural. As one woman said: "When you're separated, it's so unnatural. Your friends are all girls. You walk into a boy's dorm and they all stare at you. When you're all living together, the boys look at girls less as sex objects." Another remarked:

> The point is that we want to know boys as friends and companions, as well as dating objects. . . . It used to be, a guy kept trying to get the girl to bed, and she kept trying to stay out. Now they both want a good, honest relationship first. . . . And I'm not talking about promiscuity. Sometimes I think parents think so much dirtier than we do. I'm talking about the total relationship, as opposed to sex roles.

The primary objection from an adult point of view is that coed dorms lead to promiscuity. However, students who want to have sex together find ways of doing so under any arrangement. But more important, students form relationships other than those based exclusively on sex. They go beyond sexual attraction to a more encompassing relationship. They participate less in structured, one-to-one dating and more in informal group activities. They plan more group activities and events. Administrators report that students spend as much time studying as those in single-sex residences, that the level of conversation is intellectually higher, and that there is less vandalism.

Not all students want or choose coed living when given the option. Some find it too much of a strain to "get dressed before walking down the hall" or "having to be on your best behavior all the time." Generally, the cautious or socially immature student (one who could benefit most from coed living) is most likely to choose a single-sex residence. When Lambda Nu, a fraternity at Stanford University, went coed, four men quit but ten joined. Forty-two women applied, and twenty were picked by lot. The men and women live in separate sections of the house, but there are few rules. Students admit there is little promiscuity.

Although coed living is not for everybody, it has many advantages in promoting natural heterosexual development and relationships.

kind of marriage, companionate marriage, can be distinguished from ordinary marriage:

> First, that there should be for the time being no intention of having children, and that accordingly the best available birth control information should be given to the young couple. Second, that so long as there are no children and the wife is not pregnant, divorce should be possible by mutual consent. And third, that in the event of divorce, the wife would not be entitled to alimony. (Russell, 1961)

In defending Lindsay's position, Russell espoused several arguments. He felt that companionate marriage would do a great deal of good because it would eliminate incompatible couples, particularly sexually incompatible couples. He wrote: "It seems absurd to ask people to enter upon a relation intended to be lifelong, without any previous knowledge as to their sexual compatibility. It is just as absurd as it would be if a man intending to buy a house were not allowed to view it until he had completed the purchase." He argued also that marriage should never be considered consummated until the wife's first pregnancy because children rather than intercourse are the true purpose of marriage.

Margaret Mead on Two-Step Marriage

Anthropologist Margaret Mead (1966) caused a stir in 1966 with a proposal for marriage in two steps. Mead outlined two forms of marriage. The first was **individual marriage,** which was a business union between two individuals who would be committed to each other for as long as they wanted to remain together but not as parents. This first step would be marriage without children and would give two young people a chance to know each other more intimately than would be possible through a brief love affair. If their relationship deepened and was compatible, they could agree to move on to the second step, **parental marriage.** If they decided to separate, however, the husband would not be responsible for the continued financial support of his wife, so there would be no alimony.

individual marriage

parental marriage

Mead emphasized the seriousness of both steps. Individual marriage should be considered a serious commitment, entered into in public, validated and protected by law and religion, in which each partner would be looking toward a lifetime relationship (though not yet bound to it) and concerned deeply for the happiness and well-being of the other. Parental marriage would be allowed only after a good individual marriage; it would be difficult to contract and would be entered after a period of preparation. The couple would have to demonstrate their economic ability and, perhaps, their emotional capacities to raise a child. If parental marriage did end, divorce would be arranged to offer maximum protection for the children.

In the rationale for marriage in two steps, Mead emphasized several important points. *One,* marriage is the necessary prelude to responsible parenthood, and all children born of a marriage should be wanted and properly cared for. *Two,* under the present system of dating, courtship, and mate selection, young couples enter early marriage and become parents before they know each other as husband and wife. *Three,* Americans have finally come to accept the notions that sex is a natural activity and that young Americans cannot be expected to postpone sex until their middle twenties. Society has encouraged early marriage as a way of providing a sex life for adolescents; but in doing so, it has generated new difficulties. The young couple, being inexperienced, are likely to bungle their first sex relationships. They are faced with problems of adjustment of early marriage, such as finances and making friends. Using early marriage as a means of solving the sex problems of youths raises the possibility these adolescents will be irrevocably trapped. They ought to be committed to each other when they marry, but such commitments should not be irrevocable. Individual marriage would provide the first step without the final commitment.

Michael Scriven's Three-Step Plan

preliminary marriage

personal marriage

parental marriage

Philosophy professor Michael Scriven (1967) has elaborated on Margaret Mead's two-step plan. He proposes three types of marriage: **preliminary marriage,** which would be legitimized cohabitation, entered into contractually for one year without the need for subsequent commitment; **personal marriage,** similar to Margaret Mead's idea of individual marriage, which could be entered into only after a year's trial of preliminary marriage; and **parental marriage,** the last step to be taken, and only after successful personal marriage.

Other Writers on Trial Marriage

Other writers have presented variations of the basic suggestions already made. In *The Sexual Wilderness*, Vance Packard (1968) suggests a two-year confirmation period after which marriage would become final or be dissolved. He feels that because the first two years of marriage are the most difficult, two years of confirmation would be adequate. Packard does not refer to "trial marriage," which he regards as little more than unstructured cohabitation; rather, a period of confirmation with no expectation of permanency would contribute to the success of the plan.

Family therapist Virginia Satir (1967) introduced a plan to make marriage a statutory five-year renewable contract. Like other writers, Satir felt there needs to be "an apprentice period . . . in which potential partners have a chance to explore deeply and experiment with their relationship, experience the other and find out whether his fantasy matched the reality."

So far none of these plans have been legalized by any state.

ADOLESCENT MARRIAGE

Trends and Incidence

Figure 17-1 gives a detailed picture of U.S. statistics on marriage ages between 1890 and 1987. The median age of first marriage for females stopped declining in 1956 and for males in 1959 and has been increasing slowly since. The median age of first marriage in 1987 was 25.8 for males and 23.6 for females. It appears that the steady drop in median age of marriage that was especially noticeable in the 1940s has been arrested. However, there are still numbers of youth, especially girls, who are marrying young. Census figures for 1987 show that 5.4 percent of girls and 1.4 percent of boys aged 15 to 19 are (or have been) married (U.S. Bureau of the Census, 1987). Forty percent of women and 22 percent of men aged 20 to 24 are or have been married.

Prospects and Prognosis

In order to evaluate whether adolescent marriage is wise or unwise, desirable or undesirable, one must ask how successful these marriages are. If they are strong, happy, satisfying marriages, there is no cause for complaint or alarm; but if they are weak, unhappy, frustrating marriages, causing much personal suffering and numerous social problems, there is ample cause for concern.

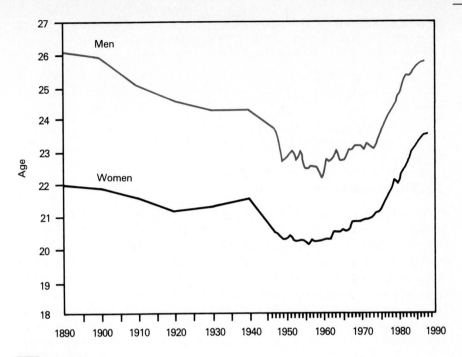

■ FIGURE 17-1

Median age at first marriage, by sex: 1890 to 1987.

From: U. S. Bureau of the Census (1987). Current Population Reports, Series P–20, No. 417. *Households, Families, Marital Status, and Living Arrangements: March 1987.* (Washington, D.C.: U.S. Government Printing Office), p. 4.

Divorce statistics are a means of measuring marriage success or failure. Using this measure, adolescent marriages do not work out well (Bishop and Lynn, 1983; Booth and Edwards, 1985). *Numerous research studies indicate that the younger people are when married, the greater is the chance of unhappy marriage and thus of divorce* (Teti, Lamb, and Elster, 1987). The older is the couple at first marriage, the greater is the likelihood the marriage will succeed. But this direct correlation between age at first marriage and martial success diminishes for men at about age 27, when the decline in divorce rates slows considerably. For women, the divorce rate declines with each year they wait to marry until a gradual leveling off occurs at about age 25. Therefore, *strictly from the standpoint of marital stability, men who wait to marry until at least age 27 and women who wait until about age 25 have waited as long as practical to maximize their chances of success* (Booth and Edwards, 1985).

Many couples marrying young may never get divorced, but some express deep dissatisfaction with their marriage. Here are some of their comments.

"I don't think people should marry young. It's hard to get along when he is going to school. Our income is rather short. We probably should have waited."

"We thought we were in love, we would get married and have good times. We had a very poor idea of what marriage was. We thought we could come and go, do as we pleased, do or not do the dishes, but it isn't that way."

"I have missed several years of important living, the dating period, living with another girl, being away from home, working, maybe. I wouldn't get married so young again."

"I would have waited to finish high school first. It has tied me down so. I've had no fun since I was married. I can't go to dances. I don't feel right here. . . . I guess I thought he was the only one in the world, I was badly mixed up."

A Profile of the Young Married

Early marriages primarily involve young wives and their older husbands. Typically, a high school girl will marry a boy who is past high school age, usually from 3.5 to 5.5 years older. Usually the younger the bride, the larger is the age difference between her husband and her. Early marriages disproportionately involve adolescents from lower socioeconomic backgrounds. Typically their parents have less education and are of a lower occupational status.

There are several good reasons why low socioeconomic status correlates with early marriage. As a group, these youths are less interested in high school and post-high school education, so they see no need to postpone marriage to finish their schooling, especially when marriage seems much more attractive than school (Cherlin, 1980). Less skilled occupations require only a minimal amount of education. In some communities marriage by age eighteen, especially for girls, is generally approved because the youths have reached a dead end in school and marriage seems the only attractive course. The parents are less often likely to object to early marriage. Furthermore, premarital pregnancy, one of the principal causes of early marriage, is much more common among youths from low socio-economic status families (Bishop and Lynn, 1983).

Similarly, adolescents who have lower intelligence and poorer grades in school more often marry early (Call and Otto, 1977). Furthermore, those who marry during school are more likely to drop out of school. It becomes a vicious circle: the academically inferior marry earlier, and once married, are less likely to continue their education (Lowe and Witt, 1984). This is especially true of those who have children soon after marriage (Haggstrom, Kanouse, and Morrison, 1986).

Place of residence seems to have some influence on age at marriage. Rural residents tend to marry a year earlier than urban residents (Hogan, 1978). Those from the South tend to marry earlier than others, those from the Northeast later, with those from the central and western states somewhere in between. Youths of foreign parentage usually marry later than those of native-born parents (Edington and Hays, 1978). Foreign-born Irish males have the highest age at marriage (29.4 years), those with Spanish surnames the earliest (25.6 years). The age is variable depending on native customs (Hogan, 1978).

There is some evidence that the less emotionally adjusted a boy or girl is, the more likely early marriage is to occur. Also, the early married are more socially maladjusted at the time of marriage than are others (Grover et al., 1985). However, young marrieds evidence the most personality improvement during the early years—more so than do the nonmarrieds—so that at the end of a few years, the personality differentials virtually disappear. If the marriages can survive, marriage itself seems to be a contributing factor in developing personal and social maturity.

Youths who marry early tend to have less satisfactory relationships with their parents. They have more disagreement with parents before marriage and less attachment to their fathers. Furthermore, wives who report problems with families in their childhood and adolescence report unhappiness, doubt, and conflict in early marriage (Friedman, 1978).

Reasons for Adolescent Marriage

The most important causes or reasons for early marriage are:

> Sexual stimulation, pregnancy.
> Early dating, acceleration of adult sophistication.
> Social pressure.
> Overly romantic, glamorous views of marriage.
> Escape; attempt to resolve personal, social problems.
> Affluence, prosperity.

The reasons deserve closer examination.

The number one reason for early marriage, particularly while still in school, is *pregnancy* (Bishop and Lynn, 1983). Pregnancy rates vary from study to study according to the age of the youths. The younger the adolescent is at the time of marriage, the more likely pregnancy is to be involved. Pregnancy rates may be as high as 50 percent when at least one of the partners is still in high school (Patten, 1981).

Research clearly indicates that within a social class, the earlier a boy or girl starts to date, the more likely early marriage is to occur. It is important to emphasize the phrase "within a social class," for adolescents from higher socioeconomic status groups start *dating earlier* than those from lower socioeconomic status groups, yet the latter marry earlier. Why? Although higher-status youths start dating earlier, they proceed at a slower pace from dating to marriage. Lower-status youths start dating a little later but are more likely to become romantically involved, go steady, and proceed more rapidly from first date to marriage (Larson et al., 1976). Age when dating starts is not itself the deciding factor. What is important is the length of the person's dating experience before marriage—generally, the longer the better.

There are other correlates to these statements. The more dates a girl has compared with others her age, the more likely early marriage is to occur (Marini, 1978). Also, the earlier a girl begins to go steady and the more steady boyfriends she has in high school, the more likely is her early marriage. But again the emphasis should be not just on how young dating begins but how rapidly the young person advances to serious dating, going steady, engagement, and other symbols of adult status.

Social pressure from parents, friends, and society pushes adolescents toward early marriage (Call and Otto, 1977). Educators report a chain reaction of early marriages in their schools. When one couple marries, there is increased pressure on others to do the same. No one wants to be left out. Pressure also comes from parents who do not want their daughters to be wallflowers or spinsters or their sons to be thought "queer."

One study of high school sophomores to determine their concepts of marriage revealed that 64 percent of them held very *magical views of marriage* (Tamashiro, 1979). Marriage was seen as a fairytale in which a man and woman fall in love, marry, and live in bliss for infinity. Even adolescents whose parents are divorced and/or remarried have idealized concepts of marriage (Ganong, Coleman, and Brown, 1981). Being in love in our culture is held to be so romantic and wonderful that many youths do not wait to enter this blissful state (Scott, 1983). The concept of marriage for love leads youths to feel that the goal of life is to find love, and that once found, one must hurry up and marry, at all costs, before it escapes. Girls who marry early often feel that marriage is their goal in life.

Marriage is sometimes used as a means of *escape* from an unhappy home situation, lack of school achievement, personal insecurities or inadequacies, or unsatisfactory social adjustment with one's peers. The less attractive one's present situation and the more attractive marriage seems, the more the emotionally insecure or socially maladjusted individual feels pushed toward marriage as an escape from an unhappy environment into something that promises to be better (Larson et al., 1976).

More early marriages occur in times of *economic prosperity* than in times of economic depression. The reason is obvious: getting married costs money; therefore, when employment is readily available, young couples feel they can afford to get married.

Adjustments and Problems

Many of the adjustments young couples must make or the problems they must solve are no different from those of other couples, but they are aggravated by *immaturity*. It is essentially the problem of immaturity that is the great obstacle to successful teenage marriage.

Immaturity creates problems in many ways. *The less mature are less likely to make a wise choice of mate.* When the time span between first date and marriage is shortened, youths have less chance to gain experience in knowing and understanding the kind of person with whom they are compatible. The young adolescent girl or boy in the throes of a first love affair is at a distinct disadvantage in making an intelligent choice of mate.

The less mature are less likely to evidence the ultimate direction of their personality growth. Youths change as they mature and may find they have nothing in common with their partners as they grow older. Two young people who might genuinely find a community of interest and a good reciprocal interaction at a particular point in their growth could easily grow away from each other in the ensuing two or three years as their personalities unfold.

The most common example is the case of a young woman who dropped out of school to work to put her husband through college only to discover afterward that he has grown away from her intellectually and they can no longer enjoy talking together. The same holds true of a boy who marries young. He may marry a girl who has not yet found herself in life and runs the risk of living with a girl different from the woman she will be several years later. Many girls marry only to discover later that they resent having to give up a promising career.

The less mature are less likely to be able to handle the difficult and complex adjustments and problems of marriage. There is ample evidence to show that emotional maturity and good marital adjustment go together (Booth and Edwards, 1985).

Many teenagers are still insecure, oversensitive, and somewhat tempestuous and unstable. Many are still rebelling against adult authority and seeking emotional emancipation from parents. If these youths marry, they carry their immaturities into marriage, making it difficult to adjust to living with their mate and making it harder to make decisions and solve conflicts as they arise. Booth and Edwards (1985) found that the principal sources of marital dissatisfaction among couples who married young were lack of faithfulness, presence of jealousy, lack of understanding, disagreement, and lack of communication. Attempts to dominate or refusal to talk made communication difficult.

Most youths have not yet become responsible enough for marriage. The average teenage boy is not ready to settle down. He wants to go out, have fun, be with the gang, and be free to do as he pleases. He may resent being tied down and possibly having to support a wife and child. He may not yet evidence a "monogamous attitude." Nor are many teenage girls ready to be wives and probably mothers, to manage a family budget, or to handle their share of the responsibility for the homemaking tasks.

One of the real problems and disadvantages of early marriage is that it is often associated with *early parenthood* (Kellam, et al., 1982). A majority of teenage couples have a baby within one year after marriage. The younger the brides and grooms, the sooner they start having children. Also, the earlier the age at marriage, the greater is the percentage of brides who are premaritally pregnant. Those who get married because of pregnancy have the poorest prognosis of marital success. Because premarital pregnancy and early postmarital pregnancy are followed by a higher-than-average divorce rate, large numbers of children of early marriages grow up without a secure, stable family life or without both a mother and a father (Gershenson, 1983). Apparently many young marrieds are not mature enough to assume the responsibilities of marriage and early parenthood, so the marriages often fail and the children suffer.

Not only do adolescent parents begin having children at an earlier age, but they also have more children (Marini, 1981; Peabody et al., 1981). The young women who are the least happily married are also the ones who experience unplanned pregnancies. Early motherhood creates many stresses in the lives of adolescents (McLaughlin and Micklin, 1983). Adolescent mothers are more likely

Physicians have emphasized the medical risks of early pregnancy. Babies born to adolescent mothers are more likely to be premature and to have low birth weights, physical and neurological defects, and higher mortality. (John Telford)

to be out of school, unemployed, poor, and on welfare (Rindfuss and St. John, 1985). They experience loneliness and isolation from friends, with little time for themselves. Many are able to cope only by asking family members and community agencies for assistance (Barth et al., 1983; Colletta, Hadler, and Gregg, 1981). Many live with their parents after the baby is born (Nathanson, Baird, and Jemail, 1986).

Physicians have emphasized the medical risks of early pregnancy. Children born to adolescent mothers are more likely to be born premature, with low birth weight and with physical and neurological defects than are infants born to mothers in their twenties (McKenry et al., 1979). Perinatal, neonatal, and infant mortality have been found to be higher for children of young mothers (McKenry et al., 1979; "Substantially Higher," 1984).

The higher incidence of physical defects in children born to adolescent mothers is not due solely to the age of the mother. It is related also to the fact that these mothers may be pregnant out of wedlock and of low socioeconomic status and so receive inadequate nutrition and poor or inadequate prenatal care ("Social Factors," 1984). Early pregnancy is also a medical risk for the young teenage girl. If she becomes pregnant while her own body is still growing and maturing, the growing fetus imposes an additional strain on her system, and she is more prone to complications of pregnancy.

One of the major problems of early marriage is *financial worry*. The primary difficulties are inadequate income and the fact that income has not reached the level expected. Little education, inexperience, and youth do not bring high wages (Grindstaff, 1988). Some couples marry without any income.

With little or no income, couples receive part or all of their financial assistance from parents. Families usually give some assistance to their children in the first year of marriage, such as wedding gifts, clothing, home furnishings and equipment, food, loans of household equipment and car, baby-sitting services, money, and other gifts.

Not only low income but also inexperience in financial management and naively optimistic expectations get young marrieds into financial trouble. Teen-agers usually expect to be able to purchase immediately many of the items that probably had taken their parents years to acquire.

One of the expensive obsessions of adolescent males is to have a car. In spite of their low income, 86 percent of young heads of families (ages 18 to 24) have cars (U.S. Bureau of the Census, 1985). This heavy outlay for cars and transportation is a major drag on the budgets of young families that need funds for current expenses or for household goods to begin marriage.

There is often a marked *decrease in sexual satisfaction* after marriage, especially after the first baby is born. Disagreements are common over the quality and frequency of sex relations.

One of the most frequent complaints of wives is the husband who goes out with his friends and leaves her home alone.

In-law problems are more likely if young couples live with parents or accept financial help from them. When parents give assistance to married children, they often expect continual affectional response, inclusion in some of their children's activities, personal service and attention, and compliance with parental wishes. The more immature the young marrieds, the more likely parents are to try to "help," to direct and interfere in their children's lives, and the more likely the young couple is to enact the residues of late adolescent conflicts over autonomy and dependence.

MARRIAGE AND PUBLIC SCHOOLS

Early marriage diminishes educational attainment among those attending high school (Kerck-hoff and Parrow, 1979). Not only do young marrieds make less educational progress during the four-year period, but they also tend to have lower educational aspirations for the future (Lowe and Witt, 1984). The converse is also true: those with lower educational aspirations tend to marry earlier than those with higher aspirations (Marini, 1978).

Drop-out rates among married high school couples are high. The rates reflect the fact that the great majority of the girls are pregnant before marriage, and school administrative policies and programs fail to keep the students in school. Once she has dropped out, the chances of the adolescent mother's returning to continue her education are relatively small, especially if she keeps her baby and receives little encouragement or help in returning (Ewer and Gibbs, 1976). Boys who drop out most often do so for economic reasons. Figure 17-2 shows the mean educational attainment for women by age at which they had their first child. If the girl was less than 15 when she had her first child, her average years of education was only 8.9. If her first baby was born when she was 24 years old, her average years of education was 13.5 (Dillard and Pol, 1982).

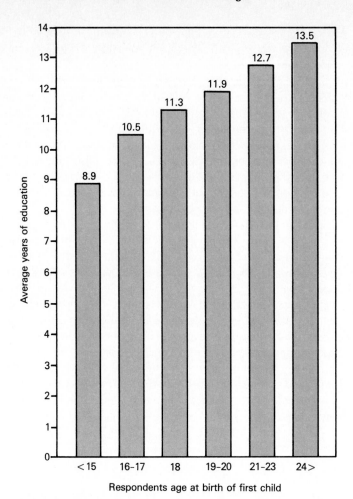

Average years of education

Respondents age at birth of first child

FIGURE 17-2

Mean educational attainment for women by age at which they had their first child.

From: Dillard, K. Denise, and Pol, L. G. (April, 1982). "The Individual Economic Costs of Teenage Childbearing." *Family Relations,* 31, 255. Copyrighted 1982 by the National Council on Family Relations, 1910 West County Road B, Suite 147, St. Paul, Minnesota 55113. Reprinted by permission.

What are high schools legally permitted to do when a student marries? What are they permitted to do when they discover a student is pregnant out of wedlock? What are the student's constitutional rights? What are the rights of the school board? What does the law say?

With the implementation of the regulations issued under Title IX of the Education Amendments of 1972, *all married students and unmarried girls and young mothers are entitled to complete their education with full access to the resources and facilities provided by the public school system* (Henderson, 1980). Specifically, these regulations require that any school system receiving federal funds shall not (a) apply any rule concerning a student's actual or potential parental, family, or marital status that treats students differently on the basis of sex; or (b) discriminate against or exclude any student from its education program or activity on the basis of such student's pregnancy or pregnancy-related condition. Assignment of a student to a separate portion of the program or activity of the school can be made only if the student voluntarily requests such assignment or a physician certifies inability to continue in the normal program. Any separate instructional program for pregnant students must be comparable to that offered nonpregnant students (Goldmeier, 1976).

There are legally defensible reasons for a board to remove a pregnant girl from school, but these defenses sometimes are so difficult to prove that a board may wonder if it is all worth the effort. A school district may be able to justify in court the removal of a pregnant girl from the regular school program if ("Pregnant," 1973):

1. The girl refuses to place herself under medical care.
2. The district is willing to claim and able to prove that the girl in question clearly is immoral. But pregnancy outside of marriage is not in itself proof of promiscuity or immorality. As one court ruled, "The court would like to make manifestly clear that lack of moral character is certainly a reason for excluding a child from public education. But the fact that a girl has one child out of wedlock does not forever brand her as a scarlet woman undeserving of any chance for rehabilitation or the opportunity for further education" (*Perry v. Granada*, 1969).
3. The board is able to prove that a pregnant girl causes a substantial disruption in the operation of her school. Chances are that a pregnant girl will be the object of some whispering, giggling, and pointing, but a court may not rule that such attention adds up to a substantial disruption.
4. The board is able to prove that a pregnant girl presents a clear and present danger to the health, welfare, and safety of other students. Will other students run out and become pregnant because they see one of their classmates in that condition?

Generally courts have said that the denial of regular academic education can be exercised in only the most severe cases and that marriage and pregnancy are not in themselves acceptable reasons for dismissal. This reasoning forces boards to rely on defenses such as the four just mentioned, and those defenses (except in the case of the girl who refuses to place herself under the care of a doctor) can become difficult.

If a school board is bent on restricting a pregnant student's activities, it may be able to keep her out of extracurricular activities. Courts have ruled that married students and pregnant students (married or not) can participate in extracurricular activities in those instances when:

School officials could not prove that "any inconvenience or damage was suffered" (*Wellsand* v. *Valpraiso*, 1971).

No disruption of or interference with school activities or threat of harm to other students could be linked to the appearance of a pregnant, unmarried student at extracurricular activities (*Ordway* v. *Hargraves*, 1971).

Courts could not find a reasonable relationship between legitimate school purposes and rules that deny extracurricular activities to married and/or pregnant students.

It is evident that the courts are now clearly on the side of married and/or unmarried pregnant students who want to continue their education. Some schools make a real effort at rehabilitation. Others are relieved if the girl drops out of school voluntarily, and many of these schools make no effort to get her to return, even after the baby is born (U.S. Dept. of HEW, 1974).

Probably the most successful approaches are those including special programs and services especially for expectant mothers (Holman and Arcus, 1987; MacGregor and Newlon, 1987; Roosa, 1986). The special services provided include the following:

Individual treatment plans for prenatal, obstetrical, and postnatal medical care are drawn up.

Social services include assignment of caseworkers to assist each girl.

Educational services include not only regular academic courses and assistance with these but also courses in reproductive health. Most important, the girls are helped in every way possible to continue their education during and after pregnancy.

Even if pregnant students are allowed to attend their regular school and classes, they are often too embarrassed or uncomfortable to do so, so they drop out, never completing their education. For this reason many schools have found it advisable to offer special classes and programs, usually away from the regular school building, to get the girls away from the scrutiny of other students. Often other community health or youth service agencies cooperate with the school in offering a full range of classes, programs, and services to expectant mothers. These programs are expensive, but they have succeeded in keeping many girls in school, in giving them proper prenatal, obstetrical, and postnatal health care, and in providing counseling and guidance for a wide range of academic, vocational, family, social, and emotional problems with which they are confronted.

(For a more complete discussion of the problems and adjustments of pregnant unwed mothers and of programs and services for them, see: Dillard and Pol, 1982; Held, 1981; Patten, 1981; Peabody et al., 1981).

SUMMARY

Unmarried cohabitation is defined as two unrelated adults of the opposite sex sharing the same living quarters in which there is no other adult present. According to this definition, there has been a 25 percent increase from 1980 to 1987.

There are various patterns of cohabitation and meanings associated with them. Cohabitation includes arrangements without commitment, intimate involvements with emotional commitment, living together as a prelude to marriage, living together as a trial marriage, and living together as an alternative to marriage. The most frequent pattern is intimate involvement with emotional commitment, but it does not usually include any plans for marriage.

Societal attitudes have become more permissive of nonmarital cohabitation so unmarried couples are accepted more readily and drawn more fully into the mainstream of society.

Most couples report no regret at having cohabited. Some report tension and conflict, disappointment, a feeling of being used, overinvolvement and a feeling of being trapped, a loss of identity, disagreement about chores and role performances, difficulty because of different moods, temperaments, personalities, and habits, sexual problems, and other problems similar to those married couples face. Some couples are devastated by relationships that do not work out.

Nonmarital cohabitation has a harmful effect on some and a positive effect on others. Most studies reflect no differences in marital quality between couples who have and have not cohabited before marriage.

Various persons have proposed a testing period, or trial marriage, before permanent marriage. Margaret Mead's two-step marriage is the best known of these proposals. The first step would be individual marriage; the second step would be parental marriage.

Age at first marriage is an important factor in marital success. From the standpoint of marital stability, men who wait to marry until at least age 27 and women until age 25 have waited as long as practical to maximize their chances of success. The median age of first marriage continues to rise and is now 25.8 for males and 23.6 for females.

Young married couples are more likely to be lower socioeconomic status youths, those who do poorly in school, rural rather than urban youths, especially from the South, and those who are less emotionally adjusted.

The reasons for adolescent marriage are pregnancy, acceleration of adult sophistication, social pressure, overly romantic views of marriage, or escape. It is more likely to occur in prosperous times than in periods of economic hardship.

The adjustments young couples must make are no different from those of other couples but are aggravated by the couple's immaturity. Adjustments are aggravated by early parenthood. Other adjustment problems relate to financial worry, a decrease in sexual satisfaction, tension over social activities and friends, and problems with in-laws.

School dropout rates among young marrieds run very high, but, by law, all married and unmarried students and pregnant students are entitled to complete their education. Schools cannot legally dismiss a pregnant girl unless she refuses to place herself under medical care, it can be proved that she is immoral, the girl causes a substantial disruption in the operation of the school, or it can be proved that she presents a clear and present danger to the health, welfare, and safety of other students.

Many schools try to provide special programs and services for expectant students: individual medical treatment and care, social services, and special educational services and programs.

DISCUSSION QUESTIONS

1. Have you cohabited outside of marriage, or are you cohabiting now? Would you be willing to discuss your experiences? How would you answer the following questions?
   a. How long were you |have you been| together? Why did you break up?
   b. What factors made you decide to enter into this arrangement? How did you get started?
   c. What sort of financial arrangements did |do| you have with each other?
   d. How did |do| you divide housework, cooking, laundering, food buying, and other chores in and around your living quarters?
   e. How would you describe your relationship? In love? What sort of commitment did |do| you have? Engaged? Intend to get married? Any special plans for the future? Did |do| you consider living together a trial marriage?
   f. Did |do| you go out or date others? Could |can| you? Did |do| you want to while you were |are| living together? How do you feel about this? Any jealousy problems?
   g. What would you say were |are| your biggest problems?
   h. What about your parents? Did |do| they know? Why or why not? How do you think they feel about your cohabiting? What would happen if they knew? How did |do| you keep them from finding out?
   i. Does cohabiting help you in any way to select a mate? Prepare for marriage? Do you think you have a better chance of having a happy marriage because you have cohabited?
   j. What worries you the most about cohabiting?
   k. Would you advise other young people to cohabit? How old should they be?
2. How old do you think people should be before getting married? Explain.
3. Is adolescent marriage ever justified? Explain.
4. Why are some adolescents in such a hurry to get married?
5. What special problems do married adolescents face?
6. What are some of the special problems facing adolescents who get married because of pregnancy?
7. Why do so many pregnant adolescent girls drop out of school? What can the school do to prevent them from dropping out?
8. If the school finds out a student is pregnant out of wedlock, what can they do to help the most?

BIBLIOGRAPHY

Abernathy, T. J. (Winter, 1981). "Adolescent Cohabitation: A Form of Courtship or Marriage?" *Adolescence*, 16, 791–797.

Bachrach, C. A. (1987). "Cohabitation and Reproductive Behavior in the U.S." *Demography*, 24, 623.

Barth, R. P., Schinke, S. P., and Maxwell, J. S. (December, 1983). "Psychological Correlates of Teenage Motherhood." *Journal of Youth and Adolescence*, 12, 471–487.

Bishop, S. M., and Lynn, A. G. (July, 1983). "Multi-Level Vulnerability of Adolescent Marriages: An Eco-System Model for Clinical Assessment and Intervention." *Journal of Marital and Family Therapy*, 9, 271–282.

Booth, A., and Edwards, J. N. (February, 1985). "Age at Marriage and Marital Instability." *Journal of Marriage and the Family*, 47, 67–75.

Call, V. R. A., and Otto, L. B. (1977). "Age at Marriage as Mobility Contingency: Estimates for the Nye-Berardo Model." *Journal of Marriage and the Family*, 39, 67–79.

Cherlin, A. (1980). "Postponing Marriage: The Influence of Young Women's Work Expectations." *Journal of Marriage and the Family*, 42, 355–365.

"Cohabitation by the Unmarried" (1986). *Medical Aspects of Human Sexuality*, 20, 63–69.

"Cohabiting Young Women Plan to Get Married" (1987). *Medical Aspects of Human Sexuality*, 21, 16.

Colletta, N. D., Hadler, S., and Gregg, C. H. (Fall, 1981). "How Adolescents Cope with the Problems of Early Motherhood." *Adolescence*, 16, 499–512.

Davidson, S. (November, 1983). "Proliferating POSSLQ." *Psychology Today*, 17, 84.

DeMaris, A., and Leslie, G. R. (February, 1984). "Cohabitation with the Future Spouse: Its Influence upon Marital Satisfaction and Communication." *Journal of Marriage and the Family*, 46, 77–84.

Dillard, D. D., and Pol, L. G. (April, 1982). "The Individual Economic Cost of Teenage Childbearing." *Family Relations*, 31, 249–259.

Edington, E., and Hays, L. (1978). "Difference in Family Size and Marriage Age Expectation and Aspirations of Anglo, Mexican American, and Native American Rural Youth in New Mexico." *Adolescence*, 13, 393–400.

Ewer, P. A., and Gibbs, J. O. (1976). "School Return among Pregnant Adolescents." *Journal of Youth and Adolescence*, 5, 221–229.

Friedman, J. H. (June, 1978). "Birth Order and Age at Marriage in Females." *Psychological Reports*, 42, 1193–1194.

Ganong, L., Coleman, M., and Brown, G. (Summer, 1981). "The Effect of Family Structure on Marital Attitudes of Adolescents." *Adolescence*, 16, 281–288.

Gershenson, H. P. (August, 1983). "Redefining Fatherhood in Families with White Adolescent Mothers." *Journal of Marriage and the Family*, 45, 591–599.

Glick, P. C., and Spanier, G. B. (1980). "Married and Unmarried Cohabitation in the United States." *Journal of Marriage and the Family*, 42, 19–30.

Goldmeier, H. (1976). "School Age Parents and the Public Schools." *Children Today*, 5, 19–20, 36.

Grindstaff, C. F. (1988). "Adolescent Marriage and Childbearing: The Long-Term Economic Outcome, Canada in the 1980s." *Adolescence*, 23, 45–58.

Grover, K. M., Russell, C. S., Schumm, W. R., and Paff-Bergen, L. A. (1985). "Mate Selection Processes and Marital Satisfaction." *Family Relations*, 34, 383–386.

Haggstrom, G. W., Kanouse, D. E., and Morrison, P. A. (1986). "Accounting for the Educational Shortfalls of Mothers." *Journal of Marriage and the Family*, 48, 175–186.

Held, L. (Winter, 1981). "Self-Esteem and Social Network of the Young Pregnant Teenager." *Adolescence*, 16, 905–912.

Henderson, G. H. (April, 1980). "Consequences of School-Age Pregnancy and Motherhood." *Family Relations*, 29, 185–190.

Hogan, D. P. (May, 1978). "The Effects of Demographic Factors, Family Background, and Early Job Achievement on Age at Marriage." *Demography*, 15, 161–175.

Holman, N., and Arcus, M. (1987). "Helping Adolescent Mothers and Their Children; An Integrated Multi-Agency Approach." *Family Relations*, 36, 119–123.

Honig, A. S. (1978). "What We Need to Know to Help the Teenage Parent." *Family Coordinator*, 27, 113–119.

Kaplan, H. B. (1979). "Psychosocial Antecedents of Unwed Motherhood among Indigent Adolescents." *Journal of Youth and Adolescence*, 8, 181–207.

Kellam, S. G., Adams, R. G., Brown, C. H., and Ensminger, M. E. (1982). "The Long-Term Evaluation of the Family Structure of Teenage and Older Mothers." *Journal of Marriage and the Family*, 44, 539–554.

Kerckhoff, A. C., and Parrow, A. A. (1979). "The Effect of Early Marriage on the Educational Attainment of Young Men." *Journal of Marriage and the Family*, 41, 97–107.

Larson, D. L., et al. (1976). "Social Factors in the Frequency of Romantic Involvement among Adolescents." *Adolescence*, 11, 7–12.

Lindsay, B. (October, 1926; March, 1927) "The Companionate Marriage." *Redbook*.

Lowe, G. D., and Witt, D. D. (August, 1984). "Early Marriage as a Career Contingency: The Prediction of Educational Attainment." *Journal of Marriage and the Family*, 46, 689–698.

McKenry, P., et al. (1979). "Adolescent Pregnancy: A Review of the Literature." *Family Coordinator*, 28, 17–28.

McLaughlin, S. D., and Micklin, M. (February, 1983). "The Timing of the First Birth and Changes in Personal Efficacy." *Journal of Marriage and the Family*, 45, 47–55.

MacGregor, J., and Newlon, B. J. (1987). "Description of a Teenage Pregnancy Program." *Journal of Counseling and Development*, 65, 447.

Macklin, E. D. (1980). "Nontraditional Family Forms: A Decade of Research." *Journal of Marriage and the Family*, 33, 905–922.

Markowski, E. M., and Johnston, M. J. (1980). "Behavior, Temperament, and Idealization of Cohabiting Couples Who Married." *International Journal of Sociology of the Family*, 10, 115–125.

Marini, M. M. (August, 1978). "The Transition to Adulthood: Sex Differences in Educational Attainment and Age at Marriage." *American Sociological Review*, 43, 483–507.

_____ . (February, 1981). "Effects of the Timing of Marriage and First Birth on Fertility." *Journal of Marriage and the Family*, 43, 27–46.

Mead, M. (1966). "Marriage in Two Steps." *Redbook*, 48–49.

Meer, J. (June, 1984). "Live-in Marriage Out." *Psychology Today*, 18, 73.

Moeller, I., and Sherlock, J. (1981). "Making It Legal: A Comparison of Previously Cohabiting and Engaged Newlyweds." *Journal of Sociology and Social Welfare*, 8, 97–100.

Nathanson, M., Baird, A., and Jemail, J. (1986). "Family Functioning and the Adolescent Mother: A Systems Approach." *Adolescence*, 21, 827–841.

Newcomb, M. D. (1986). "Sexual Behavior of Cohabitors: A Comparison of Three Independent Samples." *The Journal of Sex Research*, 22, 492–513.

Newcomb, M. D., and Bentler, P. M. (1980). "Cohabitation Before Marriage: A Comparison of Married Couples Who Did and Did Not Cohabit." *Alternative Lifestyles*, 3, 65–83.

Newcomb, P. R. (1979). "Cohabitation in America: An Assessment of Consequences." *Journal of Marriage and the Family*, 41, 597–602.

Ordway v. Hargraves, 323 F. Supp. 1115 (1971).

Packard, V. (1968). *The Sexual Wilderness*. New York: David McKay Co.

Patten, M. A. (Winter, 1981). "Self Concept and Self Esteem: Factors in Adolescent Pregnancy." *Adolescence*, 16, 765–778.

Peabody, E., McKenry, P., and Cordero, L. (Fall, 1981). "Subsequent Pregnancy among Adolescent Mothers." *Adolescence*, 16, 563–568.

Perry v. Granada. 300 F. Supp. 748 (Miss., 1969).

Peterman, D. J., Ridley, C. A., and Anderson, S. M. (1974). "A Comparison of Cohabiting and Noncohabiting College Students." *Journal of Marriage and the Family*, 36, 344–354.

"Pregnant Schoolgirls and Pregnant Teachers: The Policy Problem School Districts Can Sidestep No Longer." (1973). *American School Board Journal*, 160, 23–27.

Rice, F. P. (1983). *Contemporary Marriage*. Boston, Mass.: Allyn and Bacon.

Rindfuss, R. R., and St. John, C. (August, 1983). "Social Determinants of Age at First Birth." *Journal of Marriage and the Family*, 45, 553–565.

Risman, B. J., Hill, C. T., Rubin, Z., and Peplau, L. A. (February, 1981). "Living Together in College: Implications for Courtship." *Journal of Marriage and the Family*, 43, 77–83.

Roosa, M. W. (1986). "Adolescent Mothers, School Drop-Outs and School Based Intervention Programs." *Family Relations*, 35, 313–317.

Russell, B. (1961). *Marriage and Morals*. 1929. Reprint. New York: Bantam Books.

Satir, V. (Sept. 1, 1967) "Marriage as a Statutory Five Year Renewable Contract." Paper presented at the American Psychological Association 75th Annual Convention. Washington, D.C., Mimeographed.

Scott, J. W. (Winter, 1983). "The Sentiments of Love and Aspirations for Marriage and Their Association with Teenage Sexual Activity and Pregnancy." *Adolescence*, 18, 889–897.

Scriven, M. (1967). "Putting Sex Back into Sex Education!" *Phi Delta* 49.

"Social Factors, Not Age, Are Found to Affect Risk of Low Birth Weight." (May–June 1984). *Family Planning Perspectives*, 16, 142, 143.

Spanier, G. B. (1976). "Measuring Dyadic Adjustment: New Scales for Assessing the Quality of Marriage and Similar Dyads." *Journal of Marriage and the Family*, 38, 15–38.

_____ . (May, 1983). "Married and Unmarried Cohabitation in the United States: 1980." *Journal of Marriage and the Family*, 45, 277–288.

Stafford, R., et al. (1977). "The Division of Labor among Cohabiting and Married Couples." *Journal of Marriage and the Family*, 39, 43–57.

"Substantially Higher Morbidity and Mortality Rates Found among Infants Born to Adolescent Mothers." (March–April 1984). *Family Planning Perspectives*, 16, 91, 92.

Tamashiro, R. T. (December 1979). "Adolescents' Concepts of Marriage: A Structural-Developmental Analysis." *Journal of Youth and Adolescence*, 8, 443–452.

Tanfer, K., (1987). "Patterns of Premarital Cohabitation among Never-Married Women in the United States." *Journal of Marriage and the Family,* 49, 483–497.

Teti, D. M., Lamb, M. E., and Elster, A. B. (1987). "Long-Range Economic and Marital Consequences of Adolescent Marriage in Three Cohorts of Adult Males." *Journal of Marriage and the Family,* 49, 499–506.

Trost, J. (1978). "A Renewed Social Institution: Nonmarital Cohabitation." *Acta Sociologica,* 21, 303–315.

U.S. Bureau of the Census (1987). Current Population Reports. Series P–20, (No. 417). *Households, Families, Marital Status, and Living Arrangements: March 1987 (Advance Report).* Washington, D.C.: U.S. Government Printing Office.

U.S. Department of Commerce Bureau of the Census. (1987). *Statistical Abstract of the United States, 1987.* Washington, D. C.: U.S. Government Printing Office.

U.S. Department of Health, Education, and Welfare. Bureau of Community Health Services. (1974). *Family Planning Digest,* 3, 15.

Watson, R. E. L. (January, 1983). "Premarital Cohabitation vs. Traditional Courtship: Their Effects on Subsequent Marital Adjustment." *Family Relations,* 32, 139–147.

Watson, R. E. L., and DeMeo, P. W. (1987). "Premarital Cohabitation vs. Traditional Courtship and Subsequent Marital Adjustment: A Reflection and Follow-Up." *Family Relations,* 36, 193–196.

Wellsand v. Valparaiso Community Schools Corporation et al. U.S.C.C., N.D., 71 Hlss (2) (Ind., 1971).

Yllo, K., and Straus, M.A. (July, 1981). "Interpersonal Violence among Married and Cohabiting Couples." *Family Relations,* 30, 339–347.

CHAPTER
18

The Development of Moral Judgment, Character, Values, Beliefs, and Behavior

The process by which children and youths develop moral judgment is extremely interesting. A number of major theories, based on sound research findings, have been developed and will be discussed in this chapter. The work of Jean Piaget, Lawrence Kohlberg, and Carol Gilligan represents theories that emphasize the development of moral judgment as a gradual cognitive process, stimulated by increasing, changing social relationships of children as they get older. Other theories relating to moral development emphasize personality and ego-superego development and their relationship to the development of moral character and behavior. The work of Robert Havighurst and R. H. Peck will be discussed as most representative of this viewpoint. Other researchers have concentrated on an examination of various family correlates that influence moral development. Such factors as parental warmth, parent-teen interaction, discipline, parental role models, and independence opportunities outside the home are discussed in relation to their influence on moral learning. The transmission of religious beliefs and practices from parents to children is also an important consideration and depends on a number of religious and family variables. Finally, other social influences such as peer and reference groups, television, and schools will be examined. The effects of these influences on the development of values and behavior are important and need to be understood.

COGNITIVE-SOCIALIZATION THEORIES OF DEVELOPMENT

Jean Piaget

The most important early research on the development of moral judgment of children is that of Piaget (1948, 1969). Although some details of his findings have not been substantiated by subsequent research, Piaget's ideas have formed the theoretical basis for later research. And although his work was with children, the theoretical framework that outlines his stages of development may be applied to adolescents and adults as well as children. It is important, therefore, to understand Piaget's discoveries.

Piaget's (1948) work is reported in four sections. The first section discusses the attitudes of children to the rules of the game when playing marbles. The second and third sections report the results of telling children stories that require them to make moral judgments on the basis of the information given. The last section reviews his findings in relation to social psychology, particularly to the work of Durkheim (1960), who argues that the sanctions of society are the only source of morality.

morality of constraint

morality of cooperation

In studying children's attitudes to the rules of the game, Piaget concluded that there is first of all a **morality of constraint** and, second, a **morality of cooperation**. In the early stages of moral development, children are constrained by the rules of the game. These rules are coercive because children regard them as inviolable and because they reflect parental authority. Rules constitute a given order of existence and, like parents, must be obeyed without question. Later, as a result of social interaction, children learn that rules are not absolute; they learn that they can alter them by social consensus. Rules are no longer external laws to be considered sacred because they are laid down by adults but social creations arrived at through a process of free decision and thus deserving of mutual respect and consent. Children move from **heteronomy** to *autonomy* in making moral judgments.(Piaget, 1948).

heteronomy

Piaget also discusses the motives or reasons for judgments. He says there are, first, judgments based solely on the consequences of wrongdoing (**objective judgments**) and, second, judgments that take into account intention or motive (**subjective judgments**). Piaget (1948) claims there is a growing pattern of operational thinking, with children moving from objective to subjective responsibility as they grow older. Piaget would insist that although the two processes overlap, the second gradually supersedes the first. The first stage is superseded when children deem motive or intention more important than consequences.

objective judgments

subjective judgments

> The child finds in his brothers and sisters or in his playmates a form of society which develops his desire for cooperation. Then a new type of morality will be created in him, a *morality of reciprocity* and not of *obedience*. This is the true morality of intention. (P. 133)

Piaget (1948) is careful to note that obedience and cooperation are not always successive stages but nevertheless are formative processes that broadly follow one another. "The first of these processes is the moral constraint of the adult, a constraint which leads to heteronomy and consequently to moral realism. The second is co-operation which leads to autonomy" (p. 193). (By moral realism Piaget means submitting meekly to the demands of law.)

Before moral judgment moves from the *heteronomous* to the *autonomous* stage, the self-accepted rules must be internalized. This happens when, in a reciprocal relationship and out of mutual respect, people begin to feel from within the desire to treat others as they themselves would wish to be treated. They pass from *preoperational* to *operational thinking*, from premoral to moral judgment as they internalize the rules they want to follow.

In the third section of his report, Piaget discusses the child's concept of justice as the child moves from moral restraint to moral cooperation. Two concepts of punishment emerge. The first results from the transgression of an externally imposed regulation; this Piaget calls **expiatory punishment,** which goes hand in hand with constraint and the rules of authority. The second is self-imposed punishment, which comes into operation when the individual, in violation of his or her own conscience, is denied normal social relations and is isolated from the group by his or her own actions. Piaget (1948) calls this the **punishment of reciprocity,** which accompanies cooperation. An ethic of mutual respect, of good as opposed to duty, leads to improved social relationships that are basic to any concept of real equality and reciprocity.

expiatory punishment

punishment of reciprocity

In the last section of his work, Piaget (1948), following Durkheim, asserts that "society is the only source of morality" (p. 326). Morality, to Piaget, consists of a system of rules, but such rules require a sociological context for their development. Thus, "whether the child's moral judgments are heteronomous or autonomous, accepted under pressure or worked out in freedom, this morality is social, and on this point, Durkheim was unquestionably right" (p. 344).

One of the important implications of Piaget's views is that the changes in moral judgments of children are related to their cognitive growth and to the changes in their social relationships. At first children judge the severity of transgressions by their visible damage or harm. They also develop the concept of *immanent justice*

immanent justice *immanent justice*: the child's belief that immoral behavior inevitably brings pain or punishment as a natural consequence of the transgression: "If you do wrong, you will certainly be punished." Furthermore, they judge the appropriateness of this punishment by its severity rather than by its relevance to the transgression. Only as children get older are they likely to recommend that the transgressor make restitution or that punishment be tailored to fit the wrong done. Gradually, also, they come to see that the application of rules must be relative to people and situations and that rules are established and maintained through reciprocal social agreements.

As an example, if 6-year-olds are told the story of a little boy who has accidentally dropped a sweet roll in the lake, they are likely to respond: "That's too bad. But it's his own fault for being so clumsy. He shouldn't get another." For them, the punishment implies a crime, and losing a roll in the lake is clearly a punishment in their eyes. They are incapable of taking extenuating circumstances into account. Adolescents, however, make moral judgments on the basis of what

equity Piaget calls **equity,** assigning punishments in accordance with the transgressors' abilities to take responsibility for their crimes. Adolescents are as able to employ the same sort of reasoning in relation to moral dilemmas as they are in solving intellectual puzzles. Rather than being tied to concrete facts and a narrow range of possibilities (there is punishment; therefore there must be a crime), they are able to imagine a wide range of possibilities. (The roll is lost; someone may or may not be to blame.) As a result they are able to take into account the youthfulness of the child, many of the possible reasons why the roll was lost, and to show more compassion: "It may not have been his fault; he should get another treat."

Another important implication of Piaget's view is that the changes in judgments of children must be related to the changes in their social relationships. As peer-group activity and cooperation increase and as adult constraint decreases, the child becomes more truly an autonomous, cooperative, moral person.

One of the best summaries of Piaget's conclusions has been given by Kay (1969, p. 157) in a series of simple propositions about the moral lives of children.

1. Human beings develop an intelligent and informed respect for law by experiencing genuine social relationships.
2. Such social relationships are found in two basic forms. They are first characterized by child subordination and adult supremacy and then slowly change until the relationship is reciprocal. In this case it can be based on equality or equity.
3. The social relationships are functionally linked with a system of moral judgment. When the relationship is one of subordination and supremacy, then the moral judgment exercised is based on authoritarian considerations that are objective and heteronomous. And equally when the relationship is reciprocal,

moral judgments are autonomous and reflect the subjective system of morality that now activates the child from within.

4. Judgment and conduct at the final stage of moral development are based not on subscription to an external code of law or even in the regulation of rigid reciprocity in human relationships. It consists of the recognition of the rights and needs of all individuals with due regard to the situational circumstances and the moral principles expressed in them.

Although Piaget's conclusions were deduced from research with children up to age twelve, they have some relationship to the moral life of adolescents. It has been emphasized that Piaget said that children move from a morality of constraint (or obedience) to a morality of cooperation (or reciprocity); children pass from heteronomy to autonomy in making moral judgments; and they move from objective to subjective responsibility. Piaget has said that this second stage of moral development gradually supersedes the first as children grow older.

Some subsequent research questions this view. For example, it has been found that adolescents, as well as children, tend to seek justice in an authority person. There are adolescents, and even adults, who obey certain laws and rules only because of coercion and the threat of external punishment. They are constrained by authority, not by an inner conscience. If they break the rules, their concern is not remorse at doing wrong but at having been caught. In other words, they never move from heteronomy to autonomy, from objective judgment to subjective judgment, from a morality constraint to a morality of cooperation. They remain, like young children, at a preoperational, premoral stage of development, for the rules have never been internalized, and they never desire to do the right thing from mutual respect and concern for the feelings and welfare of others.

It is unreasonable, therefore, always to attach age categories to the stages of moral development. There are children, adolescents, and adults at any one stage of moral growth. This is one reason why Piaget's findings may be applied to adolescents as well as children. Researchers like Kohlberg have confirmed some aspect of Piaget's conclusions, but they would not assign each step of development to a particular age group.

Lawrence Kohlberg

One of the principal deficiencies of Piaget's work was his exclusive concern with children under the age of 12. Kohlberg compensated for this deficiency by using adolescents in a series of studies (Kohlberg, 1963, 1966, 1969, 1970; Kohlberg and Gilligan, 1971; Kohlberg and Kramer, 1969; Kohlberg and Turiel, 1972); he confirmed Piaget's conclusions and showed their validity when applied to adolescents.

Kohlberg's (1963) initial study included seventy-two boys aged 10, 13, and 16. All groups were similar in IQ; half of each group was upper middle class. Data were collected through taped interviews in which ten moral dilemmas were presented to each subject. In each dilemma, acts of disobedience to legal-social rules or the commands of authority figures conflicted with the human needs or welfare of others. Each subject was asked to select one of two acts as the more desired solution and was then questioned about the reasons for his choice. Kohlberg's material and technique were Piagetian in form. In this study, Kohlberg was concerned not with moral behavior but with moral judgment and the process of thought by which the individual made his judgment. There were no right or wrong answers expected; the individual was scored according to mode of reasoning, regardless of the direction of the given response.

From his analysis of the interviews, Kohlberg (1970, 1971) identified three major levels of moral development, each level with two types of moral orientation or judgment. The levels and subtypes are listed in table 18-1. Kohlberg found that premoral thinking declined sharply from the younger to the older age groups. Level II increased until age 13, then stabilized. Level III also increased markedly between 10 and 13 years of age, with some additional increase between ages 13 and 16.

In outlining his stages, however, Kohlberg is careful not to equate each type with a particular age. Within any one age group, individuals are at different levels of development in their moral thinking: some are retarded, others advanced. No person fits neatly into any one of the six types. Kohlberg (1971) indicates that the development of moral thought is a gradual and continuous process as the individual passes through a sequence of increasingly sophisticated moral stages.

Type 1 obeys rules to avoid punishment. Type 2 conforms in order to obtain *premoral level*   rewards or have favors returned. At Level I, the **premoral level,** which comprises

▨ TABLE 18-1

Kohlberg's levels of development of moral thought.

Level I:	*Premoral Level*
Type 1:	Punishment and obedience orientation
	(Motivation: To avoid punishment by others)
Type 2:	Naive instrumental hedonism
	(Motivation: To gain rewards from others)
Level II:	*Morality of Conventional Role Conformity*
Type 3:	Good-person morality of maintaining good relations with and approval of others
	(Motivation: To avoid disapproval of others)
Type 4:	Authority-maintaining morality
	(Motivation: To maintain law and order and because of concern for the community)
Level III:	*Morality of Self-Accepted Moral Principles*
Type 5:	Morality of democratically accepted laws
	(Motivation: To gain the respect of an individual or community)
Type 6:	Morality of individual principles of conduct
	(Motivation: To avoid self-condemnation for lapses)

From: Kohlberg, L. (1964). "The Development of Children's Orientations toward a Moral Order. I: Sequence in the Development of Moral Thought." *Vita Humana*, 6: 11–33. Used by permission.

these two types, children are responsive to the definitions of good and bad provided by parental authority figures. Moral decisions are egocentric, based on self-interest; children interpret acts as good or bad in terms of physical consequences. Type 3 is the good boy–nice girl orientation in which the child conforms to avoid disapproval and dislike by others, whereas type 4 conforms because of a desire to maintain law and order or because of concern for the larger community. Thus, Level II, the level of ***morality of conventional role conformity,*** comprising types 3 and 4, is less egocentric and more sociocentric in orientation, developing a conformity to social conventions that is based on a desire to maintain, support, and justify the existing social structure (Muuss, 1988b). Type 5 conforms in order to maintain the respect of an impartial spectator or to maintain a relation of mutual respect. At this stage, the individual defines morality in terms of general principles such as individual rights, human dignity, equality, contractual agreement, and mutual obligations. Because moral principles have been accepted by society as a whole, the individual is motivated to accept them because of a concern for human well-being and public welfare. This is the social-contract, legalistic orientation in which justice flows from a contract between the governors and the governed (Muson, 1979). Unjust laws must be changed, and individuals flexible in their approach to these laws seek to improve them through consensus. This type is represented by those who accept the official morality of the U.S. Constitution, which recognizes important moral principles. One-third of Americans have reached this level of moral development. Finally, type 6 conforms to avoid self-condemnation (Kay, 1969). The approach to moral issues is based not on egocentric needs or conformity to the existing social order but on autonomous, universal principles of justice that are valid beyond existing laws, social conditions, or peer mores. Thus, individuals governed by universal ethical principles may break unjust civil laws because they recognize a morality higher than existing law. Americans who avoided the draft and accepted the penalty, as a protest against the Vietnam war, practiced civil disobedience in the interest of what they felt was a higher moral good. They felt there were universal moral principles that should be followed even though these challenged the existing official morality of their own government (Muuss, 1988b). Martin Luther King, Jr., (1964) wrote from a Birmingham jail:

morality of conventional role conformity

> I do not advocate evading or defying the law. . . . That would lead to anarchy. One who breaks an unjust law must do so openly, lovingly, and with a willingness to accept the penalty. An individual who breaks the law that conscience tells him is unjust, and willingly accepts the penalty of imprisonment in order to arouse the conscience of the community over its injustice is, in reality, expressing the highest respect for the law. (p. 86)

Thus, Level III, the level of ***morality of self-accepted moral principles,*** is made up of individuals who accept democratically recognized principles or universal truths, not because they have to but because they believe in the principles or truths.

morality of self-accepted moral principles

Kohlberg (1966) emphasized that a stage concept such as this implies sequence: each child must go through each successive level of moral judgment before passing on to the next. Kohlberg also emphasized that a stage concept implies universality of sequence under varying cultural conditions. That is, the development of moral judgment is not merely a matter of learning the rules of a particular culture; it reflects a universal process of development. In order to test this hypothesis, Kohlberg (1966) used his technique with boys 10, 13, and 16 in a Taiwanese city, in a Malaysian (Atayal) aboriginal tribal village, and in a Turkish village, as well as in Great Britain, Canada, and the United States. The results for Taiwan and the United States, compared in figure 18-1, indicate similar age trends in boys of both nationalities.

Kohlberg (1966) says that although his findings show a similar sequence of development in all cultures, the last two stages of moral thought do not develop clearly in preliterate village or tribal communities. It seems evident from the U.S. data also, however, that the great majority of American adults never reach Level III either, even by age 24. Only 10 percent of his middle-class urban male population had reached Level III, with another 26 percent at Level II. Although Kohlberg

▉ FIGURE 18-1

Mean percentage of use of each of six stages of moral judgment at three ages in Taiwan and the United States.

From: Kohlberg, L. (1966). "Moral Education in the Schools, a Developmental View." *The School Review*, 74, 1–30. Copyright 1966, The University of Chicago Press. Used by permission.

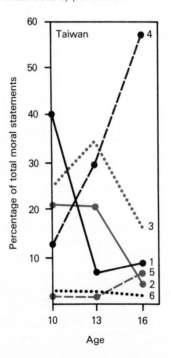
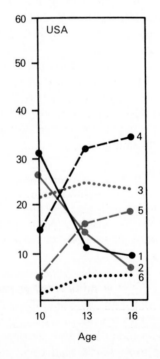
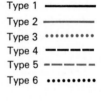

studied 10- to 16-year-olds, studies of students at Berkeley, California, showed that 72 percent were still at Level II (32 percent at stage three, 40 percent at stage four). Those who had arrived at the sixth stage were active protestors on campus. This correlation has led some writers to question the whole philosophical concept of moral maturity (Peters, 1971).

Kohlberg (1966) tested his hypothesis with children of both middle and working classes, Protestants and Catholics, popular and socially isolated children, and girls as well as boys. He found the same general stages of development among all groups but some differences in the *level* of moral development of middle- and working-class children, with the middle-class children, at all ages, in advance of the working-class children. Kohlberg emphasized that these differences were cognitive and developmental in nature, with middle-class children moving faster and farther. The explanation is not that lower-class children favor a different type of thought or hold values different from those of the middle class but that working-class children have less understanding of the broader social order and less participation in it; thus, their moral development is retarded. This explanation is further substantiated by the fact that children with extensive peer-group participation advance considerably more quickly through the successive stages of development or moral thinking.

However, whether social class has any influence must be related to culture to some extent (Corson, 1984). Research with Nigerian adolescents found no relationship to socioeconomic background, since all children, irrespective of background, were expected to be humble and obedient (Maqsud, 1980). In the United States, moral development is particularly dependent on the type of training children receive, and this may vary with class.

One other variable should be mentioned. Moral judgment also correlates highly with IQ, indicating that it is more cognitive in nature than either the "good habits" or "early emotions" views. As children participate more in social groups, they lose some of their cognitive naiveté and adopt a more sophisticated view of authority and social relationships (Berkowitz, Gibbs, and Broughton, 1980). This does not necessarily mean that they become better persons; they acquire a greater capacity for moral thinking, but whether such knowledge leads to better behavior depends on emotional and social influence in their backgrounds and relationships (Kupfersmid and Wonderly, 1980).

Kohlberg's theories have been tested by researchers (Kurdek, 1981; Rybash et al., 1981; Wonderly and Kupfersmid, 1980). Weinreich (1970, 1974) has shown that the rapidity and extent of progression through the sequence of stages are related to intelligence. This is in keeping with other research that shows that moral judgment is significantly and positively associated with chronological age and with IQ; older, brighter youngsters evidence greater maturity of moral judgment than do younger, less intelligent children. Rowe and Marcia (1980) have produced some evidence that achievement of a particular moral stage depends on reaching certain Piagetian levels and that the ability to perform certain logical operations seems to be a prerequisite to performing certain moral operations. Parental attitudes toward children are significant, as in Gfellner's (1986) conclusion that

HIGHLIGHT   Gilligan's Theory of Sex Differences in Moral Reasoning

Carol Gilligan (1977), an associate of Kohlberg, has pointed out that Kohlberg conducted his research on moral development on male subjects. The scoring method was developed from male responses, with the average adolescent female attaining a rating corresponding to stage 3 (the good boy–nice girl orientation). The average adolescent male was rated at stage 4 (the law-and-order orientation). To Gilligan, the female level of moral judgment is not "lower" than that of the male, but reflects the fact that females approach moral issues from a different perspective. Men emphasize justice—preserving rights, rules, and principles. Women emphasize concern and care for others and sensitivity to their feelings and rights. Women emphasize responsibility to human beings rather than to abstract principles. Thus, men and women speak with two different voices (Gilligan, 1982). In summarizing 6 studies, including four longitudinal, Gilligan (1984) revealed that men rely more heavily on a justice orientation, and women on an interpersonal network or care orientation (Muuss, 1988).

As a result of the difference in the way men and women think, Gilligan proposed a female alternative to Kohlberg's stages of moral reasoning. Table 18-2 compares Kohlberg and Gilligan.

At level I, women are preoccupied with self-interest and survival, which requires obeying restrictions placed upon them. Gradually they become aware of the differences between what they want (selfishness) and what they ought to do (responsibility). This leads to the next higher level, II, in which the need to please others takes precedence over self-interest. The woman becomes responsible for caring for others, even sacrificing her own preferences. Gradually she begins to wonder whether she can fulfill the needs of others and still remain true to herself. Still, she does not give her own needs full equality with others. At level III, which many never attain, the woman develops a universal perspective, in which she no longer sees herself as submissive and powerless, but active in decision making. She becomes concerned about the consequences for all, herself included, in making decisions.

Obviously, Kohlberg's and Gilligan's stages are parallel. Gilligan does not argue that her theory should replace Kohlberg's. She argues that her theory is more applicable to the moral reasoning of females and that the highest form of moral reasoning can utilize, combine, and interpret both the male emphasis on rights and justice and the female emphasis on responsibility and interpersonal care (Muuss, 1988).

children's ego and moral development are enhanced by parental warmth in the parent-child relationship. The stage at which the individual finally arrives at adulthood is related to family environment.

Later Developments and Critique of Kohlberg

One of the problems researchers have had in testing Kohlberg's theory has been the difficulty of determining at what stage an individual is. In one study of 957 individuals, more than 45 percent could not be placed in one stage or another;

TABLE 18-2

Kohlberg's versus Gilligan's understanding of moral development.

KOHLBERG'S LEVELS AND STAGES	KOHLBERG'S DEFINITION	GILLIGAN'S LEVELS
Level I. Preconventional morality Stage 1: Punishment orientation	Obey rules to avoid punishment	*Level I. Preconventional morality* Concern for the self and survival
Stage 2: Naive reward orientation	Obey rules to get rewards, share in order to get returns	
Level II. Conventional morality Stage 3: Good-boy/good-girl orientation	Conform to rules that are defined by others' approval/ disapproval	*Level II. Conventional morality* Concern for being responsible, caring for others
Stage 4: Authority orientation	Rigid conformity to society's rules, law-and-order mentality, avoid censure for rule-breaking	
Level III. Postconventional morality Stage 5. Social-contract orientation	More flexible understanding that we obey rules because they are necessary for social order, but the rules could be changed if there were better alternatives	*Level III. Postconventional morality* Concern for self and others as interdependent
Stage 6. Morality of individual principles and conscience	Behavior conforms to internal principles (justice, equality) to avoid self-condemnation, and sometimes may violate society's rules	

From: Hyde, J. S. (1985). *Half the Human Experience.* Lexington, MA: D. C. Heath. Reprinted with permission.

most of the groups were in transition between two stages, and some gave responses that straddled three stages (Muson, 1979). Moreover, Kohlberg and his associate Kramer (1969) found that many who had been in stage 4 in previous interviews had regressed to stage 2, indicating that stage change was not always just upward, and in orderly sequence (Walker, 1982). Individuals may make moral judgments at one stage in one situation and at another stage in another situation. One circumstance may require a stage 4 response; another, a more universally applicable response. Also, Kohlberg's scale evaluates the motivation for making judgments, which can vary under different circumstances.

Furthermore, Kohlberg's original scale for measuring stages lacked standardization in administration and scoring (Hogan and Schroeder, 1981; Rest, 1983; 1986). In response, Kohlberg and colleagues completed a five-part manual that he promised will provide the consistency and reliability critics are looking for.

Stage 6 (or type 6) has been dropped from the new manual entirely, for Kohlberg has estimated that only about 7 percent of 16-year-olds in the United States and Mexico and less than 1 percent of the same age group in Taiwan used stage 6 reasoning. None of those studied in Turkey or Yucatán had ever reached stage 5 (Muson, 1979).

Critics have also argued that it is not true or fair to say that the higher the stage, the greater the level of morality (Callahan and Callahan, 1981). Stage 6 reflects liberal and radical political reasoning. Does this mean that liberals are more advanced morally than conservatives? It has little basis in empirical fact (Gutkin and Suls, 1979; Wonderly and Kupfersmid, 1980). Also, there is some indication that more women end up in stage 3 and more men in stage 4. Women were more desirous of pleasing others, which enabled them to smooth tensions and bring people together. Men were more concerned about maintaining law and order. Why should stage 4 be considered superior to stage 3? This criticism has led Kohlberg to emphasize stage 4 more as concern for the larger community rather than the concern for law and order. More and more, Kohlberg has suggested that an important goal of moral-education should not be to reach stage 5, but rather "a solid attainment of the fourth stage commitment to being a good member of a community or a good citizen" (Muson, 1979, p. 57).

No evaluation of levels of moral judgment can be used to predict moral behavior; to know does not mean to do. Two people at the same level of reasoning might act differently under the pressure of circumstances. In fact, investigation of students at the University of California revealed large numbers of persons in stages 5 or 6, but also a large percentage of students who were in the relatively primitive stage 2 (Muson, 1979).

PERSONALITY TYPES, EGO THEORY, AND MORAL CHARACTER

Personality Type as the Key to Motivation and Behavior

A number of writers and researchers, particularly Robert Havighurst and his colleagues, have sought to show the relationship between personality types and morality, between moral character and behavior, between the ego-superego balance and moral maturity. From this point of view, developing moral character is not so much a matter of learning fixed moral virtues such as honesty but of developing emotional maturity and balance: love instead of hate for others, guilt instead of fear, self-esteem and trust instead of inadequacy and distrust. This point of view seeks to define and describe personality types and their characteristic affective responses as they might be revealed by projective personality tests or described by people's judgments of the child's moral character. This viewpoint emphasizes that personality type controls moral behavior. Thus, personal traits are *the* motivational factor in behavior.

Peck and Havighurst

Peck and Havighurst (1960) have been the most influential contemporary exponents of this point of view. Early in their study, they decided to place their emphasis on the predictability of moral conduct as revealed by persistent attitudes and traits the individuals manifested in their relationships with other people. The researcher's chief source of information about individual subjects, ages ten to seventeen, was the opinions others held about them. The authors defended their method when, after reviewing previous research, they concluded "that 'popular opinion' about the generality of moral character [was] . . . not so far wrong at all" (Peck and Havighurst, 1960). To ensure continuity in their research, they also studied the adolescents who had been surveyed earlier by Havighurst and Taba in order to draw upon earlier findings to supplement their own research.

They ask the all-important question "What is moral character?" and go on to describe it not only according to five character types but also in terms of the various environmental influences that affect its development. By paying particular attention to the family, the peer group, and the social environment, they show how each makes its contribution to the moral development of the individuals studied.

The five character types they identify are: *amoral, expedient, conforming, irrational-conscientious,* and *rational-altruistic.* The authors emphasized that their categories were descriptive devices only; no one character fits exactly the description for one type. The writers even go further and suggest that these developmental stages may be located from infancy to adulthood, as follows (Peck and Havighurst, 1960, p. 3):

> Amoral type: infancy
> Expedient type: early childhood
> Conforming type: later childhood
> Irrational-conscientious: later childhood
> Rational-altruistic: adolescence to adulthood

It must be recognized that there are some adolescents and adults at each of these stages of development; not everyone shows the same degree of moral growth.

Amoral persons are those who are completely egocentric. Their goal is self-gratification. They have little ego strength, cannot define their own personal goals, and are disorganized and unhappy. They have weak superegos and cannot control their impulses, lacking an integrated system of internalized moral principles. As a result they have trouble in interpersonal relationships, are hostile to themselves and others, and are antisocial persons.

Expedient persons are still egocentric because they are self-centered and selfish, but they seek to mask their socially unethical conduct and to appear moral. They have a weak ego, conscience, and superego. The only internalized principle of control is self-gratification but by taking the easy way out. They lead a drifting, fear-ridden, conscienceless life. In public life they are the persons whose greed corrupts and exploits the community about them.

Conforming persons are controlled by a single internalized principle: desire to conform to the norms of the group. Their actions are based on the rules of the group so that they can do what others do, and their only worry is that they may attract public disapproval for some action. Their behavior is "other-directed." Such persons are uncomfortable when they break rules. They have strong super-egos and are unable to control the harsh punitive effect of their consciences. Such people are usually depressed and unhappy, for they live under the strain of self-deprecation.

Irrational-conscientious persons are distinguished from conforming persons by degree. They too have weak egos and strong superegos, but they are distinguished from conformers by an even more powerfully developed superego. They do not want to violate the moral conventions incorporated in the process by their own superego development. Irrational-conscientious persons are literal-minded and rigid and therefore difficult to live with, particularly because they demand that others abide by their codes. They are ruled by the dictates of conscience, firmly established as a body of rules, but their motivations for morality are not human welfare but a compulsion to follow the rules. Life's only pleasure seems to be the cold satisfaction of living an impeccable life. Such persons possess little warmth, are unattractive to others, and have missed the joys of living.

Rational-altruistic persons are at the highest level of moral behavior; they are motivated by consideration for the welfare of others. Their behavior is rational because they consider each situation on its own merit. The essential element in the motivation of the conduct of these persons is an altruistic impulse. They have a high regard for others. They cannot enjoy themselves at the expense of others and are unhappy at the prospect of harming others.

One interesting result of the research of Peck and Havighurst (1960) was their conclusion that basic personality structure, or character type, tends to persist, to remain fairly stable between the ages to ten and seventeen. The conduct of the individual is, therefore, relatively predictable:

> As the children were studied from age ten to seventeen, each individual tended to show a stable predictable pattern of moral character. Many of their overt actions changed, of course, as they grew older, learned new social and intellectual skills, and developed through puberty. However, each child appeared to maintain very persistently his deeply held feelings and attitudes toward life, and the modes of reacting which we call his character structures. (p. 155)

The evidence of these researchers supports the view that there is an enduring basic pattern of moral character, which means that any effort to modify antisocial attitudes is a difficult educational task, as many moral educators have discovered. These difficulties can be partly overcome by attacking the developmental tasks appropriate to each stage of development with the awareness that, when success-ful, moral education can create socially desirable attitudes that are equally enduring.

Some research efforts have shown the relationship between ego development and the various stages of moral development (Gfellner, 1986). Lutwak (1984) found a positive correlation between ego development and moral development. Overall, the studies indicate that moral judgment and moral behavior are also influenced by ego development (Windmiller, 1976).

Rational-altruistic persons are motivated by their consideration of others. Persons at this stage of moral development spend time working for outside causes such as these adolescents who are addressing envelopes for a political candidate. (© The Christian Science Monitor/Melanie Stetson Freeman)

FAMILY FACTORS AND MORAL LEARNING

All the important research in the moral development of children and adolescents emphasizes the importance of parents and the family in the total process (Schab, 1980). A number of family factors correlate significantly with moral learning:

1. The degree of parental warmth, acceptance, mutual esteem, and trust shown the child.
2. The frequency and intensity of parent-teen interaction and communication.
3. The type and degree of discipline used.
4. The role model parents offer the child.
5. The independence opportunities the parents provide.

Each of these factors needs elaboration, clarification, and substantiation. (For additional information on parent-adolescent relationships, see chapter 17.)

Parental Acceptance and Trust

One important aid to moral learning is a warm, accepting relationship of mutual trust and esteem between parent and child (Hoge, Petrillo, and Smith, 1982; Tudor, Petersen, and Elifson, 1980). Young children who are emotionally dependent on their parents and have a strong emotional attachment to them develop strong consciences, whereas nondependent children grow up more lacking in conscience.

There are a number of explanations for the correlation between parental warmth and moral learning. In a warm, emotional context, respected parents are likely to be admired and imitated by youths, resulting in similar positive traits in the adolescents. Youths learn consideration for others by being cared for, loved, and trusted by their parents. In an atmosphere of hostility and rejection, youths tend to "identify with the aggressor," taking on the antisocial traits of a feared parent. In Sutherland's (1966) theory of ***differential association,*** which outlines conditions that facilitate moral and criminal learning, the impact of a relationship varies according to its *priority, duration, intensity,* and *frequency.* The all-important parent-child relationship (high priority) over many years (long duration), characterized by close emotional attachment (high intensity) and a maximum amount of contact and communication (high frequency), has the maximum positive effect on the moral development of children. Similarly, a negative parent-child relationship existing for many years in an intense, repetitive way will have a disastrous and negative effect.

differential association

Frequency and Intensity of Parent-Teen Interaction

Role-modeling theory maintains that the degree of identification of the child with the parent varies with the amount of the child's interaction with the parent. Sons who have more frequent and intensive interactions with their fathers are more likely to be influenced by them. Similarly, daughters with frequent, close relationships with their mothers are more likely to identify with them. Frequent interaction offers opportunities for the communication of meaningful values and norms, especially if the exchange is democratic and mutual. A one-sided form of autocratic interaction results in poor communication and less learning for the adolescent. It is important, therefore, for the channels of communication between parents and youths to be kept open.

Studies of father-absent homes, where there is a minimum of interaction with a male parent, show that paternal absence has an adverse effect on the moral development of adolescents (Parish, 1980).

Type of Discipline

Research on the influence of parental discipline on the moral learning of youth indicates that discipline has the most positive effect when it is consistent rather than erratic, when it is accomplished primarily through clear, verbal explanations to develop internal controls rather than through external, physical means of control; when it is just and fair and avoids harsh, punitive measures; and when it is democratic rather than permissive or autocratic (Zelkowitz, 1987). Each of these factors needs to be examined.

One of the most important requirements is that discipline be consistent, both *intraparent* (within one parent) and *interparent* (between two parents). Erratic parental expectations lead to an ambiguous environment and so to poor moral learning, anxiety, confusion, instability, restlessness, disobedience, and sometimes hostility and delinquency in the adolescent.

Inconsistency alone is not the sole determinant. If accompanied by family cohesiveness and parental love, support, and warmth, it is less likely to produce antisocial behavior than if the parents are also rejecting (Gfellner, 1986). If parents are inconsistent, harsh, and rejecting, the effect is most damaging. (See chapter 16.)

Parents who rely on clear, rational, verbal explanations to influence and control behavior have a more positive effect than those who use external controls (Eisikovits, 1982), primarily because cognitive methods result in the internalization of values and standards, especially if explanations are combined with affection so that the adolescent is inclined to listen and to accept them. Reasoning or praise used to correct or reinforce behavior enhances learning, whereas physical means of discipline, negative verbal techniques such as belittling and nagging, or infrequent explanations are more often associated with antisocial behavior and delinquency.

Parents who rely on harsh, punitive methods are defeating the true purpose of discipline: to develop a sensitive conscience, socialization, and cooperation (Herzberger and Tennen, 1985). Cruel punishment, especially when accompanied by parental rejection, develops an insensitive, uncaring, hostile, rebellious, cruel person. Instead of teaching children to care about others, it deadens their sensitivities, so that they learn to fear and hate others and no longer care about them or want to please them. They may obey, but when the threat of external punishment is removed, they are antisocial. Many criminal types fit this description (Piaget and Inhelder, 1969; Weinreich, 1970).

Parents who are overly permissive also retard the socialization process and the moral development of their children, for they give the children no help in developing inner controls. Without external authority, the child will remain amoral. Adolescents want and need some parental guidance. Without it they may grow up as "spoiled brats," disliked by their peers because of their lack of consideration for others and lacking self-discipline, persistence, and direction (Peck and Havighurst, 1960).

Parental Role Models

It is important for parents to be moral people themselves if they are to offer positive role models for their children to follow. A thirty-year follow-up study of adults, mostly from lower-class homes, who as children were referred to a clinic because of antisocial behavior, found that antisocial behavior of the father correlated significantly with deviance of the subjects in adolescence and adulthood. Furthermore, the father's antisocial behavior was the most significant factor in predicting the consistent antisocial behavior of the individual between adolescence and the midforties (Robins, 1966). Adolescents who identify with and strongly value the esteem of parents and teachers are less likely either to cheat or to become delinquent than are nondependent boys who do not esteem parental and teacher models.

Independence Opportunities

Peer influences are also important to the child's development, particularly in the lives of youths who are given maximum opportunity for varied social experiences outside the home. Social contacts with those from different cultural and socio-economic backgrounds facilitate moral development (Kohlberg, 1966).

Numerous research studies show that the development of moral autonomy and judgment is faster among boys than among girls, apparently because boys are less dependent on parental controls: parents give them more freedom than girls, and so they have greater opportunities for social experiences outside the home. However, though less independent, girls measure much higher on ratings of empathy, helping others, being more caring, supportive, and sensitive to the needs of others. In this sense, they are more morally mature because they are "other-centered" (Gilligan, 1977; Ornum et al., 1981). More discussion of some of the social influences outside the home is in the next section.

TRANSMISSION OF RELIGIOUS BELIEFS AND PRACTICES

Religious Variables

A number of factors influence the transmission of religious beliefs and practices. Religious variables influencing beliefs and practices include the content of theological beliefs, consistency of parental religious beliefs, church attendance, and frequency of discussions of religion within the family (Clark, Worthington, and Danser, 1988). These items constitute a "religious salience," or a prominence of religious thought, behavior, or external stimuli within the family (Hoge and DeZuleta, 1986).

Family Variables

Transmission of religious beliefs and practices is also facilitated by parental agreement (Clark and Worthington, 1987). Consistency promotes value salience. When parents differ substantially, fathers usually influence their children's beliefs more than mothers. When parents agree, children usually adopt the same denominational membership as parents (Hoge, Petrillo, and Smith, 1982). High frequency of church attendance and family discussion of religion are influential in shaping religious beliefs and practices of adolescents (Ozorak, 1986). This is especially true in relation to sons. If fathers frequently attend church, discuss religion, and are committed to their religion, their sons will do likewise. If fathers do these religious activities infrequently, the sons and fathers will likely not agree on church attendance (Clark, Worthington, and Danser, 1988).

Furthermore, family relationships create a climate that promotes or inhibits adolescents' adoption of their parents' values. Parents who are highly supportive and controlling (authoritative) have children whose values are similar to their own. Parents high in support and low in control (permissive) and low in support and high in control (authoritarian) tend to have children whose values differ from their own (Clark, Worthington, and Danser, 1986). Marital and parent-child conflict can inhibit transmission of religious values to adolescents (Acock and Bengtson, 1980).

SOCIAL REINFORCEMENT, INFLUENCES, VALUES, AND BEHAVIOR

Social Reinforcement

One of the important ingredients of moral development is to acquire knowledge and respect for the existing values and rules of one's social milieu (Hogan, 1975). Once known, these values and rules must be internalized. According to Piaget (1948), this internalization brings about a qualitative transformation in character structure and a sense of "moral realism"; as a result individuals follow the rules regardless of the difficulty in doing so. According to psychoanalytic theory, parents who are nurturant and responsive to children encourage identification and conscience development. As a result of this total "introjection" or "incorporation" of the parent, the child's superego becomes the internal construct that governs morality.

According to Bandura (1971) and other social learning theorists, internalization of values and rules comes through identification and modeling: children observe a relevant adult model acting according to a social norm and discover that the adult is praised or otherwise rewarded (Norcini and Snyder, 1983). Being natural imitators, the children strive to do likewise, particularly because the parents are the chief source of love or hate, physical gratification or deprivation, comfort or pain, and security or anxiety, and the children desire rewards and satisfaction. Gradually they become socialized to adopt the expected behavior themselves, even when the external rewards stop; compliance becomes a reward in itself (Hogan, 1975).

Thus, social learning theory (see chapter 3) emphasizes the acquisition of values through a process of *identification*, *internalization*, and *reinforcement*. Much has already been said about identification and internalization, but *reinforcement* needs to be discussed in more detail. **Reinforcement** is used in a particular context here to mean those social influences that parallel parental influences and enhance the learning and acceptance of particular values. When the peer group, school, church, or mass media emphasize values similar to those found in the family, learning of those values is enhanced. However, when the school, church, and other community agencies teach values different from those of the parents, the inconsistency of influence creates conflict. This is often the case with lower-class youths: the community teaches middle-class values, and the parents incompletely accept or cannot afford to accept these values and substitute their own. One outcome of this inconsistency is moral confusion. Another outcome may be rigidity or authoritarianism. Values must be adhered to rigidly if they are to be maintained at all.

reinforcement

Reference Groups

Studies of parent versus peer influence show that most parents still exert a tremendous influence over the moral development of their children (deVaus, 1983). However, these studies also show that peer influence has increased, particularly in the last ten years, and especially in those families in which parental influence has declined (Bart, 1981). As described in chapter 12, adolescents turn primarily to peers as a reaction against parental neglect and rejection. In such cases, the values of the peer group are particularly important in influencing adolescent behavior (Brown, 1982).

Youths may be members of many formal organizations, each of which has an influence, but they are just as likely to be influenced by neighborhood gangs or by the general cultural environment around them. Adolescents who are surrounded by deviant moral values may become delinquent because of their environment. Such delinquency has its origin in the values represented by the surrounding subculture. In a study of individual values, peer values, and subcultural delinquency, Lerman (1968) identified six deviant value items common among male delinquents:

1. The ability to keep one's mouth shut to the cops.
2. The ability to be hard and tough.
3. The ability to find kicks.
4. The ability to make a fast buck.
5. The ability to outsmart others.
6. The ability to make connections with a racket.

Lerman went on to say that these values were basic elements of the delinquent subculture in which the boys grew up. Boys who scored high on these six values were more likely to engage in illegal behavior. Furthermore, these values were shared values; 50 percent of boys who chose a deviant value were associated with peers who also were high in deviant values. Attraction to these deviant values began early, increased especially at age 12 to 13, and persisted as a counterattraction to school and work. But on an individual level, without the support of a delinquent peer group, deviant values were unstable and were likely to shift to a conforming value. Without the support of a peer group, individuals rarely held deviant values. If they were to maintain their values, they generally sought out those who could share and support their values. It has been shown also that boys who associate with greatest frequency, duration, and intensity with delinquent peers are more likely than other youths to report delinquent behavior. Also, a high rate of delinquency in a neighborhood provides numerous opportunities for youths to learn deviant skills and values and offers support for deviant activities.

Television

Surveys indicate that the average American child aged 2 to 11 views television 27.5 hours per week (Tooth, 1985). A survey of adolescents aged 12 to 17 in urban, two-parent families in southern Louisiana revealed that these youths viewed television an average of 17.25 hours per week (Lawrence, et al., 1986). By age 18 children will have watched television approximately 22,000 hours compared with 11,000 hours in the classroom. During 5,000 of these hours, they will have been exposed to about 35,000 commercials (Gunter and Moore, 1975; LeMasters, 1974).

Television can have a significant impact on adolescents in the formation of value systems and behavior (Davis and Abelman, 1983). In one survey, 1,043 adolescents, most under 16, reported that they had seen between one and nine television shows in the past week or so that pressured them about sex (stimulated them and motivated them to want sex) (Howard, 1985).

Public concern over the content of television shows has focused on the effect on children and youths of watching so much violence. By the time adolescents are 14 and in the eighth grade, they will have watched 18,000 human beings killed on television and violent assaults on thousands more. Thomas Radecki, a psychiatrist who is head of the National Coalition on Television Violence, reports a recent deluge of high-action, violent cartoon shows (Tooth, 1985). The coalition reports that violent acts on television increased 65 percent from 1981 to 1985.

What effect does television violence have on the moral behavior of children and youth? A 1982 study by the National Institute of Mental Health concluded that "violence on television does lead to aggressive behavior by children and teenagers who watch the programs" (Tooth, 1985, p. 65). A new study by the Task Force on Children and Television of the American Academy of Pediatrics says television contributes not only to violence but also to a high rate of drug and alcohol abuse (Tooth, 1985, p. 65). Tucker (1985) found that adolescents who were heavy television viewers also consumed the most alcohol.

Most of the classic studies on the relationship between television violence and aggression in children and adolescents support this correlation. (For more complete information, see the discussion of the research of Bandura and Walters in chapter 3.)

Television violence not only increases aggressiveness in children but also influences moral values and behavior. The Great American Values Test was administered by television to millions of Americans. The researchers concluded that even a single thirty-minute exposure to television could significantly alter basic beliefs, attitudes, and the behavior of large numbers of people for at least several months (Ball-Rokeach, Rokeach, and Grube, 1984). LeMasters (1974) lists six predominant values portrayed by the media that are in conflict with those of most parents attempting to prepare their children for the future:

Sex: Usually presented in movies and TV on a physical level, both visually and verbally, yet is presented to viewers as "love."

Violence: By age fourteen the average American child has seen 18,000 human beings killed on television.

The idealization of immaturity: Idols are not Abraham Lincolns but are often as juvenile and immature as is the viewer and seem to have gained "early wealth and fame . . . with a little talent and beauty and a hard-driving agent."

Materialism: The implication is that happiness comes with success, and success comes with houses, cars, and rugs . . . and it all seems free—on the easy credit plan.

Hedonism: Exposure to an unreal world to which one can quickly escape and be entertained.

Commercialism of the media.

HIGHLIGHT   Sexual Violence in the Media

Researchers at the University of Wisconsin are seeking to discover how repeated exposure to films with sex and violence makes viewers insensitive to real violence. Male subjects were asked to watch five feature-length films for ten hours (one a day for five days). The films were either R rated, depicting sexual violence, or X rated, showing consenting sex. After a week of viewing, the men watched another film of an actual rape trial and were asked to render judgments about how responsible the victim was for her rape and how much injury she suffered.

The men began to perceive the films differently as time went on. By the last day, after viewing graphic violence against women, the men rated the material as significantly less debasing and degrading to women and more humorous and more enjoyable, and they claimed a great willingness to see this type of film again. More significantly, the victim of rape was rated as significantly more worthless and her injury significantly less severe by men who had been exposed to filmed violence than by a control group who saw only the rape trial and did not view any of the films.

The researchers concluded that viewing the films resulted in the men becoming desensitized to violence, particularly against women.

Other researchers have shown that even a few minutes of sexually violent pornography, such as rape, can lead to a viewer's acceptance of rape myths (that the woman wanted to be raped), to an increased willingness of a man to say he could commit rape, and to a decreased sensitivity to rape and the plight of a rape victim.

Donnerstein, E., and Linz, D. (January 1984). "Sexual Violence in the Media: A Warning," *Psychology Today*, 18, 14, 15.

The corresponding parental values on these issues are sexual restraint (and association of sex with love), lifelong monogamy, avoidance of violence, developing responsibility, industry, and maturity, and planning for the future as opposed to enjoyment now (Gunter and Moore, 1975).

One immediate criticism of LeMaster's analysis is that he presents television values as all negative and parental values as all positive, when the lines cannot be so neatly drawn. Many parents, by their behavior and example, portray many of the negative values of which LeMasters speaks. There are some positive social values taught on television along with the negative. Nevertheless, the analysis is partly true, though its findings cannot be applied to all television programs or to all parents.

Television advertising has also been criticized for portraying superficial views of social and personal problems and their solution. Problems of romance, engagement, marriage, child rearing, employment, and neighborhood relations can be solved by chemical means: use this headache remedy, nasal spray, deodorant, or toothpaste, and find happiness. Gunter (1975) asked ten students in a social problems course to watch for such claims on television. The students listed forty-two such claims from the commercials in a two-hour period (p. 202).

Daytime serial soap operas are watched by thousands of adolescents after school. These programs portray distorted and negative social images. The families portrayed are all upper-middle class with expensive tastes, comfortable or lavish homes, housekeepers and nurses for the children, expensive wardrobes and who take expensive vacations. No primary male characters have working class occupations. The women are primarily affluent housewives who do their own housework because they "love it." Only a minority of female characters are professional. The characters are constantly confronted with problems: rape (often by relatives), whether to have an abortion, infertility, whether to employ artificial insemination, genetic defects, illegitimacy, divorce, death, extramarital lovers, drug addiction, juvenile delinquency, social drinking and alcoholism, illnesses and operations, and mental illness. Certainly the social values of these images that are presented to millions of viewers must be questioned.

Others have pointed to the fact that television puts children in an extremely passive position. They experience constant stimulation from the outside with little activity themselves. This may lead to the expectation that their needs will be met without effort and to a passive approach to life. Some evidence has shown that watching television reduces the time that children spend reading and doing homework. Television watching also decreases family interaction and communication. Family members are able to avoid one another and tense family interactions by watching television. This may sometimes reduce overt conflict, but it does nothing to help solve family problems through personal communication (Rosenblatt and Cunningham, 1976).

Some television programs have positive influences on youths, awakening social consciousness and encouraging social concern and reform. (See chapter 1.) Television can be an important social influence for evil or for good.

Moral Education

Discussion has been going on for years about whether schools should or can teach moral values (Mills, 1987a; Sebes and Ford, 1984). In one sense, it is almost impossible *not* to teach values. Schools emphasize sharing, cooperation, and punctuality, for example. Authors like Allport (1961) advocate the deliberate inculcation of ideas and values as a goal of education:

> If the school does not teach values, it will have the effect of denying them. If the child at school never hears a mention of honesty, modesty, charity, or reverence, he will be persuaded that, like many of his parent's ideas, they are simply old hat. . . . If the school, which to the child represents the larger outside world, is silent on values, the child will repudiate more quickly the lessons learned at home. He will also be thrown into peer values more completely, with their emphasis on the hedonism of teen-age parties or the destructiveness of gangs. He will also be more at the mercy of the sensate values peddled by movies, TV, and disc jockeys. (p. 215)

Allport feels that teachers should select those values from the whole of American ethics, particularly those based on the "American creed," and Judeo-Christian ethics. Allport feels that teachers ought to teach what they themselves stand for, so that the teacher's enthusiasm and interest are ensured and "the teacher's self-disclosure leads the student to self-discovery" (p. 216).

One of the problems of moral education is that inculcating values does not necessarily result in moral behavior: there is a difference between *knowing* what is right and *doing* it (Kupfersmid and Wonderly, 1980; Maqsud, 1980; Schab, 1980). Traditional moral and religious education emphasized memorization of Bible verses, proverbs, and principles of conduct. This version of moral education constitutes what Kohlberg calls a "bag of virtues"—honesty, service, self-control, friendliness, and other moral virtues. Aristotle proposed a list that included temperance, liberality, pride, good temper, truthfulness, and justice. The Boy Scouts added that a scout should be honest, reverent, clean, and brave.

As a result, some writers, including Kohlberg (1966), face the issue more flexibly. Kohlberg feels the proper role of the teacher is neither to moralize individual, personal principles nor to indoctrinate state-defined values but to stimulate development of the individual's moral judgment by encouraging free discussion, participation, and thought about real-life issues (Englund, 1980). Kohlberg feels the teacher ought to be able to evaluate the maturity of the child's moral judgment and, regardless of whether the child's values agree with his or her (or society's) own moral values, stimulate the child to develop a higher stage of moral judgment. (Kohlberg suggests his own stages of moral judgment as a basis for evaluation.) The effort would be made to help the child judge the rightness or wrongness of moral action based on "universal, consistent, objective, impersonal, ideal grounds." Kohlberg admits that it is not certain that advanced moral judgment will automatically produce more moral action (the child may know what is right but not want to do it), so the teacher also has to get the children to examine the pros and cons of their conduct in their own terms.

In this type of teaching the primary method used is to present case studies, or moral dilemmas for the students to solve (Mills, 1987b; Mills, 1988). Here is one dilemma used to promote thinking and discussion:

> Joe is a 14-year-old boy who wanted to go to camp very much. His father promised him he could go if he saved the money for it himself. So Joe worked hard at his paper route and saved the $40 it cost to go to camp and a little more besides. But just before camp was going to start, his father changed his mind. Some of his friends decided to go on a special fishing trip, and Joe's father was short of the money it would cost, so he told Joe to give him the money he had saved from the paper route. Joe didn't want to give up going to camp, so he thought of refusing to give his father the money. (Pagliuso, 1976, p. 126)

The students are then presented with several questions:

> Should Joe refuse to give his father the money? Why? Why not?
> What do you think of the father asking Joe for the money?
> Does giving the money have anything to do with being a good son?
> Should promises always be kept?

The students might also be asked to respond to the following:

> Joe wanted to go to camp but he was afraid to refuse to give his father the money. So he gave his father $10 and told him that was all he made. He took the other $40 and paid for camp with it. He told his father the head of the camp said he could pay later. So he went off to camp, and the father didn't go on the fishing trip. Before Joe went to camp, he told his older brother, Alexander, that he really made $50 and that he lied to his father and said he'd made $10. Alexander wonders whether he should tell his father or not. (Pagliuso, 1976, p. 128)

This dilemma raises a number of important issues: whether lying, withholding the truth, or tattling is justified; whether it is more important for Alex to be a loyal son or a loyal brother.

> Should Joe have lied?
> Should Alex tell his father?
> What should the father do if he finds out (Rice, 1980, p. 160)?

Teachers need to invent other situations that relate to students' own lives and are meaningful to them.

There is considerable evidence to support the conclusion that public schools are not having much effect on the values of youth, at least during high school. As a result of the failure of moralizing as a method of teaching values, schools are now using an approach called **values clarification** (Arcus, 1980). The values clarification approach is not concerned with the *content* of values but with the *process* of valuing. It does not aim to instill any particular set of values; rather, the goal is to help students become aware of the beliefs and behaviors they prize and would be willing to stand up for, to learn to weigh the pros and cons and consequences of various alternatives, to choose freely after considerations of consequences, and to learn to match their actions with their beliefs in a consistent way. A limited amount of research and a lot of experience with this approach indicate that students who have been exposed to it become less apathetic, less flighty, less conforming, less overdissenting, more energetic, more critical in their thinking, and more likely to follow through on their decisions (Simon, 1972).

values clarification

A number of authors have developed numerous exercises and strategies that may be used in the classroom to facilitate the process of values clarification.* Here are a few of the strategies that have been used (Rice, 1980).

Either-or forced choice. The teacher asks: Are you

_____ more of a saver or a spender?
_____ more of a loner or a grouper?
_____ more physical or mental? etc.

---

* Much of the material in this section is from my book, *Morality and Youth* (Philadelphia: Westminster Press, 1980). Used by permission.

Values continuum. Students are asked to arrange themselves in relation to an entire group of students to indicate their values position along a continuum. They might be asked, for example: How far would you go to be popular with your group? The students would place themselves anywhere along a continuum ranging from "Do anything, including risking safety" to "Do nothing at all."

Write down twenty things you would like to do, and indicate beside each the cost (in dollars and cents) of doing it, whether you like to do it alone or with other people, whether planning is required, and when you did it last. Then from the twenty items, list the five most important. Discuss with the class your selections and the reasons you made them.

Rank order. Students are asked to rank various items in order of preference; for example:

Where would you rather be on a Saturday afternoon?

_____   at the beach

_____   in the woods

_____   in a discount store

What would you give the lowest priority to today?

_____   space

_____   poverty

_____   defense

_____   ecology

In *Advanced Value Clarification*, Kirschenbaum (1977) describes the value clarification process in terms of five important dimensions:

Thinking about value decisions.

Feeling: becoming aware of one's feelings so as to enable one to achieve goals more readily.

Choosing: considering alternatives and doing achievement planning.

Communicating: listening and talking with others and resolving conflicts, which helps in establishing goals and values.

Acting repeatedly, consistently, and skillfully in achieving one's goals.

Values clarification has not been without critics. For example, can anyone really be objective about what he or she values? Psychologists would say it is difficult. Does the act of clarifying one's values improve morality? Not if the values held are unworthy or superficial and not if they remain unchanged. What are the real objectives of the program? Sharing one's personal values with others may bring a person into open conflict with parents or teachers.

In spite of weaknesses, "The values clarification approach to moral education is being widely used and with some success in stimulating thinking. Students are reported to be less apathetic, less conforming, and more energetic and critical in their thinking" (Rice, 1980, p. 156). Studies conducted at the college level in the late 1950s showed little change in the value orientation of students from their freshman to senior years. Most recent research, however, emphasizes that modern college students improve significantly in their ability to think critically, and become less dogmatic, less traditional in their morals and more willing to accept new ideas over the four-year college span (White, 1980). For example, in previous generations, college students tended to favor the same political parties as their parents. Today, however, nearly as many students deviate from their parents' political views as conform to them (Green, Bush, and Sahn, 1980). This is some indication that influences outside the home are influencing the value orientation of modern college students, so that these youths no longer automatically adopt the values of their parents.

SUMMARY

This chapter has discussed five major aspects of moral development:

1. Theories of development of moral judgment, represented by Piaget, Kohlberg, and Gilligan.
2. The relationship of the development of personality types to moral character and behavior as discussed by Peck and Havighurst.
3. Family correlates to moral development.
4. Transmission of religious beliefs and practices.
5. The social influences of peers, television, and education on moral values and behavior.

Several important factors need to be emphasized. First, there are marked similarities among the theories of Piaget, Kohlberg, Gilligan, and Peck and Havighurst. Kohlberg's research and theory is actually Piagetian in method and content and a substantiation of part of what Piaget said, though the number and titles of the stages of development of moral judgment are different. Piaget outlined only two stages of moral development: a morality of constraint (or obedience) and a morality of cooperation (or reciprocity). In between is a transitional stage during which rules become internalized as the individual moves from heteronomy to autonomy. Kohlberg and Gilligan outlined three major levels of moral development: a premoral (or preconventional) level, a morality of conventional role conformity, and a morality of self-accepted moral principles (postconventional morality). Like Piaget, Kohlberg emphasized that the level of morality at which individuals operate depends on their *motives* for doing right. Piaget says that as children become more moral, they depend less on outside authority to constrain them and more on an inner, subjective desire to cooperate and to consider the rights and feelings of others. Essentially, Kohlberg says the same thing: children's motives change gradually from a desire to avoid punishment, gain the reward of others, and avoid disapproval or censure, to a more positive motive of desire for individual and community respect and a desire to avoid self-condemnation. Amoral people do what is expected only if they have to avoid punishment or gain rewards. The most moral people depend upon inner controls because certain principles and values have been incorporated into their cognitive structures through socialization with others. In between are people who maintain a morality of convention to avoid disapproval or censure. They are not immoral because they do conform, but they are not moral either, for their motives are selfish and their control is external. Gilligan describes the changes in women's motives. Their motives change from self-interest and survival to the desire to please and be responsible for others to a more universal perspective in which the woman becomes concerned about the consequences for all, including herself.

Peck and Havighurst's view concerns the relation among personality type, character, and moral behavior. They were not concerned about the cognitive development of moral judgment as were Piaget and Kohlberg. However, there is some similarity between their views. Peck and Havighurst say that people behave the way they do because they are certain types of people. Because amoral people are completely egocentric and selfish with a weak ego and superego, their whole goal is self-gratification. At the opposite extreme are the rational-altruistic people whose motivation is the welfare of others. These types of people are similar to those at Piaget's, Kohlberg's, and Gilligan's highest level of moral development. Thus, the moral progression is similar in all four theories: from amorality to outer control to inner control; from negative, selfish motivations to positive, altruistic motivations; from a desire to escape external punishment to a desire to escape self-condemnation. Also according to all four theories, there are individuals of a particular age group in each of the stages of moral growth and development, although children tend to move to more advanced stages of development as they get older. All the theories emphasize also the importance of the socialization process, peer-group participation, and the parent-child relationship in moral development.

A second important conclusion needs to be emphasized: moral growth and development cannot be isolated from other aspects of the adolescent's life. They have many correlates in the parent-child relationship especially, and to a lesser extent in the childhood peer relationship. What happens to children at home, with peers, and in the neighborhood will affect their moral development.

Third, moral growth and development begin in early childhood and are not as amenable during adolescence to outside influences and change as is sometimes thought. Such socializing influences as television, which can have a measurable effect on youths, begin very early, and these early influences can still be measured during adolescence. The public senior high school seems to exert little measurable influence on morals; values change little during four years. At college age, the situation is similar but not quite as static. The greater independence and autonomy of college students, especially of those away from home, makes them more amenable to school and peer influences; as a result some of their basic values and moral principles are changed during these years. Essentially, however, even this stage of their moral growth and development is the culmination of years of socialization rather than the result of the influences of a few years of college.

DISCUSSION QUESTIONS

1. Explain the difference between:
   a. Morality of constraint and morality of co-operation
   b. Objective judgments versus subjective judgments
   c. Objective versus subjective responsibility
   d. Expiatory punishment versus punishment of reciprocity
   e. Immanent justice versus equity according to Piaget

2. Explain Kohlberg's three levels of moral thought.

3. What are some criticisms of Kohlberg's model?

4. Do you agree or disagree with Gilligan's theory that women ought to be judged by different standards than men?

5. How does personality type influence moral behavior?

6. What family factors contribute positively to moral learning?

7. How does the type of discipline influence moral development?

8. Explain the following as related to moral development:
   a. Modeling
   b. Identification
   c. Internalization
   d. Reinforcement

9. What do you believe about the effect of television violence on children?

10. What do you believe about the effect of pornography on children?

11. What values are taught:
   a. Through television ads?
   b. Through soap operas?

12. Does the public school influence moral development? values? moral behavior? Explain.

13. Should the schools teach moral values?

14. What do you think of the values clarification approach to moral education?

BIBLIOGRAPHY

Acock, A. C., and Bengtson, V. L. (1980). "Socialization and Attribution Processes: Active Versus Perceived Similarity among Parents and Youth." *Journal of Marriage and the Family*, 42, 501–515.

Allport, G. W. (1961). "Values and Our Youth." *Teachers College Record*, 63, 211–219.

Arcus, M. E. (April, 1980). "Value Reasoning: An Approach to Values Education." *Family Relations*, 29, 163–171.

Ball-Rokeach, S. J., Rokeach, M., and Grube, J. W. (November, 1984). "The Great American Values Test." *Psychology Today*, 18, 34–41.

Bandura, A. (1971). *Social Learning Theory*. Morristown, N.J.: General Learning Press.

Bandura, A., and Walters, R. H. (1959). *Adolescent Aggression*. New York: Ronald Press Co.

———. (1963). *Social Learning and Personality Development*. New York: Holt, Rinehart and Winston.

Bart, W. M. (Summer, 1981). "Attention Structure, Anti-Social Behavior, and Peer Group Regulation of Behavior among Adolescent Students." *Adolescence*, 16, 433–442.

Berkowitz, M., Gibbs, J., and Broughton, J. (1980). "The Relation of Moral Judgment Stage Disparity to Developmental Effects of Peer Dialogues." *Merrill-Palmer Quarterly*, 26, 341–357.

Brown, R. B. (April, 1982). "The Extent and Effects of Peer Pressure among High School Students: A Retrospective Analysis." *Journal of Youth and Adolescence*, 11, 121–133.

Callahan, D., and Callahan, S. (April, 1981). "Seven Pillars of Moral Wisdom." *Psychology Today*, 84ff.

Clark, C. A., and Worthington, E. V., Jr. (1987). "Family Variables Affecting the Transmission of Religious Values from Parents to Adolescents: A Review." *Family Perspectives*, 21: 1–21.

Clark, C. A., Worthington, E. L., Jr., and Danser, D. B. (1988). "The Transmission of Religious Beliefs and Practices from Parents to First Born Early Adolescent Sons." *Journal of Marriage and the Family*, 50, 463–472.

Comstock, G. A. (1986). "Sexual Effects of Movie and TV Violence." *Medical Aspects of Human Sexuality*, 20, 96–101.

Corson, D. (Summer, 1984). "Lying and Killing: Language and the Moral Reasoning of Twelve- and Fifteen-Year-Olds by Social Group." *Adolescence*, 19, 473–482.

Davis, D. K., and Abelman, R. (1983). "Families and Television: An Application of Frame Analysis Theory." *Journal of Family Issues*, 4, 385–399.

deVaus, D. A. (Spring, 1983). "The Relative Importance of Parents and Peers for Adolescent Religious Orientation: An Australian Study." *Adolescence*, 18, 147–158.

Donnerstein, E., and Linz, D. (January, 1984). "Sexual Violence in the Media: A Warning." *Psychology Today*, 18: 14, 15.

Durkheim, E. (1960). *Moral Education*. New York: Free Press.

Eisikovits, Z., and Sagi, A. (June, 1982). "Moral Development and Discipline Encounter in Delinquent and Nondelinquent Adolescents." *Journal of Youth and Adolescence*, 11, 217–230.

Englund, C. L. (January, 1980). "Using Kohlberg's Moral Developmental Framework in Family Life Education." *Family Relations*, 29, 7–13.

Gfellner, B. M. (1986). "Changes in Ego and Moral Development in Adolescents." *Journal of Adolescence*, 9, 281–302.

Gilligan, C. (1977). "In a Different Voice: Women's Conceptions of Self and of Morality." *Harvard Educational Review*, 47, 481–517.

Gilligan, C. (1982). *In A Different Voice: Psychological Theory and Women's Development*. Cambridge, MA.: Harvard University Press.

Gilligan, C. (1984). "Remapping the Moral Domain in Personality Research and Assessment." Invited address presented to the American Psychological Association Convention, Toronto, 1984.

Green, J. J., Bush, D., and Sahn, J. (December, 1980). "The Effects of College on Students' Partisanship: A Research Note." *Journal of Youth and Adolescence*, 9, 547–552.

Gunter, B. G., and Moore, H. A. (1975). "Youth, Leisure, and Post-Industrial Society: Implications for the Family." *Family Coordinator*, 24, 199–207.

Gutkin, D. C., and Suls, J. (December, 1979). "The Relation between the Ethics of Personal Conscience-Social Responsibility and Principled Moral Reasoning." *Journal of Youth and Adolescence*, 8, 433–441.

Herzberger, S. D., and Tennen, H. (1985). "The Effect of Self-Relevance on Judgments of Moderate and Severe Disciplinary Encounters." *Journal of Marriage and the Family*, 47, 311–318.

Hogan, R. (1975). "The Structure of Moral Character and the Explanation of Moral Action." *Journal of Youth and Adolescence*, 4, 1–15.

Hogan, R., and Schroeder, D. (July, 1981). "Seven Biases in Psychology." *Psychology Today*, 8ff.

Hoge, D. R., and DuZuleta, E. (1988). "Salience as a Condition for Various Social Consequences of Religious Commitment." *Journal for the Scientific Study of Religion*, 24, 21–38.

Hoge, D. R., Petrillo, G. H., and Smith, B. I. (August, 1982). "Transmission of Religious and Social Values from Parents to Teenage Children." *Journal of Marriage and the Family*, 44, 569–580.

Howard, M. (1985). "Postponing Sexual Involvement among Adolescents: An Alternative Approach to Prevention of Sexually Transmitted Diseases." *Journal of Adolescent Health Care*, 6, 271.

Hyde, J. S. (1985). *Half the Human Experience*. Lexington, MA.: D. C. Heath.

Kay, A. W. (1969) *Moral Development*. New York: Schocken Books.

King, M. L. (1964). *Why We Can't Wait*. New York: Harper & Row.

Kirschenbaum, H. (1977). *Advanced Value Clarification*. LaJolla, Calif.: University Associates.

Kohlberg, L. (1963). "The Development of Children's Orientations toward a Moral Order." *Vita Humana*, 6, 11–33.

———. (1966). "Moral Education in the Schools, a Developmental View." *School Review*, 74, 1–30.

———. (1969). *Stages in the Development of Moral Thought and Action*. New York: Holt, Rinehart and Winston.

———. (1970). "Moral Development and the Education of Adolescents." In *Adolescents and the American High School*. Edited by R. F. Purnell. New York: Holt, Rinehart and Winston.

Kohlberg, L., and Gilligan, C. (Fall 1971). "The Adolescent as a Philosopher: The Discovery of the Self in a Postconventional World." *Daedalus*, 1051–1086.

Kohlberg, L., and Kramer, R. (1969). "Continuities and Discontinuities in Childhood and Adult Development." *Human Development*, 12, 93–120.

Kohlberg, L., and Turiel, E., eds. (1972). *Recent Research in Moral Development*. New York: Holt, Rinehart and Winston.

Kupfersmid, J. H., and Wonderly, D. M. (June, 1980). "Moral Maturity and Behavior: Failure to Find a Link." *Journal of Youth and Adolescence*, 9, 249–261.

Kurdek, L. A. (August, 1981). "Young Adults' Moral Reasoning about Prohibitive and Prosocial Dilemmas." *Journal of Youth and Adolescence*, 10, 263–272.

Lawrence, F. C., Tasker, G. E., Daly, C. T., Orhiel, A. L., and Wozniak, P. H. (1986). "Adolescents' Time Spent Viewing Television." *Adolescence*, 21, 431–436.

LeMasters, E. E. (1974). *Parents in Modern America*. Rev. ed. Homewood, Ill.: Dorsey Press.

Lerman, P. (1968). "Individual Values, Peer Values, and Subcultural Delinquency." *American Sociological Review*, 33, 219–235.

Lutwak, N. (Fall, 1984). "The Interrelationship of Ego, Moral, and Conceptual Development in a College Group." *Adolescence*, 19, 675–688.

Maqsud, M. (August, 1980). "Relationships between Personal Control, Moral Reasoning, and Socioeconomic Status of Nigerian Hausa Adolescents." *Journal of Youth and Adolescence*, 9, 281–288.

Matteson, D. R. (1975) *Adolescence Today: Sex Roles and the Search for Identity*. Homewood, Ill.: Dorsey Press.

Mills, R. K. (1987a) "Traditional Morality, Moral Reasoning and the Moral Education of Adolescents." *Adolescence*, 22, 371–375.

_____ . (1987b). "The Novels of S. E. Hinton; Springboard to Personal Growth of Adolescents." *Adolescence*, 22, 641–646.

_____ . (1988). "Using Tom and Hank to Develop Moral Reasoning in Adolescents: A Strategy for the Classroom." *Adolescence*, 23, 325–329.

Muson, H. (February, 1979) "Moral Thinking: Can It Be Taught?" *Psychology Today*, 48ff.

Muuss, R. E. (1988a). "Carol Gilligan's Theory of Sex Differences in the Development of Moral Reasoning during Adolescence." *Adolescence*, 23, 229–243.

_____ . (1988b). *Theories of Adolescence*. 5th ed. New York: McGraw Hill.

Norcini, J. J., and Snyder, S. S. (April, 1983). "The Effects of Modeling and Cognitive Induction on the Moral Reasoning of Adolescents." *Journal of Youth and Adolescence*, 12, 101–115.

Ornum, W. V., Foley, J. M., Burns, P. R., DeWolfe, A. S., and Kennedy, E. C. (Winter, 1981). "Empathy, Altruism, and Self-Interest in College Students." *Adolescence*, 16, 799–808.

Ozorak, E. W. (1986). *The Development of Religious Beliefs and Commitment in Adolescence*. Paper presented at the meeting of the American Psychological Association. Washington, D. C. (August).

Pagliuso, S. (1976). *Understanding Stages of Moral Development: A Programmed Learning Workbook*. New York: Paulist Press.

Parish, T. S. (Fall, 1980). "The Relationship between Factors Associated with Father Loss and Individuals' Level of Moral Judgment." *Adolescence*, 15, 535–541.

Peck, R. H., and Havighurst, R. J. (1960). *The Psychology of Character Development*. New York: John Wiley and Sons.

Peters, R. S. (1971). "Moral Development: A Plea for Pluralism." In *Cognitive Development and Epistemology*. Edited by T. Mischel. New York: Academic Press.

Piaget, J. (1948). *The Moral Judgment of the Child*. 1932. Reprint, Glencoe, Ill.: Free Press.

Piaget, J., and Inhelder, B. (1969). *The Psychology of the Child*. Translated by Helen Weaver. New York: Basic Books.

Rest, J. R. (1983). "Morality." In *Handbook of Child Psychology*, III., 4th ed. Edited by P. H. Mussen. New York: Wiley.

Rest, J. (1986). *Moral Development: Advances in Research and Theory*. New York: Praeger.

Rice, F. P. (1980). *Morality and Youth*. Philadelphia: Westminster Press.

Robins, L. N. (1966). *Deviant Children Grown Up*. Baltimore: Williams & Wilkins.

Rosenblatt, P. C., and Cunningham, M. R. (1976). "Television Watching and Family Tensions." *Journal of Marriage and the Family*, 38, 105–111.

Rowe, I., and Marcia J. E. (April, 1980). "Ego Identity Status, Formal Operations, and Moral Development." *Journal of Youth and Adolescence*, 9, 87–99.

Rybash, J. M., Roodin, P. A., and Lonky, E. (February, 1981). "Young Adults' Scores on the Defining Issues Test as a Function of a 'Self' versus 'Other' Presentation Mode." *Journal of Youth and Adolescence*, 10, 25–31.

Schab, P. (Winter, 1980). "Cheating in High School: Differences between the Sexes (Revisited), *Adolescence*, 15, 959–965.

Sebes, J. M., and Ford, D. H. (March, 1984). "Moral Development and Self-Regulation: Research and Intervention Planning." *Personnel and Guidance Journal*, 62, 379–382.

Simon, S. B., et al. (1972). *Values Clarification*. New York: Hart Publishing Co.

Sutherland, E. H., and Cressey, D. R. (1966). *Principles of Criminology*. 7th ed. New York: J. B. Lippincott.

Tooth, G. (February 18, 1985). "Why Children's TV Turns Off So Many Parents." *U.S. News & World Report*, p. 65.

Tucker, L. A. (1985). "Television's Role Regarding Alcohol Use among Teenagers." *Adolescence*, 20, 593–598.

Tudor, C. G., Petersen, D. M., and Elifson, K. W. (Winter, 1980). "An Examination of the Relationship between Peer and Parental Influences and Adolescent Drug Use." *Adolescence*, 15, 783–798.

Walker, L. (1982). "The Sequentiality of Kohlberg's Stages of Social Development." *Child Development*, 53, 1330–1336.

Weinreich, H. E. (1970). "A Replication and Evaluation of a Study by Lawrence Kohlberg of the Development of Moral Judgment in the Adolescent." Master's thesis, University of Sussex.

_____ . (1974). "The Structure of Moral Reason." *Journal of Youth and Adolescence*, 3, 135–143.

White, K. M. (Spring, 1980). "Problems and Charac-

teristics of College Students." *Adolescence*, 15, 23–41.

Windmiller, M. (1976). "Moral Development." In *Understanding Adolescence*. 3d ed. Edited by J. F. Adams. Boston, Mass.: Allyn and Bacon.

Wonderly, D. M., and Kupfersmid, J. H. (Fall, 1980). "Promoting Postconventional Morality: The Adequacy of Kohlberg's Aim." *Adolescence*, 15, 609–631.

Zelkowitz, P. (1987). "Social Support and Aggressive Behavior in Young Children." *Family Relations*, 36, 129–134.

CHAPTER
19

Education and School

TRENDS IN AMERICAN EDUCATION

Traditionalists versus Progressives

traditionalists

progressives

During the past fifty years, the emphasis in American education has shifted from one extreme to the other. **Traditionalists** have argued that the purpose of education is to teach the basics—English, science, math, history, and foreign languages—to increase student knowledge and intellectual powers. **Progressives** have urged that the purpose of education is to prepare students for all of life: citizenship, home and family living, a vocation, physical health, the effective use of leisure time, effective personality growth.

The debate has continued partly because of the insistence that education has an important role in reforming society and solving social problems. Each time a social problem has arisen, a new school program has been designed to deal with it. When traffic fatalities rose, driver education was introduced. A rise in premarital pregnancies and in divorce rates was followed by courses in family life education. Demands for racial integration led to black studies and school busing. Feminists' demands for equality and liberation resulted in women's studies. Rise in crime rates resulted in new social problems offerings. Since social needs change from time to time, the educational pendulum has been pushed first in one direction and then another.

Rise of Progressive Education

Until the 1930s, traditionalism was the dominant emphasis in American schools. Then came the Depression, which destroyed the job market for adolescents, so that many who would have gone to work stayed in school instead (Ravitch, 1983). Most of these youths were noncollege bound, uninterested in traditional academic subjects, and in need of different programs to deal with their own problems. Educational philosophers like John Dewey felt the schoolroom should be a laboratory of living, preparing students for all of life. Under the progressive influence, many schools introduced vocational and personal service courses, restricting academic courses to the college-preparatory program. Life adjustment education centered around vocations, leisure activities, health, personal concerns, and community problems. Principals boasted that their programs adjusted students to the demands of real life, freeing them from dry academic studies. Developing an effective personality became as important as improving reading skills (Ravitch, 1983; Wood, Wood, and McDonald, 1988).

Sputnik and After

The nation was shocked when the Soviet Union launched Sputnik, the first space satellite, in the 1950s. Almost overnight, the nation became obsessed with the failure of the schools to keep pace with the technological advances of the Soviet Union. The schools were blamed for a watered-down curriculum that left American youth unprepared to face the challenge of communism. As a result, Congress passed the National Defense Education Act and appropriated nearly $1 billion in federal aid to education, which supported the teaching of math, science, and foreign languages. Schools modernized their laboratories. Courses in physical sciences and math were rewritten by leading scholars to reflect advances in knowledge.

1960s and 1970s

By the mid-1960s, the cold war had abated. The United States was swamped with the rising tide of social unrest, racial tension, and antiwar protests. Once again, society was in trouble, and the schools were called upon to rise to the challenge. Major school aid legislation was passed, primarily to benefit poor children as part of the Johnson administration's War on Poverty. Once more the educational clamor was for relevance. Educators claimed that schools were not preparing young people for adult roles and demanded that adolescents spend more time in community and work settings, as well as in the classroom. Academic programs gave way to career and experimental education so that adolescents could receive "hands-on" experience. Elementary schools adopted open education, knocked down classroom walls, and gave students more choices as to what to do each day. High schools lowered graduation requirements. Enrollments in science, math, and foreign languages fell as traditional subjects gave way to independent study, student-designed courses, and a flock of electives. By the late 1970s, over 40 percent of all high school students were taking a general rather than college preparatory or vocational course of study, and 25 percent of their educational credits came from work experience outside school, remedial course work, and courses aimed at personal growth and development (National Commission on Excellence in Education, 1983).

By the mid-1970s, thoughtful persons became more alarmed at the steady, slow decline in academic indicators. **SAT** scores had shown a steady decline from 1963 to 1980. Verbal scores fell over fifty points and average math scores nearly forty points. The College Entrance Examination Board administering the tests cited such in-school reasons* as grade inflation, absenteeism, frivolous courses, the absence of homework, and a decline in reading and writing assignments as reasons for falling test scores. It became obvious that high school students were taking more nonacademic courses and fewer courses necessary for college preparation.

SAT

1980s

Parental and public outcry grew, resulting in the appointment of the National Commission on Excellence in Education (1983). This commission found that:

> The number and proportion of students demonstrating superior achievement on the SATs (those with scores of 650 or higher) had declined.
> Scores on achievement tests in such subjects as physics and English had declined.
> There was a steady decline in science achievement scores of U.S. 17-year-olds by national assessments in 1969, 1973, and 1979.

---

* Psychologists and educators cite other reasons also such as family tensions, disorganization, and instability.

Average achievement of high school students on most standardized tests was lower than when Sputnik was launched.

Nearly 40 percent of 17-year-olds could not draw inferences from written material; only one-fifth could write a persuasive essay; and only one-third could solve a mathematics problem requiring several steps.

About 13 percent of all 17-year-olds in the United States could be considered functionally illiterate. Functional illiteracy among minority youth ran as high as 40 percent (National Commission on Excellence in Education, 1983).

This time, the reason given for demanding a back to basics education was not a threat from the Soviets but a fear that the nation was falling behind the economic competition from Japan and Western Europe and was losing its competitive edge in world markets. Educational reformers demanded more academic rigor in the schools, more required courses, particularly in math and science, longer school days, and tougher standards for graduation. Thus, the pendulum has again swung back to a more traditionalist posture.

By the time the commission issued its report, however, the American Association of School Administrators (1983) pointed out the following:

The decline in SAT scores had stabilized and appeared to be reversed.

Students had been taking an increasing number of academic courses in each of the last six years.

Many states had already adopted stricter graduation requirements.

Many school districts had already raised expectations for students.

The percentage of adolescents enrolled in school continued to climb, and American schools were educating a larger percentage of 17-year-olds than any other educational system in the world.

The average citizen was better educated and more knowledgeable: more literate and exposed to more math, literature, and science than the average citizen of a generation ago.

According to the United Nations, the United States had one of the highest literacy rates in the world (American Association of School Administrators, 1983, p. 14).

Any attempt to evaluate the effectiveness of American education has to consider what should be evaluated and by what standards. In addition to providing training in academic basics, the schools have been called upon to assist with vocational and job training, to help integrate racial groups, to help individuals mature emotionally and socially, to develop positive self-concept and personal-social skills in relation to others, to develop patriotism, good citizenship, and responsible civic participation, to assist in character building and in developing and modeling appropriate behavior, to provide social experience within school settings through clubs, extracurricular activities, and athletics, to assist in developing adjustments with peer groups, to improve home and family relationships, to prepare for marriage, homemaking, and parenthood, and to provide basic instruction in sex education. Although there seems to be little doubt that school effectiveness in teaching the basics declined for a number of years, there has not been sufficient evaluation of the extent to which schools have measured up to expectations in these other ways.

ADOLESCENTS VIEW THEIR SCHOOLS

Students Grade Their Schools

A nationwide survey of 1,175 students from Maine to Alaska in grades seven through twelve revealed some significant findings (Solorzano et al., 1984).

Twenty-eight percent gave their schools an A rating; 57 percent gave a letter grade of B to the overall quality of education they were receiving. Just over 13 percent issued C grades. Hardly any gave their schools a D or F. Students who gave their schools an A felt that students had an excellent chance for a good education. They felt that there was a lot of academic pressure to succeed and that everyone was concerned that they get as good an education as possible.

Students who graded their schools B felt that not enough is expected of students: that there ought to be harder tests to help motivate students to learn, that not all courses are as interesting or challenging as they should be, and that there ought to be a stronger emphasis on the importance of education for the sake of excellence. Students felt that there should be stiffer regulations for participation in extracurricular activities, such as sports and music events. Forty-five percent said participation should be limited to those maintaining at least a C average in their studies. Students felt that schoolwork was most important but that extracurricular activities were also educational.

Quality of Teachers

In response to questions regarding how their education could be improved, one-half the students said that the most important way would be to *upgrade the quality of teachers*. Only 14 percent gave their teachers an A, 55 percent gave a B. Students commented:

> It's the minority of teachers who can't or don't try to give it their best who are destructive to the system.
> Some of the older teachers don't seem concerned if you learn their subject or not. Some teachers are not caring about kids, but just doing a job.
> I feel challenged in the majority of my classes, but there are those that are lacking and, in effect, are wasted time every day. (p. 50)

When asked what was the biggest problem with the quality of teaching, over one-half the students said that teachers *failed to make the subject matter interesting*, 22 percent of students said teachers *did not challenge students to work hard enough*, and 11 percent complained about a *lack of classroom discipline*. Many students felt that teachers' *salaries were too low to attract the best teachers*. One student remarked: "Your

HIGHLIGHT   What Makes Great Schools Great

The secretary of education has cited 354 public secondary schools across the country as outstanding role models, representing exceptionally fine schools. The following highlights show what is exceptionally fine about three of the schools.

Katahdin High School, Sherman Station, Maine
The secret of success of this small, consolidated high school in rural Maine is mutual respect and caring. Classes are small, allowing teachers to know students' potentials. Emphasis is placed on building good teacher-student relationships. Any rudeness to a teacher, however, means a trip to the principal's office. "We have order and discipline, but I've always tried to couple that with a little warmth and a positive approach," the principal explains. A wall containing a "Big E" board gives weekly recognition to individual students for classroom effort and behavior. Another display, "Teachers Are People Too," contains articles on the pressures and problems of teachers. The principal is there if a student needs to cry on his shoulder, but he will also dismiss a student for bad behavior. Teachers are encouraged to give their best and report that their requests for supplies and books are never turned down. Students are encouraged to take job internships throughout the state that will prepare them for opportunities not locally available.

Thomas Jefferson High School, Los Angeles
The secret of this school of 2,000 predominately Hispanic and Black students is no-nonsense discipline, school pride, and special attention to learning problems.

Tardiness has been minimized by locking the gates promptly at 8 A.M., sending late students to a holding room for one period so they will not disrupt classes, and requiring twenty minutes of clean-up work if they are late three times in one month.

The principal repaired the graffiti-marred buildings, sealed off administrative offices that had been gutted by fire, and installed a fire and security system. Gang fights were eliminated. Students felt safe and proud of their school again.

A school-within-a-school program was started to assist students with low academic and reading scores. They sign contracts accepting responsibility for their own progress in exchange for individual instruction. Local businesses are providing support and training programs for teachers and students alike.

Bellaire Senior High School, Houston, Texas
The secret of success of this mixed racial school is keeping expectations high and offering unusually fine, special programs.

The school ranked second in the nation in the number of National Merit Scholarship semifinalists. The average test scores of the class of 1984 were more than three years above their twelfth-grade level. The school's team placed first in the national Junior Engineering Technology Society contest. Superior students want to come to the school because of quality education.

The school's strong academic tradition is enhanced by two special programs: a foreign language center that offers intensive training in seven languages and an advanced study program for juniors and seniors. Students and teachers are motivated by pride in excellence.

Solorzano, L., et al. (August 27, 1984). "What Makes Great Schools Great," U.S. *News & World Report*, pp. 46–49.

smarter students become doctors, lawyers, engineers, and other things with higher-paid salaries. If teachers were paid better, the quality of education might become better" (Solorzano, 1984, p. 50).

Youths blamed themselves, their schools, and their teachers for failing to earn an A for American education. Students say they want to work harder and to be challenged more, but most admit they will not do it without greater motivation from interested, competent teachers.

DROPOUTS AND UNDERACHIEVEMENT
Enrollment Figures

Education for all youths has not always been the philosophy of the American people. The famous Kalamazoo decision in 1874 established the now-accepted principle that public education need not be restricted to the elementary schools. Prior to that, in 1870, American youths could choose from among only 800 public high schools. Most youths who were preparing for college attended private secondary schools, then called preparatory schools. In 1950, only 33 percent of those 25 and over completed four or more years of high school; by 1983, the number was 72 percent. Figure 19-1 shows the rise since 1950. Figure 19-2 shows the percentage of dropouts from school by age and race during 1985. Until age 17,

FIGURE 19-1

Percentage of adults who have completed four years of high school or more: 1950–1985.

From: U.S. Department of Commerce, Bureau of the Census (1987). *Statistical Abstract of the United States, 1987* (Washington, D.C.: U.S. Government Printing Office), p. 121.

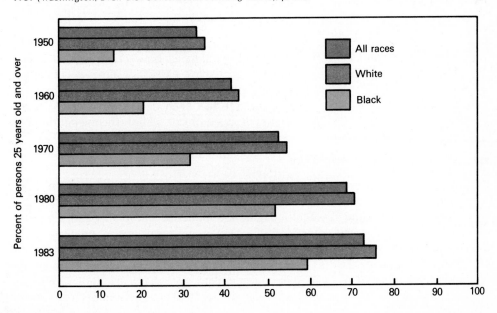

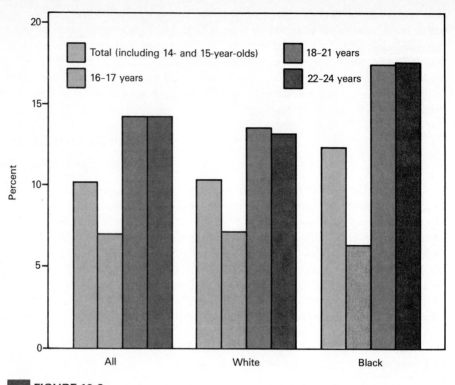

FIGURE 19-2

High school dropouts from 14 to 24 years old, by race and age, 1985.

Source of statistics: U.S. Bureau of the Census (1987), *Statistical Abstract of the United States*, 1987 (Washington, D.C.: U.S. Government Printing Office), p. 136.

attendance figures are very high, with little difference between whites and blacks. The dropouts occur during the high school years, especially after age 17, with a greater percentage of blacks than whites leaving school. The total number of dropouts is considerable, though the rate has been decreasing over the years. During 1985, over 4.5 million youths dropped out of school. The overall dropout rate in 1985 was 10 percent (U.S. Bureau of the Census, 1987).

Who Drops Out and Why

There is a constellation of causes for youths' dropping out of school or underachieving (Zarb, 1984). Socioeconomic factors, racial and ethnic prejudice and discrimination, family background, parental influence and relationships, personality problems, social adjustments, activities and associations, financial problems, health problems, intellectual difficulties or retardation, reading disability, school failure, misconduct, low marks, and lack of interest in school are all important factors. Usually problems accumulate over the years until withdrawal occurs, often only after the legal requirements of age or number of years of schooling have been met. The actual event or circumstance that precipitates withdrawal may be minor: a misunderstanding with a teacher, a disciplinary action, difficulty with peers, misunderstanding at home, or other reasons. One boy withdrew in the last semester of his senior year because his foster parents would not buy him a suit for graduation. Another boy was refused admittance to a class until a late excuse was obtained from his gym teacher in the prior period. The gym teacher would not give an excuse; the boy got angry, quit school, and never came back. In each incident like this, a whole series of prior events led to the final withdrawal: poor marks, grade retardation, conduct problems at school, strained family relationships, social maladjustment or isolation, and others. The following are some signs of possible early school withdrawal:

1. Consistent failure to achieve in regular school work
2. Grade level placement two or more years below average age for grade
3. Irregular attendance
4. Active antagonism to teachers and principals
5. Marked disinterest in school with feeling of not belonging
6. Low scholastic aptitude
7. Low reading ability
8. Frequent changes of schools
9. Nonacceptance by school staff
10. Nonacceptance by schoolmates
11. Friends much younger or older
12. Unhappy family situation
13. Marked differences from schoolmates with regard to size
14. Inability to afford the normal expenditures of schoolmates
15. Nonparticipation in extracurricular activities
16. Inability to compete with or ashamed of brothers and sisters
17. Performance consistently lower than potential
18. Serious physical or emotional handicap
19. Being a disciplinary case
20. A record of delinquency

These signs must be interpreted cautiously; the presence of one or more of these symptoms of early school withdrawal may be a false alarm. But at other times only one symptom may be present yet be a real indication of possible withdrawal. When as many as eight of these symptoms appear together, a prognosis of school withdrawal is more reliable.

Socioeconomic Factors

Research overwhelmingly indicates that low socioeconomic status correlates positively with early withdrawal from school (Manaster, 1977). Why is the dropout rate higher among students from low socioeconomic families? There are a number of considerations.

Students from these families often lack positive parental influences and examples. Many low socioeconomic parents want their children to have more education than they did. But if parents finished only fifth grade, they may consider graduating from junior high school sufficient. Sons still receive more encouragement to finish school than daughters do.

Teachers are often prejudiced against youth from low socioeconomic families, showing preferential treatment to students from higher status families. Students of higher social class backgrounds are chosen more often for little favors—running errands, monitoring, chairing committees—whereas students from lower status groups receive more than their share of discipline. Teachers are usually from middle-class backgrounds and therefore often find it difficult to understand and accept the goals, values, and behavior of pupils from other social backgrounds.

Low socioeconomic students receive fewer rewards for doing well and for staying in school than do students from higher status families. Rewards may take the form of academic grades, favors by teachers, social acceptance by peers, offices in school government, participation in extracurricular activities, or school prizes and awards. Lower status students less often receive any of these rewards than do higher status students. They do not get as good grades or enjoy as much social acceptance and prestige by peers; they seldom are elected to positions of leadership, are nonjoiners in extracurricular activities, and are not often given special prizes and awards by the school.

Lower socioeconomic students do not as often possess the verbal skills of their middle-class peers. This in itself presents a handicap in learning to read or in almost all other academic work. Insofar as lack of verbal skills is associated with low socioeconomic status, lower status youths do not do as well in school and are therefore more prone to drop out.

Peer influences on low socioeconomic youth are often antischool and delinquency prone, emphasizing early marriage for the girls and gang activities for the boys. Low socioeconomic youths often have severed their ties with adult institutions and values, becoming involved instead with groups composed of jobless dropouts.

Ethnic Considerations

Black and other minority group students have a much higher dropout rate than white students do (U.S. Bureau of the Census, 1987). The highest rates are among nonwhite students from inner-city high schools. The value orientation and the trying economic, social, and familial conditions are not conducive to continuing education. Youths from such neighborhoods are frequently truant and tend to drop out as soon as they reach age 16.

Family Relationships

The quality of interaction among members of the adolescent's family has a marked influence on school success (Hurrelman, et al., 1988). Studies of the family relationships of bright, high achieving versus underachieving high school students show that the high achievers more often than underachievers describe their parents as typically sharing recreation and ideas, as understanding, approving, trusting, affectionate, encouraging (but not pressuring) with respect to achievement, and not overly restrictive or severe in discipline (Thornburg, 1975). Youths who come from conflicting family environments are more likely to be underachievers and school dropouts than those who come from cohesive, nonconflicting families. (Wood, Chapin, and Hannah, 1988).

Personality Characteristics

Dropouts are more likely to be emotionally immature and less well adjusted than high school graduates. They may manifest symptoms of defective ego functioning: rebellion, negativism and alienation, deep-seated feelings of hostility and resentment, low self-esteem, feelings of inferiority, excessive fear and anxiety, or emotional instability. What is so often described as laziness or a lack of will power may actually be sullen resentment toward punitive parents, social rejection, or unfair treatment at school, which cause such feelings of rebellion that the adolescent refuses to do anything demanded by authority. Some students develop a real phobia in relationship to school (Paccione-Dyszlewski and Contessa-Kislus, 1987).

Five traits have been identified as common among underachievers: (1) negativism, (2) inferiority feelings, (3) high anxiety, (4) boredom, and (5) overprotectedness (Stevens and Pihl, 1987).

Social Adjustment, Peer Associations

Peer influences often are a major factor in influencing a particular student to stay in school or not. Most adolescents want to do what their friends are doing. If friends are dropping out of school to get jobs earning "big money" or to get married, the individual may be persuaded to do likewise. Similarly, the student who becomes acculturated into a lower-class pattern of life that rejects education or into a delinquent group rebelling against the established system of education is strongly influenced by his or her peers to drop out of school.

Employment, Money

Financial considerations are important in individual decisions about whether to stay in school. Even high school is expensive. This factor plus financial pressures at home force some adolescents to leave school to go to work. Sometimes parents pressure youths to go to work to help support the family. At other times there is the lure of being financially independent, having spending money for social activities or to buy a car. The desire for clothes, a car, or other symbols of status in an affluent society lures many youths to accept early employment.

School Failure, Apathy, Dissatisfaction

Many school factors have been associated with dropping out of school. Among these are poor reading ability, grade retardation, repetition, misplacement, low or failing marks, inability to get along with teachers, misconduct, and low IQ or mental retardation. There is also a general, vague category that might be labeled apathy, lack of motivation, or a feeling that school is irrelevant. Some students are not necessarily emotionally or socially maladjusted but simply lack interest in school work, feel it is a waste of time, and would rather get married or go to work. Such youths may be capable of doing acceptable work but have no interest in doing so. Sometimes such a student has been placed in the wrong type of program (Knoff, 1983). A switch to a vocational course that the student finds appealing is of help to the adolescent wrongly placed in the college prep program. Students who have had to repeat grades and who thus miss friends and feel themselves to be social misfits may develop an intense dislike for school and lose all interest and desire to learn. Similarly, students who have a history of low marks and failure find school an unrewarding, painful experience and cannot wait to get out (Deci, 1985).

Many students do not drop out but are thrown out or given a temporary suspension, which they turn into a permanent absence. Students who are disciplined by temporary suspension are tempted not to return if they have experienced much long-term dissatisfaction or difficulty at school. Administrators and teachers often breathe a sigh of relief when the student does not come back. At other times a student is expelled and not allowed to return, so he or she has no choice in the matter.

Schools that establish effective intervention programs for potential dropouts can reduce the rate considerably. What is needed is a determined effort to correct the conditions that cause the student to drop out (Caliste, 1984). One study of juvenile delinquents and school dropouts revealed four factors that predicted drop out: misbehavior in school, disliking school, negative influence of peers, and poor relationships with parents (Dunham and Alpert, 1987). Specific interventions are needed to correct these conditions if the likelihood of dropping out is to be reduced.

Pregnancy, Marriage

Leaving high school to get married is seldom a reason boys drop out of school, but *pregnancy and marriage are among the most common reasons for girls.*

HIGHLIGHT   Middle-Class Parenting and Underachievement

Metcalf and Gaier (1987) studied patterns of parenting among middle-class parents of underachieving eleventh and twelfth graders and found four patterns that contributed to academic underachievement.

Upward striving parents—parents pressure adolescents to get good marks; they criticize and nag.

Overprotective parents—parents are overrestrictive, overdirecting, domineering, compulsive perfectionists, constantly expecting their children to do better.

Indifferent parents—parents set low standards, show little interest, set no consistent limits.

Conflicted parents—parents have blatantly inconsistent ideas on child rearing.

Apparently, excessive pressure, criticism, indifference, and conflict all contribute to academic underachievement.

THE SECONDARY SCHOOL TEACHER

What Makes a Good Teacher?

One of the important keys to fruitful secondary school education is having good teachers in the school system (Aptekar, 1983). But what constitutes a "good" teacher? There is little agreement on the answer. Are good teachers those who are selected according to certain personality traits characteristic of mature, mentally healthy people? Are good teachers best defined by the degree of understanding, rapport, and warmth of the relationships they are able to establish with pupils, colleagues, and administrators? Or are they best defined by their professional backgrounds, qualifications, and abilities to use appropriate materials and methods in motivating learning in students? Although various educators emphasize one category or another, there is sufficient evidence to justify emphasizing all three categories: (1) personality, (2) relationships, and (3) professional qualifications and performance.

Personality Traits and Character

Teachers who are emotionally secure people free from excessive fears, worries, and anxieties, with an adequate self-concept, do not have to overcompensate for their failures or rationalize them or have to protect their own egos by projecting their inadequacies on others or blaming them for their own failures. They can be confident, accepting, trusting people who feel and act secure and mature. In one study of what high school dropouts thought of their teachers, the students listed

One important key to fruitful secondary school education is finding good teachers who are professionally qualified and who have rapport with their students. (Alex McMahan)

self-confidence as the most important attribute of an effective instructor because such teachers would not need to belittle others in order to feel secure themselves.

It is also beneficial to students' emotional development if teachers are emotionally stable people with high frustration tolerances and fairly even, pleasant dispositions and temperaments, free of excessive emotionalism or extremes of mood. They are not always patient but are usually so and behave in a controlled manner.

Emotional security enables teachers to keep an open mind on questions and issues, to be willing to entertain different points of view, to let students air their opinions and not pressure them to come up with the "right" answer (the teacher's answer). They can be flexible in scheduling, administering, and teaching their classes and not mind innovation or change if it makes a contribution to the learning process (Fisher, 1976). They are relatively free of racial, ethnocentric, religious, political, and other prejudices and biases so that they can present issues honestly from different points of view. Thus, they can be as tolerant, impartial, and fair as possible.

Emotional maturity also enables teachers to show kindness, love, and genuine warmth and regard for other people. This enables them to find close personal attachments in their own lives and to build rapport with adolescents. Thus, they can communicate that they like adolescents, understand them, and enjoy being with them. Students also like teachers who are generally happy, pleasant, cheerful people.

Although there are "successful" teachers who are fairly self-centered, the better ones are unselfish and altruistic to the point of being pupil centered, with a genuine concern for them and their welfare. Teachers need to be honest, sincere, caring, socially responsible people who strive to set a good example of personal conduct in their own lives and who are aware and sensitive to the social and ethical mores of the culture in which they live. This requires not only concern about individual ethics but also social morality.

Teaching is an exhausting profession, often requiring almost unlimited reservoirs of physical, emotional, and mental energy. It is not a profession for the sickly. Therefore, teachers need much drive and energy, backed up by a healthy constitution. Lethargic, phlegmatic, apathetic, bored people in poor health can neither inspire students nor meet the vigorous demands of their profession.

Teachers' Relationships with Others

It is helpful if teachers enjoy satisfying social relationships outside school so that there is no need to work off negative feelings on their pupils or to use students to fulfill their own emotional and social needs. Teachers who get along well with their colleagues, who have satisfactory personal lives as individuals or members of a family, who are accepted and liked by others and have found social acceptance in adult society make better teachers.

Furthermore, teachers need to like adolescents, to be able to relate to them as growing people who are becoming adults, and to treat them with admiration and respect as individuals. The teacher who hates youths, who is supercritical and rejecting of them, has no business in the classroom.

The best teachers evidence real understanding of youths, the developmental tasks of adolescence, and the particular problems, adjustments, and interests of young people. Thus, the basic teacher-pupil relationship is one of adult to growing adult, with genuine concern, tolerance, friendliness, and respect evident in their relationship, with the teacher manifesting understanding of adolescents' lives and needs and an ability to relate and communicate with them.

Professional Qualifications

One of the major criticisms of teacher candidates is that they are intellectually the poorest in the universities. This impression is commonly held among students outside colleges of education but can also be found among faculty members in universities across the nation. However, since the range of test scores overlaps among all college majors, there are some education majors scoring very high as well as low. Also, test scores vary from institution to institution.

Another criticism of teachers has been that they are too middle class and thus are not able to relate to lower socioeconomic class students. Although it is desirable from one point of view to employ more teachers from lower socioeconomic families, the likelihood of hiring teachers with lower scholastic ability becomes greater, for there is a positive correlation between performance on scholastic aptitude tests and the socioeconomic status of the family. However, a large number of those growing up in poor families are also of superior intelligence, so it is sometimes possible to find both brains and the ability to relate to all students in the same teacher.

It is important that teachers, once trained, keep abreast of the times in attitude, instructional knowledge, and skills. This means that teachers need to take advantage of numerous opportunities for professional improvement, participate in learned societies, attend workshops and conferences, take graduate courses, and keep up in their field by reading professional journals, new books, and research literature—not just in teaching methods, but in subject matter as well.

A *good teacher is willing to spend necessary time in preparation*, plans carefully, and understands and uses sound principles of learning through a variety of appropriate teaching methods and techniques. Students are highly critical of teachers who are "never prepared," are "lazy," "aren't interested in teaching," who "don't care if we learn," or who "use films as a substitute for a good lesson."

CURRICULUM CONSIDERATIONS
Three Curricula

The average comprehensive high school today offers three basic curricula.

College Preparatory   The most prestigious is the college preparatory curriculum, enrolling about one-half the students. It has one goal: to prepare the student for success in the type of college that leads to graduate school. Some high schools, particularly in middle- and upper middle-class suburban communities, are particularly successful, boasting 80 to 90 percent of their students going to college. Other schools, though enrolling large numbers of students in the college prep program, are unsuccessful because the majority of these students do not get into college. In such cases the college prep program does not meet the needs of the majority of students; even if they graduate, they do not go to college, yet they are not employable without additional training.

Vocational   The vocational curriculum is the one curriculum designed for preparing students for gainful employment. Students spend about one-half their time in general education, the rest in specialized courses and, in some cases, on-the-job training (Panel on Youth, 1974). Vocational teachers usually have work experience in the vocation they are teaching. The quality of the program varies from superb to mediocre. However, the number of exclusively vocational high schools is limited, and because vocational enrollments in comprehensive high schools are typically limited to 20 percent of the student body, only the ablest students are accepted. The program therefore rejects many of those who need help the most.

General   The third curriculum is the general curriculum. Its students are the castoffs from the other two curricula plus those not committed either to college or to one of the vocations taught in the vocational curriculum. It has no goals other than to provide a general education for those who may be able to go onto some type of job or some type of vocational, post-high school education. Most dropouts and unemployed youths come from the general curriculum. More of these youths might have stayed in high school and been employable if they had had more specific vocational training. (A student bulletin, put out by a large, well-known guidance firm, describes a general program as one teaching "what everybody should know." This, according to the bulletin, includes English, math, science, social studies, and a foreign language. No wonder this program does not meet all students' needs.)

Curriculum Improvement

Efforts over the years at curriculum reform have consistently confronted two major problems. One is the rigidity of course requirements, grade demands, scheduling, and the lockstep structure of schools. When certain subjects are required, when carefully chosen subject-oriented content is obligatory in any one course, and when these subjects must be taught at particular grade levels for prescribed periods of time, with the student earning certain minimum ranks, any curriculum reform has been difficult. To change would mean to overthrow the whole rigid system.

The second problem in instituting curriculum reform is the teacher and his or her methods. When teachers are required to cover so much material in a subject-centered course, when classes are overcrowded and budgets for hiring additional personnel are limited, teachers become conditioned to "coverage" and to "tell-

HIGHLIGHT   Computerized Education

Behaviorist B. F. Skinner, professor emeritus at Harvard University, Father of Operant Conditioning, has also been labeled the "father of the teaching machine." Appalled at the way his daughter was taught arithmetic in her fourth-grade class, he constructed the first crude teaching machine in 1953. The prototype used cards and levers, and correct answers were reinforced with lights.

Today computers are beginning to realize the potential Skinner envisioned three decades ago. Educators' greatest failure has been the effort to get a whole class of pupils to progress at the same rate. This is impossible, and everybody knows it. No teacher can arrange maximum learning situations for thirty pupils. In the typical classroom, students who go faster are held back, while those who do not grasp the lessons fall further behind.

The answer is the use of individual computerized teaching machines, which each student can operate at his or her own rate. The right kind of programs can interest students in almost anything. The problem now is finding sufficient software that is well designed. An algebra program can be as motivating as Pac-Man if the student is successful. The machine can make success possible. Furthermore, if teachers realize that their pupils are learning, it will eliminate much teacher burnout, increase their morale enormously, and keep more good teachers teaching.

Hall, E. (September, 1983). "A Cure for American Education," *Psychology Today*, 17, 26, 27.

ing." If a new course or new topics in an old course are introduced, the temptation is to teach the new courses like the old.

In an effort to overcome these obstacles, considerable effort has gone into making some sweeping changes in curricular approaches (National Task Force,

It is impossible for educators to get a whole class of pupils to progress at the same rate, and some students are held back while others fall behind. Computerized education may be the answer to this problem, gearing programs to individual students who learn at different rates. (Laima Druskis)

1974). The new approaches emphasize student responsibility (Stefanko, 1984), individual study and growth at individual rates; and flexibility of content, scheduling, and methods of teaching for each course.

SUMMARY

During the past fifty years, the emphasis in American education has shifted between traditionalism, emphasizing basic education, and progressivism, emphasizing education for all of life. Until the 1930s, traditionalism was the dominant emphasis. Then came the Depression and the introduction of life adjustment education centered around vocations, leisure activities, health, personal concerns, and community problems.

This emphasis changed after the Soviet Union launched Sputnik in the mid-1950s. Now the demand was for more emphasis in teaching math, science, and foreign languages. A billion dollar aid to education program financed this change. By the mid-1960s, the cold war abated, and the nation was swamped with social problems and unrest, so once more the emphasis was on education to solve society's illness. The new progressivism emphasized work-study, career and experiential education, open classrooms, independent study, and student-designed courses. Enrollments in basic education courses dropped.

By the mid-1970s, the nation became alarmed by the seventeen-year drop in SAT scores and other indicators of declining proficiency. As a result, the National Commission on Excellence in Education was created in the 1980s and made numerous recommendations to return to basic education. The pendulum had swung full cycle.

Nationwide surveys among students reveal a general approval of their school programs. Suggestions for improvement include making courses more interesting and challenging, putting more emphasis on excellence, stiffening requirements, and upgrading the quality of teachers.

Students dislike other aspects of school: the emphasis on grades, the rigidity of requirements, the irrelevance of courses, the failure of the program to challenge brighter students, the need for more emphasis on vocational education.

There are a number of reasons why pupils drop out of school: socioeconomic factors, racial and ethnic prejudices and discrimination, disturbed family situations and negative parental influences, emotional problems, negative social adjustments and peer associations, financial reasons, school failure, apathy, and dissatisfactions, and pregnancy and marriage.

One of the most important keys to superior secondary education is to have good teachers—those who have mature, well-adjusted personalities and are emotionally secure and stable. Teachers must be well adjusted socially and enjoy satisfying social relationships with others. They must be professionally qualified to teach: intelligent, well trained, with a good grasp of subject matter, and willing to spend the necessary preparation time to teach.

The average comprehensive high school offers three basic curricula: the college preparatory, vocational, and general. Efforts at curriculum reform have consistently confronted two major problems: the rigidity of course requirements, grades, demands, and scheduling in the lockstep school structure; and the teacher and his or her methods, which emphasize content coverage and a lack of willingness to adopt new courses, emphases, and methods. Computerized education may be one answer to gearing programs to individual students who learn at different rates.

DISCUSSION QUESTIONS

The subject of school lends itself to animated and provocative classroom discussion. The following major subjects and some questions under each are only suggestive; the instructor may want to add others or ask members of the class to write out some questions they would like to see discussed.

Personal Experiences with School

1. Describe the type of high school you attended, evaluating the good and bad things about it.
2. What curriculum options were available in your school? Did these meet the needs of the students?
3. What courses were offered that you feel were unnecessary? What courses were not offered that you feel should have been?
4. What types of vocational education were offered in your school? Did these programs prepare students for jobs? What other types of vocational courses and programs should be offered?
5. In what ways did your high school program prepare you for college? In what ways was it deficient in preparing you for college?
6. What do you think of the guidance program and counselors in your school? How could the guidance program have been improved?
7. What place do you feel extracurricular activities have in the school program? How are they beneficial? How are they harmful? Was there too much emphasis on competitive athletics in your school? What benefits are derived from school athletics? Did the clubs and activities meet the needs of students from lower-class families?
8. What did you think of your teachers? What qualities did you most admire? What qualities did you like least? What are the most important attributes of a good teacher? What characteristics do you admire least in teachers? What training or preparation should be given to teachers to enhance their abilities and qualifications to teach?

9. Did your school have many dropouts? Why did these students leave school? What kept you in school sometimes when you felt you would rather leave and go to work?

Grading and Evaluation

1. What are the purposes of grading and evaluation? Does the present system serve these functions? Should grades be given at all? Why? Why not?
2. What do you think of standardized tests such as the SAT as a means of evaluating ability to do college work? What changes would you make in college selection criteria?
3. What factors encourage cheating? What can be done to minimize cheating?

Student Options

1. Do you think students should have a voice in the organization and selection of high school curricula? How can the program become more relevant to student needs?
2. How much voice should students have in deciding the specific subjects to be studied as part of a course?
3. What subjects do you feel are most unnecessary in the average high school curriculum?
4. What should be the role of the student council in high school? What roles does it usually perform?
5. What are the advantages and disadvantages of vocational education in high school? Should there be separate vocational schools? Comment on vocational education as it now exists. How could it be improved?
6. Do you think high schools cater to college prep students while neglecting those in other programs?
7. Should students have any freedom in selecting their teachers? What do you think of team teach-

ing versus teaching by one person for such courses as English, science, math, and history? What are the advantages of each method?

Discipline

1. Are high schools too strict or too lax in discipline?
2. What forms of discipline should schools use?
3. What should schools do about such problems as drinking, smoking (cigarettes or pot), cheating, or vandalism in school?
4. Who should do the disciplining in school? Should parents be involved in school discipline?
5. For what reasons should students be expelled from school?

Teaching Methods

1. In what ways should the school library be used as a multimedia center to contribute to the learning process?
2. What are learning packages? How do they contribute to individualized instruction?
3. How can the computer contribute to the educational process?

4. What are dial-access and push-button learning systems? What is programmed instruction and how does it work?
5. What sort of teaching machines can be used in the high school?
6. How are electronic learning laboratories used in teaching foreign languages?
7. In what ways can commercial, public, and closed-circuit television contribute to the learning process?

Building and Design

1. What types of building designs facilitate learning?
2. What do you think of architecturally open classrooms?
3. What different types of spaces are needed in the most up-to-date high school building?
4. How do interior decor, acoustics, soundproofing, furnishings, carpets, and other design features influence the learning process?
5. How can the high school building best serve adolescents after school hours?

BIBLIOGRAPHY

American Association of School Administrators. (1983). *The Excellence Report: Using It to Improve Your Schools*. Arlington, Va.: AASA.

Aptekar, L. (Summer, 1983). "Mexican-American High School Students' Perception of School." *Adolescence*, 18, 345–357.

Buxton, C. E. (1973). *Adolescents in School*. New Haven, Conn.: Yale University Press.

Caliste, E. R. (Fall, 1984). "The Effect of a Twelve-Week Dropout Intervention Program." *Adolescence*, 19, 649–657.

Carter, E. B. (June, 1984). "A Teacher's View: Learning to Be Wrong." *Psychology Today*, 18, 35.

Deci, E. L. (March, 1985). "The Well-Tempered Classroom." *Psychology Today*, 19, 52–53.

Dunham, R. G., and Alpert, G. P. (1987). "Keeping Juvenile Delinquents in School: A Prediction Model." *Adolescence*, 23, 45–57.

Fisher, R. J. (1976). "A Discussion Project on High

School Adolescents' Perceptions of the Relationship between Students and Teachers." *Adolescence*, 11, 87–95.

Hall, E. (September, 1983). "A Cure for American Education." *Psychology Today*, 17, 26, 27.

Hasset, J. (September, 1984). "Computers in the Classroom." *Psychology Today*, 18, 22–28.

Hurrelmann, K., Engel, U., Holler, B., and Nordlohne, E. (1988). "Failure in School, Family Conflicts, and Psychosomatic Disorders in Adolescence." *Journal of Adolescence*, 11, 237–249.

Kipms, D., and Resnick, J. H. (1971). "Experimental Prevention of Underachievement among Intelligent, Impulsive College Students." *Journal of Consulting Clinical Psychology*, 36, 53–60.

Knoff, H. M. (Fall, 1983). "Learning Disabilities in the Jr. High School: Creating the Six-Hour Emotionally Disturbed Adolescent?" *Adolescence*, 18, 541–550.

Manaster, G. J. (1977). *Adolescent Development and the Life Tasks*. Boston, Mass.: Allyn and Bacon.

Metcalf, K., and Gaier, E. L. (1987). "Patterns of Middle-Class Parenting and Adolescent Underachievement." *Adolescence*, 23, 919–928.

Miller, D. D. (1976). "What Do High School Students Think of Their Schools?" *Phi Delta Kappan*, 57, 700–702.

National Commission on Excellence in Education (1983). *A Nation at Rest: The Imperative for Educational Reform*. Washington, D.C.: U.S. Government Printing Office.

Paccione-Dyszlewski, M. R., and Contessa-Kislus, M. A. (1987). "School Phobia: Identification of Subtypes as a Prerequisite to Treatment Intervention." *Adolescence*, 22, 277–384.

Panel on Youth, President's Science Advisory Committee. (1974). *Youth: Transition to Adulthood*. Chicago: University of Chicago Press.

Ravitch, D. (October, 1983). "The Educational Pendulum." *Psychology Today*, 17, 62–71.

Solorzano, L. (August, 27, 1984). "Students Think Schools Are Making the Grade." *U.S. News & World Report*, pp. 49–51.

Solorzano, L., Hogue, J. R., Peterson, S., Lyons, D. C., and Bosc, M. (August 27, 1984). "What Makes Great Schools Great." *U.S. News & World Report*, pp. 46–49.

Stefanko, M. (Spring, 1984). "Trends in Adolescent Research: A Review of Articles Published in Adolescence—1976–1981." *Adolescence*, 19, 1–14.

Stevens, R., and Pihl, R. O. (1987). "Seventh-Grade Students at Risk for School Failure." *Adolescence*, 22, 333–345.

Svec, H. (1986). "School Discrimination and the High School Dropout: A Case for Adolescent Advocacy." *Adolescence*, 21, 449–452.

Thornburg, H. D. (1975). *Development in Adolescence*. Monterey, Calif.: Brooks/Cole Publishing Co.

U.S. Bureau of the Census, Department of Commerce (1987). *Statistical Abstract of the United States, 1987*. Washington, D.C.: U.S. Government Printing Office.

Wattenberg, W. W. (1973). *The Adolescent Years*. 2d ed. New York: Harcourt Brace Jovanovich.

Wirth, P. (1970). "My Ideal School Wouldn't Be a School." *Teachers College Records*, 72, 57–59.

Wood, J., Chapin, K., and Hannah, M. E. (1988). "Family Environment and Its Relationship to Underachievement." *Adolescence*, 23, 283–290.

Wood, N. L., Wood, R. A., and McDonald, T. D. (1988). "Integration of Student Development Theory into the Academic Classroom." *Adolescence*, 23, 349–356.

Zarb, J. M. (Summer, 1984). "A Comparison of Remedial Failure, and Successful Secondary School Students across Self-Perception and Past and Present School Performance Variables." *Adolescence*, 19, 335–348.

CHAPTER

20

Work and Vocation

The choice of a vocation is one of the most important decisions that the adolescent has to make (O'Hare, 1987). This chapter examines the process of that choice: factors that influence choice and other factors that should. It discusses the major theories of vocational choice that have grown out of research discoveries and goes on to discuss the influence of parents, peers, school personnel, sex-role concepts, intelligence, aptitudes, interest, job opportunities, job rewards and satisfactions, socioeconomic status, and prestige factors.

IMPORTANCE OF VOCATIONAL CHOICE

Pressures to Choose

Adolescents are constantly pressured by other people to choose a vocation. Parents have asked for years: "What do you want to be when you grow up?" Peers inquire: "What are you going to do after you graduate?" School personnel want to know: "Which program do you want to enroll in?" The television announcer proclaims: "Stay in school if you want to get a good job." "But which job, which vocation?" is the question the adolescent asks.

There are also societal pressures stemming from work values inherent in Western culture. The puritan work ethic is geared to four principles: (1) it is a person's duty under God to work and to work hard (industry is blessed; idleness is sinful); (2) success in work is evidence of God's favor and a person's worth; (3) the measure of success is money and property; and (4) the way to success is through industry and thrift. This ethic permeates the culture in which adolescents are brought up (some youths reject the ethic and are criticized); it is inevitable that they be influenced by these values.

Adolescents are constantly pressured to chose a vocation, partly because once they stop going to school, many adolescents are expected to start supporting themselves. (© The Christian Science Monitor/Melanie Stetson Freeman)

Additional pressures arise from within adolescents themselves. Indecision and uncertainty regarding the future create anxiety, and adolescents must face the decision if they are to find relief. Failure to do so results in turmoil, instability, and a sense of personal failure. Most adolescents are confused and unhappy until future plans begin to take shape. (See the section on Erikson in chapter 3.)

Part of the pressure to choose arises from environmental circumstances. Once adolescents stop going to school, they are expected to start supporting themselves and, in some cases, a whole family. Parental financial support, even if offered during college, is now usually withdrawn. Marriage plans provide additional motivation to get jobs. The longer adolescents are out of school and unemployed, the more they are criticized by parents and acquaintances for not going to work.

Motives for Choice

There are sound psychological reasons why this task of vocational choice is important. All people need to meet their emotional needs for recognition, praise, acceptance, approval, love, and independence. One way individuals do this is by taking on a vocational identity, by becoming "somebodies" whom others can recognize and by which others grant them emotional fulfillment. Through identifying with a particular vocation, they find selfhood, self-realization, and self-fulfillment. To the extent that they succeed in their own and others' eyes, they gain self-satisfaction and recognition. In their search for identity and self-satisfaction, they are strongly motivated to make a vocational choice that will contribute to their fulfillment. (See chapter 9.)

For adolescents who are of a philosophical frame of mind, their vocation is one channel through which their life goals and purposes might be fulfilled. It is the reason for their existence, the niche they feel compelled to fill in the world. If they believe life has meaning and purpose, they strive to find and to live out that meaning and purpose by the way they spend their time, talents, and energy. One way is through the work they perform. Vocational choice not only involves "How can I make a living?" it also implies "What am I going to do with my life?"

For adolescents whose concern is one of service—for meeting the needs of people or bettering the society in which they live—the choice of vocation will depend on the needs they recognize as most important and can best satisfy through their work. So they seek a vocation in which they can be of service. For adolescents who try to be "practical," the choice involves discovering the types of work in which there are the most vacant positions, which pay the best money, in which they are most interested, and for which are best qualified. Such choices are based primarily on economic motives, practical considerations, and personal interests and qualifications. For other youths, seeking a vocation becomes a means by which they show they are grown up, financially independent, emancipated from parents, and able to make it on their own. For them, going to work becomes a means of gaining entrance into the adult world.

Sometimes, however, no rational choice of vocation is made at all. Adolescents just go out and get the first job they can find that pays well; or they accept a job because a friend has recommended them for it or because it happens to be the only one that opens up and that they hear about. Under such circumstances vocational choice is happenstance rather than a thoughtful process. Adolescents may temporarily enjoy economic and other benefits such employment brings. Only later do they discover they are unhappy, ill suited to the tasks, and sacrificing their freedom and lives for doubtful benefits. They need to back up, reassess their goals, talents, and opportunities, and discover the ways these might be combined in meaningful, rewarding work.

A minority of adolescents choose not to work at all, at least no more than they can help. Their rebellion against the values exemplified in the lives of adults and the values of their society has convinced them that they should reduce their need for money as much as possible and lead simple but impoverished lives to give them the freedom to do as they please. Sometimes this means doing absolutely nothing; at other times it means engaging in what they feel are self-fulfilling activities, even though not remunerative. This kind of "dropping out" became almost epidemic during the 1960s, when adolescents began packing their bags and drifting throughout the country. This trend slowly abated during the 1970s.

Under the best of circumstances choosing a vocation is an increasingly difficult task as society becomes more complex. The Dictionary of Occupational Titles now lists more than 47,000 different occupations, most of which are unfamiliar. But if at all possible, adolescents need to make rational, considered choices of vocations. If they fail to identify themselves with the kind of work for which they are suited and in which they can find satisfaction and fulfillment, their vocational nonidentity reflects their larger failure to discover their own identity. In a sense they will have failed to discover what their own lives are all about.

THEORIES OF VOCATIONAL CHOICE

A number of theorists have sought to describe the process of vocational development. The particular theories that will be discussed are those of Ginzberg (1972), and Holland (1985).

Ginzberg's Compromise with Reality Theory

compromise with reality theory

In their ***compromise with reality theory,*** Eli Ginzberg (1972) and associates emphasize that making a vocational choice is a developmental process that occurs not at a single moment but over a long period. It involves a series of "subdecisions" that together add up to a vocational choice. Each subdecision is important because each limits individuals' subsequent freedom of choice and their abilities to achieve their original goals. For example, a decision not to go to college and to take a commercial course in high school makes it difficult later to decide to go to college. Extra time, effort, and sometimes money must be expended to make up for deficiencies. As children mature, they gain knowledge and exposure to alternatives; they learn to understand themselves and their environment and are better able to make rational choices. Ginzberg divides the process of occupational choice into three stages.

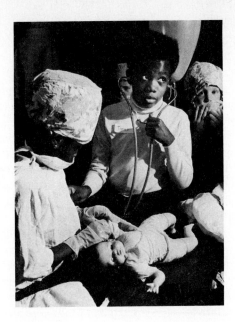

Eli Ginzburg has divided the process of occupational choice into three stages. During the fantasy stage that occurs up to age eleven, children imagine what they want to be, without regard to needs, ability, training, employment opportunities, or any realistic considerations. (© Ellis Herwig/Taurus Photos)

Fantasy Stage   The fantasy stage occurs up to age 11. During this time children imagine workers they want to be without regard to needs, ability, training, employment opportunities, or any realistic considerations. They want to be airline pilots, teachers, doctors, nurses, and so forth.

Tentative Stage   The tentative stage spans ages 11 through 18 years and is subdivided into four periods or substages. During the *interest period*, from 11 to 12, children make their choices primarily in the light of their likes and interests. The stage represents a transition between fantasy choice and tentative choice. The second period, the *capacities period*, occurs between about 13 and 14 years of age. During this period adolescents become aware of role requirements, occupational rewards, and different means of preparation. However, they are primarily thinking of their own abilities in relationship to requirements. During the third period, the *value period*, from ages 15 to 16, adolescents attempt to relate occupational roles to their own interests and values, to synthesize job requirements with their own values and capacities. They consider both the occupation and their own interests (Panel on Youth, 1974). The fourth and last stage, between ages 17 and 18, is a *transition period*, in which adolescents make transitions from tentative to realistic choices in response to pressures from school, peers, parents, colleges, and the circumstance of graduating from high school.

Realistic Stage   During the realistic stage, from age 18 on, adolescents seek further resolution of their problems of vocational choice. This stage is subdivided into a period of *exploration*, during which they make an intensive search to gain greater knowledge and understanding; a period of *crystallization*, in which they narrowly define a single set of choices and commit themselves; and a period of *specification*, in which a general choice, such as physicist, is further limited to a particular type of physicist.

Ginzberg's interviews were conducted primarily with adolescents from upper-income families, who no doubt had a considerably greater range of choices. The process would take longer for these youths than for others because their education is extended. Lower-income youths often have an earlier crystallization of occupational choice, though their choices still seem to parallel those of the theoretical model. Also, Ginzberg's observations were primarily of boys, although he concluded that girls parallel the first two stages, fantasy and tentative. Other research indicates that the transition to realism applies to both boys and girls but that girls tend to keep their vocational plans more tentative and flexible than boys do (Matteson, 1975).

Ginzberg's theory suffers from rigidity with respect to the exact sequence, nature, and timing of the stages; thus, it may be too artificial and contrived. One recent study found no significant difference in career maturity between ninth and twelfth grade students (Post-Kammer, 1987). *Some research, however, generally supports the broad outlines of the hypothesis, although it does not always support the chronological ages associated with Ginzberg's different stages.* For example, a study of ninety-one adolescent boys in a "potential scientist pool" showed that after eleventh grade, thirty-four moved out of the program and seventeen moved in, but only five of those who moved in after grade eleven stayed in. One boy moved in after graduation and stayed in (Wattenberg, 1973). This finding indicates that some boys made relatively stable vocational choices before grade eleven, whereas others had not made up their minds even after high school. It is difficult, therefore, to apply exact chronological ages to the periods Ginzberg outlines. Some relatively young adolescents show a high degree of maturity in making vocational choices; others evidence emerging maturity; while still others never seem to show the maturity necessary to match interests with capacities and training with job opportunities. Some people continue to change vocations throughout adulthood.

Ginzberg has made some recent reformulations of his theory to take these factors into account. He now acknowledges that career choices do not necessarily end with the first job and that some people remain occupationally mobile throughout their work histories. He also now emphasizes that some people—the economically disadvantaged and minority races especially—do not have as many choices as the upper classes do (Ginzberg, 1972).

Holland's Occupational Environment Theory

occupational environment theory

According to Holland's (1985) ***occupational environment theory*** of vocational choice, people select occupations that afford environments consistent with their personality types; they are more likely to choose and remain in a field when personal and environmental characteristics are similar.

Holland outlined six personality types—*realistic, intellectual, social, conventional, enterprising,* and *artistic*—and occupational environments compatible with these types. Holland measures personality types with a *self-directed search system*. This system has six scales, each corresponding to one of Holland's personality types. Holland believes that responses to the lengthy inventory of items on each scale

HIGHLIGHT   Developmental-Contextual Concepts

The latest thinking on career development emphasizes the dynamic interaction between individuals and their environment in their vocational quest (Osipow, 1983). Specifically, there are three types of influences on development (Vondracek and Schulenberg, 1986).

1. *Normative, age-graded influences* that vary with chronological time. These influences might be biological or environmental. For example, certain types of careers, such as professional sports, require requisite physical characteristics.
2. *Normative, history-graded influences* that also reveal individuals' vocational environmental preferences. Thus, individuals striving for a suitable career seek out those environments compatible with their patterns of personal orientations and exhibit these inclinations through their responses to the personality test items. According to Holland (1985), then, it is possible to ascertain occupational orientations by the scores on the personality scales.

may be biological or environmental in nature. They could include such historical events as depression, war, famine, or even the launching of Sputnik.
3. *Nonnormative, life-event influences.* These might include an unexpected death of a family breadwinner, an illness, injury, or loss of scholarship forcing alteration of career plans.

   In other words, there may be significant influences on career choice over which the individual has minimal control.

Subsequent research offers only partial support to Holland's theory (Brown, 1987). Even though personality often influences vocational choice, individuals sometimes elect and stay in occupations even when their personalities do not match the vocational environment. Thus, individuals may stay in a job because it offers more security, higher wages, less travel, requires less education, because they are close to retirement, or because they don't want to move geographically. Many workers stay on jobs for which they are not perfectly fitted because of personal or family obligations (Salomone and Sheehan, 1985).

There is a need also to formulate theories that can be applied specifically to women, who may behave differently vocationally than do men (Astin, 1984; Forrest and Mikolaitis, 1986).

PEOPLE INFLUENCING CHOICE*

Parents

Parents influence their adolescent's choice of vocation in a number of ways (Lopez and Andrews, 1987). *One way is through direct inheritance*: a son or daughter

---

* Once married, people can be significantly influenced by their spouse as well as by parents (Wilson, 1986).

inherits the parents' business, and it seems easier and wiser to continue the family business than to go off on their own.

Parents exert influence by providing apprenticeship training. A father who is a carpenter teaches his trade to his son by taking him with him on the job or by asking a carpenter friend to let him serve an apprenticeship under him. In the case of low socioeconomic status families, the adolescent may not have any other choices. Many mothers or fathers of such families have taught their skills to their children.

Parents influence their children's interests and activities from the time they are young by the play materials provided, by the encouragement or discouragement of hobbies and interests, by the activities they encourage their children to participate in, and by the total experiences they provide in the family. Sibling influence also is important in stimulating masculine or feminine interests. A parent who is a musician exerts an influence on the child to take music lessons and to like music in a way that a nonmusician parent can never do. A father who is a professional football player usually wants his son to be exposed to football from the time the boy is little. An estimated 44 percent of physicians' sons choose medicine and 28 percent of lawyers' sons choose law, a far greater percentage than mere chance would allow for (Conger, 1973).

Parents provide role models for their children to follow. Although the parent may not try to exert any conscious, direct influence, the influence by example is there, especially when the child identifies closely with the parent. Researchers have found that fathers who serve as the most positive occupational and overall role models exert the strongest and most positive influence on their sons' future occupations. Mortimer found that the combination of a prestigious paternal role model and a close father-son relationship engendered the most effective transmission of vocational values and the clearest impact on sons' occupational decisions (Mortimer, 1976). Although fathers of low socioeconomic status do not exert as positive an influence because they are not as close to their adolescents or as actively involved in their care, and their occupations are less prestigious, they nevertheless do exert an influence on the career decisions of their youth (Peterson, Stiver, and Peters, 1986).

Parents sometimes direct, order, or limit the choices of their children by insisting they not go to school, or go to a certain school, enroll in a particular major, or start out on a predetermined career. Parents who do so without regard for the talents, interests, and desires of their adolescent may be condeming the youth to a life of work to which she or he is unsuited. Often an adolescent has no strong objections and accedes to parental wishes from a desire to please them and from not knowing what else to do. One of the motives of parents for taking such a course of action is try to get the child to take up an occupation that the parents were always interested in but never got to do: the parents live vicariously through the child (Wattenberg, 1973). Or, because the parents have a vocation and have found satisfaction, they urge the adolescent to share their goals because they are sure she or he would like it too. Stories are legion of the father who insists his son attend his alma mater, join the same fraternity, play football as he did, and become a professional like himself. The father can exert pressure by offering or withholding money or by getting his son into his school and fraternity. Other parents, of course, have very low educational and occupational expectations for their children, thus limiting the possible vocational choices (Galambos and Silbereisen, 1987).

Sometimes parental influence is less direct. *Parents influence adolescents to follow an occupation in the same status category or in a status category immediately above that which they occupy.* For example, a physician mother influences a daughter to be a physician or to choose another profession offering similar prestige and rewards. A mother who is a skilled worker may urge the girl to choose either the same or another skilled occupation. A father who is a clerical worker may urge a son to seek a position in the next higher category, managerial work.

It is also true, however, that of the one-third who do not choose an occupation in their father's status category, a number circumvent the entire status structure through extensive education in order to rise far above their parents. In this way they move from blue-collar positions into professions. Others become socially mobile downward, never aspiring or able to succeed as their parents have.

Peers

Studies of the relative influence of parents and peers on the educational plans of adolescents (relating to the level of vocation rather than to the particular job) reveal somewhat contradictory findings. *Actually, the majority of adolescents hold plans in agreement with those of parents and their friends.* Thus, friends reinforce parental aspirations because adolescents associate with peers whose goals are consistent with parental goals. This is substantiated by the fact that when parents have college aspirations for their children, 65 percent of their children's best school friends also have college plans; when parents have high school plans, 66 percent of their children's best school friends also have high school plans. The adolescents' interactions with peers support the values of parents as far as educational aspirations are concerned (Panel on Youth, 1974).

It has been found that the extent of upward mobility of working-class adolescents depends on the influences of both parents and peers. Working-class adolescents are most likely to aspire to high-ranking occupations if they are influenced in this direction by both parents and peers and least likely to be high aspirers if they are subjected to neither of these influences.

School Personnel

To what extent do school personnel influence adolescents' vocational plans? A great deal, according to a study of college freshmen at the University of Maine (Johnson, 1967). In this study, students were requested to indicate from a list of nine individuals or group of individuals the ones they felt were most influential in their decision to select a particular field of study. Thirty-nine percent indicated that their high school teachers had been most influential in helping them make their decision. This represented the highest percentage of any of the alternative choices, with "other adult acquaintances" next in rank order of influence, accounting for 19 percent of the responses. The other 42 percent of responses were variously distributed in lesser amounts among the following seven alternatives: father; mother; elementary school teacher or principal; high school counselor, dean, or principal; college teacher; college counselor, dean or other nonteachers; and close friends.

Teachers exerted a major influence on the plans of college-bound students during the later part of their high school career: 75 percent of the University of Maine entering freshmen made vital decisions regarding their future after they started the eleventh grade in high school; 55 percent made their decision regarding a major field of study during the last year of high school. This study was of entering college freshmen only; studies among the general high school population reveal much greater parental influence and less influence by counselors and teachers. The college bound have a much closer rapport with teachers than do other students. Forty-one percent of the entering freshmen said they knew one or two high school teachers well enough to be personally friendly with them and to be able to talk over matters other than school affairs. Twenty-six of the students felt they knew three or four teachers this well. Twenty-four percent indicated they knew five or more high school teachers on this basis (Johnson, 1967).

These findings are in agreement with other research that shows the significant influence that school personnel and adult friends exert over vocational choice (Saltiel, 1986).

SEX ROLES AND VOCATIONAL CHOICE

Cultural Expectations

Adolescents are strongly influenced by societal expectations as to the type of work that males and females should do. Traditionally women have been far more limited than men in the number and categories of jobs available to them. In spite of gains, women still outnumber men 1.5 to 1 in service occupations, 3 to 1 in clerical jobs, and 5 to 1 in elementary level teaching. Ninety-five percent of nurses, 85 percent of librarians, and 67 percent of social and recreation workers are women. Only 18 percent of lawyers and judges and 19 percent of physicians and surgeons are women (U.S. Bureau of the Census, 1987). (See table 14-2 and the discussion of masculine-feminine roles in chapter 14.)

This picture is being modified (Gerstein, Lichtman, and Barokas, 1988). Strict government enforcement of equal employment opportunity laws is ensuring women opportunities in hitherto restricted fields. Any woman who strives for a particular position is legally entitled to it if she is qualified. Jobs that women are now occupying that before were restricted to men include commercial airplane pilots, subway train operators, baseball umpires, jockeys, and a variety of blue-collar jobs (Stringer and Duncan, 1985). The percentage of women in all jobs in the United States has increased. Figure 20-1 shows that by 1995, 46 percent of all workers in the labor force will be women; 54 percent will be men.

Female Motivations

Some women, especially the less educated, are not highly motivated to succeed in a full-time, long-term career. Some want only to prepare for an occupation before and for a time after marriage and as financial insurance in case anything should happen to their husband (Granrose, 1985). However, there is a rapidly increasing trend for females to work full time throughout much of their lives;

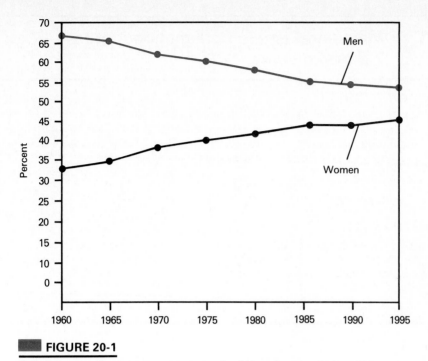

FIGURE 20-1

Percentage of men and women in the labor force, 1960–1995.

From: U.S. Bureau of the Census, Department of Commerce (1987). *Statistical Abstract of the United States*, 1987. Washington, D.C.: U.S. Government Printing Office, p. 376.

therefore, an increasing percentage of adolescent girls choose occupations that indicate a permanent, major interest in a career. Most want to balance career ambitions with marriage and raising a family (Cook, 1985).

Research on women who became wives, mothers, and career people indicates that these women more often come from higher social class backgrounds than do their conventional counterparts. Their parents are often ambitious for them. They also tend to be only children or first-born children or are separated from siblings by a large age gap, so that they manifest what has been termed the **only-lonely child syndrome.** There is often greater separation from parents or greater overall tension in their family backgrounds (Rapoport and Rapoport, 1971). The resulting picture is of highly capable, creative women who are able to find personal fulfillment through both careers and family, in response to the way they were influenced and socialized while growing up.

only-lonely child syndrome

OTHER CRUCIAL DETERMINANTS OF VOCATIONAL CHOICE

Intelligence

Mental ability has been shown to be important to vocational choice in several ways. *First, intelligence has been shown to be related to the decision-making ability of the individual.* Bright adolescents are more likely to make vocational choices in keeping

HIGHLIGHT   Male and Female College Graduates— 7 Months Later

A survey of 346 college graduates (51% men and 49% women) from an Eastern university seven months after graduation revealed the following male–female differences (Martinez, Sedlacek, and Bachhuber, 1985):

Similar percentages of men and women were employed or involved in further education.

Men were more likely than women to report they were employed in their chosen field or in a satisfactory position. Women were more likely in the process of seeking a job in their chosen field.

Men were more likely than women to enter engineering and mathematics; women were more likely to hold jobs in education, the social sciences, and clerical fields.

Men were more likely than women to have been hired by large corporations.

About the same percentage of men and women held jobs in management or business administration.

Men earned significantly more than women ($18,220 vs. $12,798).

with their intellectual abilities, interests, capacities, and opportunities to receive training. The less bright are more likely to make unrealistic choices. They more often choose glamorous or high-prestige occupations for which they are not qualified or even interested solely because of the prestige. They more often choose what they think parents want them to do or what peers consider desirable rather than what they are capable of doing.

Second, intelligence has been shown to relate to the level of aspiration. Students who show superior academic ability and performance tend to aspire to higher occupational choices than those with lesser ability (Picou and Curry, 1973).

Third, intelligence is related to the ability of the individual to succeed or fail in a given occupation. For this reason, the vocational counselor usually measures level of intelligence as a beginning in assessing the vocational qualifications of a given student because some occupations require a higher ability than others. But a high IQ is no guarantee of vocational success, nor is a low IQ a prediction of failure. The measurement may be in error. (See chapter 8.) Interest, motivation, other abilities, and various personality traits determine success as much as intelligence does. A high IQ shows only that the individual has the capacity to succeed as far as intelligence is concerned. But actual achievement must also be taken into account. Bright, high-achieving students are generally superior to bright, underachieving students in study habits, aspiration levels, and professionally oriented career expectations. A bright individual who is poorly motivated and indifferent may fail in an occupation, whereas an individual of average mental ability who is highly motivated, industrious, and conscientious may overachieve and far surpass the brighter person.

Furthermore, where do the IQ requirements for different occupations begin? There is actually a great deal of overlap in tested intelligence among workers in various jobs. How "smart" do you have to be to be a miner, an accountant, a physician? Some people who become physicians, teachers, engineers, or business executives show on tests that their intelligence is much below average for their professions.

Educational institutions are faced with a dilemma in deciding on the cutoff point below which they will not admit students. Whereas SAT scores are helpful in predicting possibilities of success or failure for groups of students, they are not sure indicators of the individual. Counselors must be extremely cautious in interpreting test results, particularly in predicting success or failure based on mental ability alone. Many individuals who are now successful in professional fields would not be admitted to the training programs if they had to pass the entrance exams today.

Aptitudes and Special Abilities

Different occupations require different aptitudes and special abilities. For example, mechanical ability tests may cover information required of mechanics: types of gears, kinds of wrenches, gauges, strengths of materials, sizes of fasteners, or certain aptitudes such as manual and finger dexterity. Some occupations require strength, others speed, others good eye-hand coordination, or good spatial visualization. Some require special talent such as artistic, musical, or verbal skills. Some fields require creativity, originality, autonomy; others require conformity, cooperation, ability to take direction. Possession or lack of certain aptitudes may be crucial in immediate job success or in the possibility of success with training and experience. Certainly, increasing technology requires more and more specialized training and abilities (Hoyt, 1987).

The exact measurement of some aptitudes, however, is not an exact science; therefore, it cannot always be determined which people are most likely to succeed in particular occupations (Graham, 1975). The fault lies generally with the tests used. Before relying too much on aptitude tests, therefore, counselors and students should be certain that the instruments used are valid measurements of the aptitudes tested.

Interests

Interest is another factor considered important to vocational success. The theory is—and it is valid—that the more interested people are in their work, the more likely they will succeed. To put it another way, the more their interests parallel those who are already successful in a field, the more likely they are to be successful too, all other things being equal. Vocational interest tests are based on this last principle: they measure clusters of interests similar to those of successful people in the field to predict the possibilities of success. The individual is counseled to consider vocations in the fields of greatest interest.

Intelligence, ability, opportunities, and other factors must be related to interests for success in a field. An individual may be interested in medicine but not have the ability or opportunity to become a physician; this person may then have to choose a career as a laboratory technician, physical therapist, or some related occupation. Whereas interests point to the field of inquiry, ability, opportunity, and other factors may have to point to the particular job choice within that field.

Strong Vocational Interest Blank

Factor analysis of the **Strong Vocational Interest Blank** (Strong, 1943) indicates that interests may be subdivided and grouped to some degree by level. There are professional-scientific, professional-technical, and subprofessional-technical groups, as well as others. Interests are related to both the field and level of occupational choice. Interests that are based on abilities are stronger and more realistic than those influenced primarily by such things as prestige factors and group values. However, there is only a low correlation between interests and aptitudes.

Job Opportunities

Being interested does not mean that jobs are available. Some employment fields, such as agricultural workers, are becoming smaller; other, such as clerical workers, are becoming larger. There has been a continued shift toward white-collar occupations. This means youths need to control interests as well as be controlled by them, for interests and job availability are not synonymous (Mitchell, 1988).

What are the employment opportunities in the professions? Table 20-1 shows projected needs to 1990 (U.S. Dept. of Labor, 1980). The primary employment opportunity in terms of total job openings per year is in kindergarten and elementary education; registered nurses are second, accountants are third, practical nurses are fourth, and lawyers are fifth. Overall, it is obvious that the greatest opportunities are in the health fields.

TABLE 20-1

Projected growth, various professions, 1990.

	AVERAGE ANNUAL OPENINGS TO 1990		AVERAGE ANNUAL OPENINGS TO 1990
Administration		Programmers	9,200
Accountants[3]	61,000	Systems analysts	7,900
Bank officers, managers[6]	28,000	Engineers	
Buyers	7,400	Aerospace	1,800
City managers	350	Chemical	1,800
Credit managers	2,200	Civil	7,800
Health administrators[10]	18,000	Electrical	10,500
Hotel managers, assistants	8,900	Industrial	8,000
Public-relations workers	7,500	Mechanical	7,500
Purchasing agents	13,400	Petroleum	900
Urban planners	800	Teachers	
Computer Specialists		College	11,000
Computer operators	12,500	Kindergarten, elementary	
Computer repairs	5,400	school[1]	86,000

TABLE 20-1

(continued)

	AVERAGE ANNUAL OPENINGS TO 1990		AVERAGE ANNUAL OPENINGS TO 1990
School counselors	1,700	Social Sciences	
Secondary school	7,200	Anthropologists	350
Mathematics		Economists	7,800
Actuaries	500	Geographers	500
Mathematicians	1,000	Historians	700
Statisticians	1,500	Political scientists	500
Scientists		Psychologists	6,700
Astronomers	40	Sociologists	600
Biochemists	900	Technicians	
Chemists	6,100	Drafters	11,000
Geologists	1,700	Engineering, science	
Geophysicists	600	technicians[7]	23,400
Life scientists	11,200	Food technologists	500
Meteorologists	300	Forestry technicians	700
Oceanographers	150	Range managers	200
Physicists	1,000	Soil conservationists	450
Soil scientists	180	Surveyors, technicians	2,300
Health Services		Other Professions	
Chiropractors	1,500	Actors	850
Dental assistants	11,000	Airplane pilots	3,800
Dental hygienists	6,000	Air-traffic controllers	700
Dental lab technicians	2,800	Architects	4,000
Dentists	5,500	Dancers	550
Dietitians	3,300	Floral designers	4,200
Licensed practical nurses[4]	60,000	Foresters	1,400
Medical-lab workers	14,800	Funeral directors, embalmers	2,200
Operating room technicians	2,600	Industrial designers	550
Optometrists	1,600	Interior designers	3,600
Pharmacists	7,800	Landscape architects	1,100
Physical therapists, aides	3,100	Lawyers[5]	37,000
Physicians, osteopaths[9]	19,000	Librarians	8,000
Podiatrists	600	Musicians	8,900
Registered nurses[2]	85,000	Newspaper reporters	2,400
Veterinarians	1,700	Personnel, labor relations	17,000
X-ray technologists	9,000	Photographers	3,800
Merchant Marine		Radio, TV announcers	850
Officers	700	Singers	1,600
Sailors	250	Social workers[8]	22,000

Note: Superscripts indicate rank order.

From: U. S. Bureau of Labor Statistics, Department of Labor (1980). *Occupational Outlook Handbook, 1980–1981* (Washington, D.C.: U.S. Government Printing Office).

HIGHLIGHT   The Changing Work Force: Projections 1986 to 2000

According to Hoyt (1988), the following changes will be taking place in the work force up to the year 2000:

1. Skill levels required for occupational success will increase with both the content and complexity of jobs being modified by technological change.
2. When compared with current jobs, a higher percentage of the new jobs to be created during the period will demand some form of post-secondary education while a sharp decline will occur in the percentage of new jobs requiring less than a high school education.
3. Almost 5 in 6 of the 21 million new labor market entrants will be minority persons, women, or immigrants. Only 8 percent of this 1986–2000 increase will be nonminority white men.
4. Women and minority persons are currently less well prepared for occupational success by the existing educational system than are non-Hispanic white men.
5. Blacks, Hispanics, and Asians account for a rising proportion of the school population; 23 of the 25 largest city school systems enroll more minority than nonminority pupils.
6. Minority youth and family households headed by women under age 25 are likely to find employment problems greatly compounded by the fact that they are poor.
7. Both black and Hispanic youth have higher dropout rates than nonminority youth and this contributes to their difficulties in career development (Hoyt, 1988, pp. 32, 33).

Job Rewards and Satisfactions

One factor to consider in selecting a vocation is the financial reward. Table 20-2 shows an estimated starting pay for 1988 graduates with bachelor's degrees in different fields. Actual salaries vary in different parts of the country.

Young people are interested in job satisfactions other than money, however. Yankelovich (1974) has listed the top ten job criteria for young working people according to a nationwide survey:

Friendly, helpful coworkers (70 percent)
Work that is interesting (70 percent)
Opportunity to use your mind (65 percent)
Work results that you can see (62 percent)
Pay that is good (61 percent)
Opportunities to develop skills/abilities (61 percent)
Participation in decisions regarding job (58 percent)
Getting help needed to do the job well (55 percent)
Respect for organization you work for (55 percent)
Recognition for a job well done (54 percent)

TABLE 20-2

Average starting salary for 1988 graduates with a bachelor's degree.

FIELD	AVERAGE SALARY, 1988
Engineering	$29,820
Computer science	28,331
Physics	24,276
Economics, finance	23,136
Accounting	22,838
Chemistry	22,647
Marketing; sales	21,471
Mathematics	21,346
General business administration	20,335
Journalism	19,843
Social science	19,672
Agriculture	19,401
Personnel administration	19,319
Liberal arts; arts and letters	19,213
Advertising	18,963
Education	18,850
Hotel/restaurant management	18,693
Communications	18,120
Human ecology; home economics	17,398
Natural resources	17,271
Retailing	17,035
Geology	16,649

From: *The World Almanac and Book of Facts*, 1989 edition, copyright © Newspaper Enterprise Association, Inc., 1988, New York, NY.

Many of these job criteria cannot be ascertained before a vocation or a particular job is selected but become important once the individual is on the job.

SOCIOECONOMIC STATUS AND PRESTIGE FACTORS

Choosing the Familiar

A study of the occupations chosen by over 1,000 boys and girls in a rural county in New York State and about 250 boys and girls from a school in Brooklyn showed that only 150 occupations were chosen by boys and even fewer by girls (Ramsey, n.d.). The occupations chosen could be grouped into two categories: those that were familiar to the rural community and those that were glamorous and prestigious.

Socioeconomic status tends to influence the knowledge and understanding youths have of different occupations. Middle-class parents are more able than working-class parents to develop broad vocational interests and awareness of opportunities beyond the local community. Socially disadvantaged adolescents have seen less, read less, heard less about, and experienced less variety in their environments in general and have fewer opportunities than the socially privileged.

As a result low socioeconomic status males and females are inclined to take the only job they know about at the time they enter the labor market.

The socioeconomic and cultural background of youths influences their job knowledge and their job preference. Furthermore, local variations in occupational choice tend to correspond with variations in the economic structure: the larger the proportion of people employed in a particular kind of job in a city, the larger is the proportion of youths who desire to go into that occupation. Whether an adolescent lives in a rural or urban environment is also a factor in vocational choice. Urban boys have higher occupational expectations than do rural boys. One reason is that youths in rural areas lack immediate contact with persons holding high-status positions.

Prestige and Value

Adolescents may also say they want to go into an occupation simply because it sounds glamorous or has high prestige (Borow, 1976). There are at least five commonly accepted assumptions about occupational values in our culture: (1) white-collar work is superior; (2) self-employment is superior; (3) clean occupations are superior; (4) the importance of a business occupation depends on the size of the business; and (5) personal service is degrading: it is better to be employed by an enterprise than to do the same work for an individual.

There have been other attempts at classifying values. One method has been to group values into three major value clusters: people oriented, extrinsic reward oriented, and self-expression oriented. Vocational selection will depend partly on which values are considered more important. Community values also influence youth. Jobs considered most prestigious and with the highest status are more desired by youth than those with lower prestige and status.

Social Class and Aspirations

Middle-class youths tend to choose occupations with higher status than do lower-class youths. There are a number of considerations in determining why this is so. To aspire to a position is one thing; really to expect to achieve it is another. Lower-class youths more often than middle-class youths aspire to jobs they do not expect to achieve, but the fact that lower-class youths realize the remoteness of reaching their goal makes them lower their level of aspirations. Of course, sometimes guidance counselors, teachers, parents, or others try to persuade lower-status youth from aspiring to higher occupational levels, when—given sufficient incentives and help—they might be able to succeed at them (Yogev and Roditi, 1987). A large number of lower socioeconomic status youths are of superior ability and could succeed at high status jobs if they had a chance.

The individual's preference hierarchy may also be at odds with the general consensus. This is another way of saying that some lower-class youths do not ascribe the same status to job success and work as do middle-class Americans. Also, people with a lower-class background sometimes consider certain kinds of blue-collar work more desirable than white collar.

Still another factor enters in: a correlation between academic ability and socioeconomic status. The higher the status, the higher the academic performance; and the better the students' academic performances, the more prestigious the occupations to which they aspire. Apparently students see their high academic ability as providing them access to high-prestige occupations. Occupational aspiration is related to both social class and academic aptitude.

Race and Aspirations

When race is considered apart from social class, there is no conclusive evidence that race alone is the determinative factor in occupational aspirations. However, black youths of lower socioeconomic status have lower aspirations just as do white youths of lower status. Regardless of aspirations, there are fewer employment opportunities for youths than for adults and fewer opportunities for blacks than for whites. In his study of low-class delinquent and nondelinquent black adolescent males, Picou and staff (1974) found that both the delinquent and nondelinquent respondents had rather high-prestige occupational goals, but the majority of both groups felt that lack of financial resources for higher education was a major impediment to the attainment of their goals. More delinquents than nondelinquents felt that their race, their lack of intellectual capability, and poor job opportunities would have a deleterious effect on the attainment of their occupational aspirations. The researchers emphasized that the occupational aspirations of many of these black youths were unrealistic. They concluded:

> This finding may reflect the vicious circle of poverty of all racial and ethnic categories. It can be summarized as follows: the lower class youngster is reared in an environment that emphasizes occupational and economic success. Being inculcated with these cultural values, he develops goals and values that imply future social mobility and achievement. However, because his parents lack the financial resources to insure the most important prerequisite for attainment—higher educational training—the youngster fails to realize his goals and plans for his future. Thus, he is forced to seek employment in low-paying unskilled occupations and once again the vicious circle of poverty begins with his children. (Picou et al., 1974)

ADOLESCENTS AND UNEMPLOYMENT

Numbers

One of the major social problems in the United States is unemployed youths. If just youths 16 to 19 who are in the labor force are considered, the unemployment rates in 1985 were 16 percent for whites and 40 percent for blacks (U.S. Bureau of the Census, 1987, p. 39). Figure 20-2 shows the figures plus comparable ones for young adults 20 to 24 years of age. Altogether, this means that 3.2 million young people, aged 16 to 24, were out of work. The highest unemployment is among non-white teenagers, and this is true whether they are in school or not. Also, the jobless rate of Hispanic youths is well above the rate for their white counterparts but much lower than that for blacks. These statistics probably underestimate the extent of the problem, for many adolescents who get discouraged and stop looking for work are not counted as unemployed. This high rate of joblessness means more crime, more drug addiction, more social unrest, and less income for many poor families.

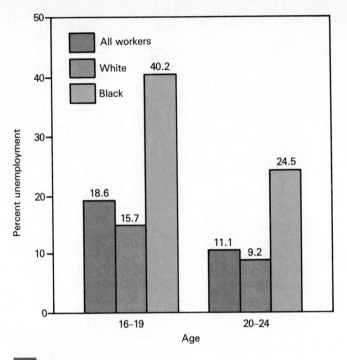

FIGURE 20-2

Civilian labor force employment, by race and age, 1985.

From: U. S. Bureau of the Census, Department of Commerce (1987). *Statistical Abstract of the United States,* 1987 (Washington, D. C.: U.S. Government Printing Office), p. 390.

Causes of Unemployment

Why is the rate of unemployment among youths so high? One reason for the high unemployment rate among youths is that they have little training and skill, little experience, and many are able to take only part-time jobs while in school. They are confined to a narrower range of the less skilled occupations, at which many car. work only part time. Youths with high school diplomas have better chances on the labor market than do dropouts, as is reflected by lower unemployment rates among graduates. Figure 20-3 shows the percentages of high school graduates and dropouts in the labor force. Many employers require educational degrees that have little relationship to job skills; dropouts are often denied work not because they cannot do the job but because they do not have the necessary credentials.

State licensing boards often operate to restrict entry into business. The Colorado Board of Cosmetology, for example, requires that a prospective hairdresser take 1,650 hours of instruction, including 100 hours of supervised practice at shampooing ("Why It's Hard," 1976). Such requirements hit hardest at the young, especially those who seek to combine work with schooling. Union requirements also limit participation of the young. It takes time and experience to acquire

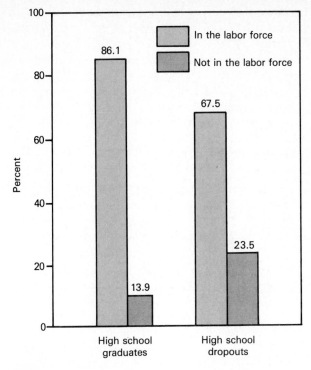

■ **FIGURE 20-3**

**Percentages of high school graduates and drop-
outs in and not in the labor force and not enrolled
in school, 1985.**

From: U.S. Bureau of the Census, Department of Commerce
(1987). *Statistical Abstract of the United States, 1987* (Washington,
D.C.: U.S. Government Printing Office), p. 136.

membership in a union; therefore, adolescents are not able to accept jobs in the
construction industry, for example, which could be an important source of part-
time and summer employment. Many unions also limit the number of apprentices
that can be trained ("Why It's Hard," 1976). In cases of layoffs, seniority rules work
in favor of the older, more experienced workers; youths are the first to lose
their jobs.

Minimum wage legislation may sometimes affect unemployment. When the
minimum wage goes up relative to the low productivity of inexperienced youths,
employers hesitate to hire them, often preferring older people if they are available
("Jobs," 1976). Furthermore, job turnover among youths is higher than among
older, more stable workers. Some employers will not hire anybody under 21 for a
regular job; they want those who have a greater degree of maturity ("Why It's
Hard," 1976).

Many jobs in transportation, construction, manufacturing, and agriculture
are closed even to youths available for full-time year-round work because of the
legal minimum ages for hazardous work. Although state laws differ, the general

standard is that all wage employment is barred to those under 14, all employment during school hours is barred to those under 16, and certain hazardous jobs and industries are barred to youths under 18.

On the other hand, the average period of unemployment among youths is shorter than among older workers. Females average somewhat shorter periods of unemployment than males and whites shorter periods than non-whites. The fact that half of all unemployed youths have no more than four weeks without work reflects the seasonal and intermittent nature of their unemployment.

EDUCATION AND EMPLOYMENT

The educational background of youths continues to improve. Studies of dropouts consistently show that the high school graduate is superior to the early dropout in each of the following: (1) number of promotions and raises, (2) holding onto one job, (3) fewer and shorter periods of unemployment, (4) higher job satisfaction, (5) more recreational pursuits, (6) more hobbies, and (7) greater frequency of additional training (Bernard, 1971).

SUMMARY

Choosing and preparing for a vocation is one of the most important developmental tasks of adolescence. Done wisely and realistically, it enables individuals to enter vocations for which they are well suited, in which they find satisfaction and fulfillment, and which are needed by society. Done haphazardly and foolishly, it leads to frustration, discontent, unhappiness, and social disapproval.

The process is often a complicated one. Ginzberg shows insight in emphasizing that it is a long-term process comprising many small decisions, each of which affects the next decision and further limits subsequent choices. Choices made early in high school affect the availability of later options. Thus, there is a fatalistic element to the process: individuals do not have complete freedom but are limited by what they have already done and are also subject to many influences in the present. This is more true of low socioeconomic status adolescents, who are caught in a series of circumstances, some of which they are powerless to control. Adolescents from higher socioeconomic status groups are more fortunate because they have more options open and more resources to use in taking advantage of options.

Ginzberg divides the process of occupational choice into three stages: fantasy stage (up to age 11), tentative stage (11 to 18 years), and realistic stage (from 18 on). Research generally supports the broad outlines of this theory, though the sequence, nature, and timing of the stages may not always be the same. Also, career choices do not always end with the first job.

Holland theorizes that people select occupations that afford environments consistent with their personality types. He outlined six personality types: realistic, intellectual, social, conventional, enterprising, and artistic.

There are numerous influences on vocational choice: parents, peers, and school personnel. Concepts of sex roles, cultural expectations, and female motivations also influence vocational choice. Other crucial determinants of vocational choice are intelligence, aptitude, and special abilities, interests, job opportunities, socioeconomic status and prestige factors, and race.

One of the major problems in the United States is unemployment among youths. Rates among black and other minorities are even higher than among whites. There are numerous causes: the massive youth population, lack of training, skill, and experience of youth, restrictive licensing and union requirements, minimum wage legislation and lack of education.

DISCUSSION QUESTIONS

1. Why is making a wise vocational choice considered one of the most important developmental tasks of adolescence?

2. Why do so many adolescents make poor vocational choices?

3. Two theories of vocational choice have been outlined: those of Ginzberg and Holland. Explain the major emphasis of each. Which do you find most appealing? Which seems the least true to life? Explain.

4. Should parents have any voice about the vocation their adolescent chooses? What is the parental role in this regard?

5. How influential are peers over vocational choice?

6. Has any person at school been particularly influential in your choice of vocation? Describe.

7. Just because a person is interested in a particular vocation, does this mean he or she should go into it? What other factors ought to be taken into consideration?

8. Should vocations be chosen on the basis of job rewards? What other factors are important?

9. Is job prestige and status a valid consideration in choosing a vocation?

10. What can be done about the high unemployment rate among adolescents?

11. Is a good education necessary to get a good job?

BIBLIOGRAPHY

Astin, H. S. (1984). "The Meaning of Work in Women's Lives: A Sociopsychological Model of Career Choice and Work Behavior." *Counseling Psychologist*, 12, 117–128.

Bernard, H. (1971). *Adolescent Development*. Scranton, Pa.: Intext Educational Publishers.

Borow, H. (1976). "Career Development." *Understanding Adolescence*, 3d ed. Edited by J. F. Adams. Boston, Mass.: Allyn and Bacon.

Brown, D. (1987). "The Status of Holland's Theory of Vocational Choice." *The Career Development Quarterly*, 36, 13–23.

Conger, J. J. (1973). *Adolescence and Youth*. New York: Harper & Row.

Cook, E. P. (1985). "Sex Roles and Work Roles: A Balancing Process." *The Vocational Guidance Quarterly*, 33, 213–220.

Forrest, L., and Mikolaitis, N. (1986). "The Relationship Component of Identity: An Expansion of Career Development Theory." *The Career Development Quarterly*, 35, 76–88.

Galambos, N. C., and Silbereisen, R. K. (1987). "In-come Change, Parental Life Outlook, and Adolescent Expectations for Job Success." *Journal of Marriage and the Family*, 49, 141–149.

Gerstein, M., Lichtman, M., and Barokas, J. U. (1988). "Occupational Plans of Adolescent Women Compared to Men: A Cross-Sectional Examination." *The Career Development Quarterly*, 36, 222–230.

Ginzberg, E. (1972). "Toward a Theory of Occupational Choice: A Restatement." *Vocational Guidance Quarterly*, 20, 169–176.

Graham, R. (1975). "Youth and Experiential Learning." In *Youth: The Seventy-fourth Yearbook of the National Society for the Study of Education*. Part I. Edited by R. J. Havighurst and P. H. Drever. Chicago: University of Chicago Press.

Granrose, C. K. (1985). "Plans for Work Careers among College Women Who Expect to Have Families." *The Vocational Guidance Quarterly*, 33, 284–295.

Holland, J. L. (1985). *Making Vocational Choices: A Theory of Vocational Personalities and Work Environments*. 2nd ed. Englewood Cliffs, N.J.: Prentice-Hall.

Homan, K. B. (1986). "Vocation as the Quest for Authentic Existence." *The Career Development Quarterly*, 35, 14–23.

Hoyt, K. B. (1987). "The Impact of Technology on Occupational Change: Implications for Career Guidance." *The Career Development Quarterly*, 35, 269–278.

———. (1988). "The Changing Workforce: A Review of Projections—1986 to 2000." *The Career Development Quarterly*, 37, 31–39.

Johnson, E. G. (1967). "The Impact of High School Teachers on the Educational Plans of College Freshmen." Testing and Counseling Service Report No. 32. Orono: Univ. of ME mimeo.

Lopez, F. G., and Andrews, S. (1987). "Career Indecision: A Family Systems Perspective." *Journal of Counseling and Development*, 65, 304–307.

Martinez, A. C., Sedlacek, W. E., and Bachhuber, T. D. (1985). "Male and Female College Graduates—7 Months Later." *The Vocational Guidance Quarterly*, 34, 77–84.

Matteson, D. R. (1975). *Adolescence Today: Sex Roles and the Search for Identity*. Homewood, Ill.: Dorsey.

Mitchell, C. E. (1988). "Preparing for Vocational Choice." *Adolescence*, 23, 331–334.

Mortimer, J. T. (1976). "Social Class, Work, and the Family: Some Implications of the Father's Occupation for Familial Relationships and Sons' Career Decisions." *Journal of Marriage and the Family*, 38, 241–256.

O'Hare, M. M. (1987). "Career Decision-Making Models: Espoused Theory vs. Theory-In-Use." *Journal of Counseling and Development*, 65, 301–303.

Osipow, S. H. (1983). *Theories of Career Development*. 3rd ed. Englewood Cliffs, N.J.: Prentice-Hall.

Panel on Youth, President's Science Advisory Committee. (1974). *Youth: Transition to Adulthood*. Chicago: University of Chicago Press.

Peterson, G. W., Stiver, M. E., and Peters, D. F. (1986). "Family versus Nonfamily Significant Others for the Career Decisions of Low-Income Youth." *Family Relations*, 35, 417–424.

Picou, J. S., and Curry, E. W. (1973). "Structural, Interpersonal, and Behavioral Correlates of Female Adolescents' Occupational Choices." *Adolescence*, 8, 421–432.

Picou, J. S., et al. (1974). "Occupational Choice and Perception of Attainment Blockage: A Study of Lower-Class Delinquent and Non-Delinquent Black Males." *Adolescence*, 9, 289–298.

Post-Kammer, P. (1987). "Intrinsic and Extrinsic Work Values and Career Maturity of 9th- and 11th-Grade Boys and Girls." *Journal of Counseling and Development*, 65, 420–423.

Ramsey, C. E. "A Study of Decision-Making of Adolescence." Unpublished data.

Rapoport, R., and Rapoport, R. N. (1971). *Dual Career Families*. Baltimore: Penguin Books.

Salomone, P. R., and Sheehan, M. C. (1985). "Vocational Stability and Congruence: An Examination of Holland's Proposition." *The Vocational Guidance Quarterly*, 34, 91–98.

Saltiel, J. (1986). "Segmental Influence: The Case of Educational and Occupational Significant Others." *Adolescence*, 21, 615–622.

Stringer, D. M., and Duncan, E. (1985). "Nontraditional Occupations: A Study of Women Who Have Made the Choice." *The Vocational Guidance Quarterly*, 33, 241–248.

Strong, E. K. *Vocational Interests of Men and Women*. Palo Alto, Calif.: Stanford University Press, 1943.

U.S. Bureau of the Census. (1987). *Statistical Abstract of the United States, 1987*. Washington, D.C.: U.S. Government Printing Office.

U.S. Department of Labor, Bureau of Labor Statistics. (1980). *Occupational Outlook Handbook, 1980–1981*. Washington, D.C.: U.S. Govt. Printing Office.

Vondracek, F. W., and Schulenberg, J. E. (1986). "Career Development in Adolescence: Some Conceptual and Intervention Issues." *The Vocational Guidance Quarterly*, 34, 247–254.

Wattenberg, W. W. (1973). *The Adolescent Years*. 2d ed. New York: Harcourt Brace Jovanovich.

"Why It's Hard to Cut Teen-Age Unemployment." (May 17, 1976). *U.S. News & World Report*.

Wilson, J. B. (1986). "Perceived Influence of Male Sex Role Identity on Female Partner's Life Choices." *Journal of Counseling and Development*, 65, 74–77.

The World Almanac and Book of Facts, 1989. New York: Pharoe Books.

Yankelovich, D. (1974). *The New Morality: A Profile of American Youth in the 70's*. New York: McGraw-Hill.

Yogev, A., and Roditi, H. (1987). "School Counselors as Gatekeepers: Guidance in Poor versus Affluent Neighborhoods." *Adolescence*, 22, 625–639.

Glossary

Accommodation—modifying a current mode or structure of thought to deal with new features of the environment.

Acculturation—the process of adopting or teaching the cultural traits or social patterns of a particular social group.

Acne—pimples on the skin caused by overactive sebaceous glands.

Activism—involvement in trying to achieve political goals and social change.

Adolescence—the period of growth from childhood to maturity.

Adolescent culture—sum of the way of living of adolescents.

Adolescent society—structural arrangements of subgroups within an adolescent social system.

Adolescent subculture—values and way of life that are contrary to those found in adult society.

Adrenal glands—ductless glands located just above the kidneys that secrete androgens and estrogens in both men and women in addition to their secretion of adrenalin.

Age-grade society—adolescent society composed of those in the same grade level.

Alcohol abuse—excessive use of alcohol so that functioning is impaired.

Alcoholism—chemical dependency on alcohol accompanied by compulsive and excessive drinking.

Anabolic steroids—the masculinizing hormone testosterone taken by athletes to build muscle mass.

Anal stage—the second psychosexual stage in Freud's theory of development: the second year of life, during which the child seeks pleasure and satisfaction through anal activity and the elimination of waste.

Androgyny—a blending of male and female characteristics and roles.

Anglos—English-speaking Americans of European ancestry.

Anorexia nervosa—an eating disorder characterized by an obsession with food and with being thin.

Anovulatory—without ovulation.

Anxious runaway—a runaway who comes from a multi-problem family.

Argot—language or slang of a particular group.

Assimilation—incorporating a feature of the environment into an existing mode or structure of thought.

Authority crisis—that point in life where one begins to question who has control over one's life.

Autonomy—independence or freedom.

Autosociality—period during which a child plays alongside other children, not with them.

Bartholin's glands—glands on either side of the vaginal opening that secrete fluid during sexual arousal.

Bulimia—an eating disorder characterized by binging and purging.

Chicano—term for Mexican Americans.

Clitoris—a small shaft containing erectile tissue, located above the vaginal and urethral openings, that is highly responsive to sexual stimulation.

Cognition—the act or process of knowing.

Coitus—sexual intercourse.

Colonia or barrios—colonies or districts of Spanish-speaking people.

Compromise with reality theory—theory of vocational choice proposed by Eli Ginzberg.

Concrete operational stage—the third stage of cognitive development according to Piaget.

Conversion disorder—a somatoform disorder in which anxiety becomes so severe that it causes physical symptoms such as temporary blindness or paralysis. Also called conversion hysteria.

Corpus luteum—yellow body that grows from the ruptured follicle and becomes an endocrine gland secreting progesterone.

Cowper's glands—small twin glands that secrete a fluid to neutralize the acid environment of the urethra.

Crystallized intelligence—arises from acculturation and education, general knowledge.

Cultural determinism—the influence of a particular culture in determining the personality and behavior of a developing individual.

Cultural relativism—variations in social institutions, economic patterns, habits, mores, rituals, religious beliefs, and ways of life from one culture to another.

Date rape—forcing unwanted sexual intercourse while on a date.

Deductive reasoning—beginning with an hypothesis or premise and breaking it down to see if it is true.

Defense mechanisms—according to Freud, unrealistic strategies used by the ego to protect itself and to discharge tension.

Depersonalization and **derealization**—becoming detached emotionally from the self.

Depression—a mental illness characterized by feelings of sadness, despair, melancholia, listlessness, and a reduction of mental activity and physical drive.

Developmental tasks—the skills, knowledge, functions, and attitudes that individuals have to acquire at certain points in their lives in order to function effectively as mature persons.

Differential association—Sutherland's theory that outlines conditions which facilitate moral or criminal learning.

Disorders of impulse control—mental illnesses in which the individual has an uncontrollable urge to steal, set fires, or to engage in other impulsive behavior.

Ectomorph—tall, slender body build.

Ego—according to Freud, the rational mind that seeks to satisfy the id in keeping with reality.

Ego-dystonic homosexuality—homosexuality that the individual cannot accept in himself or herself, so he or she desires to be heterosexual.

Endomorph—short, heavy body build.

Epididymis—a system of ducts, running from the testes to the vas deferens, in which sperm mature and are stored.

Equity—assigning punishments in accordance with ability to take responsibility for a crime.

Estrogen—feminizing hormone produced by the ovaries and to some extent by the adrenal glands.

Expiatory punishment—punishment that results from an externally imposed regulation.

Extrinsic values—rewards that are received outside of a thing or activity that are not inherent in it: for example, receiving money for work.

Fallopian tubes—tubes that transport the ova from the ovaries to the uterus.

Femininity—personality and behavior characteristics of a female according to culturally defined standards of femaleness.

Flaming youth—a term used during the 1920s to describe "wild" adolescents of the day.

Follicle-stimulating hormone (FSH)—a pituitary hormone that stimulates the maturation of the follicles and ova in the ovaries and of sperm in the testes.

Foreclosure—according to Marcia, those adolescents who have established an identity without search or exploration, usually according to what has been handed down by parents.

Formal operational stage—the fourth stage of cognitive development according to Piaget during which people develop abstract thought independent of concrete objects.

Fluid intelligence—ability to think and reason abstractly.

Gender—one's biological sex plus psychosocial components that characterize one as male or female.

Gender identity—one's internal sense of being male or female.

Gender role or sex role—the outward manifestation and expression of maleness or femaleness in a social setting.

Generalized anxiety disorder—a mental illness in which individuals make an enormous catastrophe out of the smallest mishap and believe that perceived catastrophe exists. It is an overexaggeration of anxiety out of proportion to the situation.

Genital stage—the last psychosexual stage of development according to Freud during which sexual urges result in seeking other persons as sexual objects to relieve sexual tension.

Gonadotropic hormones—sex hormones secreted by the gonads.

Gonadotropin-releasing hormone (GnRH)—a hormone secreted by the hypothalamus that controls the production and release of FSH and LH from the pituitary.

Gonads—the sex glands: testes and ovaries.

Hermaphroditism—condition in which an individual has the gonads of both sexes.

Heteronomy—control of conduct external to the self.

Heterosexuality—sexual orientation to those of the opposite sex.

Heterosociality—period during which adolescents prefer company of both sexes.

Homosexuality—sexual orientation to those of the same sex.

Homosociality—period during which children prefer company of those of same sex.

Hormones—biochemical substances secreted into the bloodstream by the endocrine glands that act as an internal communication system telling the different cells what to do.

Human growth hormone (HGH)—a pituitary hormone that regulates body growth.

Hymen—tissue partly covering the vaginal opening.

Hypothalamus—a small area of the brain controlling motivation, emotion, pleasure, and pain in the body; that is, it controls eating, drinking, hormonal production, menstruation, pregnancy, lactation, and sexual response and behavior.

Id—according to Freud, those instinctual urges

that a person seeks to satisfy according to the pleasure principle.

Ideal self—the kind of person an individual would like to be.

Identification—the process by which an individual ascribes to himself or herself the characteristics of another person.

Identity achieved—according to Marcia, those adolescents who have undergone a crisis in their search for an identity and who have made a commitment.

Identity crisis—a point in life at which one begins to question one's roles, values, personality, and orientation to life.

Identity diffused or **identity confused**—according to Marcia, those adolescents who have not experienced a crisis and explored meaningful alternatives nor made any commitments in finding an acceptable identity.

Imaging—being on best behavior to make a good impression.

Immanent justice—the child's belief that immoral behavior inevitably brings pain or punishment as a natural consequence of the transgression.

Individual marriage—according to Mead, the first step in marriage during which a couple are committed to one another without children.

Individuation—the formation of personal identity by the development of the self as a unique person separate from parents and others.

Induction—parental control through offering alternative choices.

Inductive reasoning—gathering individual items of information and putting them together to form hypotheses or conclusions.

Inhibin—a hormone produced in the testes to regulate FSH secretion and sperm production.

IQ (intelligence quotient)—calculated by dividing the mental age (MA) by the chronological age (CA) and multiplying by 100.

Intrinsic values—values that are inherent in a thing or activity because of its very nature.

Juvenile—in the legal sense, one who is not yet considered an adult in the eyes of the law.

Juvenile delinquent—a juvenile who violates the law.

Klinefelter's syndrome—XXY chromosomes in males resulting in feminine appearance and mental impairment.

Labia majora—major or large lips of tissue on either side of the vaginal opening.

Labia minora—smaller lips or tissue on either side of the vagina.

Latency stage—the fourth psychosexual stage in Freud's theory of development: from about 6 to 12 years of age, during which sexual interests remain hidden while the child concentrates on school and other activities.

Long-term storage or long-term memory—also called secondary memory (SM), the process by which information is perceived and processed deeply so it passes into the layers of memory below the conscious level.

Low socioeconomic status—those persons w io are low social class and status, including cultural deprivation, and low income.

Luteinizing hormone (LH)—a pituitary hormone that stimulates the development of the ovum and estrogen and progesterone in females and of sperm and testosterone in males.

Luteotropic hormone (LTH)—a pituitary hormone that contains the hormone prolactin that stimulates milk production by the mammary glands of the female breast.

Machismo—means maleness or manhood in Spanish.

Masculinity—personality and behavioral characteristics of a male according to culturally defined standards of maleness.

Masturbation—self stimulation for purpose of sexual arousal.

Matrilineal—descent through the mother's line.

Maturation—the biological or genetic components to development.

Maturity—the time in life when one becomes an adult physically, emotionally, socially, intellectually, and spiritually.

Menarche—first menstruation.

Mesomorph—medium, athletic body build.

Metabolism—the rate at which the body utilizes food and oxygen.

Modeling—learning by observing and imitating the behavior of another.

Mons veneris—mound of flesh or mound of Venus in the female located above the vagina, over which pubic hair grows.

Morality of constraint or **morality of obedience**—conduct is coerced by rules or authority.

Morality of conventional role conformity—second level of development of moral thought based on desire to conform to social convention.

Morality of cooperation or **morality of reciprocity**—conduct regulated by mutual respect and consent.

Morality of self-accepted moral principles—third level of development of moral thought based on adherence to universal principles.

Moratorium—according to Marcia, those adolescents who are involved in a continual crisis and who continue to search for an identity who have not made any commitments.

Nocturnal emissions—male ejaculation during sleep.

Obese—overweight, excessively fat.

Objective judgment—judgments based solely upon the consequences of wrong doing.

Obsessive-compulsive disorder—a mental illness in which an anxiety state is characterized by overwhelming obsessive thoughts and compulsive behavior.

Occupational environment theory—theory of vocational choice proposed by Holland.

Only-lonely child syndrome—refers to the characteristics of an only child in a family.

Oral stage—the first psychosexual stage in Freud's theory of development: from birth to one year, during which the child's chief source of pleasure and satisfaction comes from oral activity.

Ovaries—female gonads or sex glands that secrete estrogen and progesterone and produce mature egg cells.

Parental marriage—according to Mead, the second step in marriage during which a couple have children.

    —according to Scriven, the last step of marriage only after successful personal marriage.

Penis—the male sexual organ for coitus and urination.

Personal marriage—according to Scriven, couple marriage after the year's preliminary marriage; marriage without children.

Phallic stage—the third psychosexual stage in Freud's theory of development: from about the fourth to the sixth year during which the genital area is the chief source of pleasure and satisfaction.

Phobia—an anxiety disorder characterized by excessive, uncontrolled fear of objects, situations, or living creatures of some type.

Physical addiction or physical dependency—develops from abusing a drug that forms a chemical dependency.

Pituitary gland—master gland of the body located at the base of the brain.

Pluralistic society—a society in which there are many different competing standards of behavior.

Preliminary marriage—according to Scriven, contractual cohabitation for one year.

Premenstural syndrome (PMS)—typified by nervousness, irritability, anxiety, and unpleasant physical feelings and mood swings that occur just before menstruation.

Premoral level—first level of development of moral thought according to Kohlberg, based on reward and punishments.

Preoperational stage—the second stage of cognitive development according to Piaget, lasting from 2 to 7 years of age.

Privatism—concern with one's own self, life, and problems as distinguished from activism, which is concern for social and political issues.

Problem-finding stage—a fifth stage of cognitive development characterized by the ability to be creative, to discover, and to formulate problems.

Progesterone—female sex hormone produced by the corpus luteum of the ovary.

Progressives—educators who emphasize that the purpose of education is to prepare pupils for all of life.

Proprium—the self identity that is developing in time.

Prostate glands—two glands that secrete a portion of the seminal fluid.

Pseudohermaphroditism—condition in which either a male or female has incompletely developed organs of both sexes.

Psychological dependency—developing an overpowering emotional need for a drug.

Psychological factors affecting physical condition—emotional or psychological factors that contribute to ill health; also called psychosomatic reactions.

Psychosocial moratorium—a socially sanctioned period between childhood and adulthood during which the individual is free to experiment to find a socially acceptable identity and role.

Puberty—that whole period during which the person reaches sexual maturity and becomes capable of reproduction.

Pubescence—that whole period during which the physical changes related to sexual maturation take place.

Punishment of reciprocity—self-imposed punishment.

Reinforcement—positive reinforcements are influences which increase the probability the preceding response will occur again. Negative reinforcements are influences which increase the probability the preceding response will stop.

Rootless runaway—one who runs away from home for fun and to seek pleasure and gratification.

SAT—Scholastic Aptitude Test.

Schizophrenia—a mental illness characterized by emotional and cognitive disturbance and social withdrawal.

Scrotum—the pouch of skin containing the testes.

Secular trend—the trend to mature sexually at earlier ages.

Self—a person's personality or nature of which one is aware.

Self-concept—conscious, cognitive perception and evaluation by individuals of themselves; it is their thoughts and opinions about themselves.

Self-esteem—one's impression or opinion of oneself.

Self-reinforcement—learners reward themselves for activities or responses that they consider of good quality.

Seminal vesicles—twin glands that secrete fluid into the vas deferens to enhance sperm viability.

Sensorimotor stage—the first stage of cognitive development according to Piaget, lasting from birth to about 2 years of age.

Sensory storage or sensory memory—the process by which information is received and transduced by the senses, usually a fraction of a second.

Sexual identity—one's characteristics as a sexual being.

Short-term storage or short-term memory—also called primary memory (PM); the process by which information is still in the conscious mind being rehearsed and focused on.

Social cognition—how people think and reason about their social world as they watch and interact with others: their understanding and ability to get along with other people.

Social-evaluative anxiety—shyness.

Socialization—that process by which individuals learn and adopt the ways, ideas, beliefs, values, and norms of their culture.

Social role taking—according to Selman, the various social roles that individuals assume which reflect their understanding of themselves, their reaction to others, and their ability to understand others' points of view.

Somatoform disorders—disorders in which the individual experiences physical health problems that have psychological rather than physical causes.

Spermatogenesis—process by which sperm are developed.

Stereotype—a broad, oversimplified conception or idea held about persons of a particular group usually based on prejudiced ideas and feelings.

Steroids—the hormone testosterone.

Strong Vocational Interest Blank—a test that measures suitability for different vocations according to interests.

Subjective judgment—judgments that take into account intention or motives.

Subsystem—a smaller segment of adolescent society within the larger social system.

Superego—according to Freud, that part of the mind that opposes the desires of the id by enforcing moral restrictions that have been learned to try to attain a goal of perfection.

Syncretism—trying to link ideas together.

Teenager—in a strict sense includes only the teen years: 13 to 19.

Terrified runaway—a runaway who is escaping sexual or physical abuse.

Testes—the male gonads that produce sperm and male sex hormones.

Testosterone—masculinizing sex hormone produced by the testes and to a lesser extent by the adrenals.

THC—the active ingredient in marijuana.

Throwaways—adolescents who have been told to leave home.

Traditionalists—educators who emphasize that the purpose of education is to teach the basics.

Transductive reasoning—proceeding from particular to particular in thought, without making generalizations.

Turner's syndrome—female with X0 chromosomes.

Unmarried cohabitation—two unrelated adults of the opposite sex sharing the same living quarters in which there is no other adult present.

Urethra—the tube carrying the urine from the bladder to the outside; in males it also carries the semen to the outside.

Uterus—womb in which the baby grows and develops.

Vagina—canal from the cervix to the vulva that receives the penis during intercourse and acts as the birth canal through which the baby passes to the outside.

Values clarification—method of teaching values that helps students become aware of their own beliefs and values.

Vas deferens—the tubes running from the epididymis to the urethra that carry semen and sperm to the ejaculatory duct.

Vestibule—the opening cleft region enclosed by the labia minora.

Vicarious reinforcement—learning from observing the positive or negative consequences of another person's behavior.

Vulva—collective term referring to the external genitalia of the female.

Author Index

Subject Index